THE
EASTERN
EUROPE
COLLECTION

HISTORY

OF THE

HOUSE OF AUSTRIA

Volume III

William Coxe

ARNO PRESS & THE NEW YORK TIMES

New York - 1971

Reprint Edition 1971 by Arno Press Inc.

Reprinted from a copy in
The Columbia University Library

LC# 72-135801

ISBN for Volumes I, II, III: 0-405-02743-5

ISBN for Vol. III: 0-405-02792-3

The Eastern Europe Collection
ISBN for complete set: 0-405-02730-3

Manufactured in the United States of America

HISTORY

OF THE

HOUSE OF AUSTRIA,

FROM THE

Foundation of the Monarchy

BY RHODOLPH OF HAPSBURGH,

TO THE DEATH OF

LEOPOLD THE SECOND:

1218 TO 1792.

BY WILLIAM COXE, F.R.S. F.A.S.

ARCHDEACON OF WILTS, AND RECTOR OF BEMERTON.

THIRD EDITION.

IN THREE VOLUMES.

VOL. III

LONDON:

HENRY G. BOHN, YORK STREET, COVENT GARDEN.

1847.

CONTENTS

OF

THE THIRD VOLUME.

HISTORY

OF

THE HOUSE OF AUSTRIA.

CHAP. LXXII.—JOSEPH I.—1705, 1706.

JOSEPH, eldest son of Leopold, was born at Vienna in 1678, and owed his christian name, which none of his ancestors had ever borne, to a vow made by his father, that if by the intercession of St. Joseph, God would bless him with another son, he should be called Joseph. The young prince gave early signs of an active and aspiring mind, and perhaps no heir of an extensive empire was educated with greater care, or provided with more excellent governors and preceptors. Leopold conferred the charge of governor on Charles Dietrich, prince of Salm, who proved himself worthy of his high office by his zeal in promoting the improvement of his pupil, and by inculcating rational and liberal principles both of religion and policy. Knowing that the Jesuits sacrificed all other considerations to the interests of their society, and sensible that they had abetted the intolerance and persecution which, since the death of Maximilian II. had equally disgraced and disturbed the administration of the Austrian sovereigns, he prevailed on Leopold to exclude their order from all share in the education of his successor. This liberal education, so different from that which had been usually bestowed on the Austrian princes, excited the envy of the Jesuits, and though unable to shake the authority of the governor, they obtained the dismission of the preceptor Rummel, a secular priest, whom the prince of Salm had selected on account of his profound learning and pure morals. But their intrigues were counteracted by the young prince himself, who defended his preceptor with a spirit above his years, and boldly declared to his father, that if Rummel was dismissed he would decline all further application.

Crowned sovereign of Hungary in 1687, and king of the Romans in 1690, Joseph was not induced by these splendid titles to arrogate a share in the administration; but continued to exhibit a laudable example of filial respect and obedience, till his father himself, during the latter months of his reign, was induced by sickness and infirmity to consign to him the reins of government.

As he advanced in years his great qualities expanded themselves. During the first campaign of the war, Joseph, then twenty-two, extorted from his reluctant father the permission to serve in the German army, and repaired to the siege of Landau. On his arrival he hastened to the trenches; and when his attendants entreated him to withdraw from a place so much exposed, he replied, " Let those who are afraid retire." To Melac the governor, who sent a herald to know the situation of his quarters, that he might respect his person, he answered, " My quarters are wherever I am called by necessity or danger. Attend to your own honour, and omit nothing which your master's service and your duty prescribe." Nor was this an empty vaunt. The king of the Romans shared the fatigues and risks of the common soldiers, and was always observed in the most dangerous posts. He was no less humane and generous than brave and intrepid: he exhorted and animated the soldiers, visited the sick and wounded, and distributed presents among the widows and orphans of the slain. The valour which he displayed, the address by which he inspired the troops with courage and good will, and the generals with activity and vigilance, infused such energy into the besiegers, that Landau capitulated after an obstinate siege, and he returned in triumph to Vienna. The year ensuing, he again repaired to the siege of Landau, which had been retaken by the French, and exhibited new proofs of heroism, courtesy, generosity, and beneficence. He displayed the highest marks of esteem towards Labadie, the intrepid governor, whose brave defence protracted the siege sixty-nine days, granted him an honourable capitulation, and assured the gallant chief that he deemed it his highest glory to subdue such an enemy.

Joseph was twenty-five when the death of Leopold called into action all his talents, activity, and resources. The first object of his reign was to reduce the number of courtiers and officers of the household, who, without adding to the lustre, had contributed to exhaust the revenues of the crown ; and on the same principle of economy he introduced various regulations into the civil and military departments. He at the same time gave a proof of the liberal principles by which he intended to govern, by removing the ministers who were devoted to the Jesuits, and discountenancing an order which, for so long a period, had reigned paramount at the court of Vienna. He displayed equally his gratitude and judgment, in consigning the conduct of the state to his governor the prince of Salm, and in raising his precep- tor Rummel to the bishopric of Vienna, with the principal direction of ecclesiastical affairs.

The embarrassments of a new reign produced no change nor essential delay in the exertions against the common enemy. The great object of the allies was to push the war on the Moselle, to recover Loraine, and from thence to attack the defenceless provinces of France. The project was settled by Eugene, Marlborough, the margrave of Baden, and Joseph himself, during the last siege of Landau, and the arrangements for opening the campaign were made before the departure of Marlborough from the scene of action. Magazines were formed at Coblentz and Treves, and the operations were to commence with the siege of Saar Louis. The Dutch consented to maintain the de- fensive on their own frontier, to strengthen the army of Marlborough ; and the margrave of Baden promised to take the field early in the spring, and detach a part of his force to concur in the attack. It was confidently hoped that the general consternation in France, joined to the civil war which persecution had excited among the Protestants of the Cevennes, would cripple all the efforts of the enemy, and contribute to render the success of the present as brilliant as the close of the last campaign.

But Louis, however we may condemn his arrogance and presumption in prosperity, possessed, in an eminent degree,

that fortitude which rises superior to adversity. He redoubled his exertions to repair his losses ; and called forth
all the spirit of his subjects, and all the resources of his
powerful monarchy. The elector of Bavaria, assisted by
Villeroy, was to act offensively on the side of the Lower
Countries with 75,000 men ; Villars, with 55,000, to protect
the country watered by the Moselle ; Marsin, with 30,000,
to maintain the defensive on the Upper Rhine ; troops,
under the duke of Berwick, were detached to awe the insurgents in the Cevennes ; and great reinforcements were
poured into Italy, to complete the subjugation of the duke
of Savoy.

Yet all these exertions would have been made in vain,
had not the divisions of a vast and heterogeneous confederacy, and the discordant interests which arise from success,
palsied the efforts of the allies. The Maritime Powers themselves spent the winter in discussions relative to their
respective contingents, and in contests for the supreme
command ; but the most fatal obstacle to the intended
invasion was derived from the tardiness and jealousy of the
German princes, who, in the humiliation of France, again
dreaded the revival of the imperial authority, and the ascendency of Austria. When, therefore, Marlborough led
the reinforcements to the army on the Moselle, he found
neither provisions, artillery, horses, nor carriages. None
of the German contingents were arrived, and the margrave himself, after attempting to evade an interview,
left the few troops which had been assembled, and retired
under a real or affected indisposition to the baths of
Schwalbach.

Thus mortified and abandoned, Marlborough was unable
to push the intended attack in opposition to Villars, who
had taken a strong position at Sirk on the frontiers of
Loraine, where he equally covered Luxemburgh, Thionville,
and Saar Louis. After earnest and repeated, though vain
appeals to the German States, he left 7000 Palatine
auxiliaries to cover Treves, and hastened towards the
Meuse, where the French had taken Huy, reduced the town
of Liege, and threatened to carry the war into Holland, or
cut off the communication between the United Provinces
and the Upper Rhine. He joined the Dutch troops on the
5th of July, recovered Huy and Liege, overruled the oppo-

sition of Slangenberg and other generals, broke through
the lines which the French had formed to cover their frontier from Antwerp to the Mehaigne, at Heilesheim, and
defeated a part of the troops, which had been hastily assembled to oppose him. He drove back the enemy from
the Deule on the 29th of July, and followed them to a
position which they took behind the Ysch; but, when he
had reduced them to a situation in which they could not
avoid an engagement, he was again opposed by the cabal
of Slangenberg and the Dutch deputies, and saw all his
measures frustrated at the very moment of execution.
Thus curbed in his operations, he employed the remainder
of the campaign in demolishing the French lines, and after
reducing Leewe, and drawing his troops into quarters, he
quitted the army to make preparations for more strenuous
and effectual exertions in the ensuing year.

After the departure of Marlborough towards the Meuse,
Villars sent strong succours to the army in the Low Countries, left 10,000 men on the Moselle, and with the remainder of his force joined Tallard to overwhelm the small corps
of Germans collected for the defence of their lines. But
this design was frustrated by general Thungen, who retiring to an entrenched camp under the walls of Lauterburgh, maintained his position till he was joined by the
margrave of Baden, with the rest of the contingents, on the
30th of June. Yet though the German army was now
superior in number to the enemy, the margrave, disheartened by his languishing disorder, or still under the
influence of that jealousy which had frustrated the grand
system of attack, continued unmoved by all the remonstrances of the allies and the imperial court, and the campaign was principally wasted in marches and countermarches
on both sides of the Rhine. The French secured Loraine
and the three bishoprics, by the re-occupation of Treves,
Saarburgh, and Hornberg; and the Germans forced the
lines formed by Marsin on the Motter, and recovered
Haguenau and Drusenheim. After these movements, the
two armies, who had suffered chiefly from fatigue and the
severity of the weather, gradually retired into winter-
quarters.

The campaign was scarcely closed before a sudden and
general insurrection of the Bavarian peasantry gave new

alarms to the court of Vienna. From a desire to appropriate Bavaria, no less than from resentment against the elector, the Austrian court had treated the country with great rigour, dismembered several districts, and compelled the natives to take an oath of allegiance. These measures, joined to the loyalty of the people, gave rise to a conspiracy for throwing off the Austrian yoke, in which the electress herself was implicated. The plot being accidentally discovered, the emperor deprived her of the regency, removed her children into the Austrian territories, disarmed the natives, made forced levies, and imposed heavy contributions. The peasantry thus driven to despair, rose almost at the same instant, when the troops were principally drawn to Italy and the Rhine, seized the important posts of Brauna, Burghausen, Scharding, and Kelheim, and even surprised the suburbs of Munich. Their numbers rapidly augmented to 30,000 men, and their enterprise would have produced the most alarming consequences, had they not consented to an armistice of ten days. This fortunate delay enabling the Austrians to concentrate their forces and recall part of their troops, they soon gained the superiority over a disorganised and ill-armed multitude, defeated them with great slaughter, reduced them to submission, and punished this attempt to recover their independence with redoubled severities.

In the midst of these operations the attention of Europe was arrested by the appearance of a new champion on the theatre of action, who threatened to suspend the triumphs of the allies. This champion was Charles XII., king of Sweden.

The glory, influence, and acquisitions, which Sweden had acquired by her arms, had long excited the envy of the northern powers. The enmity of Denmark was fomented by the support which Sweden gave to the dukes of Holstein Gottorp; Peter, czar of Russia, was anxious to acquire the Swedish provinces of Ingria and Carelia, in order to establish himself on the shore of the Baltic; Augustus, king of Poland and elector of Saxony, was desirous to re-annex Livonia to his newly-acquired kingdom. These potentates, who had been kept in awe by Charles XI., availed themselves of the accession of a minor king to humble a nation whose superior splendour obscured their glory. They entered into a secret league for the abasement of their common rival, and at the commencement of 1700, broke out into open hostilities. The king of Denmark directed his attacks against the duke of Holstein, the ally and brother-in-law of Charles; and Augustus burst into Livonia. This sudden and unprovoked hostility, without a declaration of war, struck terror into the Swedish court. The ministers, who dreaded a contest under a young and inexperienced monarch, proposed to avert the storm by negotiation; but Charles, who had listened with silent contempt to their discussions, astounded the whole council by exclaiming, with an air of decision and gravity above his age, " I have resolved never to undertake an unjust war ; yet I will never finish a just war, except with the ruin of my enemies."

He followed this declaration by an instantaneous change in his habits and manners, from which he never afterwards swerved. Full of enthusiasm for his ancient models, he devoted himself to war, by renouncing all the pleasures and luxuries of civilised life ; and voluntarily undergoing the hardships and privations of a Spartan. He abstained from wine, shunned the company of woman, slept on the bare ground, with no other covering but his cloak, accustomed his body to incessant exercise, and habituated himself to the extreme of abstinence in sleep and food. The whole machine of government, and every district of his country, instantly felt the impulse of his powerful hand. Troops were despatched to assist the duke of Holstein, whose territories had been nearly subjugated by the Danes; and urgent appeals made to the houses of Hanover and Brandenburgh, and to the Maritime Powers, for the assistance stipulated by ancient treaties. With a spirit of enterprise equal to his great models, he carried the war into the territories of his enemies. He detached a light squadron to intercept the communications of the king of Denmark, who was employed in Holstein, and sailed with a powerful force to attack Copenhagen itself. While his fleet, assisted by an English and Dutch squadron, blockaded that of the Danes, and bombarded the capital, he headed the descent of his troops. Impatient to reach the shore, he leaped into the sea, sword in hand, led forward his soldiers in the face of the Danish batteries, and invested the town by land.

The promptitude and vigour of this enterprise reduced the king of Denmark to immediate submission. Within eleven days after the descent of the youthful hero, he deserted his alliance against Sweden, by a separate treaty at Travendahl, on the 18th of August, 1700, gave a compensation to the duke of Holstein, and confirmed all former engagements.

Having thus humbled one enemy, Charles turned with the same promptitude and decision against Peter, czar of Muscovy, who had invested Narva with 40,000 men. On the 30th of November, in less than two months after he had reached the shores of Denmark, he landed at Pirna, marched rapidly to Narva, amidst the severities of winter, attacked the Russians, though covered with formidable entrenchments, gained a complete victory, and dissipated the whole army. The moment the approach of spring allowed him to act, he entered Livonia, forced the passage of the Duna, obtained another decisive but bloody victory, in the neighbourhood of Riga, on the 9th of July, 1701, and subjugated Courland and Livonia. Pursuing the same principle of ruining those enemies who had planned his destruction, he entered Poland, roused the factions which always distracted that unhappy country, routed in numerous conflicts the partisans of Augustus, and on the 12th of July, 1704, procured the election of Stanislaus Letzinski, a Polish noble, whom accident brought to his notice. He had no sooner witnessed the coronation of the sovereign to whom he had given a throne, than he hastened to complete his work, by annihilating all the resources and hopes of Augustus ; bursting through Silesia into Saxony with 20,000 men, in contempt of all the remonstrances of the emperor, he, on the 4th of September, 1706, forced Augustus, in the centre of his own dominions, to resign the throne from which he had been driven, and acknowledge the title of his rival.

Charles took up his residence at Alt Ramstadt, in a state of momentary inactivity ; and while he held in his hands the balance of Europe, courted or feared by all parties, he kept the various candidates for his favour in suspense, though he displayed a partiality to the French and Bavarian ministers, and treated the remonstrances and menaces of the empire with pride and contempt.* He laid a list of grievances before the emperor, demanded redress for a real or fancied insult to his envoy by an imperial chamberlain, required the surrender of 1500 Russian fugitives who had taken refuge in the Austrian territories, and the recall of the German officers who had entered into the service of the czar, and insisted on the restoration of the Protestant churches in Silesia.

It was highly dangerous to provoke a monarch who held in his hand the balance of the war, who was courted by France to imitate the example and emulate the exploits of Gustavus Adolphus, whose resentment was implacable, whose decisions instantaneous, whose spirit was rendered inflexible by the slightest opposition. Joseph therefore acted with consummate address. He soothed the diet, which had imprudently threatened to avenge the aggressions of Sweden by a declaration of war ; he stifled his own ardent feelings, opened a friendly negotiation, and laboured, by every mark of attention, and every proof of acquiescence, to conciliate the haughty Swede. But the mysterious conduct of Charles, and the presence of so enterprising a prince, with a veteran and victorious army in the heart of the empire, made a deep impression on Joseph, whose hereditary dominions were principally threatened, awed the neighbouring states, and detained a considerable force from the scene of action.

CHAP. LXXIII.—1706.

TOWARDS the beginning of May the two armies assembled in the Netherlands : the French under the elector of Bavaria and Villeroy, behind their lines near Louvain,

* England was so conscious of the danger to be apprehended from the king of Sweden's junction with France, that the duke of Marlborough recommended the emperor to deliver up the Russian fugitives to Sweden ; but the emperor rejected with scorn so degrading a proposal, as contrary to the law of nations and the honour of his crown. Letter from count Wratislaw to the duke of Marlborough, May 14. 1707.

amounting to 70,000 men; the allies, nearly equal in numbers, at Borchloe, on the borders of the bishopric of Liege.

Marlborough, anxious to open the campaign with an engagement, employed a spy to alarm the French generals with rumours of a design to surprise Namur, or pillage the town and rich abbey of St. Amand. Having by this stratagem, induced them to quit their lines, and advance to Tirlemont, he suddenly pushed towards the sources of the Gheet, either to force them to a battle, or cut them off from Namur. But on approaching Ramilies, he found that they had at the same time marched to anticipate his design, and on the dispersion of a thick fog, which had concealed their movements, he discovered their army occupying a position beyond the Little Gheet. Their line stretched from near Tavieres, on the Mehaigne, to the village of Anderkirk. In their front before the right of their infantry was Ramilies, which was defended by several battalions, a little beyond was Offuz, situated at the sources of the Little Gheet. On their right were Tavieres and Franquenies, which at the commencement of the battle were occupied only by a regiment of dragoons; their left, with a considerable part of their centre, was posted between the two branches of the Little Gheet; and the only point of their line not defended by nature, was an open space of 1200 paces, between Ramilies and Tavieres, stretching from the source of the Gheet to the Mehaigne.

Marlborough hastened to bring on an engagement before they could recover from the confusion of their sudden march, or secure themselves in their advantageous post. As their right and part of their centre were the only vulnerable points, he added to his left wing twenty squadrons of Danish horse from his right, drew twelve battalions from his infantry, to form an attack against Ramilies, and four to assault Franquenies and Tavieres. Soon after mid-day, on the 23rd of May, the engagement began. The four battalions having carried Tavieres, the cavalry of the left instantly advanced beyond the village, cut to pieces a body of dismounted dragoons, in their way to recover it, and, forming in two solid lines, attacked the right of the French, which was composed of the household troops, and the best soldiers of France. The confederate

cavalry, twice driven back, was again rallied by Marlborough himself, who was exposed to the same danger
from which he had so narrowly escaped at Blenheim; and
being supported by fresh squadrons from the right, broke
the enemy with great slaughter. During these charges,
the attack was made against Ramilies; the twelve battalions, sustained by the whole line of infantry, assailing
the village in front and flank, carried it with far less difficulty than had been expected from the strength of the
post. The infantry, advancing beyond the village, broke
the French, and drove them in disorder towards Judoigne.
The left of the enemy, which, from its position between
the two branches of the Gheet, could neither attack or be
attacked, began to retire with the artillery, favouring the
retreat of the fugitives; but being bravely charged by
some regiments of English horse, at a moment when their
march was accidentally interrupted, they were struck with
a panic, took to flight, and were pursued as far as Meldert,
five leagues from the scene of action.

The French lost in killed and prisoners 13,000 men, 50
pieces of cannon, and almost all their baggage, while the
allies had scarcely 2000 killed or wounded.* The elector
of Bavaria and Villeroy, after narrowly escaping in the
rout, fled to Louvain, where they held a tumultuary
council of war by torch-light, abandoned the unfortified
towns and open country, and retreated with their discomfited army behind the canal of Brussels.

The allies did not allow the enemy time to recover from
their panic. They occupied Louvain the day after the
battle, and received the submission of the sovereign
council, and the states of Brussels. They "pressed the
enemy while confusion continued among them†;" followed
them in their retreat to Ghent; by throwing bridges over
the Scheldt and threatening their rear, forced them to fall
back to Courtray, and compelled them to distribute a considerable part of their army for the defence of the frontier
places, particularly Mons, Tournay, Lille, Ypres, and

---

* From more accurate accounts, it appears, that the loss of the
allies was 1066 killed, and 2667 wounded. Memoirs of the duke of
Marlborough, chap. xlv., to which we refer the reader for a description
and plan of the battle.

† Letter from the duke of Marlborough.

Menin. Meanwhile the principal towns in the Netherlands followed the example of the capital, or were reduced
by detachments from the victorious army; Mecklin surrendered, Alost declared for Charles, Dendermond was
blockaded, Lierre was occupied by a detachment, Antwerp,
Bruges, Ghent, and Oudenard submitted without delay.

Marlborough was desirous to invade the French frontier
by the Lys and the Scheld, while their army was in confusion, and the towns ill provided for resistance ; but was
again thwarted by his Dutch colleagues. He therefore
hastened to the Hague as well to overrule this opposition
as to concert measures for the government of the reduced
territories ; yet notwithstanding all his remonstrances, he
was necessitated to undertake the siege of Ostend, before
that of Menin, which he proposed as the first step of his
intended invasion.

The most active exertions were made by both parties.
Reinforcements poured in to the French army ; detachments were drawn from the Rhine, and Vendome, recalled
at the most critical juncture from Italy, was appointed to
the command, as a general "who could gain the confidence
of the soldiers, and restore the troops to that spirit of
fortitude and enterprise so natural to the French nation."
On the other hand, the confederate army was strengthened
with 12,000 men from the neighbouring garrisons, and
the troops of Hanover and Prussia advanced by rapid
marches towards Brabant. Plassendael was taken by
storm, Ostend invested by Overkirk, while an English
squadron blockaded the harbour, and the main army at
Rousselaer covered the siege. After some delays, the
attacks were begun, and this important fortress, which had
formerly withstood a siege of three years, surrendered in
July, only eight days after the opening of the trenches.

Although the delay occasioned by this siege, and the
requisite preparations, had given the enemy time to recover
from their consternation, yet Marlborough resumed his plan
of attacking the French frontier. He embarked a regiment
at Ostend, to join an expedition, which was fitting out in
England, to alarm the opposite coast, sent a detachment to
occupy Courtray, crossed the Lys to unite with the Prussian,
Hanoverian, and Palatine auxiliaries, destroyed the sluices
with which the enemy had dammed up the Deule and the

Lys, to prevent the navigation from Ghent, and invested Menin, the key of Flanders, a masterpiece of the art of Vauban. With the main army at Helchin, he protected the siege, and Vendome, notwithstanding he had assembled and re-organised the French troops, was reduced to remain on the defensive behind the Deule, and witness its capture. The subsequent surrender of Dendermond, on the 23rd of August, having opened the whole course of the Scheld, Marlborough crossed that river, and closed this splendid campaign with the reduction of Ath. After some movements for the sake of forage, he repaired to the Hague, and the troops, in the beginning of November, took quarters in the principal posts of their new conquests from the sea to the Meuse.

On the Rhine, Villars, as before, was opposed to the margrave of Baden. The campaign was opened by the French, who forced the lines formed by the Germans on the Motter, drove them back to the Lauter, and reduced Drusenheim and Haguenau, which contained their principal magazines. But the fatal battle of Ramilies debilitated their efforts in every quarter; the reinforcements drawn to the Netherlands reduced the French commander to the defensive ; while the tardiness of the German princes, and the march of the imperial cavalry against the rebels in Hungary, prevented the margrave from profiting by the weakness of his antagonist.

In consequence of the civil war in Hungary, and the exertions of the imperialists in other quarters, the affairs of the emperor, and his ally the duke of Savoy, had rapidly declined in Italy. On the other hand, Louis made vast preparations to achieve the conquests of Piedmont, or detach the duke of Savoy. Reinforcements were sent by sea from Provence ; and a corps of 10,000 men, under la Feuillade, bursting from Dauphiné, opened a passage through the Alps along the Doria, by the capture of Exilles and Susa, with their dependent forts. By these accessions of force the French army was increased to 40,000 men ; and Vendome leaving his brother, the grand prior, to clear the country south of the Po, and close the passages into Italy, crossed the Po at Trino, in the face of the combined army, and subjugated all the principal fortresses of Piedmont,

gradually circumscribing the duke of Savoy to the vicinity
of his capital.

Fortunately this career of success was checked before
the small but strong fortress of Verrua, which commands
the navigation of the Po, and by its position forms an out-
work of Turin. The garrison, succoured by continual reinforcements from Victor Amadeus, who took post at Crescentino, on the opposite side of the river, held out with
incredible bravery and perseverance, till the opening of the
ensuing spring ; they did not surrender till March 11. 1705,
when the French had dearly purchased the place, by the
loss of 18,000 men, and the exertions of a whole campaign,
and rendered the capture of little value, by blowing up the
fortifications. The losses of the French, and the fatigues of
a winter siege, prevented Vendome from pursuing his
operations ; and after allowing his troops to repose till the
middle of June, he advanced to the attack of Civasso,
(behind which the combined army had retired), as a prelude to the siege of Turin.

He was, however, suddenly called from this enterprise
to succour his brother, who was unequally opposed to the
superior talents of Eugene. While Vendome was occupied
in Piedmont, the grand prior, favoured by the connivance of
the papal officers in the Ferrarese, had driven the remnant
of the imperialists into the Trentin, with the loss of all
their baggage, shut up the principal passes into Italy, and
blockaded Mirandola, the last place held by an imperial
garrison. In this state of affairs, Eugene reached the Trentin, followed by 8000 Prussian auxiliaries, who had been
subsidised by England. Failing in his attempts to drive
the French from the Mincio, he suddenly crossed the Lago
di Garda, joined the imperial corps, who during the winter
had maintained themselves on its western shore, anticipated,
by a rapid march, the French commander, who took post
before him, gained the passage of the Oglio at Urago, advanced to Romanengo in his way to the Adda, and would
probably have carried to the duke of Savoy that succour
which his multiplied distresses rendered so necessary, had
not his progress been checked by the arrival of Vendome
with considerable reinforcements.

Eugene spent the rest of the campaign of 1705 in
marches and counter-marches, in which he exhausted all

his resources to gain a passage over the Adda or the Po; but was baffled by the vigilance of his antagonist, and the difficulties of a country abounding in defiles, and intersected by innumerable canals and torrents. The only striking event of the campaign was the short but desperate battle of Cassano, which took place during one of these marches. On the 16th of August, Eugene attacked a part of the French infantry, while separated from the cavalry, which had been pushed across the Adda, to oppose his passage; but the strength of the enemy's position, and the sudden arrival of Vendome, with the rest of the troops from the opposite side of the river, robbed him of the victory. Yet, though foiled in his principal design of joining the duke of Savoy, he succeeded in maintaining his footing in Italy, by establishing his quarters on the skirt of the mountains, between the Lago di Garda and Brescia; while by drawing off so considerable a portion of the French force, he relieved, though he could not assist, the duke of Savoy, and suspended the siege of Turin.

The exertions of Eugene could not, however, prevent the success of different enterprises at a distance from the scene of action. Mirandola was captured after a long blockade; on the side of the Alps, Villafranca and the citadel of Nice were reduced, and the fortress of Montmelian, the only remaining post in Savoy, surrendered after an investment of eighteen months. The only compensation obtained by the confederates for those losses, was the recovery of Asti, which being evacuated by an erroneous order, was instantly occupied by Staremberg, and maintained against all the efforts of la Feuillade.

Although the campaign of 1706 in Italy opened with a sinister event, the arms of the allies were ultimately crowned with success still more brilliant than even in the Netherlands. Early in the year Vendome silently and gradually assembling his choicest troops, surprised the imperialists in their quarters, attacked and broke the forces who were hastily assembled near Calcinato, drove them back into the Trentin, and afterwards dislodged them from the quarters which they occupied between the Adige and the Po. He profited by this bold and successful enterprise to shut up all the avenues by which they could descend into Italy. Count Medavi, with 8000 men guarded the passes to the west of the Lago di Garda ; an intrenchment, defended by 15,000 men, extended from Garda to the Adige ; 12,000 were distributed along the river, as far as St. Pietro di Legnago ; and St. Fremont, with 6000, was intrusted with the defence of the Lower Adige.

While Vendome was thus employed in closing the passes, the most active preparations were made for reducing Turin. Immense magazines were formed at Susa, Casale, Crescentino, and Civasso, and an army collected for the siege, under the command of La Feuillade, exceeding 50,000 men. The city was invested in May, and trenches opened in the commencement of June against the citadel and a work stretching towards the Doria. The duke of Savoy remained in Turin till after the investment, to mature the necessary arrangements ; but before the circumvallation was completed he left the command of the town to the marquis di Carail, and of the citadel to count Daun, with a garrison of 10,000 men, took the field with his cavalry, baffled or eluded the French commander by successively retreating to Villestellone, Coni, Civasso, and Saluzza, along the borders of the mountains, and at length threw himself into the valley of Lucerna, where he dismounted his troops, and sent his horses to the pastures in the Alps. His retreat having left the open country in the power of the enemy, Asti was besieged by the militia of the Milanese, Mondovi and Ceva surprised, and the duchess, with her infant family, sought refuge in the Genoese territories.

Early in the spring Eugene hastened to the frontiers of Italy, with the intention of resuming the plan on which he had acted the preceding campaign. But, on arriving at Salo, he had the mortification to find his designs disconcerted by the unexpected defeat of the imperialists in their quarters, and with difficulty secured the retreat of the fugitive army, which was reduced to 11,000 men. His future operations were attended with embarrassments which would have discouraged an inferior general. To attain the object of his expedition, it was necessary to traverse a country above two hundred miles in extent, full of strongholds, watered by four navigable rivers, abounding in defiles, and intersected by innumerable rivulets, canals, and torrents, in the face of a superior enemy who guarded every avenue. Deeming it, therefore, impossible in this situation to force his way through the district north of the Po, Eugene drew his troops by Riva round the northern point of the Lago di Gardi, and suddenly descended, as before, by the sources of the Brenta into the Veronese. Being joined by 10,000 of the auxiliaries from Germany, he left 6000 men under Wetzel at San Martino, to secure the junction of 6000 Hessians, yet on their march, and to divide the attention of the enemy. He amused the French, as on the former occasion, with feint attacks along the course of the Adige, while a strong detachment secured a passage and constructed a bridge at Ruotanova. The whole army promptly passed without opposition, pushed the corps of St. Fremont beyond the numerous canals and streams between the Adige and the Po, passed the Po near Biaggio, secured Finale and Biondena, dislodged the enemy from the Panaro and the Canale di Modena, and followed them to the river Parmegiana.

In this situation of affairs Vendome was recalled from Italy to head the army in Flanders, dispirited by the defeat of Ramilies, and the command was intrusted to the duke of Orleans, under the direction of Marsin. The new general having obtained a reinforcement of 15,000 men from la Feuillade, left a corps of 10,000, under Medavi, to observe the imperialists at San Martino, and, with the rest of the army, crossing the Po, joined the retreating body on the Parmegiana to arrest the progress of Eugene.

The imperial general, too weak to force the position of the enemy, employed himself in securing Carpi, Reggio, and Corregio, till the junction of the Hessians enabled the corps beyond the Po to approach the Mincio, and open a passage by the capture of Goito. This diversion, reducing the French to abandon their design of making a stand on the Parmegiana, and again fall back beyond the Po, he pushed forward with unexpected celerity. Notwithstanding his troops were exposed to the burning rays of an Italian sun, and suffered equally from drought and want of provisions, he anticipated the movements of the French, though their march was facilitated by carriages from the Milanese. While he allowed his army to repose and wait for supplies, he pushed forward detachments by night to secure the passes, and throw bridges over the

numerous rivers which swell the waters of the Po,
anticipated the enemy at Placentia and the pass of
Stradella, crossed the Tanaro above Isola ; and after a
march of thirty-four days, one of the most memorable
in the military annals of modern Europe, united at
Villastellone with the duke of Savoy, who, on his approach
had quitted the mountains, roused his faithful peasantry,
and collected a respectable force. They crossed the Po
near Moncaliere, and advanced to the neighbourhood of
Chieri, in the vicinity of the capital, on the very day in
which the duke of Orleans with Marsin reached the lines
before Turin.

Never was an event more opportune than this junction ;
for the city was reduced to the utmost extremity. Every
means of attack and defence had been exhausted by both
parties during a contest of near twelve weeks, till the
resources possessed by the assailants, and the advantage
of numbers gained the superiority. The outworks, in
spite of a brave defence, were successively carried ; the
body of the place was assailed ; the provisions reduced,
the ammunition exhausted ; that part of the town which
was exposed to the enemy's batteries presented only a heap
of ruins ; and the brave garrison, worn out by incessant
exertions, were threatened with an assault without the
means of resistance.

The duke of Savoy and Eugene ascended the heights of
Superga *, above Chieri, which commands a view of
Turin and the circumjacent territory. They looked down
upon the vast circumference of intrenchments which invested the capital, and formed a circuit of thirty miles ;
and saw or heard the repeated signals of distress made
by the besieged. They watched, with a mixture of hope
and anxiety, the movements of the enemy, whom they

* Superga is a striking feature, as well in the history as the geo-
graphy of Savoy. On this spot, from whence Victor Amadeus and Eugene
surveyed the lines of the enemy, the former erected one of the most
splendid churches in Italy, in consequence of a vow which he made on
the occasion ; and, in memory of the relief of Turin, the royal family
were accustomed to go annually in procession, and return thanks in
this church for the almost miraculous deliverance of the capital. Few
strangers visit this part of Italy without repairing to this church, as
well on account of its historical importance, as the magnificent prospect
which it commands.

expected to quit their posts, concentrate their forces, and prepare for a contest in the open field, in which they could employ all the advantages derived from superior numbers. But the spirit of the French army seems to have subsided, and the effects of the victory at Ramilies were felt in Italy. The allies had the satisfaction to see them continue in their posts, and hailed their caution as the signal of victory. With that decision, promptitude, and energy which characterised the operations of Eugene, he selected as the point of attack that part of the lines which crossed the peninsula formed between the Doria and the Stura, where the two rivers at once secured his own flanks, and presented considerable obstacles to the movements of the enemy. On descending from the height, orders were instantly given for the march ; the allies crossed the Po near Moncagliere, intercepted a considerable convoy which the enemy were anxiously expecting from Susa, passed the Doria, reduced the castle of Pianessa, and extended themselves between the Doria and the Stura. Having collected a force of 10,000 militia to throw succours into the place, should the enemy quit or weaken any part of their lines, they made preparations for an immediate assault.

At sunrise, on the morning of September 7., the confederates advanced towards the intrenchments in several columns preceded by all the grenadiers in a body. When arrived within cannon-shot the infantry formed in two lines, with the artillery in the intervals between the battalions, and the cavalry in the same order behind, though exposed to a heavy cannonade. They then moved to the attack. The first line of the Prussian infantry on the right, commanded by the prince of Anhalt, made the assault against the left of the French, which was flanked by the Doria and the castle of Lucento. Being thrown into disorder by a sudden sally of the French cavalry, Eugene rushed forward to rally and lead them again to the charge. In the midst of the confusion he was thrown from his horse, and two domestics killed by his side ; but he instantly revived the courage of his soldiers, by rising and waving his hat as a sign that he had received no injury. He remounted, led on the troops, who derived new spirit from his escape, and forced the intrenchment. The prince of Wirtemberg, at the same time, carried the works on the side of the Stura, and opened a way for the cavalry; but his troops, impelled by their ardour, pursued the French far beyond the intrenchment, and would have been cut off, had not the regiment of Staremberg opportunely advanced from the second line, seized the abandoned artillery, and turned it on the enemy, who began to rally. The centre, led by the duke of Savoy, succeeded also in gaining the works, after a dreadful carnage, and opened a passage for the cavalry. The enemy, however, still disputed their ground with great bravery; their cavalry broke through the ranks of the allies, and attacked them in flank and rear, and, though repulsed, again rallied and renewed the fight. But nothing could withstand the impetuosity of the troops led by Eugene and the duke, who lavishly exposed their persons. The second line with the artillery being brought up, a more desperate engagement took place, and the French finally gave way; one body fled over the Doria, and there made a stand; a second attempted to gain the Po, but was intercepted by a sally from the city; and a third, which took refuge in the inclosures of the Old Park, between the mouths of the Doria and Stura, was driven into the Po.

Beyond the Doria, the troops in the trenches continued their fire against the city during the whole action, greatly annoying the garrison with their bombs; but, perceiving the day lost, they blew up their magazines, and retired with precipitation by Moncagliere. Marsin, being mortally wounded, and taken prisoner, died at Turin the day after the battle; the duke of Orleans was likewise wounded; 6000 men, among whom were several distinguished officers, were made prisoners, and 2000 killed. The allies lost only 1500.

The duke of Savoy and Eugene, having given the necessary orders for securing the magazines and encamping the troops, entered the capital amidst a vast concourse of people, and returned thanks to God in the cathedral. The last powder left in the place was spent in the rejoicing on this occasion.

Although only part of the French army was engaged, and their utmost loss in killed, wounded, and prisoners scarcely exceeded 9000 men, the death of Marsin, and the want of an experienced chief, produced all the fruits of a total defeat, and occasioned the overthrow of that power which seemed so firmly established in Italy. The French troops having retreated in confusion toward Pignerol, and abandoned those in the Milanese, the allies hastened to profit by their victory. The militia, supported by a regular force, followed the retreating army to the frontiers of Dauphiné, secured the passes of the Alps, and frustrated all their attempts to re-enter Piedmont ; while the towns, which were dismantled or weakly garrisoned, again raised the standard of their beloved sovereign. At the same time the duke and Eugene turned against the French corps under Medavi, who, on the 9th of September, two days after the battle of Turin, had defeated the prince of Hesse at Castiglione with the loss of 4000 men. They opened a passage into the Milanese by reducing Novarra, passed the Tesino, received the submission of Milan, and blockaded the French troops in the citadel. Being joined by the prince of Hesse, who, after his defeat crossed the Lower Adige and the Po, and penetrated through the Cremonese, they drove the corps of Medavi into the Mantuan, and before the close of the campaign, recovered many of the posts occupied by the French in Lombardy, confining the remnant of their forces to the citadels of Milan and Mantua, Finale, Valencia, Mirandola, Sabionetta, and Cremona. Eugene, who was nominated governor of the Milanese, received the allegiance of the natives in the name of their new sovereign ; Joseph invested his brother with the duchy as a fief of the empire, and yielded to the duke of Savoy the provinces of Valenza and Alessandria, the Lumellina, and the Val di Sesia, which had been promised as the price of his alliance.

During these transactions the affairs of the house of Austria had likewise prospered in Spain. After landing in Portugal, Charles published a manifesto or declaration of his rights, the king of Portugal a justification of his conduct ; and both monarchs, at the head of their army, advanced to the frontier. But, as it happens in all cases of civil contest, the emigrants deceived themselves as well as their protectors, and the conquest of Spain proved a far more arduous task than it had been represented by the admiral and his adherents. The army of Portugal was ill-

disciplined, inefficient, and ill-provided ; the succours
furnished by the allies too scanty to make a permanent
impression. Above all, none of the parties had appreciated
the effects of national and religious prejudice; the proud
and spirited Castilians, however dissatisfied with the administration of the French, were indignant at having a
sovereign forced on them by the Portuguese, whom they
detested, and by the English and Dutch whom they stigmatised as heretics. At this moment they were encouraged
by a succour of 12,000 men under the duke of Berwick,
and conciliated by the recall of the princess Orsini, and
the French agents, who had rendered themselves unpopular.
Won also by the bravery and exertions of Philip himself,
they rallied round their acknowledged sovereign, and,
instead of waiting for an attack, became themselves the
assailants. After a campaign, in which both parties respectively invaded each other's territories, though the
advantage remained on the side of the Spaniards, the two
armies retired into winter-quarters within their respective
frontiers.

While the united troops attacked the western provinces
of Spain, the English fleet, which had landed Charles at
Lisbon, after a fruitless attempt to surprise Barcelona,
joined a squadron under Sir Cloudesley Shovel, sailed in
search of the French fleet from Brest, and in their way
took Gibraltar by escalade. They next attacked the French
fleet off Malaga ; and though the honours of victory were
claimed by both parties, the allies gained the advantage,
for the French retired into their ports, and did not venture
another engagement during the whole war.

The campaign of 1705 was far more favourable to the
allies. A Spanish army, after wasting several months in
the siege of Gibraltar, was compelled to abandon the enterprise ; and a French squadron, which blocked up the
harbour, was defeated. Spain was attacked on both sides ;
the combined forces of the English and Portuguese, under
the earl of Galway and the marquis das Minas, bursting
from Beyra and Alentejo, opened the frontier by the capture of Valencia, Alcantara, Salvatierre, and Albuquerque :
while, on the opposite side, Barcelona was taken by
Charles, with the assistance of the British fleet and forces
under the earl of Peterborough ; Catalonia declared for the

house of Austria, and, with the exception of Alicante and Penisola, Arragon and Valencia followed the example.

These advantages enabled the allies to make a rapid progress in the ensuing campaign. Philip, after pressing Barcelona to the utmost extremities, was compelled by the arrival of an English fleet to raise the siege, and, with great difficulty, making a circuit through the mountains of Roussillon and Navarre, again reached his capital on the 9th of December, 1705. The death of Peter II., who had been affected with an hereditary melancholy, gave new vigour to the government of Portugal; and his son, John V., a prince of great spirit and abilities, supported the cause of Charles with redoubled vigour. England and Holland poured in reinforcements, and a grand project was formed to push the war at once from Catalonia and Portugal, secure the capital, and terminate the contest by a single effort. On one side the Portuguese forces, after reducing Alcantara, penetrated through the province of Salamanca to Madrid, driving before them the small army of Spain under marshal Berwick; on the other, the army of Charles, having relieved Barcelona, took the route of Arragon, which had revolted, and pushed a corps to the vicinity of the capital; and the queen-mother at Toledo endeavoured to excite the people of New Castile, by raising the standard of Austria. Nothing could have have prevented the establishment of Charles II. on the Spanish throne but the want of promptitude and decision among the allies, and his own uncertain and dilatory spirit. Whilst he wasted much time in forms and ceremonies at Saragossa, Galway, remaining inactive at Madrid, suffered Berwick to draw reinforcements from France, and Philip with his spirited queen, to rouse the zeal of the Castilian nobles. In consequence of this impolicy and these delays, the forces of Philip, who seemed on the point of being overwhelmed, again made head, recovered the capital, drove the Portuguese to their own frontier, and confined Charles with his English auxiliaries to Catalonia, Valencia, and Arragon. Notwithstanding, however, the failure of this grand enterprise, the allies maintained a footing on both sides of Spain, and possessed the means of renewing their invasion with a still greater prospect of success the ensuing campaign, when they expected reinforcements from Italy;

they also obtained some compensation for their losses on the continent by the acquisition of Yvica, Majorca, and part of Minorca, which had been reduced by the British squadrons under the domination of Charles.

CHAP. LXXIV.—1707.

THE pride of Louis being humbled by the disasters of the preceding campaigns, he attempted to divide the allies by offering separate terms of peace. To the Maritime Powers he made a private application soon after the battle of Ramilies, by means of the elector of Bavaria. He gave Charles the option of Spain, and the Indies, or the Italian territories ; proposed to yield a barrier in the Netherlands to the Dutch, to disavow the pretender, and grant great commercial privileges to both nations. These conditions, vague in themselves, and far from affording that security and compensation for which the allies had commenced the war, were scarcely deemed worthy of a discussion. Louis afterwards made a similar application to the emperor, by means of the pope, offering the cession of the Italian territories, with the islands in the Mediterranean ; but this proposal was rejected also with disdain.

These attempts, evidently intended to divide or amuse the allies, in some measure produced the desired effect. The emperor was apprehensive lest he, like his father, should be deserted by the Maritime Powers; and his alarms were increased by the clamours for peace at this time made by the Tory party in England.* The general

---

* It is not without extreme surprise, that we still find historians and writers affecting impartiality, and boasting of information, who revive the Tory clamour, that England in 1706, might have made a safe and honourable peace, and severely censure the conduct of Marlborough, and the Whig members of administration, for rejecting the terms offered by France. The slightest knowledge of parliamentary transactions will prove, that even if the offers of Louis had been sincere, England could not have deserted the house of Austria without a breach of the most solemn engagements. Without enlarging on this hacknied question, we trust that the narrative in the text, of the events during and since the thirty years' war, will convince the impartial reader, that it would have been no less contrary to sound policy than to good faith, as well as the principles of the Grand Alliance, if England

unanimity was likewise disturbed by disputes relative to the provisional government of the conquered Netherlands: the emperor being desirous to obtain the administration, while the Maritime Powers appropriated the revenues and supreme authority, under the appointment of a council composed of their partisans, who directed the affairs of state in the name of Charles. Besides these causes of disunion, which weakened the force of the Grand Alliance, and the presence of Charles XII., the embarrassments of the emperor were increased by the successful progress of Ragotsky and his partisans, who, rising with new vigour from their recent defeats, had acquired the preponderance in Transylvania, and again began to make a progress in Hungary.

Influenced by these motives, and dreading lest the allies should sacrifice Italy as the price of an accommodation, Joseph hastily, on the 13th of February, concluded with France a treaty of neutrality for Italy, by which the French and Spanish troops, amounting to 22,000 men, evacuated all the posts from which they had not been expelled at the close of the preceding campaign. This transaction created great dissatisfaction among the allies, particularly the Maritime Powers, who objected to the liberation of a force which must have been ultimately reduced to surrender at discretion ; and nothing but the prudence of Marlborough and the caution of Heinsius prevented, at least a division, if not the dissolution of the confederacy. After some discussions, the agreement was ratified on the 16th of March by the duke of Savoy, and the allies, though reluctantly, acquiesced in the transaction. The same motives, however, induced Joseph to turn his views to the reduction of Naples, which from the depressed situation of France, and the unpopularity of the new government, was likely to become an easy conquest.

Such were the views and dispositions of all parties at the opening of the campaign. As the French were driven from Italy, a grand project was now formed to penetrate into France from the Netherlands, and from Piedmont. On the side of the Netherlands the arrangement of the plan of operations was easily settled between the two Maritime

and Holland had deserted the common cause for the sake of the illusory advantages offered by Louis.

Powers; but in Italy the greatest difficulties arose from the discordant views and interests of the different parties. The emperor and the duke of Savoy proposed to invade Dauphiné or the Lyonnais; the Maritime Powers urged the advantage of penetrating through Provence, and terminating the war at a single stroke, by the reduction of Toulon, the seat of the French naval strength in the Mediterranean, the depository of immense magazines, stores, and artillery, and from its local situation, no less than from the dilapidated state of its works, incapable of making a long resistance. At length the perseverance of the Maritime Powers prevailed. The duke of Savoy was gained by considerable subsidies, by promises of territorial acquisition, and by the offer of commanding the expedition; while Joseph could not in prudence openly oppose the importunities of England and Holland, on whom he depended for support, though he yielded with a reluctance which marked his full disapprobation of the enterprise.

The magazines were to be formed by the duke of Savoy; the Maritime Powers placed the 25,000 German auxiliaries in their pay at his disposal; a combined fleet of forty sail was to co-operate with the land forces; and Eugene, with a corps of imperialists, was to join in the expedition. The most vigorous preparations and earnest representations were made, both by England and Holland, that the forces might be ready to act at an early period, as the success of the enterprise principally depended on anticipating the enemy. But continual obstacles to the expedition arose from the conduct of the emperor. Nothing could prevail on him to suspend his intended invasion of Naples, and two months were wasted in preparations for an enterprise which diminished the forces of the allies, without weakening those of the enemy. Still further obstacles were derived from the necessity of maintaining 10,000 men in Germany, to watch the king of Sweden, and of sending reinforcements against the rebels in Hungary; these diversions, besides retarding the junction of the troops, reduced the army of Eugene to 12,000 men. This ill-fated enterprise was still further delayed by a temporary illness of the duke of Savoy, by the difficulty of embarking the artillery and provisions, and finally by the disputes of the duke with the English admiral, relative to the payment of the stipulated subsidy.   An enterprise, begun under all these disadvantages, must have been directed against an enemy far less vigilant and active than France to prove successful.

Troops being left for the security of Piedmont, the army, amounting to 35,000 men, was put in motion, towards the latter end of June, and, after a feint on the side of Susa, scaled the Col di Tende, and advanced to Nice, while the combined fleet of forty-three sail and fifty-seven transports anchored before Finale.   Four ships of war, with a detachment of seamen and marines, having dislodged a body of the enemy from the intrenchments which they had formed on the bank of the Var, the allies crossed without loss, left a corps to secure the forts and their bridges, and pushed through the rugged country which borders the Mediterranean, without any other delay than waiting for their baggage and provisions.   They passed by Antibes, beyond the range of its artillery, and, after a march of eleven days, encamped near Toulon ; while the fleet anchored before the isles of Hieres.

They had the mortification to find the enemy in a state far different from their expectations.   The French court being secretly apprised of their object, had taken measures to frustrate the enterprise.   The fortress, which had been greatly neglected, was suddenly put in a state of defence ; the forage destroyed, or carried into the towns ; the passes of the Alps secured ; and marshal Tessé, to whom the command of the army was intrusted, distributed the troops in situations to cover the frontier and accelerate their junction at the point of attack.   On the first movement of the allies towards Provence, he hastened to anticipate their arrival before Toulon.   Besides a detachment under general Dillon, which had been sent too late to defend the passage of the Var, and had retreated before the allies, his troops marched day and night in scattered parties, or were conveyed in carriages.   The first who arrived intrenched themselves under the walls, on the western side, which the allies had not occupied, and the rest pouring in every hour, the whole army assembled within the space of ten days, and formed three intrenched camps, stretching north and west from the walls to the adjacent heights.   The nobles of the neighbouring provinces marched at the head of their servants and retainers into the city, coined their plate, and pawned

their jewels to pay the workmen employed on the fortifications. Besides the force thus assembled under the walls,
which was already superior to that of the allies, an army
was collecting under the duke of Burgundy, from the troops
destined for Catalonia, and the reinforcements drawn from
Flanders and the Rhine.

On the other hand, the allies were embarrassed by the
disunion among the commanders, arising from the jealousies
which actuated the courts of Vienna and Turin ; for
Eugene, instead of the alacrity which he had displayed on
other occasions, increased the indecision of the duke of
Savoy, by continually expatiating on the difficulties and
dangers of the enterprise.* After losing some days in
bringing up the artillery from the ships, batteries were
opened, the heights of St. Catherine carried, and the fleet
began to bombard the city. It was, however, too late.
The garrison or rather the army, defended the place with
vigour, sunk ships at the entrance of the harbour, kept
up an incessant fire from the ramparts, and made several
desperate sallies, in one of which they drove the allies
from the important post of St. Catherine, on the 29th of
July. The army under the duke of Burgundy began to
draw near ; the besiegers suffered severely from the scarcity, which was the effect of Tessé's precautions, and a
corps under Medavi at Touris, which was rapidly increasing, threatened to cut off their communications with Piedmont. In this situation they relinquished their ill-fated
expedition. They completed the reduction of Fort Louis,
re-embarked their artillery and ammunition ; and while
the fleet divided the attention of the enemy by a bombardment, commenced their retreat on the night of the 21st of
August. After a march of ten days they repassed the
Var, and on the 14th of September again traversed the
Col di Tende.† The French commander, who had closely

* This expedition is circumstantially described in the Memoirs of
the Duke of Marlborough

† Besides the causes above mentioned, Lamberty asserts, on the
authority of the duke of Savoy himself, that the siege was raised in
consequence of opposition from the emperor, who was alarmed by the
declaration of Charles XII., that he would invade the hereditary
countries, if Toulon was taken. A remark of Sir Cloudesley Shovel,
recorded by the late lord Walpole, proves that the British commander
was not sanguine in his hopes of success, from the disinclination of

followed their rear, without risking an action, threw garrisons into Nice and Villafranca, and resumed the same defensive dispositions which he had adopted at the opening of the campaign.

Thus terminated an expedition in which the allies lost 13,000 men, by sickness or desertion, the failure of which occasioned great discontents in England and Holland, where the most sanguine hopes had been entertained of success. It was attributed to various causes, each nation endeavouring to throw the blame on the other ; but it appears to have been principally derived from the jealousy of the different parties, the lukewarmness of the emperor, and the division of his troops for the conquest of Naples. The allies closed their unfortunate campaign on the 4th of October, by recovering Susa, which excluded the French from Piedmont, and opened a passage into Dauphiné. After this exploit the imperial troops retired into winter-quarters in the Ferrarese and Mantuan; the palatine forces marched to the sea to embark for Catalonia, and the Hessians took the route towards Germany.

The conquest of Naples, purchased with so dear a sacrifice, was effected without difficulty. Early in the spring Count Daun, the brave defender of Turin, marching at the head of 10,000 men, through the ecclesiastical state, awed the pope into compliance, notwithstanding his attachment to the house of Bourbon. Having received a train of artillery at Ancona, he burst into the kingdom of Naples, which he found defenceless, and, seconded by the affection of the people, to whom the viceroy had imprudently distributed arms, he entered the capital without a single skirmish. The prince of Castiglione, who had retired into Apuglia with a body of cavalry, the only force capable of resistance, surrendered ; on the 30th of September, the cities and strongholds followed the example of the capital, except Gaeta, which was taken by storm ; and, before the end of three months, the whole kingdom submitted to Charles.

On the side of the Rhine great precautions were taken

Eugene, at the commencement of the enterprise. " The duke of Savoy," he said, " is heartily and sincerely for the success of the undertaking, but the disposition of the prince is the reverse, and Toulon will not be taken."—Mem. of lord Walpole, p. 6.

to secure the empire by strengthening the lines of Stol-
hoffen. They were well furnished with artillery, and defended
by 20,000 men, a part of the German troops under the
margrave of Bareith, who had recently succeeded to the
command on the death of the margrave of Baden. But no
precautions could compensate for the deficiencies of the
contingents, which, from the threatening posture of
Charles XII., were retained by the elector of Saxony and
the neighbouring princes for the protection of their own
territories, instead of being sent to the Rhine. Villars,
the French commander, forced the lines with little difficulty, on the 23rd of May seized the magazines, and demolished the dikes and sluices which strengthened the
works. Advancing into the empire, he levied contributions, which the Germans tamely suffered to pass even
through their army, for fear of exposing their country to
devastation. Having left a corps of cavalry to secure the
lines on the Lauter, he followed the margrave, who successively retreated to Sforzheim, Heilbron, and Gemund,
after throwing garrisons into Friburgh, Landau, and Philipsburgh. He reduced the petty towns in his route, levied
heavy contributions, spread terror on every side, and pushed
his party beyond the Danube, even to the plain of Hoch-
stadt. He pressed Charles XII., who was then in Saxony,
to join him at Nuremberg, and renew the attacks which
had been so successfully made against the hereditary territories in the thirty years' war. But fortunately the Swedish
monarch, soothed by the conciliating conduct of Joseph,
declined his overtures, and the detachments which were
drawn from the army of Villars, for the relief of Toulon,
checked his career till the affairs of the empire were placed
in a more favourable situation.

As these reverses were attributed to the indolence and
advanced age of the margrave of Bareith, who was still
more inactive than his predecessor, Joseph sent his general
Heister to infuse spirit into the troops. He also took measures for securing the strong places of Bavaria, awing the
partisans of the elector. To draw the French forces from
Suabia and Franconia, the margrave, by his order, made a
rapid movement behind the mountains of Wirtemberg towards Mentz, joined the troops of Westphalia and other
circles, and by this march forced Villars to return to the

Rhine. As the junction of the contingents did not yet encourage the margrave to resume offensive operations, the emperor offered the command to George Augustus, duke of Hanover, with the hope of securing the assistance of his powerful family. With some difficulty, the resignation of the margrave was procured on the 15th September, and the duke joined the army; but from the lateness of the season, this change produced no important effect; for after a few skirmishes on both sides of the Rhine, the two armies retired into quarters; the French into Alsace, the Germans along the Rhine, the Maine, and the Neckar.

While the progress of the allies was suspended in the Netherlands, Germany, and Piedmont, the Austrian arms experienced a sad reverse in Spain. Louis was enabled, by the neutrality of Italy, to strengthen the army of Berwick with 16,000 men, and the duke of Orleans was appointed to the command. On the other hand, although auxiliary troops had been sent from England, the army of Charles was still inferior to that of the enemy. This heterogenous mass, composed of Germans, English, Dutch, Portuguese, and native Spaniards, all animated by national jealousy and religious antipathy, was commanded by officers who were influenced by a similar spirit. The two chiefs, Galway and Das Minas, were continually at variance, each aspiring to the superiority; the eccentric earl of Peterborough was disgusted with both; and general Stanhope, the British envoy, aggravated the disunion by his imperious temper. The court was still more the scene of intrigue than the army. The prince of Lichtenstein, formerly governor of Charles, and now the chief of his household, the duke of Moles, charged with the conduct of political affairs, and the count of Stella, the minister of his pleasures, shared the confidence of the young monarch. Though jealous of each other, they joined in excluding the native Spaniards from a share in the government; and Oropesa, the only person whose extensive connections and former services raised him above their power, voluntarily abandoned all share in the administration, under pretence of age and infirmity; but in reality to avoid giving countenance to the measures of foreigners, which he considered as hostile to the interests of his country.

Charles himself was ill calculated to restore strength and

union to his party. Though possessing personal courage
and literary acquirements, he was distant, formal, reserved,
and without energy of mind; a mere puppet in the hands
of those who had obtained his confidence; unable to adopt
a decisive line of conduct amidst a variety of jarring
opinions, and trifling away his time in frivolous pleasures,
and scientific pursuits. With a singular degree of infatuation, he commenced the construction of a palace on the
very ground which he was still contesting with a powerful
rival; and offended his brave and faithful Catalans by the
contributions which he levied for completing this monument of thoughtless extravagance.

By these divisions in the court and army, all the designs
of the allies were counteracted. The earl of Peterborough,
disgusted with being superseded in the command, quitted
the army under the pretence of a dispute relative to the
system of operations, and indignantly retired to Italy, from
whence he again sent his advice to remain on the defensive,
backed by the opinion of Eugene. Charles, with some of
his Spanish and German counsellors, was inclined to adopt
this advice; but was overruled by the representations of
the two commanders, Galway and Das Minas, who threatened the suspension of the British subsidy, if the system
suggested by Peterborough was pursued. Charles accordingly returned in disgust to Catalonia with two regiments,
under pretence of securing that province, and left the commanders with an army of 26,000 men to execute their own
plans of operation.

The confederate generals, thus freed from control, collected their troops, and pushed on to the frontiers of Mercia,
with the hope of crushing in detail the forces of Berwick,
who were quartered along the frontiers of Arragon and
Valencia. The duke retreating, they pressed forward to
Almanza; but as he contrived to detain them till he could
concentrate his troops, by throwing garrisons into Chin-
chilla and Villena, they soon found themselves threatened
by a superior force. Confiding, however, in the courage
and ardour of their soldiers, they risked an engagement,
and gained considerable advantage, till the Portuguese
cavalry, which formed their right wing, gave way, leaving
the infantry exposed, and by this disgraceful flight involved
the allies in a defeat almost as fatal as that of Blenheim to

the French. Five thousand were slain, eight thousand English and Dutch surrendered after the battle, and the two commanders were desperately wounded. Galway taking refuge under the walls of Tortosa, was only able to collect 5000 men. The duke of Orleans joined the victorious army the following day, and completed the success which had been begun by the skill of Berwick. The loyalty of the Castilians was roused to enthusiasm by the birth of a son to Philip, and they redoubled their efforts to support a native prince. Valencia and Arragon were recovered, deprived of their privileges, and rendered dependencies on Castile; Lerida, with the contiguous district of Catalonia, was subdued; and Charles was excluded from all his conquests in Spain, except a part of Catalonia, with the towns of Alicante and Denia. To complete this series of disasters, Cuidad Rodrigo was retaken, and Alcantara reduced by the Spanish forces. The dread of an invasion of Portugal induced Galway and Das Minas to embark for Lisbon with the forces under their command; and the defence of Catalonia was left to the discouraged remnant of British and Dutch auxiliaries.*

CHAP. LXXV.— 1708.

THE disasters of the Austrian arms in Spain, the failure of the enterprise against Toulon, and the inactivity of the allies in the Netherlands, were the fatal effects derived no less from a want of concert and union, than from the suspense and anxiety which the presence of Charles XII. created in every member of the Grand Alliance. Fortunately the mutual confidence of the allies was restored by the firmness with which the Maritime Powers rejected the offers of peace; and the possession of Naples quieted the apprehensions and allayed the jealousy of the emperor. They all cordially united in conciliating Charles XII.; before the opening of the last campaign, Marlborough himself repairing to Ranstadt in April, 1707, used the influence

* For an account of the battle of Almanza, and its fatal consequences, see the Memoirs of the Bourbon Kings of Spain, chapter xv.

which a general of his talents and fame naturally possessed
over a monarch whose whole soul was absorbed in military
glory ; and Joseph himself omitted no sacrifice to soothe so
terrible an enemy. He delivered up the chamberlain who
had insulted the Swedish envoy, confirmed the family compact which nominated six successive princes of Holstein
Gottorp to the bishopric of Lubec, exempted Bremen and
Pomerania from furnishing their contingents during the
Spanish war, agreed to re-establish the Lutheran worship
in Silesia, and even permitted six new churches to be built
for the inhabitants of that persuasion. By these concessions he delivered his hereditary territories from invasion,
and the empire from a civil war ; and Charles quitted Germany to indulge his vindictive spirit against Russia, with
the hope of dethroning Peter, as he had dethroned Augustus.

A change equally favourable to the house of Austria
took place in England, where the Tories, who had been
secretly favoured by the queen, and had thwarted the operations of the war, were excluded from power, by the dismission of Harley their leader, and the re-establishment of
the Whigs in the principal departments of state. Marlborough and Godolphin, whose disgrace had been triumphantly
announced, rose from their temporary depression, and employed the resources of the country with redoubled vigour.
An additional impulse was given to the national spirit by
an attempt of the French court to land the Pretender in
Scotland, where the number of his partisans was augmented by the discontents arising from the recent union
with England. This expedition, though frustrated by the
vigilance of the English fleet, stimulated the public resentment against France, and by contributing to render the
Tories still more unpopular, strengthened the power of the
Whigs, and increased the influence of the Austrian party.

Joseph availed himself of these favourable circumstances
to make amends for his remissness during the preceding
campaign ; and, although the war still raged in Hungary,
prepared to furnish all the assistance which his exhausted
resources and numerous embarrassments would permit, to
co-operate with the Maritime Powers against the common
enemy. By his orders Eugene visited the different courts
of the empire, to call forth the exertions of the German

princes. He prevailed on Augustus of Saxony to lead his
own contingent to the army ; and by offering to the elector
Palatine the restoration of his paternal honours and dominions, which had been transferred to the Bavarian house,
obtained his promise to employ his whole force in the common cause. Eugene then repaired to the Hague, to settle
with Marlborough and the States the arrangements for the
campaign. He opened a conference held on this subject
with a pathetic detail of the injuries sustained by the imperial house ; apologised for the recent failures, by describing the difficulties of his sovereign, and announced his
resolution, by new exertions, to make ample amends for
former deficiencies. He concluded with presenting a plan
of operations. He was himself to act on the Moselle, with
a separate army of 10,000 imperialists, and 14,000 Palatine, Hessian, and Saxon auxiliaries ; while Marlborough
pursued his system of attack in the Netherlands, and
powerful reinforcements were to be sent to Spain and the
Rhine. He announced his hope that the formidable power
of the Gallic monarchy would be speedily reduced, and the
kingdom of Spain, with its dependencies, restored to the
house of Austria, in the person of Charles the lawful sovereign. He was seconded by Marlborough, who declared
the approbation of the queen, and readily obtained the
acquiescence of the States.

This plan, however, like that of Marlborough before his
memorable march to the Danube, was only an ostensible
project to deceive the enemy ; for by a secret agreement
between the two great generals, Eugene, after collecting his
troops on the Moselle, was suddenly to join the allied army
in the Netherlands, and assist in striking a decisive blow
before the enemy could draw a proportionate reinforcement
from the Rhine. The arrangements for this march being
settled, Eugene and Marlborough repaired to Hanover, and
obtained from the elector, who was to command the German
army, his consent to remain on the defensive. Marlborough then returned to the Hague; and Eugene, after
visiting Vienna to receive the last instructions of the emperor, took the route to the Rhine. Early in June he began
to assemble the auxiliaries ; and would have fulfilled the
concerted plan, had not the elector Palatine delayed the
march of the troops, by refusing his co-operation, till he

was formally invested with the fifth electorate and the Upper Palatinate.

During this unfortunate delay the campaign opened in the Low Countries with a sinister aspect. To oppose the meditated attacks of the allies, exertions no less strenuous had been made by France. The elector of Bavaria with Berwick was sent to the Upper Rhine, to watch the motions of the German army; Villars was despatched to Languedoc and Dauphiné, to oppose the duke of Savoy, and quell the disturbances which still reigned among the Protestants in the Cevennes; and in the Netherlands, whither the court purposed to turn the principal force of the war, every effort was made to collect a powerful army, which was to be commanded by the duke of Burgundy, the favourite grandson of Louis, who was assisted by the counsels of the enterprising Vendome.

In May the troops on both sides assembled, the allies to the number of 70.000 men, under Marlborough and the Dutch general Overkirk, near Brussels; the French, to the amount of 80,000, near Mons; and both parties drained the neighbouring garrisons to augment their strength. The duke of Burgundy had no sooner reached the scene of action than the two armies advanced towards Soignies, as if inclined to open the campaign with an engagement. But the French commanders, who had secured agents to facilitate the surprise of the principal towns of Flanders, made a sudden march through Neville to Braine l'Allieu, and thus drew Marlborough to the neighbourhood of Louvain. Having thus diverted the attention of the British general from the quarter of their intended enterprise, the enemy suddenly decamped on the evening of the 4th of July, detached several corps towards the places where they had established a secret correspondence, and rapidly moved to Tubise and Halle, where they purposed to cross the Senne.

One of these parties appeared before Ghent at the dawn of the 5th of July, and having by stratagem secured one of the gates, readily obtained the submission of the place, and blockaded a garrison of 300 men in the citadel; a second was equally successful at Bruges; and after a fruitless attempt to surprise Damme, took the small but important post of Plassendael, on the canal of Bruges, by storm.

Receiving intelligence of the sudden movement of the enemy towards the Dender, Marlborough broke up from the neighbourhood of Louvaine on the morning of the 5th, and crossing the Senne and the canal of Brussels, encamped between Anderlecht and the mill of Tombeck. From hence he sent a body of cavalry under general Bothmar, with orders to cross the Scheldt near Termond, and if possible to counteract the designs of the enemy on the towns in Flanders.

As the French were then traversing the Senne within a short distance of his camp, he hoped to bring them to an engagement before they could reach the Dender. He therefore sent out a detachment to harass them in their march, and prepared to move at the dawn. The promptitude of the enemy, however, baffled his design. They effected the passage of the Dender with the loss of part of their baggage and 300 prisoners, and descending the stream, took post between Alost and Oerdegem, with a view of threatening Brussels, and covering the attack against the citadel of Ghent. Marlborough accordingly advanced to Asch on the evening of the 6th, to dispel the alarm which reigned among the inhabitants of that large and opulent capital.

Here he was cheered by the arrival of Eugene, who, finding it impossible to effect a junction with his own troops, hastened from Maestricht to take a personal share in the expected conflict.

At this crisis the citadel of Ghent surrendered, and the enemy prepared to accomplish their ultimate designs, by the reduction of Oudenard, the key of Flanders, the chief avenue to the other fortresses of the allies in that province, and the only channel of communication with the coast. The place was invested on the morning of the 9th, a train of heavy artillery ordered from Tourney, and to cover the siege, they prepared to occupy the strong camp of Lessines on the Dender.

But they were exposed to a general whose resources were inexhaustible, and whose promptitude and activity were seldom paralleled. Though suffering under bodily indisposition, the vigorous mind of Marlborough was unimpaired, and he hastened to anticipate their design. The roads being previously cleared, the allied army again broke

up at two in the morning of the 9th, and while they halted
a few hours at Herfelingen, general Cadogan, with eight
battalions and as many squadrons, was sent forward to
throw bridges over the Dender, and take post at Lessines.
He effected his object at midnight, and in the morning the
whole army, which had resumed its march at the evening
tattoo, was posted beyond the Dender. The enemy, little
expecting that their able antagonist would traverse twice
the distance in the same space of time, were rapidly approaching the spot; but perceiving the allies in position,
they turned to the right, and hastened towards Gavre, with
the hope of covering themselves behind the line of the
Scheld. This disappointment aggravated the disputes
which already reigned betwen the duke of Burgundy and
Vendome, and destroyed that unity of action and counsel,
which were indispensable in so delicate and critical a
situation.

During the night of the 10th Marlborough and Eugene
prepared for an immediate engagement; although they
had yet a space of fifteen miles to traverse, and a rapid
stream to cross, before they could come in contact with the
enemy. As before, a strong detachment, with thirty-two
pieces of artillery, were sent forward under the command
of Cadogan and Rantzue, with orders to clear the roads
and throw bridges over the Scheld, in the vicinity of
Oudenard. Departing at the dawn of the 11th, the detachment was followed at eight by the whole army, in four
columns, the cavalry leading the march, and the artillery
in the rear.

About ten in the morning the allied detachment reached
the Scheld, between the town and abbey of Eename, and
commenced the construction of the bridges. The enemy
at the same moment had begun the passage of the river at
Gavre, two leagues below, and so little suspected the approach of the allies, that their advanced guard, under the
marquis de Biron, drew towards Eyne and Ruybrock, and
began to disperse for forage.

In the interim the allied detachment had completed their
bridges; and as the leading columns of the main body were
approaching, they passed the river, left four battalions to
guard the pontoons, and took post with the remainder on the
high ground between Eyne and Bevere. Discovering the

foraging parties of the enemy, Cadogan pushed forward the cavalry, who attacked and drove them towards Lynnghem, making several prisoners. The assailants were, however, repulsed in their turn by Biron; but perceiving the allied detachment in position, and the columns of cavalry crossing the river, he withdrew from a fear of being overwhelmed by superior force. Indeed his apprehensions were not without foundation, for the two confederate generals hearing that the enemy were passing at Gavre, were alarmed for the safety of their detachment, and hastening forward at full gallop, with the second column of cavalry, reached the bridges at the moment of the skirmish.

The appearance of the allies created a general sensation throughout the French ranks; but Vendome conceiving that the main body was still too far distant to form, before he could mature his preparations for an attack, directed seven battalions to occupy the village of Heurne, and part of the cavalry of the right to draw up near the windmill. Under cover of this disposition, he intended to place his left in the plain of Heurne, and extend his right across the Boxer Couter towards Mooreghem. This arrangement was, however, countermanded by the duke of Burgundy, who conceived that the high ground of Huyse, with the Norken in front, would afford a more eligible position. In the midst of the indecision created by this evolution, the seven battalions, instead of occuping Heurne, advanced and took post at Eyne, where they were placed beyond the reach of protection by the change in the direction of the main body.

Meanwhile the allied commanders hastened the march of their columns, superintended the passage of the Scheld, and posted the troops as they arrived. About two the second column of cavalry was placed in front of Bevere, and a battery of six pieces planted on the hill above Schaerken; at three, the first column of cavalry filed through Oudenard, and the infantry of the right reached the bridges. The four battalions hitherto posted to guard them joined the advance, and the first blow was struck by an attack on the insulated brigade in the village of Eyne, who were speedily broken, and three entire battalions made prisoners. A small body of cavalry left for their support were next charged, routed, and driven across the Norken, among the columns of their own army, who were forming on the other side.

The French commanders now perceived that it was impossible to retire without an engagement, and active preparations were made to repel the impending attack, by placing the army on the high ground of Lede, Huyse, and Maldeghem in two lines, with a reserve. The greater part of the cavalry was posted on the right, opposite Oyke ; the left extended to behind Mullem ; and the front was covered by the Norken and the defiles along its banks.

The same perplexity and want of concert which had marked all the preceding operations of the French commanders, prevailed also at this important crisis. By the direction of the duke of Burgundy, sixteen squadrons under general Grimaldi crossed the Norken, for the purpose of ascertaining whether the right wing could advance, and occupy the space between the two rivulets at Diepenback and Chobou ; but observing the Prussian cavalry already formed, and the British advancing, they fell back to the small plain near the mill of Royeghem. Vendome directed his left to advance at the same moment, with the view of bringing both wings into action together ; but the duke of Burgundy again countermanded the order, under pretence that an impassable morass separated the two armies on that side ; and another invaluable hour was thus lost in useless manœuvres.

These movements did not escape the attention of Marlborough. To repel the attack which appeared to be menaced on his right, he pushed forward the infantry of Cadogan's detachment into the hedges of Groenvelde, and advancing himself by Heurne with the Prussian horse, drew them up in front of the enemy. At the same time the first line of the right wing was rapidly formed on the heights of Bevere.

At this moment thirty battalions of the enemy's right debouched from the defiles in their front, and after some hesitation attacked the troops posted in the hedges of Groenvelde. A vigorous conflict ensued, and the duke of Argyle, who led the British infantry, hastened with twenty battalions and a few pieces of cannon to the assistance of the forces engaged. Still, however, the remainder of the enemy's right, following the direction of their companions gradually prolonged the line till they outflanked some Prussian cavalry on the left of the British; and driving them back, occupied Barwaen and the farm of Banlancy. They were, however, attacked in their turn by count Lottum, with the second column of infantry, who recovered the lost ground, and drove them across the rivulet.

Marlborough and Eugene, who had hitherto remained together, now separated, and Eugene repaired to the right to assume the command of that wing, comprising the British troops. Foreseeing that the stress of the action would lie on this quarter, Marlborough ordered count Lottum with twenty battalions to prolong his own right, and strengthen the wing under Eugene. The opening which this movement occasioned between the castle of Bevere and Schaerken was filled up by eighteen battalions from the right of the left wing, who had formed across the Boxer Couter, with the left in front of Mooreghem.

In the interval the corps of Cadogan had been driven from the coverts and avenues near Herlehem into the plain; but Eugene advancing with this new accession of strength, broke the first line of the enemy, and general Natzmer, with the Prussian gens d'armes and cuirassiers, charged through the second, into the small plain near the chapel of Royeghem. But his career being checked by the household troops, and his ranks thinned by the fire of musketry which flashed from every hedge, he lost half his men, and escaped himself with the utmost difficulty.

While the action thus raged on the right, Marlborough, with the Hanoverian and Dutch battalions, had pressed forward, driving the enemy from inclosure to inclosure, till he reached the hamlet of Diepenbeck. From hence he discovered that the enemy had neglected to occupy the commanding ground above the mill at Oyke, which seemed to afford an opportunity of turning their right and cutting it from the main body. He therefore requested marshal Overkirk, who had brought up the rear, with nearly all the cavalry of the left, and twenty battalions of Dutch and Danes, to execute this bold and decisive manœuvre; and the veteran hero performed this his last effort in the field with a spirit worthy of his early days. His troops having deployed, two brigades forced the ravines near the castle of Bevere; and the prince Oxenstiern immediately ascended the hill of Oyke with the remainder of the twenty battalions sustained by the cavalry. The whole mass changing front to the right, extended their left towards the Keele; and the prince of Orange, sustained by thirteen squadrons, rushed with the infantry down the height overlooking Marollen, penetrated through the defiles, dislodged a corps of French grenadiers from the hedges which skirted the extremity of the plain, and cut to pieces the greater part of the cavalry posted to sustain them.

Amidst these multiplied attacks, the enemy slackened in their resistance, and Marlborough still gaining ground, established his line between Chobon and Diepenbeck. Vendome indeed made an effort to avert the fate of his troops by leading his infantry near Mullem, to the rescue of their companions; but this body, inferior in numbers, subdued in spirit, and entangled by the intricacy of the ground, could make no impression. Darkness now enveloped the contending hosts, and the peals of musketry continued to roll round the narrowing circle of the devoted army, till the right of Eugene and the left of the prince of Orange approached the same point. They mistook each other for enemies, and a mutual carnage would have ensued, had not the commanders made prompt and effectual endeavours to stop the firing and halt the troops as they stood. To this measure many of the enemy owed their safety. Favoured by the obscurity, numbers slipped through an opening near the castle of Bevere, and fled towards the French frontier; some endeavoured to join their left wing in the direction of Mullem, and others wandering to the allied posts, were made prisoners.

Vendome perceiving the destruction of his right wing inevitable, retired with the infantry, which was still posted on the bank of the Norken, and joined the left at Huyse and St. Denast. He urged the duke of Burgundy and a crowd of panic-struck generals to take advantage of the night, and restore order; but finding his arguments nugatory, he gave the word for a retreat, and generals and privates, horse and foot, instantly hurried in the utmost disorder towards Ghent. With difficulty he persuaded twenty-five squadrons and some battalions to remain united, and with this body he covered the flight of the crowd, and repulsed the attack of an allied detachment, who were sent in pursuit the ensuing morning. At Ghent he overruled the timid counsels of the prince, who proposed to retire into France, and took post on the canal leading from Ghent to Bruges, at once to secure his recent conquests, and prevent the allies from attacking the fortresses of the Scheld or the Lys.

This victory was purchased with the loss of 3000 men on the part of the confederates, while that of the French amounted to above 15,000 in killed, wounded, and prisoners.

Distraction, mistrust, and consternation pervaded every rank of the French army ; the jealousies of the commanders were increased by ill success, the fortresses, drained of troops, seemed likely to fall an easy conquest, and an ill-defended barrier presented a feeble obstacle to the progress of the victorious army. But in this critical emergency the danger was suspended by marshal Berwick, who, following the imperialists from the Moselle, had reached the Sambre the day after the defeat of the main army. He exerted himself with uncommon activity to secure the frontier, collected the fugitives who had fled to Courtray, threw garrisons into Lille, Tournay, and the fortresses more immediately exposed to an attack, and took post with the remainder of his troops in the vicinity of Douay.

Such was the situation of the contending parties before the siege of Lille, the first and fairest of all the French conquests on the side of the Netherlands, a place on which Vauban had exhausted his skill, garrisoned by above 13,000 men, and commanded by marshal Boufflers, an officer distinguished for experience, courage, and perseverance. As the allies had now a strong though discomfited army in their rear, and a force gradually increasing in front, the design was considered as desperate both by friends and enemies ; and Vendome derided their attempts to form a siege while he was master of a post which enabled him to interrupt their supplies. But the fertile genius of Eugene and Marlborough overcame obstacles apparently insuperable. Only two days after the battle, the lines which the French had thrown up between Warneton and Ypres were razed, the army crossed the Lys, and detachments occupied the posts of Lens and La Basée. Troops were likewise sent to Oudenard and Rousselaer to cut off the supplies which the enemy drew from Tournay and Ypres, and an inundation was formed by the governor of Ostend, to deprive them of their communication along the coast. As the French, by the possession of Ghent, were masters of the principal canals and rivers, a more circuitous communication was opened through Brussels. The train of battering artillery, with all the requisites for a long siege, which had been conveyed by sea to Saas van Ghent and Antwerp, was transported to Brussels, and another drawn from Maestricht. This important convoy was protected in its march by the army of Eugene, passed the Scheld between Oudenard and Tournay, and reached the confederate camp in safety, notwithstanding the difficulties of the transport and the vicinity of the enemy. Lille was instantly invested; Eugene, with 30,000 men, carried on the siege, while Marlborough, with the main army, covered his operations.

The Duke of Burgundy and Vendome, leaving La Motte with 8000 men to maintain the post at Ghent, united with the troops of Berwick at Ninove, crossed the Scheld at Tournay, and moved towards the source of the Marque, with a view to break through the lines of circumvallation. As Marlborough followed their movements, and took a strong position between the Deule and the Marque, they opened roads through the defiles which separated the two armies, drew a train of heavy artillery from Douay, and made preparations to risk an engagement for the relief of the place. But the allies having no less actively employed the interval in strengthening their position, all the attempts of the enemy terminated in the attack of an outpost and a fruitless cannonade. Foiled in this design, they re-crossed the Scheld, extended themselves along its bank from Berken to Saulsoy, and threw up intrenchments before Oudenard, while La Motte advanced from Ghent to surprise Brussels, which was thus insulated from the main army.

These projects did not escape the vigilance of Marlborough. He ordered troops from the Dutch garrisons in Flanders to succour Brussels, sent a strong corps to Oudenard, and took post between Seers and Forêt, on the Marque. To open a new channel of communication for the supplies, he caused a corps, which had been assembled in England for alarming the coast of France to land at Ostend, and occupy Leffingen, a post commanding the passage of the canal from Bruges to Nieuport.

During these movements the siege was pushed by Eugene with great vigour and perseverance. The besiegers effected a lodgment on the outworks, though with considerable loss, and Eugene, who exposed himself like a common soldier in rallying and leading the troops to the assault, received a contusion in the head from a musket ball. Happily it was not dangerous, though it prevented him from directing the attacks a few days, during which the conduct of the siege, with the command of the army, devolved on Marlborough.

Meanwhile the vigilance and vicinity of the enemy reduced the allies to great distress for want of ammunition and supplies; and all the attention of both armies was called forth, one to prevent, the other to secure, the passage of a considerable convoy from Ostend. Detachments to the number of 8000 men were drawn from the main army to cover the road between Ostend and the camp, and Marlborough himself advanced with a corps to Rousselaer; the troops at Leffingen drained the inundations, occupied Oudenburg, formed a bridge over the canal, and the convoy began its march. On the other hand, La Motte, with a force augmented to 24,000 men, after attempting in vain to secure Oudenburg, pushed towards Tourout to intercept the convoy, on the 28th of September. He was opposed by general Webb, who, though at the head of scarcely 6000 men, posted his small corps with such skill in a defile between the wood of Wynendale and the castle of Tourout, and defended himself with such intrepidity, that the French commander abandoned the contest with equal loss and disgrace. During the action the convoy passed in safety behind the wood, and reached the place of destination.

The failure of this enterprise, with the increasing distresses of the besieged, induced the French commanders to redouble their efforts for cutting off the communication of the allies with Ostend, as they had already closed the way to Brussels. Vendome himself repaired to Bruges, assembled 30,000 men, took post on the canal between Plassendael and Nieuport, and broke the dikes to inundate the country. But Marlborough, leaving 12,000 men in his camp at Roncques, advanced with 50,000 as far as Wynendale, and compelled him to fall back behind the canal of Bruges.

From this time Marlborough kept the principal part of his force between Rousselaer and the Lys, occasionally pushing corps towards Ostend to cover the passage of the stores, which were conveyed in boats over the inundation ; and, notwithstanding all the difficulties of the transport, forwarded a constant supply of provisions and ammunition to the besieging army. As a last resource, Vendome commenced a regular attack against Leffingen, which had so greatly favoured the passage of the convoys, and gained possession of the place after a siege of eight days. But before he could complete its reduction the town of Lille surrendered. The besiegers, having pushed their works to the covered way, opened breaches in the body of the place, and made preparations for an assault, the governor agreed, on the 22d of October, to a capitulation, which Eugene generously allowed him to dictate, and retired with 5500 men into the citadel. A garrison of 7000 was sent into the town by Eugene ; after a short cessation of arms, hostilities were recommenced, and the trenches opened against the citadel on the 29th.

The French exerted themselves with unabated perseverance to maintain the advantage which they had gained by the capture of Leffingen. Having thus cut off the only communication with Ostend, and established themselves on the canal of Bruges, they strengthened their position on the Scheld, by augmenting their works, and forming inundations above and below Oudenard. Their ministers and agents confidently asserted, that the allies would ultimately be forced to abandon an object for which they had made such long and arduous exertions, and their officers even boasted that the want of necessaries would force the army to surrender. To hasten a triumph so fondly anticipated, a plan was arranged for reducing Brussels. The elector of Bavaria, marching from the Rhine with 15,000 men, commenced a formal attack against the place, hoping that his presence would encourage his partisans to declare in his favour, as his influence had delivered Ghent and Bruges into the hands of the French at the opening of the campaign.

The vigilance, activity, and resources of the allied generals increased with the difficulties of their situation. The enemy had no sooner begun to collect troops for the expedition of the elector, than reinforcements from Ostend secured Antwerp, and the governor of Brussels was encouraged with the promise of immediate support. Preparations being previously made for forcing the passage of the Scheld, the object of the elector's attack was no sooner known, than the army was put in motion; the baggage was sent to Oudenard. the troops of Marlborough crossed the Lys, and Eugene advanced from the trenches before Lille with 15,000 men. Favoured by a thick fog they, on the 27th of November, unexpectedly attacked the enemy in three points, at Elseghem, Escanaffe, and Gaveren, drove them from their position, and harassed them in their retreat towards Ghent and Tournay. After this brilliant action, Eugene returned to press the siege of Lille, and Marlborough continuing to advance, forced the elector, who had opened trenches against Brussels, to retire, with the loss of his artillery and ammunition. Marlborough returned towards the Scheld, to protect the march of the convoys from Brussels, and Eugene resuming the siege, was reinforced by the corps which had been sent to La Bassée. But although he effected a lodgement on the second counterscarp, and although the defeat of the French army on the Scheld annihilated all hopes of relief, the brave governor held out till the 7th of December, when a total want of ammunition compelled him to yield; and his garrison quitted the ramparts, which they had so intrepidly defended, with the honours of war.

On the surrender of the citadel, the French commanders deeming the season too far advanced for any further operation, distributed their troops into quarters. But Eugene and Marlborough closed this glorious campaign on the 30th of December, with the reduction of Ghent, after an investment of only three days; Bruges and Plassendael were instantly abandoned by the enemy. Having thus recovered posts which were necessary, as well to maintain their conquests as to support their future operations, they distributed their troops in quarters along the Scheld and the Meuse.

The diet of the empire commenced the year with the most vigorous resolutions for bringing a powerful army into the field at an early period; but these resolutions, though supported by threats of military execution and the admonitions of the emperor, did not stimulate the indolence or quiet the jealousies of the German princes, and their exertions were made with the usual tardiness and reluctance. In consequence of the detachments respectively drawn by the French and allies to the Low Countries, the whole campaign was spent in almost total inaction.

On the side of Italy, the duke of Savoy, at the head of his own troops and the auxiliaries, was baffled in all his attempts to penetrate into Dauphiné by the vigilance and promptitude of Villars; but he compensated for this disappointment, by capturing, in face of the French army, the posts of Exilles, Fenestrelles, and Perouse, which secured the avenues into Piedmont.

Hitherto the war in Spain had been principally maintained by the Maritime Powers, the Portuguese, and the Spanish adherents of Charles; but in this campaign, Joseph, in conformity with his promise, took a more efficient part, by sending a corps of Germans, under Staremberg. Yet notwithstanding this accession of force, and the arrival of the auxiliary Hessians from Italy, the allies were unable to make head against the enemy, abandoned Denia Tortosa and the town of Alicante, and with difficulty preserved their footing in Catalonia. But the reduction of Sardinia and Minorca, by the English forces, maintained the honour of their arms in this quarter of Europe, and completed the conquest of all the Spanish islands in the Mediterranean, except Sicily and the isle of Elba.

The French being driven from Germany and Italy, Joseph had the means as well as the opportunity of restoring the imperial authority to a portion of its former splendour, by rewarding his adherents, and punishing the princes who had leagued with his enemies. By a decree of the Aulic Council, published at Vienna with the accustomed formalities, Joseph had deprived the electors of Cologne and Bavaria of all their dignities and possessions, and set a price on the head of the elector of Bavaria; but he had been prevented from carrying this sentence into execution by the remonstrances of the king of Sweden and the German princes, who opposed this act of authority, as contrary to his capitulation. The departure, however, of Charles from Germany, and the successful events of the campaign enabled the emperor to overrule all opposition. A law of proscription was published in the diet, and Joseph formally invested, on the 21st of July, 1708, the elector palatine with the fifth electorate, and the office of cup-bearer. He also obtained the unanimous consent of the states to restore Bohemia to all its electoral rights and franchises. He at the same time reconciled the Catholics to the erection of the new electorate, in favour of a Protestant family, by agreeing that if the palatine electorate should devolve on a Protestant, the Catholics should still retain the same number of voices in the college, and he thus procured the assent of the diet to the grant made by his father to the house of Hanover.

Joseph extended his dominions and influence in Italy, by executing the ban against the dukes of Mantua and Mirandola. He appropriated Mantua, granted the Montferrat to the duke of Savoy, and conferred on the house of Guastalla, who had claimed the succession on the death of the proscribed duke, the petty districts of Sabionetta and Bozzolo. He likewise confiscated Mirandola, and transferred it by sale to the duke of Modena.

The humiliation of the pope was another consequence of his ascendency in Italy.

Clement XI., of the illustrious house of Albani, who had been raised to the papacy by the influence of France, had, under an affected neutrality, displayed an evident partiality towards the house of Bourbon, during the whole contest for the Spanish succession. By this partiality, as well as by his refusal to acknowledge Charles, he had offended the emperor, and he accelerated a breach by a continued series of petty provocations. The arrest of a Roman gentleman, attached to the imperial embassy, for striking the officers of justice, occasioned an acrimonious discussion, which ended in the abrupt departure of the ambassador from Rome, and the dismission of the nuntio from Vienna. While reparation was demanded for this insult, Clement again exposed his own weakness, by contesting the right of first petition * in the empire, and by prohibiting the chapter of Hildesheim from admitting a

---

* The right of first petition is similar to the option of archbishops of Canterbury and York, on the consecration of each bishop in their respective jurisdictions.

canon recommended by Joseph. Neither the failure of these attempts, nor the preponderance of the imperial arms in Italy, deterred Clement from continuing his impotent opposition against the head of the empire. As the German troops had spread themselves over the ecclesiastical state, committing great irregularities, had levied contributions on the clergy in the duchy of Parma, and extorted a considerable sum from the duke as a compensation for exemption from quarters, the pope annulled this agreement, and issued a bull of excommunication against those who collected these contributions. The imperial agents at Rome, having published circular letters against the ecclesiastical censures, and asserted the feudal superiority of the emperor over all the cities of Italy, the anger of Clement was roused almost to frenzy by this contempt of his authority. Incited by the representations of marshal Tessé, the French minister, and encouraged by the promises of support from the house of Bourbon, he endeavoured to revive the religious leagues. He accordingly obtained contributions from the cardinals, opened the treasures deposited in the castle of St. Angelo, made preparations for war, and imitated the example of his martial predecessor Julius II., by reviewing the troops in person. Flattering himself that his menaces and threatening posture would awe the emperor, he announced his purposes in an admonitory letter written with the usual arrogance of the papal court, in the time of its uncontested supremacy.

But the time of anathemas was past. Joseph equally despising the spiritual and temporal arms of the church, annulled the bull, confiscated the papal revenues in the Milanese and Naples, and cardinal Grimaldi, the imperial viceroy, not only declared that kingdom independent, but even claimed Benevento and Avignon. At the same time count Daun dissipated the tumultuary bands of the church, captured Commacchio, besieged Ferrara, and advanced to Bologna, while a corps from Naples threatened the frontier, and a squadron of the Maritime Powers blockaded the ports of the ecclesiastical state.

Although no succour arrived from France or Spain, and not a single state of Italy ventured to arm in his favour, Clement still maintained his impolitic firmness, assembled a conclave, and proposed once more to transfer the see to

Avignon. But the cardinals were unwilling to sacrifice the luxuries of Italy, and become dependents on France; and the dread of another sack of Rome compelled the degraded pontiff to accept the terms dictated by the court of Vienna. He agreed to continue an imperial garrison in Commacchio, till all arrangements were completed, referred the dispute relative to Parma and Placentia to arbitration, acknowledged Charles as a king; and promised to reduce his army to 5000 men, and to allow the imperialists quarters, and a free passage through his territories.

Chap. LXXVI. — 1709.

In the midst of the former campaign, Marlborough himself made private overtures for peace, through the medium of his nephew, marshal Berwick, and offered to exert his influence in procuring the consent of the belligerent powers. But this offer being tendered during the siege of Lille, when the allied army was supposed to be reduced to the greatest straits, was contemptuously rejected by the French court. The final triumph of the confederates, the distresses of a dreadful famine in France, and the increasing burdens of the war, again induced Louis himself to make new proposals during the winter, as well to gain time as to detach some of his enemies, or at least to excite the enthusiasm of his own subjects, by an affected display of moderation.

Instead, however, of a public and general offer, Louis followed the system which he had before so successfully employed, and secretly tempted the States with commercial advantages, and the formation of a strong barrier in the Netherlands. After various communications by means of his agents in Holland, he despatched Rouillé, president of the parliament of Paris, to open a formal though clandestine negotiation with the States; repeated and even enlarged his former offers; affected a readiness to agree to a partition of the Spanish monarchy, by which Philip was to retain only Naples, Sicily, and Sardinia; proposed to renew the stipulations of the peace of Ryswick, professed a disposition to meet the claims of England, made vague promises of satisfaction to Savoy and Portugal, and omitted no lure

E 2

which was likely to detach the States, or furnish them with
a pretext for deserting the common cause.

The secret conferences being interrupted by the refusal
of the States to continue the negotiation without the concurrence of the allies, Eugene and Marlborough were
admitted on the part of England and the emperor, the
former accompanied by count Sinzendorf, and the latter by
lord Townshend, a staunch Whig, and a supporter of the
Austrian interest. Their interference soon damped the hopes
which Louis had entertained of breaking the confederacy.
Eugene announced the resolution of the emperor, not to be
satisfied with less than the cession of the whole Spanish
monarchy, and the revival of those stipulations in the treaty
of Westphalia which related to Austria and the empire;
Marlborough corroborated this declaration by asserting that
England would conclude no peace in which the interests of
all her allies were not comprised. They insisted also on
the discontinuance of all secret conferences, and on the immediate dismission of Rouillé, except France would un-
equivocally agree to comply with these demands.

Still, however, the French monarch continued to keep
alive the negotiation by new promises and new offers, held
out the prospect of a partition of Spain, and redoubled his
efforts to gain the Dutch. But unable to break the unanimity of the confederates, pressed by the increasing distresses of his country, and embarrassed by the cabals of
his court and family, he affected a compliance with all
their demands, and sent his confidental minister, Torcy, in
disguise to Holland. Torcy, more plausible and more
deeply versed in the arts of negotiation, pursued the same
line of conduct as Rouillé, though with greater finesse and
duplicity. Under a seeming readiness to assent to every
reasonable claim, he evaded by equivocations and captious
explanations the demands of the emperor and the duke of
Savoy, and endeavoured to shake the resolution of the
Maritime Powers, by offering a ready compliance with the
conditions in which their interests were peculiarly concerned.

While Louis was thus publicly amusing the allies, he
omitted no private intrigue to sow suspicions among them.
His agents in England and Holland endeavoured to revive
the public jealousy of the house of Austria, and laboured

to excite animosity against the partisans of the war. He tampered with the duke of Savoy, who was disgusted with the court of Vienna, endeavoured to tempt the fidelity of the Dutch deputy Vanderdussen, and offered an enormous bribe even to Marlborough himself.* But these and other artifices were defeated by the mutual confidence and good faith of the allies, and still more by the penetration and firmness of Eugene and Marlborough, who "treated the peace as they had managed the war, and baffled the stratagems of the French ministers as well as the schemes of the French generals."

At length Torcy, foiled in all his arts, requested their ultimatum; and the ministers of the belligerent powers, to prevent jealousies or separation of interests, as well as to avoid fruitless discussions, drew up a series of preliminaries as the basis of the peace, from which they solemnly agreed not to deviate. The WHOLE monarchy of Spain was to be yielded to the house of Austria, and Charles acknowledged by Louis. To secure the fulfilment of this condition, if Philip refused his compliance beyond the term of two months, the French troops and succours were to be withdrawn, and Louis to act in conjunction with the allies for effecting its complete execution. The monarchy was to remain entire in the house of Austria, and the throne was never to be filled by a prince of the house of Bourbon. Finally France was not even to trade to the Spanish Indies; and was to restore all the places occupied in the Netherlands, except the towns which were to be given up as a barrier to the Dutch. France was to cede Strasburgh with the fort of Kehl, to the empire, to possess Alsace, according to the literal terms of the treaty of Munster, or the right of prefecture over the ten towns, restoring the fortifications to the same state as before that treaty; to relinquish Landau to the empire, Brisach to the house of Austria; and to demolish the fortifications on the Rhine from Basle to

---

* Torcy offered to Marlborough 2,000,000 livres, if he would secure Naples and Sicily, or even Naples, to Philip; the same gratification for Dunkirk or Strasburgh; 3,000,000 for Naples, with Dunkirk or Strasburgh, and Landau, or Dunkirk and Strasburgh alone; and 4,000,000 for Naples and Sicily, with Dunkirk, Strasburgh, and Landau. It is perhaps scarcely necessary to add, that Marlborough did not even deign to return an answer to this proposal. — Torcy, t. ii. p. 238.

Philipsburgh. The clause relative to religion in the treaty
of Ryswick, which had created such discontents, was to be
referred to future discussion. In regard to England, Louis
was to acknowledge the Protestant succession; cede the
French possessions in Newfoundland; restore all his conquests during the war; raze the fortifications, and fill up
the port of Dunkirk, and send away the pretender. He
was to approve the concessions made to the Portuguese
monarch; to acknowledge the king of Prussia, and acquiesce in his possession of Neufchatel and Vallengin; to
refer the affairs of Bologne and Bavaria to the empire; to
approve the cessions granted to the Elector Palatine, and
acknowledge the ninth electorate in the House of Hanover.
To the States he was to yield Furnes, Ambach, Knoque,
Menin, Ypres, Warneton, Comines, Warwick, Popernigen,
Lille, Tournay, Condé, and Maubeuge, as a barrier; to
revive the commercial privileges granted by the treaty of
Ryswick, and allow them to retain garrisons in Huy, the
citadel of Liege, and Bonn.

On the ratification of these preliminaries, Louis was to
evacuate Namur, Charleroy, Luxemburgh, Condé, Tournay,
Maubeuge, Neuport, Furnes, Knoque, and Ypres, and raze
Dunkirk. A cessation of arms was to be concluded for two
months, and the congress for the negotiation of a general
peace to commence at the Hague on the 25th of June. All
the confederates were empowered to produce new pretensions, but no future demands of either party were to interrupt the armistice; and the cessation of arms was to continue till the conclusion of a general peace, if the monarchy
of Spain was restored, and the articles of the preliminaries
duly executed.

It was not to be expected that a sovereign so ambitious,
and so long accustomed to domineer, should sacrifice his
grandson and relinquish the principal fruits of his arms
and policy till driven to still greater extremities. Louis,
therefore, rejected the preliminaries without delay, declaring, that if compelled to continue the war, he would wage
it against his natural enemies, and not against his grandson. He once more appealed to his people, displayed the
cruelty and dishonour of being reduced to dethrone his
own grandson, expatiated on the arrogance and exorbitant
demands of the allies, roused the languid spirit of the

nation, and again brought a force into the field sufficiently powerful to keep the balance of the war suspended.

In the midst of these transactions, the allies imprudently omitted to embrace an opportunity of detaching from France her only remaining ally, on terms which would have produced the greatest advantage, and accelerated the termination of the war. The elector of Bavaria, hopeless of repairing his ruined fortunes by the support of Louis, offered to join the confederacy, and surrender Luxemburgh, with the other towns which he still held in the Netherlands, either on the restoration of his own territories, or the grant of an equivalent, for which Mantua or the Netherlands were proposed. Joseph readily listened to an overture which would have secured Bavaria; and Marlborough, who was sensible that this acquisition was almost the only means of balancing the preponderance of France, promised the concurrence of England. But the Dutch, either from jealousy of Austria, or from the dread of seeing a weak prince sovereign of the Netherlands, opposing this accommodation, Joseph reluctantly rejected the overture; and Louis quieted the fears and regained the confidence of the elector by the prospect of future acquisitions, and by the most solemn promises never to desert him.

All hopes of peace being thus annihilated, the allies, to use the language of Eugene, "prepared to dictate their terms by means of 150,000 armed plenipotentiaries at the gates of Paris." Joseph was enabled by recent success in Hungary to detach a considerable portion of his force to the scene of action; and the whole confederacy purposed to make a general attack against the French frontier from Italy, the Rhine, and the Netherlands, leaving the troops in Spain to remain on the defensive.

In the Netherlands, both parties took the field towards the beginning of June. The allies, amounting to 110,000 men, full of spirits, and provided with every requisite, assembled under Eugene and Marlborough near Courtray: the French under Villars, the most fortunate and enterprising of their generals, not inferior in numbers, but in a deplorable state for want of clothing, ammunition, and provisions, took post behind the marshes, stretching from Lens to La Bassée, to cover Douay and Arras. The confederates approached their lines, and finding the position too strong to risk an attack, threatened Ypres, and affected to make preparations for an engagement. Having by these feints induced the French commander to weaken the garrisons, they silently decamped in the night of June 9, at the moment when both armies were hourly expecting the signal for battle, and on the ensuing morning invested Tournay, while their detachments surprised the posts of St. Amand on the Scarpe and Mortagne at the confluence of the Scarpe and Scheld. So rapid and unexpected was the movement, and so prevalent the expectation of a battle, that Villars had reduced the garrison to 8000 ; and a foraging party, sent out by the governor, was cut off by the corps which led the march. Thirty thousand men were appointed for the attacks, and the two armies of Eugene and Marlborough took post between the Scarpe and the Scheld to cover the siege. A flying corps of 10,000 men, which had been left in Brabant, straitened the place on the west, and the battering artillery, which had been sent as far as Courtray, to increase the uncertainty of the enemy, was remanded and brought up the Scheld.*

The attempt of Villars to replace the troops which he had drawn from the garrison, being frustrated by the vigilance of Eugene and Marlborough, he, on the 4th of July, endeavoured to divert their attention by detaching 10,000 men against Warneton, a post which covered the passage from Menin to Lille ; but a strong corps arriving at the moment when the place had been carried by storm, again wrested it from the French. A similar enterprise against Commines was repulsed by the garrison, and the march of a detachment toward St. Guislain, for the purpose of threatening Brabant, was rendered fruitless by inundations and other measures of defence. The channel of the Scheld was cleared to facilitate the transport of supplies, and fortified posts at Marchiennes and Pont à Tressin completed the chain of communications necessary to secure the passage of convoys from Menin through Lille.

Villars, baffled by the skill of his antagonists, disappointed in his efforts to reinforce the garrison or interrupt the siege, unable to make any important movement for

* For an account of the masterly manœuvres which led to the battle of Malplaquet, see Memoirs of the Duke of Marlborough, chap. lxxxii.

want of provisions and forage, abandoned Tournay to its fate. But to check the progress of the allies after its reduction, he took post between the Lys and the Scheld, placed a corps on the Haine near St. Guislain to cover his right, and another on the Lys to secure his left. He formed lines and inundations, employed every resource of the military art to strengthen his position, called out the militia of Picardy and the Boulonnois, and drew a reinforcement of 10,000 men from the Rhine.

During these preparations the town of Tournay surrendered on the 30th of July, and the governor retiring into the citadel, which was remarkable for the strength of its fortifications and numerous counter-mines, protracted his defence till the 4th of September.

Though masters of Tournay, the allied generals were unable to pursue their original system of attack by the strong position which Villars had so judiciously taken. Unwilling to risk the rash experiment of assailing a camp which he had employed several weeks to fortify, they endeavoured to draw him from his post as the only means of engaging him with advantage. Accordingly, on the very day in which the citadel surrendered, they suddenly decamped, detached a corps to drive the French from the Haine, and invested Mons, the capital of Hainault, which was defended by a weak and sickly garrison, ill provided, and, to use the expressions of the French commander, " the hospital of the army."

Their plan had the desired effect. Villars assembled his troops on the Honneau, passed the Scheld at Valenciennes, collected reinforcements from the garrisons, and occupied the post of Malplaquet, situated between the source of the Haine and the Sambre. In this situation, which was rendered strong by woods and morasses, he hoped again to check the movements of the allies, to confine their operations to the siege of places, which would contribute little to their further progress, and to protect the grand line of fortresses stretching from the Lys to the Meuse.

The allies, elated with this advantage, hastened to bring on a decisive engagement. They left a corps to blockade Mons, crossed the French lines on the Trouille, on the 9th of September, and reached Blaregnies at the moment when Villars had taken up his position. As it was then nightfall, they remained under arms till the morning. A council of war was held, and Eugene contended for the necessity of an engagement, before the enemy could render their camp as impregnable as their former position. Being warmly seconded by Marlborough, he overruled the timid opposition of the Dutch deputies ; but unfortunately it was agreed to wait the junction of 10,000 men who had been left at Tournay. These not arriving till the following night, gave time to the enemy to prepare for defence. Their right extended into the wood of Lagniere, their left was flanked by the woods of Taniere and Sart ; their centre stretched between the two woods across a plain of 3000 paces in breadth, in which were situated the villages of Aulnoit and Malplaquet. They had constructed intrenchments and formed barricadoes of trees on both flanks, thrown up one line across the plain behind Aulnoit, and commenced a second before Malplaquet, with a view to take up a new position, where they could present a more extensive front, if driven from their first line. Their infantry was partly distributed in the woods, and partly behind their intrenchments in the plain, their cavalry drawn up in two lines on the open ground beyond, their artillery commanded all the approaches, and the whole presented the appearance of a fortress rather than a camp.

Notwithstanding the difficulties of the attack, the allies did not shrink from their original determination. A detachment reduced St. Guillain, on the Haine, which was necessary to favour their retreat in case of a reverse, and preparations were made for the engagement. At break of day of the 11th of September, the generals drew up their troops, and rode between the two armies to examine the ground, under a heavy cannonade, which swept away numbers in their presence. As they passed they were received with repeated acclamations ; and the soldiers, loudly demanding the signal for battle, expressed the firmest confidence in the skill of their leaders and their own intrepidity. Their forces, drawn up before Aulnoit and Blaregnies, stretched from the wood of Lagniere to the village of Sart ; the infantry in two lines in front, the cavalry in the same order in the rear. As Eugene had been the first to propose an engagement, he took on himself the duty of dislodging the enemy from the woods of Sart and Taniere,

which was the most arduous part of the contest ; his troops,
therefore, consisting of Austrians and Germans, were
placed on the right, and those of England and Holland,
under Marlborough, on the left. With loud huzzas, and
the discharge of all the artillery, the signal was given for
battle. Eugene at the head of his infantry, assisted by a
corps of the British, penetrated by three attacks through
the wood of Sart ; but in addition to the obstacles of the
ground, he experienced the most desperate opposition from
the enemy. Animated by the ardour of the contest, he
repeatedly rallied his troops, exposing himself like the
meanest soldier, and in the foremost ranks was struck by a
musket ball in the head. As the blood streamed from the
wound, he was entreated to retire and suffer it to be
dressed ; but, determined to conquer or die, he replied,
" If we fall, what will it profit; if victorious, we shall
have time sufficient to attend to our wounds." After a
bloody contest, continually renewed, his troops, animated
by his example, dislodged the enemy from the woods, drove
them from their works, and flanked the intrenchments on
the plain. But as the French again rallied in the open
ground, and presented a new and formidable front, he was
unable to emerge from the thickets, and suspended his progress to wait the event of success on other points.

During this conflict, the attack was begun at the extremity of the left. The young prince of Orange, impatient to emulate the glory of his ancestors, led forty Dutch
battalions against eighty of the French, posted on the skirt
of the wood of Lagniere, and dislodged them from two of
their intrenchments. Repulsed at a third, he rallied his
troops, and planted with his own hand the standard on
their works ; yet though no exertions of personal valour
could avail against so superior a force, he disdained to retreat, and occupied the attention of the enemy by maintaining himself behind the neighbouring inclosures.

In the centre the vigilant eye of Marlborough watched
the progress of the conflict to regulate his own movements.
Perceiving that the enemy, to oppose Eugene, had thinned
the troops which defended their works on the plain, he
seized the critical moment to commence his attack, pushed
forward his infantry, and burst through the formidable intrenchment. While Eugene, on the skirt of the wood, with

his artillery poured down destruction on the hostile ranks, the cavalry advanced, and formed under the protection of the infantry ; though frequently repulsed, they as often rallied, and at length broke the squadrons of the enemy, and the whole mass pushing forward separated the right of the French from the left. Victory, which had hovered in suspense, now declared for the allies. Villars, being dangerously wounded at the commencement of the action, Boufflers, on whom the command devolved, gave orders to quit the field. Part of the infantry on the right, skirting the wood, fell back through Bavay towards Maubeuge ; and on the left, Boufflers himself heading the cavalry, covered the fugitives, and retired with the artillery to Valenciennes, unmolested by the victors, who were too much exhausted to interrupt his retreat. Thus terminated, after a desperate struggle of seven hours, one of the most furious battles during the memorable war of the Succession; of the French 14,000 were killed and wounded, and of the allies no less than 20,000 were swept away in this dreadful carnage.*

Although their loss was far greater than that of the enemy, yet so imposing is the name of victory, so discouraging even a voluntary retreat, that the French suffered the remainder of the campaign to pass without a single effort, dividing their army into two flying camps to cover Maubeuge, Valenciennes, and Quesnoy. The victorious generals returned to their former camp the day after the engagement, prosecuted the siege of Mons without interruption, and forced the town to surrender on the 30th of October. As the season was far advanced, the roads broken up by the continual rains, and the forage become scarce, they did not commence the siege of Maubeuge, which had been designated as the next object of attack, but took up winter-quarters, to recruit their forces, and

* The Dutch, who suffered most severely in this engagement, and lost nearly two thirds of their infantry, accused both Eugene and Marlborough of having sacrificed their troops ; and this accusation occasioned great discontent on the part of the States during the remainder of the war. But in reality their loss was derived from the imprudent impetuosity of their youthful commander, who, contrary to the general system of the battle, lavished the lives of his soldiers in an unnecessary attack. — See Memoirs of the Duke of Marlborough, ch. lxxxii.

make the necessary preparations for opening the campaign at an early period in the ensuing year.

On the side of the Rhine, and in Italy, the operations were planned with unusual boldness, and if successful would have given the last blow to the declining greatness of France. The army of the empire was to invade Alsace, while the troops of the emperor and the duke of Savoy were to penetrate into Dauphiné. The two bodies were then to unite in Franche Comté, where the natives were ready to receive them, and commence the ensuing campaign with invading that quarter of France, which was not covered with a formidable line of fortresses, like the frontier on the side of the Netherlands. But this plan, however well concerted, failed in the execution. The same delays as before took place in all the movements of the Germanic body; and the military operations were still farther retarded by the disinclination of the elector of Hanover to resume the command. In Italy, likewise, the duke of Savoy, disgusted with the emperor for withholding the territory of the Langhes, which he claimed as a part of the Montferrat, not only relinquished the command, but refused the co-operation of his troops. Though at length soothed by the urgent representations of the Maritime Powers, he did not take the field; and the army was intrusted to the imperial general count Daun.

These delays gave time to the French to complete their measures of defence. When, at length, the armies were put in motion, the superior skill and vigilance of the dukes of Harcourt and Berwick arrested the progress of the allies, and deprived them of the advantages which they possessed from superior numbers. On the side of Alsace the elector was prevented from establishing a passage over the Rhine; on that of Italy Daun was entangled among the Alps, and, after a fruitless struggle of two months, measured back his steps into Piedmont, lest the winter should close the passage, deprive him of subsistence, and preclude his return.

Chap. LXXVII. — 1710, 1711.

THE success of the allied armies in the Netherlands, the loss of the great barrier fortresses Lille and Tournay, the cabals of the court, the exhausted state of the finances, and the universal cry of the country for peace, induced Louis to renew his overtures. After various secret endeavours to obtain some modification of the former preliminaries, he affected to receive them as the basis of the negotiation, with the single exception of a change in those articles which related to the evacuation of the Spanish dominions. Having by this seeming compliance obtained the consent of the Dutch to renew the negotiation, he sent the marshal d'Huxelles, with the Abbé de Polignac, as his plenipotentiaries, to confer with the two Dutch deputies employed on the former occasion ; and the village of Gertruydenburg was rendered memorable as the place where the conferences were held.

This acquiescence afforded the French monarch an opportunity to amuse the allies with a repetition of the same expedients and cavils as in the preceding year, and again to rouse the zeal of his people by a new display of his numerous concessions, and a new appeal to the national feeling. At the same time this separate negotiation contributed to weaken the mutual confidence of the allies. As the importunities of the French plenipotentiaries extorted from the Dutch deputies a kind of tacit acquiescence, in the proposal of ceding Naples and Sicily, or at least Sicily to Philip, and as this condition found supporters among the members of the States, the jealousy of Joseph was again awakened. To prevent a departure from the grand principle laid down in the preliminaries, count Sinzendorf presented to the pensionary and to Marlborough two memorials, discussing the different expedients offered by the French for securing a compensation to Philip ; namely, the cession of Naples and Sicily, Sardinia, with the places on the coast of Tuscany, and the kingdom of Aragon, either jointly or separately. His arguments, supported by the influence of England, overruled the inclination of the Dutch. They declared that Louis, either by persuasion or force, should procure the complete evacuation of Spain and its dependencies, and they even announced the intention of the allies to produce further demands as a compensation for the prosecution of the war, since the rejection of the preliminaries. These demands seem to have been an addition to their barrier, the cession of Alsace to the duke of Loraine, and the reintegration of Loraine, and the three bishoprics with the empire. Louis, thus pressed, made additional offers; he tendered four towns in the Netherlands as pledges; he proposed to cede Alsace, to yield Valenciennes to the Dutch, and even to furnish a monthly subsidy, as far as 1,000,000 livres, to be employed in the expulsion of Philip; but he clogged these offers with requiring the complete restoration of the electors of Cologne and Bavaria, the renunciation of all further demands, and the mutual reduction of troops; he likewise declared his inability to persuade and his resolution not to force his grandson to abandon the Spanish dominions, and accept the compensations which he had himself proposed.* As therefore, none of these offers were conformable either to the letter or spirit of the preliminaries, and as the invariable duplicity of Louis destroyed all confidence in his professions, they rejected his offers, and closed the conferences on the 25th of July.

The States-general justified the conduct of their plenipotentiaries by a resolution, declaring that the king of France had departed from the basis of the negotiation, by evading the execution of the capital point, the complete restitution of the Spanish territories; and had no other view than to sow jealousies among the allies. The queen of England approving this resolution, gave new assurances that she would prosecute the war with vigour; and the emperor expressed his satisfaction in a letter of thanks, giving the States the title of " High and Mighty," which

---

* The same remarks may be applied to the account of this negotiation as to that of the former. The Tory writers re-echo the pathetic declamations and invectives with which the French authors abound, give implicit credit to the professions of Louis, adduce his offers as not clogged with any condition, and without adverting to the steps by which France had attained her aggrandisement, accuse the allies, and Marlborough and Eugene in particular, of prolonging the war from motives of private interest.

they had long demanded in vain from the court of Vienna.

These negotiations did not retard the operations of the campaign. As the French in the preceding years had disconcerted the plans of the allies, by taking strong positions behind the numerous streams and rivers which intersect the frontiers of Artois and Hainault, Eugene and Marlborough conceived the design of breaking this system of defence, by occupying, before the enemy could assemble, the lines which they had formed behind the Deule and the Scarpe, to cover the fortresses on the course of the Lys and the Scheld. At the close of the preceding campaign, they had accordingly concerted the necessary arrangements for taking the field at an earlier season than in any former period of the war. The troops quartered in Brabant and Flanders, being suddenly assembled in the neighbourhood of Tournay, the two generals joined the army in the middle of April, distributed the requisite supplies for a forced march, and, during the night of the 20th, headed the troops, who were divided into two columns, crossed the Deule at Pont à Vendin, and Oby, before the French were apprised of their approach, and drove two corps which had been hastily collected at St. Amand, beyond the Scarpe, and behind the marshes of Lens. They took post on both sides of Douay, a fortress connected by navigable communications with the Lys and the Scheld, and from its strength and position admirably calculated to form a place of arms for supporting their intended inroad into the heart of France.

The ensuing days were employed in forming lines of circumvallation, in preparations for the siege, and in securing the requisite posts. The castle of Mortagne having been previously captured by a detachment, and St. Amand, Marchiennes, with the abbey of Hênon abandoned by the enemy, the communication by the Scheld was opened with Tournay, the sluices on the Deule were repaired, and the same facility given to the communication with Lille. The junction of 20,000 auxiliary Prussians, Palatines, and Hessians, raised the number of the allied forces to 90,000 men, and the two armies were posted in situations best adapted for favouring the passage of convoys, and forming on the right or left of the Scarpe to cover the siege. Forty battalions under the princes of Anhalt and Nassau were appointed for the attacks ; and the batteries opened on the 11th of May. The approaches were pushed with that vigour which had already distinguished all their operations ; and as the want of necessaries prevented Villars from assembling his army before the beginning of May, they anticipated all his movements for the relief of the place, and reduced the garrison of 8000 men to surrender on the 26th of June.

After remaining several days, as well to give repose to their troops as to level the trenches, and put the place in a posture of defence, they recalled their detachments, and advanced to the ground between Lens and the source of the Lave. Deeming it impracticable to dislodge the French commander from the lines which he had formed on the Crinchon for the protection of Arras, they abandoned their design of besieging that fortress, and directed their march to Bethune. The place was invested by 18,000 men on the 16th of July, a strong detachment stationed between Lens and La Bassé to secure the passage of convoys from Lille and Tournay, and the trenches opened on the 27th, while the main army took post at Berle, to cover the siege.

The French general having thrown a garrison of 9,000 men into the place, under the command of Monsieur de Puy Vauban, a nephew of the celebrated engineer, and having reinforced the neighbouring places, St. Venant, Aire, and Ypres, left Bethune also to its fate. He drew reinforcements from Condé, Valenciennes, and Cambray, followed the movements of the allies, and intrenched himself between the sources of the Canche and Scarpe. By this position he covered Arras and Hesdin, and was ready to occupy any point of a barrier formed equally by nature and art, from the sea to the Meuse, by the Canche, the Scarpe, the Senset, the Scheld, the Honneau, and Sambre, strengthened or connected with intrenchments, and supported by the fortresses of Hesdin, St. Pol, Arras, Bouchain, Valenciennes, Condé, Maubeuge, and Charleroy. In this formidable situation he remained without risking any enterprise, except desultory skirmishes or the attack of convoys, till the reduction of Bethune, which yielded on the 29th of August, after a siege of thirty-seven days.

As the allies were still unable to draw the French to an engagement, and unwilling to risk the desperate enterprise of again forcing their lines, they employed the remainder of the campaign in reducing Aire and St. Venant, the sieges of which they covered by the same position. Success, as before, crowned their arms; for Villars quitting the army to repair to the waters of Bourbonne, the command was intrusted to Harcourt, who remained inactive during the rest of the campaign. St. Venant surrendered on the 29th of September, thirteen days after the opening of the trenches, and Aire, which from its marshy situation, as well as the strength of its works, was capable of a longer defence, resisted till the 8th of November. After the completion of this enterprise, the confederates returned to the plains of Lille, and followed the example of the French, in distributing their troops into quarters. Eugene and Marlborough repaired to the Hague; and having made the necessary arrangements for the subsistence of their forces during the winter, returned, one to Vienna, the other to London, with the hope of completing the humiliation of France in the ensuing campaign.

The duke of Savoy being still dissatisfied with the emperor, the command in Italy was again intrusted to count Daun, who was at the head of 45,000 men. While he penetrated through the valley of Barcellonette, Seissan, a Protestant refugee of Languedoc, was to land with a body of troops at Cette, and rouse his persecuted brethren in Provence and Dauphiné, who were no longer awed by a military force. These insurgents were to form a point of union at Die, open a communication with the allies by the Drome and the Vivarais, and thus excluded the French army from Provence. But Berwick, by adopting the same system of operation as in the preceding campaign, prevented Daun from establishing himself beyond the Alps; Seissan had no sooner landed than he was defeated and compelled to re-embark; the Protestants were overawed; and the allies, after an arduous campaign, again forced to retire into Piedmont.

On the side of the Rhine the two armies continued, as before, wholly on the defensive.

Chap. LXXVIII. — 1709–1711.

While the possession of Spain was contested in negotiations at Gertruydenberg, and by arms on the frontiers of France, the sceptre itself was wrested from the Austrian grasp.

In consequence of the strenuous efforts made by the allies against France, the war in Spain had been suffered to languish. Since the fatal battle of Almanza, Charles had maintained himself in Catalonia ; and on the opposite side of Spain the united army of Portuguese and English, after being defeated in their attempts to capture Badajoz, remained on the defensive. On the other hand, the diminution of the French forces, which were withdrawn for the defence of their own country, and the discontents excited among the Castilians, by the negotiations for peace, prevented Philip from profiting by the weakness of his antagonist. His embarrassments were also aggravated by divisions in his court. The princess of Orsini with her adherents, who had been dismissed to conciliate the natives, had been reinstated in favour, resumed her former authority, and, assisted by the councils of the financier Amelot, directed the civil and military administration of Spain. By her influence ministers and generals were appointed or displaced; even the duke of Orleans was deprived of the command, and two of his confidential agents arrested, under the pretext of a real or pretended attempt to supplant Philip. With her influence, and the predominance of her counsels, the antipathy of the nation revived in its full force, and fears were entertained of a general insurrection ; some of the grandees even advised Philip to declare war against France, and the French and Spanish troops even treated each other as enemies.

To regain the confidence of his subjects, Philip assembled the cortes of Castile and Arragon at Madrid, and presented to them his infant son Louis, as prince of Asturias, and heir to the crown. He also placed the administration in the hands of the duke of Medina Celi, an ardent Spaniard, vested the command in native generals, and in con-

formity with the dying advice of Portocarrero* dismissed
as before, all his French adherents, except the princess of
Orsini, who regained her lost popularity by appearing as
the promoter of this change. He likewise profited by the
publication of the preliminaries to appeal to the feelings of
his subjects, to excite their pity for the hardships of his
situation, alarm them with the fear of dismemberment, and
announce his resolution never to abandon a throne endeared
to him by the affections of his people, but rather to perish
at the head of the last Spanish troop, and tinge with his
blood the beloved soil of Castile.

By this pathetic appeal, he flattered the pride, and revived the hopes of the Castilians. The nobles sent their
plate to replenish his treasury, and led their vassals to recruit his armies ; and the wealthy ecclesiastics poured out
their treasures in support of a monarch, distinguished for
his piety, and against a prince whose title was defended
by heretics. His resolution was strengthened by the
promise of Louis never to abandon his cause, and his
necessities were relieved by the fortunate arrival of a considerable treasure from America. But, at this moment, the
renewal of negotiations for peace, and the proposals of
Louis to abandon Spain, revived the national ferment, and
forced him to dismiss the few French troops who remained
in his service, at the time when their bravery and discipline were necessary for the maintenance of his crown.

Meanwhile the Austrian party had been gaining strength
to renew the contest. Being joined by reinforcements,
Charles himself, accompanied by count Staremberg,
advanced against Philip, and raised the siege of Balaguer,
which had been reduced at the close of the preceding year.
Strengthened by the arrival of general Stanhope, with

* This extraordinary prelate experienced a series of vicissitudes not
unusual in the lives of intriguing statesmen. After commencing his
career as a partisan of the house of Austria, he suddenly turned to the
house of Bourbon. Having been the principal agent in procuring the
crown for Philip of Anjou, he had the mortification to find that he
bore the name, without enjoying the substance of power, and he retired
in disgust. On the ascendency of Charles, he endeavoured to make
amends for his former defection, by again embracing his cause, thun-
dered out a Te Deum, and consecrated his standards ; but on the reverse of circumstances, he closed his versatile life by again enlisting
under the banners of the house of Bourbon. He died Sept. 4. 1709.

succours from Italy, he pressed on the retreat of the
enemy, and drew near them, soon after they had passed
the Noguera, in the neighbourhood of Almenara, on the
27th of July, 1710. Here, from natural indecision, or
deference to the advice of Staremberg, Charles would have
suffered his rival to escape ; but his reluctance was overruled by Stanhope, who at the head of an advanced corps,
gained the passage of the Noguera, and threatened, if he
declined a battle, to withdraw the troops in British pay.
The consent of Charles being extorted, Stanhope attacked
a body sent by the enemy to secure the passage over the
river, killed one of the Spanish generals with his own
hand in the first charge, and totally routed the enemy.
The approach of evening alone saved the main army ; for
the defeat spread dismay through the Spanish ranks, and
Philip himself, with his guards and attendants, sought refuge in Lerida. Charles passed the night on the field, and
the ardour of Stanhope still continuing to animate his
movements, the neighbouring posts were secured, the
allies followed the enemy in their retreat, and notwithstanding the extreme heat of the season, the badness of
the roads, and want of water and provisions, again overtook
them soon after they had passed the Ebro at Saragossa.
Without delay they crossed the river, approached the
troops of Philip, who were posted on a rising ground near
the walls, continued all night under arms, and at break of
day commenced the engagement. Stanhope, as before,
leading his men to the attack, was seconded by Staremberg,
and, after a short, but severe conflict, the allies gained a
complete victory over troops who, though superior in
number, were confounded by the rapidity of their pursuers,
and considered themselves as sacrificed to the insidious
policy of the French court. The amount of slain and
prisoners was considerable ; the army was dispersed ; part
fled to Lerida, with the marquis de Buy the commander ;
and Philip himself, with a disheartened remnant, hastened
to Madrid. Charles entered Saragossa in triumph, amidst
the acclamations of the citizens, and gained their affections
by restoring their ancient constitution and privileges,
which had been abolished by Philip.

Had Charles been capable of improving his victory,
this successful day might have again restored the crown to

the house of Austria. But those sad jealousies between the commanders, which had before occasioned his reverses, and had broken out even during the march, again revived. Stanhope and Staremberg were continually contesting for pre-eminence. The one frank, impetuous, enterprising, and overbearing; the other cool, formal, and cautious, indignant at the superiority assumed by his rival, and priding himself on his military experience, and the favour of his sovereign. In the discussions for arranging the plan of future operations, Staremberg proposed to reduce the neighbouring provinces before they advanced, and, by the capture of Pampeluna, to shut up the principal passage by which French succours could enter Spain. Stanhope was anxious to crown his brilliant enterprise, by conducting Charles a second time to Madrid; and both relied on the junction of the Portuguese army. The importunities and threats of Stanhope at last prevailed, and Charles reluctantly directed his march to Madrid, on the 28th of September. But instead of the welcome, which a victorious prince might have expected to receive in his capital, a sullen silence reigned in the deserted streets; those, who by bribes or compulsion were induced to mingle their shouts with the acclamations of the soldiery, were shunned as traitors to their lawful king, and enemies to their country, and although a few necessitous or disaffected nobles offered their homage, the body of the people gave signal proofs of dislike to his person, and aversion to his cause. The same disappointment attended his hope of support. Stanhope in vain advanced to Toledo, to facilitate a communication with the Portuguese; no instances could induce them to quit their own frontier, and the king even refused to weaken his forces by sending the troops in the pay of the Maritime Powers.

While Charles remained in a state of indecision, Philip actively employed the interval in repairing his losses. He removed the tribunals and court to Valladolid, sent the queen and the young prince of Asturias to Victoria, collected his scattered troops, and raised new levies; while the fugitives, who had taken refuge in Lerida, assisted by the natives, cut off all the communications of the victorious army between Barcelona and Madrid. That jealousy of France which the nation had cherished in prosperity subsided in adversity ; the grandees themselves joined Philip in soliciting Louis to furnish succours, and send Vendome, whose services they recollected with gratitude and admiration, to assume the direction of the war. Demands which had been anxiously expected were fulfilled without delay. The duke of Noailles, with the forces in Roussillon, prepared to penetrate into Catalonia; Vendome, at the head of 3000 horse, joined Philip at Valladolid, roused the enthusiasm of the troops, rapidly assembled 30,000 men, and advancing to Almarez on the Tagus, became master of the only communication by which the Portuguese could unite with the allies.

During this interval Charles saw his army mouldering away for want of provisions, from excesses, and from assassinations by the natives. Hopeless of support from the Portuguese, and exposed to the enterprises of the Spanish partisans, who pushed their incursions to the capital, he was again distracted by the diversity of opinions among his generals. Some proposed to continue in the heart of Castile ; some to transport the court to Saragossa ; others to regain Catalonia ; and all exhorted him no longer to trust his own person among a hostile people, but to retire to Barcelona. While he was yet hesitating, a deserter brought him a letter from his queen, announcing that the advance of Noailles with 15,000 men threatened to cut off his retreat. This intelligence, with the approach of Philip and Vendome, extorted the consent of Charles. Madrid was evacuated amidst the execrations and outrages of a people, whose prejudices had been wounded, and whose religion violated ; and on quitting the capital, November the 11th, the ears of the fugitive monarch were assailed with the sound of bells, and acclamations of the inhabitants proclaiming the triumph of his rival. After waiting a few days between Madrid and Toledo to assemble the troops and secure his passage, Charles, with an escort of 2000 horse, took the route to Barcelona, and was followed by his army, who hoped to pass the chain of mountains which separate Castile and Arragon, before they were overtaken by the enemy. Influenced by mutual jealousy, or compelled to divide for want of quarters, they marched in different columns, all dissatisfied and dispirited, spreading into the villages, and retarded by the badness of the roads, and the

F

extreme severity of the weather. Staremberg led the van with the main body, and Stanhope, at the head of 4000 English, closed the rear with no other means of communication than a few scattered corps, ignorant of the country, and deprived of all intelligence by the hostility of the natives.

In this state Staremberg reached Cifuentes, while Stanhope cantoned his troops in Brihuega, another town on the Tagus, north-east of Guadalaxara. But, as he was preparing to resume his march on the ensuing morning, he was surprised with the appearance of the enemy, who had crossed the Tagus at Guadalaxara, and posted themselves between Brihuega and Cifuentes. Though shut up in a small place, with no other defence than a slight wall, without artillery, without provisions, and with little ammunition, he disdained to surrender, and made preparations to defend his post till he could be relieved by Staremberg, to whom he sent repeated messengers. He maintained himself three days against the continued assaults of the Spanish army, and did not yield till he had exhausted his scanty means of defence, till the enemy had burst into the town, and till even the inhabitants had risen against his troops.

It was late in the evening before the account of Stanhope's danger reached Cifuentes. Staremberg, after passing a night in preparations for his march, waited several hours to collect his scattered forces; and did not take his departure till mid-day. In consequence of these delays, and the difficulty of clearing a rugged country in so advanced a season, the troops were overtaken by darkness. After lying under arms all night, they pushed forwards to within a league of Briehuga, with the hopes of yet preserving the flower of their infantry. But the silence with which their signals were received announced the reduction of the place, and Staremberg observed the Spanish army in battle array, crowning the gentle eminences above the plain of Villa Viciosa. Though his troops were inferior in numbers, and fatigued with a long march, he was too far advanced to retreat in the face of an active enemy. He had scarcely formed his order of battle before the attack began. Conducted by Vendome, and animated by the presence of Philip, the Spaniards rushed to the charge with irresistible fury, cut to pieces or dispersed his left wing, and took his baggage. The centre and right, however, repulsed all their assaults, and, after an obstinate and bloody contest, which was only interrupted by darkness, maintained their ground, and captured part of the enemy's artillery. Staremberg passed the following day on the field ; but his baggage lost, his army reduced to 9000 men, harassed by the victorious cavalry, and dreading a new attack, he rendered useless the artillery which he could not convey for want of horses, and took the route of Saragossa. The victory was claimed by both parties, and Te Deum was sung both at Barcelona and Madrid ; yet whatever honour or advantage Staremberg might have gained in this well-fought conflict, he suffered all the consequences of a defeat. He made a slow and orderly retreat ; but he with difficulty forced his way through a rugged and hostile country, in the face of an active and vigilant enemy, and after an arduous march reached Catalonia with no more than 7000 men, the dispirited remnant of that army which, a few months before, seemed master of Spain.

Chap. LXXIX.—1705–1711.

While the principal force of the Grand Alliance had been turned against France, tranquillity was restored in Hungary, so long the scene of commotion.

Joseph had seen and lamented the fatal effects of the intolerance, cruelty, and impolicy exercised in Hungary by his father, and had in vain used his influence to promote an accommodation. He had no sooner ascended the throne than he turned his attention to terminate a rebellion which distracted his counsels, divided his forces, and exposed the most vulnerable part of his dominions to the open attacks or secret machinations of his enemies. By the constitutional intervention of the Palatine, he declared to the states that, as in conformity with his oath, he had never interfered in the government during the life-time of his father, he disclaimed all participation in the persecutions of which they complained. But having now assumed the supreme authority, he promised, on the word of a sovereign, to fulfil the articles which he had sworn to observe at his coronation, and summoned a diet for the confirmation of their privileges and the redress of their grievances. He gave likewise a proof of his sincerity by dismissing those ministers who had advised the measures pursued by Leopold, and appointing others more inclined to lenity and toleration ; he even removed general Heuster, notwithstanding his eminent services, and conferred the command in Hungary on d'Herbeville, a native of Loraine, and an officer of a more mild and conciliating character.

These offers, however, made little impression on the malecontents, who suspected the sincerity of the court, and deemed themselves in a situation to enforce the acceptance of the preliminaries proposed to Leopold. They did not yet venture to throw off their allegiance ; but for the purpose of cementing their union and regulating their proceedings, Ragotsky summoned a diet at Setzim. The magnates, prelates, and deputies from the insurgent provinces and royal cities, not in the possession of the imperialists, assembled in a tent erected between the two lines of the army ; and after the usual celebration of mass by the bishop of Gran, instituted a regular confederacy similar to those of Poland. The administration was assigned to a senate or council of twenty-four members, and the direction of the league, in conjunction with the senate, intrusted to Ragotsky with the title of *Dux,* or leader. Ragotsky, being elevated on a buckler by the principal magnates, all the members took an oath of fidelity to the government thus provisionally established, and engaged not to conclude peace except on the restoration of their ancient rights. In reply to the offers of the emperor they demanded the cession of Transylvania to their chief, the total abolition of the hereditary sovereignty, the revival of the oath of St. Andrew, with their other religious and civil immunities ; and they affected as a favour to permit Joseph to retain his crown, as an elective king, on giving security for the restoration of the elective monarchy after his decease. Joseph, however anxious to turn his whole force against France, could not accept such degrading conditions ; and both parties renewed the war with redoubled vigour.

The insurgents were encouraged to provoke a continuation of the contest by the favourable situation of their affairs. They had recovered from their defeat at Tirnau, had driven the Austrian army of 12,000 men to take refuge in the isle of Schut, blockaded Leopoldstadt, Pest, Buda, Peterwaradin, and Great Waradin, and spread themselves along the frontiers of Austria, Styria, and Moravia; in Transylvania they had also confined general Rabutin to Hermanstadt, and a few neighbouring posts. Their forces were still the same desultory hordes, averse to discipline, and headed by the feudal lords, with little skill or experience; but they possessed essential advantages in their habits of life and knowledge of the country, and were rendered formidable by their numbers, amounting to 75,000 men.

In this desperate crisis the ministers advised Joseph to abandon so distant a country as Transylvania; but, sensible that it was the focus of rebellion, and afforded the principal means of communication with the Turks, he rejected a proposal equally weak and impolitic, and ordered Herbeville to use his utmost exertions for its recovery. The general executed these orders with admirable skill and promptitude. He marched behind the Danube, as far as Buda, crossed to Pest, gained the passage of the Teiss at Segedin, though harassed by parties of the insurgents, raised the blockade of Great Waradin, deceived by feints the vigilance of Ragotsky, who had hastened to defend the chain of mountains between Transylvania and Hungary, forced the intrenched pass of Sibo, and, on the 22nd of November, 1705, invaded Transylvania with an army augmented by desultory bands of Rascians, and other hordes still attached to the house of Austria. After relieving Hermanstadt, and uniting with Rabutin, he reduced the whole country, and re-established the Austrian government.

While the imperial army was engaged in this expedition, Austria, Moravia, and Styria were exposed to the devastations of the insurgent hordes, who pushed their incursions to the very walls of Vienna, and spreading terror through the neighbouring provinces, were joined by crowds of peasants, lured by the hopes of plunder. Joseph collected troops from all quarters, and drew lines along the most exposed parts of the frontier, to restrain these predatory inroads. He also redoubled his efforts to pacify the insurgents. He opened a new negotiation through the intervention of the English and Dutch ministers, at Tirnau, endeavoured to conciliate Ragotsky by offering him the margraviate of Burgau, as an equivalent for Transylvania, and the restoration of his patrimony in Hungary, with the dignity of a prince of the empire; and even employed the agency of his wife and sister, whom he liberated from their confinement. He also acknowledged the Hungarian confederacy, and renewed his promises of confirming all the privileges which he had engaged to maintain at his coronation. By means of these concessions, as well as at the instances of the mediating powers, he, in May, 1706, obtained a temporary cessation of arms, which enabled him to furnish supplies for the blockaded fortresses; but no lures could tempt Ragotsky to make a separate accommodation; and the confederate states still refused to accept peace on any other terms than those which they had already proposed.

Ragotsky, in June, 1707, held a diet in the open air at Onod, in imitation of ancient custom, and with the unanimous suffrages of the whole confederacy, declared Joseph a tyrant and usurper, who was animated by the innate despotism of the Austrian family. Perceiving that all attempts to accommodate the disputes by the intervention of the diet, would be fruitless, Joseph again had recourse to arms. He drew reinforcements from the Netherlands and the Rhine, made forced levies in the hereditary countries, and sent his most experienced generals to command in Hungary. His efforts were now crowned with repeated successes, because the malecontents, unaccustomed to regular warfare, were divided by jealousies, disappointed of those succours which France had so lavishly promised, and discouraged by a bull of excommunication, issued against them by the pope.

In this situation of affairs, general Heuster, who was reappointed to the command, commenced a brilliant career, by suddenly marching from the isle of Schut, crossing the Wag, on the 17th of August, 1708, and surprising the main body of the malecontents, under Ragotsky, who had invested Trentschen, to open a way into Silesia and Moravia, where he expected to be joined by numerous partisans.

The irresistible shock of disciplined troops broke, at the first onset, the tumultury bands of insurgents, who were unskilfully posted, without confidence in their officers, and commanded by chiefs at variance with each other, or secretly inclined to Austria. The combat was short, but the victory was bloody and decisive: 6000 men were left on the field, as many captured; Ragotsky, stunned by a fall from his horse, escaped with difficulty, and the whole army was dispersed. From this period the fortune of Austria triumphed. Ragotsky could scarcely collect a force sufficient to engage in desultory skirmishes; the misintelligence increased among the chiefs; many of the officers deserted with whole regiments to the Austrians; suspicion and despondency reigned among those who from fear, interest, or desperation, remained under his standards. The towns and district of the mines in the mountains were the first fruits of this victory; all Lower Hungary, except Neuhasel, was next reduced; other enterprises, of less importance, brought daily new advantages; and a body of imperialists restored the Austrian government in Transylvania, where the natives were jealous of their new prince, and hailed the victorious cause. A desultory army, the forlorn hope of the insurgent party, which had been collected with extreme difficulty by Bertzeny, was defeated by general Seckingen at Zadock, on the frontiers of Poland, on the 22nd of January, 1710; Neuhasel surrendered before the close of the year; Ragotsky and Bertzeny sought an asylum in Poland; and Karoly, on whom the command devolved, was left with only 7000 dispirited troops.

During this career of victory Joseph acted with equal prudence, lenity, and vigour. To hasten the dissolution of the confederacy, he denounced the penalty of high treason against Ragotsky and all his adherents, who did not return to their allegiance within a limited time; though, instead of retracting his concessions and imitating the impolitic severity of Leopold, he still continued to allure those with forgiveness whom rigour might have driven to desperation, and he omitted no effort to bring his rebellious subjects to a sense of their duty. At the last moment he employed Palfy to enter into a negotiation with Ragotsky; to the discomfited remnant of his party he condescended to propose the same terms which he had held forth to the insurgents in the height of prosperity. During the absence of Ragotsky in Poland, Karoly listened to the lenient offers of the emperor; and the convention which gave peace to Hungary was arranged at Zatmar, in January, 1711, between Palfy, the imperial general and plenipotentiary, and Karoly, as head of the confederate party. The principal conditions of this celebrated treaty were, a general amnesty; the restitution of confiscated property; the liberation of prisoners; and the exercise of the Protestant religion, as stipulated by the constitutions of the kingdom; with the confirmation of all rights and immunities approved by Joseph at his coronation, and liberty to propose other grievances for redress at the ensuing diet.*

* The confederacy being now entirely dissolved, and all hopes of exciting a new insurrection frustrated, Ragotsky dismissed his most faithful retainers, sailed from Dantzic to Hull with a few attendants and from thence embarked for France. He was gratified with a pension of 100,000 livres, under the honourable name of a subsidy, and 40,000 for the support of his adherents; but he was probably disgusted with this splendid servitude in France, and repaired in 1718 to Spain, whither he was lured by the turbulent Alberoni, with the prospect of assistance to effect a new revolution in Hungary. From hence he went to Constantinople, to encourage the Turks to continue the war against Charles VI.; but he found the Ottoman court astounded by the recent defeat of their army under the walls of Belgrade, and on the eve of concluding the peace of Passarovitz. By an article of that peace, Ragotsky, with Bertzeny, and some of the other chiefs, who remained faithful to his cause *, were allowed to take up their residence in Turkey, at a distance from the Hungarian frontiers; and from this period he remained tranquil, at the castle of Rodosto, on the sea of Marmora, although his name was made use of by some turbulent Hungarians to foment a conspiracy against the government in 1723.

Ragotsky left some curious memoirs of his life and actions, from his birth to the termination of the rebellion in Hungary, which are written with candour, and dedicated to Eternal Truth; and contain a curious narrative of the memorable struggle in Hungary. He gave the strongest marks of attachment to his religion, though accompanied with great liberality of sentiment, and exhibits the uncommon character of the chief of a party acting from principles of honour, and what he deemed motives of patriotism.

His wife emulated his constancy and firmness. When released from her confinement, and sent by Joseph to gain her husband, she used her influence in persuading him not to desert his cause. On her return

* Windisch, p. 195.

Joseph, who esteemed the talents and respected the intrepidity of Ragotsky, offered to receive him as a generous enemy to whom peace is given, not as a rebel to whom pardon is offered. But the inflexible chief, influenced by an imperious sense of honour, or inspired by republican pride, refused to approve a treaty which had been concluded without the participation of the senate, and passed the remainder of his days in exile, rather than owe his honours and estates to a sovereign against whom he had rebelled, but who was worthy of his attachment and emulous of his friendship.

This negotiation was scarcely brought to a conclusion, and Joseph was beginning to feel the proud satisfaction of giving tranquillity to a country so long distracted by civil commotions, and of being able to turn his whole force against France, when death arrested him in the midst of his short but brilliant career. He expired in the thirty-third year of his age, on the 17th of April, 1711, of the small-pox, a victim to the ignorance of his physicians.*

This great and amiable monarch was of the middle stature; his countenance beautiful and animated; his address and deportment uncommonly pleasing and dignified. Blue eyes, yellow hair, and a complexion remarkably fair, gave him, in early youth, a delicacy of appearance which did

she was again confined, but escaping, repaired to the quarters of Charles XII., then in Saxony. She afterwards passed into Poland, and from thence into France, and died in Paris in 1722.

Ragotsky being of a religious disposition, passed great part of his retirement in penitence and devotion, and wrote meditations, hymns, soliloquies, and a commentary on the Pentateuch, the original of which is preserved in the library of St. Germain des Pres, as we are informed by the authors of the Art de Verifier les Dates.

He was father of two sons, Francis and George, who were both educated in the Austrian court, and not permitted to assume the family name, though they were gratified with other titles. Francis was appointed marquis of St. Carlo in the kingdom of Naples, and George marquis of St. Elizabeth in Sicily. The former died unmarried in 1728, and the latter at Paris, in 1726, leaving no issue by his wife Susanne, of Bois Lippe, and lady of Clere in the Vexin.

* The late prince of Auersperg, who was a page to the emperor at the time of his decease, informed Mr. Wraxall, that his physicians, according to the practice of the times, not only excluded the air from his apartment. but swathed him in twenty yards of English scarlet broad cloth, when the disorder was at its height.

not announce his native activity or vigour of sentiment; but as he advanced to manhood, the labours of two trying campaigns, and the incessant fatigues of the chace, wore away this semblance of effeminacy, and brought out a look and deportment more analogous to his real character.

Generous, complacent, and benevolent, he found no pleasure greater than that of hearing and relieving the distressed. He had such an aversion to flattery, that he suppressed even the compliments generally introduced into birth-day odes. "I come," he said on these occasions, "not to listen to praises, but to hear music." Though educated in the midst of a bigoted court, and under the auspices of a superstitious father, Joseph was tolerant both in principle and practice. He experienced the most heart-felt satisfaction in alleviating the restraints which his pre-decessors had imposed on his Protestant subjects. He banished from his presence those who had excited the for-mer persecutions, and forbade the Catholic priests to em-ploy in their sermons their customary invectives against other religious sects. Yet this liberality of sentiment was not accompanied with lukewarmness towards the faith in which he was educated, or even with the slightest neglect of religious rites.

He gave a proof of judgment and moderation seldom exhibited by a young monarch, of an ardent temper, and impassioned for military glory. Although he had already distinguished his talents in two campaigns, and often ex-pressed his envy at the military career in which his bro-ther was engaged, yet, from the time of his accession, he never put himself at the head of his armies, nor interfered in the conduct of the war; but left the command of his troops and the arrangement of military operations to his great generals, Heuster, Staremberg, and Eugene, while he more beneficially employed himself in promoting the wel-fare of his country, by superintending the civil administra-tion, and infusing order and justice in every department of government.

As a lover and patron of the arts and sciences, Joseph may be classed among the most distinguished of his pre-decessors. Without the pedantry of his father, he pos-sessed that general knowledge and liberal taste which best becomes a sovereign. He spoke, besides his native tongue,

Spanish, French, Bohemian, and Hungarian, with considerable fluency, was master of the Italian dialects, and wrote Latin with facility and elegance. He was versed in different branches of art and science, remarkable for knowledge of music, and for skill in civil and military architecture; he excelled in personal accomplishments and manly exercises; and was intimately acquainted with the history and constitutions of the states which he was born to govern.

Wilhelmina Amelia, wife of Joseph, was daughter of John Frederic, duke of Hanover, by Benedicta Henrietta, princess Palatine of the line of Simmeren. She was born at Hanover, in 1673, and bred up in the Catholic religion, which her father had embraced during his travels in Italy. She became, in 1700, the mother of a son, Leopold Joseph; but the joy which the birth of an heir gave to the father and to the aged Leopold, was soon converted into grief by his death, before he had completed his first year. She bore besides two daughters, Maria Josepha and Maria Amelia.

Maria Josepha, who was born in 1699, married Augustus, third elector of Saxony and king of Poland; and Maria Amelia, born in 1701, espoused Charles Albert, elector of Bavaria and emperor of Germany. By the family compact, concluded in the reign of Leopold, and confirmed both by Joseph and his brother Charles, the succession to the Austrian dominions, in failure of issue male, was entailed on these princesses; but the death of their father frustrated their hopes; for Charles VI. obliged them, on their respective marriages, to renounce all their claims to the Austrian succession in favour of his own daughters.

These princesses were destined to experience singular vicissitudes of fortune. Maria Josepha was left to lament the flight of her husband into Poland, and the occupation of Dresden by the Prussians, at the commencement of the seven years' war, and died in November, 1757, of grief and agitation, the consequences of the harsh treatment which she experienced from the king of Prussia. Maria Amelia, after reluctantly sharing with her husband the transitory honours of queen of Bohemia and archduchess of Austria, saw him driven from his capital, and living in nominal sovereignty, but real dependence on France. On his death

she persuaded her son to make his peace with her cousin
Maria Theresa ; and during the remainder of her life enjoyed uninterrupted tranquillity. She died in December,
1756.

CHAP. LXXX.—CHARLES VI.—1685–1712.

On the death of JOSEPH the hopes of the house of Austria
and the future destiny of Germany rested on CHARLES,
who was the only surviving male of his illustrious family.
By that event the house of Austria, Germany, and Europe
were placed in a new and critical situation. From a principle of mistaken policy the succession to the hereditary
dominions had never been established according to an
invariable rule ; for it was not clearly ascertained whether
males of the collateral branches should be preferred to
females in lineal descent, an uncertainty which had frequently occasioned many vehement disputes.

To obviate this evil, as well as to prevent future disputes, Leopold had arranged the order of succession : to
Joseph he assigned Hungary and Bohemia, and the other
hereditary dominions ; and to Charles the crown of Spain,
and all the territories which belonged to the Spanish inheritance. Should Joseph die without issue male, the whole
succession was to descend to Charles, and in case of his
death, under similar circumstances, the Austrian dominions
were to devolve on the daughters of Joseph in preference
to those of Charles. This family compact was signed by
the two brothers in the presence of Leopold.

Joseph died without male issue ; but left two daughters,
to whom the natural affection of a father might have
prompted him to transmit the succession ; yet his prudence
and justice prevailed over the sentiments of paternal affection : appreciating the danger of conferring the sceptre on
his eldest daughter, who had not yet completed her twelfth
year, he confirmed the family compact, and consigned to
his mother the temporary administration of affairs.

Charles, who now succeeded to the Austrian dominions,
was son of the emperor Leopold, by his third wife Eleonora
Magdalen, a princess of Palatine Newburgh : he was born

in 1685, and educated in the court of his father, under the direction of Anthony prince of Lichtenstein, his governor, and Lavigni, an ecclesiastic of exemplary morals, and of profound and elegant learning

He was at this juncture in Spain, defending the crown against his competitor the duke of Anjou, who had assumed the title of Philip V. On the 12th of September, 1703, he had been proclaimed king of Spain, at Vienna, by the title of Charles III. ; being acknowledged by the allied powers, he took his departure on the 19th, and passed through Holland landed at Portsmouth, where he was received by the dukes of Marlborough and Somerset, and conducted by prince George of Denmark to an interview with queen Anne at Windsor. He was then in the eighteenth year of his age, and is thus described by the continuator of Rapin : " The court was very splendid, and much thronged ; the queen's behaviour towards him was very noble and obliging. The young king charmed all who were present ; he had a gravity beyond his age, tempered with much modesty. His behaviour was in all points so exact, that there was not a circumstance in his whole deportment that was liable to censure. He paid an extraordinary respect to the queen, and yet maintained a due greatness in it. He had the art of seeming well pleased with every thing, without so much as smiling once all the while he was at court, which was only three days. He spoke but little, and all he said was judicious and obliging."

In the ensuing year the young monarch sailed from Portsmouth with a large fleet, commanded by Sir George Rooke, and a considerable body of land forces under the duke of Schomberg ; but being driven back by a violent tempest, did not reach Lisbon till after the death of the Infanta of Portugal, to whom he was betrothed.

Having made several ineffectual attempts on the Spanish coasts, Charles at length landed in Catalonia, where he had numerous partisans, at the head of 12,000 men, under the command of the brave and eccentric earl of Peterborough, and prepared to commence the siege of Barcelona. Although a revolt had taken place among the Catalans, and sanguine hopes were entertained of immediate success, yet the English commander found the scene of affairs far different from his expectations. " Instead of 10,000 men in arms," to use his own words, "to cover his landing, and strengthen his camp, he found only so many higglers and sutlers flocking into it; instead of a city in a weak condition, and ready to surrender upon the appearance of his troops, he found an orderly garrison, and a force almost equal to his own army."

In this hopeless situation of affairs, it was unanimously resolved in several councils of war to re-embark the troops; but this determination was overruled by the spirited resolution of Charles to "stay and die with his brave Catalans." The siege was accordingly commenced, the fort of Montjoy was taken by storm, and Charles entering Barcelona in triumph was proclaimed king.   Catalonia joyfully received her new master; and the kingdoms of Arragon and Valentia were overrun by his arms. But the party of his rival Philip having regained the ascendency, a combined army of French and Spaniards, led by Philip in person, and commanded by the duc de Noailles, drove back his troops, and laid siege to Barcelona.

Charles resolved to stand by his capital, and showed more concern for the security of the place than for the safety of his own person.

On the advance of the French army, lord Peterborough, alarmed at the danger of the archduke, threw seven or eight hundred men into the town; the garrison of Guione, with a number of miquelets, also forced their way into the place; while the English general, with 2500 troops and miquelets, occupied the heights surrounding the enemy's camp, cut off their supplies of provisions, and even prevented all correspondence by land between Philip and Madrid; so that the only mode of communication was by sea through Alicant.   With all these reinforcements, however, the garrison of Barcelona did not exceed 2500 regular troops, including 800 or 900 English, 600 of whom defended the fort of Montjoy.

In April, 1706, the French and Spanish army, amounting to 20,000 men, commenced the siege by attempting to storm the fort of Montjoy; but being repulsed with great slaughter, proceeded by regular approaches, and did not compel the garrison to surrender till after a siege of twenty-two days.

In consequence of this protracted defence, the troops in

Barcelona were enabled to repair the works of the town, to remount the artillery, and prepare for the approaches of the French, which were carried on with little skill and great caution.   By means, however, of their formidable artillery, the enemy in thirty-five days made two breaches in the rampart, one of which was practicable, and advanced even to the covered way.   The garrison, reduced to 2000 men, were wholly employed behind the breaches, while the inhabitants guarded the remainder of the works.

In this situation the enemy might have carried the town by assault, had they not been intimidated by the desperate resistance of the garrison of Montjoy, and by the loss of their best engineer, Lapara, who had been killed in the attack of that fort.

The resolution of Charles rather to be buried under the ruins of his capital than to yield, preserved Barcelona, as the inhabitants were animated by his presence and example to make a desperate resistance.   His prudent and spirited conduct on this memorable occasion is described by Mr. Walpole, who witnessed the relief of Barcelona : " The king's presence and example, who frequently showed himself in places of most danger, and made all his family work at a great intrenchment behind the breaches, gave life and vigour to them ; and from the confession of all his people, had the king withdrawn himself, which many advised him to do, they would have surrendered immediately."

Notwithstanding his unshaken firmness and extraordinary exertions, Charles was reduced to the most desperate situation, and to use the words of Mr. Walpole, " not a speck of blue appeared to give any hopes of the preservation of the town, nor even of the king's person, and consequently of the whole monarchy. "   On one side the besiegers hourly threatened an assault, on the other a French squadron of twenty-eight ships of the line blocked up the harbour ; while the English fleet, on which his deliverance depended, was detained by contrary winds.   At length the wind became favourable ; the long-expected succours drew near ; the French squadron quitted the harbour, and on the 8th of May the English fleet, amounting to fifty sail of the line, with a considerable body of land forces, anchored before the town.

On the 11th of May, the troops were landed with the utmost expedition, and passed great part of the night under arms behind the breaches. On the ensuing morning the French army broke up the siege, and retreated with precipitation, leaving their sick and wounded, great part of their artillery, with immense magazines and stores. Their retreat was harassed by the small but enterprising body under lord Peterborough, and their march being overcast by a total eclipse, the superstitious favourers of the house of Austria portended the eternal setting of the Bourbon sun.

The wonderful spirit and activity of Charles, which formed a striking contrast to his natural phlegm, subsided on the relief of the place ; he wasted much time in religious ceremonies, and in making a procession to the shrine of the Holy Virgin at Montserrat. In answer to the urgent remonstrances of general Stanhope, he excused his delay by alleging that his equipage was not ready ; and was not roused by the animated reply of the English ambassador : " Sir, king William entered London in a coach with a cloak bag behind it, and was made king not many weeks after."*

The deliverance of Barcelona was followed by a series of alternate successes and defeats, in which Charles twice entered Madrid in triumph, and was twice compelled to retreat ; he was at one period master of all the eastern parts of Spain ; and at another reduced to the single province of Catalonia. In the midst of this struggle, he espoused Elizabeth Christina, princess of Brunswick Wolfembuttel †, and resided at Barcelona, hoping to realise his expectations on the crown of Spain, rather from the astonishing successes of the allies in Germany, Italy, and Flanders, than from the efforts of his own heterogeneous army, divided among themselves, and led by generals of different nations and principles, equally at variance with each other.

Charles was awakened from his dreams of visionary grandeur by the intelligence of his brother's death, which happened April 17. 1711, and which secured to him the

* Mr. Walpole to Mr. Robert Walpole, Barcelona, June 23., N. S. 1706.

† He had offered his hand to Wilhelmina Carolina, princess of Brunswick Blankenburgh ; but from attachment to the Protestant religion, she rejected his offer, and afterwards espoused George II.

whole inheritance of the house of Austria, and opened the prospect of the imperial dignity.

In consequence of the arrangements made by Joseph, the empress mother, as regent, assumed the reins of government, proclaimed Charles king of Hungary and Bohemia, and archduke of Austria, without opposition, notified his accession to the courts of Europe, and took every precaution, in concert with Eugene, to secure for him the imperial crown. From the sudden death of Joseph, the throne was vacant, and the struggles for that dignity might have occasioned new and dangerous convulsions, had not the most prudent and vigorous measures been instantly adopted. Prince Eugene had reached Nuremberg in his way to assume the command of the imperial army in Flanders, before he received information of the emperor's death. He hastened to the Upper Rhine, and gained the electors of Mentz, Treves, and Palatine; he then repaired to the Hague, and after concerting the plan of future operations with the English and Dutch ministers, returned to Germany, gave an impulse to the circles of the empire, and collected a considerable force in the vicinity of the Rhine, both from the detachments of the Austrian troops, and from the contingents of the German princes and states. Having assumed the command in quality of generalissimo, he placed himself in a position to prevent the interference of France, and to awe the diet of election, and despatched a messenger to his royal master, urging his instant presence in Germany.

Charles sanctioned the proceedings of his mother, and enlarged the term of her regency; he intrusted Eugene with full powers to manage his interests at the approaching election; established a council, under the direction of his consort, for the conduct of his affairs in Spain, and gave the strongest hopes of support to his faithful subjects in Catalonia. Embarking at Barcelona on the 27th of September, he landed in the vicinity of Genoa, had a public interview with the duke of Savoy in the neighbourhood of Pavia, and received on his arrival at Milan, the 16th of October, the joyful tidings of his unanimous election to the imperial throne; after a short stay at Milan, where he was congratulated by the Italian powers, the new emperor proceeded through Inspruck to Frankfort, and was crowned on the 22nd of December. In addition to the usual titles of emperor and king of the Romans, and to those of Hungary and Bohemia, he styled himself king of Spain, and in proof of his determined resolution to assert his right to that crown, he conferred the order of the Golden Fleece on several of his adherents.

The election of Charles VI. formed a new epoch in the political annals of Germany. Hitherto the capitulation ratified by each emperor was considered as a temporary act, only binding the sovereign who swore to its observance ; but the despotic proceedings of Leopold and Joseph, in putting the princes and electors to the ban of the empire, confiscating their territories, and granting new fiefs, without the consent of the diet, gave rise to a Perpetual Capitulation, which had been originally proposed at the peace of Westphalia, and was now to be ratified by each succeeding emperor, confirming the privileges of the Germanic body, limiting the authority of their chief, and unchangeable except by consent of the diet.

By this capitulation the emperor was not to assemble any diet or council relating to the affairs of the empire, without summoning all the princes and states : he was not to wage war, conclude peace, or enter into alliances without their consent. He was not to put any prince under the ban of the empire by his own authority ; not to appropriate to himself, or confer on his own family, any confiscated territory, and he was bound to restore the possessions of which the members of the empire had been forcibly deprived. It was also stipulated that no election of the king of the Romans should take place during the life of the reigning emperor, unless he was long absent from Germany, or the infirmities of age rendered him unable to conduct the helm of affairs. This instrument likewise ratified the privilege of election secured to the electors by the Golden Bull, precluded the head of the empire from conferring a vacant electorate without the consent of the college, and confirmed to each prince and state the right of concluding separate alliances, either among themselves or with foreign powers, which were not contrary to the interests of the empire.

At the conclusion of the ceremony, the new emperor hastened to Vienna, to take possession of his hereditary dominions. After a residence of only two months in the capital, which was employed in the necessary regulations at the commencement of a new reign, he directed his attention to Hungary, and repairing to Presburgh, in May, 1712, he ratified the pacification of Zatmar, and was crowned with the usual solemnities.

Chap. LXXXI. — 1711-1714.

HAVING pacified Hungary, Charles returned to Vienna to resume, with increasing vigour, his military preparations for prosecuting the war ; and the state of the enemy gave hope that the house of Austria would once more regain her ancient ascendency.

France itself exhibited the most striking scene of misery and desolation. Even the very seasons seemed to war against the monarch and his people. The sudden vicissitudes of weather destroyed the vines and corn in the germ ; every city and every province was threatened with impending famine ; commerce and manufactures, the nerves of a nation, were also annihilated ; the population swept away by the ravages of war. The finances, rapidly decreasing, were yearly becoming more and more unequal to support the enormous burdens of protracted hostilities : the forcible circulation of fictitious money, and the anticipation of the revenues by every species of fraud and artifice, blasted the honour of the government at home, and sunk its credit abroad ; the public sale of military rank, and the prostitution of honours, hitherto the venerated badge of merit, and other expedients the most disgraceful to a high-spirited people, proclaimed at once the distresses of the nation and the reduced situation of the court. In the midst of these calamities, the court was the scene of intrigues and feuds : the very house of Louis was divided into parties ; and the monarch who, in his prime, had awed, astonished, and terrified his contemporaries, in his decline sunk in the opinion of his subjects, his family, and Europe by the indecision of his counsels, the failure of his measures, the ill choice of his ministers, and the effects of his degrading connection with Madame de Maintenon, his supposed mistress and real wife.

By the disastrous events of five campaigns, and the three desperate defeats of Ramilies, Oudenarde, and Malplaquet, the barrier which had hitherto defied all the efforts of Europe was broken through; and the fortresses, the result of such art, expense, and labour, diverted, but could not resist, the tide of war. The army, which had risen like the hydra from its repeated discomfitures, and the generals who had exhausted in vain all the resources of the military science, were driven to the last line of the formidable frontier. That stupendous colossus, which had over-shadowed and overawed the world, was smitten to its foundations ; the loss of a single battle, or the capture of a single fortress, would have opened a passage into the defenceless provinces of France, and scarcely left the monarch, who, for half a century, had given law without control, a place of security even within his own capital.

The continuance of the same vigour, skill, and unanimity for a single campaign would have secured to the allies all the objects of the Grand Alliance; and all the advantages for which they had made such numerous sacrifices and such astonishing exertions. But unfortunately their hopes were frustrated by that principle of dissolution which is inherent in all great confederacies; and it is with the deepest concern we reflect, that England was the primary cause of this change, so fatal to Europe and so disastrous to the civilised world.

Although Anne had obtained a crown by the Revolution she was invariably inimical to its principles, and adverse to the succession in the Hanover line ; and she was affected with scruples of conscience, in accepting a throne, from which she had seen her father excluded. Overborne by the spirit of the nation, and dazzled by the splendid victories obtained over its natural enemy, she had hitherto supported in public the Whig administration, but was secretly disgusted by the political thraldom in which she was held by her great and powerful ministers, and was still more alienated by the caprice and insolence of her former favourite, the duchess of Marlborough. Thus circumstanced, she transferred her confidence to Mrs. Masham, a relation and dependent of the duchess, who gradually supplanted her benefactress. Her scruples revived, and she gave way to the sentiments of affection towards her brother, whom she had been compelled to stigmatise as illegitimate. She was desirous to restore a Tory administration, by whose means she hoped to set aside the Hanover line, and to introduce her brother as her successor, provided he would embrace the Protestant religion, to which, notwithstanding the bigotry of her family, she was invariably and ardently attached. With these feelings she entered into a secret negotiation with Harley, which ended in the gradual dismission of the Whig ministry, and the appointment of a Tory administration, of which Harley was the chief.

Anne, as well as the nation, looked with a more favourable eye towards France; the new ministry intrigued with the court of St. Germain; caballed with the Jacobites, and privately renewed the negotiations for peace. The party of Austria rapidly declined; and the death of Joseph unfortunately furnished a plausible pretext for breaking the Grand Alliance. The dangers arising from the union of the empire, Bohemia, Hungary, Austria, and Spain, in the same person, were exaggerated; and the nation was alarmed with the apprehension of seeing the exorbitant power of Charles V. revived in the person of the new emperor.

A relaxation accordingly took place in the prosecution of hostilities; and Marlborough, weakened by the departure of Eugene to cover Frankfort, and checked in his grand design by the sinister manœuvres of the English ministry, confined his operations to the capture of Bouchain, which was effected on the 13th September, 1711.* On the side of Italy the attempts of the duke of Savoy to penetrate into France, were defeated by marshal Berwick; in Spain the imperial arms were unsuccessful; and Philip circumscribed the Austrian adherents and the empress almost within the walls of Barcelona.

In this situation of affairs the British ministry pressed the negotiations for peace. Preliminaries were signed at London on the 8th of October, 1711, by which Louis agreed, in general terms, to take measures for preventing the union of the crowns of France and Spain on the same head, to secure a barrier in the Low Countries for the

---

* For this masterly campaign of 1711, see the Memoirs of the Duke of Marlborough, ch. ci. cii.

States-general, and on the side of the empire for the house of Austria, and to give a reasonable satisfaction to the other members of the Grand Alliance.

Charles, aware of these negotiations, exerted all his efforts to prevent the conclusion of the preliminaries, and made warm representations in the different courts of Europe against so dishonourable a desertion of the Grand Alliance. He despatched circular letters to the electors, exhorting them to persist in their engagements, and urged the States-general to join in his exhortations to the queen, not to trust the immortal glory which she had gained in the war, and the welfare of her people, to the insincerity of French promises. At the same time count Gallas, his minister in London, made the strongest remonstrances against this breach of faith, and even printed in the public papers the preliminary articles, which had been communicated to him in confidence, with a severe and violent comment. The queen, irritated at this appeal to the people, and his cabals with the Whigs, ordered him to withdraw from England, though she softened this mark of resentment, by informing the emperor that she would receive any other minister.

Encouraged by the representations of the Dutch, and the clamours of the Whig party in England, the emperor, in the commencement of 1712, despatched Eugene to London, hoping either to induce the queen to continue the war, or to rouse the spirit of the nation against the peace. But the presence of Eugene produced a contrary effect. His friendly visits to the duke of Marlborough and the leaders of the Whigs offended the queen; and he was charged by the Tories with forming the most diabolical as well as ridiculous plots against the government. Among other projects, he is said to have proposed the assassination of the earl of Oxford, also to set fire to London in the night, par·ticularly to the palace, while in the midst of the confusion, the duke of Marlborough was to head an armed force, take possession of the Tower, the Bank, and the Exchequer, and seize the person of the queen. Thus was prince Eugene, whose known character for integrity and honour ought to have shielded him from such imputations, degraded into a leader of banditti; and so great was the alarm and ferment that he was publicly insulted by the populace. After a continuance of three months, he returned with the mortification of having witnessed the disgrace of the duke of Marlborough, the defeat of the Austrian party, and of having failed in his efforts to prevent the meeting of the congress of Utrecht, which assembled early in 1712.

The emperor was resolved to prosecute the war although deserted by England; and therefore despatched his chancellor, count Sinzendorf, to Utrecht, with a view to break off, or at least to retard the negotiations. Sinzendorf claimed the full execution of the Grand Alliance; demanded, in the name of his master, not only the entire possession of the Spanish monarchy, but the restitution of all the cessions which had been made to France by the treaties of Munster, Nimeguen, and Ryswick, and encouraged the ministers of the other allies to advance similar claims. This conduct, indeed, suspended the proceedings at Utrecht, but enabled the French to accelerate their private negotiations with the court of England.

Meanwhile Charles made the most active preparations for the prosecution of hostilities, and hoped to break up the conferences at Utrecht by some splendid enterprise against the French in the Netherlands. His views were warmly seconded by the States, and the other allies, who were equally averse to the terms of peace. Early in the spring, prince Eugene took the command of the allied army, which amounted to 120,000 men, and was soon afterwards joined by the British forces under the duke of Ormond.

Although the duke of Ormond declared that he had orders to co-operate with the allies, the effects of the private negotiation between England and France were soon manifest. Eugene having proposed to attack the French army under Villars, was thwarted by Ormond, who had private orders neither to risk a battle nor undertake a siege. Eugene next turned his attention to the siege of Quesnoy, which he invested, and by urgent remonstrances at length prevailed on Ormond to furnish a corps of the auxiliaries in British pay to cover his operations But when the town was nearly compelled to surrender, the British commander concluded an armistice with Villars, and communicated to prince Eugene his orders to separate from the confederates. He then prepared to march towards Dunkirk, which had been yielded to England as a cautionary deposit.

The emperor and the States made the most urgent remonstrances to the queen against this desertion of their cause ; and the discontents in the army rose to the most dangerous height. The duke of Ormond was refused by the States a passage through Douay and Tournay ; was deserted by all the auxiliary troops, except two regiments ; and the princes by whom those troops were furnished declared their resolution to support their contingents one month, and after that period to share the expense with the States and the emperor. Ormond increased the general indignation by seizing the towns of Ghent and Bruges in the name of the queen of England, and by these measures gave the deathblow to the Grand Alliance. Notwithstanding, however, this base desertion, the emperor and all the other allies disdainfully rejected a suspension of arms, which was proposed by the British plenipotentiaries, and unanimously determined to prosecute hostilities.

Eugene, having taken Quesnoy, invested Landrecy, on the 4th of July, 1712, but the loss of the British forces was severely felt. Villars advancing to its relief, attacked a body of troops posted near Denain, under the earl of Albemarle to cover the convoys, stormed their intrenchments, and after a bloody conflict, forced seventeen battalions, with the commander-in-chief, and all the officers, to surrender prisoners of war. Eugene, who was on the other side of the Scheld, marched to support Albemarle, but by the breaking of the bridge was unable to furnish any succour, and was only a melancholy witness of this fatal catastrophe, which compelled him to raise the siege. This misfortune was the prelude to greater disasters, and was followed by the captures of Denain, Marchiennes, St. Amand, Douay, Quesnoy, and Bouchain.

In the course of these events, the armistice between France and England was prolonged, and the duke of Savoy and the king of Portugal were induced to desert the cause of the emperor. The Dutch, terrified by the progress of the French arms, alarmed by the threats of England to conclude a separate peace, and lured by the favourable conditions of the barrier treaty, soon followed their example ; and the negotiations were carried on with such earnestness and zeal, that treaties of peace between France and all the belligerent powers, except the emperor, were signed at Utrecht on the 11th of April, 1713. Spain acceded to these treaties on the 13th of July.

Louis acknowledged the title of the queen to the crown of England, and the Protestant succession, agreed not to allow the pretender to reside in France, to raze the fortifications of Dunkirk, and to cede Nova Scotia or Acadia, with the exception of the isle of Cape Breton, also Hudson's Bay, Newfoundland, and St. Christopher's. Spain likewise yielded to England Gibraltar and Minorca, and by an engagement called the Assiento, granted the right of supplying the Spanish colonies with negroes for thirty years, which had been before enjoyed by France.

Charles was highly dissatisfied with the terms imposed upon him by France and England; and, without consulting his own strength, disdainfully persisted in rejecting all overtures. Having obtained the co-operation of the empire, he determined to prosecute the war alone against the French, who had sustained during twelve years the efforts of the greater part of Europe. Conscious, however, that he could not equally maintain the contest in all parts without allies, he concluded with France and England a treaty of neutrality for Spain, Italy, and the Low Countries, in consequence of which the Austrian troops evacuated Catalonia and the islands of Majorca and Ivica, and he concentrated his force on the banks of the Rhine. He flattered himself that his brave troops, led by Eugene, would still perform wonders; that one important victory would obtain more advantageous terms; and that at all events it would be far more honourable not to owe a peace to the allies who had deserted him, under the humiliating conditions of acknowledging his rival Philip V., but to conclude a separate treaty with France, without renouncing his pretensions to the crown of Spain.

The whole campaign passed without a general action, and was principally confined on the side of the imperial troops to defensive operations. The great military talents of Eugene being unable to cope with the superior numbers of the French, led by marshal Villars, the capture of Landau and Friburgh, the exhausted condition of the Austrian finances, and the unwillingness of the German states to continue the war, compelled Charles to enter into a negotiation with France. On the 26th of November,

1713, prince Eugene and marshal Villars opened conferences at Rastadt; on the 6th of March, 1714, the preliminaries were signed, and a congress assembled at Baden
in Switzerland. Charles, indignant at the conduct of
England, rejected her mediation, and refused to admit the
British plenipotentiaries at the congress ; the ministers of
the Pope, the duke of Loraine, the electors of Cologne and
Bavaria, were likewise excluded; and as Charles was intrusted with full powers by the German diet, the terms of
peace were adjusted between himself and the empire on
one side, and France on the other, and signed on the 7th
of September.

The treaty of Ryswick was made the basis of the peace.
Charles was also guarantied in the possession of Naples,
Milan, Mantua, Sardinia, and the Low Countries, under
the condition of ratifying the barrier treaty ; he obtained
the restoration of old Brisac, Friburgh, and Kehl ; in return he reinstated the electors of Bavaria and Cologne in
their dominions and dignities ; he agreed to leave the
princes of Italy in the peaceable enjoyment of the territories which they actually possessed, and permitted the important fortress of Landau to be retained by France.

" Thus," justly exclaims marshal Villars, " after a war of
fourteen years, during which the emperor and the king of
France had nearly quitted their respective capitals ; Spain
had seen two rival kings in Madrid, and almost all the
petty States of Italy had changed their sovereigns ; a war
which had desolated the greater part of Europe, was concluded almost on the very terms which might have been
procured at the commencement of hostilities."

CHAP. LXXXII. — 1706–1719.

AMONG the most difficult points which remained for future
adjustment, was the transfer of the Netherlands in the possession of the Dutch, to the emperor, and the final ratification of a barrier treaty.

The pretensions of the two parties were so opposite and
contradictory, and the mediation of England so lukewarm,
that all compromise seemed impracticable ; even the death

of Anne during these negotiations, though it changed the conduct of England, did not overcome the reluctance of the emperor, and George I. in vain despatched generals Stanhope* and Cadogan to Vienna, the first from his personal credit with the emperor, and the other from his friendship with prince Eugene, who had the greatest preponderance in the Austrian cabinet.

Many motives influenced the conduct of the emperor in declining to ratify this treaty. Towards the close of the reign of Anne he had entertained an opinion that the party of the pretender was paramount in England, and had affected to listen to overtures for a match between the exiled prince and one of his nieces. Even the accession of George I. did not wholly dissipate this illusion; Charles imagined that his establishment on the British throne would be but of temporary duration, and was unwilling to involve himself in an engagement to guaranty the Protestant succession. He therefore dismissed Mr. Stanhope with great marks of personal regard, but without gratifying him in the object of his mission.

Both the emperor and his ministers treated lord Cobham, who succeeded general Stanhope, with studied neglect; and prince Eugene testified the utmost reserve and indifference to his friend and fellow-soldier, general Cadogan, who repaired to Vienna in the character of ambassador. In various conferences he bitterly inveighed against the harsh and degrading conditions which the Maritime Powers attempted to impose on his imperial master, and declared that the revenues of the Netherlands would be inadequate to the support of the civil establishment, after the payment of the subsidies to the Dutch.

Charles, aware of the weakness of the Dutch government, and of the embarrassments of England by the rebellion of 1715, which was magnified almost into a new revolution, and encouraged by the secret overtures of France, deli-

* General, afterwards earl Stanhope, had served under Charles in Spain with great credit. On the accession of George I. he was appointed secretary of state, and some letters are still preserved among the Walpole Papers, which passed between Mr. Stanhope and the emperor. Among these is one written by Charles in his own hand, highly expressive of his esteem, and of his regret for the fate of the Catalans, which does honour to his head and heart.

vered an ultimatum, by his minister, count Konigsegg, to
the congress at Antwerp, and threatened to march his
troops into the Netherlands, unless in six weeks his demands were complied with.   These disputes delayed the
conclusion of the treaty until the total defeat of the rebels
in England, the death of Louis XIV., and the dread of a
Turkish war, changed the politics of the emperor ; while
prince Eugene suddenly promoted the ratification, from a
jealousy of the Spanish council, who obstructed the treaty,
and from resentment against the deputies of the Low
Countries, who desired an archduchess for their governess.
The treaty was accordingly concluded on the 15th of November, 1715.   Prince Eugene was appointed governor,
and the Dutch, on the 4th of February, 1716, delivered the
Netherlands to count Konigsegg, as plenipotentiary of the
emperor.

By the barrier treaty the states agreed to yield to the
emperor the provinces possessed by Charles II., as well as
those ceded by France at the peace of Utrecht.   A corps
of from 30,000 to 35,000 men was to be maintained in those
countries, of which the emperor agreed to furnish three
fifths, the States the remainder ; and in case of war, a
further augmentation was to be arranged by the two parties.
The emperor allowed the States the sole right of garrison
in Namur, Tournay, Menin, Furnes, Warneton, Ypres, and
the fort of Knocque ; but the garrison of Dendermond was
to be furnished jointly, the governor to be nominated by
the emperor, and to take an oath that he would do nothing
to the prejudice of the States.   In like manner, in the
garrisons belonging to the States, their officers were to
preserve to the house of Austria the sovereignty of the
places committed to their care, and not to intermeddle in
civil affairs.   The Dutch troops were also allowed the free
exercise of their religion in the different garrisons ; but
were to establish no churches, nor annex any exterior distinctions to their places of worship.

The States were permitted to repair the fortifications of
the different towns, but not to erect new works without
previous notice to the governor-general, nor to charge the
emperor with the expenses without his consent.   Different
cessions also were made to the States for the security of
their frontiers ; and the emperor engaged to pay the annual

sum of 500,000 crowns for the maintenance of the Dutch troops, and charged himself with the debts of Charles II. to the United Provinces. Their rights and privileges of commerce were to remain on the same footing as established by the treaty of Munster, in 1648, and the ships, commodities, and merchandises from Great Britain to the Netherlands, or from the Netherlands to Great Britain, were to pay the same duties of export and import as were established at the conclusion of the treaty, till new regulations should be made by the three powers in a treaty of commerce which was to be arranged as early as possible. The emperor also engaged that these provinces should never be transferred to a prince of the house of Bourbon by marriage, sale, or otherwise. England guaranteed this treaty, and engaged, should the Netherlands be attacked, to furnish 10,000 men, with twenty ships of war, if necessary, or to act with her whole force.

But notwithstanding the signature of the treaty, the mutual jealousy of the emperor and the Dutch did not subside ; the emperor deemed the conditions on his part too severe, and exhibited evident signs of a resolution not to fulfil the articles ; while the Dutch, on theirs, retained possession of the districts which were restored by France.

A general consternation also prevailed among the natives of the Low Countries, who complained that the Dutch, jealous of their prosperity, wished to exclude them from all commerce. The states of Brabant and Flanders made strong remonstrances by deputies sent to Vienna; they represented the treaty as derogatory to the emperor's dignity, and fatal to the dearest interests of his subjects. They stated the impossibility of executing the treaty without annihilating their immunities, because subsidies were granted to the Dutch as a fixed revenue, whereas, according to their constitution, no subsidies could be granted without the consent of the States.

Hence the scruples of the emperor returned, and he opened new conferences with the States-general, in the hopes of obtaining a modification of the conditions ; but the negotiation was protracted by the discussions relating to the appointment of the magistracy in several of the towns garrisoned by the Dutch troops, the toleration of religion, the extension of the limits, the arrears of the sub-

sidies; and the convention which finally settled these and
a few other contested points was not concluded till the 22nd
of December, 1718, by the Imperial and Dutch plenipotentiaries at the Hague.

Chap. LXXXIII.—1715–1718.

During the negotiations for the barrier treaty, several
events occurred of great importance to the house of Austria.
Among those the most remarkable was the peace of Passarovitz, which terminated the war with the Porte, and, by the
acquisition of Belgrade, secured the frontiers of Hungary
from Turkish invasion.

The good effects of the fortunate change which had
taken place in the minds of the Hungarians, from the pacification of Zatmar, were displayed in this war; when the
native troops had no inconsiderable share in driving the
Turks beyond the Danube, and in conquering the Bannat
of Temeswar, and the territory of Belgrade.

In 1715 the Turks broke the peace of Carlovitz, declared
war against the Venetians, conquered the Morea, and laid
siege to Corfu. These rapid successes, which recalled to
recollection the former preponderance of the Ottoman
power, spread general alarm among the princes of Europe;
and the king of Sardinia projected a confederacy of the
Italian states under the protection and guidance of France.
But Charles, jealous lest this confederacy should give pre-
eminence to the houses of Bourbon and Savoy, counteracted the league; and when the Venetians appealed to
him as a guarantee of the treaty of Carlovitz, made preparations for immediate hostilities. After an offer of
mediation, which the Porte rejected with disdain, he despatched prince Eugene into Hungary at the head of a
small, but well-disciplined army, flushed with victories in
the Netherlands and on the banks of the Rhine. Eugene
passed the Danube in sight of the Ottoman army of
150,000 men, and encamped near Peterwaradin behind the
very intrenchments which he had occupied in his former
campaign, and which, by an unaccountable negligence, the

Turks had not destroyed. Without delay he led his troops against the enemy, routed their numerous and undisciplined forces, who could only oppose to the military skill of Eugene, and the deliberate courage of the imperial army, a blind and impotent valour, killed the grand vizir and 30,000 Turks, took 50 standards, 250 pieces of heavy artillery, and an immense booty. This action was fought on the 5th August, 1716, near Carlovitz, in the very camp wherein, seventeen years before, the Turks had signed the truce of twenty years, which, by attacking the Venetians, they now broke. The capture of Temeswar, the last of the ancient dependencies of Hungary retained by the Turks, secured the possession of the Bannat and the conquest of Wallachia.

These conquests, which distinguished the campaign of 1716, were followed by still greater successes in the ensuing year. In the month of June, Eugene invested Belgrade, the key of the Ottoman dominions on the side of Hungary. The place, which contained a garrison of 30,000 men, was vigorously defended, and supported a blockade of two months, till the arrival of an immense army under the command of a new grand vizir, gave hopes to the besieged, and alarmed the besiegers. The Turkish troops advancing, intrenched themselves in the form of a semicircle, stretching from the Danube to the Save, and thus confined the imperial army in the marshy grounds between those two rivers.

In this exposed and unwholesome situation, numbers of the imperialists daily perished from the fire of the enemy, and more fell victims to the ravages of a contagious disorder. Yet the troops supported these accumulated evils with the most exemplary patience, anxiously expecting that the Turks would be compelled, for want of provisions and forage, to break up their camp ; but these hopes were frustrated by the perseverance of the enemy, who pushed their lines and batteries to an eminence commanding the bridge over the Save. Eugene now found himself in a critical situation ; the enemy by destroying the bridge might prevent his retreat, or might send a corps across the Save to surprise the detachments intrenched at Semlin, and cut off the parties employed in bombarding the lower town of Belgrade. The imperial troops also, daily di-

H 3

minishing in number, would be soon unable to guard the lines ; and the emperor and empire exhausted by the war which they had just concluded with France, could not support the enormous expense of another campaign. The danger was still further increased as the enemy had advanced their trenches and raised batteries within musket-shot, and were even preparing to storm the lines. Eugene was therefore aware that a decisive victory alone could relieve the army from their dangerous situation, and preserve Hungary and Transylvania.

Under these circumstances Eugene summoned a council of war, and being unanimously supported in his opinion, issued orders for a general engagement. During the anxious night preceding this action he visited the posts, instructed the officers, exhorted the soldiers, and distributed with his own hands refreshments to fortify them against the fatigues of the ensuing fight, and as he passed from post to post, cries of exultation resounded from every quarter. " Lead us," they exclaimed, " against the enemy! Eugene commands! the safety of our country, and the interests of our religion are at stake ; we will conquer or die !"

The imperial army consisted of 60,000 men ; but as 20,000 were stationed to keep in check the garrison of Belgrade ; and as several detachments were posted on the opposite bank of the Save, not 40,000 could be brought into action, to storm intrenchments mounted with a numerous artillery, and defended by not less than 200,000 men, the most complete army which the Porte had ever sent into the field since the siege of Vienna.

Before midnight Eugene was on horseback ; three bombs were discharged as a signal, and the whole army was instantly in motion. About two, the right wing, advancing in order and silence under cover of the darkness, burst upon the enemy's works, and surprised the guard, who were reposing in negligent security. But the same darkness which had at first favoured their attack, was so much increased by a thick fog, that part of the right wing fell by mistake upon some intrenchments which the enemy had raised that night, and meeting with a desperate resistance were thrown into confusion. As long as the fog lasted this confusion was irreparable, and the imperialists, ignorant of the ground, and harassed by the impetuous assaults of the enemy, suffered extremely. At length the sun rose and dispelled the mist; Eugene discovered part of the right wing separated from the centre, taken in flank and rear, and exposed to imminent danger. To see and remove the danger was the effort of a moment. Placing himself at the head of the second line, and followed by a corps of volunteers, he charged the enemy sword in hand, and though wounded, forced his way through their ranks, mowing down all before him. The troops alarmed for the safety of their intrepid leader, pressed forward, redoubled their efforts, and drove the Turks back to their intrenchments. At this moment, Eugene surveyed the lines with awful apprehension. Aware that the spirit of the army had led them to be too precipitate in the attack, he endeavoured to curb their impetuosity, and to give a more certain and solid direction to their force. But his own example overbore a deference even to his orders. The impulse was given, and nothing could restrain the ardour of the troops. The infantry made the attack with irresistible violence, forced the intrenchments, carried the batteries, and turned the Turkish cannon against the banners of the crescent. From that moment all was rout and dismay; before midday the imperialists were in possession of the intrenchments, artillery, and camp ; and the enemy fled with such disorder and precipitation, that those who were in the rear killed those who were before, not to be impeded in their flight.

The immediate consequence of this defeat was the surrender of Belgrade, which was followed the next year by the peace of Passarovitz, so called from a small town in Servia, where Eugene and the grand vizir opened the conferences, and signed the preliminaries, on the 21st of July, 1718, under the mediation of Great Britain and the United Provinces. This treaty established a truce of twenty-five years, and secured to the house of Austria the Bannat of Temeswar, and the Bannat or western part of Wallachia and Servia, together with the town and territory of Belgrade and part of Bosnia.

Chap. LXXXIV. — 1715-1720.

While Charles was embarrassed with the war against Turkey, he was occupied in a series of complicated negotiations with France, England, and Holland, and involved in hostilities with Spain.

Although the principal powers of Europe were comprehended in the treaties of Utrecht and Rastadt, yet the two sovereigns, principally interested in the event of those negotiations, were not reconciled. The emperor did not acknowledge Philip, king of Spain, and Philip did not renounce his pretensions to the kingdom of Naples, the Milanese, and the Low Countries, which the peace of Utrecht had transferred to the house of Austria. Hence those treaties contained the seeds of immediate rupture, and could be considered as little more than establishing a temporary suspension of arms; Europe accordingly was kept in a state of perpetual agitation during a period of sixteen years, before the disputes concerning the Spanish succession could be finally terminated.

Charles, though too much exhausted to meditate the renewal of hostilities, was compelled by the threatening aspect and ambitious views of Spain to take measures for his own security.

On the death of Maria Louisa of Savoy in 1714, Philip espoused in the same year Elizabeth Farnese, princess of Parma. This turbulent and ambitious woman gained a prodigious ascendency over the mind of her hypochondriac and doting husband, and not only fomented the enmity which Philip entertained against the emperor; but by adding her own pretensions to the duchies of Tuscany and Parma, contributed to widen the breach, and remove still further the prospect of an accommodation. The views of Elizabeth were seconded by the daring genius of Alberoni, whom she had raised to the office of prime minister, and who, infusing a new spirit and activity into the counsels of Spain, made active preparations both by sea and land. The emperor, alarmed at these preparations, dreading lest the French monarch should assist his grandson, and aware that Naples would fall an instant sacrifice to the attacks of the

two powers, was induced to listen to the overtures of
George I., which he had before rejected, as the alliance of
England was the only counterpoise he could secure to the
vast weight and power of the house of Bourbon. He
accordingly lent a willing ear to the claims of George, as
elector of Hanover, on the duchies of Lauenburgh, Bremen,
and Verden, and hastened the conclusion of a defensive
alliance, which was signed at Westminster on the 5th of
May, 1715.

But the death of Louis XIV. in the following September,
greatly changed the situation of affairs. He was succeeded
by a minor of an infirm constitution ; and the duke of
Orleans, who governed France first as regent, and afterwards as prime minister, was anxious to recover his country
from the exhausted state to which it had been reduced by
the numerous wars of Louis XIV., to repress the national
spirit of conquest, which had given umbrage to the powers
of Europe, and to secure his own succession to the crown,
which had been guaranteed by the treaty of Utrecht,
should Louis XV. die without issue.

The court and kingdom were divided into two parties ;
one favoured the rights of the duke of Orleans, the other
the claims of Philip, who, notwithstanding his renunciation,
aspired to the reversion of the French crown. With a view,
therefore, to support his rights, the duke of Orleans was
desirous to form a connection with England, who was
equally interested to prevent the accession of Philip, and
whose assistance was necessary to repress the efforts of his
numerous partisans in France.

The British cabinet no less appreciated the great advantages of an alliance with France, which would counteract
the intrigues of the pretender abroad, deprive him of the
only power whose interposition they had just reason to
apprehend, and awe his adherents into submission at home.
The interests of the two parties equally concurring in the
same object, the negotiation was speedily brought to a successful issue; and on the 4th of January, 1717, a triple
alliance was concluded at the Hague between England,
France, and Holland, for maintaining and guaranteeing the
order of succession to the crowns of France and England,
as settled by the peace of Utrecht.

The emperor was highly averse to the spirit and tenor

of this alliance, which, by ratifying the treaties of Utrecht,
secured Spain to Philip, and confirmed the galling conditions of the Barrier.   His pride was likewise mortified, as
he foresaw that the connection with the house of Austria
would now become a secondary consideration with England.

During the negotiations his minister at London endeavoured to prevent the conclusion, by declaring that the
signature of such an engagement should instantly annul
the treaty of Westminster.   Some trifling modifications
were accordingly made, but as they were not sufficient to
appease the emperor, he declined acceding to the alliance.
Conscious, however, that he could not break the connection
between France and England, and alarmed by the vast preparations of Spain, while he was involved in a war with
the Turks, he was compelled to yield to the necessity of his
affairs.   But he temporised and protracted his accession
till he had extorted a secret promise, from France and
England, to effect the exchange of Sardinia for Sicily; as
he was well aware that while Victor Amadeus retained
that island, the possession of Naples would be rendered
extremely precarious.

These engagements, however secret, were not concealed
from Philip and Victor Amadeus, and they both united to
frustrate the plan.

Although Spain was scarcely recovered from the devastations of a long and bloody war, Philip was roused into
action by the importunities of his ambitious consort, who
was anxious to assert her claims to the duchies of Tuscany,
Parma, and Placentia.   These claims were encouraged and
supported by her favourite Alberoni, whose vast and enterprising genius aspired to realise greater projects than the
acquisition of two petty territories in Italy. He had gained
Victor Amadeus by the offer of the Milanese in exchange
for Sicily; he had, through the means of baron Gortz,
negotiated a peace between Charles XII. and Peter the
Great, who were both irritated against George I.; and at
his instigation the Swedish monarch agreed to make a
descent into England at the head of a formidable body
of Swedes and Russians, to collect the Jacobites to his
standard, and march to the capital.   He prevailed on the
Turks to continue the war against the emperor, and carried
on secret negotiations with prince Ragotski and the male-

contents of Hungary. He tried to amuse the court of London with the proposal of a marriage between the prince of Asturias and the princess Anne, while he was secretly endeavouring to excite an insurrection among the Jacobites, and had actually promised to support the pretender with the whole force of Spain.

In regard to France, he intrigued with the malecontents in Brittany, and attempted to foment troubles in the Cevennes by exciting the Protestants to rebellion. He insisted that the exclusion of Philip from the crown of France was invalid, because contrary to the Salic law, which no act could annul; and that if Louis XV. should die without issue male, Philip was the undoubted heir, and not the duke of Orleans, who had usurped the regency. To support his master's right he formed, by intrigues and money, a powerful party in France, composed of the Jesuits, and a considerable number of the nobility devoted to the old system of Louis XIV., who were disgusted with the regent, and headed by the duke and duchess of Maine. He even despatched emissaries into France to secure the person of the duke of Orleans, and to convey him to Spain; and, covering his ambitious projects with the appearance of public good, he proposed to convoke the states-general, for the appointment of a new regent, reforming the state, and paying the national debt. The magnitude of his preparations being not inadequate to the execution of this gigantic project, Europe waited in anxious suspense the bursting of the storm.

Alberoni commenced the execution of his plan by the invasion of Sardinia. On the 22nd of August, 1717, the marquis de Leda at the head of the Spanish army disembarked at Cagliari, and soon effected the conquest of the whole island. In the following year he invaded Sicily with a still more numerous armament, and in a short time made himself master of the principal fortresses except Syracuse, which he closely blockaded.

These acts of hostility and the impending danger united the emperor, France, and England for their common safety. Charles being delivered from the dread of the Turks by the victory of Belgrade, despatched a body of troops to the defence of Naples, and hastened the conclusion of the peace of Passarovitz. He also reluctantly renounced his preten-

sions to Spain ; and on the 2nd of August, 1718, concluded
a treaty with Great Britain and France, which, from the
expected accession of the United Provinces, was termed
the Quadruple Alliance. By this arrangement the emperor
agreed to acknowledge Philip king of Spain, and to give
to Don Carlos Tuscany, with the eventual investiture of
Parma and Placentia, and in the mean time to secure the
reversion by garrisoning the fortresses of those duchies
with neutral troops.   In return for these renunciations,
Sicily was to be yielded by Victor Amadeus to the emperor,
in exchange for Sardinia, and Philip was to renounce his
pretensions on the Netherlands, the duchy of Milan, and
the two Sicilies. By a separate article, the three allies
bound themselves to enforce the acceptance of this treaty,
and the kings of Spain and Sardinia were allowed three
months only to notify their acquiescence to these conditions.

Victor Amadeus, exposed to the attacks of France, acceded to the treaty on the 2nd of November ; but Philip
disdainfully rejected all overtures of accommodation, although his fleet had been defeated and almost totally destroyed by admiral Byng off the coast of Sicily, on the 11th
of August.

Towards the commencement of the ensuing year, a
French army, under marshal Berwick, crossed the Pyrenees, and penetrated into Spain ; the coasts of Gallicia
were ravaged by the English squadrons, and a remnant of
the Spanish navy destroyed in Vigo. The fleet which
carried the pretender to Scotland was dispersed by a
storm ; the regent, duke of Orleans, quelled the conspiracy
fomented by the Spanish faction in France ; Peter the
Great was awed by the appearance of an English fleet in
the Baltic ; and Charles XII., on whose co-operation
Alberoni had founded the most sanguine hopes, was killed
at the siege of Fredericshall, on the 13th of November.
The English fleet having prevented the Spaniards from
reinforcing their army in Sicily, the imperial general, count
Mercy, landed at the head of 13,000 troops, and being reinforced with 10,000 men, took Massena after an obstinate
resistance of three months, recovered the greater part of
the island, and confined the enemy almost under the walls
of Palermo.

This rapid success gave weight to the demands of the allied powers; the fall of Alberoni was the prelude to the pacification of Europe, and on the 25th of January, 1720, Philip acceded to the terms of the Quadruple Alliance, which was moulded into a treaty of peace, and signed at the Hague on the 17th of February. By this treaty it was stipulated that the duchies of Tuscany, Parma, and Placentia should never be united with the crown of Spain; and the emperor promised to expedite the letters expectative of the reversion, called, in the diplomatic language of the times, the Eventual Investiture, within two months after the ratification.

On the 2nd of August, 1718, soon after the signature of the Quadruple Alliance, Charles promulgated a new law of succession, for the inheritance of the house of Austria, under the name of the Pragmatic Sanction. According to the family compact formed by Leopold, and confirmed by Joseph and Charles, the succession was entailed on the daughters of Joseph in preference to the daughters of Charles, should they both die without issue male. Charles, however, had scarcely ascended the throne, though at that time without children, than he reversed this compact, and settled the right of succession, in default of his male issue, first on his own daughters, then on the daughters of Joseph, and afterwards on the queen of Portugal and the other daughters of Leopold. Since the promulgation of that decree, the empress had borne a son who died in his infancy, and three daughters, Maria Theresa, Maria Anne, and Maria Amelia. With a view to insure the succession of these daughters, and to obviate the dangers which might arise from the claims of the Josephine archduchesses, he published the Pragmatic Sanction, and compelled his nieces to renounce their pretensions on their marriages with the electors of Saxony and Bavaria. Aware, however, that the strongest renunciations are disregarded, he obtained from the different states of his extensive dominions the acknowledgment of the Pragmatic Sanction, and made it the great object of his reign, to which he sacrificed every other consideration, to procure the guaranty of the European powers.

CHAP. LXXXV. — 1718.

BEFORE we proceed in the history of Charles VI., it is necessary to pause and review his political situation, in regard to the internal state of his dominions, and his relations with foreign powers.

At the conclusion of the Quadruple Alliance, Charles seems to have attained the summit of his power and splendour ; and if we estimate his power from his possessions he would appear the greatest monarch in Christendom. He was by election emperor of Germany, by hereditary right sovereign of Hungary, Transylvania, Bohemia, Austria, Styria, Carinthia, and Carniola, the Tyrol, and the Brisgau, and he had recently obtained Naples and Sicily, the Milanese and the Netherlands. The population of these extensive dominions did not amount to less than 24,000,000 of souls. But if we consider the effective strength of these territories and their disjointed state, we shall find that Charles was rather weakened than strengthened by his new acquisitions.

The Netherlands, though the richest and most populous district of Europe, were distant from his other dominions ; part of the revenues was appropriated to the repairs of the fortifications, and the maintenance of Dutch garrisons ; and the remainder, which, by the constitution of the country, he could not augment or alienate, was inadequate to their defence in time of war. His authority also was extremely limited and precarious, as the country was divided into provinces forming separate and independent states, which possessed different privileges, and could not be reduced to a uniform system of government. Having recently experienced a tumultuary opposition to some innovations which he was desirous of introducing into the forms of government and the collection of the revenue, he was obliged to quell the refractory spirit of the natives by exemplary punishment, and could only keep them in awe by a military force.

In addition to the ancient causes of enmity which subsisted between the houses of Austria and Bourbon, the possession of the Netherlands furnished a new source of future contention by inflaming the natural jealousy arising from the proximity and jarring interests of rival nations.

The Barrier Treaty contained the seeds of inevitable dissension, and the tenure on which those countries were held gave rise to continual bickerings with the Maritime Powers, who, jealous of their commercial interests, had bound him by the strongest engagements not to permit any foreign trade from the Netherlands which might interfere with theirs. Hence the acquisition of these territories was the source of continual dissensions, and weakened instead of cementing the union of the house of Austria with England and Holland.

The kingdom of Naples and its appendage Sicily, which Charles acquired in exchange for Sardinia, did not furnish a military force sufficient for their own defence. Hence they were likely to become the point of attack from France and Spain; and the emperor could not furnish adequate succours from his German territories without the assistance of the Maritime Powers.

The duchies of Milan and Mantua were likewise isolated from his other dominions by the interposition of the Grisons and the territory of Venice; and Mantua, the only place capable of resisting a long siege, required a numerous garrison and immense magazines. The revenue of the country, though more adequate to the maintenance of the civil establishment, was yet too scanty to furnish resources for war; and that duchy, separated from his other possessions, was exposed to invasion from the arms of France or Spain, unless it was protected by the king of Sardinia, who held in his hands the key of Italy.

In these circumstances, Charles derived his only certain and permanent sources of strength from his hereditary dominions; but these were greatly inadequate to the grandeur of his ideas and the extent of his projects.

In point of numbers, and when headed by such generals as Eugene and Staremberg, the imperial army might have been extremely formidable, had the finances been sufficient for their maintenance. The amount of the peace establishment exceeded 100,000 men; but all these troops were necessary to occupy his numerous fortresses, to secure the tranquillity of his distant territories, to supply his contingent of 18,000 men for the Low Countries, and to repress the discontents in Hungary. Their pay was extremely small, because, when stationary, they were supplied with provisions and forage from the hereditary countries.

During the whole reign of Charles VI. the war establishment never exceeded 160,000 men ; of these not more than 70,000 could be brought into the field, who, being deprived of their customary supplies of provisions from the hereditary countries, and unable to maintain themselves by their scanty pay, could scarcely be kept on foot without subsidies from foreign powers, except in a war with the Turks, when they drew their subsistence from Hungary.

His revenues, which amounted to 30,000,000 of florins*, were scanty in comparison with the extent of his dominions, and in a state of almost irreparable disorder. The original cause of this dilapidation was principally derived from the burdensome wars in which Leopold and Joseph had been engaged for the Spanish succession. Although the finances had been improved by the establishment of the bank of Vienna, and the wise measures adopted under the administration of count Gundaker Staremberg for the liquidation of the arrears ; yet the good effects of that plan had been thwarted by the expenses of the campaigns against the Turks, the warlike preparations occasioned by the perpetual contests with Spain, and the defective management of the revenue under the auspices of count Altheim.

Another great cause of the disorder in the finances arose from the practice of the emperor himself, who drew annually from the governors, both of his hereditary and foreign provinces, sums to a considerable amount for his private purse. These sums being taken from the revenues appropriated to the maintenance of the civil and military establishments, injured the public service, and occasioned the neglect of the most urgent affairs. The governors were anxious to gain the favour of the emperor by making large remittances, which supplied him with the means of bribing foreign courts, gratifying his Spanish and Italian adherents, and purchasing jewels, of which he was more fond than any of his predecessors.

The imperial dignity gave splendour to the house of Austria, as well as the influence which was derived from the power of conferring ecclesiastical dignities and honorary

---

* Not more than 3,000,000*l.* sterling.

distinctions; but, as emperor of Germany, Charles possessed rather a nominal than a real sovereignty. He had no permanent revenue, nor any settled military force; and his principal influence arose rather from his weight as head of the house of Austria, than as chief of the empire and president of the diet. In case of war in which the empire took part, he was indeed assisted with men and money by the contingents of the princes and states, according to the resolutions of the diet; but even when the whole body was unanimous the contingents fell far short of their nominal amount; the supplies of money voted under the name of Roman months*, were scanty and ill paid; and the army, which on paper was stated at 120,000 effective men, seldom exceeded 20,000 in the field, consisting chiefly of raw and undisciplined troops, actuated by the petty interests and discordant views of the states to which they belonged, and rarely in a condition to act before the middle of the campaign.† But whenever the states were divided in opinion, and particularly in a war with France, the emperor was feebly supported; and part of the Germanic body either adopted a neutrality, or joined in hostilities against their chief.

Charles was not gifted with the talents of his brother Joseph, had not enjoyed the same advantages of education, and was by nature so cold and phlegmatic, that it was said he was serious even when he smiled; but he was by no means deficient in abilities. His conception though slow was clear; his political knowledge was extensive, and he expressed himself in various languages with great elegance and facility. His intentions were honest and upright; and he was anxious to govern his subjects with wisdom and justice. His religion was less tinctured with bigotry

---

* These subsidies were called *Roman months*, because formerly the states of the empire were obliged to furnish an army of 20,000 foot, and 4000 horse, to accompany the emperor in his expedition to Rome; and those who did not choose to provide soldiers paid a monthly equivalent in money. This mode of contribution was afterwards extended to all other cases where men and money were required for the service of the empire, and hence the term Roman months was applied to subsidies in general.

† As these troops seldom made their appearance before the month of August, by a pun on the imperial title of *Augustus* they were termed the *August* troops.

than that of his father Leopold, or even of his brother Joseph. Though sincere in his belief of the Roman Catholic faith, and attached from principle to the see of Rome, he yet preserved himself in great points uninfluenced, always retained the clergy in due subjection, and never suffered them to intermeddle in matters of state. Strict in his morals, he was ever remarkable for great propriety of character and decorum of manners; and even in the ardour of youth never deviated into any glaring excess. But these solid qualities and upright intentions were counteracted by a narrow jealousy, a love of adulation, and a punctilious obstinacy, which induced him to maintain an inflexible perseverance in measures once adopted; these natural defects were aggravated by the ascendency which an artful favourite, count Altheim, had acquired over his mind.

It was a great misfortune to Charles, that of all the ministers and attendants whom Leopold had placed about his person on his departure for Spain, and at an age when the deepest impressions are made, not one was worthy either of his esteem or imitation. His governor, prince Lichtenstein, who accompanied him in the character of grand master of his household, and to whose guidance he was peculiarly intrusted, was a nobleman of mean intellects, pedantic knowledge, and wholly devoted to the wild pursuits of alchemy; hence, at a time of life when friendships are easily formed, Charles contracted a partiality for count Altheim, from whom he imbibed principles which unfortunately regulated his future conduct, and influenced the events of his reign.

Count Altheim, the nephew of prince Lichtenstein, first attracted the notice of Charles by an open variance with his uncle, and soon improved the favourable opinion of the young monarch by the elegance of his address and the insinuation of his manners. Under the semblance of a frank and open behaviour, he concealed great cunning and intrigue. To perpetuate his influence he prejudiced Charles against the court and ministers of Vienna; he insinuated that the sole aim of Joseph and his cabinet was, to exclude him from the throne of Spain, to annex the Milanese to the Austrian dominions, to secure to him only the kingdom of the two Sicilies with the Low Countries, and to render him entirely dependent.

When Charles became head of the house of Austria, the artful favourite availed himself of his master's vanity to suggest that his glory was interested in being his own minister; that he was superior to his servants in abilities as in dignity; that he ought to prove himself greater than either his father or brother, by supporting alone the weight of empire, and should principally consult those who were indebted to him for their elevation, and had his honour only at heart. By instilling such doctrines, and by appearing totally subservient to the will of the emperor, Altheim acquired an undue influence over the counsels of his phlegmatic and suspicious master. But though he might have aspired to the situation of prime minister, he was so conscious of his own incapacity to direct the helm of government, that he never accepted an office of responsibility. He refused to be a member of the secret conference or cabinet council, and in the post of master of the horse, became the real though not the ostensible minister, and contented himself with the substance, while he left to others the shadow of authority. He gradually appropriated to himself the disposal of all places except in the military line, new modelled the board of finances, and filled the several departments of government with his creatures.

He availed himself of the predilection which Charles always professed for Spain, and his sanguine hopes of recovering that crown, and prevailed on him to institute a council composed entirely of Spaniards or Italians, for the purpose of governing the Low Countries, Naples, and the Milanese; and this council became the private cabinet which, during his life, swayed the helm of state. He also availed himself of the discontents which had taken place between counts Sinzendorf and Staremberg, two ministers of the conference, and by sometimes supporting the one and sometimes the other, he held the balance in his own hands, and prevented them from uniting against his own authority.

Having diminished the influence and credit of these ministers, Eugene alone remained a barrier to his ambition, and an object of his jealousy. The rank and dignity, the high consideration in which the prince was held by persons of all stations, his power as president of the council of war, and member of the secret conference, led the favourite to spare no cabals, and to employ intrigue upon intrigue, to undermine his credit and obtain his dismission.

Under the pretence of general reformation in the departments of government, Altheim insinuated to the emperor, that the power of Eugene was too great for a subject, and even shackled the authority of the sovereign. He therefore proposed as a remedy against what he called a government within a government, to establish an independent committee of war, and he hoped, that as the high spirit of the prince would not brook this affront, his remonstrances would offend the emperor, and he\would either resign or be dismissed. The conduct of Eugene justified this supposition ; for when informed of the intended alteration in the council of war, he declared that if a single servant was dismissed, he would instantly retire.

The efforts of Altheim were seconded by his brother-in-law, count Nemsch, who submitted to the emperor daily reports highly unfavourable to the prince. Before the scheme was matured, a valet of count Nemsch having stolen the minutes of these informations, carried them to Eugene, who instantly appealed to his sovereign. This unexpected discovery disconcerted the whole project. Charles could not refuse attending to the just remonstrances of his general on the eve of a war with Spain ; and the favourite himself had not courage to carry his plan into execution. Nemsch was arrested, tried, deprived of all his employments, and imprisoned for two years in the citadel of Gratz ; and one of his principal agents, the Abbé Todesqui, was whipped by the common executioner and banished.

But though Eugene thus triumphed over the cabals of his enemies, he never acquired the full confidence and friendship of Charles. The recollection of past services, the disgrace which would be incurred by dismissing him, and the dread of driving him into the service of France, preserved him in his posts, but with more ostensible than real power. During a war indeed, or when hostilities seemed unavoidable, Eugene possessed considerable authority, and was permitted to regulate the military operations with almost absolute sway ; but in peaceable periods his counsels had little weight, and the emperor consulted his own prejudices and suspicions, and followed the importunate representations of his other ministers, who envied the high distinction enjoyed by the great supporter of the house of Austria. Hence his audiences of his sovereign were always cold and short, each mistrusting the other ; the emperor from jealousy, Eugene from a recollection of the many attempts which had been made to remove him. He gave his advice plainly and frankly in the cabinet whenever it was demanded; but never enforced his opinion, or condescended to court the approbation of his sovereign, or the concurrence of the ministers. In his own department alone he preserved his authority without the smallest control even from the emperor himself.

Not long after the failure of this intrigue, Eugene was relieved from further attempts by the decease of count Altheim, who died in 1722, to the great regret of the emperor. Charles testified his friendship for the favourite, by declaring himself guardian of his children, and, to use the words of a contemporary writer, " gave orders in what manner they should be educated, and treated them more like his own children than his subjects."

On the death of count Altheim, the principal ministers of the cabinet were prince Eugene, count Gundaker Staremberg, and count Sinzendorf, emphatically called ministers of the secret conference, and the marquis de Realp, who was at the head of the council of Spain.

The marquis de Realp, a native of Catalonia, who had attached himself to the interests of Charles, while struggling for the crown of Spain, owed his promotion to the influence of count Altheim, to whom he always continued devoted. Though not a member of the conference, he had at this period great personal credit with his master, as well because he had been recommended by Altheim, as because he was intrusted with the principal management of the Spanish and Italian affairs. He was visionary and indiscreet, wholly ignorant of the political system of Europe, and, ill qualified for negotiation ; but was consulted by the emperor in commercial regulations, particularly those relating to his foreign dominions.

Since the death of Altheim the emperor had lived with Realp in greater familiarity than with any of his other ministers ; Charles admitted him in his hours of retirement, which were passed in the society of Spaniards and Italians,

who had attached themselves to his fortunes in Spain, and
with whom he shook off that solemnity of deportment
which he uniformly maintained in public.

Count Sinzendorf, chancellor, and secretary for the direction of foreign affairs, had been principally recommended
by the marquis de Realp, as a counterpoise to the interests
of prince Eugene. Realp, well acquainted with the suspicious character of the emperor, described him as a man
not remarkable for eminent talents, and of an interested
and supple disposition, but of great experience in foreign
affairs. Yet Sinzendorf, though at first he acted a subordinate part, afterwards gradually supplanted his patron,
and rose to the highest confidence by flattering the
chimerical schemes of the emperor, and by affecting an
entire deference to his will.

His character formed a singular contrast of opposite
qualities. He united the extremes of flattery and blunt-
ness, suppleness and obstinacy, phlegm and impetuosity,
humility and arrogance. He was highly elated with the
most trifling incident in his favour, and sunk into the
deepest despondency on the smallest reverse. From his
devotion to the luxuries of the table, he is justly termed by
the royal historian the Apicius of the imperial court;
from his fondness of the pleasures and enjoyments of
society, and his attachment to play, he was unable to attend
to the multiplicity of business; and by his dilatory and
procrastinating spirit increased the natural tardiness of the
cabinet of Vienna. The magnificence of his establishment, and love of parade, involved him in expenses which
far exceeded his income ; and he was not backward in accepting presents from foreign courts as the price of his
good offices. He did not, however, conceal from the emperor the amount of these gratifications, or the offers
which were made to him, and in some instances was
authorised by his master to accept the presents, and to
employ part of the money in gaining foreign ministers, or
in promoting his favourite schemes.

Count Gundaker Staremberg possessed high integrity
and an elevated mind, and was well acquainted with the
financial department, of which he had the direction. He
despised the arts of flattery, by which Sinzendorf and
Realp conciliated their master ; and, like Eugene, always
delivered his opinion with frankness and sincerity. He

was, however, cold, formal, reserved, and contemptuous, jealous of Eugene, but despising his other colleagues. He therefore extorted the esteem, but did not possess the confidence of the emperor ; was disliked by the other ministers, and had little credit out of his department.

These were the ministers who were intrusted with the ostensible direction of foreign affairs ; and their discordant views and characters increased the difficulty of transacting business with a court which had been long remarkable for its dilatory and overbearing conduct. The change which had taken place in the habits and disposition of the emperor contributed still further to augment this embarrassment.

At the commencement of his reign Charles was sedulous in the transaction of business, constantly attended the conferences of state, toiled through the mass of diplomatic papers, and even wrote numerous despatches to his ambassadors with his own hand. But this assiduity gradually subsided, he devoted great part of his time to music and to the pleasures of the chace, and wasted the remainder in ceremonies and parade, or in the company of his Spanish and Italian favourites. He still, however, affected great attention to business, and would suffer no measure to be executed which he had not previously examined and sanctioned. He also received the result of each conference, which was drawn up by count Sinzendorf, secretary for foreign affairs, and counter memorials were often presented by the other ministers.

From this mode of conducting business, papers and documents continually accumulated, which the emperor had neither leisure nor inclination to examine ; and the most important negotiations were continually neglected. Even the copy of the Quadruple Alliance remained three months on his table before he could be induced to sign it.

CHAP. LXXXVI.—1718-1722.

THE external relations of the house of Austria towards foreign powers were essentially changed on the conclusion of the Quadruple Alliance.

I 4

A bloody war, which had continued for the space of
eighteen years, had totally changed the political situation
of the North.   It originated in the contest for the
possession of Livonia, which had been alternately occupied by the Poles and Russians, and had been assigned
to the Swedes at the peace of Oliva.   Augustus II.,
king of Poland, with the hopes of recovering Livonia,
formed a confederacy with Russia and Denmark, against
Charles XII., who had recently succeeded to the crown of
Sweden in the fifteenth year of his age.   But the views of
the confederates were baffled by the vigour and intrepidity
of the young monarch: Charles compelled the king of
Denmark to desert the confederacy, and conclude the
peace of Travendahl; he forced Augustus to abdicate the
throne of Poland, which he conferred on Stanislaus Letzinski; defeated the czar in several encounters, and
threatened him with the same fate as Augustus.   But after
having raised his military glory to the greatest height, he
lost by the single battle of Pultawa all the fruits of his
former successes, sacrificed his veteran troops amidst the
wilds of Russia, and wasted several years as a fugitive and
suppliant at the mercy of the Porte.

During his absence, Augustus regained the throne of
Poland; and the confederacy was renewed and strengthened by the accession of the electors of Brandenburgh and
Hanover.   The emperor, anxious to prevent the war from
spreading into the empire, joined with the other members
of the Grand Alliance to secure a neutrality for the Swedish
provinces in Germany.   This proposal, however, being
scornfully rejected by the king of Sweden, the confederates
burst upon his dominions, overran Pomerania, Bremen, and
Verden, involved his nephew, the duke of Holstein, in his
misfortunes, and Charles XII. only returned to experience
new defeats, and to witness the loss of his fairest provinces.

Though at length reconciled to his rival, Peter the
Great, he still breathed war and vengeance, led his army
into the heart of Norway, and fell a sacrifice to his daring
spirit, on the 11th of December, 1718, at the instant when
he was preparing to second the wild schemes of Alberoni,
and in concurrence with Russia, to turn his arms against
the emperor, and the powers confederated by the Quadruple
Alliance.   His death was a fortunate event to Europe;

for although he had exhausted his country, and occasioned its dismemberment, yet being still adored by a people emulous of military glory, and animated with a recollection of their former deeds, his eccentric valour might have again turned the tide of success.

Peter the Great had made considerable progress in civilising his vast empire, and by creating a navy, disciplining his army, and concentrating his force on the side of the Baltic, had converted Russia from an Asiatic into an European power. He had consolidated his conquests from Sweden, and began to take an active part in the political transactions of Germany and the North. Although from a dread of the Turks he had courted the alliance of Austria, yet he was greatly displeased with the emperor for supporting the nobles of Mecklenburgh against their sovereign Charles Leopold, who had espoused Catherine, his niece; and he was still further irritated by his interference in the affairs of Sweden to the exclusion of the duke of Holstein, who was betrothed to his daughter, the princess Anne. From these causes of disgust, Peter was readily induced to concur in the schemes of Alberoni, and to co-operate with his rival, Charles XII., in taking vengeance on the emperor.

Alarmed at the threatening aspect of Russia, the emperor, on the 5th of January, 1719, concluded a defensive alliance with the king of England as elector of Hanover, and the king of Poland as elector of Saxony. Fortunately, however, the hostile designs of Russia were frustrated by the events which occasioned the disgrace of Alberoni, and by the death of Charles XII.; but Peter still retained his dislike, and even after the peace of Nystadt prepared vast armaments by sea and land, to interfere in the affairs of Mecklenburgh, and to place his intended son-in-law on the throne of Sweden.

The Turks, fallen from their former grandeur, and humbled by the peace of Passarovitz, were kept in continual alarm by their dread of the Russians and the troubles of Persia; and Sultan Achmet III., who had exchanged the restless and baneful activity of his ancestors for the indolence of the seraglio, was neither able nor willing to infringe the treaty of Passarovitz, which he had recently concluded.

At this period the influence of the emperor seemed to preponderate in Italy, and its heterogeneous states were split and divided by different interests, and not likely to unite in one compact league against the house of Austria.

Those parts of Italy which did not acknowledge the sovereignty of the house of Austria, were the republics of Venice and Genoa, the dominions of the pope, the territories of the king of Sardinia, and the duchies of Modena, Parma, and Tuscany.

During the contests between France and Spain, after the death of Charles V., as well as during the war for the Spanish succession, Genoa maintained for the most part a wise neutrality, and purchased from the emperor the marquisate of Finale, which was guarantied by the Quadruple Alliance. But in 1715, the Genoese having offending Charles by arresting an imperial officer who wore his sword, contrary to the ordinances of the state, a corps of Austrian troops marched to the gates of Genoa, and compelled the republic to liberate the prisoner, to pay 300,000 dollars, and to depute a senator to Vienna, for the purpose of expressing their regret and requesting forgiveness. From their local situation the Genoese were attached to France, and jealous of the king of Sardinia, who had pretensions to the marquisate of Finale ; but, deriving experience from their recent humiliation, were afraid and unwilling to offend the emperor.

Although the peace of Passarovitz deprived Venice of the Morea, which had long been an object of contention with the Turks, yet it secured her trade, and ensured to her the possession of the Dalmatian territory and the valuable islands of Corfu, Cephalonia, Zante, and Cerigo. Since that pacification the republic relinquished its ambitious designs of making conquests in Greece, and preserved a state of uninterrupted neutrality in regard to the affairs of Europe. From her position on the Adriatic and the frontiers of the Milanese, as well as from dread of the Turks, Venice was closely united with the house of Austria, and was treated with the respect due to an ancient ally by the emperor, who looked forward to the assistance of her fleet, in case of a rupture with the Turks.

The thunders of the Vatican, which had long awed the princes of Europe, had lost their terrors; and the pope, hemmed in between the Milanese and the kingdom of Naples, was of still less weight as a temporal power.

Next to the emperor, the king of Sardinia was the most powerful prince in Italy, less from the extent than from the situation of his dominions, which formed a barrier on the side of France.

Victor Amadeus possessed the ambition, courage, and talents which had raised his predecessors from petty princes of Savoy to a secondary sovereignty in Europe, and had increased his dominions by a similar policy, in alternately swaying the balance between the houses of Austria and Bourbon in Italy, and selling his service to the highest bidder. By the treaty of Utrecht he had obtained from France the forts of Exiles and Fenestrelles, the valleys of Oulx, Sezane, Bardonache, and Chateau Dauphin, and the confirmation of the territories in the Milanese, promised by Leopold as the price of his accession to the Quadruple Alliance, the greater part of which Charles had been reluctantly compelled to yield. These territories consisted of part of the duchy of Montferrat, the provinces of Alexandria and Valencia, with the district between the Po and the Tanaro, of the Lumellina and the valley of Sessia. But these acquisitions did not gratify his ambition; he aspired to the possession of the whole Milanese with the title of king of Lombardy, and was disgusted with the emperor, who refused to fulfil the promises made by Joseph in seconding his views, and withheld the Langhes and the Vigenvenasco, which had been promised by Leopold. He was still more irritated at the compulsory exchange of Sicily for the barren island of Sardinia.

Victor Amadeus at this period had recovered his country from the calamities of war, had improved his finances, and possessed a well-disciplined army, by whom he was adored. Hence the house of Austria became deeply interested to secure his assistance, or at least his neutrality; but Charles had conceived a peculiar jealousy of the king of Sardinia. He was indignant that the reversion of the crown of Spain was entailed, by the peace of Utrecht, on the descendants of Victor Amadeus, in preference to his own line; and he beheld with the strongest aversion the attempts of the British cabinet to negotiate a marriage between the prince of Piedmont and one of the daughters of Joseph, which might render the house of Savoy a claimant of the Austrian succession. He knew also that the assistance of Victor Amadeus could not be gained without sacrificing a part of Lombardy, and was not ignorant of his customary remark, " I must acquire the Milanese piece by piece, as I eat the leaves of an artichoke."

From its insignificance and weakness, Parma would not deserve notice among the powers of Europe, had it not given a queen to Spain, and been distinguished by the disputes for the Succession. The ducal throne was occupied by Francis, the seventh prince of the house of Farnese, who was without issue, and the presumptive heir was his brother Anthony, who was likewise childless. They were both of an inferior capacity, and wholly subservient to the counsels of Spain.

Tuscany, which under the first princes of the house of Medici had risen to such distinction and splendour, was sunk into a state of decline under Cosmo III., whose advanced age and extreme bigotry weakened every nerve of government. His only surviving son, John Gaston, was without any prospect of issue, and in character both·indolent and licentious. Princes of such talents were incapable of supporting the claims of the princess Anna Maria Louisa, daughter of Cosmo III., and wife of the elector Palatine, or of making any effectual resistance to the eventual disposal of Tuscany.

The small territory comprising the duchies of Modena, Reggio, and Mirandola was principally remarkable for its position between Tuscany, Parma, Mantua, and the ecclesiastical states, which rendered its acquisition of importance during an Italian war. The sovereign, Rinaldo d'Este, was a prince of an enterprising spirit, and during the war of the Succession had continued inflexible in his attachment to the house of Austria, although his dominions were overrun by the French. The battle of Turin having restored the preponderance of the imperial arms in Italy, he recovered his possessions, and received, in reward for his fidelity, the investiture of Mirandola from the emperor Joseph. Gratitude and inclination bound him to the interests of the house of Austria, and he was a firm adherent to Charles VI.

The relative situation of England and the house of Austria always depended on the connection of England with

France. During the ambitious projects of Louis XIV., England courted the house of Austria as the great counter-poise to the house of Bourbon, and their interests were still more closely united in the war of the Spanish Succession. Anne first tore asunder the bands of amity by de-serting the principles of the Grand Alliance and concluding a separate peace with France, which wrested the crown of Spain from Charles VI., and guarantied it to a prince of the house of Bourbon.

Although the breach occasioned by this desertion was in some measure healed by the accession of George I., and the mutual interests of the two powers, to withstand the ambitious designs of Elizabeth Farnese, had renewed their connection, yet the coolness which had arisen was never wholly removed. Charles was offended with the recent alliance of England and France, because it rendered his co-operation of less value; he was displeased with the onerous terms of the Barrier Treaty, and his resentment was still further excited by the petty discussions relative to the German interests of the king of England as elector of Hanover. Long accustomed to blind complaisance from England, he expected that an elector of Hanover upon that throne would be still more subservient to his views and de-sires, and was both disappointed and chagrined when the conduct of George I. dissipated the illusion. England, though willing to conciliate the head of the house of Aus-tria, was more anxious not to lose the lucrative commerce with Spain, and was too attentive to her own interests not to enforce the strict execution of that part of the Quadruple Alliance which related to the eventual investiture of the duchies of Parma and Placentia in favour of Don Carlos, and which the emperor was desirous to elude.

The republic of the United Provinces was in a state of weakness and disunion; the government was a confederacy of discordant states without a stadtholder, loaded with debts, and incapable of active exertion. After the death of pensionary Heinsius, whose influence had long been predominant, it was still more distracted by different parties, equally jealous of France and of the house of Austria. The States had been recently alienated by the prevarications of the emperor in concluding their favourite object, the Barrier Treaty, and were chiefly swayed by the united influence of England and France.

The duke of Orleans, who held the reins of government
in France, had already made one step towards a reconciliation with Spain, by affiancing Louis XV. with the infanta
Mary Anne, eldest daughter of Philip and Elizabeth Farnese, and by the marriage of Elizabeth, his fourth daughter,
with the prince of Asturias.   This marriage, however, did
not affect the union between France and England, or occasion any essential change in the situation of France with
regard to the house of Austria ; for the infanta Mary Anne
being only four years of age, the consummation of her
marriage with Louis XV. was distant, and the eventual
succession to the crown of France still open.

Spain, though humbled by the loss of her fleet and the
defeat of her projects, retained a spirit of pride and bound-
less ambition.   Philip V. seemed to have relinquished his
personal enmity to the duke of Orleans by the conclusion
of the double marriages ; but being reduced to a state of
morbid melancholy, he was wholly governed by Elizabeth
Farnese, who directed her ambitious views to secure the
eventual succession to the crown of France for her descendants by Philip.   This, however, being a distant contingency, she was still more anxious to procure the reversion
of Tuscany, Placentia, and Parma, the hopes of which had
alone induced her to accede to the Quadruple Alliance ;
well aware of the emperor's repugnance to confirm the
reversion, she employed her utmost efforts to extort his
acquiescence by obtaining the concurrence of England and
France.

Portugal was governed by John V., a prince of a violent
and haughty disposition, but who possessed more talents
than any of his predecessors of the line of Braganza.   He
was attached to the house of Austria as well from his
enmity to France, and his rivalry to Spain, as from his
marriage with Mary Anne, sister of Charles VI.

Germany was at this period agitated by religious dissensions, which divided the empire into two parties, the
Catholics and the evangelical body, or Protestants.   Fruitless attempts had been made to terminate these dissensions
by the treaties of Westphalia and Nimeguen ; and the
peace of Ryswick, which concluded the war between the
empire and France, furnished new motives of dissension,
as by the influence and threats of France a clause was

introduced in the fourth article, stipulating that the Roman Catholic religion should be continued in the places restored by France as it was then exercised. This clause, which was contradictory to the treaty of Westphalia, was agreed to by the emperor and the Catholic states, but rejected by the Protestants; and the treaty was ratified by the emperor Leopold without any reference to their remonstrances and claims. Violent disputes accordingly arose in the diet; and, after much altercation, the Protestants seem to have acquiesced, with the hopes that the treaty itself would be invalidated by the war which was on the point of breaking out for the Spanish succession. These disputes, though suspended by the war, were renewed after the peace of Baden, in which the obnoxious clause was not formally repealed. The Protestants were persecuted by the elector Palatine, and deprived of many of their churches; and reprisals were made on the Catholics by the king of Prussia and the elector of Hanover.

In addition to these religious disputes, the diet was agitated by the rival claims of the electors of Bavaria, Palatine, and Hanover.

The troubles of Mecklenburgh contributed also to divide the states of the empire, and embarrass the emperor. Violent disputes arising between Charles Leopold the reigning sovereign, and the states of the duchy, respecting the imposition of provincial taxes, the excise, and the right of garrison in the town of Rostock, they appealed to the emperor, and were warmly supported by the elector of Hanover. Letters of protection were accordingly granted to Rostock, and an imperial decree of sequestration was issued against the duke, the execution of which was intrusted to the elector of Hanover and the duke of Brunswick. The duke, however, assisted by Peter the Great, whose niece he had espoused, collected a considerable force, and prepared to resist the execution. At the same time the king of Prussia, who had claims on the eventual succession, complained that the decree had not been intrusted to him as director of the circle of Saxony, and the czar declared that he would never suffer a prince who had married into his family to be oppressed.

These different claims and declamations greatly embarrassed the emperor, and induced him to lay the affair before

the diet.   The duke, however, derived less advantage from
the czar than he expected from so powerful an ally, as the
Russian troops only served to increase his enemies without
enabling him to resist them.   He therefore disbanded his
forces, and retired to Dantzic ; the army of execution overran the duchy, established an imperial administration,
sequestered the ducal revenues, and restored the privileges
and possessions of the nobles.   But this settlement was of
temporary duration, the troubles were soon renewed; and
the affairs of Mecklenburgh continued to embarrass the diet
and the emperor during a considerable part of his reign.

The authority of the emperor, which was thus thwarted
by the contests of opposite parties, was still further controlled by the ascendency which the elector of Hanover
had acquired on his accession to the throne of Great Britain,
and by the increasing strength of the house of Brandenburgh.

The house of Brandenburgh is descended from the petty
counts of Hohenzollern in Suabia, one of whom obtained,
in 1200, the burgraviate or presidency of Nuremberg.
Frederic II., or, according to some, the third burgrave, is
distinguished in the history of Germany, during the thir-
teenth century, as having greatly contributed to the election
of his relation Rhodolph, of Hapsburgh, to the imperial
throne ; having, partly by marriage, partly by purchase,
and partly by investiture, obtained an independent sovereignty in Franconia, he laid the foundation of the rising
greatness of his family.   His lineal descendant, Frederic IV.,
possessed the principalities of Culmbach and Bareith, with
the margraviate of Anspach, and contributed to the aggrandisement of his house, by purchasing from the emperor
Sigismond the mark or marquisate of Brandenburgh, with
the electoral dignity.   He received the investiture of his
new dominions and dignity from the emperor in 1417, at
the city of Constance ; and, from that period, his family
was called the electoral house of Brandenburgh.

Under the successors of Frederic, the margraviates of
Anspach and Bareith were transferred to the younger
branches; and the power of the reigning house did not rise
into consequence till the beginning of the seventeenth century.   The principal events which contributed to its aggrandisement were, the introduction of the reformation, by which

the bishoprics of Brandenburgh and Havelburgh were se-
cularised and annexed to the electoral dominions; the
acquisition of Prussia, which was originally a Polish fief;
and the succession to the counties of Cleves, La Marc, and
Ravenstein, as part of the inheritance of the house of
Juliers, in virtue of the marriage of Sigismond, elector of
Brandenburgh, with Anne, eldest sister of John William,
the last duke.

The power of the house of Brandenburgh was still farther
augmented and consolidated by Frederic William, who for
his distinguished civil and military talents was surnamed
the Great Elector. His son and successor Frederic assumed
the regal title; and though it did not add to his power, it
contributed to the aggrandisement of his family, by rescuing it from that state of servitude in which the house of
Austria had hitherto kept the princes of Germany.

Frederic dying in 1713, was succeeded by his son Frederic
William, who, instead of continuing the splendour of his
father's establishment, made economy the great basis of
his administration. The first object of the new king was,
to suppress the numerous charges of his father's court,
to sell his jewels, horses, and furniture; and by reducing
the establishment almost to that of a private individual,
he laid the foundation of that treasure which he bequeathed
to his successor.

Frederic William next directed his attention to the improvement of his finances: he equalised the land tax,
raised the excise, augmented the tolls, improved agriculture by suppressing the feudal tenures; and, by simplify-
ing and improving the mode of collection, nearly doubled
his annual revenues. He also established a more simple,
though despotic form of government, suppressed the council
of state, reduced the ministers to mere clerks, and directed
every department with the same ease and order as a colonel
governs his regiment, or a steward regulates his accounts.

But the great political end of all his interior arrangements was, to render himself formidable by the maintenance
of a large army. He had learned, from the example of his
ancestor George William, that a prince without troops was
liable to be oppressed both by his allies and enemies; from
that of the great elector, that an effective and well-disciplined army had raised the house of Brandenburgh to a high

degree of eminence among the powers of Europe. He had
beheld with indignation his father receiving foreign subsidies, and the Prussian troops acting under the direction of
the sovereigns by whom they were paid; and, in the campaign which he served in Flanders, had been heard to
declare that, by a proper administration of the finances, a
king of Prussia could maintain 40,000 men from his own
resources alone. He proved the truth of his assertion;
for, in the very first year of his reign, he increased his
army from 28,000 to 50,000 men, notwithstanding he augmented the pay of his soldiers. He published military
regulations for every officer, enforced subordination and
regularity by the severest penalties, annually inspected
every regiment, directed their evolutions in great reviews,
acted the part of a non-commissioned officer at the ordinary
parades, and, from his attention to the most trifling manœuvres, was sarcastically called the serjeant king.

But his love of detail did not fetter his genius, or draw
him from weightier matters; for he formed a military
system till then unknown in Europe. He first established
that discipline which every other power has been striving
to imitate, and that mechanism in the infantry by which
the parts are firmly connected, and become one uniform
and simple whole. He established warehouses and magazines of corn in all his provinces, which might supply his
troops with immediate subsistence in time of war, or serve
to ease his subjects in time of scarcity, and he furnished
the magazines with large trains of artillery, and all sorts of
military stores.

In the prosecution of his military arrangements, Frederic
William united all the companies or schools of cadets,
which the great elector had founded for the children of the
poor nobility, in different cities and towns, and formed
them into a corps of cadets in the capital. In this academy,
the cadets were instructed in all the arts and sciences with
which an officer ought to be acquainted; and, being trained
to military discipline, furnished never-failing supplies for
the officers of the army. He also founded at Potsdam an
hospital for 3000 orphans of soldiers.

By means of his effective and well-disciplined army,
Frederic William became the arbiter of Germany; and his
alliance was warmly courted by the European powers.

Hitherto, either from inclination or policy, he had generally
concurred with George I., whose daughter Sophia Dorothea
he had espoused. With him he had zealously joined in
supporting the Protestant interest in the empire, and,
naturally jealous of the house of Austria, had evaded every
connection which seemed likely to promote its aggrandisement in Germany. But his capricious and unstable temper,
agitated by every gust of passion, and his aversion to the
reality, notwithstanding his love of the image of war, rendered him incapable of adopting any coherent system of
policy.

Chap. LXXXVII. — 1718-1727.

The eagerness of Charles to obtain possession of Sicily
had induced him to sign the Quadruple Alliance, and to
agree to terminate his disputes with Spain at the congress
of Cambray, under the mediation of England and France.
But he had no sooner acquired Sicily, than he testified his
repugnance to fulfil his engagements. The principal motive of his conduct was, an aversion to bestow the succession to Tuscany, Parma, and Placentia on a prince of the
house of Bourbon, which he foresaw would endanger the
security of his dominions in Italy. In fact, he had only
signed this article with a resolution to evade it, and with
the hope that England would be equally interested to prevent the execution. But when he found that George I.
was unshaken in fidelity to his engagements, he gave way
to his indignation against England, and not only procras-
tinated the meeting and conclusion of the congress, but
entered into desperate projects to injure the commerce of
the Maritime Powers ; and in direct contradiction to the
spirit, as well as the letter of the barrier treaty, established
the East India Company at Ostend, in 1722.

Philip was equally averse to fulfil the articles of the
Quadruple Alliance, and from his accession to that treaty
on the 25th of January, 1720, nearly three years were
passed in frivolous delays and ridiculous discussions on the
titles assumed by the two monarchs, before any progress
was made in the business to be deliberated at the congress

of Cambray. Count Sinzendorf, the imperial plenipotentiary, successfully employed those arts of chicanery of
which he was so consummate a master; but the pretensions of Philip being warmly supported by Great Britain
and France, the emperor could not withhold the act of investiture longer than the beginning of 1724, and the congress was at length formally opened in the beginning of
April.

In addition to the embarrassments arising from these
contrary pretensions, and the captious dispositions of the
two sovereigns, the proceedings of the congress were now
delayed by the sudden abdication of Philip V., who, on the
10th of February, 1724, resigned his crown to his son Don
Louis, made a solemn vow never to resume it, and retired
to St. Ildefonso.

It is needless to inquire into the motives of this extraordinary resolution, whether from constitutional melancholy,
from religious scruples, or from the hope of succeeding to
the crown of France on the death of Louis XV., who had
been recently attacked with a dangerous disorder. This
sudden change gave birth to new difficulties, and divided
the administration of Spain into two parties; for Philip, in
his retirement, swayed the reins of government, and the
orders, which were to convulse or pacify Europe, still issued from Elizabeth Farnese. The new king, though he
at first bowed before paternal authority, was not equally
submissive to the dictates of his step-mother; he was,
therefore, gradually wrought upon by his adherents, who
urged him to emancipate himself from the shackles in
which he was held by the court of St. Ildefonso, and to
assume the real, as he possessed the nominal power.

This motley species of divided government could not
long subsist; derangements and delays took place in every
part of the administration, and foreign affairs were neglected, even beyond the usual procrastination of the dilatory court of Madrid. The abdicated sovereign, instigated
by his ambitious consort, was unwilling to relinquish his
long-established authority; Louis was disgusted with acting
the part of a puppet on the throne; and these royal jealousies and discordant views seemed likely to excite a con-
vulsion, which must have ended in the deposition of the
son, or the imprisonment of the father.

Fortunately for Spain, this dreadful alternative was avoided by the sudden death of Louis. He was seized with the small-pox, and, being unskilfully treated by his physicians, was, on the 31st of August, hurried to the grave, in the eighteenth year of his age, and only the eighth month of a nominal reign. The queen was eager again to seize the reins of government, which seemed likely to be wrested from her grasp; and Philip himself, after a few affected scruples, was easily induced to resume the crown.

This event seemed to remove one of the principal obstacles which had embarrassed the proceedings of the congress, and the conferences were resumed with new spirit, under the mediation of Great Britain and France. Philip required the emperor to renounce the title of king of Spain and the great mastership of the Golden Fleece, to settle the disputes which still continued concerning the succession to Parma and Tuscany, and to restore to their rightful owners the states of Mantua, Mirandola, Montferrat, and Sabionetta, which Joseph had of his own authority appropriated or conferred.

The emperor, on the contrary, expressed his resolution to retain the title of king of Spain, though he demanded that Philip should renounce that of archduke of Austria; he claimed the sole right to the grand mastership of the Golden Fleece, as being founded by the ancient dukes of Burgundy, of whom he himself was the lineal heir and descendant; he also insisted that the pretensions of the duke of Parma, and of the other princes, had no relation to the objects treated of in the articles of the Quadruple Alliance, and should be referred to the Aulic council, or the diet of Ratisbon.

In attempting to adjust these complicated objects of dispute, the mediating powers dipleased both parties; the two monarchs privately made overtures to each other, and the baron de Ripperda was secretly despatched from Madrid to negotiate with the court of Vienna.

This extraordinary man was a native of Groningen; and, having served as colonel in the Dutch army, during the war of the Succession, was personally known to prince Eugene. At the peace of Utrecht, he was deputed as envoy from the States-general to Spain; and having, by his talents and address, acquired the favour of Alberoni, em-

braced the Catholic religion, and settled at Madrid, where
he was employed in affairs of a secret and delicate nature.
Venal and rapacious, he, at the same time, received bribes
from England and a pension from the court of Vienna,
and seems at an early period to have formed the project
of uniting Philip with the emperor, and to have lured the
queen of Spain with the hopes of an archduchess for one of
her sons. During the latter part of Alberoni's administration, Ripperda excited his jealousy, and was disgraced; but
again rose into favour on his fall. Being strongly recommended by the duchess of Parma, at the suggestion of the
imperial court he became the channel of communication
between the queen and her mother, and, in the private
audiences to which he was admitted, found means to dazzle
the visionary imagination of Philip with splendid schemes
for the improvement of the finances, the augmentation of
the army, and the amelioration of commerce; he likewise
gained the implicit confidence of the queen, by his affected
solicitude for the establishment of her sons in Italy.

At length he availed himself of the disgust and resentment entertained by Philip and his queen at the dilatory
proceeding of the congress of Soissons, and offered to proceed to Vienna, and open a negotiation with the emperor,
which, from his intimacy with the ministers, and his knowledge of the court, he promised to bring to a speedy and
successful termination. His offer was eagerly accepted;
and, in 1724, he departed with great secrecy to Vienna,
and took up his residence in the suburbs, under the fictitious name of the baron Pfaffenberg. For a considerable
time his arrival was known only to the emperor, the marquis de Realp, and to count Sinzendorf, who was intrusted
with the negotiation. Their conferences were held by
night, and the mystery was not even suspected by the
foreign ministers till the middle of February.

In these private meetings the claims of the respective
sovereigns were agitated with scarcely less obstinacy and
perseverance than at the congress of Soissons; and the
negotiation was protracted for several months. Charles,
anxious to separate the two branches of the house of Bourbon, and to secure the largesses of Spain, lured the queen
with the hopes of bestowing the eldest archduchess on Don
Carlos, and securing to the young prince a splendid esta-

blishment in Italy, and the reversion of the Austrian succession. He does not, however, seem to have been sincere in this proffer, and much time was passed in urgent demands on one side, and quibbling evasions on the other.

At length the conclusion of this tedious negotiation was accelerated by the dissolution of the temporary union which had been effected between Spain and France, under the administration of the duke of Orleans. During his life the infanta was treated as the future queen; but his successor, the duke of Bourbon, actuated by different interests, and anxious to secure an heir to the crown of France, sent back the young princess to Spain, and married Louis XV. to Maria Letzinsky, daughter of Stanislaus, titular king of Poland. This insult roused the proud and irritable court of Madrid almost to frenzy. In the first paroxysm of resentment the queen tore off a bracelet, ornamented with the portrait of the king of France, and trampled it under foot; and Philip exclaimed that Spain could never shed sufficient blood to avenge the indignity offered to his family. He declared his resolution to separate France and Spain for ever, and offered to submit the final settlement of his disputes with the emperor to the sole mediation of England. This offer being declined by George I., the Spanish monarch turned his resentment against England, broke up the congress of Cambray, and ordered Ripperda to conclude, on any terms, an immediate accommodation with the court of Vienna.

But although the negotiation seemed now brought to a successful issue, the emperor experienced the greatest difficulties from the repugnance of his family and ministers. Eugene and Staremberg were violent in their opposition; the former contemptuously stigmatised the petty intrigues of the emperor with some of his ministers unknown to the others, and the latter petulantly observed that the marquis de Realp would ruin his master with his visionary schemes, and expressed astonishment that Sinzendorf, who was by birth an Austrian, should wish to render Austria a province of Spain. Count Windisgratz, president of the Aulic council, inveighed against the partisans of the treaty as traitors; and the empress herself, disappointed in her favourite object of bestowing the hand of her daughter, Maria Theresa, on the duke of Loraine, gave way to her indignation, and reproached count Sinzendorf with sacrificing her dearest hopes to an alliance with a foreign family.

Charles, on this occasion, laid aside his ungracious deportment and characteristic phlegm, and even condescended to employ artifice in order to extort the approbation of his own family and ministers. He paid unusual deference to the cold and formal Staremberg, solicited Eugene in person, and even bribed the countess of Bathiani to obtain his acquiescence; he lured the ostentation of count Windisgratz by representing that the subsidies of Spain would enable him to give law to the empire, and render the decrees of the Aulic council irresistible. He reconciled the empress by the prospect of a brilliant establishment for their daughters, whose posterity he urged, in addition to the empire and the Austrian dominions, might wear the crowns of France and Spain. Proud of the success of his petty intrigues, Charles could not refrain from expressing a childish exultation, and boasted that he had now overcome the repugnance of all his ministers, and matured a plan which was to revive in his person the ancient splendour and power of the house of Austria; and to give effect to his negotiations, he increased his army by taking 30,000 foreigners into pay.

The alliance, concluded at Vienna between the emperor and Spain, consisted of three separate treaties. The first, signed on the 30th of April, 1725, confirmed the articles of the Quadruple Alliance: the emperor renounced his pretensions to the crown of Spain, and Philip acknowledged his right to the Netherlands, the duchy of Milan, and the kingdom of Naples and Sicily; Charles also obtained his favourite object, the guaranty of the Pragmatic Sanction. Both sovereigns agreed to retain the titles which they had assumed; and stipulated that the honours conferred on their respective subjects, during the war, should be confirmed; an article which highly gratified the Spanish and Italian favourites of the emperor, many of whom had been created grandees of Spain and knights of the Golden Fleece. The second and third treaties were signed on the first of May. The second was a treaty of commerce, which opened the ports of Spain to the subjects of the emperor, sanctioned the establishment of the Ostend Company, and gave to the Hanseatic towns the same privileges of trade as were enjoyed by the English and Dutch. The third was a treaty of mutual defence, by which the emperor promised his good offices for the recovery of Gibraltar, and the two sovereigns specified their respective contingents, and agreed to support each other with their whole force if necessary.

In addition to these treaties, secret articles were also supposed to be arranged, though not formally executed, relative to the marriage of the two archduchesses with Don Carlos and Don Philip, the support of the Ostend Company, the recovery of Gibraltar by force, and the restoration of the pretender to the throne of Great Britain, should George I. refuse to accede to the treaties of Vienna.

The first treaty alone was soon communicated to the public, the others were gradually made known ; but the secret articles were never formally divulged, and were solemnly denied by the emperor and his minsters; although the conduct of the two courts, and the subsequent avowal of the king of Spain, fully established the proofs of their existence.*

The emperor, deluded with visionary hopes of governing the counsels of Spain, and commanding the wealth of the Indies, trusted that the other powers of Europe would be awed by this alliance. His allusion was increased by the ready accession of the empress Catherine, who, anxious to place her son-in-law, the duke of Holstein, on the throne of Sweden, received large remittances from Spain, and made vast preparations by sea and land to co-operate with the allies of Vienna against England. Charles also expected that France, torn by factions, loaded with debt, and under the weak administration of the duke of Bourbon, could not engage in hostilities, when awed on one side by Spain, and on the other by the whole German empire, which he hoped to unite in his cause. He flattered himself that England, for the sake of her commerce, would deprecate a war with Spain, relinquish Gibraltar and Minorca, and acquiesce in the establishment of the Ostend Company ; and he entertained no dread from the opposition of the United Provinces, who were in too feeble and disordered a state to act without the impulse of France and England.

* For a proof of these facts, the reader is referred to the Memoirs of Sir Robert Walpole, ch. xxvii., and of Lord Walpole, p. 139.

The demand of Gibraltar, made by the king of Spain, was the signal of hostile preparations; and England, against whom the force of the confederacy was principally directed, made exertions equal to the magnitude of the danger. George, having obtained the aid of his parliament, and the co-operation of France, hastened to Hanover, where he baffled the schemes of the emperor in Germany and the north; he detached Sweden and Denmark, gained the king of Prussia, and other princes of the German empire, and on the 30th of September, 1725, concluded a defensive alliance between England, France, and Prussia, which was called the treaty of Hanover, and to which the United Provinces, Sweden, and Denmark, afterwards acceded.

But Charles was not daunted by this powerful confederacy; his hopes were excited by the liberal remittances at first made by Philip, while his pride was inflamed by the reception of his minister, count Konigsegg, whose arrival at Madrid was hailed with acclamations of unbounded joy, and who swayed without control the counsels of Spain. He therefore treated the preparations of the allies with the utmost contempt; he boasted that he would crush the Protestant interest in Germany, and raise a new house of Burgundy from the younger branch of the house of Bourbon, which should again humble the pride of the elder line. He styled the government of the United Provinces a company of pedlars and merchants, and declared that unless George would restore Gibraltar and Minorca to Spain, he would sow such dissensions between him and his parliament as should end in his expulsion from the throne.

The conduct of the emperor was conformable to these declarations; he treated the British agent at Vienna with scorn and neglect, gave continual audiences to the duke of Wharton, who was deputed by the pretender; he caballed with the opposition in England, and ordered his minister count Palm to present a memorial to the king, reflecting on the speech from the throne, and denying the existence of the secret articles with which he was charged, and to publish it as an appeal to the nation at large, against the conduct of the king.

While the emperor thus insulted the king and the nation he made the most active exertions to form a confederacy against the allies of Hanover. He had concluded with the king of Portugal a commercial treaty, by which he obtained the freedom of trade to the Brazils in preference to all other nations.   He entered into a defensive alliance with Catherine empress of Russia, in virtue of which, both the contracting parties agreed to furnish 30,000 men in case of an attack, and he secured her accession to the treaty of Vienna, and her guaranty of the pragmatic sanction.   He gained the electors of Mentz, Treves, Cologne, and Palatine, extorted the neutrality of Saxony, and prevailed on the duke of Wolfembuttel to consent to the introduction of an Austrian garrison into Brunswick, which would open to his arms the electorate of Hanover.

But the circumstance which most distressed the allies of Hanover and strengthened the party of the emperor, was the defection of the king of Prussia.   The petty disputes relative to recruiting parties, and the claims to some inconsiderable districts on the frontiers of Hanover, had long agitated the irritable mind of Frederic William; and the superiority which George assumed over him aggravated his disgust.   To these motives were added his apprehensions of being exposed to an attack from the Russians for his adherence to the Hanover alliance.   Charles availed himself of this change in his disposition, and lured him with the promise of supporting his pretensions to the remainder of the succession of the house of Juliers on the death of the elector Palatine, or of investing him with an equivalent, should that inheritance fall to the collateral branch of Sultzbach.   Count Seckendorf, who had served in Flanders with Frederic William, was privately despatched to Berlin, and by humouring the temper, and flattering the prejudices of the capricious sovereign, secured his concurrence, and concluded, on the 12th of October, 1726, the treaty of Wosterhausen.   The king of Prussia guarantied the Pragmatic Sanction; the emperor agreed to secure the succession of Juliers, Berg, and Ravenstein, or an equivalent, to the house of Brandenburgh; and both parties promised a reciprocal succour of 10,000 or 12,000 men in case of an attack.

Encouraged by this success, the allies of Vienna prepared to execute their projects.   In February, 1727, Spain commenced hostilities by the siege of Gibraltar; the czarina assembled her forces by sea and land, and Charles collected a formidable army in the Netherlands, for the invasion of Holland. A combination of unfavourable circumstances, however, prevented the emperor from fulfilling his designs. In vain he attempted to reconcile the discordant interests of the German states, and to draw the empire into the quarrel ; he was only able to obtain the renewal of the defensive association from the circles of Austria, Franconia, Suabia, and the Rhine, but they refused to take part in the great disputes which were then pending between the allies of Hanover and Vienna.

In England all parties were indignant at the insults of the emperor : the parliament supported the king in all his engagements ; a British squadron in the Baltic awed the empress of Russia ; another in the Mediterranean threatened the coasts of Spain, and a third blocked up the galleons in the ports of the Indies. A subsidiary army of Danes, Swedes, and Hessians, to the number of 42,000 men, was taken into British pay, and France collected a numerous force on the frontiers of Spain and Germany. The death of the czarina frustrated the expectations of the emperor in the North ; the irresolute spirit of the king of Prussia at the same time began to waver ; and many of the German states, awed by the formidable aspect of the Hanover allies, deserted the cause of the house of Austria. The detention of the galleons in America prevented the court of Madrid from remitting such vast supplies as the unbounded promises of Ripperda had led him to expect ; his own revenues were in too scanty and in too disordered a state to maintain a force sufficient to resist his enemies, and his hereditary dominions were threatened with an immediate attack. Even in his own court, and among his own ministers, he found the strongest opposition to his favourite measures. Notwithstanding all his endeavours, he could not succeed in reconciling his consort and ministers to the union with Spain ; count Windisgratz was the only ardent supporter of it ; while Eugene and Staremberg did not affect to conceal their disapprobation, declared that they only signed it in obedience to the emperor, and, from a jealousy of count Sinzendorf, endeavoured to retard its execution.

The empress also, when the first illusion was dissipated, turned again with affection to the prince of Loraine, and saw with displeasure the estrangement between the houses of Austria and Brunswick. Even Sinzendorf, though he durst not openly disavow the work of his own hands, was alarmed at the difficulties in which his master was involved, and was anxious to relieve him from his embarrassments, by secretly thwarting that alliance which he had been so anxious to conclude.

At this juncture an important change took place in the court of Spain. Ripperda, after concluding his negotiations at Vienna, and prodigally distributing the Spanish largesses to the emperor and his ministers, departed on the 9th of November, 1725, and passing through Italy, embarked at Genoa and landed at Barcelona. At this place, with that presumption and violence which marked his character, he boasted of his transactions at Vienna; and declared that Spain and the emperor united would give law to Europe. "The emperor," he said, "had 150,000 troops under arms, and in six months could bring as many more into the field; France shall be pillaged, the king of Prussia crushed in one campaign, and George I. driven from his German and British territories."*

On his arrival at Madrid, he was instantly appointed minister and secretary of state, and vested with uncontrolled authority. But his talents and character soon appeared unequal to his elevated situation. His caprice and vanity disgusted all parties, and being unable to fulfil his promise of supplying the court of Vienna with the expected subsidies, he alienated the imperial ambassador, count Konigsegg, by his indiscretion and arrogance, and even paid assiduous court to the English and Dutch ministers. Having thus lost the favour of the queen, who was governed by Konigsegg, he was disgracefully dismissed within four months after the elevation, and his departments were filled by Grinaldo, the marquis de Paz, and Don Joseph Patinho, who engaged to fulfil the treaty of Vienna, and to supply the promised subsidies.

Aware of the general indignation, and apprehensive of being imprisoned, Ripperda took refuge in the house of the British ambassador, Mr. Stanhope, to whom he disclosed the secret engagements between the king of Spain and the emperor; and to ingratiate himself with the king of England, developed their plans and magnified the danger to

* Memoirs of Sir Robert Walpole, chap. xxxv.

which Europe was exposed by the union of Spain and
Austria. He was, however, forcibly taken from the house
of the British ambassador, and transferred to the castle of
Segovia.*

Although the dismission of Ripperda was principally
owing to the intrigues of the imperial cabinet, yet the
protection which he received from the British ambassador
filled the court of Vienna with alarm and consternation;
and the disclosure of the secret articles compelled the
emperor to have recourse to the meanest subterfuges.
The character and abilities of Ripperda were now as much
decried as they had been before exalted, and the emperor
and his ministers affected surprise at being accused of
placing their confidence in so indiscreet and contemptible a
man.

The disclosure of the engagement for the proposed
marriages involved the imperial court in the greatest
embarrassment. Hitherto the report was only founded on
conjecture; but from this time it seemed to be confirmed:
a general dissatisfaction prevailed, and the danger of
uniting the Spanish and Austrian dominions in one family
was re-echoed from one quarter of Europe to the other.
Charles was therefore obliged to tranquillise the king of
Prussia, the elector of Bavaria, and the other princes of
the empire, who were alarmed at the prospect of a Spanish
successor on the imperial throne, by a public denial of his
supposed engagements, and yet he was to continue to lure
the queen of Spain with the prospect of the marriages, by
which alone he could secure her support. †

The scandalous venality of the imperial court was also
publicly exposed. In the account of the money which he
had distributed at Vienna, Ripperda had stated 400,000
florins as given to the imperial ministers. Philip, justly

* For the rise, fall, and subsequent adventures of Ripperda, see
the Memoirs of Sir Robert Walpole, ch. xxv., and Kings of Spain,
ch. xxxvii.

† From a candid review of the numerous documents relative to
these engagements, it appears probable that Charles had no other
intention than to lure the queen of Spain, and render her the dupe of
his schemes; he therefore never gave a written promise, though he did
not scruple, through the medium of his ministers, counts Sinzendorf
and Konigsegg, to make the most solemn assurances of his intention
to gratify her wishes. — Mr. Robinson's Despatches.

surprised at the magnitude of the sum, appealed, for the truth of the statement, to the court of Vienna, who acknowledged the receipt, but avoided an explanation of the particulars, because the emperor had shared in the gratification.

These transactions greatly affected the credit of the court of Vienna; and no event in the reign of Charles involved him in more embarrassment and disgrace. In the subsequent negotiations he was compelled to have recourse to prevarication and duplicity, and to affirm on one side what he as positively denied on the other. Thus humbled and disappointed, Charles sacrificed Spain to his own safety; and his plenipotentiary signed at Paris, on the 31st of May, 1727, the preliminaries of peace with England, France, and the United Provinces. A general armistice was concluded for seven years; the charter of the Ostend Company was suspended for the same term; and the disputes subsisting between the allies of Vienna and Hanover were to be settled by a general congress. The king of Spain, thus deserted by Austria, acceded to the preliminaries on the 30th of June, and peace again appeared on the eve of being restored to Europe.

In the midst of these events, a material change had taken place in the administration of France. The duke of Bourbon had flattered himself with the hopes of governing the young king by the influence of the queen; but he was disappointed. Fleury, the king's preceptor, had silently and gradually gained the full confidence of the sovereign; and a struggle for power ensued, which terminated in the dismission of the duke, and the elevation of Fleury to the helm of state.* Although this event occasioned no immediate change in favour of the emperor, yet it ultimately led to the re-establishment of the connection between France and Spain, and the re-union of the house of Austria with England.

* For the account of this change of administration, see Memoirs of Lord Walpole, ch. xii.

CHAP. LXXXVIII.—1727–1731.

As the emperor and the king of Spain had finally arranged their disputes by the treaties of Vienna, and signed the preliminaries with England, France, and the United Provinces, on the basis of the Quadruple Alliance, it was expected that Spain would instantly raise the siege of Gibraltar, that the emperor would grant the investiture of Parma and Tuscany to Don Carlos, and suppress the Ostend Company. But these hopes were disappointed, by the death of the king of England, who suddenly expired on his journey to Hanover on the 22nd of June, 1727.

This event revived the visionary hopes of the emperor : he expected that George II. would be embarrassed with the attempts of the Jacobites, who would be supported by cardinal Fleury ; or at all events that Townshend and sir Robert Walpole, to whom he attributed the alienation of England, would be driven from the helm, and succeeded by a new administration more favourable to the house of Austria. The counsels of Spain were actuated by the same motives ; Philip delayed, under various pretences, to raise the siege of Gibraltar, and both sovereigns resumed their warlike preparations with increasing vigour. But the accession of the new sovereign was undisturbed ; cardinal Fleury refused to support the Jacobites, and, by means of his friend Mr. Walpole*, the British ambassador at Paris strongly recommended to the king of England the continuance of the ministry, and expressed the resolution of his master to cultivate the union between the two crowns. This disappointment did not produce any material change in the disposition of Spain and the emperor ; and the allies of Hanover were reduced to the same state of uncertainty, with respect to peace or war, as before the signature of the preliminaries.

Irritated by this equivocal and hostile conduct, France and England determined to anticipate the intended aggressions of the emperor, on the side of Hanover and Holland, by attacking him in Germany. As a prelude to this aggression, George II. by a subsidiary treaty, signed

* Memoirs of Lord Walpole, ch. xv.

on the 25th of November, 1727, detached the duke
of Brunswick Wolfembuttel, and secured the possession of
Brunswick, which frustrated the plan of the emperor to
invade the Hanoverian dominions.* Charles was thus
reduced to a state of inaction, and Spain, unable to cope
with France and England, ratified the preliminaries by an
act signed at the Pardo, a royal palace near Madrid, on
the 5th of March, 1728, and a congress was opened at
Soissons on the 14th of June. At this place the ministers
of the empire, Spain, and the Hanover allies assembled,
and the negotiations were conducted under the management
of cardinal Fleury, who occasionally repaired thither from
Paris.

During the continuance of the congress the emperor
threw fresh difficulties on the suppression of the Ostend
Company, and on the investiture of the duchies, that he
might attain his favourite object, the formal guaranty of
the Pragmatic Sanction, from the European powers.
Cardinal Fleury opposed this guaranty, and succeeded in
preventing the other plenipotentiaries from accepting it as
the basis of the definitive treaty ; and this opposition increased the obstinacy of the emperor.

In these circumstances the conduct of the Austrian
cabinet was involved in contradictions and inconsistencies.
When the emperor flattered himself with hopes of the
arrival of the galleons, and the receipt of Spanish subsidies,
he was anxious not to offend the queen of Spain, and
affected to abide by his engagements. But when France
and Great Britain threatened hostilities, and particularly
when his hopes of Spanish gold were less sanguine, his
demeanour became as meek as it was before haughty and
imperious. During the delays which were derived from
this fluctuating state of mind, the mistrust and diffidence,
which had been gradually increasing between the courts of
Madrid and Vienna, were revived ; and the queen of Spain,
as a proof of the emperor's sincerity to secure the succession
of Parma and Tuscany for Don Carlos, insisted that the
article of the Quadruple Alliance, relative to the neutral
garrisons, should be changed, and Spanish troops substituted in their stead. This proposition, to which the court
of Madrid obstinately adhered, became the principal object

* Memoirs of Sir Robert Walpole, ch. xxxiii.

of the negotiation, which the emperor, by every species of artifice and chicanery, endeavoured to evade, or to make the guaranty of the Pragmatic Sanction the price of his assent.

Fnding the queen of Spain obstinate in her resolution, the emperor redoubled his efforts to divide the allies of Hanover, by secret and insidious propositions made to each ; and count Sinzendorf even suggested the plan of a provisional treaty, on the basis of tbe preliminaries, to settle the objects in dispute without the intervention of Spain. This plan being digested, was signed by Sinzendorf and transmitted to Madrid by the allies of Hanover for the accession of Spain, but rejected by the queen, who was determined not to recede from the demand of Spanish garrisons.

In this interval the provisional treaty being despatched to the emperor, who was making a progress through his dominions, Eugene, Staremberg, and even Realp, joined in opposing it. Charles, on his return, lured by new overtures from Spain, disavowed it, recalled Sinzendorf from the congress, and a general opinion prevailed at Vienna that the plenipotentiary would be disgraced. The emperor, however, received him with marks of the greatest cordiality, apologised for his apparent disapprobation, and Sinzendorf even joined in decrying the treaty which he had himself concluded.

But the emperor still avoided any positive engagement, either with Spain or the allies, although he did not desist from his private overtures. The suspicions of the queen of Spain being artfully fomented by France and England, she at length demanded a specific declaration of his intention in regard to the marriage of an archduchess with Don Carlos. Irritated by his equivocal answer, she prevailed on the king to conclude a separate treaty with England and France, which was signed at Seville on the 9th of November, 1729, and acceded to on the 21st by the United Provinces.

Thus terminated the frail connection between the house of Austria and Spain, from which the emperor had reaped nothing but chimerical hopes and continual disappointments, and in consequence of which, notwithstanding the largesses of Ripperda and the subsidies of Spain, he incurred an additional debt of not less than sixteen millions of florins.

By the alliance of Seville, the contracting powers confirmed the treaty of Utrecht; guarantied each other's possessions in all quarters of the globe; settled their respective contingents for mutual defence in case of an attack, for securing the succession of Parma and Tuscany to Don Carlos, and defending him in his possession against any power who might attempt to disturb him; they also agreed to support the introduction of 6000 Spanish instead of neutral troops, into the fortresses of Leghorn, Porto Ferraio, Parma, and Placentia, within six months from the signature of the treaty.

This compulsory clause, which in the public treaty only alluded to the emperor, without mentioning his name, formed the subject of a secret article, wherein the contracting parties bound themselves to make war in case of opposition, and not to lay down their arms till the whole was executed. The king of Spain also revoked the privileges of trade granted to the subjects of the emperor by the treaties of Vienna, restored the exclusive rights enjoyed by the English and Dutch, in consequence of the fifth article of the treaty of Munster, and relinquished his claims on Gibraltar and Minorca.

Charles was highly indignant at the conclusion of this treaty; not only because he was made the duke of Spain, and disappointed in the guaranty of the Pragmatic Sanction; but because he considered the engagements of the allies of Seville, for the abolition of the Ostend Company, and the compulsory admission of Spanish troops into Italy, as violating his rights of sovereignty in the Low Countries, and infringing his imperial authority. His pride was still more wounded by the contemptuous silence with which his person and rights were passed over, and the peremptory manner in which he was required to give a prompt and speedy accession without negotiation. He upbraided the allies with omitting even his very name; and his ministers, with their usual captiousness; asked how their imperial master could give an answer when no proposal was made, or how his concurrence could be required, without specifying with what he was to concur? Count Sinzendorf stigmatised the manner in which the treaty was concluded as an unheard-of affront, of which no instance could be adduced even among barbarians.* The emperor accordingly gave no other answer than that he would abide by his engagements, and would send instructions to his plenipotentiaries at the congress at Soissons; he at the same time issued instant orders for his troops to hold themselves in readiness to march.

In a paroxysm of despair Charles declared his resolution rather to risk a general war, and stand singly against the united powers of Europe, than agree to such humiliating conditions. If driven to extremities he could, he said, effect a reconciliation with Spain, by giving his daughter in marriage to Don Carlos; and the queen would purchase that object on any condition. It would be far more honourable to make concessions by an act of his own, than to have them extorted by compulsion. He would break off all connection with England and Holland, and leave them to regret their own folly, in having contributed to the preponderance of the house of Bourbon in Europe. He threatened to evacuate the Low Countries, to inundate Italy with troops, and to bring into the field an army of 165,000 men; he demanded the contingent of Russia, drew from the king of Prussia a promise of 10,000 men, and appealed to the diet of the empire against the infraction of his prerogative, and the infringement of their privileges, by alienating the feodality of Tuscany and Parma without the concurrence of the empire and its head. He employed his usual artifices to divide the allies, and, notwithstanding his recent disappointment, still flattered himself with the hopes that the British nation would not support the king in a German quarrel.

But he found both his threats and allurements ineffectual; the British nation, pleased with the renewal of their lucrative commerce with Spain, warmly supported the treaty of Seville; the allies were active in forming a plan of hostile operations, and meditated a descent on Sicily, which was ill provided for defence. Charles was coldly supported by the states of the empire, and deserted by the king of Sardinia, who entered into engagements with the allies of Seville;

---

* From an interesting despatch of lord Waldegrave to lord Townshend, dated January 1. 1730, in which he relates the effects produced by the communication of the treaty on the imperial court and ministers.

the king of Prussia shrunk from the contest, and Russia, in the beginning of a new reign, was unwilling to engage in a war.   Thus abandoned by his allies, his finances exhausted, his countries impoverished, and his army inefficient and dispirited, Charles was unable to support the contest alone.   He therefore yielded to the necessity of his affairs; but availing himself of the rising misintelligence among the allies of Seville, succeeded in detaching the Maritime Powers from France.

Fortunately for the house of Austria, England had already testified a disposition to renew the ancient confidence by the mission of earl Waldegrave to Vienna.   From the accession of George I., except during the temporary missions of lords Stanhope, Cadogan, and Cobham, no regular minister had resided at Vienna; and the British affairs were principally conducted by St. Saphorin, a native of Switzerland, who, though a man of abilities and integrity, was of a caustic and presumptuous temper, and had contributed, by his exaggerated discourses, to aggravate the discontents subsisting between the courts of London and Vienna.

The mild and insinuating manners of lord Waldegrave were well calculated to heal the breach; he found the emperor and his ministry highly prejudiced against the British administration, and jealous of the king's ascendency in the German empire; and although he was treated by Charles with extreme coldness, yet he conciliated the reserve of prince Eugene, the blunt and honest frankness of Staremberg, and the caprice of Sinzendorf.   He was no less successful with the Spanish favourites, particularly the marquis de Realp, and thus laid the foundation of the new union with England, which was completed by Mr. Robinson.*

The allies of Seville were at this period divided in their views and interests, and the bonds of amity which had connected England and France were relaxed.

The house of Brunswick, firmly established on the throne of Great Britain, no longer felt the necessity of cultivating a strict union with France to check the hopes of the disaffected and prevent internal commotions.   In France the

* For an account of lord Waldegrave, see Memoirs of Sir Robert Walpole, ch. xxxviii.

birth of a dauphin, in 1729, having annihilated the hopes
of Philip V., cardinal Fleury had effected a reconciliation with Spain; and, though from his pacific principles, he was inclined to maintain the system of Europe
according to the Quadruple Alliance, he now directed his
views to alienate Spain from England, and to reunite the
two branches of the house of Bourbon.　Hence a spirit of
delay and irresolution was infused into the counsels of the
allies ; Spain, from disappointment and revenge, urged the
necessity of an immediate breach with the emperor, and
was eager to dismember Parma and Tuscany from the empire, and France was desirous of carrying the war into
Flanders, to which England and Holland were averse.
Fleury availed himself of these discordant views, thwarted
every scheme of hostility, and insinuated to the queen of
Spain, that the difficulties and delays in carrying the treaty
of Seville into execution by force arose from the English
and Dutch.

The emperor was not unacquainted with this growing
disunion among the allies ; and his ministers, with the connivance, though without the avowal of their master, made
secret overtures to England.　In a tone of unusual humility,
they adverted to the former friendship between the two
powers, and trusted that England would not concur in the
ruin of an ancient ally, to raise the house of Bourbon to a
pre-eminence in Europe.　They insinuated that the emperor would sacrifice the Ostend Company, and permit the
introduction of Spanish garrisons, provided England would
guaranty the Pragmatic Sanction, which was necessary for
the preservation of the balance of Europe.

At this crisis Spain, impatient of delay, declared herself
free from all engagements contracted by the treaty of
Seville ; and England, apprehensive of losing the commercial advantages recently obtained, accepted the overtures of
the emperor, and opened a negotiation to renew her ancient
connection with the house of Austria.　Although the imperial ministers were unanimous* for this reconciliation,

---

* Lord Waldegrave has recorded an anecdote of prince Eugene's
extreme aversion to this war, in a letter to lord Townshend, Vienna,
March 18. 1730. " The prince, after having won a game of piquet of
me, and was saying that what I had lost would help to pay for the
foils that were brought home to him the same morning, and that in

the conclusion was delayed by the pride and obstinacy of
the emperor, who from his jealousy of the house of Hanover, was averse to allow the claims of George II. in
Germany. But his reluctant consent was at length obtained by postponing the German affairs to a future discussion ; and a treaty was concluded on the 16th of March,
1731, between the king of England and the emperor, which
is denominated the treaty of Vienna. By this treaty the
emperor engaged not to oppose the introduction of 6000
Spaniards into the fortresses of Tuscany and Parma, and
to abolish the Ostend Company. In return, England
guarantied the Pragmatic Sanction, on the condition that
the archduchess, who succeeded to the Austrian dominions,
should not be married to a prince of the house of Bourbon,
or to prince so powerful as to endanger the balance of Europe.

Anthony Farnese dying on the 20th of January, 1731,
in the midst of the negotiation, the emperor had taken
instant possession of Parma, under the pretence of securing
that duchy to his heir, should the duchess, who declared
herself pregnant, be delivered of a posthumous son. But
on the conclusion of the treaty, he declared, that he had
only adopted this measure to secure the peace of Italy, and
would give immediate possession to Don Carlos, should the
duchess be delivered of a daughter, or prove not pregnant.

Spain having revoked her declaration against the peace
of Seville, acceded to the new treaty on the 6th of June,
and on the 22nd of July, the emperor concluded another
treaty at Vienna with Great Britain, Spain, and the United
Provinces, which terminated the disputes concerning the
Spanish succession. And thus, at the close of these negotiations, Charles derived no other advantage from his complicated intrigues and mighty preparations, than the single
guaranty of the Pragmatic Sanction, and a reconciliation

the summer I should have my share of the diversion he proposed by
them, ' Si cette fichüe guerre ne nous empêche pas :' he added, ' Je n'ai
jamais eu si peu de plaisir de ma vie dans les apparences d'une guerre,
c'est l'unique dans les arrangemens de laquelle je ne puis prendre
plaisir.   Il n'y a point d'object, il n'y a pas assez de sujet pour faire
tuer une poulet.' This he spoke aloud, and repeated his words. There
were ten or a dozen men and women standing round the table, and our
game was going on ; so that there was no laying hold of any thing he
had said to carry the discourse farther."

with the Maritime Powers; both of which he might have
acquired at an easier rate, and with greater advantages, had
he yielded to the urgent instances of Great Britain to accede to the treaty of Seville.

Chap. LXXXIX. — 1731–1733.

HAVING obtained the guaranty of the Pragmatic Sanction
from Spain, Prussia, Russia, England, and Holland, the
emperor directed all his efforts to procure the accession of
the other European powers, particularly the states of the
German empire.   In pursuing this object he experienced
extreme difficulty, from the religious disputes between the
Catholic and Protestant bodies, and from the discordant
views of the German princes.

The religious disputes, which arose from the obnoxious
clause in the treaty of Ryswick, still continued undiminished.
At length the emperor, though inclined to favour the Catholics, was induced to yield to the just remonstrances of
the Protestants, and in consequence of a convention between
the Catholics and Protestants, issued an edict, dated November 14. 1720, enjoining the Elector Palatine, who had
persecuted the Calvinists, to redress their grievances, and
to restore them to the same situation in which they stood
on the conclusion of the peace of Baden.   By this convention it was also proposed to reinstate the Protestants in the
privileges secured to them by the peace of Westphalia.

The Catholics, however, not only evaded the performance
of the convention, but insisted that it established the clause
in the treaty of Ryswick ; because the edict only enjoined
the restoration of the privileges possessed by the Protestants at the peace of Baden ; and had no retrospect to the
rights of which they had been deprived between the treaties
of Ryswick and Baden.

This disunion was augmented by disputes concerning an
article in the treaty of Westphalia, stipulating, that in case
of a division between the two religions, the point should be
amicably decided, and not carried by a majority of voices.

The emperor having always favoured the cause of the
Catholics, was secure of the majority of that body in sup-

port of the Pragmatic Sanction ; but he experienced great
difficulty in his attempts to gain the concurrence of the
Protestants ; because he had offended them by not obtaining
the repeal of the obnoxious clause in the treaty of Ryswick ;
and because he had been opposed by the elector of Hanover,
who possessed the chief influence in the Protestant body.
By his recent alliance with the king of England, Charles
had gained the support of Hanover ; and he had found
means to conciliate the king of Prussia, by yielding to his
representations in the affairs of Mecklenburgh, and by affecting to promote his views on the inheritance of Juliers
and Berg.

Since the establishment of an imperial commission in
Mecklenburgh, the troubles of that country had again broke
out with increasing violence.   The duke braved the multiplied decrees of the Aulic Council, regained possession of
part of the duchy, and renewed his exactions on his subjects.
He was accordingly deposed by a provisional rescript ; the
administration was given to his brother Christian Louis,
and the king of Prussia, as conservator of the circle of
Lower Saxony, was joined in the commission.   The opposition of the princes of the empire, supported by France,
Sweden, and England, compelled the emperor to revoke
his provisional rescript ; but he still continued the government in Christian Louis, by investing him with the office
of imperial commissary.   The duke was soon afterwards
driven from his dominions by the Hanoverian forces ; and
the king of Prussia availed himself of these contests to introduce his troops into the duchy.   The emperor also renewed his promises of favouring the claims of Frederic
William on the succession of Juliers, which, in consequence
of the advanced age of Philip William, Elector Palatine,
seemed likely to become vacant.   Having thus succeeded
in conciliating the elector of Hanover and the king of
Prussia, he, on the 11th of January, 1732, obtained the
guaranty of the Pragmatic Sanction by the suffrages of the
whole Germanic body, except the electors of Bavaria, Palatine, and Saxony.   In consequence of their claims to the
Austrian inheritance, the electors of Saxony and Bavaria
were induced to protest against this act, and the Elector
Palatine, from a suspicion that the emperor had guarantied
the succession of Berg and Juliers to the king of Prussia.

This opposition was fomented by France, who encouraged the elector of Bavaria to submit his pretensions to the states of the empire, and promoted a league between the electors of Saxony and Bavaria, which was concluded on the 4th of July, 1733, in support of their respective rights and prerogatives.

This opposition to the guaranty of the Pragmatic Sanction, joined to the disputes relative to Parma and Placentia, portended the renewal of hostilities between the houses of Austria and Bourbon. Charles, alarmed at the intrigues of France in the empire, and apprehensive of her growing influence at the court of Dresden, strained every nerve to procure the guaranty from the protesting electors, and to form alliances, as if on the eve of a general war, and was warmly supported in his views by the king of England.

Augustus II., persisting in his refusal of the guaranty, the emperor warmly opposed his views of rendering the crown of Poland hereditary in his family; and with this intention renewed the ancient alliance of the house of Austria with Poland, which furnished a pretext for his interference in the affairs of the republic. As Augustus was rapidly declining in health, Charles was no less interested to exclude any competitor, who might be supported by France in the expected vacancy. He therefore entered into negotiations with Russia and Prussia, and a formal treaty was drawn up, by which the succession of Berg and Dusseldorf was to be guarantied to the king of Prussia, and the duchy of Courland to be secured to a Prussian prince. With a view to the establishment of an hereditary monarchy in Poland, as well as to exclude Stanislaus, or any prince dependent on France, the contracting powers agreed to concur in placing Emanuel, prince of Portugal, on the throne, and to support his election with troops and money. But the death of Augustus prevented the signature and execution of this engagement.

At this period Poland was in a state of confusion and anarchy. In consequence of the numerous employments which Augustus had filled with his Saxon adherents, he had become extremely unpopular; the diet had even annulled the election of his natural son Maurice count of Saxe to succeed to Courland, on the death of Ferdinand the reigning duke without issue; declared that duchy a fief of the republic ; and proposed, on the death of Ferdinand, to incorporate it with the possessions of the crown. The opposite party had also thwarted the attempts of the king to fill the vacant offices of Great General and Great Chancellor, and even prevented the meeting of a diet.

Augustus having at length succeeded in conciliating many of his opponents, summoned a diet in January ; and with a view to complete his design of rendering the crown hereditary in his family, hastened from Dresden in the midst of a severe winter, and in an infirm state of health. In answer to the advice of his physicians, and the remonstrances of his friends, he replied, " I am aware of my danger, but I owe more to my subjects than to myself." Soon after his arrival at Warsaw, the fatigues of the journey, and a gangrene in his foot, hurried him to the grave on the first of February, 1733, in the sixty-fourth year of his age. This event hastened the bursting of that storm which the lowering aspect of affairs seemed to portend, and, from the disposition and connections of the other powers of Europe, placed the house of Austria in a new and dangerous situation.

Denmark was governed by Christian VI., a prince devoted to the arts and sciences, and distinguished by his aversion to war, and his taste for splendour and magnificence : and Sweden continued, under the reign of Frederic, a prey to factions, and of too little weight in the balance of Europe to render her accession or opposition an object of much importance.

Russia had changed her line of sovereigns; but her internal state and external relations continued the same. In consequence of her vicinity and contests with the Turks, her interests were inseparably united with those of the house of Austria ; and in every instance since the death of Catherine I., Charles found Russia his most stable ally. Peter II., who was nearly related to the empress of Germany*, had succeeded to the throne, and his short reign was principally distinguished by the fall of Mentchikof and the favour of the Dolgoruckis. On the demise of Peter, in 1730, the crown was transferred to Anne, youngest daughter of Ivan, and niece of Peter the

---

* Elizabeth Christina, princess of Brunswick Blankenburgh, wife of Charles VI., was sister of Charlotte Christina, mother of Peter II.

Great. She was raised to the throne by the council of state, in preference to her eldest sister Catherine, duchess of Mecklenburgh, on the condition of consenting to the limitation of the royal prerogative, which she broke, by the assistance of the guards, and resumed the unlimited authority of her predecessors.

In the alliance which Charles had concluded with Catherine in 1726, he obtained the guaranty of the Pragmatic Sanction, on condition that he should assist in procuring the restitution of Sleswick to the duke of Holstein. Peter II., being less inclined to favour the claims of the duke of Holstein, the article relative to the restitution of Sleswick was annulled, and a new one substituted, by which the emperor, the czar, and Spain agreed to pay an annual pension of 300,000 florins to the duke of Holstein, until he received an equivalent for his pretensions. Anne was jealous of the duke, and careless of his interests; and therefore only promised in general to fulfil the engagements of her predecessors, in regard to the Pragmatic Sanction, and the emperor was satisfied with this declaration, without proposing a new treaty.

On the side of Europe the Turks were disposed to maintain the same state of peace and tranquillity, and were wholly occupied with the progress of Kouli Khan, who had taken Bassora, and invested Babylon.

Louis XV. was at this period devoted to his pleasures, and wholly governed by cardinal Fleury, under whose wise administration France had recovered from her dependent and exhausted condition. The nation, pleased with the renewal of the connection with Spain, began to resume their ancient schemes of conquest; and the ardent spirit of the nobles looked forward to a new war, to retrieve the honour of the country, which they considered as sullied by the subordinate part it had acted since the death of Louis XIV. France was the head of the league in opposition to the guaranty of the Pragmatic Sanction, and agitated every court of Europe with her intrigues.

Philip still continued in the same state of hypochondriac melancholy, from which he could only be roused by the bustle and occupations of war. He had renounced all hopes of succeeding to the crown of France, and directed his whole views to gratify his queen, who was eager for the renewal of a contest with the house of Austria, that she might gain a settlement for another of her sons in Italy. France and Spain were engaged in warlike preparations both by sea and land, and seemed only to wait for a pretext to commence hostilities.

Spain and Portugal had apparently renounced their ancient enmity, by the double marriages of Joseph prince of Brazil, and Mary Anne, Infanta of Spain, and Mary Barbara, princess of Portugal, with Ferdinand prince of Asturias, on the 19th of January, 1729. But this connection did not remove the spirit of national antipathy; and the proud and captious tempers of John and Philip were ill calculated to promote their union. John, who was brother-in-law of Charles, still retained his partiality for the house of Austria, and fostered an equal aversion to the house of Bourbon.

During the disputes concerning the succession of Tuscany and Parma, the king of Sardinia was courted by the houses of Bourbon and Austria. Lured by the offer of part of the Milanese, Victor Amadeus concluded, in June, 1730, a treaty with the emperor; but he had scarcely signed it before he was induced to enter into an alliance with Spain on more advantageous conditions. Soon after this event, this ambitious monarch astonished Europe by a voluntary abdication of his dignity. The motives which occasioned this unexpected resolution have never been ascertained; it was attributed to the embarrassments arising from his contradictory engagements, to the decline of his health, and to a fit of devotion, or to a desire of recognising his marriage with the countess of St. Sebastian, who had long been his mistress, and whom he had recently espoused.

He performed the ceremony of his abdication on the 3rd of September, 1730, at his favourite palace of Rivoli, and after an eloquent and affecting discourse, in which he represented the decline of his age, the infirm state of his health, and his desire to pass the remainder of his days in retirement and devotion, he expressed his satisfaction in being able to resign the crown to a son, who, from his age and capacity, was equal to the cares of government. On the ensuing day he repaired to Chambery, where he passed several months with apparent satisfaction, in company with the countess of St. Sebastian, who was created marchioness of Sphingy, and whom he avowed as his wife. The abdicated monarch, however, soon regretted the loss of power; his discontent was fomented by his wife, and his intellects being affected by a stroke of apoplexy, he was instigated to attempt the resumption of the crown.

The mode in which he endeavoured to re-ascend the throne seemed rather the project of a madman, than the act of a sovereign grown grey in the affairs of state. Under pretence of change of air, he returned to Montcallier, a royal palace near Turin, and was received by his son with great marks of respect and deference. Soon after his arrival, he sent for the marquis del Borgo, the prime minister, and ordered him in a high tone of authority to bring the paper, by which he meant the act of abdication. After the departure of the marquis, he became greatly agitated. Starting up at midnight, he exclaimed, "My resolution is taken!" and mounting his horse, accompanied by a single attendant, rode to the gate of the citadel of Turin, and demanded admittance, which being refused by the governor, he returned to Montcallier in a state of fury and despair. Meanwhile, a privy council being held before the king, the ministers unanimously urged the necessity of securing the person of the abdicated monarch, and extorted from Charles Emanuel his reluctant consent for the arrest of his father.

Victor Amadeus had retired to rest, and, exhausted with his efforts, fell into so profound a sleep, that he did not awake when the doors of his apartment were forced open. After much ineffectual resistance, he was separated from his wife, and conducted to Rivoli, under a military escort. During his conveyance he descended from the carriage, under various pretences, and ineffectually endeavoured to excite the compassion of the soldiers, by reminding them of the dangers they had mutually shared, and the victories which they had gained under his command. He was deeply affected with the view of apartments which had been the scene of his former grandeur, and where he had signed his abdication, which he never recollected without the most indignant emotions. Notwithstanding his wife was permitted to reside with him, the natural violence of his temper, irritated by confinement, overpowered his reason, and, at his own request, he was again removed to Montcallier, where he died on the 20th of October, 1732.

Charles Emanuel was in the thirty-first year of his age when he succeeded to the crown. His education had been much neglected, and he had been assiduously removed from all share in the administration of affairs; but he soon proved that he possessed the talents, though not the spirit of his father. Finding an excellent minister in the marquis d'Ormea, the Richelieu of Savoy, he pursued with equal address and judgment the system of aggrandisement which had been adopted by his predecessors, and held the balance of power in Italy, by taking advantage of the disputes between the houses of Austria and Bourbon, and adding his weight to the side from which he hoped to reap the greatest advantage. During the short time in which he had held the reins of government, he had considerably improved the revenue; his army was in a high state of order and discipline; and, trained in the military school of his illustrious father, he was ambitious to signalise his arms, and emulate the glory of his predecessors.

The United Provinces, sunk into the lowest state of weakness and imbecility, were the prey of contending factions. The views of the States were principally directed to the preservation of their commercial advantages; and although guaranties of the Pragmatic Sanction, were indifferent to the safety of any part of the Austrian dominions except the Low Countries. They were alienated from the emperor by the disputes relative to the Barrier Treaty, as well as by the haughty conduct of the Austrian ministers; and suspiciously regarded the connection between the emperor and England as likely to involve them in a war with France.

Since the accession of the house of Brunswick England had increased in wealth and commerce, and enjoyed a greater degree of tranquillity at home and a longer duration of peace abroad, than during any period since the reign of queen Elizabeth. This prosperous state of affairs was derived from the establishment of septennial parliaments, which enable the crown to pursue a permanent system of policy, and from the judicious measures and pacific principles of the British administration.

George II. was in the fiftieth year of his age, and was a prince of high integrity, honour, and veracity. He possessed good sense, and a sound judgment; but was of a warm and irritable temper, not easily appeased, and impatient of remonstrance. He was no less rigidly attached to etiquette and punctilious forms than Charles himself, and was of a warlike disposition, and fond of military parade. In regard to the general interests of Europe, his views were enlarged and correct: but from an attachment to his German dominions, he often suffered the prejudices of an elector to bias his judgment and did not sufficiently appreciate the great commercial and naval principles of the English government. On his accession to the crown, he found England in amity with France, and at variance with the house of Austria; and, from principles of prudence and policy, acquiesced in a system which secured the tranquillity of his British dominions. He was however, aware that the house of Austria was the natural ally of England, and hastened the conclusion of the treaty of Vienna, as soon as the emperor had promised to gratify him in his electoral claims. From that moment he steadily adhered to the emperor, and beheld with indignation the efforts of France to humiliate the house of Austria.

Although impatient of control, and jealous of being governed, yet he was greatly influenced by queen Caroline, whose mild, prudent, and conciliating manners were more congenial to the character of the English nation. She maintained a correspondence with the empress, to whom she was distantly related, and constantly expressed her own wishes, and the desire of the king, to cement the union between the two nations. Her views, however, being principally directed to maintain the prosperity and peace of England, she was swayed by the advice of sir Robert Walpole, whose dismission she had prevented, on the accession of her husband, and whom she continued to support with all her influence.

Sir Robert Walpole, who was now considered as prime minister, had risen from a private station, by his abilities as a parliamentary orator, and knowledge of finance. He commenced his political career at an early period, and distinguished himself during the whole reign of queen Anne, as well in a public as in a private station, by his strenuous support of the cause of the house of Austria, in the war of the Succession, and by his aversion to the house of Bourbon. He signalised himself by his opposition to the peace of Utrecht, as well as by his zeal for the Hanover succession, and soon after the accession of George I. was placed at the head of the treasury. On the schism of the Whig ministry in 1717, he resigned his post, and continued in opposition until, on the failure of the South Sea scheme, the inclinations of the king and the voice of the nation recalled him to his former station. From this time the interior administration of the kingdom was intrusted to his care; and the foreign affairs were principally managed by his brother-in-law, lord Townshend, who was secretary of state; but in consequence of a disagreement, lord Townshend having resigned in 1730, Walpole became the chief minister, and had the principal share in directing the counsels of England, both in domestic and foreign transactions.

From his early youth he had imbibed the principles of the Revolution, and continued invariable in his aversion to the Stuarts, and in his zeal for the Hanover line. To support that succession, and to promote the commerce of his country, were the great objects of his policy; and to attain those objects, he adopted a system of pacific and preventive measures, from which he never swerved. With this view he had promoted the alliance with France, in order to prevent her interference in the cause of the Pretender; but when the emperor, in league with Spain, threatened to support the dethroned family, and, in opposition to the commercial interests of England, established the Company of Ostend, he did not hesitate to break off the connection which had long subsisted between the Maritime Powers and the house of Austria. On the rupture between Spain and the emperor, and the change in the political situation of Europe, he was one of the earliest advocates for renewing the union with the house of Austria, and for securing the indivisibility of that succession, as a counterpoise to the house of Bourbon. To his counsels, therefore, was principally owing the treaty of Vienna; and though he fully appreciated the danger of admitting a prince of the house of Bourbon into Italy, yet he was bound to support the Quadruple Alliance, though made in opposition to his sentiments, as well for the honour of his country as from the fear of losing the commerce with Spain.

The foreign affairs were ostensibly directed by the duke of Newcastle, secretary of state for the southern, and lord Harrington for the northern department. The duke of Newcastle was little more than a cipher in the administration, and he derived his principal consequence from his ascendency among the Whigs, and his attachment to sir Robert Walpole, to whom he owed his official situation.

Lord Harrington, on the contrary, was personally attached to the king, had imbibed his notions of war and glory, and deemed it for the honour and interest of England to support the house of Austria, even at the hazard of a rupture with France. As he usually accompanied the king to Hanover, he had great influence in the conduct of foreign transactions, particularly in the negotiations with the court of Vienna, which belonged to his department, and both at home and abroad he warmly exerted himself to rouse the spirit of the British cabinet.

Walpole was also thwarted by a strong and violent party in the kingdom, who reprobated his pacific measures, as a temporising system, and a dereliction of the national honour, calculated to aggrandise the house of Bourbon, the natural enemy, and to depress the house of Austria, the natural ally of England. These clamours were supported by men of the highest character for wit and eloquence, some of whom maintained an intimate union with the imperial ambassador in England, and corresponded with the emperor or his ministers abroad.

Chap. XC.—1733, 1734.

SEVERAL competitors started up for the vacant throne of Poland, but were soon reduced to two ; Stanislaus Letzinski, and Augustus elector of Saxony, son of the deceased monarch.

Stanislaus Letzinski, son of the great treasurer of Poland, was born 1677, and had been placed on the throne by Charles XII. on the forced abdication of Augustus II. ; but being deprived of his dignity soon after the battle of

Pultawa, he retired into Swedish Pomerania, exerted himself in favour of his benefactor, and headed the Swedish troops in that province. The progress of the Russians having alarmed Frederic I., king of Prussia, he formed the plan of a league between Charles XII. and Augustus, which was to be cemented by the abdication of Stanislaus. The exiled monarch himself consented; but having failed in obtaining by letters the acquiescence of Charles, quitted the army, and proceeded towards Bender, with the hopes of softening his inflexible spirit. Being arrested on the confines of Moldavia, he was conducted to Bender, and received a message from Charles, enjoining him never to make peace with Augustus. Stanislaus was soon afterwards restored to liberty, and repaired to Deux Ponts, which Charles assigned to him as the place of his residence, with the whole revenue of the duchy.

On the death of Charles XII., the duchy was transferred to another branch, and Stanislaus, compelled to seek a new asylum, took up his abode at Weissemburgh in Alsace, where he resided in humble circumstances, but with the title of king, till the marriage of his daughter with Louis XV. On that event he was gratified with a considerable pension, maintained a brilliant court, and received all the honours due to a sovereign. When the death of Augustus again vacated the throne of Poland, Stanislaus became a candidate for the crown, and was supported by a strong party in the kingdom, and by all the influence of France.

The death of the Polish monarch changed the sentiments of the emperor. His son and successor Augustus testifying a readiness to guaranty the Pragmatic Sanction, Charles warmly espoused his pretensions to the throne, and gained the concurrence of Russia, who was equally interested in excluding Stanislaus Letzinski, the dependent of France. Charles therefore declared his intention to promote a new and free election, according to the constitution of Poland, which he had guarantied, and to support such a candidate as might be unexceptionable both to the republic and the neighbouring powers. In this declaration, which was a virtual exclusion of Stanislaus, he mentioned the concurrence of the czarina and the king of Prussia, in consequence of their mutual engagements for the support of the constitution and liberty of Poland. He at the same time despatched additional troops into Silesia, and displayed his resolution of co-operating with Russia and Prussia in the exclusion of Stanislaus by force.

In consequence of these movements, and the language held by the imperial ministers in every court of Europe, the king of France announced his intention, as guarantee of the treaty of Oliva, to oppose the intervention of foreign powers in the choice of a king ; while his agents in Poland exerted the influence, and lavished the treasure, of France to secure the election of Stanislaus. The emperor, however, was not intimidated by these threats. Relying on the support of Russia, Prussia, and the Maritime Powers, he issued a counter-memorial, in which he inveighed against the conduct of France, as endeavouring to limit the choice of the Poles to a single person, and stigmatised the French declaration as couched in unbecoming terms, and dispersed throughout Europe with indecent affectation.

In this interval, the diet having assembled under the auspices of the primate, who was gained by France, entered into a confederacy to elect none but a native of Poland ; and the majority testified a decided resolution in favour of Stanislaus. In opposition to this powerful party, the emperor concerted with the czarina and the king of Prussia a plan for the march of their respective armies into Poland. Being, however, deterred by the lukewarmness of England, the defection of the United Provinces, and the wavering conduct of the king of Prussia, he suddenly changed his intentions, recalled the greater part of his troops from Silesia, and declared that he would not influence the diet of election by an armed force. But in consequence of the earnest representations of Russia, and his desire to assist the elector of Saxony, he soon afterwards ordered 6000 men to reinforce the camp in Silesia ; and although the king of Prussia declared his intention to remain neutral, the imperial ambassador accompanied the Russian minister at Warsaw, when he notified to the grand marshal of the diet the resolution of his mistress to exclude Stanislaus by force.

These threats, and the approach of a Russian army, roused instead of intimidating the Poles ; the diet of election assembled in the plain of Wola, and chose Stanislaus king on the 12th of September. The new sovereign, accompanied by a single adherent, after escaping a series of imminent dangers in his passage through Germany, had arrived on the 9th at Warsaw, made his appearance in the field of election, and was received with loud acclamations.

According to the custom of Polish elections, a party, headed by prince Viesnovitzki, seceded from the diet, and crossing the Vistula, joined the Russian army, which was in full march to the gates of Warsaw. Under the protection of these troops the seceders, with other parties, formed a new diet of election at Kamien*, in the vicinity of Prague; and on the 5th of October chose the elector of Saxony, who assumed the title of Augustus III. Meanwhile Stanislaus had retired from Warsaw, and taken refuge in Dantzic, where he sustained a siege against the Russian and Saxon troops. The remaining part of Poland submitting with little opposition to the Russian arms, Augustus was crowned on the 25th of December, at Cracow, and took quiet possession of the throne.

Thus the emperor succeeded in placing Augustus on the throne, and securing his guaranty of the Pragmatic Sanction. Although he did not send a single soldier into Poland, and left the whole management of the election to the czarina; yet the declarations of his ministers, his treaty with the elector of Saxony, and decided opposition to Stanislaus, involved him in a war with France, Spain, and Sardinia, in which, notwithstanding the solemn guaranty of the Pragmatic Sanction by the principal powers of Europe, he was left with no other ally than Russia, and the feeble support of the German empire.

Charles had flattered himself, that the timid and cautious Fleury would not venture to attack the house of Austria in defiance of numerous guaranties and formidable alliances; and, at all events, deemed himself secure of a cordial support from the Maritime Powers, Russia, Denmark, Prussia, and the king of Sardinia. But he was disappointed in his expectations. Walpole would not involve England in a war on the eve of a general election, and in the midst of the discontents arising from the excise; and Holland, gained by France, refused to arm in defence of the house

* Prague is the suburb of Warsaw, and Kamien is a village distinguished by the election of Henry of Valois.

of Austria for the sake of a Polish election. The king
of Prussia, induced by personal aversion to Augustus
III., by the dread of seeing his dominions in Westphalia
overrun by the French, and suspecting the insincerity of
the emperor, in his promise to guaranty the inheritance of
Juliers, seceded from the alliance, and continued neutral.
Russia was sufficiently occupied with keeping the Poles in
subjection, and guarding against the inroads of the Turks;
while Denmark was unable to send a sufficient force in
support of her ally.

Notwithstanding these disappointments, Charles still
relied on the co-operation of the king of Sardinia for the
safety of his dominions in Italy. But France had now
matured her great scheme of humbling the house of
Austria; and having secured the concurrence of Spain,
and entered into a negotiation with the king of Sardinia,
issued a declaration of war, and prepared to attack the
Austrian dominions in Germany and Italy.

The emperor, jealous of the king of Sardinia, was unwilling to purchase his alliance by yielding to demands
which he considered as exorbitant. He therefore resisted the urgent representations of the British cabinet,
and, under pretence of consulting the Aulic council and
the senate of Milan, gave evasive and unsatisfactory
answers. Meanwhile the courts of France and Spain lured
Charles Emanuel, who was indignant at these delays, with
more specific and advantageous conditions than he had
even demanded from the emperor. They engaged to
assist him in conquering the Milanese, which he was to
possess with the title of King of Lombardy, and to intrust
him with the command of the combined armies in Italy.
With such impenetrable secrecy was this intrigue conducted, that the court of Vienna viewed with satisfaction
the military preparations of Charles Emanuel, and count
Daun, governor of Milan, supplied him with grain and
implements of war. Even while the king of Sardinia arranged the plan of operations with France and Spain, he
deceived the imperial minister at Turin; and when the
French army under marshal Villars crossed the Alps, the
governor of Milan offered to assist him with a corps of
troops in impeding their march. Nor was the imperial
court undeceived till Charles Emanuel, having joined his

army to the French and Spaniards, assumed the command, and burst into the Milanese. From the suddenness of his attack, and the weakness of the imperial force, he overran Austrian Lombardy in less than three months, seized the magazines and artillery, and Mantua was the only place in that part of Italy which remained to the emperor at the close of the campaign.

The emperor was taken unawares in Italy by this un-expected defection of the king of Sardinia, and the want of an efficient force; but on the side of Germany he had time to prepare for resistance, and to oppose the arms and intrigues of the house of Bourbon. France had suc-ceeded in isolating the house of Austria from the other powers of Europe, for the purpose of attacking the distant parts of her extensive dominions at one and the same moment; and now exerted all her efforts either to divide the German empire, or to obtain its neutrality. At the same instant in which the French troops passed the Alps to join the Sardinians, another army occupied Loraine, and took possession of the fort of Kehl. But to calm the apprehensions of the empire, and to palliate these acts of hostility, the French minister declared to the diet, that his master would molest no prince who did not enter into hostile engagements against France ; and that the seizure of Kehl was no less directed to secure the empire against the oppressions of their chiefs, than to attack the house of Austria, with whom alone the king of France was at enmity.

The approach of winter preventing the march of the enemy into Germany, the emperor availed himself of this respite to form the lines of Etlingen, which covered Phi-lipsburg and defended the passage of the Rhine. He also made the strongest representations to the diet against the aggression of France. He easily gained the majority of the Catholics, and secured the Protestant party, by pro-mising to obtain the repeal of the obnoxious clause in the treaty. of Ryswick. The diet accordingly voted a con-siderable supply of money, and an army of 120,000 men, notwithstanding the remonstrances of the electors of Co-logne, Bavaria, and Palatine, who declared their intention of adopting an exact neutrality.

Charles was deeply affected with the disastrous state of

his affairs in Italy, and directed his first and principal efforts to preserve the important fortress of Mantua. He therefore sent into Lombardy the greater part of the levies drawn from his hereditary dominions, and gave the supreme command to count Merci, the most enterprising of his generals, with positive orders to undertake offensive operations. In February, 1734, Merci, at the head of 6000 men, hastened to Mantua, and having reconnoitred the position of the allies, returned to Roveredo, to press the march of the troops who were assembled in the Tyrol and the bishopric of Trent. At this critical juncture he was seized with an inflammation in his eyes, which was followed by a stroke of apoplexy, and was reduced to a state of almost total blindness. His intended operations were thus retarded till the beginning of May, when, being convalescent, he put himself at the head of 60,000 men, and drew towards the Oglio and the Po. The Sardinian troops were posted on both sides of the Oglio, and the French on the southern bank of the Po, from Guastalla beyond Revere. Merci reached the northern bank of the Po, and by a bold and skilful manœuvre, effecting a passage near St. Benedetto, surprised the French troops, drove them, with the loss of their magazines and baggage, to Parma, and occupied the cities of Guastalla, Novellara, Mirandola, and Reggio. But in the midst of this success being seized with a return of his complaint, he retired for a short time to Padua, to obtain relief from the physicians of that place.

During his absence the Austrian generals attempted to drive the French from the strong post of Colorno, and to cut off their communication with the Sardinian forces. After a bloody engagement they succeeded, but were again driven back by the king of Sardinia with considerable loss. The ill success of this enterprise, undertaken without orders, roused the indignation of the commander in chief, and he had no sooner rejoined the army, than he retired in disgust to St. Martino, where he passed several days. Being at length appeased, he repaired to the camp, resolved to signalise his return by an important enterprise ; and, from the situation of the allied army, entertained sanguine hopes of success. The king of Sardinia was at Turin on a visit to his queen, who was indisposed,

and had left orders to undertake no offensive operations
until his return; Villars had also recently quitted the
army, in consequence of his advanced age, and the command of the French troops had devolved on marshal de
Coigny, who was embarrassed with the cabals of Broglio
and Maillebois.   Eager to avail himself of the embarrassments of the enemy, Merci advanced as far as St. Prospero, halted a few days ; and on the 28th of June, crossing
the Parma, south of the city, encamped between that
river and the Braganza.

During his approach the allied forces were not inactive,
marshal Coigny, aware of his intentions, had already
selected a strong position, which he occupied on the evening of the 28th.   His troops were posted along the causeway leading to Placentia ; the left wing was flanked by the
city of Parma, the right covered by the village of Crocetta
and by morasses which extended to the Tarro.   He enlarged the fosses on each side to the depth of twenty-seven
feet, strengthened his position by additional entrenchments
and abbatis, and occupied with detachments the casines
scattered on the south of the causeway.   This position was
skilfully chosen ; for the nature of the ground, and the
depth of the trenches, rendered the numerous cavalry of
the imperialists totally useless.

On the 29th in the morning, Merci crossed the Braganza,
and leaving Parma to the east, directed his march in two
columns to Crocetta.   After making a short harangue to
his soldiers, he gave the command of the left column to
the prince of Wirtemberg, and at the head of the right,
rode within musket-shot of the causeway.   Without waiting for the left column, he ordered two regiments of
infantry to begin the attack ; they intrepidly advanced to
the foss, and began to fill it with fascines, but were mowed
down by the well-directed fire of the enemy, with the loss
of their grenadiers, and most of the officers and men
were wounded.   Those who survived giving way, Merci
ordered other regiments to advance, and these troops being
supported by the left column, filled up the ditch with
fascines, and even the dead bodies of their companions,
and were on the point of carrying the entrenchment.   At
this moment Merci was mortally wounded by a musket-
shot, and the soldiers, astounded at the loss of their

general, and the incessant fire of the enemy, were thrown into the utmost confusion. Being encouraged by the arrival of the prince of Wirtemberg, who assumed the command, they gained the summit of the causeway, and rushed forward to the second foss, which they filled with the dead bodies of the French and Sardinians. During this carnage the prince of Wirtemberg had two horses killed under him, and was obliged to quit the action by a severe contusion. The troops, though left a second time without a chief, fought with incredible fury, and forced the allies from six successive entrenchments. Here the French made a desperate stand at a farm-house, and, though driven from it with great slaughter, recovered possession, and mowed down whole companies of the imperialists with grape and musket shot. This dreadful conflict had now lasted ten hours without intermission, when the enemy retired in good order towards the walls of Parma. The imperialists remained masters of the intrenchments ; yet, being without a commander, without provisions, discouraged by their loss, and apprehensive of another attack, fell back towards St. Prospero, and on the following day retreated to Reggio. Thus ended this memorable engagement, in which not less than 10,000 men fell on the field of battle, accompanied with this unparalleled circumstance, that not a prisoner or standard was taken on either side. The allies lost many of their bravest generals and officers, and the imperialists their commander in chief, and seven generals, with more than 340 officers killed and wounded.*

Although Merci risked this attack in opposition to the remonstrances of all the generals, and although the manner in which it was made exposed him to the censure of ex-

---

* The account of this engagement is principally taken from Consul Skinner's Report, written from Reggio, July 1., Orford Papers, and Muratori Annali d'Italia.

List of German officers of the first rank killed and wounded : — killed, the marechal count de Merci, the prince of Culmbach, the prince de Lichtenstein, the colonel d'Harrach, count Formentini, colonel Nicolo Palfi, serjeant general de Wins. Wounded, prince of Wirtemberg, prince Leopold of Hesse Darmstadt, the marquis Gabriel d'Este, general Palfi, count de Castelbarco, (who is imagined to have died on being removed) the marquis d'Est di Santa Christina, the deputy marechal Diesbach, the serjeant general Walsech. — Consul Skinner's Account.

treme rashness*, yet, had he survived, the allies would
probably have been driven from Parma, and the affairs of
the emperor retrieved. The imperialists, however, retreated unmolested behind the Secchia, to preserve their
communication with Mantua and Mirandola; but a garrison of 1200 men in Guastalla, being left without provisions, artillery, or ammunition, surrendered themselves
prisoners of war to the king of Sardinia, who rejoined his
army the morning after the engagement.

The French posted themselves on the opposite side of
the Secchia, and the king of Sardinia took up his head
quarters at St. Benedetto; and thus the allies, having
occupied Modena, with Carpi, Ribiera, and Reggio, commanded the whole duchy, and confined the imperialists in
the district between Mantua and Mirandola. While the
imperialists were waiting the arrival of count Konigsegg,
their new commander, the loss at the battle of Parma, the
divisions which began to take place between the French
and Sardinians, and the cabals among the French generals,
reduced the allies to a state of inactivity and supineness.

In July the imperialists received considerable reinforcements, and Konigsegg, who had assumed the command,
advanced to Quingentolo. Here he was separated from
the enemy only by the Secchia until the 14th of September, when he commenced his military operations by a
brilliant enterprise. While a detachment kept in check a
French corps at Questello, 10,000 men fording the Secchia
in the night with rapidity and silence, surprised the head
quarters of marshal Broglio, who had only time to escape
in his shirt. By this enterprise they spread an alarm
through the French army, routed several corps assembled
in haste, took 2000 prisoners; and their success would

---

* " Pray God pardon the marechal de Merci, who is slain ! All the
officers that are come to this place from the field, both well and wounded,
with one voice cry out upon his conduct; protesting, that they were
led to slaughter to no end or purpose; insomuch that they affirm, the
whole army would have been sacrificed had it not been for the bravery
of the grenadiers, who, by their death, saved the rest from destruction.
In fact, no one can commend the disposition of the order of battle made
by him.   Perhaps it was never heard of, that when there was a strong
intrenchment to be forced, the cannon should be left behind.   But he
has paid for his miscarriages, though with the loss of the bravest men
that his imperial majesty had in his army."—Consul Skinner's Account.

have been still more complete had not the soldiers fallen to pillage, and given the French time to recover from their surprise, and the king of Sardinia to fly to their assistance.

In consequence of this action the allied army fell back to Guastalla, and took post between the Crostolo and the Po, near the intrenchments at the head of one of their bridges. They were followed by the imperialists, who, eager to improve their success, attacked them on the 19th of September. The action was maintained for eight hours with the greatest obstinacy, and the imperialists were at length repulsed through the exertions of the king of Sardinia, who rode from rank to rank encouraging the soldiers, and led them repeatedly to the charge. The loss on both sides was considerable, and nearly equal; but the allies remained masters of the field, and in possession of four standards and some artillery; the French lost three generals, and the imperialists the prince of Wirtemberg, general Colmenero, and the prince of Saxe Gotha, besides many inferior officers. The imperialists, though repulsed, retreated in good order, without being pursued, and occupied a strong position on the north of the Oglio and the Po. The remainder of the campaign was distinguished by no event, except the relief of Mirandola, which was invested by Maillebois, and from which he was driven with the loss of all his artillery. The imperialists kept the field until the beginning of January, and the allied troops, encamped in the midst of morasses, suffered greatly by epidemic disorders, till the king of Sardinia drew them into winter quarters. The Germans, availing themselves of their absence, passed the Oglio, and obtained possession of Bozzolo, Castel Maggiore, Sabionetta, and other places which lie between the Oglio and the Po.

Thus terminated the campaign in Lombardy, in which the emperor reaped little advantage from his great exertions, except the preservation of Mantua, and the possession of Mirandola; and count Konigsegg returned to Vienna, to form a plan for the next campaign, in which he expected to be overwhelmed by a still greater force.

During these events Don Carlos declared himself of age, and assumed the government of Parma and Placentia. A Spanish army commanded by the duke Montemar, under the orders of Don Carlos, assembled in Tuscany, and passing through the territories of the church advanced to the northern frontier of the kingdom of Naples; while a Spanish squadron, having on board a considerable military force, appeared before Civita Vecchia. Part of the ships remained on that station, and the rest sailed to the bay of Baiæ, and took possession of the islands of Ischia and Procida, on the 20th of February, 1734.

At this period the imperial army was scattered in different fortresses, and only two bodies remained in the field; one corps of 6000 men was intrenched at St. Angelo della Canina on the northern frontier, and the other stationed in Apulia. The viceroy Don John Julio Visconti quitting the capital, retired to Rome, and a fatal disagreement took place between the German and Italian generals, who commanded the body at St. Angelo. General Caraffa proposed to withdraw the different garrisons, to unite the troops in one body, and to risk the fate of Naples on an engagement, rather than suffer the enemy to advance to the capital, and cut off the army in detail. The Austrian general Traun*, on the contrary, persisted in occupying the fortress, and pursuing a defensive plan † until the arrival of a reinforcement of 20,000 men, which he expected from Germany.

This plan being unfortunately adopted, occasioned the rapid subjugation of Naples and Sicily. The Spanish army having forced the lines of St. Angelo, left a detachment to blockade Capua and Gaeta, whither the imperial troops had retired, and marched towards Naples. On the approach of the Infant to Aversa, he received the keys of the capital ; and on the 10th of April 3000 Spanish troops entered Naples without opposition. In less than a month the few forts which defended the city and the port of Baiæ surrendered, and the garrisons, to the number of 2000 men, became prisoners of war. On the 10th of May, Don Carlos made his triumphal entry amidst the acclamations of the

* As the names of Daun and Traun are not dissimilar, this general has been confounded with Wyrich, count of Daun, the father of the celebrated field marshal. This general was Juliers John William, count of Arunsperg and Traun; he was born in 1670, and died in 1739.

† According to Muratori, the emperor ordered the generals to risk an engagement; while a letter from the council of war enforced defensive operations; tom. xii. P. i., p. 271.

natives, and on the 27th the duke de Montemar secured his conquests by defeating a corps of 9000 men, the last remnant of the imperial force, who took post under the walls of Bitonto.   In this conflict 2500 were killed, and the remainder having taken refuge in Bitonto and Bari, were compelled to yield themselves prisoners of war. Gaeta surrendered on the 6th of August ; and Capua was defended by Traun till the 24th of November.

In the midst of these events Don Carlos was crowned by the title of Charles III., and experienced a ready submission from the natives, who, disgusted with the government of a German viceroy, hailed the accession of a prince likely to fix his residence among them.   Montemar, created duke of Bitonto in reward for his services, landed on the 29th of August, at the head of a considerable force in the neighbourhood of Palermo ; and in the course of the ensuing summer, subjugated the whole island of Sicily, except Messina and Syracuse.

On the side of Germany the emperor made great levies, and obtained large supplies from his hereditary countries. Expecting England to declare in his favour, and relying on the spirit displayed by the empire, he entertained sanguine hopes of bringing an army into the field, under the command of Eugene, sufficient to oppose the progress of the French at the opening of the campaign.   But these hopes were disappointed ; the supplies voted by the diet were greatly deficient ; and of the nominal army of 120,000 men, only 12,000 made their appearance, when the duke of Bevern took the command.

On the 9th of April, 1734, the French army under marshal Berwick opened the campaign, and after forcing Traerbach to capitulate, passed the Rhine in three columns, and directed their march to turn the lines of Etlingen. The duke of Wirtemberg finding the lines untenable, retired precipitately to Heilbron, and resigned the command of the army to prince Eugene, who had recently arrived from Vienna.

That great general had taken his departure from the capital, with little hopes of retrieving the affairs of his master.   He had in vain remonstrated against interference in the Polish election, from a conviction that the emperor would be deserted, or feebly supported by his allies, and exposed singly to all the efforts of the house of Bourbon. Eugene had the mortification to witness the evacuation of the lines of Etlingen, the hasty retreat of the German troops, and the siege and capture of Philipsburgh, which, though bravely defended by baron Wotgenau with only 4000 men, surrendered on the 18th of July to the marquis d'Asfield, as marshal Berwick had been killed by a cannon ball during the siege. The arrival of Eugene infused a momentary spirit into the imperial army; but notwithstanding his great military skill, the inferiority of his force compelled him to remain on the defensive. On his arrival at the head-quarters the army did not amount to 25,000, and during the whole campaign never exceeded 60,000, although many princes served in person, and even the king of Prussia himself, with the hereditary prince, afterwards Frederic II., led his contingent under the standard of Eugene. This army, however, ill resembled those veteran forces whom Eugene had so often led to victory; it consisted of a motley multitude of raw peasants, unused to discipline; foreigners, animated by no spirit but the hope of pay and plunder; and the German contingents, actuated by the discordant principles and views of their leaders. Concord, unanimity, and subordination were banished from such an assemblage, and the different commanders were less attentive to the success of their operations than to their contests for rank and precedence.

The situation of Eugene was embittered by the captious conduct of the duke of Bevern, who accused him of inactivity and peevishness. The prince, he insinuated to the emperor, was only the shadow of what he was; his memory began to fail; he was broken both in body and mind; from a diffidence of his own powers, was governed by men of inferior capacities, and had reduced the imperial army to a state of dishonourable inactivity. In consequence of these suggestions the emperor despatched a spy to watch the conduct of Eugene; but the prince, though deeply affected with these unjust suspicions, would not hazard the fate of the house of Austria, by exposing the weakness of his army in a rash attack against an enemy far superior in number and resources. His great name still awed his antagonists; with a weak and divided army he curbed the exertions of the French, and the capture of Philipsburgh terminated the offensive operations of the year.

During this arduous campaign Eugene acted with a magnanimity worthy of his great mind; he repressed the feelings of indignation at the aspersions of his conduct and military skill, and seemed alive only to the dangers which menaced his imperial master. Convinced, from past and present experience, that without the assistance of the Maritime Powers, the emperor could no longer resist the formidable combination against him, he exerted his personal influence over George II. to rouse England from her supine indifference. He wrote a series of letters to general Diemar, his confidential agent at London, which were laid before the king, and which displayed the situation, and support the cause of the house of Austria, with equal spirit and strength of argument. In the last of these letters, in which he reiterates all his former arguments, he urged that the imperial forces were insufficient alone to resist France and her allies; that the emperor, at the time he had it in his power to secure the attachment of the house of Bourbon, on his own terms, had sacrificed his advantages to public liberty, and to his inclination for a union with the two maritime powers; that he had cheerfully complied with every demand of the king as elector, and for his sake had deprived himself and his subjects of all the advantages to be derived from the commerce of the Indies. He enforced, also, the impolicy of increasing the power of the house of Bourbon; described the formidable state of the French and Spanish marine; and endeavoured to alarm England, by expressing his conviction that should any disaster happen to the English fleet, the kingdom would not be secure for a single day from a debarkation of French troops on its coasts:—for how, said he, could the king believe that the attachment of the house of Bourbon to the family of the pretender was extinct, when his eldest son was about to serve in the Spanish armies in Naples and Sicily?

The spirited remonstrances of Eugene, however, were ineffectual; the king acknowledged the strength of his arguments, and was warmly disposed to succour the emperor; but the sentiments of sir Robert Walpole having gained the ascendency, the British cabinet would not plunge the nation in a war, and the emperor was left to his fate.

Chap. XCI. — 1733-1739.

The whole conduct of the emperor relative to the Polish election, and the subsequent contest with the house of Bourbon, displays such a series of rashness and timidity, caution and violence, as were wholly incompatible with his character and principles.

This fluctuation was principally derived from the proceedings of the Maritime Powers, and particularly from the conduct of England. On the death of Augustus II. the British cabinet warmly approved the measures adopted by the emperor, in concert with the czarina and the king of Prussia, for the exclusion of Stanislaus, and the election of a prince agreeable to the neighbouring powers. With a view also to procure the guaranty of the Pragmatic Sanction from the new elector of Saxony, they encouraged the emperor to support his pretensions to the crown of Poland, and did not even disapprove the violent manifesto against the court of France.

But when the Dutch were lulled by the French into a state of inactivity, and when the court of Versailles demanded a specific answer from the king of England, whether he intended to take part with the emperor, the British ministry, apprehensive of a war, instantly changed their language, and despatched courier after courier to Vienna, to prevent the emperor from employing force in the Polish election. The emperor complied with these instances, recalled his troops from Silesia, and affected to leave the whole conduct of the election to the czarina. He had nevertheless taken too decisive a part to recede ; and although he did not march a single soldier into Poland, his ambassador at Warsaw concurred with the Russian minister in his declarations against Stanislaus. Aware at the same time that his conduct would not soften the resentment of France, he was buoyed up with the hope of receiving assistance from England ; and in a memorial to the British cabinet, urged that hostilities might be prevented, or at least repelled, if the Maritime Powers would declare in his favour. But England being deaf to these representations,

France was encouraged to declare war against the house of Austria.

From the defenceless state of the Netherlands, the imperial troops being withdrawn from the barrier towns to Luxemburgh, the States-general were alarmed, and on the 24th of November, 1733, concluded a neutrality with France, by which they agreed not to interfere in the contest relative to the Polish election. This treaty, by which the Dutch first abrogated their guaranty of the Pragmatic Sanction, furnished the pacific members of the British cabinet with an excuse for declining to assist the emperor. On the 12th of November, count Kinsky, the imperial ambassador in London, delivered a memorial, claiming the succours stipulated by the treaty of Vienna. The king, in answer, declared, that as the rupture related solely to Polish affairs, in which he had only used his good offices, he must be satisfied that the demand was founded on positive engagements before he involved his people in a war. He must therefore carefully examine the question, consult his allies, particularly the States-general, and take proper measures to provide for his own security, as well as to execute his engagements.

As this reply did not amount to a positive refusal, the emperor still entertained the most sanguine hopes of assistance from the Maritime Powers; and his hopes were flattered by the secret assurances of the king, through the medium of the correspondence between queen Caroline and the empress, and by the inclination of the greater part of the cabinet. In order to alarm sir Robert Walpole, and the pacific part of the British cabinet, the emperor affected to open a private negotiation with Spain; and count Kinsky, after requiring from the king a peremptory answer to the demand of succours, insinuated, that if the emperor did not receive immediate assistance, he had no other alternative to prevent the total destruction of himself and his family than to give his second daughter in marriage to Don Carlos.

Charles anxiously waited for the result of this expedient, and for the opening of parliament, when he expected a declaration of war against France and Spain. It is difficult to express his astonishment, disappointment, and despair, when a letter from lord Harrington announced the impossibility of assisting the emperor that campaign ; and declaring, that in the disastrous situation of his affairs, the king could not in justice object to the marriage of his second daughter with Don Carlos. When Mr. Robinson communicated this answer, the imperial ministers received it with marks of the highest astonishment and indignation, and treated the alternative of the marriage, said to be proposed by count Kinsky, as a pretext invented to excuse the desertion and injustice of England ; the emperor himself positively disavowed his ambassador, and in a sensible and spirited memorial, justified his conduct in the affairs of Poland, and bitterly inveighed against the British cabinet for the breach of the most solemn engagements.

Soon after the delivery of his memorial, England and the States tendered their good offices for an accommodation, and endeavoured to persuade the emperor to acquiesce in the neutrality of the Netherlands. In this instance Charles consulted his magnanimity rather than his strength, disdainfully rejected the proposed neutrality, and even threatened to remove the war into Flanders, by attacking France on the side of Luxemburgh. He still, however, deceived himself with respect to the intentions of the Maritime Powers, as England displayed some appearance of spirit, by a trifling augmentation of the marine force, and by the mission of Mr. Walpole to the Hague to counteract the influence of France.

Finding at length that the whole summer was wasted in equivocal negotiations, and that his repeated and peremptory demands of succour were only answered by offers of mediation, he was irritated at the conduct of England ; and his indignation was still farther excited by suspicions that a plan of pacification was arranging between the Maritime Powers and France. He attributed this conduct wholly to the influence of sir Robert Walpole and his brother, who principally managed the negotiations at the Hague ; and relying on the divided state of the cabinet and the secret inclinations of the king, he attempted to renew the chimerical project which he had adopted in 1726, of appealing to the nation against the minister.

"I have been confirmed," he wrote to count Kinsky, " in the opinion which I before entertained of the sentiments of the English court. I had good reasons to

mistrust the conduct of the Walpoles soon after the conclusion of the treaty with England on the 16th of March,
1731 ; but the strong and repeated assurances which I
received, that it was intended to fulfil the guaranties,
removed my doubts. From that time I had never
failed in a due attention to the king and the royal
family, and in doing every thing which could be agreeable to the present administration. On the death of
the king of Poland, my first care was, to communicate to
the king of England the principles on which I acted. I
took no step without making a previous and confidential
overture to him, and I followed, in every instance, his
advice.   *   *   *

"England has never failed to give me promises both
before and since the commencement of the war ; but instead
of fulfilling those promises, she has even favoured my enemies. This behaviour, however, has not induced me to
address myself to the king of England otherwise than in
the most amicable terms ; and to represent to him, in the
most affecting manner, the imminent danger which threatens
to overwhelm not only the house of Austria, but all Europe,
and more particularly his royal family, as well as the honour
and prosperity of the English nation. But these representations have not hitherto had any effect. This fatal
inactivity has now continued for eleven months ; and
although the evil might have been easily prevented, yet the
whole is left exposed to the most dangerous extremities.
These very extremities, of which England is the occasion,
are made a pretext to palliate and excuse the want of
assistance ; and this want of assistance is urged as an inducement to compel me to accept an unjust and dishonourable peace.   *   *   *

"You have done right in counteracting, there, where
it was necessary, the insinuations of the Walpoles against
me, and in developing to all the real state of the question, and by whose means affairs have been brought
into their present dangerous situation. The king will
have no difficulty in judging whether I or the house
of Bourbon are most inclined to court his friendship.
Let him know that I never will consent to the plan of
pacification now in agitation ; that I had rather suffer
the worst extremities than accede to such disadvantageous

proposals; and that, even if I should not be able to prevent them, I will justify my honour and my dignity, by publishing a circumstantial account of all the transactions, together with all the documents, which I have now in possession.

"If these representations fail, and if the Walpoles continue their unjustifiable conduct, means must be taken to publish and circulate throughout England our answer to the proposal of good offices, which was not made till after the expiration of nine months. You will concert with count Uhlfeld * the best method to effect that purpose, and contrive that the answer shall appear to have been first published in Holland without our concurrence. But should the court of London proceed so far as to make such propositions of peace as are supposed to be in agitation, you will not delay a moment to circulate throughout England a pro memoria, containing a recapitulation of all negotiations which have taken place since 1718, together with the authentic documents, detailing my just complaints, and reclaiming in the most solemn manner the execution of the guaranties." †

Failing in this attempt to alarm the minister, and compel him to act offensively against France, the emperor redoubled his cabals with the opposition, and endeavoured to remove sir Robert Walpole by means of a meddling emissary whom he despatched to England. This agent was Strickland, an English Roman Catholic, and an adherent of the pretender, by whose interest he had been promoted to the abbey of St. Pierre de Prou in Normandy. During the quarrel between the emperor and George I. in 1726, he maintained a correspondence with the opposition, and through their interests with the emperor was appointed bishop of Namur. He was afterwards a spy to the English minister, and by order of George II., lord Harrington strongly solicited the court of Vienna to obtain for him a cardinal's hat, that he might reside at Rome for the purpose of watching the pretender. With this strong recommendation he repaired to Vienna, and improved the good opinion already entertained of him by the emperor from the

* The imperial minister in Holland.

† A copy of this letter from the emperor to Kinsky is preserved in the Walpole Papers.

reforms which he had introduced into his diocese. Having attracted the notice of the empress, he gained her confidence by his plausible manners, and was admitted to a private audience of the emperor. He conciliated the suspicious character of Charles by strictures on his ministers, and by presenting plans for reforming the government. He boasted of his influence in England, availed himself of lord Harrington's recommendation, and represented himself as able either to force sir Robert Walpole into the war, or to obtain his removal by means of the king and queen, and of the party attached to the house of Austria.

The emperor, fond of new schemes, embraced this proposal, supplied the bishop of Namur with credential letters to the king and queen, and furnished him with numerous documents justifying the measures of his own cabinet, and criminating the conduct of sir Robert Walpole. He was despatched to England without the knowledge of any of the imperial ministers, except Sinzendorf and Bartenstein, under pretence of thanking the king for having procured the emperor's promise to nominate him a cardinal. On his arrival in London, under a feigned name, he had a long and secret conference with Lord Harrington, was graciously received by the king and queen; and reports began to circulate that he had been successful in his endeavours to obtain the dismission of the Walpoles. But these attempts served only to strengthen the influence of the prime minister, and to frustrate the schemes of the emperor. At his representations the meddling emissary was civilly dismissed; and the queen, in a letter to the empress, contradicted the erroneous reports of Kinsky and the bishop of Namur, and declared that England could not enter into hostilities. The emperor, at length undeceived, defeated in all his attempts, and disappointed in all his hopes, reluctantly agreed to accept the good offices and admit the mediation of the Maritime Powers.

In consequence of his consent, the Maritime Powers proposed an armistice, and produced a project of pacification, which had been secretly concerted with France. The principal articles were the abdication of Stanislaus, who was, however, to retain the title of king, with the disposal of his estates in Poland ; in return for the restitution of the conquered states, the guaranty of the Pragmatic Sanction by

France and the king of Sardinia, and the immediate posses-
sion of Parma and Placentia, with the reversion of Tuscany,
Leghorn excepted, which was to be made a republic, the
emperor was to acknowledge Don Carlos king of the two
Sicilies, and cede to the king of Sardinia the provinces of
Tortona, Novarra, and the Vigenevasco.

To this project the emperor proposed many alterations
which were inadmissible ; but, in the spring of 1735, accepted the plan as a basis for an accommodation, on condition
that Leghorn should not be separated from Tuscany, and
that the allies should declare their approbation in two
months. He was induced to give this assent, though reluctantly, from the hopes of being able to delay, if not
frustrate, the project ; and his hopes were encouraged by a
series of events which seemed to announce the approach of
a general war. A great coldness had taken place between
England and France, relative to the pacification. During
the negotiation, Fleury affected to demand no compensation
for France ; but the plan, being divulged, excited general
indignation among the French ; and it was considered as
highly dishonourable to their monarch to desert his father-
in-law, in support of whom the war had been undertaken,
merely to obtain the transfer of some dominions in Italy for
Don Carlos and the king of Sardinia. The cardinal therefore availed himself of the premature disclosure of the plan,
in the speech made by George II. at the opening of the
new parliament, and, after much complaint, prevarication,
and delay, refused to fulfil his promise. *

The queen of Spain was equally averse to a project which
wrested from her family Parma, Placentia, and Tuscany,
at the moment when the expulsion of the emperor from
Italy seemed inevitable, and had made several overtures
to the court of Vienna to renew the engagements for the
marriage of an archduchess with the Infant. The king of
Sardinia was scarcely less alarmed than the emperor with
the progress of the combined army in Lombardy ; he was
aware that the expulsion of the house of Austria would
destroy the balance of Italy, and leave him solely in the
power of the house of Bourbon. As early as June, 1734,
he had made overtures to the king of England, in which he

* Memoirs of Sir Robert Walpole, ch. xliv. and Memoirs of Lord
Walpole, ch. xvii. xviii.

disclosed his secret treaty with France, inveighed against the conduct and plans of cardinal Fleury and the court of Spain, displayed his own danger, and requested the king's mediation to negotiate a separate peace with the emperor. He afterwards even exhorted the emperor to deliver him from the servitude in which he had involved himself by his union with the house of Bourbon, and offered to join his troops with the imperialists, if the Maritime Powers would enter into the war, and a sufficient force could be brought into Italy to secure him from the resentment of France and Spain. In consequence of this disunion among the allies, the emperor carried on secret negotiations with the respective courts, occasionally with the connivance of the British cabinet, but sometimes without their knowledge; and with a view to alarm the Maritime Powers, his ministers declared, in different courts of Europe, that their master had the means of concluding a separate accommodation.

The affairs of the North wore a favourable aspect. Stanislaus, besieged in Dantzic, where he had taken refuge, made a desperate defence for several months against the combined armies and the Russian fleet which blockaded the harbour. Perceiving resistance to be ineffectual, he made his escape, and, after a series of romantic adventures, arrived at Marienwerder in Prussia. Dantzic instantly submitted, and all Poland acknowledged Augustus. Hence the king of Poland was enabled to reinforce his Saxon contingent in Germany; the czarina despatched a corps of 16,000 troops to the Rhine, and was preparing to march a still greater force; the king of Denmark had recently concluded a subsidiary treaty with England, and seemed inclined to take an active part against the house of Bourbon.

In the midst of these transactions, a violent dispute between Spain and Portugal seemed to announce an immediate rupture. The servants of Don Cabral de Belmonte, the Portuguese minister at Madrid, were imprisoned for rescuing a malefactor from the officers of justice. The ambassador having complained of this insult as an infraction of the law of nations, was warmly supported by the court of Lisbon, who retaliated by sending nineteen domestics of the Spanish ambassador to prison. As neither of the violent and punctilious monarchs would give the satisfaction reciprocally demanded, the two ministers retired from their respective embassies ; both nations prepared for hostilities ; the king of Portugal demanded assistance from England and from the emperor in virtue of subsisting treaties, and exhorted them to conclude an offensive alliance. He publicly said, the time is now arrived to reduce Philip to reason ; Spain is without troops, a small number of Portuguese will overrun the country ; and Philip will be compelled to recall his armies from Italy for the defence of his own kingdom. By this diversion the force of the allies will be weakened, the imperial troops may again acquire the ascendency, and the attempts of the house of Bourbon to humiliate the house of Austria be frustrated.   These sentiments were too congenial to the opinion of Charles not to be received with avidity ; he made unbounded promises of assistance, and privately encouraged the king of Portugal to agree to no accommodation with Spain, " because," he said, " the British ministry dare not leave Portugal destitute of help, and in that case must, however unwillingly, come forward to the assistance of the house of Austria. "

England seemed to awaken from her pacific lethargy ; and sir Robert Walpole himself was foremost in recommending and enforcing the necessity of the most active exertions.   On the 7th of February, 1735, he carried two motions through the House of Commons " for taking 30,000 seamen and 26,000 soldiers into pay, in addition to 12,000 men in Ireland, and 6000 Danes, according to the subsidiary treaty with Denmark."   A squadron of twenty-five ships of the line was preparing to sail for the protection of Portugal ; Mr. Walpole exerted all his influence at the Hague to rouse the Dutch to similar exertions ; the States-general recommended an augmentation of troops, and the British ministers, in every court of Europe, inveighed against the perfidy of France.

Impressed with new hopes of drawing the Maritime Powers into the war, the emperor, on the 23rd of May, delivered a memorial to the British and Dutch ministers at Vienna, written in a high tone of confidence.   This memorial recapitulated and justified the several pieces delivered by the emperor since the publication of the project for an accommodation, and expatiated on his readiness to concur in the armistice, and on his inclination for peace.   It inferred, from the delays and warlike prepar-

ations of the allies, the extent and danger of their ambitious designs, and urged the necessity of preventing or
opposing them, for which the situation of Portugal seemed
to present a favourable opportunity. He still, however,
disclaimed any intention to recede from his pacific declarations, and offered to conclude an armistice, and open a
negotiation for a general peace, provided it could be
settled without delay, or prejudice to his affairs or pretensions. The plan of pacification was to be adopted as
the basis of the peace, except the separation of Leghorn
from Tuscany. The conferences were to be held at the
Hague, under the mediation of the Maritime Powers ; and
the discussions confined to those matters alone which
immediately concerned the contracting parties. An armistice was to be concluded for two months, during which
all the dominions of the neutral princes were to be evacuated, and no military contributions to be levied on the
states of the empire. Charles also required from the
Maritime Powers a secret declaration, to be signed at the
same time as the preliminaries, that they would indemnify
him for all infractions of the armistice, and should the
negotiation prove unsuccessful, would fulfil the guaranty
stipulated by the treaty of 1731.

The emperor was aware that these terms were inadmissible ; because his enemies would never consent to
relinquish their conquests, without being secure of a
general peace ; but from the recent events, and the appearance of vigour displayed by the Maritime Powers, he
hoped to draw them into his views, and looked forward to
the renewal of a grand alliance against the house of
Bourbon.

Although these hopes were dissipated, yet the spirited
appeal of the emperor brought his affairs to a crisis. The
leading members of the United States resisted all the
attempts of Mr. Walpole to rouse them to exertion, and,
while their own country was not attacked, finally declared,
that not only the loss of the emperor's dominions in Italy,
but even the invasion of his hereditary countries, would
not induce the republic to enter into a war. In consequence
of this resolution, lord Harrington, who accompanied the
king to Hanover, delivered to count Kinsky a verbal
answer to the emperor's memorial. After displaying the

ineffectual attempts to induce the Dutch to arm, he said,
" his majesty thinks himself bound in honour, justice, and
affection, to represent the true state of the case, and is
with regret compelled to undeceive the emperor in his
hopes of engaging England separately, at least for the
present. Our engagements in the treaty of Vienna being
reciprocal with those of the Dutch, are considered in
England as an obligation to be fulfilled by both. The
apprehension also of driving Holland into the arms of
France, the great and unequal burden required for the
support of such a war, the small probability of success,
and above all the danger of irretrievably diverting the
most valuable branches of our trade into other channels,
render it a matter of the most extreme difficulty, if not
impossible, to extort the consent of the English nation.
In these circumstances, as the emperor cannot prosecute
the war beyond this campaign, the king can only serve
him by negotiation ; and if his imperial majesty can
extricate himself from his present difficulties by a separate
agreement with any of his enemies, as his ministers have
frequently insinuated, and will open himself in confidence,
the king will readily give his assistance, and thinks he can
answer for the concurrence of the States." Mr. Robinson
was at the same time instructed to make a similar communication to the ministers at Vienna.

The surprise and indignation of the imperial court was
still greater at this communication than at the first refusal
of the Maritime Powers to fulfil their engagements in the
beginning of 1734. Mr. Robinson could only draw from
them sullen and violent declarations of astonishment and
affliction, on seeing their master abandoned by the only
power on whom he principally relied for assistance. They
disavowed the assertions of the imperial ambassadors, that
the emperor had the means of extricating himself from
his distress, and protested that, deserted as he was by his
friends, he had no other alternative but to submit to the
mercy of his enemies. He must give up the Low Countries, and all his foreign possessions, and concentrate his
force within his hereditary dominions, where he would be
great enough for himself, though not useful to others.
Count Sinzendorf passionately exclaimed, " What a severe
sentence have you passed on the emperor ; no malefactor

was ever carried with so hard a doom to the gibbet; I would burn Amsterdam, and give up Flanders. There neither is nor can be any separate negotiation."

In the midst of this suspense the armies had taken the field. In Germany, Eugene had reluctantly resumed the command of the imperial forces. At the commencement of the year he had declared to the emperor that he could not undertake to carry on the war without the assistance of the Maritime Powers. " To find myself," he said, " in the same condition as last year will be only exposing myself to the censure of the world, which judges by appearances, as if I were less capable in my old age to support the reputation of my former successes." But his scruples were overruled by his attachment to his master, and with a force of no more than 30,000 men he kept in check the French army, which amounted to 100,000.

In Italy, the imperial army experienced a series of disasters ; the conquest of Sicily was completed by the captures of Messina and Syracuse, and on the 3rd of July Don Carlos was crowned king of the Two Sicilies. In Lombardy, count Konigsegg, unable to resist the French and Sardinian army, who were joined by a considerable number of Spanish troops under the duke de Montemar, retreated beyond the Adige, into the passes of the Tyrol and the bishopric of Trent ; Mirandola surrendered to the Spanish general, and Mantua, the only remnant of the imperial possessions in Italy, was menaced with a blockade.

The distress of the emperor, at the disastrous state of his affairs and the desertion of his allies, was aggravated by the divisions in his court between the Austrian and Spanish ministers, who mutually accused each other as the cause of his misfortunes. In consequence of the absence of prince Eugene and count Konigsegg, the Spanish party had gained great ascendency, and, being apprehensive lest the loss of the Italian dominions might occasion the abolition of their places and salaries, they strongly recommended the emperor to make a separate accommodation with Spain, by giving the eldest archduchess to Don Carlos, or even both his daughters to the Spanish princes.

The repeated remonstrances of Maria Theresa, his eldest daughter, who had now attained her eighteenth year, and

was passionately attached to the duke of Loraine, to whom
she was betrothed, increased the emperor's embarrassment.
To use the words of the English minister, " She is a princess
of the highest spirit ; her father's losses are her own.   She
reasons already ; she enters into affairs ; she admires his
virtues, but condemns his mismanagement ; and is of a
temper so formed for rule and ambition as to look upon him
as little more than her administrator.   Notwithstanding
this lofty humour by day, she sighs and pines all night for
her duke of Loraine.   If she sleeps, it is only to dream of
him ; if she wakes, it is but to talk of him to the lady in
waiting ; so that there is no more probability of her forgetting the very individual government, and the very individual husband which she thinks herself born to, than of
her forgiving the authors of her losing either."

The empress also incessantly re-choed the remonstrances
of her daughter, and the complaints of the German ministers,
and exhorted the emperor to follow other counsels, and
adopt other measures.   Charles was distracted with the disastrous state of his affairs, harassed by the remonstrances
of his family, and distrusting all his ministers, was reduced
to the most abject state of despondency.   During the dead
of the night, and while alone with the empress, he gave a
loose to his affliction ; his life was endangered, and even
his understanding affected by the contending passions.

Under these impressions of alarm and despondency,
Charles adopted the desperate resolution, which he had
before rejected with abhorrence, of effecting a separate and
secret accommodation with France.   While he had entertained the smallest hopes of assistance from the Maritime
Powers, he had, by means of the pretender, the papal
nuntio at Brussels, and even of the pope himself, made
illusory overtures to cardinal Fleury.   But finding that he
should be compelled, even by acceding to the mediation of
the Maritime Powers, to yield a considerable portion of his
Italian dominions, he deemed it more honourable and more
advantageous to close with the offers of France without
their intervention.   A secret negotiation was opened through
the means of count Niewied, and La Beaume, a confidential
agent of cardinal Fleury, was despatched to Vienna.   The
emperor hastened the conclusion of the treaty by alarming
the cardinal with pretended negotiations with Spain and

the king of Sardinia ; and while he amused the Maritime
Powers, who were attempting to divide the allies, and pro-
jecting schemes of accommodation, the preliminaries with
France were suddenly signed at Vienna on the 3rd of
October, 1735.

By these preliminaries the emperor consented to the
immediate cession of the duchy of Bar to France, and the
reversion of Loraine when the duke should be put into
possession of Tuscany.   The other articles were conformable to the original plan of pacification by the Maritime
Powers, except in regard to some of the cessions offered to
the king of Sardinia.   The signature of the preliminaries
had been preceded by a virtual though not a formal armistice in Germany, and no material event had taken place,
except a skirmish at Claussen between a corps of imperialists, under count Seckendorf, and a detachment of the
French army on the Moselle, which was the last action of
the war in Germany.

In Italy, the siege of Mantua had been retarded by the
jealousy of the king of Sardinia, and the intrigues of cardinal Fleury, both of whom were averse to suffer that
important fortress to fall into the hands of Spain.   In consequence of these sentiments, the king of Sardinia discontinued his offensive operations, though he did not accede
to the armistice till the 22nd of February ; but the court of
Spain irritated at the secession of France, and disappointed
in their hopes of obtaining Parma and Tuscany, and acquiring Mantua, refused to ratify the suspension of arms ;
and the duke de Montemar, deserted by the French and
Sardinians, could not maintain his conquests in Lombardy ;
Konigsegg recrossed the Po, drove the Spaniards from the
walls of Mantua, and pursuing his success, compelled them
to retreat into Tuscany.   At length Montemar, threatened
by the imperial army, and alarmed for the safety of Naples
and Sicily, consented to a provisional suspension of arms,
which was afterwards ratified by the court of Madrid.

Thus terminated the events of the war ; but it was long
before the definitive treaty was finally arranged.   Delays
arose from the avidity of the king of Sardinia to increase
his dominions on the side of the Milanese, and from the
captious and irritable temper of the queen of Spain, who
was unwilling to relinquish the possession of Parma and

Tuscany. France also was eager to obtain the immediate cession of Loraine in addition to Bar ; while the emperor retained his unwillingness to admit a prince of the house of Bourbon into Italy, and to cede the districts in the Milanese required by the king of Sardinia. His ministers were no less intractable ; and Vienna exhibited a motley scene of cabal, intrigue, impatience, and procrastination.

Another difficulty arose from the duke of Loraine, who was unwilling to renounce his family inheritance, and required an adequate compensation if Loraine was ceded to France before the death of the grand duke of Tuscany.

Mr. Robinson, in one of his despatches, gives a pathetic and interesting account of his extreme distress and agitation on this occasion. " In an audience which I demanded of him, to announce the marriage of the prince of Wales with the princess of Saxe Gotha, he interrupted me in the midst of his compliments to pour out his joy at the marriage, and his respect and veneration for the king, which he first expressed aloud ; but lest any of his attendants in the next room might overhear, he retreated with me to the window of an adjoining apartment and said, with the greatest emotion, ' Good God, where are you ? where are the Maritime Powers ? As for my part,' he continued, ' I rely upon the king singly, and not upon treaties ; not upon formal promises, but upon what his majesty has told me over and over by word of mouth.' If his words expressed the highest agony and distress, his gestures and actions expressed no less : he threw himself in a reclining posture, and in an inconsolable manner, upon the arms and end of an adjoining table and chair." " Such also," adds Mr. Robinson, "is the extreme agitation of his mind, that his health is affected by it ; he owns he has no friend to look up to, and that next to God and the emperor, all his fortune depends on the king of England."

These complicated disputes would have still further prolonged the final arrangement of the definitive treaty, had not the pacific spirit of sir Robert Walpole and cardinal Fleury interposed ; and had not the emperor, eager to join Russia in a war against the Turks, with the hopes of indemnifying himself on the side of Bosnia for the loss of Naples and Sicily, found it necessary to secure the peace of Italy.

Charles therefore prevailed on his son-in-law to consent

to the immediate cession of Loraine, in consequence of receiving from France an annual pension of 450,000 livres, until he obtained possession of Tuscany, and agreed to satisfy the king of Sardinia.   But the definitive treaty was not signed with France until the 8th of November, 1738 ; the king of Sardinia acceded on the 3rd of February, 1739, and the kings of Spain and Naples on the 21st of April.

By this treaty Stanislaus renounced the crown of Poland, retaining only the title, and obtained the duchies of Loraine and Bar, which, after his death, were to be united to France. Tuscany was to be secured to the duke of Loraine, who had been permitted to take possession of that duchy on the death of the great duke, July 29. 1737.   Don Carlos was acknowledged king of Naples and Sicily ; the king of Sardinia obtained the provinces of Novarra and Tortona, the lordships of St. Fidele, Torre de Forti, Gravedo, and Campo Maggiore, and the territory of the Langhes.   In return the emperor acquired Parma and Placentia, and received from France and Sardinia the guaranty of the Pragmatic Sanction.

Chap. XCII.—1736, 1737.

Charles had long designed his eldest daughter for Francis Stephen duke of Loraine and Bar, grandson of his sister Leonora, and son of the benevolent Leopold, duke of Loraine, by Elizabeth Charlotte, daughter of Philip duke of Orleans.   He was born in 1708, and was educated under the auspices and at the court of Charles VI.   The emperor had protracted the declaration of the match to lure the queen of Spain with the hopes of an union between their two families, and from an apprehension, lest France should avail herself of that pretext to seize the duchy of Loraine.   But no longer influenced by these motives, the nuptials were solemnised at Vienna on the 12th of February, 1736, soon after the conclusion of the preliminaries. Charles, however, omitted no precaution to secure the succession to his dominions in the male line of his family.   By the contract of marriage Maria Theresa ratified the Pragmatic Sanction, and engaged to form no pretensions to the inheritance of the house of Austria should her father have male issue ; and the duke solemnly promised never to assert personally any right of succession to the Austrian dominions. By this marriage the two branches of the ancient house of Alsace, which are said to have derived their respective origins from duke Eticho, in the seventh century, and to have formed the lines of Hapsburgh and Loraine, were re-united in the same stock.

The joy of this auspicious event was soon overcast by the death of prince Eugene. That great man preserved his abilities and spirits, even in a very advanced age ; and after having personally braved the most imminent perils in many battles and sieges, in which he was often the first to mount the breach, he died tranquilly at Vienna in the night of the 20th of April, 1736, in the 73rd year of his age.

Every honour was paid to the memory of Eugene which the gratitude of the sovereign could dictate. The body was embalmed, and the heart sent to Turin to be deposited in the royal tomb with the ashes of his illustrious ancestors. The corpse lay in grand state for three days, with the coat of mail, helmet, and gauntlets hung over its head, and was interred in the metropolitan church of St. Stephen. Charles himself, with his whole court, assisted incognito at the cere-mony ; the pall was supported by sixteen general officers, and the funeral was solemnised with the same honours as were paid to the remains of the imperial family.

The loss of Eugene was highly unfortunate at this period, not only on account of the approaching war with Turkey, but in consequence of an essential change which had taken place in the conduct and sentiments of the emperor. Prince Eugene was the only person who would venture or was able to take the lead, in matters of state, and it was observed by a person capable of appreciating his talents and influence, that " during the two last years of his life, even the remainder of what he had been kept things in some order, as his very yes or no, during his sounder age, had kept them in the best." *

In addition to the former ministers, the conference had been increased by the admission of count Harrach, who had filled the post of ambassador at Madrid, and viceroy of Naples, and count Konigsegg, commander in chief of

* Mr. Robinson to Mr. Walpole, June 27. 1736. — Walpole Papers.

the army in Italy, who was vice-president of the council
of war, and appointed president soon after the death of
Eugene. But the emperor was more than ever distrustful
of his principal ministers, and placed his chief confidence
in Bartenstein, referendary of the conference.

John Christopher Bartenstein was son of a professor at
Strasburgh, and came to Vienna in 1714. Being an
agent or solicitor in one of the tribunals, he gained the
good will of count Staremberg by the successful management of a lawsuit, and made himself so useful in drawing
memorials, that in 1730 he was introduced into the
chancery, or office for foreign affairs, and became referendary, or secretary to the conference. The complicated
negotiations at the period of his introduction, and the
absence of the chancellor, count Sinzendorf, at the congress
of Soissons, gave him an opportunity of displaying his
talents and knowledge of foreign affairs; and the customary
mode in which the emperor transacted business with his
ministers, by writing, brought him into notice as the
channel of communication.

Charles, though haughty and reserved with his principal
ministers, was familiar and condescending with those of
a lower station, who had frequent access to his person ;
and Bartenstein possessed penetration, talents, and temper,
which enabled him gradually to acquire the full confidence of his sovereign. He was lavish in flattering the
personal vanity of the emperor, and cherished his notions
of romantic glory and pre-eminent dignity. He possessed,
in a high degree, all the arts of cavil and chicanery; and
the quality which most endeared him to the emperor
was his dexterity in starting subtleties and difficulties
without end. He furnished Charles with materials to
refute and perplex his own ministers, and was the agent
of a secret correspondence which his master maintained
with his foreign ambassadors.

By these means Bartenstein rapidly increased his influence, and at this period principally swayed the counsels
of the emperor. Though only in a subordinate situation,
he received communications from the foreign courts, in the
same manner as the members of the conference, and was
even able to humble or disgrace those ministers who
refused to submit to his control. He contrived to remove

the bishop of Bamberg from his post of vice-chancellor of
the empire, for saying in a conference, "that his business
was not to speak but to write;" and would have obtained
the dismission of count Konigsegg from the council of
war, for advising the emperor "to trust his military
affairs rather to his generals than to his clerks," had not
Konigsegg been supported by prince Eugene, and afterwards humbled himself to the favourite.   He even behaved
with extreme haughtiness to the duke of Loraine; and
when his highness objected to the cession of Loraine
without an equivalent, replied, " *Monseigneur, point de
cession, point d'archiduchesse.*" *   He was of a sanguine,
jealous, and implacable temper, which he concealed under
an exterior of composure and politeness; and as he rose
by his pen, was vain of his writings, and fond of argumen-
tation and invective.   He possessed uncommon volubility
of tongue, and frequently overwhelmed with a deluge of
words those ministers to whom he was unwilling to give a
specific answer, and whom he dismissed without allowing
them the smallest respite to introduce their business.†   It
is but justice, however, to the character of Bartenstein to
add, that he was incorruptible, and both sincerely and enthusiastically attached to the glory and interests of the house
of Austria.   Bartenstein was at first favourably inclined
towards the Maritime Powers, and promoted with all his influence the treaty of 1731; but, being disgusted with
their refusal to fulfil their engagements, and moved by the
complaints of the emperor, had earnestly supported the
alliance with France.

In these circumstances great confusion pervaded the

* Mr. Robinson to lord Harrington, Dec. 31. 1738.

† Mr. Keith gives a singular instance of Bartenstein's behaviour in
his account of his first interview: —

" I told your grace in my former letter that I was going to Bartenstein's.   I went accordingly; and, after the first compliments were over,
I began to talk about the orders I had received, in relation to the project; but instead of answering, he entered into a dissertation upon
treaties, negotiations, preliminaries, &c., and, without stopping, talked
on for near an hour, without my being able to get in one word, though
I endeavoured several times to interrupt him; so I left him as wise as
I went.   This may seem very odd; but, I do assure your grace, it is
literally true; and, from that behaviour of his, I begin to have a very
bad opinion of the success of my commission, for I am very far mistaken if he does not in a great measure direct the counsels of this court. "

councils of the imperial cabinet; the emperor, affecting to
be his own minister, treated the members of the conference
with reserve, and blamed them separately to each other;
they became timid and diffident, their zeal slackened from
the consciousness of not giving satisfaction; and, in this
weak, divided, and inefficient state of the cabinet, the
emperor was involved in the war which took place
between the Russians and the Turks, at a time when the
army was diminished, and the finances exhausted. This
war was occasioned by the avidity of Russia, which was
excited by the apparent decline of the Ottoman power.

In the commencement of the century, Peter the Great
had attempted to form a settlement on the sea of Azof,
and to open a communication with the Euxine; and seemed
on the eve of realising his favourite project by the acquisition of Azof, and the construction of Taganroc. But his
plan was frustrated by the unsuccessful campaign of 1711
against the Turks; and, at the peace of Pruth, he was
compelled to cede those fortresses, and to relinquish the
commerce of the Euxine. From that period the attention
of Russia was diverted from this object by the construction
of St. Petersburgh, the establishments on the side of the
Baltic, and interference in the affairs of Europe.

Anne, on her accession, was anxious to revive the
project of Peter the Great, but was prevented by the war
relative to the Polish election. She had no sooner established Augustus on the throne, than she seized a pretext,
from the incursions of the Tartar hordes, to turn her arms
against the Turks, then engaged in hostilities with Persia,
with a view to recover the possessions ceded by Peter the
Great, and even to conquer the Crimea. The campaign,
which opened in March, 1736, was highly successful on the
side of the Russians. Marshal Munich, at the head of the
principal army, forced the lines of Precop, penetrated into
the Crimea, as far as Batcheserai, the residence of the
Khan, and overran the whole country; a second body
under general Lacy took Azof, after a siege of twelve
days.

The Turks, alarmed at these successes, made overtures
of peace, under the mediation of the emperor, and a
congress was assembled at Nimerova in Poland, where the
plenipotentiaries assembled in June, 1737. But the

emperor, instead of being a mediator, became a party in the quarrel. The czarina had demanded the succour of 20,000 infantry and 10,000 cavalry, stipulated by the treaty of 1726, with which he could not comply while embarrassed with the European war. But he had no sooner signed the preliminaries with France, than he submitted to a council of his principal ministers and generals the question, whether it would be most expedient to declare war against the Turks, or only to despatch the succours stipulated by treaty to the assistance of Russia? The answer was in favour of the latter, and the council represented the danger of involving himself in a new war before the definitive peace was signed with France, Spain, and Sardinia, and before the army and finances were recovered.

But the emperor had already embraced the rash resolution to enter immediately into the war; and even before he affected to consult his ministers and generals, had given to the czarina a promise to attack the Turks with his whole force in the ensuing spring; although the exhausted condition of his finances, and the reduced state of his army might have afforded him a plausible pretext for declining to engage again in hostilities. He was induced to adopt this resolution as well from gratitude for the assistance which Russia had afforded him in the late contest with France, as from the hopes of compensating for his losses in Italy by new acquisitions on the side of Turkey; and he was encouraged by the declaration of his confessor, that it was the duty of a Catholic prince to extirpate the enemies of the church of Christ.

He accordingly drew his forces towards the frontiers of Turkey, and subsidised 8000 Saxons to be employed in the same quarter. The duke of Loraine was at first destined for the command; but, declining so arduous a post, it was conferred on general Seckendorf, and the duke served as a volunteer.

Seckendorf at this period enjoyed a high reputation for military skill, and had been designated to the emperor by prince Eugene, as the fittest person to succeed him in the command of the army, if his religion, which was Lutheran, was not an insurmountable obstacle. He was also warmly recommended by the prince of Saxe Hil-

burghausen, who was in high favour with the emperor.
But neither the dying eulogium of Eugene, nor the powerful
recommendation of prince Hilburghausen, nor even the
inclination of the sovereign himself, would have availed
against the opposition of Bartenstein, whom he had offended
by refusing to disclose a secret note which he had received
from the emperor, concerning the succession of Juliers
and Berg, during his mission to Berlin; nor was Bartenstein
appeased until Seckendorf had made the disclosure.   The
favourite being conciliated, the emperor summoned the
general into his presence and offered him the command.
Seckendorf, aware of the number and power of his enemies,
declined the honour, but was overcome by the kind solicitations of the emperor, who embraced him, and promised
his support.

Being despatched into Hungary to inspect the military
force, Seckendorf found the army and fortifications in a
deplorable state.   He drew a lamentable picture of the
situation and misery of the troops, and made the most
bitter complaints against the negligence and peculation of
the generals and contractors, both to the emperor and the
council of war.   "I cannot," he declared, "consistently
with my duty to God and the emperor, conceal the
miserable condition of the barracks and hospitals.   The
troops, crowded together without sufficient bedding to
cover them, are a prey to innumerable disorders ; and are
exposed to the rain and other inclemencies of the weather,
from the dilapidated state of the casernes, the roofs of
which are in perpetual danger of being overthrown by the
wind.

" All the frontier fortresses," he added, "particularly
Gradiska, Bioc, Ratscha, Szabatch, and even Belgrade, are
incapable of the smallest resistance, as well from the
dilapidated state of the fortifications, as from a total want
of artillery, ammunition, and other requisites.   The naval
armament also is in a state of irreparable disorder.   The
evil is enhanced by absurd impositions and prohibitions of
trade, which render provisions and fuel so dear, that the
scanty pay of the soldier is unequal to his support."

He had even the courage to remonstrate with Bartenstein:
" Some companies," he said, " of my regiment in Belgrade,
are thrust into holes, where a man would not put even his

favourite hounds, and I cannot see the situation of these miserable and half-starved wretches without tears." With a prophetic spirit, he concluded, " these melancholy circumstances portend, in case of war, the loss of these fine kingdoms with the same rapidity as the states of Italy. A remedy, however, is not impossible; but no time must be lost, and a different system pursued; for it is impossible that the council of war at Vienna can issue proper decrees and resolutions on subjects which they neither see nor understand." He also boldly declared to the emperor, that many of his generals were so incapable of fulfilling the duties of their station, as to endanger the loss of his crown and sceptre; and that the different governors, instead of inspecting their provinces, were employed in hunting and diversions. The emperor was pleased with the freedom of these remonstrances, and promoted the improvements suggested by Seckendorf; and although his representations excited opposition in the council of war, as well as among the generals and governors of provinces, and many obstacles were thrown in his way, yet, as the emperor did not withhold his support, Seckendorf greatly improved the state of the army ; the casernes and hospitals were put into a better condition, the price of provisions was considerably reduced, the troops disciplined, and the fortifications repaired under the superintendence of general Schmettau.

The plan of operations was judiciously formed by Seckendorf. He proposed that the Russians, after taking Bender, should direct their march along the Danube towards the Pruth ; while the imperialists should commence their operations with the siege of Widdin, concentrate their forces on the banks of the Danube, and advance through Turkish Wallachia, either to form a junction with the Russians, or to inclose the Turks between the two armies. The prince of Hilburghausen was also to be despatched with a large body of forces to drive the Turks from Bosnia, and advance through Servia to join the main army on the Danube.

Before his departure from Vienna, Seckendorf, aware that a party in the cabinet wished to commence hostilities by the siege of Nissa, a fortress at the extremity of Servia, obtained from the emperor the most positive promise that no change should be made in the plan of operations. He was nominated field marshal, and at the same time received assurances from the council of war and the treasury, that the army amounted to 126,000 men, provided with every requisite, and that a monthly remittance of 600,000 florins should be made for the pay of the troops. But on his arrival on the frontiers he found the troops greatly deficient in numbers, composed of recruits, many of whom from infirmities were incapable of service, and destitute of provisions, horses, carriages, arms, and the necessary implements of war. He was also disappointed in the promised remittances, and for the month of May received only 100,000 florins. These deficiencies were owing partly to the intrigues of his enemies, partly to the exigencies of the state, and principally to the false notion prevailing in the cabinet, that the Turks were too much occupied with the Russians to bring a formidable army into the field on the side of Belgrade.

By the most arduous exertions, Seckendorf could only collect a force of 26,000 infantry, 15,000 cavalry, and 4000 irregulars, which assembled in the vicinity of Belgrade at the latter end of July. Two other bodies were destined to co-operate with the main army, one in Bosnia, under prince Hilburghausen, and the other in Wallachia, under marshal Wallis, but the whole force did not exceed 70,000 men ; and the greater part of these were raw troops in a state of sickness, misery, and dejection, as the veterans had mostly fallen a sacrifice to unhealthy quarters and bad provisions, more fatal than the sword of the enemy. With this small and inefficient force, Seckendorf had to encounter a much more numerous and formidable army than he had reason to expect. It abounded with veterans inured to service in the Persian wars, and had been brought into a state of discipline and subordination by the celebrated renegado count Bonneval, who principally directed the operations of the campaign. *

In consequence of various obstacles, the campaign was

* To remedy the weakness of the infantry, and to strike terror into the Turks, who dread the effects of artillery, general Schmettau proposed to provide each battalion with two field-pieces ; but this judicious advice was arrogantly rejected, on the absurd principle that the infidels would be beaten, as hitherto, without artillery.

not opened till the latter end of June, when Seckendorf prepared to march, and invest Widdin.   In the midst of his preparations he was thunderstruck with an order from the emperor, delivered by the duke of Loraine himself, commanding him to quit the banks of the Danube, and to march against Nissa.   This injudicious change frustrated the whole plan of operations ; the troops, instead of continuing on the banks of the Danube, on which their magazines had been formed, were compelled to march to the distance of fifty leagues from that river, across a morassy and mountainous country, without carriages to convey their provisions, and without the means of supplying their wants in so inhospitable a district.

After a march of twenty-eight days, in an intemperate season, during which numbers perished from fatigue and hunger, the army arrived, in an exhausted and dispirited state, before the walls of Nissa ; but fortunately meeting with no resistance, obtained possession of the place on the 28th of July.   Kevenhuller was instantly despatched with a strong corps to invest Widdin on the south, while marshal Wallis occupied the opposite bank of the Danube ; but Seckendorf himself remained in the neighbourhood of Nissa, waiting for orders from Vienna ; sending different detachments to reduce the petty fortresses, and seize the passes of the surrounding mountains.

During this period the disunion among the generals, and the discontents of the army, rose to the highest pitch ; Seckendorf being of a rough, overbearing, and parsimonious temper, was illcalculated to conciliate his army, and baffle the cabals to which he was exposed as a Protestant and a stranger.   He also placed his principal confidence in two generals, who were both foreigners, the prince of Saxe Hilburghausen, and general Schmettau.   The prince was a brave, but young and inexperienced officer, who aspired to become another Eugene.   From his talents and agreeable manners, he was in high favour with the emperor, had conciliated the good will of Bartenstein, and had exerted his influence with both in favour of Seckendorf. Although he had recently abjured the Protestant religion, yet his former tenets, his youth, and the favour of the commander-in-chief, rendered him an object of jealousy to the other officers ; and count Esterhasy, bannat of Croatia,

would neither act under him nor with him, and refused
to render him the smallest assistance. General Schmettau
was distinguished for his steadiness and kill in the department of the artillery; yet, being a foreigner and a
Protestant, he was likewise involved in the odium which
was excited against the commander-in-chief.

From the unpopularity of this triumvirate, an opposition
was formed, which was headed by Philippi and Kevenhuller, the two next in command, and supported by the
duke of Loraine, who, though only a volunteer, interfered
in all military operations. The irksome situation of the
commander-in-chief was aggravated by the clamours of the
troops, who, being shut up in an unwholesome situation,
and deprived of their customary supplies, attributed their
misery to his incapacity and avarice, and accused him of
carrying on an infamous commerce, by monopolising the
provisions of the country.

While Seckendorf was thus perplexed with the cabals
of his officers and the clamours of his army, unable to
pursue his success for want of provisions, and waiting for
specific orders from Vienna, the prince of Hilburghausen
was compelled to raise the siege of Banjaluka, and was driven
back towards the Save. The emperor, therefore, alarmed
for his hereditary countries, ordered Seckendorf to suspend
his operations against Widdin, and march through Servia,
to effect a junction with prince Hilburghausen at Zwornick
on the confines of Bosnia. In pursuance of these orders
Seckendorf wholly relinquished his plan for the campaign,
and after despatching a strong reinforcement to Kevenhuller, with an army reduced to 20,000 men, directed his
march through the heart of Servia. He made himself
master of Uzitza, after a short though vigorous siege; but
on approaching Zwornick, was prevented by the inundation
of the Drina from besieging the place. Being thus frustrated in his attempts to penetrate into Bosnia, he retreated
rapidly towards the Save, and, on the 16th of October,
encamped at Szabatch, on the southern bank of that river.

During these operations marshal Wallis had advanced to
Wadovil, on the bank of the Danube, opposite Widdin, to
prevent the Turks from throwing succours into the town on
that side. Kevenhuller, at the same time, directed his
march along the Timoc, and passed the defiles without opposition. But his progress was considerably delayed by

want of provisions and other obstacles ; and, when he drew near Widdin, he found the town in a better state of defence, and occupied by a more considerable force than he expected. He therefore remained inactive on the banks of the Timoc, till the retreat of Seckendorf compelled him to abandon his views on Widdin, and direct his efforts to cover Transylvania ; as the Turks, who had hitherto appeared only in detachments, had assembled a considerable force in the neighbourhood of Widdin. After a severe action near the conflux of the Timoc and Danube, Kevenhuller, though harassed by the Turks, made good his retreat towards Orsova ; his troops effected the passage of the Danube near Cladova ; and, being joined by the corps of marshal Wallis, retired to take up their winter quarters in the bannat of Temeswar.

Thus terminated this unfortunate campaign on the side of the imperialists; while the efforts of the Russians, though more successful, were insufficient to balance the discomfiture of their allies. The campaign was principally distinguished by the capture of Otchakof, which was purchased with the loss of 11,000 regulars and 5000 Cossacs. The change of the plan of operations prevented Munich from advancing on the Danube ; the campaign was closed in the beginning of September without any material advantage, and the Turks were left, unmolested, to continue their successful operations in Servia and Wallachia.

The failure of the plan being wholly attributed to marshal Seckendorf, he received orders of recall on the 14th of October, at Szabatch, and the command of the army was given to general Philippi. After having rejected the advice of several of his friends to seek his safety by flight, Seckendorf pursued his journey to the capital, and was selected as a victim to quiet the clamours of the people, and to gratify the vengeance of his numerous enemies. Among the most powerful of these were the Jesuits, who had publicly arraigned his appointment, and in their sermons declared that a heretic general, at the head of a Catholic army, would draw down the indignation of heaven, and avert the benediction of Providence from the imperial arms. Repeated complaints were likewise transmitted from the army, and he was stigmatised with incapacity, negligence, and treachery. In consequence of these

clamours and prejudices, he was arrested on his arrival at
Vienna, confined to his house under a guard of fourteen
men, and articles of impeachment exhibited against him.
Those persons in whom he had principally confided were
involved in his disgrace, particularly generals Schmettau
and Diemar; and Doxat, the commandant of Nissa, was
beheaded for surrendering that town to the Turks, though
unprovided with proper means of defence.

The articles exhibited against Seckendorf formed a series
of malicious imputations, in which every part of his conduct was arraigned; and even the scarcity of provisions, the
deficiency of the troops, the changes in the plan of the
campaign, and the consequences of contradictory orders,
were imputed to him. But he defended himself with great
spirit and ability, and refuted the principal charges, though,
from delicacy to the emperor, he was not permitted to
reveal the secret orders which he had received, in his own
justification. Although the emperor was favourably inclined towards Seckendorf, yet the clamours of the people,
the exhortations of the Jesuits, and the cabals of his
enemies, prevented his release. In consequence of a tumult
which took place in the ensuing summer, on a gleam of
success to the imperial arms, the populace threatened his
life, and he was transferred to the castle of Glatz, and
lingered in confinement during the reign of Charles VI.

On reviewing the incidents of this unfortunate campaign, little blame seems to attach to Seckendorf; but the
discomfiture of the imperialists was owing to the deficiency
and unprovided state of the army, to divisions among the
generals, and, above all, to the contradictory orders which
emanated from the council of war and the private cabinet
of the emperor.

Charles, from his natural presumption, entertained a
high opinion of his own abilities, and imagined that his
campaigns in Spain, and his desultory conversations with
prince Eugene, had qualified him to direct the operations
of the field. He was flattered in this opinion by Bartenstein and Webber; and he even consulted one of his inferior
servants, who had been formerly a common halberdier and
door-keeper. With these agents the emperor digested
military plans, which were issued by Webber as resolutions
of the council of war. Hence arose those endless orders

and counter-orders, which perplexed the commander-in-chief, and contributed, more than any other cause, to the disgrace of the imperial arms.*

Chap. XCIII. — 1738.

In consequence of the clamours against Seckendorf and the Protestant generals, and the popular outcry, as if the assistance of heaven had been averted by the employment of heretics, not only the favourites of the emperor, but even the empress was accused of concurring in a design to render the court of Vienna dependent on the Protestant powers of Europe. Bartenstein diverted the storm from himself by sacrificing Seckendorf, whose appointment he had promoted, and by advising his son-in-law Knore, a favourite servant of the empress, who was implicated in this accusation, to abjure his religion. The emperor yielded to the general clamour, and endeavoured to pacify the people, by changing his former plan, entering into Catholic alliances and appointing Catholic generals.

He accordingly nominated the duke of Loraine general-issimo of the forces, and under him marshal Konigsegg ; but with that narrow jealousy which characterised all the pro-

---

* " The most secret orders," observes Mr. Robinson, " for military dispositions, had for some years past been issued out of the imperial cabinet through the hands of Bartenstein, Webber, and, as is said, of one Carl Dier, formerly a common halberdier and door-keeper, and now a kind of private purse-keeper to the emperor. And even what could not, for form's sake, escape passing through the channel of the president, used, after having been intimated verbally by him to Webber, to be executed and despatched by the latter, without ever bringing the minutes to the former ; the custom being for the referendary to write at the bottom of every dispatch ' Commission,' or ' Instruction, *par ordre du president et du vice-president*,' instead of their signing actually, either of them, their names. Count Konigsegg, who, though president at war, could not hinder, or was indolent enough not to oppose in that quality these underhand practices, would, however, as minister of the conference, be often blaming most of the measures so taken, in a manner to exculpate himself of consequences, which has given room to believe that the very command of the army was given him only to ruin him. His friends told him as much when he accepted it."— Mr. Robinson to lord Harrington, Vienna, Dec. 31. N. S. 1738.

ceedings of the imperial cabinet, neither was intrusted with full powers ; the duke was to do nothing without the advice of a majority in a council of war, and, if the voices were equal, he was to incline to the opinion of count Konigsegg.

The character and talents of count Konigsegg were ill calculated to supply the want of experience, steadiness, and military skill in the duke of Loraine. He was a nobleman of the most amiable manners, winning address, and of an excellent capacity, both for the cabinet and the field, but greatly deficient in activity ; and though he affected a stoical indifference, was apt, on the least reverse, to sink into despondency. One of his admirers justly observed, " that he wanted only an additional grain of salt in his composition to be one of the greatest men of his age."

The Turks opened the campaign long before the imperialists. In the beginning of March, the bashaw of Widdin took the field at the head of 20,000 men, and directed his operations to the siege of Orsova, a fortress of great importance, on an island of the Danube. By the surrender of Uzitza the Turks had secured the possession of great part of Servia, and by the capture of Old Orsova were able to approach the southern bank of the Danube, from whence they opened their batteries against the fortress. But finding their efforts ineffectual, a body of 2000 men took Meadia in the bannat of Temeswar, which commanded the passes on the north of the Danube, and thus formed attacks on both banks against Orsova. From the strength and nature of the works, however, and the spirit of the garrison, the besiegers made little progress, and the place continued to hold out, though the imperialists did not commence hostilities before the middle of June.

The plan of the campaign was formed by the emperor and his junto, and as they attributed the ill success of the preceding year to the dispersion of the forces, the army was ordered to act in one body, and the generals were forbidden to undertake any separate operation. The principal objects were, to relieve Orsova and besiege Widdin, and sanguine hopes were entertained that the son-in-law of the emperor, and so distinguished a general as count Konigsegg at the head of an army, said to be more efficient than any hitherto sent against the Turks, would drive the infidels from the provinces on the Danube.

The first incidents of the campaign seemed to give a foundation to these hopes ; the two bodies of the army which were assembled at Temeswar, under count Neuperg, and at Belgrade under marshal Wallis, united at Lagus, and being there headed by the duke of Loraine, directed their march towards Meadia. They easily passed the defiles of Slatina and Terrasowa, and on the 3rd of July encamped between Donaschy and Cornia. The following morning the imperialists were attacked with great fury by the Turks, who, having seized a height which commanded the left wing, penetrated almost to the centre of the camp, and even to the tent of the duke. They were, however, repulsed, and being seized with a panic, not only abandoned their camp at Meadia, but even relinquished their attacks against Orsova, and recrossed the Danube.

This gleam of success was hailed at Vienna as the harbinger of certain victory ; the duke of Loraine was extolled as another Eugene* ; the populace, irritated by the recollection of former defeats, tumultuously rose, and threatened the life of Seckendorf; while the Catholic priests triumphantly announced that the favour of heaven had returned to the imperial arms, which were no longer directed by a heretic commander.

This transient advantage, however, was soon overbalanced ; the imperial troops, after recovering Meadia, had scarcely reached the neighbourhood of Orsova, before they were surprised by the grand vizier, and driven back with as much rapidity as they had advanced. While passing the defile of Meadia they were attacked by a considerable body of Turks ; but the enemy being repulsed by the bravery and skill of prince Charles of Loraine, with the loss of 3000 men, the imperial army secured their retreat, and reached Lagus on the 24th of July. The grand vizier resumed the siege of Orsova, into which Konigsegg had thrown some reinforcements and provisions, and the

---

* " The important and singular success of our great duke," writes Mr. Robinson to lord Harrington, July 16. 1738, " gives a high opinion of him in the minds of the people ; and a letter dated from the field of battle, says, ' his royal highness, perceiving that the enemy had pierced the line, exposed himself greatly, and gave his orders with a coolness and wisdom which would have done honour to an old soldier.' "

misfortunes of the imperial army were aggravated by sickness, and even by the plague, which spread through the
whole bannat of Temeswar, and threatened farther ravages.

In this moment of distress the duke returned to Vienna,
either from chagrin or ill health, and the supreme command
of the army devolved on marshal Konigsegg. He continued the retreat, passed the Danube at Viplanka on the
18th of August, and hearing of the capture of Orsova,
which had surrendered to the grand vizier, retired within
the lines at Belgrade. This precipitate retreat disheartened the troops; a general panic pervaded the army; and
even the distant appearance of a Turk spread dismay
through the ranks. Equal consternation prevailed at
Vienna, and the duke of Loraine, having recovered from
his illness, was sent to Belgrade to treat with the grand
vizier, who had made overtures for peace. He reached
that place on the 11th of September; but as the Turks
pursued their advantage, took Semendria and Viplanka,
and seized the heights which commanded the lines, the imperial infantry retired within the walls of Belgrade, the
cavalry passed the Save, and the duke himself proceeded as
far as Essec, at which place he received orders of recall
from the court of Vienna, alarmed for his personal safety.

The troops, confined within the lines and walls of Belgrade, were swept away by a pestilential distemper. These
accumulated disasters being principally imputed to count
Konigsegg, he was recalled in disgrace, and Kevenhuller
appointed to the command, with the hopes of retrieving the
misfortunes of the campaign. The Turks having retired
from the heights round Belgrade, the new general put his
army in motion on the northern side of the Danube, but
could only drive the enemy from Viplanka, and on the 8th
of November retired into winter quarters.

On their side the Russians made no effectual progress.
General Lacy stormed Perekop, overran the Crimea, and
defeated a corps of 20,000 Tartars; but being unable to
take Caffa, was compelled by the approach of winter to retire into the Ukraine. Munich passed the Dnieper and
the Bog, and defeated the enemy in three encounters; but
being stopped by an army of 60,000 Turks, strongly intrenched on the banks of the Dniester, and disappointed in
all his attempts to besiege Bender, he also marched back to
the Ukraine.

The disastrous events of this campaign excited no less intrigue and clamour at Vienna, than the misfortunes of the preceding year.   Count Konigsegg was deprived of his command, removed from the presidency of the council of war, and appointed grand master to the empress.   The duke of Loraine was involved in his disgrace ; he had irritated the emperor by intercepting an order for the recall of Konigsegg on his first return to Vienna, by the spirit with which he had defended his conduct, and by imputing the disasters of the campaign to the weakness of the army, and to the want of carriages and the necessary implements of war.   He had irretrievably offended Bartenstein by his continual reproaches on the cession of Loraine, and being a foreigner, was exposed to the ill-will and jealousy of the nobles, and to the prejudices of the people.   His most trifling defects were exaggerated into vices ; he was charged with sacrificing the duties of his station to hunting and trifling diversions, and accused of returning to Vienna to avoid the dangers of the field.   In consequence of this unpopularity, and the displeasure of the emperor, he was sent, with his consort, into a kind of exile, under the pretence of taking possession of his new dominions in Tuscany.   During his absence the discontents of the people arose to the most alarming height, and reports were publicly circulated that the emperor would give his second daughter to the elector of Bavaria, and change the order of succession in his favour.

At this period there was not a single minister whose weight was equal to the very shadow of prince Eugene, except, perhaps, count Staremberg, and he was suspected of being inclined to the elector of Bavaria, because his estates were contiguous to the Bavarian dominions.   The precipitate measures, adopted by the emperor without the communication of his principal counsellors, and the unpopularity of his subordinate agents, rendered him equally odious to the nobility and the people.   Even the supple and submissive count Sinzendorf, though no friend to count Konigsegg, complained of the manner and circumstances of his disgrace, and observed, that in so important a transaction the emperor ought to have consulted his principal ministers.

In the midst of the general dissatisfaction, and the contest between the Loraine and Bavarian interests, the emperor was violently agitated, and in the agony of his mind he exclaimed, " Is the fortune of my empire departed with Eugene !" The retreat to Belgrade haunted him day and night ; and he manifested his discontent to every officer who had returned from the army, by his execrations of "that unfortunate, that fatal retreat !" He was deeply affected with the absence of his eldest daughter ; he dreaded lest, in case of his own sudden death, her return from Tuscany might be prevented by the elector of Bavaria, and that France might be enabled to realise her favourite scheme of breaking the indivisiblity of his succession.

Chap. XCIV.—1739.

With a view to remedy the negligence and inactivity of the last campaign, the emperor gave the command of the army to marshal Wallis, whom he considered as a general of more spirit and decision than those whom he had formerly employed. Wallis had conciliated the good-will of the emperor by his invectives against the pusillanimity and want of enterprise, which had marked the former campaign ; by the boldness of his remonstrances to the duke of Loraine, and by his contumelious expressions against count Konigsegg, no less than by the proofs he had displayed of his military skill and enterprise. But the choice of Wallis was ill-calculated to retrieve the desperate state of the Austrian affairs. Though vigilant and exact, even to minuteness, in maintaining discipline, he was of a morose, jealous and overbearing temper, equally presumptuous and desponding, and is well designated by the royal historian as " a man hating all, and detested by all."*

The main army having assembled in the neighbourhood of Peterwaradin in May, 1739, marshal Wallis assumed the command ; but found the magazines extremely deficient, and the troops, from the losses of the former campaigns, reduced to about 30,000 effective men, even when joined by the Bavarians and other auxiliaries. A corps of 10,000 men was also formed at Temeswar, under count

* Œuvres Posthumes du Roi de Prusse, tom. i. p. 35.

Neuperg, who was second in command, with a view to co-operate with the main army on the north of the Danube. It was proposed to commence hostilities by the siege of Orsova; and Wallis received positive orders from the emperor to engage the enemy with his whole force on the first opportunity.

On the 11th of June the army encamped near Semlin, and being joined by the auxiliaries, and the flotilla of the Danube being ready to act, they crossed the Save on the 27th, notwithstanding a violent inundation, and encamped at Mirowa, near the lines of Belgrade. On the 20th of July they reached Vinza, a small village on the bank of the Danube, and were informed that part of the Turkish army was arrived at Crotzka. With a view to surprise this body, and to prevent the Turks from obstructing his attempts on Orsova, Wallis put his whole army in motion ; and, at the close of the evening, marched along the high road towards Crotzka. He himself accompanied the advanced guard which consisted of two regiments of hussars, one regiment of cuirassiers, and another of dragoons, and eighteen companies of grenadiers; the main body followed under prince Hilburghausen, and count Neuperg was to cross the Danube, and be ready to co-operate in case of necessity.

On approaching Crotzka the road gently ascends to a defile half a league in length, bounded by steep and woody acclivities ; and beyond, scarcely broad enough to admit more than a single carriage, leads to a height planted with vines, where the ground becomes more open. From hence it descends to Crotzka, between two hills, and across a deep torrent which falls into the Danube. At the break of day, the cavalry of the vanguard had scarcely reached the ' end of the defile before they were attacked by the Turkish infantry, who were posted in the vineyards and wood. The hussars immediately took to flight ; but Wallis putting himself at the head of the cuirassiers, hastened through the narrow road, formed them on the open ground, and bravely withstood the attacks of the enemy, till the other regiment had cleared the defile, and the grenadiers had driven the Turks from the vineyards.

Meanwhile the grand vizier, who with his whole force had marched from Semendria, and occupied the heights above Crotzka, during the night, crossed the rivulet, and took post on the two hills between the defile and that village. The regiment of Savoy, struck with a panic at the appearance of such a numerous host, fled back into the defile; and being followed by a party of Turks, threw the cavalry of the main body, which had nearly reached the place of action, into disorder. Notwithstanding this confusion, the troops continued to advance; the prince of Hilburghausen formed the first battalions, which had cleared the defile, into a square, and charged the enemy; the left wing, passing along a narrow path, extended itself on the heights towards the Danube, and the cavalry was posted on the right, where the ground was favourable for action. In this position the imperial troops withstood the repeated assaults of the Turks, who attacked them with incredible fury, and with far superior numbers, from five in the morning till after sunset, when Wallis ordered a retreat, under cover of the approaching darkness. Had the Turks pursued their advantage, the imperial army might have been cut off, particularly as Wallis, from a spirit of jealousy, would not admit count Neuperg to take any part in the action, or to send more than two regiments, which, however, checked the enemy at the entrance of the defile. In this desperate conflict both parties sustained considerable loss; and, on the side of the imperialists, four generals were killed, five wounded, and four hundred officers with seven thousand men fell on the field of battle.

In this action the Turks seem to have displayed new skill in the art of war; instead of tumultuary and unconnected attacks, they fought in the greatest order, and in regular bodies, and, when broken, rallied with speed and alacrity. During the engagement the imperial flotilla, under admiral Pallavicini, had fallen down the Danube, and co-operated with the army; but, on the retreat of the troops, was compelled to warp up the stream, under the fire of the Turkish batteries, and arrived at Belgrade on the 24th in a dilapidated condition.

The imperial army regained their camp at Vinza; where they took so strong a position, and placed their artillery with such skill, that they repulsed, on the ensuing day, a considerable body of Turks headed by the grand vizier. Wallis, however, concentrated all his force, and, with a despondency equal to his former presumption, retreated in

silence during the night, and occupied the lines of Belgrade.   On the following day he was alarmed by the appearance of the Turkish irregulars, and, deeming himself
unequal to the defence of this strong position, recrossed the
Danube during the night.   The Turks instantly opened
their batteries against Belgrade; the soldiers exclaiming, "Let us take advantage of the panic and blindness
with which God has inflicted the infidels for violating the
peace of Passarovitz;" the grand vizier was impelled, by
the ardour of his troops, to commence the siege in form,
and on the 29th of July, summoned the garrison to surrender.   But the infatuation of marshal Wallis seems to
have increased in proportion to the valour and promptitude
of the enemy.   Although he repulsed a considerable body
of Turks which had assembled at Panczewa, he did not continue in the vicinity of Belgrade, to harass the besieging
army, or succour the garrison, but exhausted his troops by
useless and circuitous marches, repassed the Danube, and
stationed his army at Salankemen, on the frontiers of Hungary.   The Turks availed themselves of his retreat, occupied the northern bank of the Danube, and carried on their
approaches against the redoubt of Borzia, which commanded the fortress on that side.

The irresolution of Wallis, being aggravated by the
effects of an ague, he remained in total inaction; and made
no attempt to prevent the operations of the enemy on the
Save, who prepared to cross the river, that they might
attack Belgrade on the third side.   In this situation of
affairs, he sent repeated accounts to Vienna, that the army
was daily diminishing by desertion and sickness, that the
southern provinces were ravaged by the plague, that the
force of the enemy was rapidly increasing, and that his
own troops were discouraged, and could no longer be depended on.   In the midst of this despondency, he was still
farther alarmed by a report from general Suckof, commandant of Belgrade, that a breach was made in one of
the bastions, and an assault hourly expected, which the
garrison, diminished and enervated by sickness, would be
unable to resist.   Without waiting for the return of an
officer whom he despatched to examine the state of the
fortifications, Wallis sent colonel Gross to the camp of the
grand vizier to purchase a peace by the cession of Bel-

grade, dismantled, and renewed his representations to the emperor. The danger, he urged, was becoming more and more imminent; Belgrade was untenable, and, should that fortress fall, he could not, with a diminished and dispirited army, withstand a superior force of the enemy, nor prevent them from carrying their excursions even to the capital. At the same time he sent a resolution, subscribed by the other generals, stating the necessity of retreating to Peterwaradin. He also requested that the defence of Belgrade, or at least of Peterwaradin, might be committed to general Schmettau, who had been unemployed since the disgrace of Seckendorf.

The defeat of Crotzka, the flight of the imperial army, and the progress of the Turks spread consternation among the people and at the court of Vienna, which was aggravated by the desponding accounts, transmitted by Wallis, concerning the state of the army and the danger of Belgrade. The general terror was increased by the intrigues of Sweden, whose agents were employed in negotiating an offensive alliance with the Porte, by the tumultuous attempts of the malecontents in Poland to recall Stanislaus, and by the movements of prince Ragotski's partisans in Hungary. In the height of their consternation, the people saw, in their affrighted imaginations, the Turks almost at the gates of Vienna, and looked with anxious expectation to marshal Munich, as Leopold had done to Sobieski, to deliver the house of Austria from impending destruction.

Instead of acting with spirit and unanimity, the ministers gave way to mutual reproaches, and each was more anxious to exculpate himself from the blame of having advised the war, than to provide a remedy for the distress of the moment. Bartenstein, to whose all-powerful influence the origin and direction of the war were imputed, and who had recommended and removed generals at his pleasure, shrunk from responsibility, declared that he had even given a written opinion against the war; and endeavoured to procure, from the elector of Mentz, the reversion of the post of referendary to the empire, as a security against the resentment of the successor to the Austrian dominions.

Many of the nobles were disaffected to the house of Loraine, and turned to the elector of Bavaria, a native

of Germany, connected by blood with the house of
Austria, whose principles and manners were more congenial
to their own. The people, loaded with taxes, and dissatisfied
with the ill-success of the war, deprecated the continuance
of hostilities, and an universal clamour was raised for a
speedy peace.

In the midst of the general consternation, the emperor alone seemed to maintain any degree of firmness.
He had been induced by the representations of Wallis, and
the urgent remonstrances of his court, to intrust him with
full powers to offer the cession of Belgrade in case of
extreme necessity. But, convinced that the despondency
of the general had aggravated the distress of his affairs,
and irritated at his want of resolution, he transferred the
full powers for concluding peace to count Neuperg, and
ordered Wallis to direct his attention only to military
transactions. At the same time he sent general Schmettau
to inspect the situation of the army, and to prevent the
intended retreat to Peterwaradin, and the cession of Belgrade.

On delivering his last orders, Charles, graciously pressing the general's hand, said, "Use the utmost diligence to
arrive before the retreat of the army, projected by marshal
Wallis ; assume the defence of Belgrade, and save it, if not
too late, from falling into the hands of the enemy."

Schmettau fulfilled the wishes of his sovereign, and
reached the imperial camp at the moment the troops were
preparing to retreat. He undeceived Wallis with regard
to the situation of Belgrade, the fortifications of which were
without a breach, and defended by a garrison of 13,000
effective men ; and by the most urgent remonstrances prevailed on him to advance with the whole army, and employ
his utmost exertions for the relief of the place.

Schmettau then hastened to Belgrade, and in the latter
end of August, being assisted by a detachment, drove the
Turks from the redoubt of Borzia ; by his exertions he
animated the garrison, and soon compelled the besiegers to
abandon above a hundred paces of their works. Encouraged by his example, marshal Wallis resumed his
spirit ; he visited Belgrade, bitterly reproached Suckof for
his falsehood and pusillanimity, prepared to bring his
whole force into the fortress, and hoped to recover the

lustre of the imperial arms by a victory similar to that gained by prince Eugene on the same ground. The whole army were actuated by one spirit, and eager to repair the disgrace of their flight by new exertions, when the news arrived of the signature of the preliminaries between count Neuperg and the grand vizier, which stipulated the cession of Belgrade, and the immediate delivery of one of the gates to the Turks.

Count Neuperg had no sooner received full powers from the emperor than he hastened to fulfil his commission. He went through Belgrade, without even examining the state of the fortifications; left orders that no letters should be forwarded to him, and even desired the Turkish officers to prevent the passage of any courier. He also imprudently ventured into the Turkish camp, without requiring hostages, with the expectation of meeting the marquis de Villeneuve, the French ambassador at the Porte, by whose mediation the terms were to be adjusted.

But he had soon reason to repent his imprudence, for the indignities to which he was exposed were almost unexampled. Villeneuve, either not being arrived, or having purposely concealed himself, Neuperg was instantly arrested, and put under a guard of twenty-four janissaries. When the grand vizier, in company with the bashaws of Romelia and Bosnia, demanded the conditions he was ordered to propose, he exhibited his full powers, and offered the cession of Wallachia, provided Orsova was dismantled. On this proposal the bashaw of Bosnia spit in his face, and exclaimed, " Infidel dog! thou provest thyself a spy, with all thy full powers. Since thou hast brought no letter from the vizier Wallis, and hast concealed his offer to cede Belgrade, thou shalt be sent to Constantinople to receive the punishment thou deservest." After enduring these indignities, Neuperg was closely confined, and was not allowed to hold any communication with colonel Gross, until the 26th of August, when Villeneuve made his appearance, and obtained permission to lodge him in his tent.

Neuperg was reproached by the French ambassador for his precipitancy in entering the camp without obtaining hostages, and was now first informed that Wallis had already offered the cession of Belgrade, without which the grand vizier would not even commence a negotiation for peace. Neuperg, however, persisted in refusing to make this disgraceful cession, until he was overcome by the persuasion of Villeneuve, who affected to be alarmed with apprehensions of a mutiny in the Turkish camp. The troops, he urged, were in the act of rising, and threatened to massacre the grand vizier and the bashaws, for holding a traitorous correspondence with infidels, to deprive the Porte of so important a conquest. The imperial plenipotentiary reluctantly yielded to these representations, and signed the preliminaries on the 1st of September, under the mediation and guaranty of France.

The principal conditions were, the restoration of Belgrade and Szabatch, after the demolition of the new fortifications, with the cession of Servia, and all the districts yielded by the Turks at the peace of Passarovitz. The Porte was also to retain the fortress of Orsova, which had been erected by the imperialists, and the emperor agreed to demolish the fortifications of Meadia. As a security for the execution of these preliminaries, one of the gates of Belgrade was to be immediately delivered to a corps of janissaries.

Neuperg instantly despatched colonel Gross, and announced the signature of the preliminaries by a laconic note, addressed to the commandant of Belgrade. " Peace was signed this morning between the emperor our master and the Porte ; let hostilities cease, therefore, on the receipt of this. In half an hour I shall follow, and announce the particulars myself." On his arrival, however, Gross only expressed his surprise and indignation to general Schmettau that hostilities had not ceased ; and, as if ashamed of the conditions which he had subscribed, did not make them public until the following morning. General Schmettau acted with becoming spirit ; he urged Neuperg to suspend the cession of Belgrade, under pretence that he had exceeded his full powers ; and used all his influence with Wallis not to deliver the gate to the Turks, until the preliminaries had been ratified by the emperor. Wallis, however, could not venture to evade his positive orders to obey the plenipotentiary in what regarded the conclusion of peace ; and, when he suggested to the count the proposal of Schmettau, Neuperg indignantly replied, " If you choose rather to yield to the advice of the general than to obey the orders of the emperor, and retard only twenty-four hours the execution of the article relative to Belgrade, I will instantly despatch a courier to Vienna, and charge you with all the misfortunes which may result; I had great difficulty in diverting the grand vizier from the demand of Sirmia, Sclavonia, and the bannat of Temeswar; and when I have expedited a courier, I will return into the Turkish camp, and protest against the inexecution of the treaty."

The gate was accordingly delivered on the 4th of September to the bashaw of Romelia, at the head of 800 janissaries; and the imperialists had the mortification to see the Turkish officers ride into the town with the standards taken at the battle of Crotzka. All the arrangements being made for the demolition of the new fortifications, the main body of the imperial army retired towards Peterwaradin, and the Turks towards Nissa.

Count Neuperg had now the mortification to find that the Turks had been more anxious to conclude the peace than the emperor; and that nothing but the precipitate retreat and panic of the imperialists had encouraged the grand vizier to prosecute hostilities without tendering offers of accommodation, which he had been enjoined to do by the Porte. His chagrin was increased by the reception of two letters from the emperor, dated the 21st and 22nd of August, which arrived at Belgrade on the 27th, and were not forwarded by marshal Wallis, who literally obeyed the orders, that no messenger should be suffered to pass to the Turkish army. These letters stated that the emperor had only yielded to the surrender of Belgrade on the supposition that the fortress was in imminent danger; but learning the falsity of the report, he had no doubt that his troops would still be able to drive the enemy from their conquests, as they would be seconded by the Russians, who had already defeated the Turks in several encounters, and had advanced into Moldavia. He therefore enjoined Neuperg to declare that Wallis had exceeded his powers, in offering the cession of Belgrade, to represent to Villeneuve the real state of the fortress, and entreat him not to disclose the offers with which he had been intrusted.

The account of this dishonourable peace was received

by all ranks with grief and indignation; a general murmur arose among the troops, who exclaimed, "Belgrade must not be yielded; we are ready to sacrifice our lives, if the generals will lead us against the enemy." The populace of Vienna rose tumultuously; assaulted the houses of several officers, and would have demolished those of Bartenstein and Webber, had they not been prevented by the military. The Jesuits were enraged by the loss of their estates in the ceded provinces, and the dissolution of their splendid establishments in the town of Belgrade; and by their clamours and exhortations increased the agitation of the public mind.

But no one was more affected with the conclusion of the peace than the emperor himself, and he appeared under more agitation of mind than he had ever displayed in the midst of his greatest disasters. His chief embarrassment consisted in the difficulty of extenuating his conduct to the czarina. In an audience which he gave to her ambassador, he appeared under the pressure of the deepest affliction, and in a letter to the czarina seems to have wanted words to express the agony of his mind.

"While I am writing this letter to your imperial majesty," he observed, "my heart is filled with the most excessive grief; I was much less touched with the advantages gained by the enemy, and the news of the siege of Belgrade, than with the advice I have received concerning the shameful preliminary articles concluded by count Neuperg."

After reprobating the conduct of marshal Wallis and count Neuperg, he adds, "The history of past ages exhibits no vestiges of such an event. I was on the point of preventing the fatal and too hasty execution of these preliminaries, when I heard that they were already partly executed, even before the design had been communicated to me; thus I see my hands tied by those who ought to glory in obeying me. All who have approached me since that fatal day, are so many witnesses of the excess of my grief; and, although I have many times experienced adversity, yet I never was so much afflicted with any thing as with this event. Your majesty has a right to complain of some people who ought to have obeyed my orders; but I had no part in what they have done. Though all the

forces of the Ottoman empire were turned against me, I
was not disheartened; but still did all that lay in my power
for the good of the common cause. I shall not, however,
fail to perform in due time what avenging justice requires.
In this dismal series of misfortunes I have still one comfort left, which is, that the fault cannot be thrown upon
me. It lies entirely on such of my officers as ratified the
disgraceful preliminaries, without my knowledge, against
my consent, and even contrary to my express orders. But,
nevertheless, I ought to conform to what has once been
ratified, though unjustly; we must keep faith inviolably
even with infidels, while they observe it on their part.
However, the happy success of your majesty's arms before
Chotzim ought to procure you more advantageous conditions than you could have obtained before; and I do
not doubt but the peace between your majesty and the
sublime Porte will be concluded at the same time with
mine. It is what I have most at heart at present, as also
to perpetuate the ties which so fortunately attach me to
your majesty, notwithstanding all the machinations of
those who wish to see them dissolved. I am the first to
own that Wallis and Neuperg are highly guilty; but your
majesty will discover more and more the sincerity of my
sentiments for you, in which I have not failed, nor ever
will fail in the least."

This letter was soon followed by a circular rescript, addressed to the imperial ambassadors in the different courts
of Europe, which was drawn up by Bartenstein, and filled
with acrimonious reproaches against the conduct of marshal
Wallis and count Neuperg. It bitterly and indiscrimi-
nately censured all the operations of Wallis, particularly
dwelt on his false statements concerning the situation of
Belgrade, and condemned him for the precipitate execution
of the article relating to the delivery of the gate. The
censures against Neuperg were solely confined to his conduct in regard to the peace, and consisted of vague accusations on the progress of the negotiations, and the conclusion of the preliminaries. It exculpated the emperor
from any part in the transaction, and not only charged
count Neuperg with exceeding his powers, but accused
him of acting in direct contradiction to the most positive

instructions, and particularly of not including Russia in the treaty.

This rescript drew from marshal Wallis and count Neuperg a justification of their conduct. After attempting to vindicate his military operations, Wallis declared that he had strictly conformed to his instructions, and that his ill success in negotiating a peace was derived from the want of instructions, which he had in vain demanded. In regard to the conclusion and premature execution of the preliminaries, he threw the whole responsibility on count Neuperg, to whom he had transferred his full powers by order of the emperor. Neuperg, on his part, justified the concessions he had made on the plea of urgent necessity; and asserted that no other measures could have prevented the immediate invasion of Hungary, and the total loss of the imperial army.

The imperial rescript contained such a jumble of jarring facts, and such an apparent confusion in the dates, that even the populace discovered its fallacy, and exclaimed that it could impose on none but children. It was deemed impossible that any negotiator, in so jealous and severe a court as that of Vienna, would venture to exceed his full powers, still less to act in direct contradiction to positive instructions; hence suspicions were even formed that the emperor, or his ministers, had given orders which they now denied, and sacrificed the negotiator to exculpate themselves from the disgrace of submitting to such dishonourable terms.

If any thing could aggravate the folly and inconsistency of the imperial court, it was their conduct at the conclusion of this unfortunate negotiation. While they were thus criminating their plenipotentiary in the eyes of all Europe, and even while Bartenstein was publicly declaring that the man who exceeded his powers ought to be hanged, but that he who acted contrary to them ought to be impaled, Neuperg was sent back to the Turkish camp to settle the definitive peace, and to supply his omission in not including Russia in the treaty.

In terminating the negotiation, Neuperg proved that he had before acted from imperious necessity, and that he did not deserve the aspersions cast on his character; for he refused with great dignity and firmness to sign any treaty between the emperor and the Porte, unless an accommodation was at the same time concluded with Russia. This spirit baffled the intrigues of Villeneuve, and overcame the obstinacy of the Turks, who began to be alarmed at the victory of Chotzim, gained by marshal Munich, and the rapid progress of the Russian arms. The two treaties were accordingly signed on the 18th of September, before the departure of the grand vizier, and the stipulations for Russia were referred to the future approbation of the court of St. Petersburg. The honour of the emperor was also in some measure retrieved, by a declaration annexed to the treaty, stating, that he did not derogate from the alliance with Russia ; and reserved to himself the right of assisting Russia with 30,000 troops, should the war be continued between her and the Porte.

The articles of the peace at Belgrade were nearly similar to the tenor of the preliminaries. The emperor ceded Servia, with the fortresses of Belgrade and Szabatch ; he also yielded Austrian Wallachia, with the fortress of New Orsova, with a small district on the north bank of the Danube, and retained the bannat of Temeswar, on condition of demolishing the fortifications of Meadia.

By the stipulations arranged for Russia, Azof was to be demolished, and its territory to remain a desert, and to serve as a barrier between the two empires ; the city of Taganroc was not to be re-established, and the czarina was to relinquish her pretensions to the navigation of the Black Sea, and restore her recent acquisitions to the Porte. Anne, however, disapproved these conditions, and thought that the success of her arms entitled her to more advantageous terms ; but as she was left without an ally, as the Swedes were making preparations to co-operate with the Porte, as insurrections were brooding in Poland, and as she was alarmed with a dangerous conspiracy among her own nobles, she prudently ratified the treaty with some modifications, which increased the limits of her empire on the side of the Ukraine.

The peace of Belgrade was scarcely signed before Wallis was arrested and confined at Zigieth, and Neuperg sent to the castle of Halitz, where they remained during the life of Charles VI.

It is difficult at this distance of time to develop the

whole mystery of this extraordinary transaction ; but sufficient evidence is not wanting to trace the principal causes
which occasioned the conclusion of this precipitate peace.
At the close of 1736, attempts were made to negotiate an
accommodation between Russia and the Porte, under the
mediation of the emperor, and a congress was opened at
Memerow in Poland ; but the emperor having taken part
against the Turks, the congress was dissolved, and the
Porte requested the mediation of France, which, after
some difficulties and delays, was also accepted by the allied
powers.   Conferences were accordingly opened at Constantinople, between the Turkish ministers, and Villeneuve
the French ambassador, a man of cultivated talents and
consummate address, versed in all the arts of negotiation,
and well calculated to carry into execution the refined
views of the French cabinet.   He was instructed, while
he acted the ostensible part of an impartial mediator, to
divide the emperor from the czarina, to prevent any dismemberment of the Turkish dominions, and above all to
counteract the aggrandisement of the house of Austria.
Villeneuve secretly encouraged the Turks to reject the
exorbitant demands at first made by the allied powers,
which were no less on the side of the emperor, than the
entire cession of Bosnia, Moldavia, and Wallachia ; and,
on the side of Russia, to retain possession of Azof, Otchakof, and the Kuban, with the free navigation of the Black
Sea.

The negotiations were renewed at the close of each
campaign ; but though the allies lessened their pretensions,
the Turks rose in their demands, in proportion to their
successes ; and Villeneuve being trusted by the emperor,
to the exclusion even of his own ministers, was enabled to
obstruct the negotiation, until he had sown jealousy between the two powers, and effectually fulfilled the views
of France.   His efforts were unfortunately promoted by
the distracted state of the imperial court, and the divisions
between Wallis and Neuperg, who were more anxious to
ruin each other, than to promote the interests of their
master.

After the defeat of Krotzka, and the retreat of the
imperial army, the emperor disclosed to Villeneuve, in
confidence, the disastrous situation of his affairs, and his

readiness to conclude a separate peace, even with the cession of Belgrade, in a state of demolition. The duke of Loraine and Maria Theresa, also alarmed at the declining state of the emperor's health, and dreading lest, on his decease, the house of Bourbon should excite a contest for the Austrian succession, urgently exhorted Neuperg to yield to any terms which might terminate the embarrassments of a Turkish war. These circumstances favoured the efforts of Villeneuve; he availed himself of the confidence of the emperor; and when Neuperg was confined in the Turkish camp, he alarmed his fears, concealed the rapid successes of the Russians, magnified the strength of the Turks, and did not cease his artifices and intrigues until he had extorted the cession of Belgrade. This being the only point in dispute, the other articles were arranged without much difficulty; and Villeneuve boasted that, in making the peace of Belgrade, he had rendered a more effectual service to France than if he had gained a complete victory.

The efforts of this refined negotiator were equally promoted by the secret manœuvres of Bartenstein, who while he affected to admire and animate the spirit of the emperor, exaggerated the bad state of his affairs, and incessantly urged the necessity of an immediate peace. General Suckof, who was intrusted with the command of Belgrade, was his creature, and under his direction; and, though he could not ostensibly oppose the mission of Schmettau, to defend that fortress to the last extremity, yet he endeavoured to prevent his appointment. With this view, notwithstanding the positive orders of the emperor, Schmettau was not furnished with written instructions, but was referred to marshal Wallis, to whom he carried despatches. On arriving at the camp, Schmettau was apprised by Wallis that these despatches contained no instructions; but a private letter from Bartenstein, in which he said, " As his imperial majesty had given a promise, under his own hand, to general Suckof, to promote him to the rank of general of artillery, and the government of Servia, if he preserved Belgrade, the defence of that place could not be intrusted to any other general; and, therefore, the intention of the emperor was, that Schmettau should be employed in the army, or at Peterwaradin, to defend that

fortress should it be besieged." But although Wallis could
not venture to supersede Suckof, yet he found means to
elude the orders of "this scribe," as he called him, "who
abused the name of the emperor to favour his creatures,"
by appointing Schmettau commander-in-chief of Belgrade,
in virtue of his power as governor of the province.   It is
not easy to trace the motives which influenced the conduct
of this upstart favourite; whether to secure the favour of
the successor to the Austrian monarchy, whether from
dislike to the Maritime Powers, who had abandoned his
master in the hour of danger, or, whether from the disastrous state of the emperor's affairs, he dreaded the continuance of so unfortunate and ruinous a contest.

But although the signature and execution of the preliminaries were shamefully precipitated, and a short delay
might even have procured honourable and advantageous
terms, yet a peace at all events was absolutely necessary
for the salvation of the house of Austria.   Nor can it be
deemed a matter of surprise, that even a sovereign of so
proud and unbending a spirit as Charles VI. should ratify
so dishonourable a peace, when his situation is thus described by an eye-witness and competent judge.

" Everything in this court is running into the last confusion and ruin; where there are as visible signs of folly
and madness as ever were inflicted upon a people whom
heaven is determined to destroy, no less by domestic divisions, than by the more public calamities of repeated
defeats, defencelessness, poverty, and plague."

In a word, the deplorable state in which Charles left, on
his death, his army and finances, is the best apology for
the peace of Belgrade.

Chap. XCV.—1739, 1740.

Although the emperor had concluded a definitive peace
with the Porte, yet the vague terms of the treaty gave
rise to new cavils and long discussions concerning the demarcation of the limits, which were artfully protracted by
the intrigues of France, who thus maintained her ascendency over the contracting powers.

France, at this period, had attained an enormous pre-
ponderancy among the powers of Europe, not only from a
dread of her strength and resources, but from the character
and system of the prime minister.

Cardinal Fleury was in the 84th year of his age ; he was
of a circumspect and cautious temper, and possessed the
art of winning mankind by an unaffected air of candour
and simplicity. His great prudence and sagacity enabled
him to distinguish the precise bounds to which he could
push his intrigues, and to conceal his designs under the
semblance of moderation; his progress was, therefore,
more dangerous, as it was silent and unobserved. From
temper and principle he was anxious to maintain his
country in peace; but, as his great aim was to remove
every obstruction to the ascendency of France, he directed
all his efforts to divide, though he avoided provoking, the
other powers of Europe.

In pursuit of his plan, he had imperceptibly brought
the emperor to an entire dependence on France, and had
more reduced the house of Austria by his intrigues, than
his predecessors by the sword. Although France had
guaranteed the Pragmatic Sanction, yet he looked forward
to the prospect of dividing the Austrian dominions between
the two archduchesses, and thus hoped to diminish the
weight of a power which had hitherto been the rival, and
might again become the enemy, of the house of Bourbon.
With this view he filled all the courts of Europe with his
intrigues, and endeavoured to isolate the house of Austria,
by uniting her enemies, and paralysing the efforts of her
friends.

France wholly governed the councils of the Porte ; and,
by means of reciprocal treaties and guaranties, secured a
pretext for interference in the future disputes of the Turks
with the Christian powers.

She had effected an essential change in the administration of Sweden, by removing the ministers who were
favourable to England, and maintained the king in total
subjection, by swaying the parties which agitated that
distracted government. By her influence, also, the Swedes
were induced to arm on the side of Finland, and to make
an offensive alliance with the Porte.

Notwithstanding the subsidiary treaty, which Denmark

had concluded with England, France endeavoured to alienate the court of Copenhagen from the house of Austria; and the fluctuating conduct of the Danish cabinet seemed to favour her views. With their consent, she despatched a squadron into the Baltic, under a frivolous pretence; which, parading through the Sound, intimidated the enemies and encouraged the friends of France.

Russia, alarmed on one side with the preparations of the Swedes, and on the other kept in suspense by the protracted negotiation with the Turks, was inclined to temporise; and, unwilling to provoke the resentment of France, unless a grand combination of the European states could be formed capable of resisting the alarming power of the house of Bourbon.

Although Augustus III. owed his crown to the united efforts of the emperor and Russia, yet, as king of Poland, he was unable to suppress the domestic cabals excited by the intrigues of France, or to turn the united forces of his kingdom in favour of the house of Austria.

Germany was divided in interests, and distracted by parties. France had gained many of the Catholic princes, and in particular the elector of Bavaria, with the hopes of sharing in the Austrian succession. She also artfully availed herself of the resentment entertained by the king of Prussia against the emperor for his prevarication in regard to the succession of Berg and Juliers. By these intrigues she detached Frederic William from the house of Austria; and, by fomenting his prejudices against the house of Hanover, succeeded in weakening and dividing the efforts of the Protestant body.

The king of Sardinia was in entire subjection to the dictates of the French cabinet.

John V. king of Portugal, began to lose that spirit and vigour of intellect which had distinguished the former part of his reign; his faculties were impaired by a stroke of apoplexy, and in his character and conduct he blended the extremes of devotion and licentiousness. Scrupulously adhering to the ceremonies of the church, the bigoted monarch paid as much attention to the arrangement of a procession, and to the election of an abbot, as to the most important concerns of government. Hence the whole power fell into the hands of confessors and friars; immense sums were expended in religious establishments instead of being employed in the maintenance of an army and navy, and Portugal daily declined in power and consideration.

The king of Spain was involved in a war with England, on account of the depredations in America; and, alarmed for the safety of his colonial possessions, importunately required the interference of France, and looked forward for the active assistance which he was openly encouraged to expect.

The United Provinces still exhibited the same weak and divided government; alarmed at the increasing preponderance of France, yet without vigour to resist her encroachments; dreading the interference of England in favour of the prince of Orange, who had espoused the daughter of George II.; and though without any other ally, to whom they could look for support, considering the war with Spain as wholly foreign to their interests. They were irritated against the emperor for the haughty conduct of his ministers, and involved in interminable disputes concerning the commercial regulations of the Barrier Treaty.

England, the only power capable of consolidating a grand combination against France, was engaged in the prosecution of the Spanish war, which had been excited by the clamours of the merchants, and the madness of the people, wild with dreams of conquest and plunder. But the illusion had been dissipated by the ill success of their armaments, and by the hostile preparations of France. The nation was distracted by contending parties; the cabinet divided; and the minister, becoming more and more unpopular, was compelled to pursue a temporising policy, ill adapted to the circumstances of the times. Numerous schemes of alliance and co-operation against France were formed; but they were counteracted by the discordant views of the cabinet, and the inveterate antipathy of George II. to the house of Brandenburgh, whose concurrence was indispensably necessary for the establishment of a permanent confederacy against the house of Bourbon.

In this situation of Europe, the emperor, debilitated by his recent disasters, was bound by France with the most galling fetters. Her numerous partisans were continually representing to him the weakness of his exhausted country, and the danger of provoking the resentment of so for-

midable a power. His court was beset by her spies ; every
motion was watched, and Fleury made urgent complaints
whenever the duke of Loraine, who indignantly bore this
state of dependence, had an interview with the British
minister.   This humiliating subjection chagrined the most
upright and independent ministers of the conference ; and
counts Staremberg and Harrach, in particular, lamented
the influence of France in the counsels of their sovereign.

The emperor himself felt and appreciated his danger;
he regretted the precipitation with which he had concluded
the preliminaries at Vienna with La Beaume, and still
more his acceptance of the mediation and guaranty of
France in the treaty of Belgrade.   He saw that his ministers had been deceived by the artifices of Villeneuve,
and that the peace had been dictated at Paris.   He was
sensible that the French, by their manœuvres with the
Porte, were delaying the execution of the treaty, and was
aware of their schemes for the division or dismemberment
of his succession.   He considered a war between France
and England as inevitable, and foresaw the destruction of
the house of Austria, should England be crushed by the
united efforts of the house of Bourbon.

In this dangerous crisis, overtures were made by England,
who was alarmed at the hostile preparations of the French
by land and sea ; and at the march of their troops towards
the coast of the British channel.   The English ministry
endeavoured to rouse the imperial cabinet, with the prospect of an approaching war on the Continent, which might
be opened by the invasion of Germany, or an attack on
the Netherlands, and requested the emperor to assume a
posture of defence, and provide for the security of the
Barrier Towns.   The emperor, who was not unwilling to
act according to the extent of his power and resources,
and was anxious to consolidate the whole force of the
German empire against the aggressions of France, despatched count Ostein to Hanover to adjust the terms of a
reconciliation with England and Holland ; but the good
effects of this mission were counteracted by the secret
manœuvres of Bartenstein, whose aversion to the Maritime
Powers induced him to throw obstacles in the way of an
accommodation.   At the suggestion of the referendary,
who drew up the instructions, count Ostein was ordered to

inveigh against the former desertion of the Maritime
Powers, and to express the diffidence of the emperor to
enter into new engagements, for the fulfilment of which he
had, from past experience, no sufficient security.   Impracticable proposals, relative to German disputes, were also
introduced, and Bartenstein artfully availed himself of the
former contentions relative to the conditions of the Barrier
Treaty, which were again revived.   To the continuance of
the commercial restrictions imposed by the 26th article, the
imperial cabinet attributed the most fatal consequences,
and Bartenstein drew up a memorial, exhibiting the grievances which the people of the Netherlands suffered from
the state of their trade in Great Britain and Holland.

"The Netherlands," he said, "are at present reduced to
a most deplorable situation ; the commerce to the Indies
interdicted ; debts enormously increased during the course
of a long war; the revenues absorbed by the maintenance
of the military establishment ; the deficiency in the revenue,
already amounting to an enormous sum, is annually increasing ; and the only source to obviate these evils almost
wholly exhausted."   "The manufacturers," he added, "are
daily declining, and, without a speedy remedy, will be
annihilated.   The best workmen emigrate for want of employment, and the richest merchants threaten to quit the
country.   Hence arises an alarming decrease in the duties
on consumption, as well as those of export and import, and
even in the ordinary contributions ; and the balance of
trade having been long unequal, the inference is natural,
that it will be totally overthrown if the same principle is
pursued, of lowering the duties on the side of the Low
Countries, and raising those on the side of England."

Hence the imperial ministers contended, that the Maritime Powers had eluded their engagements contracted by
the Barrier Treaty and the treaty of Vienna, by which the
alteration of the tariff was to be settled before the expiration of a new treaty of commerce within two years, and
they urged the justice and necessity of a reciprocity of
duties.

These statements were combated on the part of England,
by insisting that the duties settled by the tariff being appropriated for the liquidation of the debt incurred for the
conquest of the Low Countries from France, could not be

changed till the debt was discharged ; and that the emperor, having accepted the Netherlands on the terms settled by the Barrier Treaty, had no right to expect an alteration of the system established by that treaty.

These discordant principles became a never-failing source of disagreement, and furnished Bartenstein with endless pretexts to inveigh against the narrow policy of the Maritime Powers.   In consequence of this dissatisfaction on the side of Austria, and the perseverance of the Maritime Powers to retain the privileges to which they were entitled by the treaty of Barrier, no compromise could be made ; and the conferences which had been opened at Antwerp in 1737, for adjusting the new treaty of commerce, produced no effect.

Chap. XCVI. — 1740.

The alarming designs of France, the danger to which the Maritime Powers were exposed, the representations of the duke of Loraine, and the instances of the ministers, at length outweighed the influence of Bartenstein ; and the emperor became more zealous than ever to renew his connection with England, and to unite the German empire against the incroachment of the house of Bourbon.   The obstacles which hitherto prevented the union of the Protestant body, arising from the disputes between the houses of Hanover and Brandenburgh, seemed now to be removed by the death of Frederic William, king of Prussia, in April, 1740 ; and hopes were entertained that his successor would be induced to pursue a different line of conduct.

Charles Frederic, who, under the name of Frederic II., was destined to give a new lustre to the crown of Prussia, and to become the formidable rival of the house of Austria, was son of Frederic William, by Sophia Dorothea, daughter of George I., king of England, and was born at Berlin, on the 24th of January, 1712.   Although Frederic William disliked magnificence, literature, and foreign manners, and was desirous of giving his son an education more calculated for a sergeant than a prince ; yet Berlin abounded with refugees and other natives of France, drawn to the capital by

Frederic I., who emulated the court of Louis XIV. To some of these foreigners, distinguished for elegance of manners and acquaintance with polite literature, the early education of the young prince was entrusted; and from them he imbibed that fondness for the French language and French manners which influenced his future life.

His governor, lieutenant-general count Finkenstein, was a man of high probity and distinguished courage, but stiff in his address, and cold in his manners; and his sub-governor, Kalkstein, was principally distinguished for his rigid economy, and perfect knowledge of military details; qualifications, which, in the opinion of Frederic William, superseded every other accomplishment. As neither of these persons was calculated to gain the confidence of a young prince, endowed with quick intellects, and a lively genius, he conceived an attachment to his preceptor du Han, a French refugee, who had served under Frederic William at the siege of Stralsund. Du Han was of a captious and sarcastic temper, and a free-thinker in matters of religion; but possessed a general knowledge of polite literature, and encouraged his royal pupil in that prepossession for French authors which he had already imbibed, and which was strengthened by the prevailing taste of the times, by the low state of German literature, and by the prohibition of his father, that his son should not be instructed in the learned languages.

Frederic William, who had employed his whole reign in the formation of that great military establishment which afterwards rendered Prussia the arbitress of Germany, was most anxious to give to his son the education of a soldier: at an early age the young prince was appointed chief of a corps of cadets, and daily practised with his pigmy troops, the military evolutions which his father performed with his tall regiment; and he made so considerable a progress in these manœuvres, that in his twelfth year he surprised the king of Great Britain, during a visit to Berlin, by exercising three hundred cadets with a dexterity above his age.

Notwithstanding his progress, the king was dissatisfied with his attachment to music, and to what he called outlandish literature, dismissed his preceptors when he had attained the age of fifteen, and assumed the principal direction of his employment. He made him his companion in most of his journeys, and gave him incessant lectures on finance, agriculture, and military discipline. But, as the young prince did not listen to such dry details with sufficient attention, the king bitterly reproached him with his passion for music and letters, and treated him with excessive rigour. For petty breaches of military order, Frederic William frequently put his son under arrest, and confined him to bread and water; he also threw his music into the fire, and broke his flute. This opposition to his favourite pursuits only increased the inclination of the young prince for the arts and polite literature ; he passed whole nights in reading by stealth, and held concerts in forests and caverns, during his hunting excursions, with musicians privately supplied by his mother.

At length, exasperated by this tyrannical treatment, Frederic formed the design of escaping into England, to seek the protection of his uncle George II. He made this attempt at a village near Frankfort ; but, being discovered, was arrested and confined at Wesel. Interrogated by his father, who demanded his reasons for deserting, he replied, "Because, sire, you have not hitherto treated me as your son, but as your slave." — "You are a cowardly deserter," exclaimed the king, "without courage, and without honour !" — "I have no less courage," answered the prince, "and honour than yourself; and I have only done what you have frequently said you would do, if you were in my place." The king, inflamed with this reproach, drew his sword, but general Mosel holding his arm, and throwing himself between them, exclaimed, "Kill me, sire ; but spare your son !" This seasonable exclamation recalled the king to reason ; and Mosel conveyed the prince into another apartment, and from thence to the prison which was destined for his reception.

Frederic was afterwards transferred to Berlin, and from thence to the palace of Mittelwalde, where he was interrogated by a committee of four persons, presided by general Grumbkow, minister of state. Having presented to the prince the interrogatories and answers of Katt, his favourite page, who was tried for assisting his escape, they questioned him on some points of which the king required information. Frederic replied with firmness, and showed that his spirit was greater than his misfortunes. On being

told that it was the king's pleasure he should be transferred
to Custrin, "Be it so," he said, "I consent; but if I am
to recover my liberty by entreaties, I fear that I shall remain there a considerable time." At Custrin he was confined six months in a cell, without furniture, without a bed,
and without a single attendant; received an allowance of
only sixpence a day, and was deprived of all books, except
a bible and a psalter. He was here repeatedly interrogated;
and as the crime alleged against him was high treason, he
had every reason to expect that his obdurate father would
imitate the example of Peter the Great towards his son,
the unfortunate Alexey. In this state of suspense he one
morning observed the window of his cell enlarging, and a
communication formed with a scaffold, covered with black
cloth, erected in the court of the citadel, on a level with
the cell in which he was confined. Being convinced that
these preparations were making for his own execution, he
prepared for his fate; and was only undeceived when the
commandant of the citadel announced the condemnation of
Katt. Four grenadiers entered the cell, and forcibly conveyed the prince to the window, holding his head towards
the scaffold, on which the unfortunate victim now made his
appearance. The sentence being read, Frederic earnestly
exhorted the executioner to defer the stroke, that he might
write to his father, and obtain the pardon of his friend, by
renouncing his right of succession to the crown. But his
tears, his entreaties, and his cries being ineffectual, he exclaimed in an agony of grief, "Would to God that I were
in your place!"—"Oh! sir," replied the unfortunate victim, "had I a thousand lives I would sacrifice them all for
you." He then knelt down; one of his attendants advancing to cover his face, "It is needless," he said; and lifting
up his eyes to heaven, "My God," he added, "to thy
hands I commit my soul!" Before the executioner could
perform his office, the prince fainted; and when he recovered saw the headless trunk of his affectionate servant,
which was exposed the whole day.

But this victim did not appease the fury of Frederic
William, and he still persisted in the resolution of immo-
lating his son to military justice. He bitterly reproached
the court martial because only one of the twenty-four
judges appointed to try the prince had condemned him to

death. To his ministers, who had the courage to represent that the heir-apparent could not be capitally convicted,
he exclaimed, " I consider my son as a soldier who dis-
obeys orders, or as a deserter who quits his post !" To
the emperor, who wrote to him with his own hand, that he
had no authority to try his son, and still less to put him to
death, because the prince, as a member of the empire,
could only be heard and judged at a full diet, he replied,
" I am a king, and in that capacity will bring my son to
judgment, by sending him into Prussia, where I acknowledge
no power except God alone."

The delays, however, which these remonstrances occasioned gave time to his paternal sentiments to regain their
influence. Great Britain, Sweden, and the States-general
joined their intercession to that of the emperor. The
queen, continually repulsed, never intermitted her solicitations, and at length prevailed. The king relented, and
released his son from prison, after obliging him to take a
solemn oath, not to entertain any resentment against the
ministers ; never to undertake any journey without permission ; to live in fear of God ; to fulfil the duties of his
religion ; and not to marry any princess whom he did not
approve. But though he released the prince from confinement, he would not permit him to return to court. He
compelled him to continue at Custrin, not to wear his uniform, and not to speak French ; he was obliged to attend
the boards of police and finance, to audit the accounts, and
to copy memorials. So minute were these orders, and so
exactly fulfilled, that when the president of the board
transmitted to Frederic William three memorials, two of
which were copied by the prince, and the third only signed,
the king wrote on the margin, " the signature of Fritz is
not sufficient, he ought to have transcribed the whole
himself." *

The king's resentment at length subsided ; he recalled
the prince to court, but did not relax his rigorous treatment, and compelled him to marry Elizabeth Christina,
daughter of the duke of Brunswick. Although Frederic
entertained an invincible aversion to his consort, with whom
he never cohabited, yet this event procured him a separate
establishment, and enabled him to fix his residence at the

* Poelnitz, tom. ii. p. 225-254.

castle of Rheimsberg. He here devoted himself to his favourite studies, and passed his time in convivial intercourse with a chosen society* of men of letters, either natives of France, or devoted to French literature. He was indefatigable in the perusal of works on ancient and modern history, particularly translations of the classics; and blended his literary occupations with concerts and theatrical representations. He also maintained an intercourse with the philosopher Wolff, who had been driven from Halle for his metaphysical tenets, and held constant correspondence with the French literati, particularly Rollin, Henault, Maupertuis, and Voltaire. His active mind was animated by the most ardent love of fame; but being excluded from affairs of state, he endeavoured to distinguish himself in the republic of letters, and composed a commentary on the prince of Machiavel, with a view to refute the political principles of that work. This piece, called the Anti-Machiavel, he submitted to the correction of Voltaire, and was preparing it for the press, when the death of his father opened a new field to his exertions.

On the accession of Frederic II., the dominions of the house of Brandenburgh consisted of provinces detached from each other; and many parts, particularly the Marck of Brandenburgh, so barren and sandy, that Frederic William had been called in derision, "the *arch sablonnier* of the German empire." The whole population did not exceed 2,400,000 souls, and the revenues, though improved by the financial system of Frederic William, amounted to no more than 8,700,000 crowns. The country maintained but little commerce, and was almost without resource, but the late king had left a treasure of 9,000,000 crowns, and an army of 76,000 men, the best disciplined troops in Europe, with artillery, magazines, and all the appointments of war in the highest state of order.

Frederic was now in the twenty-eighth year of his age; and his real character was little appreciated by his contemporaries, and scarcely known even by those who had constant access to his person. He had displayed no predilection for military affairs; had seen no service, ex-

---

* Of this select coterie, the principal were Kaiserlin, a native of Courland, Suhm, Jandum, Bielfield, Maupertuis, Algarotti, and Chasot.

cept part of the inactive campaign of 1737; and the only trait of his intrepidity, which was recollected even by his warmest panegyrists, was, that in reconnoitring the lines of Philipsburgh, he exhibited no concern in the midst of a continual discharge of cannon, the shot of which fractured some branches of trees over his head. His father was so little acquainted with his personal character, as to express apprehension lest the military establishment should be dissolved after his death; and the literary society at Rheimsberg deemed him as volatile and dissipated as themselves. They anticipated a delicious life, passed in indolence and ease, hailed the halcyon days of peace and luxury, and hoped that he would rival his grandfather Frederic I., in the magnificence of his court and the elegance of his refinements.*

But the real character of the new monarch soon developed itself in a petty transaction with the bishop and chapter of Liege, in which he displayed that prompt and decisive spirit of enterprise which afterwards marked his conduct. During an excursion to Strasburgh and Cleves (whither he repaired to have an interview with Voltaire), the inhabitants of Herstal, a small barony in the vicinity of Liege, which descended to the house of Brandenburgh as part of the inheritance of the house of Orange, refused to take the oath of allegiance. Frederic sent a corps of troops against the bishop and chapter of Liege, whom he suspected of instigating the inhabitants, and exacted from them indemnification of 60,000 rix-dollars.

Berlin now became the centre of intrigue and negotia-

---

* The voluptuous retirement of Frederic in the palace of Rheimsberg seemed rather to resemble that of Rinaldo in the palace of Alcina, than the retreat of the future hero. Baron Bielfield thus describes his mode of life: " The days glide away in tranquillity, seasoned with all the pleasures which can flatter a reasonable mind. Fare for a king, wine for the gods, music for angels, delightful walks in the gardens and woods, parties on the water, the cultivation of letters and the fine arts, spirited and pleasant conversation."—Letter 8.

" The inscription over the gate, ' Frederico tranquillitatem petenti,' seemed to indicate his sentiments," observes baron Poelnitz; " his behaviour and his actions render it probable that his reign will be one of those mild and peaceable reigns which procure kings the love of their people, wherein consists their true glory."— Lettres de Poelnitz, tom. i. p. 27.

tion, and the alliance of the new king was courted by the
different powers of Europe. Frederic listened to the overtures of the different powers without giving any decisive
answers; but infusing new vigour into every department of
government, improved the economical system of his father,
maintained the discipline of the army, raised fifteen new
battalions, and waited in silence till a scene of action should
present itself worthy of employing those talents for the
cabinet and the field, with which nature had endowed him,
and which education and reflection had matured.

Meanwhile the emperor was employed in supplying the
losses of his army, and repairing the disorders in his
finances; and seemed to be animated with equal zeal and
sincerity in his approaches towards the Maritime Powers,
and in adopting a plan of reconciliation and mutual defence.

Charles, though subject to occasional attacks of the
gout, had always enjoyed a sound and vigorous constitution, but at this period his health had been greatly injured
by the violent agitation of his mind under his recent distresses.* In the beginning of October he complained of
some symptoms of a flying gout; but notwithstanding the
remonstrances of his physicians, he refused to relinquish
the pleasures of the chase, and repaired with a hunting
party to Halpthurn. The weather was extremely cold and
changeable during the whole time, with a succession of
frost, snow, and rain; and although he was seized with a
cholic soon after his arrival, he eagerly pursued his favourite diversion, until his disorder became serious in consequence of unremitted fatigue and the inclemency of the

* It appears, from many parts of Mr. Robinson's Despatches at this
period, that the decline of the emperor's health was occasioned by the
agitation of his mind; and this fact is confirmed in a letter from Mr.
Porter, who was then employed at Vienna in settling the disputes
relative to the tariff of the Low Countries, and became afterwards
ambassador at Constantinople : " The haughty behaviour of France,
joined with the natural hatred the emperor bore that nation, and the
internal combats he underwent, by a servile compliance he had reduced
himself to, preyed on his mind, and was the proximate cause of that
ill habit of body, which at last put a period to his life. And if Mr.
Leibsetter, his most confidential physician, may be depended upon, it
was not so much the loss of Belgrade, as the manner in which it was
given up, and the usage of the French, that bore heavily on the emperor, and threw him into a profound melancholy." — Mr. Porter to
Mr. Walpole, Vienna, March 29. 1741.

season. On the 10th at night his complaint was increased
by an indigestion, occasioned by a dish of mushrooms
stewed in oil, of which he ate voraciously. After passing
the whole night in repeated vomitings and the most excruciating pain, he returned to Vienna in a state of such
extreme sickness and debility, that he fainted several times
during the journey, and was conveyed on the 11th to the
palace of La Favourite, in the suburbs of Vienna, scarcely
alive.

By proper remedies and rest he was greatly relieved, and
supposed to be out of danger; but on the 12th, his disorder
returned with redoubled violence, accompanied with a high
fever and symptoms of the gout, and his life was again
despaired of. Charles bore his painful complaints with
extreme patience, and seemed unconscious of his approaching dissolution. When his disorder was declared mortal
he would not believe his danger, and sportively rallied his
physicians on the falsity of their prognostics; but when
they persevered in their declarations, his fortitude did not
forsake him, and as they were disputing in his presence
concerning the nature of his illness, he exclaimed, "Cease
your disputes at present, but open my body after my death,
and you will then be able to ascertain the cause."

He then prepared for his dissolution, submitted to all the
ceremonies of the church, and arranged the proceedings
relative to his succession, with the greatest composure.
He summoned his ministers into his presence, gave them
proper instructions, and thanked count Staremberg, in particular, for his long and faithful services. He passed the
last hours of his life in bidding adieu to his family, and exhorting each of them, according to their respective stations;
he sent his blessing and advice to his eldest daughter, who,
on account of her pregnancy, was not permitted to approach her dying father. He took a tender leave of his
consort, with whom he had always lived in uninterrupted
harmony, and who had passed six successive nights without
rest; he addressed a word of comfort even to his favourite
dwarf, and said to prince Charles of Loraine, who was
weeping at his bedside, "Do not lament, though you are
about to lose a faithful friend."

A short time before his dissolution he had an interview
of two hours alone with the duke of Loraine, and expired

on the 20th of October, at two o'clock in the morning, in
the fifty-sixth year of his age, and the thirtieth of his
reign ; and in him was extinct the male line of the house
of Austria, which had continued in an uninterrupted succession for above four hundred years.

Charles was fond of active exercises and sports of address; he excelled in shooting at the mark and riding in
the manege ; he was devoted to music, was a performer,
and even composed an opera, which was represented with
great splendour in the theatre of the palace.　The parts
were performed by the principal nobility, Charles himself
took his place in the orchestra, and his two daughters
danced in the ballet.　He was a considerable patron of the
arts and sciences ; his band was distinguished for the ex-
cellence of the musicians ; he revived the academy of
painting, sculpture, and architecture ; improved the schools,
built the public library, and endowed it with a large collection of books, particularly with that of prince Eugene,
which he purchased.　He also laid the foundation of the
noble cabinet of medals, and drew men of letters to his
court from different parts of Europe ; among these we distinguish Metastasio, whom he appointed imperial laureate,
and domesticated at Vienna.

He spared no pains to facilitate the internal communications of his vast dominions, by the construction of numerous
high roads, and repaired, at a considerable expense, the
military way formed by Trajan through Wallachia.　He
was anxious to promote the commerce and manufactures of
his country ; and though he failed in his great schemes,
from the impracticability of his plans and the jealousy of
the Maritime Powers, yet the energy of his efforts deserves
eulogium.　He meliorated the courts of justice, and reduced the government of Hungary to a better form.　His
natural disposition was compassionate, and from his cle-
mency he was called the Titus of the age.

He married Elizabeth Christina, a daughter of Louis
Rhodolph, duke of Brunswick, by whom he had a son, Leopold, who died in his infancy, and three daughters, two of
whom survived him, Maria Theresa, his successor, and Maria
Amelia, who afterwards married prince Charles of Loraine.
As there was no prospect of any ·more issue, the emperor had been repeatedly solicited, as well by the empress

herself, and his most faithful counsellors, as by the British cabinet, to obtain the title of king of the Romans for his son-in-law, Francis, duke of Loraine. And although he fully appreciated the fatal consequences which would attend his death without issue male, or without providing a successor in the empire; yet he rejected this salutary advice, and considering the death of the empress as a more probable event, entertained hopes of male issue by a future marriage. In consequence of this ill-judged policy, he endangered the loss of the imperial crown, and exposed his successor to the greatest difficulties.

Ch. XCVII.— REIGN OF MARIA THERESA.—1740.

MARIA THERESA had not completed her twenty-fourth year, when, in virtue of the Pragmatic Sanction, she succeeded to all the dominions of the house of Austria. Her person was formed to wear a crown, and her mind to give lustre to her exalted dignity; she possessed a commanding figure, great beauty, animation, and sweetness of countenance, a pleasing tone of voice, fascinating manners; and united feminine grace with a strength of understanding and an intrepidity above her sex. During her father's illness, the young princess was exposed to great danger, in consequence of her advanced pregnancy; but sufficiently recovered her spirits the day after his death, to give audience to the ministers of state, and to assume the government.

No princess ever ascended a throne under circumstances of greater peril, or in a situation which demanded more energy, fortitude, and judgment. The treasury contained only 100,000 florins, which were claimed by the empress dowager; the army, exclusive of the troops in Italy and the Low Countries, did not amount to 30,000 effective men; a great scarcity of provisions excited alarming symptoms of discontent in the capital; the vintage was cut off by the frost, and the peasants in the neighbourhood of Vienna, inflamed by agents from the town, assembled in large bodies to destroy the game; while rumours were industriously circulated that the government was dissolved, and the elector of Bavaria was hourly expected to take possession of the Austrian territories. Great apprehensions were also entertained lest the distant provinces should break out into commotion; lest the restless spirits of Hungary, supported by the Turks, should attempt to revive their elective monarchy.

Notwithstanding the solemn guaranty of the Pragmatic Sanction, different claimants on the Austrian succession were expected to arise, besides the elector of Bavaria, whose ministers publicly protested against the accession of Maria Theresa. His brother, the elector of Cologne, only acknowledged her by the title of archduchess; the elector Palatine had even sent a letter by the common post, superscribed, "To the archduchess Maria Theresa;" and the king of Spain gave her no other title than great duchess of Tuscany.

In this arduous crisis the young queen was wholly without experience or knowledge of business; and the ministers, either timorous, desponding, and irresolute, or worn out with age, sunk under the magnitude of the impending danger. To use the words of an eye-witness, " The Turks seemed to them already in Hungary; the Hungarians themselves in arms; the Saxons in Bohemia; the Bavarians at the gates of Vienna, and France the soul of the whole. I not only saw them in despair; but that very despair was not capable of rendering them truly desperate."*

The first claimant on the Austrian succession was Maximilian Emanuel, elector of Bavaria; he asserted that the will of Ferdinand I. devised the kingdom of Bohemia and the Austrian dominions to his daughters and their descendants, in failure of the male line. The late emperor, as his pretensions had been foreseen, had endeavoured to obtain his guaranty of the Pragmatic Sanction; and with a view to refute his claims, had transmitted a memorial, proving that the clause in the will of Ferdinand devised the inheritance to his daughters, only in failure of legitimate heirs, and consequently did not set aside the female descendants of the male line. In corroboration of this proof, on the accession of Maria Theresa, the will of Ferdinand was submitted to the inspection of the principal

* Mr. Robinson to lord Harrington, Oct. 22. 1740.

officers of state, as well as to the foreign ambassadors; and troops despatched to the frontiers of Bohemia to prevent any hostile aggression on the side of Bavaria. But neither these warlike preparations, nor the exposure of the will, induced the elector to desist from his claims; and Maria Theresa waited with anxiety for the replies of those foreign powers to whom she had notified her accession.

The most favourable assurances were immediately transmitted from many of the foreign powers. The king of Prussia, in a letter to the duke of Loraine, manifested his perfect friendship, and testified his readiness to serve the house of Austria on this occasion. Augustus, king of Poland and elector of Saxony also expressed the warmest affection, and tendered his assistance in favour of the Pragmatic Sanction. The death of Anne made no change in the sentiments of the court of Russia; the strongest assurances of support were given by Biren, who was appointed regent during the minority of Ivan, and after his disgrace, were confirmed by the regent Anne, mother of the young monarch. The States-general passed a resolution to fulfil their engagements, both in regard to the Barrier and the Pragmatic Sanction; and the king of England declared his intention to cultivate the friendship of the queen of Hungary, to perform his engagements, and to co-operate with her for the general good of Europe. France, to whose acknowledgment the court of Vienna looked with anxious expectation, sent no public answer to the notification of the queen's accession. Amelot, secretary of state for foreign affairs, gave only verbal assurances of his master's readiness to fulfil his engagements; and both he and cardinal Fleury, in private letters to the prince of Lichtenstein, ambassador to the court of France, expressed concern for the death of the emperor. They excused the delays of the French court by stating that they were searching the archives for the style of address to the queen of Hungary, and when the prince of Lichtenstein transmitted a memorial in reply to the Bavarian claims, polite answers were returned, but without the smallest allusion to that document. This equivocal conduct evinced the intentions of the French court to withhold their acknowledgment of the queen's title till a pretext should offer for supporting the claims of the elector of Bavaria, and proved their reso-

lution to oppose the elevation of the duke of Loraine to
the imperial throne.

But the queen, deluded by the promises of the cardinal,
coldly received the exhortations of the British cabinet to
beware of the designs of her ancient rival, and declined
the proposal of the Maritime Powers to form a grand confederacy against the house of Bourbon.   Hence the measures of the Austrian cabinet were fluctuating and contradictory, and no decisive line of conduct was adopted at
this critical juncture.

Chap. XCVIII.—1740, 1741.

IN the midst of this suspense and alarm, a new and unexpected claimant started up, and, instead of stating pretensions on paper, or answering memorials, made a direct
appeal to the sword.   This claimant was Frederic, king of
Prussia, who acted with such consummate secrecy that his
design was not divulged, and scarcely even suspected, when
his troops entered the Austrian dominions.

Many circumstances induced this young and aspiring
monarch to adopt so decisive a measure.   He was anxious
to distinguish the commencement of his reign ; and to remove the obloquy which had been cast on the Prussian
name in consequence of the pacific conduct of his father,
who, with so powerful a force, remained in what was
deemed a state of pusillanimous inaction.   He was also disgusted with the court of Vienna, for their constant prevarication in regard to Berg and Juliers; and his disgust was
still farther increased by the conduct of the young queen,
who, on liberating Seckendorf, extorted from him the orders
of Charles VI. relating to his proffered guaranty of that
succession.   He was sensible of his own force, and the
weakness of the house of Austria, and was eager to avail
himself of the favourable situation of the European powers.

Having formed the design of invading Silesia, as the
province most contiguous to his own dominions, and least
prepared for defence, he revived some antiquated claims
of his family on parts of that duchy, and carried it into
execution with equal address and celerity.   He entered

into no alliance with any foreign power; amused the court
of Vienna with vague professions of friendship; assembled
a large corps of troops in the neighbourhood of Berlin; and
concealed his views from the marquis of Botta, who was
sent from Vienna to penetrate his designs, till December,
when his army was in full march towards the frontiers of
Silesia.

Being no longer able to conceal his intentions, he despatched count Gotter, his grand master, to Vienna, to
state his claims and demands; and, after making a similar
explanation to Botta, quitted Berlin at the conclusion of a
masked ball, reached Crossen on the 21st of December,
and on the 23d entered Silesia, at the head of twenty
battalions and thirty-six squadrons. He at the same time
dispersed memorials, in which he detailed his claims, and
declared his intention to occupy the Silesian duchies for
the house of Austria, to prevent them from being seized
by any other power.

The court of Vienna was no less alarmed at this aggression, than indignant at the affected expressions of friendship with which it was accompanied, when Gotter arrived
at Vienna to execute his commission. He was a man of a
boisterous and overbearing temper, and ill calculated to
conciliate so high spirited and sensitive a princess as Maria
Theresa. He delivered his message in a private audience
to the duke of Loraine: "I am come," he said, "with
safety for the house of Austria in one hand, and the imperial crown for your royal highness in the other. The
troops and money of my master are at the service of the
queen, and cannot fail of being acceptable at a time when
she is in want of both, and can only depend on so considerable a prince as the king of Prussia, and his allies the
Maritime Powers and Russia. As the king my master,
from the situation of his dominions, will be exposed to
great danger from this alliance, it is hoped that, as an
indemnification, the queen of Hungary will not offer him
less than the whole duchy of Silesia." This extraordinary
demand was accompanied with threatening declarations:
"Nobody," he added, "is more firm in his resolutions than
the king of Prussia; he must and will enter Silesia; once
entered he must and will proceed; and, if not secured by
the immediate cession of that province, his troops and

money will be offered to the electors of Saxony and Bavaria."

The duke of Loraine replied with great calmness and temper, but with no less spirit and dignity. He declared, that the queen, however inclined, had not the power to alienate the smallest portion of that succession which was so strongly and indivisibly entailed, and was not reduced to so low a condition as to treat with an enemy in the heart of her dominions. He expatiated on the wide scene of confusion which was opening by the impatience of the king of Prussia, which might be equally destructive to himself and to others. Gotter replying, " I have no further business here, and will instantly return ;" the duke demanded, " Are your troops actually in Silesia ?" Being answered in the affirmative, he continued, " Go then, return to your master, and tell him, that while he has a man in Silesia, we will rather perish than enter into any discussion. But if he is either not entered, and will abstain from entering, or, if entered, will return, we will treat with him at Berlin ; Botta has already instructions ; others shall be forwarded this day, and the king of Prussia may be gratified, without presuming to extort what is not in our power to grant ; for my part, not for the imperial crown, nor even the whole world, will I sacrifice one right or one inch of the queen's lawful possessions."

This firm language, and the refusal of the queen to receive Gotter, disconcerted the Prussian ministers. They seemed alarmed and ashamed of their master's conduct, and acknowledged that he would abate his demands, and be satisfied with the mortgage of a few towns in Silesia, and their dependencies. These propositions, however, were indignantly rejected, and the queen persisted in her refusal to treat with the king of Prussia while his troops remained in her dominions.

A second negotiation equally failed of success. Gotter, who returned with the refusal of the queen of Hungary to listen to any overture while the Prussian troops continued in her dominions, was again despatched to Vienna with new proposals from his master. To prevent a public breach of the Pragmatic Sanction, Frederic offered to accept part of Silesia as a mortgage, for which he would pay an equivalent in money, under the condition that the mortgage should never be redeemed. But the instructions of Gotter being defective, he could not venture to accept any specific proposal, and the queen persisted in requiring the prior evacuation of Silesia.

While this negotiation agitated the court of Vienna, the king of Prussia made a rapid progress in Silesia, and was joyfully received by the natives, two-thirds of whom were Protestants. On the first of January, 1741, he entered Breslau, the capital, compelled general Brown, who was at the head of only 3000 men, to retreat into Moravia, and before the end of that month, had made himself master of the whole province except Glogau and Brieg, which he blockaded, and Neiss, the only fortress capable of maintaining a siege. He appropriated the revenues of the country ; and, after making the necessary regulations, left the command to marshal Schwerin, and returned to Berlin to collect an army for the security of his own dominions.

In this whole transaction Frederic affected to occupy Silesia as a friend to the house of Austria, for in a letter to the duke of Loraine, he said, "My heart has no share in the mischief which my hand is doing to your court," and he renewed his proposals for an accommodation. These pacific declarations, which were so contrary to his actions, inflamed the indignation of Maria Theresa. She determined to oppose force by force, and appealed to the guaranties of the Pragmatic Sanction. Her hopes of speedy assistance against the unjust aggression of Prussia were, however, disappointed ; promises indeed poured in from every quarter, but not a single man was despatched, or a single florin remitted. Russia, under the weak government of the regent Anne, declined sending the stipulated succours ; the king of Poland began to waver ; France pursued her equivocal system of policy, and, while she gave assurances of her pacific intentions to the court of Vienna, negotiated with the king of Prussia and the elector of Bavaria. The Dutch, menaced by Prussia, and in dread of France, recurred to their usual indecision ; and England, distracted with intestine feuds, and anxious to prevent, or at least to retard, a continental war, acted with a circumspection more congenial to its own situation than to the present distress of the house of Austria. In reply to the urgent demands of the queen of Hungary, for the succour of 12,000 men, the king acknowledged the casus fœderis, and testified his resolution to abide by his engagements ; but urged the necessity of an immediate accommodation with the king of Prussia. He tendered, in conjunction with the States, his good offices to effect that object : and promised, should his endeavours fail of success, to send his contingent to the assistance of the queen of Hungary.

Thus left to herself, Maria Theresa disdained to make the smallest concession ; she collected a considerable force in Moravia, and gave the command to marshal Neuperg, whom she had recently liberated from prison, and the most sanguine expectations were entertained that he would drive the Prussians from Silesia. But in consequence of the want of magazines, the bad state of the roads, and severity of the weather, the general could not pass the mountains of Moravia and Upper Silesia before the latter end of March. Meanwhile Frederic had rejoined his army, taken Glogau by assault, pressed the preparations for the siege of Neiss, and repaired to Jagerndorf to visit the quarters of his troops in Upper Silesia, when he was alarmed by the incursions of the Austrian hussars, and even narrowly escaped being taken prisoner.

Marshal Neuperg collected his forces in Moravia, passed the mountains, and entered Silesia at Hermanstadt, near the junction of the Oder and the Ostrave, with the hopes of surprising the Prussians, who were dispersed in their cantonments, and of cutting them off in detail. With a view to seize the heavy artillery deposited at Ohlau, he left his tents at Neiss ; and continuing his march, made himself master of Grotkau, despatched general Lentulus to stop the passage of the Prussians over the Neiss at Sorge, where they had constructed a bridge ; and during the evening of the 9th of April, cantoned his troops at Molwitz and two other villages in the vicinity of Brieg. He here reposed in perfect security, encouraged by the consternation which seemed to prevail among the enemy, and by the numerous deserters who repaired to his camp. His natural confidence was increased by the consciousness that his troops were equal to the whole force of the Prussians, and that his cavalry, far superior in numbers and dis-

cipline, would act with effect in the plains of **Lower**
Silesia, and drive before them soldiers who had only figured
on the grand parades of Potzdam and Berlin.   He trusted,
likewise, to his numerous hussars, who he hoped would
discover the smallest motion of the enemy, should they be
disposed to quit their cantonments, when the ground was
covered with snow.   In this situation, Neuperg was surprised by the sudden approach of the Prussian army, which
advanced at ten o'clock on the following morning.

The king leaving Jagerndorf when the Austrians entered Silesia, speedily assembled his troops, and on the 4th
of April, hastened towards Steinau, intending to pass the
Neiss at Sorge.   Being prevented by the detachment of
Lentulus, he made a forced march, and crossed at Miche-
lau, to the south of Molwitz, with a view to occupy Grotkau.   Finding that place in possession of the Austrians,
and compelled to risk an engagement for the preservation
of his artillery at Ohlau, he advanced on the 8th of April,
and took up his quarters at Pogrel and the adjacent villages,
in the vicinity of Molwitz.

On the succeeding day a thick fall of snow concealing
his movements from the enemy, prevented him from advancing; but on the 10th the weather clearing up, he
assembled his troops, consisting of twenty-seven battalions,
twenty-nine squadrons, and three of hussars, and marched
in five columns towards the enemy.   Arriving near Molwitz, he formed his army in order of battle, although no
enemy appeared.   The right wing extended towards the
village of Hellendorf, and the left to the rivulet of Lauch-
witz; but his dispositions being unskilfully made, the cavalry
of the right did not reach their destined position, and the
infantry being crowded he drew three battalions from the
first line, with which he flanked his right wing.

Neuperg, surprised by the approach of the enemy, could
not avail himself of their want of skill, and was compelled
to form his troops in haste, exposed to the continual discharge of the Prussian artillery.   Meanwhile the Austrian
cavalry of the left wing, under general Roemer, galled by
this incessant fire, threatened to retreat unless they were
led to the charge ;   Roemer instantly attacked the right ring
of the Prussians, dispersed their cavalry, and cutting his
way through the infantry, penetrated to the baggage and

the park of artillery, where his men began to pillage. In consequence of this successful charge, and the confusion it occasioned in the Prussian army, victory appeared to incline to the side of the Austrians; even the king, at the entreaties of marshal Schweren, retired from the field, and Neuperg seized this decisive moment to put his infantry in motion. But all his efforts were ineffectual; his troops, panic-struck by the regular and rapid fire of the Prussian infantry, refused to advance; and Roemer, having again formed the cavalry, was repulsed by the prince of Anhalt, who, with the three battalions drawn from the first line, had repaired the disorder on the right. Three times Roemer charged the enemy, and was three times driven back; returning a fourth time he was killed, and his troops gave way.

Animated with this advantage, Schweren advanced with the Prussian infantry, and from this moment all was rout and confusion in the Austrian army; Neuperg, who had received several contusions, in vain attempted to revive the courage of his troops; they precipitately fled from the field of battle, and did not again rally till they had passed the town of Neiss. The loss on the side of the Prussians did not exceed 2500 men, while on that of the Austrians more than 3000 were killed, and 2000 taken prisoners, with several pieces of cannon and four standards.

This memorable combat, which decided the fate of Silesia, was rendered still more remarkable by the extraordinary flight and narrow escape of the king of Prussia, who was nearly taken prisoner at the moment when his army was victorious. Retiring from the field of battle, accompanied by Maupertuis, a French valet-de-chambre, and a few hussars, he rode towards Oppelen, where he thought himself secure of an asylum; but that town had been occupied by a party of Austrian hussars. On arriving at the gate, at midnight, the valet-de-chambre demanding admittance, the hussars instantly sallied out, attacked the party, and exchanged several shots, on which the king exclaimed, "Farewell, friends, I am better mounted than you all," and rode away. Maupertuis and the greater part of the company fell into the hands of the hussars, while the monarch, returning towards Neiss, received the news that his troops had gained a complete victory, and rejoined his army the same morning, after having rode backwards and forwards not less than twelve German miles.

The consequences of this battle were as fatal to the house of Austria as they were advantageous to Frederic. The Austrians were humbled by the loss of this first engagement with troops whom they had despised, while it stamped a new character on the Prussian infantry for steadiness and discipline, and proved them superior even to veteran troops. The king learned also to appreciate the advantage of improving his cavalry, and to correct the errors which he had committed from want of experience, and from his acquaintance only with the mere theory of war. His camp at Molwitz soon became the centre of the most important negotiations; his alliance was courted from all quarters, and he seemed to hold in his hand the balance of Europe. He still affected, however, great moderation in the midst of his success, and offered to the queen of Hungary his friendship on the same terms as before his victory.

CHAP. XCIX. — 1741.

THE court of Vienna was filled with consternation at the defeat of Molwitz in proportion to their sanguine hopes of success. In consequence of the deficiency of money and men, the greatest difficulties had been overcome to bring into the field the army intrusted to count Neuperg; that army was now so much reduced as to be no longer capable of acting offensively, and no obstacle could be opposed to the progress of the Prussians.

Hitherto the firmness of Maria Theresa, in refusing the offers of Prussia, had been justified by the favourable aspect of her affairs. During the negotiation she had made urgent and repeated applications for immediate assistance to the powers who had guaranteed the Pragmatic Sanction, particularly to England. But the British minister, embarrassed with a violent opposition, and aware of the designs of France to dismember the Austrian succession, delayed taking a decisive part, with the hope of inducing the queen of Hungary to effect an accommodation with the king of

Prussia. Hence the cabinet of England pursued a dilatory and indecisive conduct; no reply was made to the demands of the queen of Hungary, dated the 29th of December, until the end of February, and no instructions reached Mr. Robinson till the beginning of April.

At that time the Austrian ministers were again inspired with full confidence; they were delivered from all apprehensions on the side of Turkey by an amicable adjustment of the limits; they flattered themselves that France would not contravene the Pragmatic Sanction; they entertained the most sanguine expectation of immediate assistance from Russia, Saxony, the circles of the empire, and the Maritime Powers; and justly hoped that their own efforts alone, and the force under count Neuperg, would wrest Silesia from the king of Prussia. They were therefore equally disappointed and irritated when, instead of effectual assistance, the British cabinet suspended all succours until the queen should deliver a specific answer whether she chose peace or war with Prussia; if war, the king of England promised to fulfil his engagements and employ his contingent of 12,000 men, as soon as a plan of operations was concerted; if peace, he tendered his good offices to procure an accommodation. At the same time Mr. Robinson was instructed to represent the dangerous situation of Europe, the uncertainty of the concurrence of Russia, the difficulties on the side of Saxony, and the divided sentiments of the Dutch. He was ordered to expatiate on the dangerous designs of France, who was luring the king of Prussia, preparing to place the elector of Bavaria on the imperial throne, consolidating a powerful combination against the house of Austria, and forming magazines and assembling troops on the side of the Rhine. From this aspect of affairs he was to urge the necessity of gaining the king of Prussia, even by an immediate sacrifice of Lower Silesia and the town of Breslau.

These proposals were received with indignation and rejected with disdain; the queen of Hungary would not submit to the humiliation of yielding one of her richest and most valuable provinces, at a moment when she expected her troops to drive the Prussians from Silesia. The whole cabinet, deceived by the insidious assurances of cardinal Fleury, refused to credit the designs imputed to France;

and the duke of Loraine and all the ministers claimed immediate succour, as the only means of serving the house of Austria should France commence hostilities. The queen of Hungary, therefore, indignantly refused to make the smallest cession to Prussia, and declared that even if deserted by her allies, she would trust the fortunes of her house to the fidelity of her subjects and the valour of her army. The defeat at Molwitz changed the sentiments of the duke of Loraine and the ministers of the conference, and gave weight to the urgent representations of England ; but the queen persisted in her refusal to make the smallest cession, although France now began to act with less reserve, and had nearly brought her designs to maturity.

From the death of the emperor France had watched the favourable moment to reduce the house of Austria, but with her usual address cajoled the cabinet of Vienna with vague assurances of friendship, and with hopes of concurring to place Francis on the imperial throne. After the battle of Molwitz, she declared her resolution not to contravene the guarantee of the Pragmatic Sanction, unless compelled to take part in the war against the queen of Hungary. Even in the midst of hostile preparations, and while French agents canvassed for the elevation of the elector of Bavaria to the imperial throne, the court of Vienna did not credit the hostile designs imputed to France ; nor was the illusion wholly dissipated till marshal Belleisle, who had been appointed ambassador to the diet at Frankfort, repaired to the camp at Molwitz, to gain the king of Prussia, and to propose a plan for the dismemberment of the Austrian territories.

Besides the elector of Bavaria and the king of Prussia, many other pretenders to the Austrian succession were encouraged by France. Philip V., king of Spain, avowed himself the direct lineal representative of Charles V. Charles Emanuel, king of Sardinia, in virtue of his descent from Catherine, second daughter of Philip II., now revived an obsolete claim on the Milanese. Even Augustus, notwithstanding his treaty with the queen of Hungary, prepared to assert the right of his wife, Maria, eldest daughter of Joseph, in virtue of the family compact, by which the succession was entailed on the daughters of Joseph, in preference to those of Charles.

According to the plan matured by France, Bohemia and Upper Austria were assigned to the elector of Bavaria; Moravia and Upper Silesia to Augustus; Lower Silesia and the country of Glatz to the king of Prussia; Austrian Lombardy to Spain; and some compensation was to be allotted to the king of Sardinia.

While marshal Belleisle remained in the Prussian camp, Frederic, unwilling to contribute to the preponderance of France in Germany, and to aggrandise the electors of Bavaria and Saxony, made repeated overtures to the king of England, and urged that, however reluctant, he must join with France, should the queen persist in refusing all offers of accommodation. But the impending danger had no effect on the lofty and unbending spirit of Maria Theresa. She considered the offers of the king of Prussia as insidious, and made only with a view to delay the assistance of the Maritime Powers; and when her consent to accept just and reasonable terms was at length extorted, she refused to specify any condition. As the king of Prussia maintained the same reserve, George II. commanded lord Hyndford to propose the cession of the three duchies of Glogau, Schweibus, and Grunberg; but Frederic, after thanking the king for making at least one step towards an accommodation, by a direct offer, answered, "At the beginning of the war I might have been contented with this proposal; but after the expense I have incurred, and the success of my arms, the offer of one duchy is too small, for I consider Schweibus and Grunberg as part of the duchy of Glogau. Shall I again give them battle, and drive them out of Silesia? You will then see that I shall receive other proposals, and the queen of Hungary will tender better conditions, not less than all Lower Silesia, with the town of Breslau. At present I must have four duchies which lie contiguous to my territories." When lord Hyndford urged that his majesty then had it in his power to conclude an honourable peace, and to show his magnanimity by restoring the tranquillity of Germany, Frederic impatiently interrupted him: "Do not, my lord, talk to me of magnanimity; a prince ought first to consult his own interests. I am not averse to peace; but I expect to have four duchies, and will have them." He then dismissed the British minister, without giving any answer to his repeated requests that he would name the four duchies to which he alluded.

When this account was transmitted to the court of Vienna, and lord Hyndford suggested that the four duchies alluded to were Glogau, Wohlau, Lignitz, and Scweidnitz, the queen of Hungary not only rejected these demands as extravagant, but even disapproved the conduct of the king of England in offering the duchy of Glogau without her consent, and expressed the highest satisfaction that the proposal had been rejected. She also persisted for a considerable time in refusing all cessions in Silesia, and only offered to purchase the friendship of the king of Prussia by a sum of money and some sacrifices on the side of Flanders and the Rhine.

It is needless to enter minutely into every event of this negotiation, which was carried on by the mediation of England, but was frustrated by the incompatible characters of Maria Theresa and Frederic, both equally inflexible; one determined to yield nothing on the side of Silesia, and the other resolved to accept no other equivalent.

While Mr. Robinson was endeavouring to rouse the court of Vienna to a sense of their danger, and to draw from the ministers of the conference the ultimatum of the queen, a courier from George II., who was then at Hanover, brought information that Frederic had signed, on the 5th of June, a treaty with France. The British minister was ordered to urge this transaction as a new and pressing motive to detach the king of Prussia before the exchange of the ratifications, and repair to the Prussian camp with the proposals of the queen of Hungary. Maria Theresa listened to the communication with profound silence ; and in reply to his representations, broke out into exclamations and sudden starts of passion, which showed the despair and agony of her mind. Adverting to his mission to the king of Prussia, she said " Not only for political reasons, but from conscience and honour, I will not consent to part with much in Silesia. I am even afraid you will not be authorised to offer Glogau, though perhaps I might be induced to part with that province, if I could be secure of peace on all sides. But no sooner is one enemy satisfied than another starts up ; another, and then another, must be contented, and all at my expense. I am convinced of your good will, but I pity you. Your mission to Silesia will be as fruitless as that of count Gotter was here; remember

my words." When Mr. Robinson represented that it was
in her majesty's power to render his mission successful,
and urged that her own fate, the fate of the duke, of her
whole family, and of all Europe, depended upon her yielding to the hard necessity of the times, she exclaimed,
" What would I not give, except in Silesia ! Let him take
all we have in Guelderland ; and if he is not to be gained
by that sacrifice, others may. Let the princes of the empire, let the king, your master, only speak to the elector of
Bavaria; he may be more flexible, and means may be
found to gain him. Oh, the king, your master ; let him
only march, let him march only ! " No other answer could
be drawn from this high-spirited woman ; and her resolution was strengthened by the arrival of another courier,
announcing the signature of a treaty at Hanover, on the
24th of June, which secured to her a subsidy of 300,000*l.*,
granted by the British Parliament. The queen, as well as
the duke of Loraine and the whole cabinet, received this
news with marks of joy equal to their former despondency,
and were lavish in their professions of friendship and gratitude. But their long-expected answer to the earnest demand of the ultimatum evinced little disposition to purchase
the alliance of Prussia. They indulged themselves in a
bitter invective against his conduct, and only declared
that the queen was not averse to purchase a peace by a
sacrifice on the side of the Low Countries, and by the payment of 2,000,000 florins. After many contemptuous expressions against Frederic, they concluded with conjuring
his Britannic majesty, both as king and elector, to assist
the queen of Hungary, and to order the instant march of
the stipulated succours, as the common danger would be
increased by delay. As if secure of the immediate co-operation of England, count Ostein, the Austrian ambassador,
delivered a note to the king, requiring his majesty to put
the auxiliary troops in motion, to pay the subsidy at the
shortest terms, to forward the association of the circles,
and to ascertain the assistance stipulated by the courts of
Russia and Saxony.

In fact, the queen of Hungary was so far from entertain-
ing the smallest inclination to gain the king of Prussia by
cessions, that she even formed the chimerical scheme to
divide his dominions ; to secure the elector of Saxony, by

the gift of Crossen and the fiefs of Lusatia, which the king had forfeited in consequence of his felony to the crown of Bohemia ; and to detach the elector of Bavaria, by yielding to him either Tuscany, the Milanese, or the Low Countries, in exchange for the district of Bavaria, between Upper Austria and the river Inn.   She even attempted to obtain the acquiescence of England in this wild project, by threatening to throw herself in the power of France, and yield Luxemburgh and part of Flanders, rather than gratify the presumptuous demands of the king of Prussia.

But as neither her remonstrances nor threats could prevail on England to declare war, without the concurrence of Holland, and as the danger from the grand confederacy became more and more imminent, her consent to offer an accommodation with Prussia was at length extorted, by the urgent representations of the duke of Loraine and of her principal ministers.   After much hesitation, and many changes and delays in arranging the terms*, she committed the proposals to Mr. Robinson, who was to repair in person to the Prussian camp in Silesia, and to offer Austrian Guelderland and Limburgh ; and, at the last extremity, the duchy of Glogau.   But, in arranging these proposals, she displayed the strongest aversion to an accommodation ; and occasionally exclaimed to Mr. Robinson, who expressed his apprehensions that some of the conditions would be rejected by the king, " I wish he may reject them ! "   When he took his leave, she recommended her interests to his care ; and said, " Save Limburgh, if possible, were it only for the quiet of my conscience : God knows how I shall answer for the cession, having sworn to the states of Brabant never to alienate any part of their country."

In consequence of these obstacles and delays, Mr. Robinson did not depart for Silesia till the 30th of July. He reached Breslau on the 3rd of August ; and, on the 5th had an audience of the king, in his tent at the camp of

* " The project of cession," writes Mr. Robinson in a letter to lord Harrington, " was drawn up, and the instructions for the proposal of terms to the king of Prussia.   The queen, after much struggle, forced to approve them, changed them with her own hand, added that she liked one thing too much, or another too little ; what with despair, what with reluctance, what with irresolution, spoiled the whole paper, and sent it back to the chancellor so mangled, then sent for it again."

Strehlen, accompanied by lord Hyndford and count Podewilz, the Prussian minister.

After some desultory and unconnected conversation, in
which Frederic stigmatised the answer of the court of
Vienna as extremely impertinent, Mr. Robinson opened
his commission with the offer of Austrian Guelderland,
and a florid description of its value and importance.   The
king, without answering, turned to count Podewilz, and
asked, " What have we yet left in Guelderland ? " and
when the minister replied, " almost nothing," he exclaimed
" Still beggarly offers!   What! nothing but a paltry town
for all my just pretensions in Silesia ? "   He here gave way
to his indignation ; and Mr. Robinson, after some hesitation, added the offer of Limburgh as the ultimatum of the
queen of Hungary, exaggerating its advantages still higher
than those of Guelderland.   But he was interrupted in his
encomiums by the king, who ironically asked, " How can
the queen of Hungary dare to think of violating so solemn
an engagement as that of the barrier treaty, which renders
every inch of the Low Countries inalienable?   I have no
desire to aggrandise myself in parts which are useless to
me, much less to expend money in new fortifications.   But
why more fortifications?   Am I not fortifying Glogau and
Brieg, which are sufficient for one who intends to live well
with his neighbours?   Neither the French nor the Dutch
have offended me, nor will I offend them by such *unlawful*
acquisitions.   Besides, who will guaranty them ? "   Mr.
Robinson answering, that the queen would obtain the
guaranty of England, Russia, Saxony, and even of the
States-general.   " Guaranties ! " contemptuously rejoined
the king, " who observes guaranties in these times?   Has
not France guaranteed the Pragmatic Sanction?   has not
England guaranteed it ?   why do you not all fly to her
succour ? "

The conversation continued for some time in the same
tone of contempt and irony on the side of the king : he
ridiculed the conduct of those powers who affected to espouse the cause of the house of Austria, and dwelt with
great energy on the advantages of his situation.   " I am
at the head," he said, " of an invincible army, already
master of a country which I will have, which I must have,
and which is the only object of my views.   My ancestors,"

he continued, "would rise out of their tombs to reproach me, should I abandon the rights they have transmitted to me. With what reputation can I live, should I lightly quit an enterprise, the first act of my reign, begun with reflection, prosecuted with firmness, and which ought to be maintained to the last extremity ? I will sooner be crushed with my whole army, than renounce my just rights in Silesia. Have I occasion for peace? Let those who want peace give me what I want; or let them fight me again, and be again beaten!"

This burst of real or affected indignation was accompanied with theatrical gestures ; and turning, as if to finish the conversation, he said to Mr. Robinson, " I will accept no equivalent in the Low Countries; and since you have nothing to offer on the side of Silesia, all proposals are ineffectual. I will not only have the four duchies ; but, as the court of Vienna has rejected that demand, I revoke it, and require all Lower Silesia, with the town of Breslau." After frequently and peremptorily repeating his last words, he added, " If the queen does not satisfy me in six weeks, I will have four duchies more."

His indignation seemed to be still farther inflamed by the offer of Glogau, which was now made by lord Hyndford ; reiterating his demand of all Lower Silesia, he said to Mr. Robinson, " Return with this answer to Vienna; they who want peace will give me what I want." Mr. Robinson, not rebuffed by his peremptory treatment, ventured to propose a negotiation with his minister ; but Frederic disdainfully added, " I am sick of ultimatums, I will hear no more of them ; my part is taken. I again repeat my demand of all Lower Silesia ; this is my final answer, and I will give no other." He then interrupted all farther representations; and, taking off his hat, precipitately retired, with looks of high indignation, behind the interior curtain of his tent.*

Thus terminated this extraordinary conference ; and Mr. Robinson returned to Presburgh without the smallest hope of bending the inflexible spirit of the king.

* The account of this interesting conference, which exhibits the character and manners of Frederic in so striking a point of view, is taken from Mr. Robinson's Despatch to lord Harrington, dated Breslau, August 9. 1741 ; and Œuvres Posthumes, tom. i. p. 180.

Chap. C. — 1741.

On his return to Presburgh, Mr. Robinson found the court of Vienna alarmed with the first explosion of the long threatened storm. The elector of Bavaria had commenced hostilities, by taking possession of Passau, and had issued a manifesto, asserting his claims to the whole Austrian inheritance; a French army, under Broglio, was preparing to cross the Rhine; while another was assembling on the Maes, under marshal Maillebois. The king of Prussia, availing himself of his success at Molwitz, had continued his operations during the progress of the negotiation; after a short siege he had taken Brieg, removed his head quarters to Strehlen, recruited his army among the natives of Silesia, by whom he was regarded as a deliverer, and had recently seized Breslau, which the Catholic party had attempted to deliver to marshal Neuperg.

Under this pressure of distress, such was the spirit or infatuation of the queen of Hungary, that she still listened to the delusive professions of France, attempted to gain the elector of Bavaria, by offering to withdraw her husband's pretensions to the imperial crown, and obstinately refused to comply with the demands of the king of Prussia. After many demurs and quibbling distinctions, concerning the meaning of the term Lower Silesia, the queen affected to offer a division of the country. A map was accordingly marked with a line of demarcation, and presented to Mr. Robinson, who was desired to repair again to the Prussian camp, and tender this new offer to the king. The British minister in vain represented that this cession was not only far inferior to the demands of Frederic, but even less than the four duchies originally required; and, when he urged that the resolution of the Prussian monarch was taken, it was replied, "The resolution of the queen is likewise taken; and, if the house of Austria must perish, it is indifferent whether it perishes by an elector of Bavaria or by an elector of Brandenburgh."*

* " The queen," writes Mr. Robinson to lord Harrington, "had put, in her own hand, in the margin of the brouillon of count Sinzendorf's letter to me, that if the convention was not signed in the terms

With this inadequate offer, and without the smallest hope of success, Mr. Robinson again repaired to Silesia; but on his arrival at Breslau, Frederic refused to see him, and ordered his minister, count Podewilz, to declare his surprise and indignation that, after so formal and serious a demand of all Lower Silesia, he had presumed to return, with so injurious, so dishonourable, and so insidious a project, without any new credentials from his own court. "The offer," it was added, "of the court of Vienna is the highest insult, and every other article of the project captious, as it tends to involve the king in a war with France, and to draw a thorn out of the side of the court of Vienna, and thrust it deeper into the side of the king of Prussia. The king, therefore, will neither see Mr. Robinson himself, nor allow count Podewilz to treat with one whom he had so much reason to be dissatisfied with, especially as the king of England has another minister at his court in whom he places the fullest confidence." This singular message was concluded with a declaration, "That, as Mr. Robinson valued the friendship subsisting, and to subsist, between the two sovereigns, the continuation of that friendship depended on the haste with which he returned; otherwise, his Prussian majesty would not only be obliged to complain but would impute such an obstinacy to a desire in the king of England, of compelling him to treat with a person against whom he entertained such a dislike." *

This contemptuous rejection of Mr. Robinson's intervention, was followed by a letter from Frederic to lord Hyndford, announcing that he had now completed his hostile engagements with France and Bavaria, which annihilated all hopes of an immediate accommodation with the queen of Hungary.

as delivered to me, she would not be obliged to stand by it : and had enjoined count Sinzendorf to tell me, that she hoped to know in fifteen days, *à quois s'en tenir.*"

* It appears, from the Works of the king of Prussia, that he entertained a personal dislike to Mr. Robinson, for his unshaken zeal in favour of the house of Austria; at the same time, the court of Saxony complained of his supposed partiality to the king of Prussia ; and the court of Vienna, of his opposition to their interests and politics. In adverting to this singularity of his situation, Mr. Robinson observes, " I am the unfortunate victim of all three, if not approved by the king my master."—Mr. Robinson to lord Harrington, Breslau, September 2. 1741.

"I have received the new project sent by the indefatigable Robinson. It is no less chimerical than the former. You will tell the court of Vienna that the elector of Bavaria *shall* be emperor, and that my engagements with the king of France and the elector are so solemn, so indissoluble, and so inviolable, that I will never quit those faithful allies to enter into friendship with a sovereign who cannot, and who will never be reconciled to me. It is no longer time to defend the queen of Hungary, and she must learn to support all the rigour of her destiny. Are these people mad, my lord, to suppose I should be so treacherous as to turn my arms in her favour against my friends ; and can you avoid seeing the grossness of the bait they hold out to me ; I entreat you not to trouble me again with similar propositions, and to believe me so far a man of honour as not to violate my engagements."

In reviewing the progress of this negotiation on the successful termination of which even the fate of the house of Austria seemed to depend, we cannot repress our astonishment at the singular infatuation of the court of Vienna; but our surprise will diminish, when we advert to the personal character and principles of the queen of Hungary, the situation of her consort the duke of Loraine, and the views and interests of her ministers and court.

Maria Theresa had been educated as heiress to the indivisible succession of the house of Austria ; and had imbibed, from her earliest infancy, high notions of the pre-eminent dignity and power of her illustrious family. Hence she determined to assert her rights with inflexible spirit, and not to relinquish a tittle of her just pretensions, on the principle, that her inheritance was a solemn trust, which she could not alienate ; and she considered herself as irrevocably bound by the oath she had taken to support the Pragmatic Sanction. The birth of the archduke Joseph also, which happened on the 13th of March, in the midst of the negotiation, still farther strengthened her resolutions, and increased her scruples not to alienate any part of his future inheritance.

Although the duke of Loraine had been appointed coregent, transacted the business of state with the ministers of the conference, and gave audience to foreign ambassadors ; yet he had little permanent influence in the direction of affairs, as well because the spirit of the government was supposed to reside in the conference, as because the queen was not disposed to admit any participation of real authority. He was, indeed, more distinguished for the comeliness of his person, and the suavity of his manners, than for strength of understanding, or brilliancy of talents; he was fully sensible of his want of influence, and did not scruple to acknowledge that his sentiments had no weight when contrary to those of the queen. At this period, likewise, he was still less inclined and less able to take an active part in the counsels of the state, in consequence of his sentiments in regard to the king of Prussia, and the peculiar delicacy of his situation. He was well aware that his elevation to the imperial throne depended principally on the concurrence of Prussia *, and had therefore been early inclined to conciliate the friendship of the king, and credited the sincerity of his professions; but he was afterwards alienated by the contemptuous behaviour and opprobrious language of Frederic, who even charged the duke with suborning an assassin to murder him. In the heat of his resentment he treated with scorn the versatility of the Prussian monarch; and exclaimed to Mr. Robinson, who was urging the weight of his alliance, "If you have him to-day, he will be at the service of France to-morrow; and, if France has him to-day, we may have him to-morrow." Even in the most alarming crisis of the queen's affairs, though convinced that the safety of the house of Austria depended on an accommodation with the king of Prussia, he could not venture to urge his opinion, in consequence of the unpopularity which he had incurred from the ill success of his military operation in Hungary, and the charges which were circulated, that he was willing to sacrifice the territories of the house of Austria to purchase the electoral vote of Prussia.

The ministers of the conference were merely the ostensible agents of government, and count Staremberg, whom Charles VI. had recommended with his dying voice to his daughter, had fallen into dotage, acted solely from visionary

---

* In an interview with Borcke, the Prussian minister, during the illness of Charles VI. he said, "There is nobody but his Prussian majesty and the king of England that I can rely upon."—Mr. Robinson's Despatches.

notions of divine inspiration, and changed his mind as
often as he conceived himself differently inspired.

In this situation Maria Theresa was attracted by the
insinuating manners and decisive language of Bartenstein,
who, full of expedients, and fertile in resources, was alone
capable of initiating her in the affairs of state and the
forms of business. His presumptuous confidence, volubility of tongue, and the facility of his pen, combined to
dazzle an inexperienced princess; while his assiduity,
affected deference to her opinion, and enthusiasm for the
house of Austria, won her esteem and confidence. He
followed the example of count Altheim towards her father,
by endeavouring to inspire her with the same jealousy of
her own power, and high opinion of her own abilities;
he persuaded her that she ought to be her own minister,
while he overwhelmed her with papers and memorials
which she had not time to consider, and scarcely to read;
he also supplied her with arguments against her ministers,
induced her to maintain a secret correspondence with her
foreign ambassadors, of which he was the agent; and as
the duke of Loraine was a mere cipher, he directed the
affairs of government with the same absolute sway as
during the lifetime of her father.

No person had greater influence in encouraging the
queen to persevere in rejecting all offers of accommodation
with Prussia than Bartenstein, who was irritated against
Frederic, for requiring his exclusion from the conferences
with Gotter. His implacable spirit being thus roused, he
did not restrain his invectives: " The friendship of the
king of Prussa," he observed, " is worse than his enmity;
nothing but mischief can be expected from him, and the
only means of security will be to disarm him. To attempt
to rectify the king of Prussia without ruining him, would
be as much lost trouble as to wash a blackamoor white."*
These sentiments coincided too nearly with those of the
queen, to be counteracted by the earnest representations of
the Maritime Powers.

The singular infatuation of the queen in giving credit to
the professions of the French, even at the very moment
when marshal Belleisle was carrying his hostile designs
into execution, was wholly owing to the baneful influence

* Mr. Robinson to lord Harrington, April 4. 1741.

of Bartenstein, who boldly answered for their sincerity, and asserted that they would engage in no war during the life of cardinal Fleury. In vain the old ministers of the conference expatiated on the inveterate antipathy of the house of Bourbon ; in vain the duke of Loraine made the strongest remonstrances, and in vain the king of England repeatedly developed the dangerous designs of the court of Versailles. The queen of Hungary, influenced by her superior antipathy to the king of Prussia, hoped in the last extremity to disarm France by cessions in the Low Countries, and by inducing her husband to forego the imperial crown ; or if those offers failed of success, that she should be supported by the Maritime Powers and Russia ; in these hopes she was encouraged by the spirit and sentiments of the British nation.

In England the unprovoked aggression of the king of Prussia had excited general indignation ; and the wrongs of a young, beautiful, and unoffending princess roused the feelings of the people, and kindled a national enthusiasm. The minister, urged by the importunities of the king, the sentiments of the cabinet, and the public voice, yielded to the torrent. On the 8th of April, the king concluded an animated speech from the throne, by requesting the concurrence of his parliament in supporting the queen of Hungary, and maintaining the liberties and balance of power in Europe, and this speech was answered by a warm address, and a grant of £300,000 to the queen of Hungary.

In transmitting the account of these resolutions, count Ostein, the Austrian ambassador, declared that this subsidy was extorted by the general voice of the king, parliament, and people, and urged the queen not to agree with Prussia, because the English would spend the last penny of their treasure, and shed the last drop of their blood in her support. Hence the queen deemed herself secure of being assisted by the whole force of England ; hence she entertained the most sanguine expectations that the example of that nation would be followed by the United Provinces, Russia, and other powers of Europe.

Chap. CI. — 1741.

During the progress of the unfortunate negotiation with Prussia, all things concurred to strengthen the firmness of the queen, and to lull her into a fatal security with regard to the designs of France. Louis XV., naturally indolent and voluptuous, was more than ever addicted to the pursuit of his amours, and to the pleasures of the chase. Cardinal Fleury, who still held the reins of government, was on the brink of the grave, and seemed averse to plunge his country in a war which would frustrate the great object of his long administration, the recovery of the finances, and disturb the last moments of his declining life. But his benevolent efforts were counteracted by the party of the marshal and count de Belleisle, who panted for military glory, and were equally skilful in the cabinet and the field. Supported by the French nobility, and aided by the feminine cabal who directed the pleasures of the monarch, they finally roused the spirit of the king, and overcame the feeble opposition of the cardinal; their plans were mighty and gigantic, tending to no less than to confine the house of Austria within the boundaries of Hungary. But even in the midst of the warlike preparations, and while marshal Belleisle was rapidly passing from one extremity of Germany to the other to mature his schemes, the cardinal had sufficient influence to circumscribe his efforts; and with real or affected sincerity, gave repeated assurances to the court of Vienna of his pacific inclinations. Even when the French army had actually passed the Rhine, Fleury declared that this aggression was not directed against the house of Austria, but intended only to awe those princes of the empire who were hostile to France; and so great was the infatuation of the queen of Hungary, that she relied on the sincerity of these professions. But the illusion was dissipated in a moment.

The king of Prussia had scarcely rejected her last offers, before the elector of Bavaria was joined by the French army under marshal Belleisle, and pursuing his success took possession of Lintz, where he was inaugurated archduke of Austria. After despatching a body of troops to

Polten, within eight leagues of Vienna, and summoning the capital to surrender, he suddenly turned into Bohemia, and marched to invest Prague, which contained numerous magazines, and was weakly garrisoned. The other French army under Maillebois passed the Maes, and forced the king of England, who was assembling troops for the assistance of the queen of Hungary, to conclude the neutrality of Hanover; by which he engaged, as elector, not to resist the operations of the allies, nor to oppose the elevation of the Bavarian prince to the throne of the empire. Russia, involved in a war with Sweden, by the intrigues of France, was incapable of sending any succour to Maria Theresa; the electors of Saxony, Cologne, and Palatine joined the grand confederacy; Spain was preparing to make a diversion in Italy, and had already secured the neutrality of Tuscany, Genoa, the duke of Modena, and the pope; and the king of Sardinia was inclined to assist the house of Bourbon.

In Silesia, the king of Prussia, master of the capital and the greater part of the duchy, was on the point of cutting off the communication between the army of marshal Neuperg and Neiss, with a view to lay siege to that fortress, the possession of which would secure the whole province, and enable him to co-operate with the armies of France and Bavaria.

On surveying this deplorable state of affairs, the cause of Maria Theresa appeared wholly desperate: attacked by a formidable league, Vienna menaced with an instant siege, abandoned by all her allies, without treasure, without an efficient army, without able ministers, she seemed to have no other alternative than to receive the law from her most inveterate enemies. But this great princess now displayed a courage truly heroic, and, assisted by the subsidies of Great Britain, and animated by the zeal of her Hungarian subjects, rose superior to the storm.

Soon after her accession she had conciliated the Hungarians, by reviving, with the exception of the thirty-first article, the celebrated decree of Andrew II.*, which had

* Voltaire has asserted, and most modern authors have done little more than copy Voltaire, that Maria Theresa swore to observe the whole decree of Andrew II., even the thirty-first article, which declares, " Should I, or any of my successors, at any time infringe your

been abolished by Leopold; and at her coronation had received from her grateful subjects the warmest demonstrations of loyalty and affection.   Mr. Robinson, who was an eye-witness of this ceremony, has well described the impression made on the surrounding multitude.   " The coronation on the 25th was *leste*, magnificent, and well ordered.   The queen was all charm ; she rode gallantly up the royal mount*, and defied the four corners of the world with the drawn sabre, in a manner to show she had no occasion for that weapon to conquer all who saw her. The antiquated crown received new graces from her head, and the old tattered robe of St. Stephen became her as well as her own rich habit, if diamonds, pearls, and all sorts of precious stones can be called clothes."

> " Illam quicquid agit quoquo vestigia vertit,
> " Componit furtim, subsequiturque decor."†

An air of delicacy, occasioned by her recent confinement, increased the personal attractions of this beautiful princess ; but when she sat down to dine in public, she appeared still more engaging without her crown ; the heat of the weather, and the fatigues of the ceremony, diffused an animated glow over her countenance ; while her beautiful hair flowed in ringlets over her shoulders and bosom. These attractions, and the firmness of her mind, kindled the zeal and enthusiasm of that brave and high-spirited people, and to them she turned as to her principal recourse.

privileges, it is permitted you and your descendants, by virtue of this promise, to defend yourselves, without being treated as rebels." But this article was expressly excepted in the oath taken by Maria Theresa. See Voltaire, Siècle de Louis XV., and Sacy, Histoire de Hungrie, tom. 11. p. 448. and 507. who has cleared up this disputed point in the most satisfactory manner.   Sacy adds, on consulting the acts of the diet, it does not appear that the states made the least attempt to obtain from their new sovereign the ratification of the *whole* oath of Andrew II. The Hungarians had already suffered too much for the right of declaring war against their monarchs.   Instructed by past misfortunes, they were by no means desirous to obtain the confirmation of an illusive privilege, which sanctioned rebellion, and placed under the safeguard of the laws those seditious citizens whom the laws ought to punish.

    * Near Presburgh is a barrow or tumulus, called the Royal Mount, which the new sovereign ascends on horseback, and waves a drawn sword towards the four cardinal points.

    † Mr. Robinson to lord Harrington, June 28. 1741.

The grey-headed politicians of the court of Vienna in vain urged, that the Hungarians, who, when Charles VI. proposed the Pragmatic Sanction, had declared they were accustomed to be governed by men, and would not consent to a female succession, would seize this opportunity of withdrawing from the Austrian domination. But Maria Theresa formed a different judgment, and her opinion was justified by the event. She felt that a people ardent for liberty, and distinguished by elevation of soul and energy of character, indignantly reject the mandates of a powerful despot, but would shed their blood in support of a defenceless queen, who, under the pressure of misfortune, appealed to them for succour.

Having summoned the states of the diet to the castle, she entered the hall, in which the members of the respective orders were promiscuously assembled, clad in deep mourning, and habited in the Hungarian dress, with the crown of St. Stephen on her head, and the scimitar at her side, both objects of high veneration to the natives, who are devoted to the memory of their ancient sovereigns. She traversed the apartment with a slow and majestic step, and ascended the tribune, from whence the sovereign is accustomed to harangue the states. After an awful silence of a few minutes, the chancellor detailed the distressed situation of their sovereign, and requested immediate assistance.

Maria Theresa then came forward, and addressed the deputies in Latin *, a language in common use among the Hungarians, and in which, as if emulous of the spirit of ancient Rome, they preserved the deliberations of the diet and the records of the kingdom. " The disastrous situation of our affairs," she said, " has moved us to lay before our dear and faithful states of Hungary the recent invasion of Austria, the danger now impending over this kingdom, and a proposal for the consideration of a remedy. The very existence of the kingdom of Hungary, of our own person, of our children, and our crown, are now at stake. Forsaken by all, we place our sole resource in the fidelity, arms, and long-tried valour of the Hungarians ;

* The Latin is so common in Hungary, that during my travels I frequently heard the servants and postilions converse and dispute with great fluency in that language.

exhorting you, the states and orders, to deliberate without delay in this extreme danger, on the most effectual measures for the security of our person, of our children, and of our crown, and to carry them into immediate execution. In regard to ourself, the faithful states and orders of Hungary shall experience our hearty co-operation in all things, which may promote the pristine happiness of this ancient kingdom, and the honour of the people." *

The youth, beauty, and extreme distress of Maria Theresa, who was then pregnant, made an instantaneous impression on the whole assembly. All the deputies drew their sabres half out of the scabbard, and then throwing them back as far as the hilt, exclaimed, " We will consecrate our lives and arms ; we will die for our queen, Maria Theresa!" Affected with this effusion of zeal and loyalty, the queen, who had hitherto preserved a calm and dignified deportment, burst into tears of joy and gratitude ; the members of the states, roused almost to frenzy by this proof of her sensibility, testified, by their gestures and acclamations, the most heartfelt admiration, and, repairing to the diet, voted a liberal supply of men and money.

A similar and not less affecting scene took place, when the deputies assembled before the throne, to receive the oath of the duke of Loraine, who had been appointed co-regent of the kingdom, by the consent of the diet. At the conclusion of the ceremony, Francis waving his hand ex-

---

* I have principally drawn this account from the archives of Hungary, to which I had access by the kindness of count Koller, and from his communications. He was keeper of the archives, and present at the diet. With his permission I copied the speech, which is here subjoined. — " Allocutio Reginæ Hungariæ Mariæ Theresiæ, Anno 1741. Afflictus rerum nostrarum status nos movit, ut fidelibus perchari regni Hungariæ statibus de hostili provinciæ nostræ hereditariæ, Austriæ invasione, et imminente regno huic periculo, adeoquè de considerando remedio propositionem scripto faciamus. Agitur de regno Hungariæ, de personâ nostrâ, prolibus nostris, et coronâ, ab omni us derelicti, unicè ad inclytorum statuum fidelitatem, arma, et Hungarorum priscam virtutem confugimus, impensè hortantes, velint status et ordines in hoc maximo periculo de securitate personæ nostræ, prolium, coronæ, et regni quanto ocius consulere, et ea in effectum etiam deducere. Quantum ex parte nostra est, quæcunque pro pristinâ regni hujus felicitate, et gentis decore forent, in iis omnibus benignitatem et clementiam nostram regiam fideles status et ordines regni experturi sunt."

claimed, "My blood and life for the queen and kingdom!" and at the same moment the queen exhibited the infant archduke to the view of the assembly. A cry of joy and exultation instantly burst forth, and the deputies repeated their exclamations, "We will die for the queen and her family; we will die for Maria Theresa!"

The vigorous resolutions of the diet, animated by the presence of their sovereign, were supported by the nation at large; and numerous tribes, pouring from the banks of the Save, the Teiss, the Drave, and the Danube, flocked to the royal standard. These troops, under the names of Croats, Pandours, Sclavonians, Warasdinians, and Tolpaches, exhibited a new and astonishing spectacle to the eyes of Europe; by their dress and arms, by the ferocity of their manners, and their singular mode of combat, they struck terror into the disciplined armies of Germany and France. In addition to the Hungarian bands, troops were collected from all quarters, and every nerve was strained to make a grand and vigorous effort. Under the direction of general Kevenhuller, Vienna was put in a state of defence; and the burghers and students vied with the garrison in their resolution to make a desperate resistance.

In this favourable situation of the queen's affairs, divisions began to arise among her enemies. The haughty deportment of marshal Belleisle, who treated the German princes as vassals of his master, and Germany as a province of France, alienated the allies; the electors of Bavaria and Saxony, eager to share the spoils of the house of Austria, were jealous of each other's pretensions, and the elector of Bavaria, either counteracted by France and Saxony, or desirous of obtaining immediate possession of Bohemia, had turned his forces from the siege of Vienna, and hastened to the attack of Prague. The king of Prussia also was alarmed with the rapid progress of the elector of Bavaria, who, if he obtained the crown of Bohemia, might claim Silesia; he was displeased with the imperious conduct of France, and suspicious that the cabinet of Versailles was attempting to prevent his farther acquisitions. This jealousy hastened an accommodation with the queen of Hungary; he not only listened with complacency to the proposals conveyed through lord Hyndford, but even made overtures himself to marshal Neuperg; and the house of

Austria was saved by the very hand from which it had received the first wound. *

On the return of Mr. Robinson from his second journey into Silesia, the queen of Hungary was sensible of her danger, and convinced of the necessity of gaining the king of Prussia. And as Bartenstein, who had alone encouraged her obstinacy, was irritated by the perfidy of France, and urged that there was no safety to the house of Austria but in an immediate accommodation with Prussia, full powers were despatched to lord Hyndford, to offer the cession of Lower Silesia, and the town of Breslau.

After some delays and negotiations, Frederic finally delivered his ultimatum, in that brief and decisive style which marked his character. " All Lower Silesia ; the river Neiss for the boundary. The town of Neiss, as well as Glatz. Beyond the Oder the ancient limits to continue between the duchies of Brieg and Oppelen. Breslau for us. The affairs of religion in *statu quo.* No dependence on Bohemia ; a cession for ever. In return, we will proceed no farther. We will besiege Neiss for form. The commandant shall surrender and depart. We will pass quietly into winter quarters, and the Austrian army may go where they will. Let the whole be concluded in twelve days."

This negotiation was protracted by his refusal to enter into formal engagements, and the unwillingness of the court of Vienna to yield the same territory for a bare neutrality, with which they might have purchased his alliance. In the mean time, the progress of the French and Bavarian arms, the conclusion of the neutrality of Hanover, and the manœuvres of the king of Prussia, who had compelled marshal Neuperg to retire from Neiss, hastened the decision of Maria Theresa, and full powers were sent to Neuperg to cede all Lower Silesia, with the towns of Breslau and Neiss, and to secure the best conditions in return. As both parties were equally desirous of

* In the account which the king of Prussia gives of this transaction, he affects to consider all the overtures as coming from the court of Vienna ; whereas he was extremely impatient to conclude an accommodation, and even made proposals to general Lentulus, by means of colonel Goltz ; though at the same time, Goltz declared, that if the negotiation did not succeed, and was divulged, his master would disavow the proposal.—Lord Hyndford's Despatches.

a respite, the arrangements were soon made. Frederic, accompanied by colonel Goltz, met marshal Neuperg, general Lentulus, and lord Hyndford, at Ober-Schnellendorf, on the 9th of October, and a convention was drawn up and signed by lord Hyndford, to which the king only gave his verbal assent. It contained the cession of Lower Silesia, with the towns of Breslau and Neiss, and the limits specified in the king's ultimatum. It was also settled, that this convention was to be kept an inviolable secret, and if divulged by the court of Vienna, should be considered as null. To preserve appearances, it was agreed, that skirmishes should not be immediately discontinued, and that the siege and surrender of Neiss should proceed in the usual forms. Part of the Prussian army were to take up winter quarters in Upper Silesia, but were not to exact contributions, or make forced enrolments. The king promised never to demand from the queen of Hungary the cession of any other territory than Lower Silesia, and the town of Neiss; not to act offensively either against the queen, the king of England, as elector of Hanover, or any of her allies, after the surrender of Neiss; and not to molest marshal Neuperg in his march into Moravia. It was likewise agreed to endeavour to conclude a definitive treaty before the end of the year.

The king of Prussia affected great anxiety to conceal this transaction from his allies, and even exacted a written declaration from lord Hyndford, that the negotiation had proved fruitless. But although the conduct of Frederic evinced his intention to amuse the court of Vienna, and to renew hostilities whenever it suited his interests, yet this convention was highly advantageous to the queen of Hungary, as it gave her a respite from an active and enterprising enemy, and enabled her to concentrate all her efforts against the French, Bavarians, and Saxons.

Chap. CII. — 1741, 1742.

At this period all Silesia was occupied by the king of Prussia; Upper Austria, and the greater part of Bohemia, were in the possession of the French, Bavarians, and

Saxons. But the armistice with Prussia was scarcely concluded before the queen of Hungary assembled a considerable army to succour Prague, which was menaced by the
allied forces. With this view the duke of Loraine drew
together the new Hungarian levies at Znaim, and was
joined by marshal Neuperg, with the remains of the Silesian army; by count Kevenhuller, with two regiments
from the garrison of Vienna; and soon afterwards by a
corps under prince Lobcowitz, who had been stationed at
Pilsen, to observe the enemy. Being, by these accessions,
at the head of 60,000 men, he hastened to Prague; but on
the 26th of October, arrived within three leagues of the
capital only to have the mortification of hearing, that the
enemy had surprised it the preceding night, and that
general Ogilvy, the commandant, with a garrison of only
3000 men, had surrendered the citadel. On the same day,
the elector of Bavaria made his triumphant entry into the
town; was crowned king of Bohemia on the 19th of December; and, after appointing a council for the administration of affairs, took his departure for Frankfort, where the
diet of the empire was assembled.

France was now enabled to secure one of her great
objects, to wrest the imperial dignity from the house of
Austria. Maria Theresa had flattered herself with the
hopes of placing that crown on the head of her husband;
and with a view to secure for him the vote of Bohemia,
which, according to the constitutions of the empire, could
not be vested in a female, conferred on him the co-regency
of that kingdom. The legality of this transfer, however,
had been contested by the majority of the electoral college;
but as the elector of Bavaria was acknowledged king of
Bohemia, the vote was suspended for that election, by
unanimous consent.

In consequence of the neutrality of Hanover, by which
George II. was precluded from the exercise of his suffrage
in favour of the house of Austria, of the defection of
Augustus, and of the hostility of Prussia, the choice of the
college fell unanimously on the elector of Bavaria, who
was crowned at Frankfort on the 12th of February, 1742,
by the title of Charles VII.

But while Charles thus acquired an empty dignity, he
was despoiled of his hereditary dominions. The duke of

Loraine, being foiled in his attempt to relieve Prague, had retired behind the marshes of Budweiss, a position occupied by the celebrated Ziska, during the Hussite wars; where he covered the march of the Austrian detachments, which were preparing to penetrate into Bavaria. The plan of the subsequent operations was judiciously arranged, and ably executed, by Kevenhuller, the most fortunate and enterprising of all the Austrian generals. The main army, divided into two bodies, under the duke of Loraine and prince Lobcowitz, remained in Bohemia, to keep the enemy in check; while Kevenhuller, at the head of 30,000 men, advanced rapidly into Upper Austria, and blockaded Linz, whither a corps of 10,000 French, under general Segur, had been driven by the impetuous assaults of the irregulars under Mentzel, the celebrated partisan. Meanwhile general Berenclau seized the important post of Scharding on the Inn, the key of Bavaria, and routed a corps of Bavarians, detached to succour Linz. Segur, thus deprived of all hopes of relief, was compelled to surrender; and Kevenhuller, pursuing his success, obtained possession of Passau, and became master of all the passes leading into Bavaria.

These advantages were the prelude to still greater successes. Kevenhuller, pursuing his plan to cut off the resources of the enemy in Bavaria and Saxony, advanced into Bavaria, and let loose on that country the numerous irregulars which swarmed round his army. He was also assisted by a diversion from the Tyrol. The brave natives, in the most arduous crisis of the queen's affairs, had taken upon themselves the defence of their own country; and now, bursting from their mountains, ravaged the southern parts of Bavaria, and penetrated to the neighbourhood of Munich : while Kevenhuller entered the capital, without opposition, on the very day in which the unfortunate elector was chosen emperor.

In the midst of these events the king of Prussia abruptly broke the convention of Ober-Schnellendorf. He was alarmed at the progress of the Austrians in Bavaria, and apprehensive lest the queen of Hungary should again turn her arms to recover Silesia. He had previously entered into a treaty with the elector of Bavaria, and had purchased of him, as king of Bohemia, the country of Glatz for 400,000 crowns. With a view to secure this new acquisition, and consolidate his conquest of Silesia, he suddenly recommenced hostilities, entered Moravia early in 1742, he despatched marshal Schwerin to seize Olmutz, and laid siege to Glatz, which surrendered after a desperate resistance.

Frederic proved himself on this, as on all occasions, the most active and enterprising enemy of the house of Austria. Repairing to Dresden, he endeavoured to rouse the sluggish spirit of Augustus, and passed through Prague in his return to Moravia to concert a plan of operations with marshal Broglio. Having rejoined his army soon after the surrender of Glatz, he endeavoured to drive the Austrians from their advantageous position in the southern parts of Bohemia, which would have delivered the French troops in the neighbourhood, and checked the progress of Kevenhuller in Bavaria: he advanced to Iglau on the frontiers of Bohemia, occupied the banks of the Taya, from Znaim to Goedingen, made irruptions into Upper Austria, and his hussars spread terror even to the gates of Vienna.

Meanwhile the Austrians were not inactive ; a corps of 10,000 men was drawn from Bavaria to cover the capital, and the military force of Hungary assembling on the frontiers of Moravia, threatened the Prussian magazines in Upper Silesia, while prince Charles of Loraine, who was appointed commander-in-chief, prepared to advance at the head of the main army. These movements compelled Frederic to detach a considerable force for the preservation of his magazines, to evacuate Moravia, and retire to the neighbourhood of Chrudim in Bohemia. He was at this juncture quitted by the Saxons; and deriving no assistance from the French, although they had taken Egra and advanced to Piseck, he was left to support singly the whole burden of the war.

From the rupture of the armistice to the present juncture, Frederic had not ceased proposing terms of accommodation to the court of Vienna, through the intervention of lord Hyndford ; but as he increased his demands on every trifling advantage, and even required the cession of Konigsgratz and Pardubitz in Bohemia, as well as the county of Glatz, the queen of Hungary indignantly rejected all his overtures, and both parties determined to risk the event of a battle. In these circumstances prince Charles of

Loraine advanced from Moravia, whither he had marched
to relieve Brunn, passed the frontiers of Bohemia, and arrived in the neighbourhood of the Prussian quarters on the
15th of May. The two armies encountered early on the morning of the 17th. The Austrians, by a forced march, gained
the village of Czaslau on the 16th, and the following morning
advanced in four columns to attack the Prussians, posted
near Chotusitz, who were scarcely formed before the cannonade began. The numbers were nearly equal, and the
action was warmly contested on both sides; the Austrians
displayed numerous proofs of exalted courage; the infantry
retrieved the disgrace which they had incurred at the battle
of Molwitz, and the cavalry did not belie their former exertions, but lost the decisive moment by their eagerness for
plunder. At length the steadiness and discipline of the
Prussian infantry, the improved manœuvres of the cavalry,
and, above all, the activity of Frederic, decided the fortune
of the day. The Prussians remained masters of the field
of battle, with eighteen cannons, two pair of colours, and
1200 prisoners; but the Austrians retreated in good order,
and carried away fourteen standards, two pair of colours,
and 1000 prisoners. The loss on both sides was considerable: the king of Prussia computes that of the Austrians
in killed, wounded, prisoners, and deserters, at 7000 men;
his own was not inferior, and was more sensibly felt, as his
cavalry was almost ruined.

Although the victory was on the side of the Prussians,
yet the immediate consequences of this battle were highly
favourable to the queen of Hungary, as it rendered both
parties sincere in their desires for peace. The king was
disappointed of the expected advantages; and the queen of
Hungary saw the necessity of detaching an enemy who
crippled all her efforts; particularly as a corps of 10,000
men was advancing to reinforce the French army in Bohemia. Frederic lowered his demands, and made overtures of accommodation, in a manner which evinced his
extreme anxiety for peace; and lord Hyndford, in consequence of his full powers from the queen of Hungary,
signed the preliminaries at Breslau, with Podewilz, the
Prussian minister, on the 11th of June, which were afterwards ratified by both sovereigns. The queen of Hungary

ceded to the king of Prussia in full sovereignty all Upper
and Lower Silesia, with the county of Glatz, except the
towns of Troppau and Jagerndorf, and the high mountains
beyond the Oppau.   These preliminaries were formed into
a definitive treaty, which was signed at Berlin on the 28th
of July, under the guaranty of the king of England.
Augustus, as elector of Saxony, was also included in the
treaty, and agreed to withdraw his troops from the French
army, and to acknowledge the Pragmatic Sanction, which
he afterwards fulfilled.

The Austrian arms began now to be successful in all
quarters.   Just before the signature of the preliminaries,
prince Lobcowitz, who was stationed at Budweiss with
10,000 men, made an attack on Frauenberg ; Broglio and
Belleisle advanced from Piseck to relieve the town, and
a combat took place at Sahay, in which the Austrians were
repulsed with the loss of 500 men. This trifling affair was
magnified into a decisive victory ; and, according to the
words of the royal historian, " the battle of Pharsalia did
not occasion more sensation at Rome, than did this little
combat at Paris."   Marshal Broglio, elated with this advantage, and relying on the immediate junction of the king
of Prussia, remained at Frauenberg in perfect security.
But his expectations were disappointed ; Frederic had
already commenced his secret negotiations, and prince
Charles was enabled to turn his forces against the French.
Being joined by prince Lobcowitz, they attacked Broglio,
and compelled him to quit Frauenberg with such precipitation, that his baggage fell into the hands of the light
troops, and the French retreated towards Branau, harassed
by the Croats and other irregulars. The garrison of Piseck,
refusing to surrender to a detachment under Nadasti, a
body of Croats swam across the river with their sabres in
their mouths, and climbing on each other's shoulders scaled
the walls, and made the garrison prisoners of war.

The Austrians, pursuing their success against the
French, drove Broglio from Branau, and followed him to
the walls of Prague, where he found Belleisle, returned
from an unsuccessful journey to prevent the peace of Breslau, and to animate the court of Dresden.   After several
consultations, the two generals called in their posts, and
secured their army partly within the walls, and partly

within a peninsula of the Moldau, the front of which was fortified by a strong line of entrenchments.

Prince Charles occupied the White Mountain on the side of the Little Town, and general Festetitz, with 18,000 fresh men from Silesia, was stationed opposite the New Town, and completed the blockade. Soon afterwards the duke of Loraine joined the army, which now amounted to 70,000 men, and the arrival of the heavy artillery enabled the Austrians to commence the siege. Thus, except the Saxons, who were on the point of quitting the allies, and a small corps of Bavarians, the forces, which at the commencement of hostilities had threatened the extinction of the house of Austria, were shut up within the walls of Prague; while a body of 10,000 French, under the duke d'Harcourt, who had attempted to advance to the relief of their countrymen, were kept in check on the banks of the Danube, by the superior skill and activity of Kevenhuller.

Besides the success of the armies and the zeal of the people, the cause of Maria Theresa was favoured by an established prejudice prevailing in the empire, England, Holland, and even in Russia and Denmark, that the liberties of Europe depended on the destiny of the house of Austria, as the only power capable of counterbalancing the house of Bourbon. Maria Theresa, with great address, availed herself of this impression, and negotiated in every court of Europe which was not devoted to her enemies. The first and principal impulse in her favour among foreign nations was given by Great Britain, whose zeal seems to have been increased by a change in the administration. Sir Robert Walpole, whom the court of Vienna had always considered either as an enemy, or at best as a lukewarm partisan, was driven from the helm, and the management of affairs principally intrusted to lord Carteret, who had proved himself a stanch friend to the house of Austria. The new minister hastened to convey the strongest assurances of his intention to support the queen of Hungary with the whole power of the British empire; nor where his promises belied by the event. Large supplies of men and money were almost unanimously voted by parliament, the subsidies to the queen of Hungary, Denmark, and Hesse Cassel were continued, England displayed a resolution to enter with vigour into the continental war; and 16,000 men were embarked to form an army in Flanders, in conjunction with the subsidiary troops of Hanover and Hesse, and a large corps of Austrians. The dilatory spirit of the Dutch was roused by these preparations; the States resisted the repeated solicitations of the French ambassador to adopt a neutrality, augmented their army and navy, and granted a subsidy of 840,000 florins to the queen of Hungary.

A change had also taken place in the government of Russia, which afterwards proved highly favourable to the interests of the house of Austria.   Elizabeth, on the 6th of December 1741, had overturned the weak and capricious government of the regent Anne, imprisoned the infant emperor, and occupied the throne of her father, Peter the Great; but although she was assisted in this revolution by the intrigues of the marquis de la Chetardie, the French minister, the event was not less disadvantageous to the enemies of Austria.   The king of Prussia lost an able adherent by the arrest and banishment of marshal Munich; and the Russians, roused by the accession of this popular princess, redoubled their efforts against the Swedes, who had experienced a total defeat at Williamstadt, with the capture of 10,000 men.

In Italy a change equally favourable and unexpected had taken place in the affairs of the queen of Hungary. In consequence of the danger which threatened her hereditary dominions, Maria Theresa had been compelled to abandon the defence of Italy, where she could not oppose the great force assembling against her; but the subsidies of England and the zeal of her Hungarian subjects, had no sooner enabled her to stem the torrent on the side of Austria, than she turned her attention to the situation of Italy. She had contrived to retain 15,000 men, and prepared large magazines in Tuscany and the Milanese; but she placed her principal reliance on the friendly disposition of the king of Sardinia, who was alienated by the grasping ambition of the queen of Spain, and perceived that he was to support the burden of the war, to. secure the Milanese with the title of king of Lombardy for Don Philip, without reaping for himself any equivalent advantage.   To detach so important an ally from the grand confederacy, the queen of Hungary, by the instances of England, was induced to promise some cessions in the Milanese, and to transfer to the king of Sardinia her claims on the marquisate of Finale, while he engaged to prevent the introduction of foreign troops into Lombardy. But so ambiguous were the terms of this engagement, and so reluctant was the queen to comply with the demands of the king of Sardinia, that a secret article was added to the convention, by which, on the previous notice of a month, he reserved the power of receding from the alliance.

In consequence of this temporary agreement, the king of Sardinia espoused the party of Maria Theresa, at the very moment when the duke de Montemar, at the head of the Spanish and Neapolitan forces, had secured the neutrality of the pope and the concurrence of the duke of Modena, and was hastening to invade the Milanese ; while a French army was preparing to march through Savoy into Italy. By this fortunate event the French were prevented from passing the Alps during the whole campaign by a part of the Sardinian forces, while the king himself, at the head of the remainder, and assisted by the Austrians, overran the duchy of Modena, and checked the progress of the Spaniards. These operations were effectually supported by an English fleet in the Mediterranean ; and a squadron under the command of commodore Martin, by threats of an immediate bombardment, compelled the king of Naples to withdraw his troops from the Spanish army, and to engage for the maintenance of a strict neutrality.

This event weakened the Spanish forces in Italy, and prevented them from pursuing their advantages. But as the king of Sardinia drew part of his troops from the combined army to resist the Spaniards, who had entered Savoy under Don Philip, and to defend the passes of the Alps, the remainder of the campaign on the side of Modena was not distinguished by any remarkable event, and the two armies began to take up winter-quarters as early as October; the Spaniards occupying the Bolognese and Romagna, and the Austrians and Sardinians the duchies of Modena and Parma.

Chap. CIII. — 1742.

The joy and exultation of the court of Vienna at these successes were equalled only by the consternation and despair of cardinal Fleury. The aged minister, worn out with infirmities, seemed to sink even below his natural timidity; he was deeply affected by the internal distresses of the nation, the great scarcity of provisions, the increasing derangement of the finances, and the clamours of the people, who were irritated at the total defeat of those wild schemes of glory with which the war had been commenced, and trembled at the dangers gathering on their own frontiers.

He saw the king devoted to his pleasures, and governed by a violent and dissolute faction; he saw the troops under the duke d'Harcourt mouldering away on the marshy banks of the Danube; and that army which, in the preceding year, had given law to Germany, cooped up within the walls of Prague, a prey to disease and famine, and with little hopes of escaping from destruction, except by surrendering themselves prisoners of war. He saw his country deserted by Prussia and Saxony, and left without a single ally in Germany, except the new emperor, who was stripped of his territories, and draining the exhausted coffers of France for his subsistence. He saw the hostile spirit of England pervading every part of Europe, and the house of Austria rising with fresh vigour from its late depression, and forming the centre of a grand confederacy against the house of Bourbon.

Under these impressions he endeavoured to evade the storm by submission, and to purchase the deliverance of the armies in Germany by an immediate peace. He accordingly made proposals, in a letter to count Konigsegg, who commanded the army under the duke and prince Charles of Loraine, in which he exculpated himself, and threw the blame of the war on Belleisle. The only answer to this weak and humiliating offer was, the circulation of the letter, by order of the queen of Hungary; and a second, in which the cardinal remonstrated against this breach of confidence, was likewise given to the public.*

* These two letters are given in the Annals of Europe for 1742, p. 422–425.

Notwithstanding this insult, the conferences were after-wards renewed. Marshal Belleisle, who at first despised the efforts of the Austrians, and deemed himself secure of an honourable retreat, was alarmed at the distress of the army, and appeared sincere and anxious for an accommo-dation. He offered to evacuate Prague, and to quit the territories of the queen of Hungary, on the condition of retaining the arms, artillery, and baggage. On the other hand, these offers were favourably received by the duke of Loraine, who was desirous to secure the title of king of the Romans by a peace with France. In these sentiments he was confirmed by prince Charles and count Konigsegg, from their apprehensions of the difficulties which would result from a protracted siege against a considerable army, resolved to hold out to the last extremity, and inspired with the hopes of speedy relief.

But all overtures were disdainfully rejected by Maria Theresa. In answer to the further solicitations of car-dinal Fleury, she said, in the presence of the whole court, " I will grant no capitulation to the French army ; I will receive no proposition, no project from the cardinal : let him address himself to my allies." Adverting to the offers of Belleisle, she exclaimed, " I am astonished that he should make any advances ; he who, by money and pro-mises, excited almost all the princes of Germany to crush me. I have acted," she added, " with too much condescen-sion to the court of France ; compelled by the necessity of the times, I debased my royal dignity, by writing to the cardinal in terms which would have softened the most ob-durate rocks ; he insolently rejected my entreaties ; and the only answer I obtained was, that his most Christian ma-jesty had contracted engagements which he could not violate. I can prove, by documents in my possession, that the French endeavoured to excite sedition even in the heart of my dominions ; that they attempted to overturn the fun-damental laws of the empire, and to set fire to the four corners of Germany ; and I will transmit these proofs to posterity, as a warning to the empire."

The queen of Hungary was encouraged to reject all overtures from France, by the example of the British cabinet, as well as by the counsels of her own ministers. Lord Carteret warmly promoted the views of George II.

to engage in the continental war, and to dismember the territories of France. He was seconded by the zeal of lord Stair, commander-in-chief of the forces in the Low Countries, who, inspired with an equal antipathy against France, suggested schemes of aggrandisement to the court of Vienna, and proposed that the house of Austria should retain Bavaria, and indemnify the emperor by conquests from the enemy. The ministers of the conference warmly entered into these views, which were congenial to the character and temper of the sovereign; and Bartenstein, the soul of the cabinet, from disappointment and indignation, was no less violent than count Staremberg, "whose Austrian inveteracy against France was petrified through the course of fourscore years." Hence Maria Theresa not only expected to recover Loraine, and the dominions which had been wrested from her father in Italy, but also to recover Alsace, and to retain Bavaria.

As a prelude to these successes, she looked forward to the capture of the French armies in Bavaria and at Prague, who seemed abandoned to their fate, by the despondency and weakness of cardinal Fleury. Like her enemies, at the commencement of the war, she indulged herself in dreams of conquest and dismemberment, and parcelled out the territories of the emperor, and of the house of Bourbon, to herself and her allies, as France had divided the inheritance of the house of Austria. She was, however, disappointed in these sanguine expectations; the party in France which had supported the war gained the ascendency, and strained every nerve to retrieve their affairs, and to extricate the armies from their perilous situation. Secure of the neutrality of the Dutch, and aware that England, without their concurrence, would not venture to commence offensive operations on the Continent, the French cabinet formed the bold project of marching the army of Maillebois, which was stationed in Westphalia, towards Prague, a distance of 600 miles, through a country full of defiles, and overrun by the troops of the enemy. This plan was executed with equal promptitude and resolution. A corps being collected in Flanders, to watch the motions of the English, Maillebois advanced by rapid marches towards Bavaria, and arrived, on the 14th of September, at Amberg, in the Upper Palatinate. Here he was joined by marshal Seckendorf, at the head of the Bavarians; and the duke of Harcourt's army, under the command of count Saxe, who, deceiving Kevenhuller by his masterly manœuvres, had extricated the troops from their dangerous position, and formed a junction with the main army at this critical moment. With this force, amounting to not less than 60,000 men, Maillebois directed his efforts to the side of Prague; after detaching Seckendorf to take possession of Bavaria, he continued his march to Egra, and received the pleasing intelligence that Broglio, with 12,000 men from Prague, had advanced to the neighbourhood of Leutmeritz, to effect a junction.

During this period the trenches had been opened before Prague, and the siege pushed with great vigilance, but with little skill or effect. The French were reduced to great extremities from the scarcity of provisions; and for several weeks the soldiers subsisted almost on bread and water, and even horseflesh was considered as a delicacy for the officers and the sick. In this distress they made continual sallies, and though they retarded the operations of the Austrians, and on the 12th of August, in one instance gained a decided advantage, yet they were still shut up within the precincts of the town.

On the approach of Maillebois new overtures were made by the duke of Loraine; and his proposals were even transmitted to the French cabinet. But the queen of Hungary issued orders to forbid all conferences, " that count Konigsegg might be no longer amused by the fulsome speeches and insidious confidences of Belleisle." Jealous of the authority which her husband seemed disposed to assume, she declared, " she would not suffer a council at the army and a council at Vienna; she disclaimed, disallowed, and disavowed all such pernicious and unsanctioned proceedings, let the blame fall where it would;" she even ordered the duke of Loraine to reject any proposal from France, which did not comprehend cessions in Bavaria, and to elude any condition, however conformable to his own offers, as her whole view and determined resolution were, to destroy the French in Germany.

In obedience to this mandate, the Austrians continued their operations; but on the approach of Maillebois, prince Charles, leaving a corps of irregulars in the vicinity of the town, advanced to check the progress of the French army. Broglio had seized this opportunity to quit Prague, and hastened to Leutmeritz with his corps of 12,000 men ; but prince Charles, being joined by Kevenhuller, occupied the passes of Satz and Caden, and thus obstructed the advance of the army of Maillebois to Prague.

The troops of Maillebois, reduced and debilitated by the fatigues of their long march, were incapable of forcing the defiles ; and being deprived of provisions from Saxony, were compelled to quit an exhausted country, and fall back into the Upper Palatinate. From hence the French general endeavoured to alarm the enemy for Upper Austria, and turned towards the Danube, which he passed on the 12th of December; but prince Charles, having anticipated his design by occupying Passau, which covered that country, Maillebois relinquished all hopes of relieving Prague, and took up his winter quarters between the Iser, the Inn, and the Danube. Broglio, unable to effect a junction with Maillebois, collected provisions and necessaries, and led his troops back to Prague ; from whence, escaping in disguise, he reached the French army, and on the 18th of December assumed the command, in place of Maillebois, who was recalled.

The Austrians being left masters of Bohemia, prince Lobcowitz, with 18,000 men, resumed the blockade of Prague. The situation of the French was soon rendered desperate by the severity of the season, and the want of provisions and fuel. The blockade continued several weeks, and the court of Vienna hourly expected the unconditional surrender of this remnant of the French forces, when they were surprised with the intelligence that Belleisle had effected a retreat.

From the severity of the weather, and the exhausted state of the adjacent country, which had been wasted by order of prince Charles, to the extent of two leagues round the city, prince Lobcowitz had taken up his quarters beyond the Moldau, at the distance of twenty miles. He left only a detachment of hussars to observe the French, whom he considered as incapable of forcing a march of a hundred miles through a country covered with snow, broken by almost impassable mountains, abounding in defiles, and infested by his irregulars ; and he was encouraged in this opinion by the state of the enemy, who were debilitated by sickness, and totally unprovided with clothing. Belleisle availed himself of these circumstances, deceived the inhabitants of the town, and forming 11,000 foot and 3000 horse into a single column, with 30 pieces of cannon, and provisions for twelve days, departed on the night of the 16th of December, leaving the sick and wounded with a guard in the citadel.

He passed through an open country, thirty miles in extent, without receiving any check, except from the desultory attacks of the hussars and light troops, avoided the defiles which were occupied by the enemy, crossed frozen morasses, penetrated through almost impassable woods, and reached Egra on the twelfth day, without losing more than an hundred men from the assaults of the enemy. But no European army ever experienced more dreadful sufferings; the soldiers, without any other subsistence than frozen bread, compelled to sleep on snow and ice, without a covering, and perpetually harassed by flying parties, perished in great numbers. "The roads," says the historian of Bohemia, "were dreadful to behold : they were overspread with corpses ; heaps of one and two hundred men each, with their officers, were found stiffened with the frost, or dead with fatigue." Twelve hundred men sunk under these distresses ; many whose members were frozen were obliged to undergo amputation at Egra, and the remainder were thinned by the ravages of a dreadful fever. During the whole retreat Belleisle himself, although severely afflicted with the rheumatism, and unable either to walk or ride, was carried in his coach or sedan to all parts where his presence was necessary ; he reconnoitred and pointed out the roads, and superintended all the detail of the march. But notwithstanding the losses of his army, he had the satisfaction of preserving the flower of the French forces, of saving every cannon which bore the arms of his master, and of not leaving the smallest trophy to grace the triumph of the enemy.

The remainder of the French troops, amounting to only 6000 men, and those mostly invalids, seemed an easy prey ; and prince Lobcowitz, who was irritated at the escape of Belleisle, insisted on their unconditional surrender. But their gallant commander, Chevert, rejected such an humili-

ating condition, and replied to the officer who bore the
summons, " Tell the prince, that if he will not grant me
the honours of war, I will set fire to the four corners of
Prague, and bury myself under its ruins." From a desire
to preserve the capital of Bohemia, this condition was accepted, and Chevert marched out with the honours of war,
and joined the army at Egra.*

This extraordinary and unexpected retreat was unjustly
attributed to collusion ; but the empress queen was unable
to conceal from her confidants the emotions of her anger
and disappointment, and was less gratified by the recovery
of the town than chagrined at the escape of her enemies.†
She did not, however, display her disappointment in public,
but celebrated the surrender of Prague by a magnificent
and gallant entertainment. Among other festivities, it was
distinguished by a chariot race in imitation of the Greeks,
in which, to exhibit the triumph of her sex, ladies alone
were permitted to contend ; and Maria Theresa herself,
with her sister, entered the lists.

Thus, at the termination of the campaign, all Bohemia
was regained, except Egra ; and on the 12th of May, 1743,
Maria Theresa was soon afterwards crowned at Prague, to
the recovery of which, says her great rival, her firmness
had more contributed than the force of her arms.

The only reverse which the Austrians experienced in
the midst of their successes was the temporary loss of
Bavaria, which on the retreat of Kevenhuller, was occupied by marshal Seckendorf ; and the emperor made his
entry into Munich on the 2d of October.

On the 2d of January Belleisle, leaving a garrison at
Egra, quitted that town, and reconducted his army to Spire,
where it was to cross the Rhine. He thus closed this
singular expedition, in which he entered Germany as a
legislator and a conqueror, at the head of 40,000 men, and
returned to France, humiliated and a fugitive, with only
8000.

* Memoires de Richelieu, tom. 6. p. 251. ; Pelzel, p. 885.
† Mr. Robinson's Despatches, 1742. In all his letters at this
period, he mentions the inveterate animosity of the queen against
the French, and the extreme agony of her mind on their escape from
Prague.

Chap. CIV. — 1743.

The commencement of 1743 was distinguished by the death of cardinal Fleury, who died at Issy on the 30th of January, in the ninetieth year of his age. He had governed France during a period of seventeen years, with the most upright disinterestedness and unblemished integrity; but he was better calculated to superintend the regulations of peace than to direct the operations of war; and by his attention to the recovery of the finances, had exposed himself to the censure of suffering the marine to fall into decay, and of repressing the military ardour of the nation.

Louis XV. seemed like an heir emancipated from a long minority, and formed the resolution of directing, himself, the helm of government. He therefore appointed no prime minister; and, in imitation of Louis XIV., transacted business with the chiefs of each department. But this transitory ardour soon subsided; his devotion to pleasure again gained the ascendency; and the conduct of affairs being left to the heads of the different offices, the kingdom was governed by the principal ministers of state, who were independent of each other, and acted with little concert or harmony.

The counsels of France were distracted at home, and her influence rapidly declining abroad, while the cause of Maria Theresa was triumphant in every part of Europe. The zeal of the king and parliament of England had not abated; the subsidy of 300,000*l*. was continued to the queen of Hungary; another of 200,000*l*. voted for the king of Sardinia; and the army in Flanders, under the command of the earl of Stair, prepared to cross the Rhine, and to act in Germany as auxiliaries. The States-general displayed their hostile disposition to France by furnishing a contingent of 6000 men, and by preparing still farther succours; the Swedes, worsted in every engagement, were unable to continue hostilities, and Russia had concluded a defensive alliance with England; Maria Theresa was therefore enabled to turn her whole force against the house of Bourbon.

The first efforts of the campaign were directed on the side of Bavaria. Prince Charles took the field early in May; and, assisted by the counsels of the enterprising Kevenhuller, disconcerted the enemy by the rapidity and decision of his movements. He drove the advanced posts of the French back on the Iser; and, suddenly turning towards Branau, routed, after a desperate attack, a corps of Bavarians strongly intrenched at Erblach, took their standards, baggage, and artillery, and made 6000 men, with the commander-in-chief, Minuzzi, and many other officers, prisoners. He then resumed his operations against the French, and compelled Broglio, though reinforced by a detachment of 12,000 men from the army of Noailles, to fall back to the Rhine. During these operations prince Lobcowitz blockaded Egra, drove count Saxe with great loss from the Upper Palatinate, and then advanced towards the Danube to co-operate with prince Charles. At the same time baron de Stenitz made an irruption from the Tyrol, and ravaged the southern parts of Bavaria.

The unfortunate emperor, alarmed by the rapid progress of the Austrians, quitted Munich with precipitation, and being hopeless of assistance from the French, ordered Seckendorf, who with a small body of troops, still held out in Bavaria, to conclude a treaty of neutrality, by which he renounced his pretensions to the Austrian succession, and yielded his dominions to the queen of Hungary, till the conclusion of a general peace. The Bavarian troops were accordingly withdrawn into Franconia; and the emperor, stripped of all his territories, retired to Ofburgh, an imperial city, and afterwards to Frankfort.

The king of England, being relieved from his apprehensions for Hanover by the march of Maillebois into Germany, prepared to take an active part against the French as an auxiliary to the queen of Hungary. The British and Austrian troops in the Netherlands, under the earl of Stair, directed their march towards the Main; and, being joined in their way by several corps of Hessians and Hanoverians, passed the Rhine on the 14th of May, and arrived on the 23rd in the neighbourhood of Frankfort. Meanwhile, a French army assembled on the Rhine under Noailles, and occupied the banks of the Neckar to retard the march of the allies into Germany, and prevent their junction with prince Charles of Loraine. With a view, therefore, to gain the Upper Main, lord Stair pushed forwards to Aschaffenburgh, where he established his head-quarters ; but his progress was arrested by the vigilance of the French general, who occupied the defiles above Aschaffenburgh, and the posts on the Upper Main ; and secured the command of the Lower Main by throwing bridges over the river at Selingenstadt. The allied army thus confined to the vicinity of Aschaffenburgh, and unable to draw subsistence either from the Upper or Lower Main, began to experience great scarcity of provisions. At this juncture, George II., accompanied by the duke of Cumberland and lord Carteret, arrived at the head-quarters to witness the deplorable situation of his troops, who were reduced to the alternative of surrendering themselves prisoners of war, or of cutting their way through an enemy superior in numbers, and masters of all the defiles.

The arrival of the king infused a new spirit into the army ; and it was resolved to force their way to Hanau, the principal depository of their magazines, where a corps of 12,000 Hanoverians and Hessians had just arrived. The army decamped at midnight on the 27th, and Aschaffenburgh was instantly occupied by the French. At the same time a large body of the enemy crossed the river at Selingenstadt, and drew up in order of battle, their right against Welmisheim and the bank of the Main, and their left, covered by a wood, behind the Beck or rivulet of Dettingen, which, flowing in a deep ravine, was passable only by a single bridge. The allies were thus cooped up in a narrow plain, closed with hills, woods, and morasses on the right, and on the left by the Main, the steep bank of which on the opposite side was planted with numerous batteries. Notwithstanding these obstacles, they continued their march, exposed to the incessant fire of the French artillery, and advancing almost to Dettingen, formed on a narrow front as well as the nature of the ground would permit. Though full of ardour, and encouraged by the presence of the king, they could scarcely have surmounted the obstacles of nature and art, had they not been extricated by the inadvertence of the enemy.

The duke de Grammont, nephew of Noailles, who commanded that part of the French army which was stationed

near the defile of Dettingen, being encouraged by the disorder into which the allies were thrown by the fire of the
batteries, and eager to signalise himself, quitted his impregnable position, crossed the rivulet, and advanced into
the plain.   This blind impetuosity frustrated all the wise
dispositions of the commander-in-chief; he thus rendered
useless the French batteries beyond the Main, while his
own troops were exposed to a heavy fire, and compelled to
engage on equal ground with superior numbers.   Lord
Stair availed himself of this fortunate circumstance, and
was seconded by the presence of the king, and the skill of
count Neuperg the Austrian commander.   The confederate
forces after a general shout, which was the omen of victory,
advanced with undaunted resolution, and by their irresistible
impetuosity, compelled the enemy to give way.   Many of
the French regiments, particularly the household troops,
displayed uncommon valour, but were repulsed with great
slaughter ; and Noailles, who hastened with a reinforcement, was compelled to recross the Main with the loss of
5000 men killed, wounded, and taken prisoners.

Though the king took no part in the dispositions of this
battle, he displayed great personal bravery, and several
times led his cavalry and infantry to the charge.   The
duke of Cumberland was wounded in the leg, and gave a
signal proof of his humanity.   After the engagement,
when the surgeon was preparing to extract the ball, he
observed a French musqueteer brought near his tent,
dreadfully wounded, " Begin," he said, " by relieving that
French officer, he is more wounded than I am ; he may
want assistance, and I shall not."   This victory, though
purchased by the allies with a considerable loss, only secured their retreat.   The king dined on the field, and the
army, leaving their sick and wounded to the care of the
French, decamped and marched to Hanau.

The battle of Dettingen may rather be considered as an
unexpected and fortunate escape, than as an important
and decisive engagement; it was however triumphantly
celebrated by the allies, and the exploits of the king com-
pared with those of Marlborough and Eugene.   At Vienna
it occasioned a delirium of joy; the queen, in returning
from an excursion by water, was hailed by multitudes of
people, who, pouring from Vienna, crowded the banks of

the Danube for the space of nine miles. She entered the
capital in a species of triumph, and celebrated the victory
by a Te Deum in the cathedral. In making an eulogium
of George II., she expressed, with a mixture of humility
and pride, a modest sense of her own unworthiness to deserve these favours from heaven, otherwise than as an
instrument in the hands of Providence to raise the house
of Austria in her person, in proportion to its recent depression.

Her sanguine expectations were at this time buoyed up
by the favourable state of her own and the allied army,
the depression of the emperor, and the despondency of
the French. The capture of Egra on the 7th of September, secured the possession of all her hereditary countries;
and prince Charles of Loraine, after forcing the emperor
to agree to a neutrality, had reached the Rhine in the
neighbourhood of Manheim, at the head of an army flushed
with success, and equal in numbers, discipline, and appointment, to any which had been hitherto assembled by the
house of Austria.

The great scheme of dismembering France was now
brought to maturity; and prince Charles, accompanied by
Kevenhuller, hastened to Hanau to concert with the king
of England a plan of operations. The combined army,
now amounting, by the junction of the Dutch, to 50,000
men, was to cross the Rhine at Mentz, and to occupy
Alsace, while prince Charles was to pass that river from
the Austrian Brisgau, and overrun Loraine, Franche Comté,
and Burgundy. The king of England accordingly crossed
the Rhine at Mentz, on the 22nd of August, and took up
his head-quarters at Worms; while prince Charles prepared to penetrate into France in the vicinity of Brisac.
But this plan was impeded by the opposite views of the
confederate powers, by the disputes which agitated the
allied army, by the secret negotiations for peace, and by
the discordant counsels of England.

The camp of the allies soon became a scene of discord
and confusion; the impetuous temper of lord Stair was
irritated by the rejection of his proposal to cross the Main,
and pursue the enemy after the late battle; while the
Austrian generals, considering their allies as mere auxiliaries, expected to direct all operations according to the

views and interests of their sovereign ; the Dutch were
dilatory and averse to action, and the British troops, jealous of the king's partiality to his German subjects, gave
way to national antipathy, and broke out into bitter invectives against the Hanoverians. An army thus composed
was not capable of acting with spirit and unanimity ; and
its operations were still more embarrassed by the complicated negotiations which had been opened for peace.

The emperor, deprived of his dominions, and disappointed of the subsidies of France, was reduced to extreme
necessity, and made overtures for a reconciliation to
George II., through the medium of prince William of
Hesse. Preliminaries were accordingly settled, by which
he renounced his claims on the Austrian dominions, broke
off his connection with France, and agreed to other conditions advantageous to the house of Austria. In return
he was to be acknowledged head of the empire, to receive
a provisional subsidy for the maintenance of his dignity,
and to be restored to his dominions. George II. even agreed
to advance 300,000 crowns within forty days, and use his
influence to gain the concurrence of the queen of Hungary.
This accommodation was prevented by the aversion of
Maria Theresa, who aspired to depose the emperor, and
retain Bavaria, and by the opposition of the council of
regency in England, who were actuated by a jealousy of
lord Carteret. But the last, and perhaps the most powerful, cause of the inactivity of the allied army, was derived from the desire of George II. to extort from the
queen of Hungary the cessions promised to the king of
Sardinia in the preceding year, which she evaded by every
possible pretence.

In Italy, hostile operations had commenced early in the
year. The queen of Spain, irritated with the ill success of
the preceding campaign, had recalled Montemar, and
given the command to the count de Gages, who had distinguished himself by his enterprising spirit. In the beginning of 1743, while the troops were in cantonments,
this imperious woman ordered the new general to attack
the enemy within three days, or to resign the command.
Gages obeyed this peremptory mandate with equal spirit
and address ; he secretly drew his troops together, and on
the 3rd of February, with his officers, slipped from a ball

with which he amused the people of Bologna, and marched at the head of his army to surprise the Austrians in their quarters. Though the strictest precaution had been taken to conceal his design, marshal Traun was fortunately apprised of the intended attack, and had assembled his troops at Campo Santo. A desperate engagement took place, which began at four o'clock in the afternoon, and continued by moonlight till after seven. The Spaniards were superior in number, and in the beginning of the action obtained some advantage over the Austrian cavalry, but were at length compelled to retreat with considerable loss. Having taken several colours, standards, kettle-drums, and cannon, they claimed the victory, which was celebrated by a Te Deum at Madrid. The advantage, however, was decidedly in favour of the confederates, and Traun receiving a reinforcement from Germany, Gages quitted Bologna in March, and retired to Rimini with his army, reduced almost to 12,000 men.

The remainder of the campaign was not equal to this successful commencement. Elated with her successes in Germany, and the hopeless situation of the French troops in Bohemia, the queen of Hungary undervalued the advantages derived from the assistance of the king of Sardinia, and did not consider that his defection might still occasion the certain loss of her dominions in Italy. She, therefore, had thrown obstacles in the way of the promised cessions; and, in answer to the repeated exhortations of George II., peevishly exclaimed, " It is the system of England to.lead me from one sacrifice to another. I must expose my troops to certain destruction for no other end than to strip myself of my own accord. Should the cessions to the king of Sardinia be extorted from me, what remains in Italy will not be worth defending, and the only alternative left is that of being stripped either by England or France." The king of Sardinia, also, with the characteristic avidity of the house of Savoy, grasped at more than he had at first demanded; while the violent and captious spirit of the marquis d'Ormea contributed still farther to alienate the court of Vienna. The queen of Hungary, therefore, persisted in her refusal of the promised cessions, and the whole summer passed in fruitless negotiation. At length the king of Sardinia, irritated by these repeated delays, threatened that without an immediate compliance with his demands, he would unite his arms with those of France, Spain, and the emperor, against the house of Austria. This threat, aided by the representations of England, extorted the reluctant consent of Maria Theresa; and on the 2nd of September, 1743, her plenipotentiary, baron Wasner, signed an offensive and defensive alliance with the British and Sardinian ministers at Worms.

The queen of Hungary ceded the city and part of the duchy of Placentia, the Vigevanesco, part of the duchy of Pavia, and the county of Angiera; she likewise yielded her pretensions to the marquisate of Finale, which had been mortgaged to the Genoese; and also engaged to maintain 30,000 men in Italy, to be commanded by the king of Sardinia. The king was to employ 45,000 men under the condition of receiving an annual subsidy of 200,000*l*. from Great Britain, and the sum of 300,000*l*. for the liquidation of the mortgage on Finale; and, in addition to these sums, Great Britain agreed to send a strong squadron into the Mediterranean, to act in concert with the allied forces in Italy.

In the midst of these negotiations the allied armies in Italy continued inactive. But on the conclusion of the treaty of Worms, prince Lobcowitz, having succeeded marshal Traun in the command, drove the Spaniards from Rimini, and compelled them to retire beyond the Foglia. In consequence, however, of the lateness of the season, both armies took up winter quarters, the Spaniards at Pesaro, Fano, and Senegallia, and the Austrians at Rimini, Forli, and Cesano.

On the side of the Alps a combined army of French and Spaniards, under Don Philip, re-entered Savoy, and having overrun the whole duchy, attempted on the 7th and 8th of October, to penetrate into Piedmont, by forcing the lines near Chateau Dauphin, which secured the pass of the Alps. Being, however, repulsed with great loss by the king of Sardinia, in person, they were compelled by the approach of winter to retire into Provence and Dauphiné.

During the negotiations for the treaty of Worms, the confederate army in Germany remained inactive, while prince Charles in vain attempted to pass the Rhine near New Brisac. From this period no effectual movement was made, and nothing passed except desultory irruptions of the Austrian irregulars into Alsace and Loraine. In October the combined army retired into winter quarters; the English, Austrians, and Hanoverians in British pay returned into Flanders; the Dutch marched into Brabant and Guelderland; and the Hessians and other Hanoverians to their respective countries; while prince Charles, leaving part of his army in the Brisgau, dispersed the rest in Bavaria, Bohemia, and Upper Austria. Toward the close of this campaign, the entire recovery of Bohemia was completed by the surrender of the French garrison at Egra, which had held out with unexampled perseverance, and in the midst of distress greater than their countrymen had suffered at Prague, till the 7th of September.

At the close of the campaign prince Charles of Loraine returned to Vienna, and espoused the archduchess Mary Anne, sister of the queen of Hungary, to whom he had been long attached; and, as a reward for his great services, was appointed, in conjunction with his consort, to the government of the Austrian Netherlands. She was a princess of a meek and amiable temper; but this happy union was of short duration, as she died in child-bed at the conclusion of the ensuing year.

Chap. CV. — 1744.

The winter was passed by the belligerent powers in vast preparations for the ensuing campaign. Hitherto England and France had engaged simply as auxiliaries, without any formal declaration of war; the one in support of the queen of Hungary, and the other in favour of the emperor and Spain. But this year the two rival nations became principals, and brought forward their whole strength by land and sea in this arduous contest.

At this period the efforts of England were debilitated, and her councils distracted by feuds in the cabinet and the violence of contending parties.

Encouraged by these domestic broils, cardinal Tencin, minister of state, who was elevated to the purple by Jacobite

interest, projected an invasion of England in favour of the
dethroned family.   Eighteen ships of the line, having on
board 4000 land forces, suddenly appeared off the isle of
Wight, and the son of the pretender, with marshal Saxe,
who commanded the expedition, came in sight of the
English coast.   Fortunately a sudden storm dispersed the
armament, and the squadron was driven back in a shattered
state to the ports of France.   This attempt, though unsuccessful, produced an instantaneous effect; terror and indignation spread through all ranks, the divisions in the
cabinet were suspended, the public clamour ceased, the
war against France became popular ; the parliament voted
larger supplies than had ever before been granted, and the
cause of the house of Austria was promoted with redoubled
enthusiasm.

Nor was France more backward in her hostile preparations; war was formally declared against Great Britain
and Austria, and, besides the arrangements for the invasion of England, 100,000 men were assembled on the side
of Flanders.   The king himself repaired to Lisle, to take
the command of this force, and in the space of two months
captured Courtray, Menin, Ypres, Fort la Knoque, and
Furnes.

This rapid progress was no less owing to the deficiency
of the allied army, and to the incapacity and divisions of
the generals, than to the military skill of marshal Saxe,
and the enthusiasm of the soldiers, who were inspired by
the presence of Louis XV.   Part of the British troops
having been drawn into England against the projected invasion, and the other confederates being deficient in their
respective contingents, the army, which ought to have
amounted to 80,000, did not exceed 50,000 men.   Marshal
Wade, the commander of the British troops, was a man of
a fretful and indolent disposition, and these defects were
heightened by his advanced age.   He was thwarted by the
duke of Aremberg, general of the Austrian forces, who was
more anxious to cover his own estates in the vicinity of
Hainault, than to act for the advantage of the common
cause.   Prince Maurice of Nassau, who commanded the
Dutch, and was shackled by private instructions, was an
equal check on his operations, from a fear of irritating the
French, whom the States were still desirous of conciliating.

These discordant views and characters produced endless divisions, and reduced the allies almost to a state of inaction; while marshal Saxe was at the head of an army almost double in numbers, provided with a train of artillery superior to any ever before brought into the field, and animated by the presence of the sovereign. Being unshackled by instructions, or thwarted by jealousies, he was enabled to give full scope to his great military talents, and to display that vigour and decision which marked all his operations; he bore down all before him, and no obstacle seemed likely to prevent the entire conquest of the Low Countries, when the Austrians burst like a torrent into Alsace.

The defence of Alsace had been intrusted to the marshal de Coigny, who posted his principal force on the Queich, while the remnant of the Bavarian troops under Seckendorf entrenched themselves on the side of Philipsburgh; and the banks of the Rhine, from Mentz to Fort Louis, were secured by every precaution. Prince Charles, however, deceived the French commander by detaching general Berenclau towards Gernesheim, as if he intended to effect a passage on that side, while Nadasti and Trenk crossed the Rhine in boats, at the head of 9000 hussars and pandours, and surprised three Bavarian regiments posted above Philipsburgh. Under the protection of this corps bridges were constructed near the village of Schreck, and prince Charles crossed the Rhine with his whole army without loss, while Berenclau effected a passage at Weissenau, near Mentz. The Austrian commander successively made himself master of the lines of Spire, Gernesheim, and Lauterburgh, secured the important post of Weissemburgh, and thus established himself in the heart of Alsace, with an army of 60,000 men.

Meanwhile Coigny retreated to Landau, where he was joined by Seckendorf. With a view to recover the important lines on the Lauter, he attacked Weissemburgh, which was occupied by Nadasti with 10,000 men, and, after a conflict of six hours, succeeded in forcing the entrenchments; but perceiving himself too weak to pursue his success, he retreated on the approach of prince Charles, threw reinforcements into Fort Louis and Strasburgh, and fell back behind the Motter. The Austrians re-occupied Weis-

semburgh, blockaded Fort Louis, and prince Charles prepared to enter Loraine; while his irregulars spread terror
to the gates of Luneville, and compelled Stanislaus to retire
with all his court.   In consequence of this rapid success,
the king of France, renouncing his projects in the Low
Countries, left marshal Saxe to maintain his conquests, despatched 30,000 men under Noailles to reinforce marshal
Coigny, and was hastening to take the command of the
army in Alsace, when he was seized at Mentz with an
illness which threatened his life.   This event, however, did
not suspend the march of the troops; Noailles passed the
Vosges and joined Coigny at Molsheim; 10,000 men under
the duke d'Harcourt advanced to Pfalzburgh, and a third
corps under Belleisle was assembling in the three bishoprics.

Prince Charles was preparing to make head against the
accumulated forces which were gathering around him,
when he was recalled to arrest the progress of the king of
Prussia, who had again resumed hostilities.

Maria Theresa had roused the indignation of many
princes of the empire; she had contemptuously rejected all
overtures of pacification, and refused to acknowledge the
emperor and the diet of Frankfort; she did not affect to
conceal her resolution to appropriate Bavaria, and had even
compelled the natives to take the oath of allegiance.   She
meditated gigantic projects of conquests in France and
Italy, and, elated with the success of her arms, gave suspicions that she had formed the plan of recovering Silesia
and dismembering the Prussian dominions in conjunction
with England and Saxony.

Frederic was too jealous of the house of Austria, and too
well acquainted with the character of Maria Theresa, to
remain indifferent to these surmises, and he became the
soul of a new confederacy, which again involved the empire
in war, and endangered the hereditary possessions of the
house of Austria.   With his usual secresy he formed the
project of a convention, which was signed on the 13th of
May, 1744, at Frankfort on the Main, with the emperor,
France, the elector Palatine, and the king of Sweden as
landgrave of Hesse.   He beheld with alarm the rapid progress of prince Charles in Alsace, and seized this critical
opportunity, when the Austrian dominions were drained of
troops, to re-commence hostilities.   He affected great dis-

interestedness; and in a manifesto, which he published on the 9th of August, when the plan of aggression was matured, required nothing for himself, and declared that he took arms only to restore to the German empire its liberty, to the emperor his dignity, and to Europe repose.

This declaration was scarcely published before he entered Bohemia at the head of a considerable army, advanced to Prague, after a short resistance forced that capital to surrender on the 16th of September, and took the garrison of 15,000 men prisoners of war. On the capture of Prague he reduced Tabor, Budweiss, and Frauenberg, and made himself master of all Bohemia to the east of the Moldau. At the same time a corps of Bavarians and Hessians under Seckendorf, making an irruption into Bavaria, reinstated the emperor in the possession of his capital and the greater part of his electorate.

Although the alarm of these irruptions spread to Vienna, the queen of Hungary was not daunted with this reverse. She recalled the army from Alsace, and, to animate the zeal of her Hungarian subjects, repaired on the invitation of the diet to Presburgh, and roused the spirit of the nation in her defence. Count Palfy, the venerable palatine of Hungary, set up the great red standard of the kingdom, as a signal for a general insurrection*; 44,000 men instantly took the field, and another body of 30,000 held themselves in readiness as an army of reserve. "This amazing unanimity," to use the words of a contemporary historian, "of a people so divided amongst themselves as the Hungarians, especially in point of religion, could only be effected by the address of Maria Theresa, who seemed to possess one part of the character of Elizabeth of England, that of making every man about her a hero."

The wildest enthusiasm in favour of this captivating princess spread from the aged palatine to the meanest vassal of the kingdom; the numerous hordes of Hungary flocked to the royal standard, and being joined by 6000 Saxons, and an Austrian corps under Berenclau, hastened to the defence of Bohemia.

At this critical juncture prince Charles having reached the frontiers of Loraine, was exposed to imminent danger, and the re-passage of the Rhine seemed almost impractica-

* A general levy is called in Hungary an army of insurrection.

ble in the face of a superior force.   Fortunately, however, the sudden illness of Louis XV. suspended the operations of the French ; and the Austrian commander was enabled to concentrate his forces and recross the Rhine in the vicinity of Spire, in the presence of the army commanded by Noailles, with no other check than a trifling attack of his rear guard.   This important passage, effected without loss or delay, enabled him to push on rapidly towards Bohemia, and he directed his march through Suabia to Donawerth, where he arrived on the 9th of September.   Leaving the command to marshal Traun, he repaired to Vienna to concert future operations, and rejoined the army on the frontiers of Bohemia.

Although the king of Prussia had secured Prague, Tabor, Budweiss, and Frauenberg, and held the greater part of Bohemia, his troops were reduced to extreme want of provisions, and his communications were totally interrupted by hordes of irregulars.   In this situation he was surprised by the arrival of the Austrian forces on the banks of the Wotawa ; who, having been joined by the Saxons, threatened to cut off his retreat to Prague.   Being thus exposed to a superior force, he was driven from post to post, and compelled to evacuate Bohemia with a considerable loss of men, who were killed and captured in various skirmishes, or who perished from the hardships of the march and the severity of the season.

Soon after the retreat of the Austrians and the recovery of Louis XV., the campaign on the Rhine was closed by the siege of Friburgh, the bulwark of Anterior Austria, which was invested by marshal Coigny on the 30th of October.   The attacks were directed by the celebrated count Lowendahl, a Swedish officer, who had recently entered into the service of France; but the town was defended by general Damnitz with such spirit, that it held out till the 28th of November, and was not taken without the loss of 18,000 men on the side of the besiegers.   In the Netherlands marshal Saxe, though weakened by the reinforcements sent to the army of Alsace, maintained his conquests with the remainder of his troops, and baffled the inefficient efforts of the allies.

In Italy the discordant views and mutual jealousies of Maria Theresa and the king of Sardinia prevented the good effects which might have been derived from their recent union. The king was anxious to secure his own dominions on the side of France, and to conquer the marquisate of Finale; while Maria Theresa was desirous to direct her principal force against Naples, and recover possession of the two Sicilies. Hence, instead of co-operating for one great object, their forces were divided; and, after an arduous and active campaign, the Austrians were nearly in the same situation as at the commencement of the year.

Prince Lobcowitz being reinforced, compelled the Spaniards to retreat successively from Pesara and Senegallia, attacked them at Loretto and Reconati, and drove them beyond the Fronto, the boundary of the kingdom of Naples.

Alarmed by the advance of the Austrians, the king of Naples broke his neutrality, quitted his capital at the head of 15,000 men, and hastened to join the Spaniards. But prince Lobcowitz pursuing his advantage, sent a detachment into the province of Abruzzo, and dispersed manifestos to excite a rebellion in favour of the house of Austria. Unable, however, to advance through so mountainous a country, the Austrian commander turned towards Rome, with the hopes of penetrating into Naples on that side; and, in the commencement of June, reached the neighbourhood of Albano. His views were anticipated by the king of Naples, who dividing the Spanish and Neapolitan troops into three columns, which were led by himself, the duke of Modena, and the count de Gages, passed through Anagm, Valmonte, and Monte Tortino, and re-united his forces at Veletri, in the Campagna di Roma. In this situation, the two hostile armies, separated only by a deep valley, harassed each other with continual skirmishes. At length prince Lobcowitz, in imitation of prince Eugene at Cremona, formed the project of surprising the head-quarters of the king of Naples. In the night of August 10th, a corps of Austrians, led by count Brown, penetrated into the town of Veletri, killed all who resisted, and would have surprised the king and the duke of Modena in their beds, had they not been alarmed by the French ambassador, and escaped to the camp. The Austrian troops giving way to pillage, were vigorously attacked by a corps of Spaniards and Neapolitans, despatched from the camp, and driven from the town with great slaughter, and the capture of the second in command, the marquis de Novati. In this contest, however, the Spanish army lost no less than 3000 men. This daring exploit was the last offensive attempt of the Austrian forces. Prince Lobcowitz perceiving his troops rapidly decrease by the effects of the climate, and the unwholesome air of the Pontine marshes, began his retreat in the beginning of November, and, though followed by an army superior in number, returned without loss to Rimini, Pesaro, Cesano, and Immola; while the combined Spaniards and Neapolitans took up their quarters between Viterbo and Civita Vecchia.

In consequence of the expedition against Naples, the king of Sardinia was left with 30,000 men, many of them new levies, and 6000 Austrians, to oppose the combined army of French and Spaniards, who advanced on the side of Nice. After occupying that place, the united army forced the intrenched camp of the Sardinians, though defended by the king himself, made themselves masters of Montalbano and Villafranca, and prepared to penetrate into Piedmont along the sea coast. The Genoese, irritated by the transfer of Finale, were inclined to facilitate their operations; but were intimidated by the presence of an English squadron which threatened to bombard their capital.

The prince of Conti, who commanded under the infant Don Philip, did not, however, relinquish the invasion of Piedmont, but formed the spirited project of leading his army over the passes of the Alps, although almost every rock was a fortress, and the obstacles of nature were assisted by all the resources of art. He led his army, with a large train of artillery, and numerous squadrons of cavalry, over precipices and along beds of torrents, carried the fort of Chateau Dauphin, forced the celebrated Barricades *, which were deemed impregnable, descended the valley of the Stura, took Demont after a slight resistance, and laid siege to Coni.

The king of Sardinia having in vain attempted to stop

---

* This pass forms the entrance of the valley of Stura, and is a chasm scarcely twenty feet broad, between two steep precipices. It was defended by a triple entrenchment with a covert way, and by the rapid torrent of the Stura.

the progress of this torrent which burst the barriers of his country, indignantly retired to Saluzzo, to cover his capital. Being reinforced by 6000 Austrians, he attempted to relieve Coni, but was repulsed after a severe engagement, though he succeeded in throwing succours into the town. This victory, however, did not produce any permanent advantage to the confederate forces ; Coni continuing to hold out, the approach of winter, and the losses they had sustained, amounting to 10,000 men, compelled them to raise the siege and repass the Alps, which they did not effect without extreme difficulty.

CHAP. CVI.—1745.

THE regret of Maria Theresa at the ill success of her arms in Italy and Flanders, the capture of Friburgh, and the prospect of still greater losses in those distant parts did not equal her exultation at the discomfiture of the king of Prussia. She considered the recovery of Silesia as certain, and regarded all other objects as secondary concerns. She even carried her views still farther, and from the spirit of retaliation formed the project of dismembering his hereditary dominions. In pursuit of this favourite scheme, she overlooked her own weakness, and expected her allies to become passive instruments in promoting her views.

At this juncture an event happened which seemed to insure success to her projects, and opened new scenes of grandeur to her aspiring mind. Charles VII., who was naturally of an infirm constitution, was worn out with grief at the depression of his own fortunes and the sufferings of his exhausted country. Though restored to a temporary possession of his capital, he was in hourly apprehension of being again driven from the seat of his ancestors and reduced to a precarious dependence on France. In this state of alarm and anxiety he was afflicted with a severe attack of the gout, when one of his domestics officiously related the defeat of a French and Bavarian corps at Neunec, which was aggravated by their dastardly behaviour. This sudden communication of a disastrous event affecting the sensitive

mind of the unfortunate monarch, the disorder remounted
to his stomach, and proved fatal.

Charles VII. expired at Munich on the 20th of January,
1745, leaving a memorable example to his posterity not to
aspire to a dangerous pre-eminence without power, without
resources, and without those transcendent abilities which
so arduous a situation required. He was a prince of an
amiable and liberal disposition, but his amiable qualities
often degenerated into weakness, and his liberality into
profusion. In his last moments he testified his regret for
having ruined himself and his country to become an imperial pageant in the hands of France ; he exhorted his son to
reject a fatal dignity, and to regain his electoral territories
by a speedy accommodation with the house of Austria.

The death of the emperor opened a new scene of intrigue and contention in every court of Europe. France,
in particular, renewed her efforts either to wrest the imperial crown a second time from the house of Austria, or to
secure an honourable peace by consenting to the election
of the duke of Loraine. With this view her agents tampered with the princes of Germany ; at the court of Munich
they exhorted Maximilian Joseph, the new elector, to
revive the pretensions of his family on the Austrian succession, and to become a candidate for the throne of the
empire. They were no less eager to secure Augustus, and
tendered every bait which could lure the ambition or avidity of that vain and profuse monarch, by offering enormous
subsidies, an increase of territory on the side of Bohemia,
and even the imperial crown.

France likewise endeavoured to secure at least the
neutrality, if not the concurrence of Russia. She alarmed
the fears of the suspicious Elizabeth, by accusing the court
of Vienna of being implicated in a conspiracy, formed by
some discontented nobles and ladies of the court, to restore
Ivan, the relative of Maria Theresa. The unguarded conduct of the marquis de Botta gave colour to this accusation.
During the regency of Ann, Botta had been Austrian
minister at the court of St. Petersburgh, and had in vain
attempted to engage Russia in support of the queen of
Hungary. Being sent to Berlin, he maintained a correspondence with the family of Lapookin and the discontented
nobles, and perhaps too warmly censured the conduct of

Elizabeth. Several of this party being arrested and tortured, confessed that they had formed a conspiracy for dethroning the empress, and had been encouraged by Botta to expect the protection of the queen of Hungary and of the king of Prussia. In consequence of this confession, several of the suspected conspirators were tried and condemned for high treason, and Lapookin, his wife, son, and sister were knooted, their tongues cut out, and sent to Siberia. The French cabinet availed themselves of this circumstance to embroil the courts of Vienna and St. Petersburgh, and again despatched the marquis de Chetardie with the hope that he would effectually exert his influence over the mind of Elizabeth. But the queen of Hungary defeated their views by imprisoning Botta, and disavowing his conduct, and by gaining the chancellor Bestuchef. Through his influence the intrigues of la Chetardie were disclosed to the empress, and he was ordered to quit St. Petersburgh in two hours, and conveyed to the frontiers almost like a criminal. Hence the plans of France were disconcerted, and the cause of the house of Austria became triumphant at St. Petersburgh.

Although the king of Prussia had hitherto outwardly affected to co-operate with the French, that he might secure the possession of Silesia, he was secretly displeased with their conduct, and unwilling to concur in placing a new sovereign on the imperial throne, who could only be a phantom of dignity, and dependent on the will and bounty of France. He therefore made overtures to George II., to renew his accommodation with the house of Austria, while he pressed his military preparations for the ensuing campaign with his accustomed energy.

The British ministers were interested to oppose the intrigues of France, and to secure the imperial crown to the duke of Loraine; but they were irritated by the unjustifiable breach of the treaty of Breslau, which had arrested the successful progress of the Austrian arms in France. On the first intelligence of the Prussian invasion, they had assisted the queen of Hungary with an additional supply of 120,000*l.*, and were disposed to co-operate in the recovery of Silesia, though not to second her impolitic and impracticable plans for the dismemberment of the Prussian territories. The nation, however, was in a state of ferment and disorder; the outcry against the Hanoverians had arisen to an alarming height; just fears were entertained of an invasion from France, in favour of the pretender; the cabinet was distracted by internal feuds; and lord Carteret, the only minister who possessed the confidence of the king, and was capable of conducting the war with energy, had been compelled to resign. The Pelham administration had succeeded; the helm of government was eagerly grasped by the duke of Newcastle, a nobleman of high honour, and not deficient in talents, but of a jealous and querulous disposition, personally disagreeable to the sovereign; opposed in the cabinet by several of the other ministers, and even occasionally by his brother Mr. Pelham, who all re-echoed the clamours of the nation for peace.

In this state, the efforts of England were ill concerted and ill directed; and though the cause of the house of Austria was still popular, the people began to be oppressed with the burdens of a continental war. The parliament, however, voted liberal supplies for the continuance of hostilities; 6000 Hessian troops were again taken into British pay; and, to allay the outcry against the Hanoverians, they were transferred to the service of the queen of Hungary, who was gratified with an additional subsidy of 200,000l.

The views of England being principally directed to the humiliation of France, vigorous preparations were made to open the campaign in the Netherlands; a fleet was stationed in the Mediterranean to co-operate with the allies in Italy, and the British cabinet endeavoured to concentrate the whole force of the house of Austria on the same object. For this purpose, attempts were made to rouse the dilatory spirit of the Austrian court, and to overcome the obstinacy of the queen of Hungary. Before the death of Charles VII., the queen had offered to effect a reconciliation with that prince; but her demands were too imperious and exorbitant; she wished to appropriate great part of Bavaria, and to give the emperor an indemnity in Italy or the Low Countries, or by an equivalent to be conquered from France. Even on the death of the emperor, when the new elector refused to assume the title of archduke, and to accept the imperial crown, the punctilious spirit of the Austrian court retarded an ac-

commodation until the 22nd of April, when, at the earnest
exhortations of the British cabinet, the queen agreed to a
treaty which was signed at Fuessen. The elector renounced his pretensions to the Austrian succession, and
engaged to guaranty the Pragmatic Sanction, to dismiss
the auxiliary troops, and to give his vote for the duke
of Loraine; while Maria Theresa acknowledged the validity
of the late emperor's election, and relinquished her claims
on the Bavarian dominions.

The same causes concurred to embarrass the negotiations with Augustus. With a view to counteract the
union of Frankfort, a quadruple alliance had been concluded at Warsaw on the 8th of January, between the
queen of Hungary, the king of Poland, and the Maritime
Powers, by which Augustus engaged to support the
Pragmatic Sanction, and to furnish 30,000 troops for the
relief of Bohemia, on the consideration of receiving a
subsidy of 150,000l. from the Maritime Powers. This
treaty had not been formally ratified, when the death of
the emperor intervened, and Augustus took advantage of
that event to sell his alliance at a higher price. To
counteract the tempting proposals of France, it became
necessary to secure his amity by offers equally liberal.
Appreciating the importance of his alliance, he demanded
some duchies in Silesia, which would secure him a free
passage between his Saxon and Polish dominions; but
Maria Theresa disdainfully rejected this proposal, and was
no less unwilling to yield a portion of Silesia, which she
could only recover by conquest, than she was to accede to
its first cession. These and other disputes, arising from
the capricious character of Augustus, and the unbending
temper of Maria Theresa, protracted the negotiation during
several months, until the progress of the Prussian arms,
and the unceasing remonstrances of England, accelerated
the conclusion of the treaty, which was signed at Leipzic
on the 18th of May.

The treaty of Warsaw was considered as the basis of
this alliance; but separate and secret articles were arranged
between the queen of Hungary and the king of Poland,
relative to the partition of the conquests which they
expected to make from the king of Prussia. The duchy
of Silesia and the county of Glatz were to be restored to

the queen of Hungary, except the circles of Zullichau and
Schweibus, which were to be assigned to the king of
Poland, with the duchies of Magdeburgh and Crossen,
and the Prussian part of Lusatia.

During these negotiations, the court of Vienna was
distracted by opposite views and discordant interests; their
great object was the recovery of Silesia; and the queen,
though anxious to raise her husband to the imperial dignity,
even declared that without Silesia the crown of the empire
would be of no value. The duke of Loraine had long
been ambitious to acquire a regal title. Humbled by the
superior dignity of his consort, and affected with the reserved and haughty deportment of the ministers, who
considered him as a stranger, without efficient power or
real consequence, he had endeavoured to obtain the title
of king of Bohemia; and as Maria Theresa was not of a
disposition to submit to a divided authority, he looked
forward to the acquisition of the imperial crown, as the
great object of his future hopes and importance. Yet,
awed by the commanding spirit of his consort, he concealed
his anxiety, and affected a resolution rather to relinquish
that high dignity, than to purchase it by the smallest
diminution of the Austrian succession. The ministers
were jealous lest this elevation should increase his influence, but could not venture openly to oppose the wishes
of the queen. They were therefore lukewarm in his
cause, repeatedly declared that the crown of the empire
ought not to be put in competition with the recovery of
Silesia, or the cession of a single province; and even
insinuated that it might be restored to the Austrian family
in the person of the Archduke Joseph, who, though a
minor, might, like Frederic II., be raised to the imperial
dignity. In consequence of these discordant views the
negotiations were conducted with more than usual dilatoriness; but all the ministers were unanimous in rejecting
overtures for an accommodation with the king of Prussia.

The campaign was first opened in Flanders. While
the allies were wasting time in negotiations, the French
took the field ; marshal Saxe assembling his forces between
Dunkirk and Valenciennes, invested Tournay on the 25th
of April, with an army of 80,000 men, and was joined by
the king and the dauphin in the beginning of May. The

allies, commanded by the duke of Cumberland, under
the direction of marshal Konigsegg, consisted of British,
German, and Dutch troops, with not more than 8000
Austrians, and scarcely amounted to 50,000 men. The
duke of Cumberland, however, collecting his forces, hastened to the relief of Tournay, and at the beginning of
May encamped between Bougines and Moubray, within
musket-shot of the enemy's advanced posts, with an intention of compelling them to engage or raise the siege.

The French army occupied an eminence, with the
village of Antoin on their right, and Fontenoy in their
centre, strongly fortified, while their left extended to the
wood of Barry, beyond Vezon, which was defended by
formidable redoubts. Along their front was a small plain,
descending gradually from their camp, and the ground was
embarrassed by defiles, coppices, and hedges, and where
it was level, intersected by lines of different heights.
Marshal Saxe had also fortified his position with numerous entrenchments, which were defended by two hundred
and sixty pieces of artillery.

Against this force, so greatly superior in numbers and
position, the allies directed their attack. On the evening
of the 10th, they dislodged the French advanced posts
from the defiles in front of their camp, and early on the
11th the action began. The Dutch on the left were to
advance on the side of Antoin, and flank the village of
Fontenoy, while the British and Hanoverians, who formed
the centre and right, were to attack the left and centre
of the French, on the side of Fontenoy and Vezon.
General Ingoldsby, with a detachment of English, was
ordered to storm the redoubt in front of the village of
Vezon, and the prince of Waldeck to attack that of Fontenoy.

This disposition was arranged with consummate skill,
and would probably have decided the fortune of the day ;
but Ingoldsby, either from negligence or misapprehension,
did not attack the redoubt, and the prince of Waldeck was
repulsed. The British and Hanoverian infantry, however,
advanced with undaunted resolution, notwithstanding the
tremendous fire of artillery, and formed in a line between
Fontenoy and the wood of Barry, while the Dutch occupied
the space between Fontenoy and Antoin. The British

and Hanoverians bore down all before them, and compelled the enemy to retire three hundred paces behind Fontenoy; but at this critical moment the Dutch were panic struck, and fled with precipitation. The English, Hanoverians, and Austrians, now exposed on every side to a tremendous fire, began to give way; when the duke of Cumberland rushing into the thickest of the action, animated them by his words and gestures; called them countrymen, reminded them of Blenheim and Ramilies, and exclaimed, "It is my highest honour to be at your head; I scorn to expose you to a danger to which I would not expose myself." He was seconded by Sir John Ligonier, "who," to use the expression of an eye witness*, "fought like a grenadier, and commanded like a general;" and marshal Konigsegg displayed equal intrepidity, though bruised at the commencement of the action by a fall from his horse. Encouraged by the presence and example of their generals, the troops rallied, directed their efforts with redoubled ardour against the centre of the French, and by the fury of their charge seemed to dissipate whole battalions. Victory had almost declared in their favour; Konigsegg even congratulated the duke of Cumberland on the success of the day; marshal Saxe gave orders for a retreat; and the French king and dauphin, enveloped in a cloud of fugitives, were in danger of being swept away in the rout, or taken prisoners.

At this moment, the victory was wrested from the allies by a trifling circumstance, which, at any other juncture, would scarcely have deserved notice. At the suggestion of the duc of Richelieu, four pieces of artillery were pointed against the troops, who continued to advance in a firm and compact body, and the rapid and well-directed fire of this small battery, at a distance scarcely exceeding forty paces, had a stupendous effect. The allies, unsupported by their cavalry, thinned in their ranks, and fatigued with slaughter, were thrown into disorder, and the French cavalry and gens d'armes, with the Irish brigade, who had been kept as a reserve, attacked them in front and flank. The contest was short but bloody; the confusion in the

* Captain Yorke, aide-de-camp to the duke of Cumberland, third son of the earl of Hardwicke, and afterwards well known as Sir Joseph Yorke and lord Dover.

allied army soon became general, and the commander-in-chief deemed it prudent to order a retreat, which was conducted with great skill and deliberation, and without the loss of a single standard. The French remained on the field, while the allies retired to Lessines near Aeth, leaving their wounded at Bruffoel, where they were afterwards made prisoners.

Few engagements have been attended with more dreadful carnage than that of Fontenoy; both parties suffered equal loss, and shared equal honour ; but the result of the battle was most fatal to the allies. Tournay surrendered on the 22nd of May, and the citadel on the 21st of June,; and this strong and important fortress was dismantled by the conquerors. The remainder of the campaign was merely defensive on the side of the allies; the duke of Cumberland, with part of the British troops, was recalled to England, to resist the invasion of the pretender ; and before he quitted the Continent, witnessed the capture of Ghent, Oudenard, Bruges, Dendermond, Ostend, Neuport, and Aeth, which all shared the fate of Tournay.

The affairs of Italy were equally disastrous; the queen of Hungary being incapable of reinforcing her army, the king of Sardinia could not cope with the superior numbers of the French and Spaniards, who were now joined by the Genoese. Indignant at the transfer of Finale, the government of Genoa had concluded the treaty of Aranjuez, as a counterpoise to the treaty of Worms, and engaged to bring 10,000 men into the field, with a train of artillery. In return the house of Bourbon guaranteed all the possessions of the republic, and agreed to furnish a monthly subsidy of 12,000l., and all the contracting parties engaged to co-operate in procuring a settlement in Italy for the infant Don Philip. The Spanish, Neapolitan, and Modenese forces under the duke of Modena and general Gages, and the confederate troops under Don Philip and Maillebois, united near Acqui, and being joined by the Genoese, amounted to 70,000 men. They then poured into Italy, on one side overran the greater part of the Tortonese and the Milanese, and on the other, forcing the passage of the Tanaro, which was defended by the king of Sardinia, drove him under the walls of his capital. At the same time, Don Philip entering Milan in triumph on the 16th of

December, received the oaths of the inhabitants. Thus, in a single campaign, Tortona, Placentia, Parma, Pavia, Cazale, and Aste were wrested from the Austrians and Sardinians, and the citadels of Alexandria and Milan closely blockaded.

These losses on the side of Flanders and Italy were not compensated by the recovery of Silesia, to secure which the queen of Hungary had abandoned her distant dominions.

Frederic at the beginning of 1745 was in a critical situation; his discomfiture in the preceding campaign had lowered his military reputation, though it had not depressed his courage. The death of the emperor had dissolved the union of Frankfort; the French, expelled from Germany, had turned their whole attention to the Netherlands; and the king of Prussia exposed alone to the united arms of Austria and Saxony, considered " the victory of Fontenoy as of no more advantage to him than a victory on the banks of the Scamander or the capture of Pekin." His treasure began to diminish ; he had with difficulty recruited and re-organised his army, and his apparent solicitude for peace had increased the intractable spirit of the court of Vienna, who considered his proposals rather as a symptom of weakness than of sincerity. His great mind, however, rose superior to the difficulties of his situation; and his prudence and valour contributed equally to rescue him from his embarrassments.

The month of April was passed in skirmishes between the advanced posts of both armies on the frontiers of Silesia and the county of Glatz; and, aware of the intention of the Austrians to penetrate by Landshut, the king assembled his principal force in the neighbourhood of Schweidnitz, and prepared to withdraw his troops from Upper Silesia. In May a considerable action took place between the forces under the margrave Charles, who were on their march from Upper Silesia, and a body of Austrian irregulars, which terminated to the advantage of the Prussians. Frederic, however, was not dazzled by this partial success ; according to his own maxim, that " in war artifice often succeeds better than force," he assumed the appearance of dejection and alarm, in order to increase the presumption of the Austrians. Deceived by this artifice, prince Charles hastened to open the campaign. At the latter end of **May** he assembled his forces in the neighbourhood of Konigs-gratz and Jaromitz, and being joined by the Saxons at Trotenau, on the frontiers of Lower Silesia, he purposed to penetrate by the passes at Friedberg and Landshut, and cut off the communication of the king with Lower Silesia and his hereditary dominions.

At the approach of the Austrians, Frederic ordered his corps at Landshut to fall back, suffered them to cross the mountains unmolested, and seemed only anxious to secure his retreat to Breslau ; but passing by Schweidnitz, he collected his army between that town and Jauernick, and drew up his main body behind the wood of Nonnen and in the neighbouring ravines. Prince Charles, from the higher ground, perceiving only a few scattered corps, was deluded by these appearances, and still more misled by the reports of spies, whom Frederic himself condescended to deceive ; he therefore hastened to gain the centre of Silesia, advanced on the 2nd of June to Hohenfriedberg, and despatched the Saxon auxiliaries to seize Strigau, which was occupied by a Prussian detachment. Arriving late in the evening, they encamped above Strigau, fatigued with their march; and at break of day were suddenly attacked by the Prussian advanced guard, and driven from the heights, which were immediately occupied with artillery. The Saxons rallied on the neighbouring hills, but were dispersed by the cavalry, and totally defeated, before the Prussian army had formed.

Prince Charles, who was encamped in the plain below Hohenfriedberg, attributed the firing to the assault of Strigau, and not believing that the whole Prussian army was advancing against him, was surprised by an attack on both his wings almost at the same instant. In the midst of the confusion, both wings were compelled to fall back ; and, at this critical moment, a corps of Prussian cavalry, which had been kept in reserve, passing through their own infantry, fell with irresistible fury on his centre, and decided the fate of the day. Notwithstanding this masterly surprise, the Austrians behaved with great gallantry and resolution, and from the avowal of Frederic himself, conducted their retreat to the mountains with consummate skill. The battle continued seven hours with great fury; the loss on the side of the Prussians did not exceed 2000 men, while that of the Austrians and Saxons was not less than 4000 killed,

7000 prisoners, with 200 officers, 4 generals, 76 colours, 4 standards, 8 pair of kettle-drums, and 66 pieces of artillery.

Prince Charles, followed by the Prussian army, continued his retreat into Bohemia, and took a strong position at the confluence of the Adler and the Elbe, while the Saxons encamped on the other side of the Elbe. The king of Prussia advanced, and posted himself between Ruseck and Divitz on the Adler. In this position the two armies remained during three months; prince Charles waiting for reinforcements, and Frederic too prudent to attack an almost impregnable camp. The king, however, was not elated by his recent victory, but renewed his proposals for peace through the mediation of the king of England, on the same terms as he had before offered. These overtures were warmly supported by George II., who appreciated the necessity of detaching the king of Prussia, and made the strongest remonstrances to the court of Vienna. But Maria Theresa was not daunted by the recent defeat, and still looked forward to the recovery of Silesia.

The cabinet of England, convinced that nothing but absolute necessity would extort the consent of the queen of Hungary, resolved to alarm her with threats of discontinuing the subsidies, unless she sent the stipulated number of troops into Italy and Flanders. With this view Sir Thomas Robinson demanded an audience, which he opened by stating the amount of the annual subsidy advanced in support of the house of Austria. "England," he said, " has this year furnished 1,078,753*l.*, not to mention the three-fourths expected by the electors of Cologne and Bavaria. The nation is not in a condition, in a war like the present, to maintain the necessary superiority in the most essential parts, and, by endeavouring to provide for so many services, will fail in all; the force of the enemy must therefore be diminished; and as France cannot be detached from Prussia, Prussia must be detached from France. This return the English nation expect for all their exertions in favour of the house of Austria. The question is not whether the king of Prussia shall be reduced, but whether the prosecution of the war against France and Prussia will not reduce the allies to accept any terms proposed by those powers. What is to be done, must be done immediately,

and at once, while France is hesitating concerning the subsidies demanded by the king of Prussia, which, if once
granted, will fix him irrevocably.   The king of Prussia,"
he continued, " cannot be driven from Bohemia this campaign;   but by his voluntary retreat, your majesty may
despatch effectual succours into Flanders to check the rapid
progress of the French, which not only threatens the Netherlands, but menaces the very existence of the Maritime
Powers, in whose fall the house of Austria will be involved."   After again exhorting her to consent to an immediate accommodation with the king of Prussia, he concluded : " This is the only inducement of the Maritime
Powers to continue the war ; and by this alone the election
of the great duke can be secured, the weight and influence
of the whole empire obtained, and France reduced to
honourable and solid terms of peace."

The queen listened to this harangue with more than
ordinary patience and complacency; she interrupted him
but seldom, and said, " Nothing can equal my gratitude to
the king and the English nation, and I will show it by
every means in my power.   I will consult my ministers
to-morrow morning, and my chancellor shall acquaint you
with my answer ; but whatever may be determined in my
council with respect to the Prussian accommodation, I cannot spare a man out of the king of Prussia's neighbourhood.
Perhaps a regiment or two of horse, and as many of infantry, may be sent into Italy ; but the rest, in time of
peace as well as in time of war, will be necessary for the
immediate defence of my person and family."

The remainder of the conversation, which consisted of
abrupt questions, replies, and rejoinders, is too interesting
to be abridged or altered, and is therefore given in the
words of the minister :

" I said, amongst 70,000 men, who were affirmed to be
employed against Prussia, enough might be found for all
purposes ; and arguing with such diffidence of the king of
Prussia was proving too much.   Treaties enough had been
made with Louis XIV., were it only out of present necessities, and in hopes of recovering." She answered, " I cannot
spare a man."   My reply was, if her troops were so necessary for her personal defence, those of England would be
found too soon more necessary at their own home.   She

asked, "What harm will there be if the Dutch accept the
French neutrality?" I replied, no other than that every
Englishman must in such a case put up his sword. She
demanded, "Why are there less hopes of detaching France
than Prussia?" I said, because the king of Prussia would
more easily make a peace to preserve what he had, than
France to give up, as she must, what she had acquired,
and was in so fair a way of acquiring, in the Low Countries. She expressed her eagerness for another blow with
the king of Prussia; and upon my showing the just diffidence of the Saxons, she affirmed, "that prince Charles
was able alone to give another battle." "That battle,
madam," I answered, "if won, would not conquer Silesia;
if lost, your majesty is ruined at home." "Were I," she
exclaimed, "to agree with him to-morrow, I would give
him battle this evening! But why so pressing now? Why
this interruption of operations by no means to be despaired
of? Give me only to October, and then you may do what
you will." That October, I said, will be the end of the
campaign in all parts, and will be that very fatal moment
when we have reason to fear we shall be obliged to accept
the conditions France and Prussia together shall think
proper to impose upon us. "That might be true," she
answered, "were the same time to be employed as you
propose in marching from Bohemia to the Rhine, and from
the Rhine to the Low Countries. But as for my troops, I
know none of my generals who would not refuse to command such marching, or rather inactive armies; and as for
the great duke and prince Charles, they shall not. The
great duke is not so ambitious as you imagine of an empty
honour, much less to enjoy it under the tutelage of the
king of Prussia; but I shall write to know his sentiments
fully. The imperial dignity! is it compatible with the fatal
deprivation of Silesia? Good God! give me only till the
month of October; I shall then, at least, have better conditions."

The British minister then delicately touched on the discontinuance of the subsidies. He urged, that unless an
accommodation was effected with the king of Prussia, no
further assistance could be expected from the parliament
or the States-general; and requested the queen to give an
immediate and specific answer. "For this reason," she

replied, "I have given you so expeditious an audience, and have summoned my council to meet so early; though, let whatever be decided there, I see what will be executed elsewhere, with or without me."*

The tenor of the answer may be collected from this audience; and it is unnecessary to repeat the equivocations by which the Austrian ministers endeavoured to soften a direct refusal. At length the British cabinet, perceiving the inflexible spirit of Maria Theresa, secretly concluded a convention with the king of Prussia, at Hanover, by which George II. guaranteed the possession of Silesia, on the terms of the treaty of Breslau, and promised his instances to procure the accession of the States-general and of the other European powers, and to obtain from the elector of Saxony the renunciation of his claims on Silesia. It was also stipulated that a mutual guaranty of each other's dominions should pass between the queen of Hungary and the king of Prussia; and Frederic agreed to support the election of the duke of Loraine. The king of England engaged to use his endeavours to gain the approbation of the court of Vienna, and to procure an immediate suspension of arms.

The communication of this convention was received at Vienna with marks of high displeasure, and the resentment of the queen was still further inflamed by the prevaricating and insulting conduct of the king of Prussia. After exacting a solemn promise of secrecy from the British ministers, he instantly spread the intelligence that peace was concluded throughout his army; proposed to prince Charles a suspension of arms, till he could receive orders from Vienna; and used every artifice to throw the odium of continuing hostilities on the queen of Hungary. Hence the mutual aversion of the contending parties was increased: the queen and her ally, the elector of Saxony, indignantly rejected the convention, and prince Charles was peremptorily ordered to risk another battle, although the greater part of the Saxons had been already withdrawn to defend their own country from a Prussian invasion.

Prince Charles, being joined by the long-expected reinforcements, drew near the Prussians, who were encamped at Jaromitz, near the confluence of the Metau, the Aupe,

* Sir Thomas Robinson to the earl of Harrington, August 3. 1745.

and the Elbe. Aware of the strength of their position, he did not venture to attack the enemy; but, surrounding them with his irregulars, cut off their communications, intercepted their convoys, and harassed them with continual alarms. At the same time a corps of Hungarians, having surprised the fortress of Cosel in Upper Silesia, extended their incursions to Schweidnitz and Breslau, where the Prussian magazines were deposited. Frederic, thus straitened on every side, after sending a detachment to retake Cosel, retreated to Staudentz, and was followed by prince Charles, who advanced to Koenigshoff, and watched the favourable moment for an attack.

The Prussian army being reduced to 18,000 men by the absence of numerous detachments, and greatly distressed for want of provisions, Frederic was preparing to quit Bohemia, and return by Trotenau into Silesia. But his design was anticipated by prince Charles, who, covering his movements by his irregulars, gained the right of the Prussian camp, and opened a tremendous cannonade before the break of day. Frederic, at this moment concerting with his generals the order of his march, was taken by surprise; and though he had sent out a detachment to reconnoitre the preceding evening, was ignorant of the approach of the Austrians till they were discovered by the grand guards of his camp. In these circumstances, prince Charles seemed secure of victory; his army was nearly double in number to the Prussians, and his irregulars were calculated to augment, by their impetuous and desultory attacks, the confusion of a surprise, or to harass a retreating enemy. But he was opposed by a rival far superior in skill and activity, and by troops remarkable for their steadiness and valour; while his own were shamefully deficient in discipline, and exhibited proofs of cowardice, which had not hitherto tarnished the Austrian arms.

The king, sensible of the danger which would attend a retreat by roads embarrassed and intricate, and in the face of so superior a force, instantly determined to risk the fate of a battle. The Prussians, though exposed half an hour to the fire of twenty-eight pieces of artillery, formed with astonishing precision, and wheeling a quarter circle to the right, presented a front parallel to the enemy, while the cavalry of the right attacked the Austrian squadrons, which were disadvantageously posted, and threw them into disorder. The Austrian cavalry, panic-struck with this impetuous charge, could not be rallied either by menaces, exhortations, or the example of the generals; and prince Lobcowitz, after killing three officers for cowardice, was jostled by his own men into a ditch, where he lay with three contusions. The irregulars also were guilty of the greatest disobedience and disorder; instead of augmenting the first surprise of the Prussians by a furious attack in flank and rear, they did not arrive in time; and the only corps of hussars who reached the camp of the enemy were employed, during the heat of the action, in pillaging the baggage.

The Prussian infantry now advanced, and after three successive repulses carried the batteries; the Austrians were driven from height to height, and a retreat, begun without orders, was covered by general Daun with a few regiments of infantry, and two of horse. The right wing of the Austrians remained quiet spectators of the whole scene, neither attacking nor being attacked by the king of Prussia, who had not brought his left into action, and drew a considerable part of his forces from that wing to support his right and centre.

In this confusion it appears rather a matter of wonder that the defeat of the Austrians was not attended with greater carnage, for not more than 4000 were killed and 2000 taken prisoners, with twenty-two pieces of artillery, ten colours, and two standards. They were pursued only to the village of Sohr, from which the battle takes its name, and threw themselves into the forest of Silva. On the side of the Prussians, the king himself owns that 1000 were killed and 2000 wounded; but his loss was undoubtedly greater, as his troops were exposed to a long and warm cannonade in forming, and experienced a spirited resistance from a part of the Austrian army. Frederic, indeed, candidly acknowledges that he committed many errors, and attributes the victory no less to the steadiness of his own troops, than to the confusion and want of discipline among the enemy. He seems to have been deeply impressed with the danger to which he was exposed, and is reported to have exclaimed, " Since the Austrians have not been able to beat me this time, they never will beat me." Prince

Charles also did not calculate on the wonderful resources of his great rival; and, too confident of success, had made his dispositions to harass the retreat of the enemy, not to resist an attack. This victory was attended with no other disadvantage to the Austrians, than the disgrace of being defeated by a far inferior force ; and it was soon followed by the retreat of the king of Prussia from Bohemia, the frontiers of which country were too much exhausted to support his army.

During the campaigns in Flanders, Italy, and Silesia, the disasters of the house of Austria were only compensated by the election of Francis to the imperial crown. An Austrian army, under the command of Francis himself, kept the French in check on the banks of the Rhine, while the diet assembled at Frankfort, and continued its sitting without interruption. All the electoral votes, except Brandenburgh and Palatine, were obtained ; even the vote of Bohemia was acknowledged as vested in Maria Theresa, with only the opposition of the two protesting electors; and as no other candidate made his appearance, the duke of Loraine was elected in the usual forms on the 13th of September, and on his coronation on the 4th of October, assumed the title of Francis I.

Maria Theresa was present on this occasion; and from a balcony testified her triumph by first crying, " Long live the emperor Francis I.!" which was re-echoed by the acclamations of the spectators. Thus she had the satisfaction of placing the imperial crown on the head of her illustrious consort, and securing its restoration to her family, by whom it had been worn for an uninterrupted period of above 300 years. From Frankfort the empress-queen visited the army at Heidelberg, amounting to 60,000 men ; was received by the emperor himself at the head of the troops ; passed between the lines, saluting each rank with her usual affability and dignity ; dined in public under a tent; and, on her departure, distributed a gratuity to each soldier.

Although the finances of the queen had long been in a state of extreme dilapidation, and although she was reluctantly compelled to appropriate the church plate in her dominions, she was unwilling to close the campaign with dishonour : she persevered in rejecting all overtures from

the king of Prussia, and meditated projects of retaliation
and vengeance.　Instead of sending her troops into winter
quarters, she formed the bold design of uniting her forces
with those of Saxony, to march to Berlin, and dismember
the territories of that formidable rival, who had first broken
the indivisibility of the Austrian succession.　She was instigated by the declaration of the empress of Russia, that
if Frederic invaded the electorate of Saxony, a corps of
Russians should make an instant irruption into Prussia.
But this bold project was disconcerted by the foresight
and activity of the Prussian monarch ; for at the very moment when she deemed herself most secure of success, she
received the intelligence that Frederic had surprised and
defeated a division of the Saxon troops at Hennendorf, and
driven prince Charles from Silesia into Bohemia, with the
loss of 5000 men ; that another army, under the command
of the prince of Anhalt, having, on the 15th of December,
totally routed the Saxons at Kesselsdorf, the king had
entered Dresden in triumph, and overran the whole electorate.　On this alarming information, the empress-queen,
whom her own disasters could not affect, and whom no enemies could intimidate, was softened by the misfortunes of her
ally ; and, though she had publicly declared she would part
with her last garment to recover Silesia, she sacrified her
own interests and desire of vengeance to the necessities of
Augustus.　She accepted the mediation of Great Britain ;
and signed, on the 25th of December, the peace of Dresden,
which confirmed to Prussia the possession of Silesia and
Glatz ; in return Frederic evacuated Saxony, acknowledged the suffrage of Bohemia, and the validity of the
imperial election.

Chap. CVII.—1746, 1747.

THE rapid progress of the Prussian arms in Saxony
was ultimately a fortunate circumstance for the house of
Austria ; as it overcame the obstinacy of Maria Theresa,
and reduced her to the necessity of concluding peace with
an enemy, against whom she had in vain sacrificed her
best troops, and who clogged all her operations for the

security of her distant dominions. This accommodation was
the more fortunate at this period, as England, embarrassed
with a rebellion at home, was compelled to withdraw great
part of her forces from the Netherlands to resist the
pretender, who, after defeating the royal troops, had
penetrated into the heart of the kingdom, and threatened
the capital itself. It was not till the 16th of April, 1746,
that the battle of Culloden, gained by the duke of Cumberland, suppressed the rebellion ; but a considerable time
elapsed before the country was sufficiently tranquil to allow
the government to turn their attention to foreign affairs,
and renew their efforts in the Low Countries.

This interval was seized by the French with their usual
alacrity. Before the Austrians could assemble a sufficient
force in Flanders, marshal Saxe opened the campaign
with the important capture of Brussels ; on the 4th of
May Louis XV. made his triumphal entry ; Mechlin,
Louvain, Antwerp, Mons, Charleroy, and Namur, were
successively besieged and taken ; and, before the end of
September, all the Austrian Netherlands, except Luxemburgh and Limburgh, fell into the hands of the French.
Prince Charles, at the head of an army, which did not amount
to less than 70,000 men, seemed a mere spectator of these
repeated losses. Severely afflicted by the death of his wife, he
was unable to pay his usual attention to the affairs of the field ;
the troops were panic-struck at the superior ascendency of
the French artillery, under the skilful direction of marshal
Saxe ; and a general apathy pervaded the confederate
army, until the arrival of sir John Ligonier, whose energy
gave animation to the military operations, and restored the
confidence of the troops.

Soon afterwards the allies engaged in the only general
action which took place during the whole campaign. After
the capture of Namur, they posted themselves between
Maestricht and Liege, with a view to cover Holland, and
harass the French, should they take winter-quarters in
Brabant. In this position they were suddenly attacked
on the 11th of October ; and after a desperate resistance,
compelled to retreat across the Maes. The loss of this
action, which was called the battle of Raucoux, from a
village occupied by the confederates, was principally owing
to the superior skill of marshal Saxe, and to the want of

artillery among the confederates; but the retreat was ably
covered by sir John Ligonier at the head of the British horse;
the army passing the Maes, took up winter-quarters in the
duchies of Luxemburgh and Limburgh, and the French
occupied the territories which they had recently conquered.

The campaign in Italy was of a far different nature. The
empress-queen having sent a reinforcement of 30,000 troops,
the Austrians and Sardinians became greatly superior to the
enemy : Asti, Milan, Guastalla, and Parma, were retaken;
and the victory of Placentia, gained on the 17th of June by
prince Lichtenstein over the the united forces of France and
Spain, commanded by Don Philip, secured their ascendency.

In the midst of these successes, the death of Philip V.
intervened; and the turbulent spirit of Elizabeth Farnese
being no longer predominant in the cabinet of Madrid, the
counsels of Spain became more moderate under the auspices
of the new monarch.

Ferdinand VI., son of Philip, by his first wife Anna
Maria of Savoy, was a prince of a meek and unaspiring
temper, and wholly governed by his consort Barbara, princess
of Portugal, who was friendly to England, and partial to her
relation the queen of Hungary; a favourable change in the
politics and conduct of Spain was therefore instantly perceived; the command of the army was taken from the active
and enterprising count Gages, and the troops were ordered
to evacuate Italy. The French and Spaniards retreated to
Nice, and crossed the Var into Provence, leaving garrisons in Vintimiglia and Antibes. Genoa, thus abandoned
to her fate, was unable to resist the forces of Austria
and Sardinia; the king occupied Finale and the Riviera di
Ponente, the imperialists took Novi, Voltaggi, and Gavi,
and seized the pass of the Bochetta, whilst the English fleet
blockaded the port by sea. The Genoese, shut up on every
side, capitulated almost at the discretion of the conquerors,
and agreed to deliver up the city to the queen of Hungary,
with the garrison as prisoners of war, and all the artillery
and warlike stores of the republic. In addition to these
rigorous terms, the doge and six senators were to repair to
Vienna, to implore forgiveness; and four senators were
to be delivered as hostages for the fulfilment of the
articles. In consequence of this capitulation, the marquis de

Botta took possession of the town in the name of the empress-queen, on the 5th of September, 1746, with a body of 15,000 men ; while the remainder of the combined army encamped in the Genoese territory.

The success of the campaign began to occasion jealousies between the allied powers, and gave rise to violent disputes concerning their future operations. The Austrian commanders, in conformity with the treaty of Worms, were desirous to invade Naples, which would have fallen an easy prey, while the greater part of the native troops were employed against the French and Spanish army in France, and the English fleet cut off all succour by sea. But this attempt was opposed by the king of Sardinia, who was jealous of the preponderance of the Austrians in Italy, and by the English, who were desirous of making a diversion in the south of France. After much delay the allies resolved to invade Provence ; but it was not until the 30th of November that count Brown passed the Var, and, with the assistance of the English fleet, laid siege to Antibes. At this juncture an insurrection at Genoa first turned the tide of success.

From the moment of the capitulation, Botta had loaded Genoa with every species of indignity and oppression. Besides putting his troops into free quarters, and other vexations, in less than three months he exacted contributions to the amount of 24,000,000 florins, and compelled the government to deliver up the jewels which had been lodged as the pledge for a loan advanced to the house of Austria. He also exiled many of the nobles, and suffered his troops to commit the most brutal excesses among the people and peasantry. At length the natives were roused to the height of fury and despair, and a petty insult occasioned a general insurrection. The king of Sardinia having refused to furnish artillery for the siege of Antibes, the Austrians had recourse to the ordnance surrendered at Genoa. A crowd being assembled on the removal of a mortar, the carriage broke down, and a German officer struck a native who refused to assist in drawing it to the harbour ; a tumult arose, the Genoese wounded the officer, and a shower of stones compelled the Austrians to retire. During the night the insurgents increased, supplied themselves with weapons by forcing the armourers' shops and magazines, barricadoed the streets, and being directed by French officers and senators in disguise, and joined by the peasantry, drove the Austrians from Genoa and its territory, with the loss of 8000 men, and all the artillery and baggage. Having secured the passes, the city re-assumed the appearance of independence and tranquillity.

This unfortunate event increased the misintelligence between the Austrians and Sardinians. Charles Emanuel had disapproved the exclusive occupation of Genoa by the Austrians; and the empress-queen was alarmed, lest after the capture of Savona he should march against Genoa, and seize the prize which had been lost by the impolitic and brutal conduct of Botta. These bickerings retarded the commencement of operations, until the inhabitants had time to place themselves in a respectable posture of defence, and were strengthened by reinforcements from France.

Notwithstanding this disastrous event, the affairs of Italy wore a more favourable aspect than since the beginning of the war; and Maria Theresa looked forward with hopes, either of reconquering Naples and Sicily, or of compensating for the cessions which she had made to the king of Sardinia, by dismembering the Genoese territories.

All the belligerent states, however, impressed with the calamities and suffering under the burdens of war, were sincerely desirous of peace, except the empress-queen, who, irritated at the loss of Silesia, and dissatisfied with the cessions required for the king of Sardina, hoped, by the prosecution of hostilities, to obtain some compensation by conquests from the house of Bourbon. England and France, on whom the continuance of the war and the fate of Europe depended, were equally anxious for peace, and endeavoured to obtain more advantageous conditions, by a strenuous exertion of their natural strength and resources. France pushed her conquests in the Low Countries, the only part where the Maritime Powers were vulnerable; England endeavoured to ruin the French marine, and, by seizing some of the colonial possessions, to secure an equivalent for the restoration of the Netherlands. The views of the two nations were respectively successful: France overcame all the force brought forward by the allies in defence of the Netherlands;

while England, by repeated victories, destroyed the French marine in detail, and captured the Isle of Cape Breton, with the important fortress of Louisbourg, which commanded the Gulf of St. Lawrence, and was the key of Canada.

Negotiations had been opened between Spain and England, and between France and the United States. Since the accession of Ferdinand, the court of Madrid had announced sincere dispositions for peace, if it could be obtained without the dishonour of abandoning their allies, and on the condition of securing an establishment for Don Philip in Italy. A negotiation was accordingly first commenced at Lisbon, under the mediation of Portugal, by means of Mr. Keene and count Rosenberg, the British and Austrian plenipotentiaries. A second was soon afterwards opened at the Hague, through the medium of Macanas, the earl of Sandwich, and count Harrack, the Spanish, British, and Austrian ministers; but both were frustrated by the artifices of the queen-dowager Elizabeth Farnese, and by the refusal of Maria Theresa to renounce her claims on Naples and Sicily. Still, however, the Spanish court continued favourably disposed towards England, and evinced a disposition to conclude hostilities on honourable terms.

The Dutch, exposed to imminent danger by the loss of the Low Countries, and threatened with an immediate invasion, proffered their interposition to effect an accommodation with the house of Austria; but this proposition, though accepted by France, being peremptorily rejected by Maria Theresa, the States, at the commencement of 1746, made private overtures to settle a plan for a general peace. France consented, and proposed to yield the Netherlands, in return for the restitution of Cape Breton, as the basis of the preliminaries. Great Britain soon became a party in this transaction; and conferences were opened at Breda in the beginning of October, between the French, English, and Dutch plenipotentiaries. The negotiations, however, were soon suspended by the refusal of the French to admit the Austrian and Sardinian ministers, and finally broken off by the discordant views of the belligerent powers, particularly by the empress-queen, who hoped that France would be humbled by the enormous preparations making for the ensuing campaign. On the 22d of May, 1746, she had concluded a treaty of

defensive alliance with Russia, for the reciprocal succour of
30,000 men in case of an attack ; and a convention had
been settled at the Hague between the allies, which, if effectually executed, would have arrested the progress, or repelled
the attacks of France. The States-general, and Great
Britain were to furnish each 40,000 men ; the empress-
queen engaged to supply 60,000 in the Netherlands, besides
garrisons, and 10,000 in Luxemburgh ; also 60,000 in
Italy, who, in conjunction with 30,000 Piedmontese, were
to attack France on that side, while 15,000 kept in check the
king of Naples. To give vigour to these preparations, England agreed to maintain a powerful squadron in the Mediterranean, and, in conjunction with the States-general, to
anticipate the payment of the subsidies to the empress-queen,
and furnish an additional sum of one hundred thousand
pounds.

This extensive plan was soon proved impracticable ; the
Dutch, though urged by the duke of Cumberland and the
earl of Sandwich, refused to publish a formal declaration of
war against France ; and, deluded with the hopes of affecting an accommodation, were tardy in their preparations.
The king of Sardinia was almost equally remiss ; and the
empress-queen herself was unable to complete her contingent, even with the addition of raw recruits and irregular
troops. In consequence of these delays and of this deficiency,
the campaign of 1747 was unfavourable to the allies. Count
Brown continued to press the siege of Antibes and to devas-
tate Provence ; and although by the loss of Genoa his communication with the English fleet was in danger of being
intercepted, and marshal Belleisle was advancing at the head
of a considerable force, yet the generals of the combined
armies unanimously resolved in a council of war to maintain
their position. But at this juncture a courier arrived with
orders from Vienna, and, on the 3d of February, count
Brown instantly repassed the Var, contrary to the opinion
of the Austrian and Sardinian generals.

The motives of this retreat, which was warmly censured
by the allies, were derived from want of provisions and the
weakness of the army, which, in consequence of the reinforcements detached to Botta, scarcely exceeded 25,000 men ;
but more particularly from the desire of Maria Theresa to

retake Genoa, and to punish, as she said, the perfidy, perjury, and rebellion of the natives, more atrocious than even the massacre of the Sicilian vespers.

An unfortunate misunderstanding with the king of Sardinia for some time obstructed the operations against Genoa. At length a compromise was effected, and 6000 Sardinians joined the Austrians ; but this succour came too late, and neither of the allied powers would furnish the heavy artillery necessary for a siege, lest it should fall into the hands of the French. The besiegers, if they may be so termed, hoped rather to reduce the town by famine than by regular approaches ; for they continued a distant blockade without raising a single battery, until they were alarmed by the approach of the French and Spanish forces under marshal Belleisle. As the speedy recapture of Genoa had been con-fidently and repeatedly announced, both the Austrians and Sardinians were unwilling to incur the disgrace of first raising the siege ; and a kind of punctilious etiquette was observed between the king of Sardinia and count Schulen-burgh ; the Austrian general refused to retire without posi-tive orders from the king, and the king declined giving those orders, because he did not consider the Austrian forces as under his command. This frivolous contest, however, was soon terminated by the advance of Belleisle ; the king with-drew his troops to defend the passes of Piedmont ; the Austrians, having gained the point of honour, followed his example ; and thus, instead of an invasion of France, Italy itself was menaced by a French army.

During these transactions Belleisle had crossed the Var in June, and made himself master of Nice, Montalbano, Villa-franca, and Vintimiglia, and thus compelled the allies to raise the siege of Genoa. He then, with his characteristic temerity, proposed to threaten Turin by an irruption on the side of Dauphiné ; and, notwithstanding the opposition of the Spanish general, and even of the French court, despatched his brother, the chevalier de Belleisle, with 15,000 men to force a passage through the valley of Susa, which was defended by almost impregnable posts, and by numerous bodies of Austrians and Sardinians. The detachment reached the Assietta, on the road to Exilles, a formidable intrench-ment occupying the summit of a steep acclivity, strengthened with palisades, furnished with a numerous artillery, and defended by eighteen Sardinian and three Austrian battalions. These obstacles did not restrain the ardour of the French; animated by the recollection of the assault of Chateau Dauphin, they advanced to the attack ; being twice repulsed with a dreadful carnage, Belleisle placed himeelf at their head, and rushing forwards, planted the French standard on the works. In attempting to pull down the palisades, he received several wounds, which disabled his arms ; he then seized the palisades with his teeth, and in this frantic effort received his death in the midst of 4000 killed and 2000 wounded. The loss of the commander decided the fortune of this rash enterprise ; the remainder of the troops retired to Briançon ; and marshal Belleisle himself fell back to Nice.

The dilatoriness, weakness, and disunion of the allies were never more conspicuous than during the campaign in the Netherlands ; and their conduct formed a striking contest with the vigour and decision of the French. The command of the army was intrusted to the duke of Cumberland, who had recently distinguished himself in the suppression of the rebellion : but the greatest military talents could not have supplied the enormous deficiency of force ; for Great Britain alone furnished her stipulated numbers, and the contingents of the empress-queen, and of the Dutch, were scarcely two-thirds of their quota. Although the duke of Cumberland put his army in motion before the French, he could not undertake any effectual operation, for want of magazines, and even of the necessary subsistence, occasioned by the negligence of the Austrian and Dutch commissaries. He thus harassed his troops without advantage ; while marshal Saxe remained quietly in cantonments between Bruges, Antwerp, and Brussels, plentifully supplied with every necessary, and preparing to carry the war into the heart of the United Provinces on the advance of the season.

In the mean time the French cabinet amused the Dutch with affected demonstrations of friendship, and hoped, by menaces and intrigues, to force the States-general into a neutrality. With this view their minister at the Hague presented a memorial, which, though filled with high professions of regard and proffers of accommodation, concluded

with announcing the intention of the French king to carry
his arms into the territory of the republic, not as an enemy
to France, but as an ally to the house of Austria, promising
to consider the countries and fortresses which the French
army should occupy, as a deposit to be restored when the
States should cease to furnish succours to his enemies.   To
enforce these menaces, the very day in which the memorial
was presented, Lowendahl, with 20,000 men, entered the
Dutch territory, and in less than a month reduced Sluice,
Sas van Ghent, and Hulst, and made 5000 prisoners.

This irruption, though successful, effected the very measure
which the French most deprecated, the restoration of the
stadtholdership.   On his first entrance into the territory of
the republic, Lowendahl declared to two Dutch officers, that
the invasion was made by the connivance of the government,
and they must not be surprised if the French met with little
resistance.   This assertion seemed to be confirmed by the
speedy surrender of the fortresses ; and the partisans of the
house of Orange availed themselves of the consternation,
occasioned by the approach of the French, to circulate the
affidavits of these two officers.   The people, who in all
popular governments naturally suspect treachery in misfortune, was roused almost to phrenzy, and exclaimed, that they
were reduced to a worse situation, even than when invaded
by Louis XIV.; and as they were betrayed by their
own rulers, it became a duty to their country to change
the form of government, and to restore the ancient constitution, under which the States had so long prospered.

The insurrection began at the town of Vere, in Zealand ;
the burghers assembled tumultuously, and required the magistrates to raise William Henry Friso, prince of Orange, to
the stadtholdership.   This demand was instantly complied
with ; the other towns of Zealand followed the example, and
the prince was the same day appointed by the States, Stadtholder, Captain-general, and Admiral of the province.
This great and sudden change was effected with little disorder ; the remaining provinces concurred in the appointment,
and, on the 15th of May, he was solemnly installed by the
States in the office of Captain-general and Admiral of the
Union.

But this revolution, though contrary to the views and

interests of France, was too late to produce any material effect on the events of the campaign. The prince of Orange, who now assumed the command of the Dutch forces, was of a sanguine disposition, pompous manners, and punctilious temper ; unskilled in military affairs, and yet unwilling to act in subservience to his brother-in-law the duke of Cumberland. His presence and interference, therefore, contributed rather to thwart than to promote the operations of the allies.

In order to cover Maestricht, which was threatened by the French, the allies took post on the Maes ; and, after several movements on both sides, were attacked in the vicinity of Maestricht, by marshal Saxe with the whole French army on the 2nd of July. He directed his principal efforts to cut off the allies from Maestricht, and the whole of the action fell on the British, Hanoverians, and Hessians, who formed the left wing, and were posted near the village of Val or Lauffeld, from which the battle received its name. This post was so obstinately contested, that the village was four times taken and retaken ; till at length the superior skill of marshal Saxe, and the persevering valour of his troops, gained the day, and the allies were compelled to retire beyond Maestricht. In the retreat, the British infantry were in imminent danger of being cut off, but were saved by the exertions of the cavalry under sir John Ligonier, who was made prisoner; and thus sacrificed his own liberty to the safety of the army. In this action both the commanders narrowly escaped being taken : the duke of Cumberland was once enveloped in a squadron of French horse ; and marshal Saxe, in directing the attack, was impelled by his ardour into the very ranks of the enemy. The French army suffered most severely in this conflict ; for the allies lost no more than 5000 men, and marshal Saxe acknowledged to sir John Ligonier, that on his part 8000 foot and 1000 horse, with 1000 officers, were killed and wounded. This defeat was erroneously imputed by the English nation to the pusillanimity of the Dutch, and even to the treachery of the Austrians; but it was owing to the want of concert among the allied forces, and to the skillful dispositions of marshal Saxe.

The success of the French, however, did not enable him to invest Maestricht, the garrison of which was considerably reinforced. But after amusing the allied army for some time, count Lowendahl was detached with 30,000 men to besiege Bergen-op-Zoom, an enterprise which was deemed so impracticable that it only exposed the commanders to public censure, and excited little alarm in the United Provences. This fortress was the master-piece of Cohorn, and had already bid defiance to the attacks of the French; it was connected with an intrenched camp, and its communication with the sea could not be intercepted; the works were defended by a numerous garrison; the lines occupied by the prince of Saxe Hilburghausen, with twenty battalions and fourteen squadrons; and a powerful reinforcement was hourly expected. The trenches were opened on the 15th of July, and after the usual advances, which were attended with considerable loss, slight breaches were effected in the rampart in the beginning of September. The governor, who was eighty years of age, presuming too much on the strength of the place, neglected the necessary precautions, and Bergen-op-Zoom was taken by surprise early in the morning of the 15th; the assailants penetrated even to the middle of the town, with scarcely any opposition, and the governor himself was almost surprised in his bed. The garrison, however, assembled in one of the squares, made a gallant defence; and when overpowered by numbers retreated through the opposite gate.

This extraordinary event was imputed to treachery; but it appears to have proceeded solely from the negligence of the sentinels, and from the great age of the governor, who was incapable of going the rounds, and inspecting the necessary arrangements. The capture of Bergen-op-Zoom was the last important event of this unfortunate campaign, and both armies soon afterwards retired into winter quarters.*

* When I was at Bergen-op-Zoom in 1771, I learned two anecdotes from colonel Douglas, concerning two natives of Scotland, then officers in the Highland regiments, which are worthy of being commemorated.
    Francis Maclaine defended the water-fort with about sixty men; he resolutely held out, though his party was soon reduced to twenty-five, refused to surrender prisoner of war, and Lowendahl allowed him to capitulate. The fire of this small party was so brisk, that the French imagined they were more numerous than they really were.
    Hector Maclaine occupied a work with only five men. Being summoned to surrender, he answered, " We shall certainly be overpowered

The ill-success of the allies was in some degree compensated by the victory of admiral Hawke, who fell in with a French squadron off Cape Finisterre, which was convoying the West India fleet, and took six ships of the line. This victory crippled the French marine, and contributed to accelerate the conclusion of peace.

Chap. CVIII. — 1748.

During this campaign proposals for a general pacification were renewed by France. After the battle of Lauffeld, marshal Saxe made overtures to his prisoner, sir John Ligonier, with a frankness and cordiality which seemed to prove the sincerity of his court; the basis of his plan was, a mutual restitution of all conquests, and an establishment for Don Philip. These overtures were communicated to the British cabinet, and by them submitted to the allies; but as the empress-queen refused to give any specific explanation of her intentions, and as the prince of Orange, who was eager to signalise his new command, vehemently protested against entering into any negotiation, the overtures were peremptorily rejected; and at the close of the year preparations were made to prosecute the ensuing campaign with increasing vigour.

But from the discordant views and relative situations of the different powers, so many difficulties occurred in forming a specific plan, as plainly indicated the approaching dissolution of the confederacy. During the preceding year constant altercations had taken place between the courts of Vienna and London; and the British cabinet had incessantly remonstrated against the deficiency of the Austrian contingents. They represented, that both in Italy and the Netherlands the Austrian armies amounted to scarcely more than half the stipulated numbers; they enumerated, with minute precision, the enormous subsidies paid by the Maritime Powers to the

by numbers, but we hope to destroy, in the attempt, a far greater number of the French; and I am determined to die rather than surrender myself and my men prisoners of war!" The French general, astonished at this spirit, allowed him to capitulate, and he and his five men marched out with a drum beating, and the honours of war. He was afterwards a colonel in the East India Company's service.

empress-queen, and dwelt on the constant failure of her promises. They therefore proposed, that in future only half the subsidies should be paid at the commencement of the year, and the remaining half reserved until the Austrian contingents were ascertained to be complete and effective, by the inspection of British officers ; they even declared their intention to make a deduction proportionate to the deficiency in the beginning of the campaign. Count Bathiani, the Austrian commander in the Netherlands, refused to accede to these propositions ; and when they were submitted to the court of Vienna, the empress-queen did not refrain from expressing her high indignation at so degrading a proposal. She declared that she had always supplied her stipulated contingent, and remonstrated against the unfairness of excluding the irregular troops, and estimating the numbers in the middle of the campaign, when the army must have experienced a considerable diminution from action, sickness, and desertion. She urged also the imprudence of draining her hereditary dominions of her best troops, while she was menaced by such neighbours as Prussia and Turkey ; disgusted likewise with repeated details of the annual subsidies, she indignantly asked, " Has one farthing of the antecedent subsidies ever been diverted ; and have I not, in every campaign, exerted my whole force to the utmost ?" She justly observed, " All the stipulations of the future convention shall be punctually fulfilled, as far as circumstances will allow ; but as the greatest expenses necessary for opening a campaign are incurred in the winter, so those preparations must be more or less effective in proportion to the subsidies advanced during that season."

It was not, therefore, without the greatest difficulty, that a convention was concluded at the Hague in the beginning of January, between Austria, and the Maritime Powers, and Sardinia. The empress-queen agreed to furnish 60,000 men in the Low Countries; Great Britain and Holland 6000 each ; in Italy, the empress-queen was to maintain 60,000, and the king of Sardinia 30,000. Maria Theresa reluctantly agreed to the proposal of making part of the subsidies depend on the completion of the stipulated contingent ; and one-fourth of the 400,000*l.* was to be deducted if the armies were not ascertained to be complete before the

end of April; the payments to the king of Sardinia were to
be made on the same terms.   In addition to the vast force
proposed for the defence of Holland and the security of the
Low Countries, 30,000 Russian auxiliaries were taken into
the pay of the Maritime Powers, by a treaty signed the
30th of November, and had commenced their march towards
the Netherlands before the end of the year.

Notwithstanding the signature of the convention, no
specific plan of operations for the campaign in Italy was
arranged, and the regulation of the affairs in that country
was attended with insuperable difficulties, in consequence of
the disputes which arose relative to the treaty of Worms,
and, in addition to the former disagreements, new disputes
arose relative to the command.   In conformity with the
letter of the treaty of Worms, the Austrians insisted that
the king of Sardinia should command the army, but not the
detachments ; the king, on his part, refused to sign the
convention, unless he was intrusted with the same authority
as the duke of Cumberland in the Low Countries.   A
modification of this article was at length effected by the
intervention of the British cabinet, and the king was invested
with the command of detachments from the main army
This accommodation, however, did not contribute to the adjustment of a plan for the ensuing campaign.   Charles
Emanuel wished to retain the principal part of his force for
the defence of his own dominions, the empress-queen was
anxious to recover Naples and Sicily, and England urged
the necessity of commencing operations with the siege of
Genoa.   Both the Austrians and Sardinians acknowledged
the expediency of this measure, but argued that it could not
be undertaken without additional subsidies ; and the king of
England could only be induced to make a verbal promise of
reimbursement at the conclusion of the campaign.   It would
be tedious to dwell on these unfortunate disagreements, which
evinced such mutual distrust, and sufficiently displayed the
necessity of a speedy accommodation, had the affairs in the
Low Countries been less unfortunate.

Maria Theresa, not dejected by these divisions, meditated
some brilliant enterprise in Italy, which she sanguinely
hoped would be crowned with success.   She anticipated the
arrival of the Russians in the Low Countries; flattered

herself that the Dutch would make a desperate resistance; and that the army under the duke of Cumberland would be enabled to commence offensive operations. But, in the midst of these sanguine expectations, she was confounded with the signature of the preliminaries.

The conferences at Breda had been transferred, by mutual agreement, to Aix-la-Chapelle, and in the mean time all the plenipotentiaries of the belligerent powers, except those of Spain and Genoa, assembled at the Hague; count Kaunitz, afterwards so long distinguished as the prime minister at Vienna, was the Austrian plenipotentiary; and the empress-queen could not have selected a more firm and able supporter of her rights. The plenipotentiaries for the other powers were, for Great Britain, the earl of Sandwich, who here opened his diplomatic career with an ability and judgment above his years; for France, the count de St. Severin, who, by his candour and affability, was peculiarly calculated for this delicate office; and for the Dutch, no less than five, at the head of whom was count Bentinck, a man of high integrity, and devoted to the party of the stadtholder and the interests of England. The ambassador from the court of Madrid was don Masones de Lima, a punctilious and formal Spaniard; and the count de Chavannes, a shrewd and supple Italian, from the king of Sardinia. For the sake of form, plenipotentiaries were also received from the republic of Genoa, and the duke of Modena. The negotiation effectually centred in the British and French plenipotentiaries; and as both parties were equally desirous of peace, it was concluded almost as soon as it commenced : for the first formal overtures were made by St. Severin to the earl of Sandwich on the 27th of March, and on the 30th of April the preliminaries were signed between England, France, and Holland.

The sudden conclusion of this negotiation was no less owing to the deplorable state of the United Provinces than to the frankness and sincerity of France. When the duke of Cumberland joined the army in the commencement of March, he was astonished at the mismanagement and un-exampled supineness of the Dutch : Instead of 50,000 men, who, according to the promise of the prince of Orange, were to assemble in the vicinity of Breda, not 10,000 could

be collected, and those in want of arms, clothing, accoutrements, and every other necessary. He was even obliged to
detach nineteen battalions for the defence of Breda, by which
means he could not gather a sufficient force on the side of
the Maes, to join the Austrians, for the protection of Maestricht. The finances also were so much dilapidated, that the
Dutch government was unable to advance the 100,000*l.*
which they had engaged to pay for the march of the Russian
troops, and had ineffectually endeavoured to raise a loan of
300,000*l.* in England. In this situation the capture of
Maestricht was inevitable, and the French, masters of that
fortress, might have penetrated into the heart of the United
Provinces, without experiencing any effectual opposition
from a weak and distracted government, and from a people
discontented, exhausted, and spiritless.

In the secret conferences between the English and French
plenipotentiaries, the principal difficulties were, the restitution of Finale, which had been guaranteed to the king of
Sardinia, and the cession of a territory in Italy for the
establishment of Don Philip. But the impending loss of
the United Provinces, and the apprehensions lest France
should raise her demands on the surrender of Maestricht,
which was invested, extorted the consent of England; the
mutual restitution of all conquests was made the basis of the
preliminaries, and Parma and Placentia were assigned to
Don Philip. These conditions were submitted to the
Austrian and Sardinian plenipotentiaries. Count Kaunitz,
however, not only refused his consent to any farther dismemberment of the Austrian territories, but insisted on the
complete execution of the treaty of Worms, and threatened
that his mistress would resume the cessions made to the
king of Sardinia, if she was compelled to give an establishment to Don Philip. Count Chavennes, with equal obstinacy, objected to the restitution of Finale, and demanded
an equivalent for Placentia, which was yielded to his master
by the treaty of Worms. In consequence of their refusal,
and of the absence of the Spanish and Genoese ministers,
the English, French, and Dutch plenipotentiaries separately
signed the preliminaries; an immediate suspension of arms
was stipulated for the Low Countries; and the French were

permitted, for the sake of form, to take possession of Maestricht.

Maria Theresa was not unacquainted with the progress of the negotiation, as the necessity of an immediate peace to save the United Provinces was repeatedly urged to her minister Count Kaunitz, and information transmitted by him to Vienna, that her concurrence was required by the three contracting powers. But the first formal notification of the intended conditions was made to the empress in person by sir Thomas Robinson, on the 1st of May. She received, with the highest marks of indignation, a proposal so contrary to her interests, her principles, and even to the repeated professions of the British cabinet, that they would require no farther dismemberment of her territories. She scarcely allowed the minister time to execute his commission, before she burst out in the most bitter reproaches : " You, sir," she exclaimed, " who had such a share in the sacrifice of Silesia ; you who contributed more than any person in procuring the additional cessions made to the king of Sardinia ; do you still think to persuade me ? No ; I am neither a child nor a fool ! Your accounts about the Dutch are exaggerated ; a countenance may be still held, and there is still force to support that countenance. If you will have an instant peace, make it ; I can accede, can negotiate for myself. And why am I always to be excluded from transacting my own business ? My enemies will give me better conditions than my friends ; at least they will not refuse a peace, which they want as much as I do, for any dispute remaining between me and the king of Sardinia, about a little territory, more or less, or for the interpretation of a treaty. And who tells you Spain so much as desires Parma and Placentia ? She would rather have Savoy : place me where I was in Italy before the war, and I will establish the Infant : but YOUR KING OF SARDINIA must have all without one thought or care for me ! The treaty of Worms was not made for me, but for him singly ! Good God ! how have I been used by that court ! THERE IS YOUR KING OF PRUSSIA ! Indeed, indeed, all these circumstances, at once, rip up too many old and make new wounds."

She listened to the asseverations of the British minister, concerning the distressed state of the Dutch, and his attempts to explain the treaty of Worms, with sullen indignation; and then ironically demanded, "Am I to hear of Limburgh too for the Palatine, or of refunding the capitals of the Genoese, which have been confiscated in these countries?" Sir Thomas Robinson, in reply, read a passage in a letter from the duke of Newcastle to this effect : " An establishment for Don Philip, which in the opinion of the king of England, cannot be more moderate, or liable to less inconvenience, than by yielding the duchies of Parma and Placentia, to revert to the present possessors, should Don Philip succeed to the kingdoms of Naples and Sicily, in consequence of the accession of Don Carlos to the crown of Spain, on the death of the present king without issue male." This intimation roused her lofty spirit still farther, and she concluded the audience with exclaiming, " What, return to the PRESENT possessors !" and, accompanying her words with a significant gesture, added, " No, no ! I will rather lose my head !"

No persuasion could bend the empress-queen until the preliminaries were signed; when, finding herself unable to resist the will of the contracting powers, she reluctantly yielded, and, after many fruitless protests, and violent remonstrances, her plenipotentiary acceded to the preliminaries on the 18th of May.

But the discussions relative to the Barrier Treaty furnished great obstacles. Kaunitz declared that the signature of the preliminaries between the Maritime Powers and France, without the participation of the empress-queen, had abrogated that as well as all preceding treaties. Numerous disputes also took place between him and the Dutch plenipotentiaries. The Dutch insisted that the Barrier towns should be delivered to them and the empress-queen, conjointly as sovereigns ; a proposition which was peremptorily rejected, as an infringement of her prerogative : on the contrary, while she acknowledged the right of garrison, she insisted that even those towns, which, from the destruction of the fortifications were rendered incapable of defence, should not be restored to the Dutch. From the perseverance of both parties the mediation of England was for a considerable time ineffectual. This dispute nearly occasioned the rupture of the negotiation ; and both the Austrian and Dutch plenipotentiaries had positive instructions not to yield. At length the influence of England prevailed; count Bentinck was persuaded to disobey his instructions, and Kaunitz consented to a convention which revived that part of the Barrier relating to the Dutch garrisons, but preserved the sovereign rights of his imperial mistress.

Besides the disputes with the house of Austria, the conclusion of peace was retarded by difficulties in which the other contracting powers were equally involved. But at length the definitive treaty was signed at Aix-la-Chapelle, on the 18th of October, by the plenipotentiaries of France, England, and Holland, and was acceded to by Spain on the 20th of November, by the empress-queen on the 23rd, and by the king of Sardinia on the 7th of December. By this treaty the election of the emperor was acknowledged; and the house of Austria obtained the guaranty of the Pragmatic Sanction. Maria Theresa recovered the Low Countries, but was obliged to restore her conquests in Italy to confirm the cession of Silesia and Glatz to the king of Prussia, and to yield the duchies of Parma, Placentia, and Guastalla to Don Philip. She likewise ratified the cessions made by the treaty of Worms to the king of Sardinia, of the Vigevenascó, part of the Parmesan, and of the county of Anghiera.

Thus terminated a bloody and extensive war, which at the commencement threatened the very existence of the house of Austria; but the magnanimity of Maria Theresa, the zeal of her subjects, and the support of Great Britain, triumphed over her numerous enemies, and secured an honourable peace. She retained possession of all her vast inheritance, except Silesia, Parma, Placentia, and Guastalla; she recovered the imperial dignity, which had been nearly wrested from the house of Austria, and obtained the guaranty of the Pragmatic Sanction from the principal powers of Europe. She was, however, so dissatisfied, that her chagrin broke out on many occasions, and on none more than when Mr. Keith requested an audience, to offer his congratulations on the return of peace. Her minister was ordered to observe, that compliments of condolence were more proper than compliments of congratulation, and insinuated that the British minister would oblige his mistress by sparing a conversation, which would be highly disagreeable to her, and no less unpleasing to him.

Chap. CIX. — 1749-1756.

Maria Theresa employed the interval between the peace of Aix-la-Chapelle and the commencement of the seven years' war, in healing the wounds inflicted on her countries during the preceding hostilities. She had felt from fatal experience the danger which had threatened her vast empire, from the weak and unprovided state in which her father had left his dominions ; she had learned, from the example of her formidable rival the king of Prussia, the advantages resulting from an efficient and disciplined army, and well-furnished treasury; she was convinced, from the superficial manner in which the treaty of Aix-la-Chapelle had glossed over various pretensions and disputes among the belligerent powers, that the peace could be considered as little more than a suspension of arms ; and that another bloody war would take place, before the equilibrium of Europe could be settled on a more permanent basis. She conceived great apprehensions from the alarming rise of the house of Brandenburgh, and from the civil and military talents of Frederic II., and was sensible that the only effectual method to maintain the respect due to her political consequence, was, by holding herself in constant readiness for hostilities. Impressed with these sentiments, she turned her principal attention to the regulation of her finances, and the improvement of her army ; the successful manner in which she carried these objects into execution is recorded by the Royal Historian, and his testimony cannot be suspected of partiality in favour of a princess, whom he styles his "ambitious, vindictive, and implacable enemy."

" Maria Theresa prepared in the secrecy of the cabinet those great projects which she afterwards carried into execution. She introduced an order and economy into the finances, unknown to her ancestors; and her revenues far exceeded those possessed by her father, even when he was master of Naples, Parma, Silesia, and Servia. Having learned the necessity of introducing into her army a better discipline, she annually formed camps in the provinces, which she visited herself, that she might animate the troops by her presence and bounty. She established a military academy at

Vienna, and collected the most skilful professors of all the sciences and exercises which tend to elucidate or improve the art of war. By these institutions the army acquired, under the auspices of Maria Theresa, such a degree of perfection as it had never attained under any of her predecessors; and a woman accomplished designs worthy of a great man."

A new system was introduced into the administration of the finances; the number of useless collectors was diminished, the mode of anticipating the revenues by assignments abolished; the ordinary and extraordinary taxes rendered permanent for a term of years; and many exemptions annulled. Hence the revenues of the house of Austria, which, in the time of the late emperor did not exceed 30,000,000 florins, were increased to 36,000,000, notwithstanding the loss of Naples and of Silesia, which duchy alone produced six millions, and a regular fund was established for the maintenance of a standing army of 108,000 men in the hereditary countries, exclusive of the forces in Italy and the Netherlands. The troops were also partly distributed in Austria and Bohemia, instead of being solely stationed in Hungary, whence they could not immediately be drawn in cases of urgent necessity.

The death of count Sinzendorf, the chancellor, which happened in 1742, was a great loss to the court of Vienna. Though indolent and voluptuous, he was easy of access; though impetuous in his manners, he was open to conviction; he derived considerable credit from his long and tried services for more than thirty years, and he was eager to counteract the malign influence of Bartenstein,

He was succeeded by count Uhlfeld, who had filled the office of ambassador at the Hague and at Constantinople; and whose unexpected promotion to this high station was a singular proof of the jealousy of the empress, and the cunning of Bartenstein. The public voice, and the wishes of the court, pointed out count Harrach; but Bartenstein found means to influence the decision of his sovereign, by insinuating that the credit and talents of count Harrach would give him greater ascendency in the council of state than became a subject; while count Uhlfeld, with inferior talents, was a man of a more pliant disposition, and would not presume to urge his opinion in opposition to the will of the sovereign. Uhlfeld was indeed a minister suited to the temper and

genius of the referendary. He was honest and well-inten-
tioned ; but slow in his comprehension, confused in his ideas,
and indolent both from habit and want of capacity ; he was
fond of mystery, and of a captious, cavilling, and suspicious
temper. To these mental disqualifications was added a difficulty of hearing, which embarrassed those who negotiated
with him. By his taste for magnificence and parade, he had
become involved in his circumstances, and was therefore
rendered dependent ; hence he was wholly governed by Bartenstein, to whom he owed his elevation, and was as submissive to him as he was overbearing to others.

The deaths of Staremberg, Harrach, and Kinsky had increased the overgrown power of the referendary ; and the
ministers of the conference, Colloredo, Kevenhuller, and
marshal Bathiani, bowed before the idol, or were unable to
resist his superior credit.

The empress, though jealous of being governed, and peremptory in her resolutions, was extremely diffident of her
abilities, from a due consciousness of her own inexperience ;
hence she assiduously examined memorials and counter-me-
morials, and spared no endeavours to form a just and decisive
opinion on every subject of importance. From the same
motive, she not only deliberated with the emperor and her
own cabinet counsellors, but listened with great patience to
the long and contradictory expositions of foreign ministers ;
and repeatedly consulted some of her own subjects who were
not in office, and in whose abilities and honesty she confided.

Among these the most conspicuous was baron Wasner,
who had long been imperial minister in England, and returned to Vienna after the peace of Aix-la-Chapelle. He
was a man of strong sense and great capacity, of a frank and
open disposition, and well versed in foreign affairs. He was
held in high estimation by the empress, and often consulted
by her, either in person, or by means of Koch, her cabinet
secretary. His known favour excited the jealousy of Bartenstein ; and the presumptuous referendary never condescended to discourse with him on business, even when sent
by the emperor himself. Wasner strongly inculcated the
necessity of an union with the Maritime Powers, whom he
represented as the best and only friends of the house of
Austria ; and exposed the folly of imagining that France

would assist in the recovery of Silesia, the bait constantly
held out by Bartenstein.

From such a motley assemblage of discordant counsellors,
and impelled by such contradictory motives in the conduct
of foreign affairs, Maria Theresa fluctuated in continual
uncertainty. She was teased by the remonstrances of the
foreign ambassadors, who were frequently referred by Bartenstein to count Uhlfeld, and by count Uhlfeld to Bartenstein, and had even condescended to request the British
minister to conciliate the friendship of Bartenstein, "that
things," as she said, "might go on more smoothly." But a
princess of her high spirit and jealous temper could not long
submit to such humiliation for a mere subaltern in office.
She was disgusted with the presumption and petulance of the
referendary ; and as she became more acquainted with
business, and acquired in the school of adversity a greater
confidence in her own powers, she perceived the weakness
and incapacity of her cabinet, and deeply felt the necessity
of intrusting the administration of affairs to a person of tried
integrity and talents, and qualified by his rank for so important a station. She accordingly fixed her choice on count
Kaunitz, who was then ambassador at Paris.

The elevation of Kaunitz to the office of chancellor and
the supreme direction of foreign affairs forms a remarkable
epoch in the reign of Maria Theresa ; because to the counsels of that minister must be principally attributed the alliance
with France, and the change of the political system hitherto
pursued by the cabinet of Vienna.

Anthony Wenceslaus, first count and afterwards prince of
Kaunitz Rietberg, who directed the counsels of Austria for
a period of almost forty years, was son of Maximilian Ulric
count of Kaunitz, governor of Moravia, and ambassador at
Rome, by Mary Ernestina daughter and heiress of Ferdinand
Maximilian, last count of Rietberg. Being eminently noticed
for his diplomatic talents, he was sent envoy to the court of
Turin ; and the first despatch which he wrote to Uhlfield
was drawn in so masterly a manner, that the count, in presenting it to Maria Theresa, said, "Behold your first minister."
In 1744, he was removed from Turin to Brussels, in the
character of plenipotentiary, and intrusted with the direction
of affairs in the Low Countries, under the archduchess Mari-

anne and prince Charles of Loraine. In 1748, he was
appointed ambassador and plenipotentiary to the congress of
Aix-la-Chapelle, and highly distinguished himself for his
skill in negotiation, and for the firmness with which he supported the interests of the house of Austria.

Soon after the conclusion of the definitive treaty, he repaired to Vienna, and obtained both the confidence of the
emperor and empress, by whom he was secretly consulted
in every affair of importance, and was frequently employed
in qualifying and altering the captious memorials of Bartenstein. But although he swayed the counsels of the court of
Vienna, he acted in so discreet a manner as not to excite
umbrage even in the suspicious mind of the referendary, and
still less among the ministers of the conference. In September 1751, he was deputed ambassador to Paris, where
his conduct contributed still farther to increase the predilection of his sovereign. At length, the empress unable to
restrain her disgust at the overweening petulance and insolence of the referendary, recalled Kaunitz, in 1753, to assume
the principal administration of affairs, and "expected his
arrival with the same impatience as Henry VIII. looked
for the return of Cranmer when he was tired of Wolsey." *
On his arrival, Bartenstein, after some ineffectual endeavours first to intimidate, and afterwards to conciliate him,
was removed, and promoted to the vice-chancellorship of
Bohemia, with the title of privy counsellor ; at the same
time count Uhlfeld was created grand master of the court,
with a pension, and the payment of his debts. The other
ministers of the conference remained in place ; Kaunitz was
installed in the chancellorship with general approbation, and
his first measure was to introduce a new arrangement into
the office for foreign affairs.

Kaunitz was in the forty-third year of his age when he
was called to the supreme direction of affairs. He possessed

---

* Despatch of sir Charles Hanbury Williams to the duke of Newcastle, Dresden July 15. 1753. Sir Charles, who was minister at Dresden, was privately despatched by the duke of Newcastle, to gain an
insight into the situation and principles of the court of Vienna, and to
remonstrate against the infractions of the Barrier Treaty. He remained
at Vienna during the arrangements for the elevation of Kaunitz, and the
dismission of Bartenstein ; and from his interesting account the particulars of this chapter are principally drawn.

great abilities, a perspicuous method of transacting business,
and explaining the most complicated affairs, an accurate
knowledge of the state of Europe, and an indefatigable zeal
for the service of his imperial mistress. To these qualities
were added incorruptible integrity, skill in negotiation,
impenetrable secrecy, profound dissimulation which he
carried even to duplicity, and a semblance of candour and
openness by which he acquired the confidence of those with
whom he treated, even while deceiving or opposing them.

Kaunitz was called to the helm of state at a time when
the relative situation of the house of Austria had been
essentially changed by the rise of the house of Brandenburgh,
and when the court of Vienna was involved in endless disputes with England.

To prevent the renewal of war, in case of the death of the
emperor Francis, and to establish the preponderance of the
house of Austria in the empire, the British cabinet were
desirous of raising the archduke Joseph to the dignity of
king of the Romans. This project, however wise in theory,
was, in the present state of Europe and the empire, equally
chimerical and impracticable. The only votes on which
they could depend were those of Bohemia, Hanover, and
Mentz; even the electors of Saxony and Bavaria, who were
most friendly to the house of Austria, could not be secured
without considerable subsidies, nor those of Palatine and
Cologne, without the concurrence of France and Prussia,
who were decidedly hostile to the measure. Yet so eager
were the English ministry to gain this point, that they even
gave subsidies to Bavaria and Saxony in time of peace,
though contrary to the established usages of the country,
and to the sense of the nation. But these subsidies were
insufficient to obtain a majority of votes; and the empress
was called upon not only to contribute their share, but to
gratify the electors in their numerous pretensions on the
house of Austria, and the extraordinary privileges which
they required from the head of the empire.

This negotiation spread into as many different branches
as there were different electors; new demands were continually started, and new cessions required, till at length the
court of Vienna declared their inability to make any additional sacrifice. Even the ministers most devoted to the
Maritime Powers complained of the eagerness with which

this object was urged, as it gave, they said, ill-intentioned
persons an opportunity of insinuating that England, by supporting these repeated demands, took a pleasure in stripping
the house of Austria; and the emperor himself frequently
hinted to the British minister, that such a precipitancy ill
accorded with the slow and cautious mode of proceeding in
the cabinet of Vienna. These gentle remonstrances only
augmented the eagerness of the English ministry : they made
remonstrances on remonstrances : expressed their surprise
that the court of Vienna should be insensible to their own
interest, and even urged that the union between the house
of Austria and the Maritime Powers depended on a speedy
concurrence. Such indiscreet and peremptory demands had
a fatal effect on the sensitive mind of Maria Theresa, whose
greatest foible was a jealous regard of her own honour; she
was unwilling to be indebted to foreign power for the establishment of the imperial dignity in her family; she declared
that in every instance her compliance had only encouraged
new demands, and that even the crown of the empire might
be purchased at too dear a price.

Another cause of dissatisfaction between the courts of
Vienna and London, was derived from the language held in
the memorials and papers of the British cabinet, who
assumed a high tone of superiority, expatiated on their great
and important services which had saved the house of Austria from ruin, and imperiously demanded a return of gratitude. Their zealous friend baron Wasner frequently represented the fatal effects of such unconciliating language;
Kaunitz exhorted them to respect the sex, and consider the
temper of the empress-queen, and not irritate her by un-
generous reproaches. The emperor remonstrated against
some harsh expressions used to the imperial minister at
London ; even the empress herself complained to Mr. Keith
of the arrogant and peremptory style of the English papers,
which, though it had no effect on her, gave a pretext to ill-
intentioned persons ; and requested that milder terms might
be employed. This complaint was too justly founded ; Mr.
Keith often declined delivering the haughty messages and
declarations which he was ordered to communicate to the
empress in person, and more than once incurred the censure
of the king and ministers for his delicacy and good sense.
The Austrian cabinet retorted with equal spirit and rancour,

and the communications between the two courts degenerated into a paper war.

In addition to the original disputes relative to the affairs of the Netherlands, new difficulties had arisen. As we have already observed, no specific arrangements had been made for a new treaty of commerce during the reign of Charles; and soon after the accession of Maria Theresa, the conferences at Antwerp were broken up without effect. The war, in which England and Holland lavished their blood and treasure in support of the house of Austria, suspended the feuds which had been excited in the discussions relative to the Barrier Treaty; but the precipitate conclusion of the preliminaries again renewed the altercations, and rendered the empress-queen still less disposed to gratify the Maritime Powers. With the intention of bringing the point to an issue, the Austrian plenipotentiary would not agree to the specification of the Barrier Treaty among those renewed by the definitive peace; and the empress-queen established a new tariff in the Netherlands, which placed the trade of her subjects on an equality with that of England and Holland. She justified this alteration by declaring, that they had forfeited the privileges which they derived from the twenty-sixth article of the Barrier, by not concluding a treaty of commerce within the two years specified by the treaty of Vienna. On the contrary the Maritime Powers urged that the twenty-sixth article of the Barrier was not a mere provisional and temporary stipulation, but absolute and permanent, though subject to be altered by common consent; and therefore still remained in full force till the three contracting parties should concur in forming a treaty of commerce.

In addition to this source of contention, the dilapidated state of the barrier towns gave rise to new disputes. The court of Vienna declined paying the arrears due to the United States before the war, and withheld the annual subsidies, on the ground that many of those towns being demolished or incapable of defence, the subsidies ought to be appropriated to the repairs of the fortifications, and the establishment of a regular military force.

All attempts to adjust these differences were ineffectual; and the negotiation was protracted, or rather languished, till Kaunitz was placed at the head of affairs. During his residence at Brussels he had paid particular attention to the resources and riches of the Netherlands, and had formed a plan for raising the revenues and extending the commerce. He had therefore exerted all his influence to procure their emancipation from the shackles of the Barrier. It was disgraceful, he urged, for so powerful a sovereign to suffer her frontier towns to be garrisoned by foreign troops, as if her own forces were insufficient to guard her territory ; and he represented the annual subsidy as a memorial of dependence and subjection ; he also proposed to employ the whole revenue for the maintenance of a large body of troops, by which the Barrier would be more effectually defended than by Dutch garrisons. By his suggestions Maria Theresa was induced to remonstrate against the Barrier Treaty at the peace of Aix-la-Chapelle, and afterwards refused to pay the annual subsidy.

At his proposal the three powers delivered their respective claims ; a project was formed, and the difference relative to the subsidies and arrears seemed nearly brought to a conclusion ; but the commercial disputes produced insuperable difficulties. The Maritime Powers contended that the Netherlands, conquered with their blood and treasure, were delivered to the house of Austria as a deposit, on the condition of defending those territories against the French ; that according to the principles of the Grand Alliance, the sovereign had no right to extend their commercial privileges. Those countries, it was urged, formed the only cement of the connection between the house of Austria and the Maritime Powers ; and, by the breach of the Barrier Treaty, that cement would be dissolved.

This mode of argument, which treated the sovereigns of the house of Austria as mere guardians of the Netherlands, was galling to the pride and spirit of the court of Vienna ; Maria Theresa was shocked with the haughty style in which these arguments were urged ; and her constant reply to the representations of the British ministers evinced her unalterable resolution not to submit to their dictates : "Am I not sovereign," she exclaimed, " in the Low Conntries ; and is it not my duty to protect my subjects, who have been too long oppressed by the Barrier Treaty, and deprived of the advantages which all other nations enjoy?" *

* Sir Charles Hanbury Williams to the duke of Newcastle, July 15. " These expressions," he observes, " she repeated so loudly as to be heard by those in the next room."

Chap. CX. — 1756.

Such, at this juncture, was the frail tenure of the long-established connection between the house of Austria and England; and a no less essential change had taken place in her relative situation, from the increasing power and resources of the king of Prussia. The rapid aggrandisement of the house of Brandenburgh, which Leopold, Joseph, and Charles had promoted as a counterpoise to the house of Bourbon, seemed likely to destroy the equilibrium of the German empire, and threatened the loss of that preponderance in Europe, which had been hitherto possessed by the house of Austria. The attention of Kaunitz was naturally directed to this new phenomenon in the political world; the humiliation of the Prussian power, so ably exerted by a great and enterprising monarch, seemed the primary object of all his plans, and he formed the bold, and seemingly extravagant design, of effecting this object by an alliance with France. His views were promoted by the change which had been gradually wrought in the mind of his imperial mistress.

At an early period of her reign, Bartenstein had succeeded in instilling into her mind suspicions of the Maritime Powers, and had artfully availed himself of the disagreeable discussions which had accompanied the various negotiations for the cession of Silesia. The loss of that valuable province had sunk deep into her mind: like Mary of England, in her regret for the capture of Calais, she might have exclaimed that Silesia was written in her heart; and she could not see a native without bursting into tears. The cessions extorted from her in Italy furnished new fuel for discontent; and her disgust was still further aggravated by the remonstrances against the infractions of the Barrier Treaty, and the disputes towards the close of the war; while the signature of the preliminaries, without her participation, contributed to render the breach irreparable.

In the course of the negotiations for the peace of Aix-la-Chapelle, the empress-queen had attempted to conciliate France, and Kaunitz had even secretly offered the cession of part of the Low Countries, provided Louis would assist in recovering Silesia. The empress-queen, not disconcerted at the rejection of this proposal, renewed her overtures to Blondel, chargé d'affaires at Vienna, and afterwards to the marquis d'Hautefort, the French ambassador; and at the same time Kaunitz was despatched to Paris with instructions to promote this great object.

During his embassy he laboured with continual assiduity and address to soften the inveterate enmity of the French court, and to loosen the connection between France and Prussia. He insinuated to the ministers that the aggrandisement of Prussia was their work, and that they had hitherto received no other return than ingratitude from a sovereign who was governed solely by his own interest. To strengthen these impressions, which gradually began to take effect, he paid assiduous court to the marchioness of Pompadour, with whom he had opened a correspondence during the negotiation for the peace of Aix-la-Chapelle, and employed every species of flattery to induce her to second his views. At his suggestion the pious and high-born Maria Theresa did not scruple to write in the most confidential terms of friendship and equality to the mistress of Louis; and when Kaunitz apologised for requiring so great a sacrifice, she replied, " Have I not flattered Farinelli? " * The low-born favourite, enraptured with the attentions and familiarity of the greatest sovereign in Europe, employed all her influence to promote the wished-for alliance. The projects and intrigues of Kaunitz seemed even on the point of being crowned with success, when they were frustrated by the insinuations of the king of Prussia, who retained many adherents at the court of Versailles, and by the timidity of the favourite, who hesitated at taking upon herself the responsibility of recommending an alliance with the inveterate enemy of France, in opposition to the opinion of the cabinet, and to the deep-rooted prejudices of the nation.

In the midst of these intrigues Kaunitz was recalled to Vienna, and placed at the head of affairs. But though

---

* Despatch of Mr. Stanley to Mr. Pitt, Paris, August 20. 1761. Farinelli, the celebrated singer, had been called to Madrid during the reign of Philip V., and was at this time in high favour with Barbara, queen of Ferdinand VI. For an account of Farinelli, and his influence with the court of Madrid, see Memoirs of the Kings of Spain, chap. xlix.

defeated in his attempts to vanquish the prejudices of the
court of Versailles, he did not for a moment lose sight of
his great object; and count Staremberg, his successor at
Paris, was instructed to pursue the same line of conduct,
and to watch for a favourable opportunity of securing the
concurrence of France. At the same time, either to lull
the suspicions of the Maritime Powers, or from the dread of
breaking off a long-established for an uncertain alliance,
Kaunitz affected a great enthusiasm for the ancient connections of the house of Austria. Before his departure for
Paris he had been the secret channel of communication
between the British minister and the empress, and had
provided for the continuance of the correspondence through
Koch, the cabinet secretary ; he also now called himself the
champion of the ancient system, and declared that his
mistress could neither expect friendship nor service from
the court of Versailles.

At this time he seems even to have fluctuated between
the fear of losing England, and the dread of being disappointed in his attempts to conciliate France. At one period
he exerted all his efforts to draw Great Britain into his
views, by expatiating on the ambitious, restless, and turbulent spirit of the king of Prussia ; he also endeavoured to
inflame the emnity between the courts of London and
Berlin, which had been aggravated by disputes relative to
the possession of East Friesland, and by the refusal of the
king of Prussia to discharge a loan advanced by the English
merchants on some districts in Silesia. But the British
cabinet refusing to break the engagements contracted by
the treaties of Breslau and Dresden, Kaunitz suffered the
causes of misunderstanding between the house of Austria
and England to operate in their full force, and resumed his
intrigues at Versailles with redoubled ardour. The disputes
which had now risen between England and France presented
to this artful minister a favourable opportunity of forwarding
his views.

By the twelfth article of the peace of Utrecht, France
had ceded to England Nova Scotia or Acadia, *according to
its ancient limits.* This vague expression had occasioned
disputes between the two countries, which were renewed by
an article of the treaty of Aix-la-Chapelle, specifying "that

all things should be placed on the same footing as before the war." England therefore claimed that territory according to the limits assigned in the commissions of the French officers, and by the preceding treaties, which comprised the whole tract lying between the River St. Lawrence, Pentagoet or Penobscot, and the Atlantic Ocean ; while the French, on the authority of some ancient maps and historians, restricted the limits of Acadia to the south-eastern part of the peninsula comprehended between the capes of St. Mary and Causo. During these discussions, the establishment of an English company trading to the Ohio, occasioned new contentions ; and the French endeavoured to confine the colonists towards the west, by building a line of forts between their settlements on the Mississippi and the province of Canada. Disputes also arose relative to the islands of St. Lucia, Dominica, St. Vincent, and Tobago. As neither court was willing to relinquish their respective claims, the contest was likely to be decided by the sword ; and a new continental war seemed inevitable.

In this state of affairs England required the house of Austria to fulfil the existing treaties, and repay the assistance so liberally furnished in the last war ; and urged the empress-queen to specify the force she would bring forwards in defence of the Netherlands and of Hanover, if attacked by France and Prussia. But Kaunitz amused the British cabinet with vague assurances and impracticable plans, was explicit in no other instance than in enforcing the necessity of dismembering the Prussian dominions ; and when the commencement of hostilities with France compelled the British cabinet to require a specific declaration from the court of Vienna, he still continued to temporise, and on the 16th of April, 1755, delivered a memorial, which he affected to call the ultimatum of his court, and a plan of mutual operations against France.

In this paper the empress declared, that she could not expose her hereditary dominions and the capital to the attacks of her implacable enemy the king of Prussia, by withdrawing her troops from Bohemia, and could only agree to complete the contingent of 25,000 men in the Netherlands. She therefore proposed to leave the principal defence of those countries to the Maritime Powers, expected the king of England to enter into a treaty with Russia for 60,000 men, and to renew the subsidiary treaties with Saxony, Bavaria, the landgrave of Hesse, and other princes; she required the United Provinces to supply their contingent of 6000 men, and England 10,000. These forces, united with the Hessians and Austrians, would, it was asserted, form an army of 70,000 men capable of resisting France; and the imperial troops, assisted by the Russians, would then be able to withstand all the attacks of Prussia.

In answer to this extraordinary proposal, which threw the whole burden of the war upon the Maritime Powers, the British cabinet declared that the king was taking 8000 Hessians into pay for the defence of the Netherlands, was inclined to join with the empress-queen in renewing the subsidiary treaties with Saxony and Bavaria, and would incur the whole expense of obtaining from Russia a corps of 50,000 or 60,000 men to be employed for the common cause. In return, the court of Vienna was required to despatch an immediate reinforcement of 25,000 or 30,000 men to the Netherlands, exclusive of the garrison of Luxemburgh, as the only means of obtaining the co-operation of the United Provinces, and to assemble a second army for the protection of Hanover, if attacked by Prussia.

In the midst of this discussion the king of England repaired to Hanover to hasten the negotiation. In the course of the journey the earl of Holdernesse, secretary of state, visited the Netherlands and the United Provinces. He learned from the governor prince Charles of Loraine, that the imperial forces consisted only of 20,000 troops, of which above 7000 would be requisite for the garrison of Luxemburgh; that, excepting the Barrier Towns, no fortress was tenable; and that, being unable to defend the whole country, he would only engage to cover those parts of the Dutch frontier which were most exposed. The situation of Holland was still more unfavourable. The Dutch, irritated with the contests relative to the Barrier Treaty, and alarmed at the defenceless state of the Netherlands, had even withdrawn their troops from the Barrier Towns, and were desirous to save their country by negotiating a neutrality.

In consequence of this intelligence, the British minister

again represented the danger which would result from
leaving the Netherlands and Holland exposed to the aggressions of France ; but all their remonstrances, and even
reproaches, being ineffectual, they recapitulated the consequences of the conduct adopted by the court of Vienna, and
declared, " should the empress decline fulfilling the conditions
required, the king cannot take any measures in concert
with the house of Austria, and the whole system of Europe
must be dissolved." *

The answer of the court of Vienna was a summary of the
grievances of which they had long complained, and exhibits
the style of altercation adopted by both parties in this
memorable controversy.†

* The earl of Holdernesse to Mr. Keith, Hanover, May 31. 1755.

† " The empress-queen has never had the satisfaction of seeing her
allies do justice to her principles ; she at least flattered herself with that
satisfaction on the present occasion, when their real interests ought to
have induced them rather to animate than to diminish her zeal in support of her cause. If the troops of the empress were in the pay of Great
Britain, the disposal of them could not be settled in a more decisive
manner than in requiring her imperial majesty to remove them from
the centre of her dominions; and send them, with little appearance of
advantage, and the prospect of certain danger, to the protection of the
Netherlands, the United Provinces, England, and the electorate of Hanover. To persuade the empress to take this step we are reproached
with the numerous efforts made by the English in favour of the house
of Austria, while to those efforts they owe their present greatness, riches,
and liberty ; and had they always persevered in the same sentiments,
they would not now be menaced with the loss of what they have acquired at the expense of so much blood and treasure. All Europe will
doubtless agree with the court of Vienna ; for if the house of Austria
has derived useful succours from her alliance with the Maritime Powers,
she has frequently purchased those advantages with the blood and ruin
of her subjects ; while her allies have opened to themselves new sources
of aggrandisement and riches. With regret, therefore, we find ourselves
under the necessity of opposing these truths to unjust and unceasing reproaches ; and could any consideration diminish our gratitude towards
the Maritime Powers, it would doubtless be their endeavours to represent those succours as purely gratuitous, which have been, and will always
be, the consequences of their alliances, and of measures dictated by their
own interests. Had they always known and consulted their true interests, England would not now blame us for the insecurity of the Netherlands, which is only a necessary effect of her conduct and system.
In time of peace England judges rightly in considering their defence as
an object which ought only to interest the Maritime Powers. How
often have they not by singular arguments attempted to weaken our

After briefly stating the origin and progress of the
negotiations, and the plans of mutual defence which had
been proposed respectively, it was added ; "having no direct
interest, either in the object, motives, or consequences of
the war, her imperial majesty engages to share the danger,
although well aware that she must defend herself against
France and Prussia, aud perhaps against the Turks.   Can
it then be imagined, that in incurring all these perils for
the cause of her allies, she will imprudently neglect the
means of her own defence, and expose the centre of her own
dominions?   In leaving her troops, which are now stationed
in the Netherlands, for the defence of England and Holland,
and in resolving to attack the king of Prussia, should he
invade the electorate of Hanover, she exposes herself to the
peril of opposing the most dangerous enemy of the allies,
and undertakes for the common cause, not only all which is
in her power to execute, but even beyond what her allies
had a right to expect.

"It has been thought necessary to detail all the consequences which will result from the loss of the Netherlands,

most pressing remonstrances on the dangers which threatened those provinces ?   They have even not scrupled to advise the empress to disband
the troops, should the expense of maintaining them prevent her from
paying the subsidy stipulated by the Barrier Treaty.   In conformity to
this dangerous system the allies of the empress have considered the
Netherlands as provinces of their own ; England and Holland have
divided the commerce ; and Holland alone has drawn annually a million
of florins ; while the house of Austria has seen her subjects exhausted,
their property pass into the hands of foreigners, their manufactures de-
caying, and the whole substance of the state dried up.   She has often
attempted to convince the allies, that their interests were involved in the
preservation of the Netherlands ; but the treaty itself (which she has
faithfully observed during forty years, to the ruin of her subjects), the
voice of equity, and the safety of the common cause, have all yielded to
the opinion, that it was the business of the Maritime Powers to defend
the Netherlands.   Holland has more than once been on the point of
acknowledging the force of our arguments, but the same impression was
never made on England.   Hence the odious negotiation of the Barrier is
not concluded ; yet England reproaches us for her own indecision.   Till
this moment it has been urged that the defence of the Netherlands was
the duty of the Maritime Powers ; and now the empress is addressed
to save them.   It is pretended that we have too few troops in those
countries ; and yet only six months ago, England exerted every effort to
reduce us to the necessity of diminishing them one half."

as if we had not long ago endeavoured to induce the
Maritime Powers to comprehend the extent of those
consequences. The only answer which now can be made
to these representations is, although we shall feel the
misfortune of losing a part of our dominions, yet we can
prefer a lesser to a greater evil. But with a view of
composing these pernicious dissensions, the empress, more
affected with the dangerous situation of her allies, than
offended at their conduct, is desirous of making her last
effort, and frankly explaining her expectations and intentions. She has therefore ordered her ultimatum to be
delivered."

In this ultimatum the empress agreed to maintain a corps
of 25,000 men, exclusive of the garrisons of Namur and
Luxemburgh, which amounted to about 12,000 more, on the
sole condition that England should likewise bring into the
field 20,000 men ; that the United Provinces should furnish
their contingent, as stipulated by the Barrier Treaty, or at
least 8000. The king was also required to specify the
succours which in virtue of existing treaties he proposed to
send to the empress-queen, both in quality of king and
elector ; to conclude as soon as possible the subsidiary
treaties ; to employ, for the defence of the empress against
the king of Prussia, the Russian troops in the pay of Great
Britain ; and, finally, to adopt all the necessary measures to
secure the king of Sardinia, so as to remove all causes of
apprehension for Italy. On these conditions alone the imperial troops should instantly march to the Netherlands, as
soon as certain intelligence was received that the 20,000
men in the pay of Great Britain were in motion, and positive
assurances given for the due performance of the other conditions.*

Before this paper reached Hanover the breach was still
further widened by a peremptory memorial which the British
envoy was commanded to deliver to the court of Vienna,
requiring an explicit and categorical answer to the following
questions ; Should the French, or any ally of France, attack
the electorate of Hanover, is the empress determined to
send assistance ? What number of troops will she send ;

* Mr. Keith to the earl of Holdernesse, Vienna, June 19. 1755.

and in what time will they be in motion to join the British and Hanoverian forces ? It was urged, "obligation of treaties, gratitude for former assistance, and self-interest combine to show the necessity of assisting the king. The proportion of that assistance, and the expedition used in rendering it effectual, will display the real intentions of the court of Vienna, which the king is induced to believe will be consonant to equity and justice."

Kaunitz coldly answered, "Our only reply is to refer the king to the ultimatum already delivered to Mr. Keith. My mistress has no doubt those declarations will appear as satisfactory and ample as can be expected in the present situation of affairs ; nor can she give any answer to the present nor to any future question, till the king shall have explained his intentions upon the points contained in that ultimatum." In consequence of this answer, George II., with becoming dignity, declared that he would not enter into a paper war with the house of Austria ; and aware that he could expect no effectual assistance from the empress-queen, turned to the king of Prussia.

Frederic had long been disgusted with the haughty and contemptuous tone of superiority assumed by the court of Versailles * ; he was not unacquainted with the intrigues of the imperial minister ; he was alarmed at the evasive conduct of France, when pressed to renew the alliance which expired in May, 1756, and was apprehensive of being exposed singly to the arms of Russia and Austria. He therefore readily entered into engagements with the king of England, and on the 16th of January, 1756, a convention of neutrality was concluded, to prevent the contests in America from disturbing the peace of Germany, and for that purpose only to resist the entrance of foreign troops into the empire. By the two secret articles the Austrian Netherlands were excepted from the operations of this treaty ; and England agreed to indemnify the Prussian merchants for the capture of vessels during the preceding war.

The empress and her minister beheld the conclusion of

* Œuvres Posthumes, tom. iii. p. 43. 65. The first overture was made by Frederic himself, by means of the duke of Brunswick, in a letter from the duke to the earl of Holdernesse, dated August 2. Sir Benj. Keene's Papers.

this convention, not only without regret, but with extreme
satisfaction. They had already matured their plan for the
alliance with France ; the marchioness of Pompadour had
gradually replaced most of the ministers adverse to the
house of Austria with her own creatures, and had succeeded
in exciting the resentment of Louis against the king of
Prussia, who had indulged himself in sarcastic reflections on
his bigoted and licentious conduct. By these and other
means the Austrian party gained an ascendency in the French
cabinet, and the negotiation between England and Prussia
hastened the accomplishment of their views.

As early as the 22d of September, 1755, the mistress,
with her favourite the abbé de Bernis, and count Staremberg
the imperial minister, met at Babiole to adjust the first out-
lines of the intended alliance ; which were afterwards
privately discussed between the imperial minister and Bernis, at an apartment in the palace of the Luxemburgh belonging to the historian Duclos.* The plan being matured, the
mistress obtained from the king the express nomination of a
committee of her creatures, among whom was Bernis, though
not a counsellor of state, to receive from the imperial
ambassador the plan of an alliance between the houses of
Austria and Bourbon.

The terms proposed by Staremberg evinced the sincerity
of the empress-queen, and were calculated to eradicate all
seeds of disunion. Mons was to be annexed to France ; the
fortress of Luxemburgh to be raised ; Brabant and Hainault
to be ceded to the infant Don Philip, in exchange for Parma,
Placentia, and Guastalla ; Poland to be declared an hereditary monarchy in the descendants of Augustus ; Prussian
Pomerania to be given to Sweden ; and such arrangements
to be made with Russia, Spain, and the Italian Powers, as
would ensure the success of the alliance. The committee
were unwilling to charge themselves with the sanction of
this new and gigantic plan, so adverse to the ancient system,
and so likely to alienate the Porte and the German princes.
Accordingly, Bernis proposed a treaty of union between the
courts of Vienna and Versailles ; a guaranty of their respective possessions in Europe, and of the Prussian dominions,

* Duclos, Memoires Secrets, tom. ii. p. 416, 417., to whom these
anecdotes were communicated by the cardinal De Bernis himself.

and, to avoid the ungrateful appearance of acting against England, the empress was permitted to observe a neutrality. Maria Theresa at first objected to the guaranty of the Prussian dominions, but at length consented ; and the treaty was on the point of being concluded, when the signature of the convention of London completed the separation of France from Prussia. The Austrian minister availed himself of this event, made new overtures with a view to avoid the guaranty of the Prussian dominions, and finally succeeded in his object.

Hitherto the negotiations with France had been conducted by Kaunitz, under the auspices of Maria Theresa, with count d'Aubeterre the French ambassador at Vienna, and by Staremberg with the creatures of the marchioness de Pompadour at Paris, without the knowledge of the emperor Francis, or the participation of the ministers. But when the treaty was matured, it became necessary to lay the plan before the council of state. The empress being unwilling to shock the prejudices of her consort, or to stem the opposition of her own ministers, affected ignorance of the whole transaction. With her connivance in a meeting of the council of state, Kaunitz proposed the plan of an alliance with France. He had scarcely announced the memorial, when the other ministers murmured disapprobation ; and Francis rising up, with great emotion, vehemently struck the table with his hand, exclaiming, " such an unnatural alliance is impracticable, and shall never take place," and instantly quitted the apartment. Kaunitz appeared to hesitate, till, encouraged by his mistress, he detailed all the advantages which the house of Austria would derive from an alliance with France. The empress listened with affected attention, and gave her approbation in so decisive a tone as to silence the other counsellors. She concluded by undertaking to persuade the emperor, and affected to express her doubts of the concurrence of France. Kaunitz answered for that power ; the acquiescence of the emperor was soon extorted, and the management of the whole negotiation assigned to the minister, who had proposed, and so ably supported, the policy of the measure.

This whole transaction had been conducted with so much secrecy, that only vague suspicions were entertained of those negotiations which had passed in September and October; and the Prussian treaty was alleged by the court of Vienna, as the sole and operating cause which had compelled the house of Austria to quit her ancient allies, and to renounce that system which she had invariably followed for the last century. The empress-queen and her minister therefore received the communication of the treaty of London with as much affected surprise and indignation, as if no previous overture had been made to the court of Versailles.

In delivering on the 7th of April, a copy of the treaty with Prussia to the Austrian minister, Mr. Keith justified it as perfectly inoffensive, calculated to maintain the peace of the empire, and to relieve the empress-queen from her apprehensions of the king of Prussia; and he concluded with demanding an explanation on the subject of the supposed negotiation with the court of Versailles. A month elapsed before any answer was returned; when Kaunitz delivered a paper criminating the conduct of England, and justifying the empress; he also peremptorily refused to give any explanation relative to the negotiation with France.

In an audience of the empress, the British minister experienced greater affability and condescension; but she expressed the utmost abhorrence of a connection with the king of Prussia; and notwithstanding her previous negotiation with France, threw the blame of first deserting the ancient alliance on the king of England. In reply to the observation of Mr. Keith, that the answer delivered by count Kaunitz contained an absolute renunciation of the ancient and true system of Europe, she said, " I have not abandoned the old system, but Great Britain has abandoned me and that system, by concluding the Prussian treaty, the first intelligence of which struck me like a fit of apoplexy. I and the king of Prussia are incompatible; and no consideration on earth shall ever induce me to enter into any engagement of which he is a party." Mr. Keith, after apologising for the treaty, and employing many arguments to reconcile the empress-queen, adverted to the supposed negotiation with the French court. She refused to explain her conduct; but asked, " Why should you be surprised, if, following your example in concluding a treaty with Prussia, I should enter into an engagement with France ? "

Affecting to disbelieve that the empress would connect herself with the inveterate enemy of her person and family, the British minister declared that nothing could convince him of the existence of such an alliance, till he saw with his own eyes the signature of MARIA THERESA at the bottom of a treaty with that crown. "I am," she replied, "far from being French in my disposition, and do not deny that the court of Versailles has been my bitterest enemy ; but I cannot conceal, that the cessions which Great Britain extorted from me at the peace of Dresden, and of Aix-la-Chapelle, have totally disabled me. I have little to fear from France ; I am unable to act with vigour, and have no other resource than to form such arrangements as will secure what remains." The British minister exclaiming, "will you, the empress and archduchess, so far humble yourself as to throw yourself into the arms of France ? " " Not into the arms," she hastily rejoined, "but on the side of France. I have," she continued, "hitherto signed nothing with France, though I know not what may happen ; but whatever happens, I promise, on my word of honour, not to sign any thing contrary to the interest of your royal master, for whom I have a most sincere friendship and regard."

The empress listened with great affability to all the remonstrances and arguments of the British minister, but continued unshaken in her resolution : and concluded : "I no longer have it in my power to take an active share in distant transactions ; I am therefore little concerned for the remote parts of my dominions, and my principal object is to secure my hereditary possessions. I have truly but two enemies whom I really dread, the king of Prussia and the Turks ; and while I and the empress of Russia continue on the same good terms as now subsist between us, we shall, I trust, be able to convince Europe, that we are in a condition to defend ourselves against those adversaries, however formidable."

The empress gave this audience on the 13th of May, and the treaty with France had been already signed on the 1st. In imitation of the convention of London, the two sovereigns agreed, by an act of neutrality, to prevent the contest in America from disturbing their mutual harmony ; and a treaty of alliance, purely defensive, renewed all former engagements since the treaty of Westphalia. The empress-queen promised to defend the French dominions in Europe, if attacked, except during the present war with England ; while the king of France was to aid the house of Austria without any exception. The two powers also stipulated to assist each other with a mutual succour of 24,000 men in case of invasion, the present war excepted.

The origin and progress of this negotiation have been thus traced from authentic documents with considerable minuteness ; because it is an event which effectually changed the system of Europe, and materially affected the interests of the house of Austria. These documents also prove, that the treaty of Versailles was not the necessary consequence of the alliance between Great Britain and Prussia, signed January 16. 1756, and that the plan of an union with France had been gradually and circumspectly matured during a long course of intrigue and negotiation.

The courts of Vienna and London accused each other of haughtiness, obstinacy, ingratitude, a renunciation of the ancient system, and a desertion of that alliance which had subsisted for more than a hundred years ; yet each demanded from the other what perhaps was equally impracticable and impolitic. The court of Vienna, if sincere, expected England to co-operate in dismembering the Prussian dominions, and required the Maritime Powers to charge themselves with almost the whole defence of the Netherlands. On the other hand, the court of London expected the empress to protect the electorate of Hanover, and to detach a considerable force for the defence of the Netherlands, which England was most interested to preserve. With such discordant expectations, and the jealousies which had so long subsisted, it was no wonder that a separation ensued. The British ministry did not consider, that the relative situation of the house of Austria had been totally changed by the treaties of Dresden and Aix-la-Chapelle ; that the empress would, during the first campaign, be compelled to concentrate her forces for the defence of her hereditary countries ; and that till the Russian troops had actually taken the field, she must become totally useless to her allies.

On her part, Maria Theresa saw France preparing to invade the Netherlands ; Frederic capable of penetrating into

Bohemia at the head of 100,000 men, the German empire divided into parties, and principally governed by the Protestants, excited and supported by the court of Berlin ; the Protestant states powerfully armed, and the Catholics without troops or money. She saw Spain disposed to neutrality ; the king of Sardinia jealous and disgusted ; Sweden and Denmark devoted to France ; the Turks at variance with Russia, and secretly excited by French and Prussian emissaries ; Holland irritated and desponding ; England incapable of protecting the Netherlands, and alarmed for the electorate of Hanover. In these circumstances many evident advantages concurred to recommend the alliance with the court of Versailles. By this new connection the house of Austria would be delivered from the distant wars in Italy, Flanders, and on the Rhine, which had always been carried on at an enormous waste of blood and treasure. The influence of France in the Divan removed all apprehensions of an attack on the side of Turkey ; the Catholic princes and states of the empire, no longer excited by the intrigues and money of France, would join the standard of their liege lord the emperor ; Sweden and Denmark would be swayed by the influence of the court of Versailles. The empress-queen hoped also to detach Russia from England, and to obtain the concurrence of Spain. Thus secure on the side of France, Flanders, Italy, and Hungary, she would be enabled to employ her whole force against her most formidable enemy the king of Prussia, the great and primary object of all her apprehensions.

But notwithstanding all these advantages, the breach with the Maritime Powers made a deep impression on the court and capital. She was accused of ingratitude to England, without whose assistance she must have been overwhelmed ; some of her ministers displayed their discontent in a sullen acquiescence ; prince Colloredo, and even the confessor of the emperor, openly disapproved an union with the inveterate enemy of the Austrian name. She had not without extreme difficulty extorted the reluctant consent of her husband ; but her favourite daughter, the eldest archduchess, assailed her with repeated remonstrances. The archduke Joseph also, encouraged by his governor Bathiani, asked her, if she deemed herself safe in trusting to France, who had so often

deceived her? Though frequently repulsed, he returned
with spirit to the charge ; and importunately urged her not
to separate from England, from whom she and her family had
derived such effectual assistance.*

Chap. CXI. — 1756.

Maria Theresa, proud of her new connection, looked forward
with confidence to the speedy accomplishment of her views
against the king of Prussia ; and the favourable state of the
French affairs gave foundation to her hopes.

In America the expeditions of the English, undertaken
the preceding year against the French settlements, had been
attended with an unfortunate issue. The flames of war had
spread into Europe, and vast preparations were made on the
coasts of Normandy and Brittany for the invasion of
England. The British ministry applied to the States-general
for the contingent of 6000 men, according to treaty ; but the
Dutch, overawed by France, refused to comply with this
demand, and acceded to a neutrality. At the same time an
expedition sailed from Toulon against Minorca, and the duke
of Richelieu, with a considerable force, laid siege to Fort St.
Philip ; admiral Byng, who was despatched with a squadron
to the Mediterranean, failed in relieving the fortress, and the
garrison capitulated on the 29th of July.

At this period England was in a state of unusual weakness
and alarm. Since the death of Mr. Pelham the cabinet had
been agitated by cabals, embarrassed by continual changes,
and was without a single minister capable of directing a continental war with vigour and effect. The public mind was
depressed by the inefficiency of the administration, and the
failure of the military enterprises in America. The continuance of Hanoverian and Hessian troops, who had been
called into the country on the appearance of an invasion,
excited great discontents ; the nation groaned under the
pressure of an alarming scarcity ; and, in the midst of these
calamities, the loss of Minorca roused the people almost to
frenzy.

* Keith to Holdernesse, May 15. and Sept. 20. 1756.

Buoyed up with hopes from the depressed situation of England, and the successes of her new ally, Maria Theresa exerted all her efforts to consolidate a general combination against the king of Prussia, equal to that which had threatened the existence of the house of Austria on the death of the late emperor. She secured the co-operation of Augustus, king of Poland, and elector of Saxony, as well by the intervention of his consort Maria Josepha, whom the ties of blood and religion attached to the house of Austria, as by the agency of his prime minister count Bruhl, who was offended by the sarcasms of Frederic. But she turned her principal attention to gain the assistance of the empress of Russia, and fully succeeded in this important object, although she had to combat the long-established influence of England.

On the first prospect of a continental war, George, alarmed for the safety of his electorate, had formed the plan of a triple alliance between England, Austria, and Russia. With this view he despatched sir Charles Hanbury Williams to Petersburgh, with the proposal of a subsidiary treaty with Elizabeth for an auxiliary force of 55,000 men, should his German dominions be invaded. To this overture the empress readily acceded, in consequence of her inveterate aversion to the king of Prussia, against whom the Russian troops were specifically destined to act, and the convention was signed on the 30th of September. But even before the signature, the politics of England had changed; the empress-queen having entered into negotiations with France, George made overtures to the king of Prussia, and concluded the treaty of London. He once again endeavoured to prevail on Elizabeth to unite with his new ally, in defence of Hanover; but Maria Theresa, conscious that without the assistance of Russia she could not fulfil her views against Prussia, used her utmost endeavours to thwart his plans. She fomented the antipathy of Elizabeth against Frederic; contrary to her usual parsimony, she bribed the venal ministers, and induced Elizabeth to break the subsidiary treaty which she had recently signed with England, and to promise a succour of 60,000 troops.

Having succeeded in forming this alliance, the empress-queen made vast preparations, and formed two considerable armies in the neighbourhood of Konigsgratz and Prague, while the Russians began to assemble on the frontiers of Livonia. The king of Prussia, alarmed at these hostile appearances, and suspecting the secret combination between the courts of Vienna, Petersburgh, and Dresden, demanded from the empress-queen an explicit declaration of her sentiments. In answer to this demand, she briefly replied, " In the present crisis I deem it necessary to take measures for the security of myself and my allies, which tend to the prejudice of no one." The king, not satisfied with so vague an answer, reiterated his demand, declaring his knowledge of the offensive projects formed by the courts of Petersburgh and Dresden, and requiring an immediate and categorical answer, " not delivered in an oracular style, ambiguous and inconclusive," concerning the armaments in Bohemia, and a positive assurance that she would not attack him either during that or the following year.

Maria Theresa no less haughtily replied, " The arrangement with Russia was purely defensive ; she had concluded no offensive alliance ; and although the critical situation of Europe compelled her to arm, she had no intention to violate the treaty of Dresden, but would not bind herself by any promise from acting as circumstances required." This reply was scarcely delivered before she was roused with the intelligence that the king of Prussia had penetrated with a formidable force into Saxony, taken possession of Dresden, and blockaded the Saxon troops, who had occupied the impregnable post of Pirna.

On the first intelligence of the Prussian irruption, marshal Brown, with the army at Prague, hastened to the relief of the Saxons; but his views were anticipated by Frederic, who, leaving 40,000 to continue the blockade of Pirna, penetrated into Bohemia with 24,000 men. On the first of October, the two armies met at Lowositz, near the banks of the Elbe, not far from the frontiers of Saxony, and a battle ensued, in which the Austrians, though superior in number, were compelled to retire behind the Eger, leaving the Prussians masters of the field. The loss amounted to only 3000 on each side, and four pieces of artillery were taken from the Austrians ; but marshal Brown was disappointed in the object of his march, the relief of the Saxons.

During these transactions the Saxon troops supported the

severities of the season, and the extremes of famine and wretchedness, with exemplary courage ; but were foiled in all their endeavours to extricate themselves by the superior vigilance and skill of the enemy. A final attempt made by marshal Brown at the head of 8000 men, to force the Prussian posts, was equally ineffectual; and Augustus had the mortification to witness the surrender, and ratify the capitulation, of his troops : 17,000 men were made prisoners of war, and eighty pieces of cannon delivered to the king of Prussia. The officers were liberated on their parole, and the standards restored ; but Frederic compelled the troops to enter into his service, appropriated the revenues of Saxony, and treated it as a conquered province. Augustus retired with his family to Warsaw ; and thus this unfortunate ally of Maria Theresa a second time experienced the fatal effects of his devotion to the house of Austria.

On the other side of Bohemia, the army of Piccolomini was kept in check by marshal Schwerin, who advancing by Glatz into Bohemia, destroyed all the subsistence, and foraged under the very cannon of the Austrian camp. After the surrender of the Saxons, the Prussian army took up winter quarters on the frontiers of Saxony and Bohemia ; and marshal Schwerin retired into Silesia.

During the winter the king of Prussia published a justification of his conduct; in which he introduced, as proofs of the combination forming against him, the copy of a treaty of partition signed the 18th of May, 1745, between the courts of Vienna and Dresden ; the secret articles of the treaty of Petersburgh, 22nd May, 1746, and various despatches written by count Bruhl and the Saxon envoys. These papers* were said to have been found in the archives of Dresden, which he had forcibly seized, but doubts were entertained of their authenticity, and the court of Vienna published a refutation of the charge.

Deeply affected by the humiliation of her ally, and irritated by the conduct of Frederic, the empress-queen passed the winter in making the most vigorous preparations for the ensuing campaign, in consolidating a grand combination against Prussia, and in separating England, his only ally,

* These papers are given by Hertzberg in his curious Receuil de Deductions Manifestes, &c.

from the other European powers. In all the catholic courts she artfully represented the alliance of Great Britain and Prussia as the league of heretics against the true faith, and held up the cause of the house of Austria as the cause of religion and justice.

At the court of Versailles, supported by the marchioness of Pompadour, and assisted by the tears of the dauphiness, daughter of Augustus, she gained a complete ascendency in the cabinet, and converted France from a mere auxiliary into a principal in the war. Her views were greatly promoted by the attempt of Damiens to assassinate the king of France on the 5th of January, 1757. This atrocious act, though only the deed of a bigoted fanatic, was attributed to the machinations of the king of Prussia and the intrigues of the Jesuits ; and even the partisans of the dauphin, who were anti-Austrian in principle, were implicated in the accusation. The mistress, by her intrigues and influence, overbore all opposition ; and France entered into new engagements to support all the views of the empress-queen. By a secret agreement, concluded towards the commencement of 1757, the king engaged to pay an annual subsidy of 12,000,000 imperial florins to the empress-queen, to maintain at her disposal 10,000 troops of Bavaria and Wirtemberg, and to send into the field an army of 105,000 men; he likewise promised never to desist from hostilities until the empress should be put in possession of Silesia, Glatz, and Crossen.*

Maria Theresa was no less successful among the principal states of the empire ; the invasion of Saxony and Bohemia was represented as a breach of the public peace, and the aggressor as punishable with the forfeiture of all fiefs, dignities, and titles. Soon after the invasion, the emperor issued a decree, demanding the aid of an army of execution ; the proposal of several states, and particularly of the electoral house of Brunswick, to proffer the mediation of the

* This convention was never acknowledged by the two courts, nor referred to in the new treaty of Versailles, signed Dec. 30. 1758. The terms are mentioned in Koch, tom. ii. p. 90. ; and the conduct of France sufficiently proves the existence of such an engagement. It is also confirmed in a despatch from lord Bristol, ambassador at Madrid, to Mr. Pitt, dated July 27. 1758.

empire, was rejected by a large majority, and an army voted with the accustomed formalities. The zeal of the Austrian party was still further excited by the declarations of France and Sweden, who announced to the diet, that in consequence of an application from several distinguished states of the empire, they had resolved to exercise their right, as guarantees of the treaty of Westphalia, to resist infractions of the public peace. Russia had now heartily acceded to the treaty of Versailles; and Sweden entered warmly into the views of the house of Austria.

Maria Theresa was also successful in neutralising those powers which she could not win over to espouse her cause. Though she failed in obtaining the co-operation of the king of Spain, she counteracted the efforts of England, and induced him to persevere in maintaining a neutrality; by threatening instant invasion, she deterred the States from joining with their ancient ally.

Of all the northern powers, Frederic V., king of Denmark, was alone inclined to co-operate with England. He had espoused Louisa, daughter of George II., and the ties of blood had been strengthened by a similarity of commercial interests. But Frederic, like his father, had embarrassed his finances by the splendour of his establishment and his devotion to the fine arts; he had therefore accepted a subsidy from France, and his connection with England was still further weakened by the death of his first wife and his marriage with Julia Maria, princess of Brunswick, a relation of the empress-queen.

George embarrassed with the feuds in the cabinet and the discontents of the people, trembled for the safety of England, and was incapable of forming any plan of active operations to counteract the attempts of the French in Germany. The king of Prussia proposed to establish Wesel, the strongest fortress in the duchy of Cleves, as a place of arms, to concentrate the forces behind the Lippe, in the vicinity of that town, in order to cover Westphalia, and protect the electorate of Hanover. But the king, unable to induce the administration to take a principal share in a continental war, rejected this plan as too extensive, adopted a defensive system on the Weser, and formed an army of observation, consisting only of the Hanoverian and auxiliary troops, under the command of the duke of Cumberland. In consequence of this refusal the king of Prussia razed the fortifications of Wesel, despatched only 6000 men to join the duke of Cumberland, and abandoned the defence of his Westphalian territories.

Chap. CXII. — 1757.

At the commencement of 1757, the grand confederacy against the king of Prussia was consolidated by the efforts and intrigues of the court of Vienna. The French had drawn together 80,000 men on the Rhine, under the command of marshal d'Etrées ; the army of execution was assembling in the empire ; the Swedes were preparing to penetrate into Pomerania, and 60,000 Russians were stationed on the frontiers of Livonia, waiting the season of action to burst into the kingdom of Prussia. With this favourable aspect of affairs, the empress prepared for the campaign by augmenting her forces in Hungary and Bohemia to 150,000 men ; the main army, stationed in the vicinity of Prague, was commanded by prince Charles, who was assisted by the skill of marshal Brown, and the other corps intrusted to count Daun.

Frederic possessed too much foresight and vigilance to remain inactive while his enemies were collecting their forces ; he therefore resolved to carry the war into the heart of the Austrian territories, and by a decisive stroke to shake the basis of the confederacy. He covered this plan with consummate address ; he affected great trepidation and uncertainty, and to deceive the Austrians into a belief that he only intended to maintain himself in Saxony, put Dresden in a state of defence, broke down the bridges, and marked out various camps in the vicinity. In the midst of this apparent alarm three Prussian columns burst into Bohemia, in April, and rapidly advanced towards Prague. The prince of Bevern from Lusatia, at the head of the first, drove Konigsegg with 20,000 men from a strong post at Reichenberg, while marshal Schwerin, leading the second from Silesia, on the side of Landshut, harassed his retreat, and cut off his rear guard of 1500 men. The king himself, joined

by prince Maurice of Anhalt Dessau, from Brix, advanced
with the third by Aussig, compelled marshal Brown to
retreat from Budin, and seized considerable magazines,
which facilitated the subsistence of his troops. The Austrians,
pressed on all sides, retreated with precipitation under the
walls of Prague, on the southern side of the Moldau, while
the Prussians advancing towards the capital formed two
bodies; one under Schwerin remaining at Jung Bunzlau,
and the other, headed by the king, occupying the heights
between the Moldau and the Weisseberg.

Expecting to be joined by marshal Daun, who was hastening from Moravia, the Austrians remained on the defensive ;
but prince Charles took so strong a position as seemed to
defy all apprehensions of an attack. His left was covered
by the Ziskaberg, a steep hill overhanging the Moldau, a
deep and craggy ravine ran along his front, and the ground
on his left was a morass intersected with hedges, drains, and
dikes; his force exceeded 70,000 men, and his position was
strengthened by works which ran along the brow of the
precipice, defended by a powerful train of artillery.

These obstacles, however, were insufficient to arrest the
daring spirit of Frederic, who resolved to attack the Austrians
before the arrival of Daun. Leaving a corps under prince
Maurice above Prague, he crossed the Moldau near Rostock
and Podabe on the 5th of May, with 16,000 men, and on
the following morning at break of day was joined by the
corps under marshal Schwerin. The troops had no sooner
formed than they moved in silence and order along the
ravine towards the right of the Austrians, while prince
Charles, drawing the cavalry from his left and part of the
second line, prepared to charge the enemy as they emerged
from the marshes and defiles. The king, however, continued
to advance his cavalry, notwithstanding the embarrassments of
the ground, pushed through the village of Bichowitz, and
forming on a plain beyond, repulsed that of the Austrians after
several successive charges ; and the infantry, emulous of this
example, hastened to join the enemy, but were broken and
mowed down by the continual fire of the Austrian artillery.

At this moment the king, almost frantic with the prospect
of a defeat, rode up to Schwerin, whose regiment had given
way, and upbraided him for the dastardly behaviour of his
soldiers. Stung with these reproaches, the veteran seized

the standard, and wrapping the colours round his body, exclaimed, "Let the brave follow me!" He led his troops to the charge under a tremendous fire of grape shot, and instantly fell pierced with several balls.* But his death opened the way to victory; the Austrian line disordered by these repeated charges, penetrated in different points, and taken in flank by the victorious cavalry, was broken and compelled to give way. In the heat of the action marshal Brown, having received a severe wound, was conveyed to Prague, and his absence increased the confusion of the troops. Meanwhile a part of the Prussian right wing, impelled by their ardour, passed the ravine, climbed up the precipices, and piercing the Austrian centre, joined their victorious companions on the left. Prince Charles, with those who had not engaged, thus attacked on all sides, retreated with equal skill and bravery, and disputed every height; but at length took refuge within the walls of Prague.

Thus victory declared on the side of the Prussians, but was purchased by the loss of their best troops, not less than 18,000, even by the avowal of the king, being killed, with many of his bravest officers, and Schwerin, the father of the Prussian discipline, and the guide of Frederic in the career of victory. Of the Austrians 8000 were killed and wounded, 9000 made prisoners, and 28,000 shut up within the walls of Prague. The defeat would have been still more complete had prince Maurice been able to pass the Moldau, and intercept the fugitives; but the river having risen, he had not a sufficient number of pontoons to form a bridge, and a column of 16,000 Austrians made good their retreat along the Moldau to join the army of marshal Daun.

Prague was instantly blockaded by the victorious army, and not less than 100,000 souls were confined within the walls, almost without the means of subsistence. They were soon reduced to the greatest extremities; but the spirit of the troops and of the inhabitants was animated by an address

---

* "Schwerin was deeply lamented by his master, and Frederic has immortalised the circumstances of his death, by erecting a statue to his memory in one of the principal squares of Berlin. Schwerin is there represented as he fell, the colours clasped in his hand, and in the act of expiring. The monument commemorates at once the frailty of the sovereign and the merits of the general."— *Wraxall's Memoirs*, vol. i. p. 162.

from Maria Theresa, brought by a captain of grenadiers, who escaped the vigilance of the besieging army.

"I am concerned," said the empress, "that so many generals, with so considerable a force, must remain besieged in Prague; but I augur favourably for the event. I cannot too strongly impress on your minds, that the troops will incur everlasting disgrace should they not effect what the French, in the last war, performed with far inferior numbers. The honour of the whole nation, as well as of the imperial arms, is interested in their present behaviour ; the security of Bohemia, of my other hereditary dominions, and of the German empire itself, depends on a gallant defence, and the preservation of Prague. The army under the command of marshal Daun is daily strengthening, and will soon be in a condition to raise the siege ; the French are approaching with all diligence; the Swedes are marching to my assistance; and in a short space of time, affairs will, under the divine Providence, wear a better aspect."

This address, from a sovereign whom they adored, excited general ardour ; the garrison, though reduced to feed on horse-flesh, held out with uncommon perseverance ; and the inhabitants supported without a murmur all the horrors of a bombardment, which destroyed one quarter of the town. Several desperate sallies were made; but the garrison was threatened with famine ; and the loss of Prague would have been followed by the most fatal consequences. The recent defeat had spread consternation throughout Germany; the elector of Bavaria and the other Catholic princes had already sent agents to treat with the king of Prussia; and almost every member of the empire was preparing to desert the cause of Maria Theresa. The flower of her armies were shut up in Prague ; the remainder defeated, dispirited, and dispersed; the capital of Bohemia reduced to the last extremity ; the whole kingdom ready to submit to the law of the conqueror; her hereditary dominions exposed ; Vienna itself threatened with a siege, and the imperial family about to take refuge in Hungary.

In this disastrous moment the house of Austria was preserved from impending destruction by the skill and caution of a general, who now, for the first time, appeared at the head of an army. This general was Leopold count Daun, a native

of Bohemia, son of Wyrich Philip Lorenzo count Daun,
and prince of Tiano, who had distinguished himself in the
campaigns of Italy during the reigns of Joseph and Charles,
and had held the high offices of viceroy of Naples, governor
of Milan, and stadtholder ad interim of the Netherlands.
Leopold was born in 1705, embraced the military profession
at an early period, and learned the art of war under Seckendorf and Kevenhuller. He distinguished himself at the
battles of Crotzka, Dettingen, and Hohenfriedberg; and from
his knowledge of tactics, was chosen to introduce the new
system of discipline into the army. Although favoured by
Eugene and Kevenhuller, he had risen slowly and silently by
merit, and without intrigue, from a subaltern rank to that of
field marshal; and after the death of prince Piccolomini, was
intrusted with the army, which, under his auspices, was to
restore the honour and credit of the Austrian arms. Sagacity
and penetration, personal bravery tempered with phlegm,
animation in the hour of battle, with extreme caution both
before and after the engagement, recommended him at this
critical juncture, like another Fabius, to check the fire and
enterprise of the modern Hannibal.

On the first intelligence of the entrance of the Prussians
into Bohemia, Daun had marched through Moravia towards
Prague, to effect a junction with prince Charles. On arriving
at Boehmischgrod, within a few miles of Prague, he was
apprised of the recent defeat, and halted a few days to collect
the fugitives, till his corps swelled so considerably, that
Frederic detached against him the prince of Bevern with
20,000 men. Daun, though superior to the enemy, was too
prudent to hazard the fate of the house of Austria on the issue
of a single battle, with dispirited and almost desponding troops,
against an army flushed with recent victory. On the approach of the prince of Bevern, he therefore retreated to
Kolin, Kuttemberg, and Haber, in order to afford a refuge
to the shattered remains of the defeated army, and to receive
the recruits which were pouring in from Moravia and Austria.

While he was thus baffling the enemy, he, like the great
general who saved Rome by delay, had to support the murmurs of his officers, and the reproaches of those impatient
spirits who are always eager to engage, and cannot dis-

tinguish prudence from pusillanimity. Among others the duke of Wirtemberg exclaimed, "If you continue this conduct, I would advise you to march to Vienna; but I will retire to my own dominions, and countermand the troops I have ordered to join you." Yet neither invectives nor murmurs could induce Daun to change his wise measures, until his army was increased, and the soldiers began to recover from their despondency. Finding himself at length at the head of 60,000 men, he made a rapid movement in front, forced the prince of Bevern to retire, and was advancing to attack the king in his posts before Prague, while prince Charles was to make a sortie with his whole force.

Frederic, conscious of his danger, had already anticipated the design of Daun; leaving the greater part of his army to continue the blockade, he marched with 12,000 men on the 13th of June in the morning, and joined the prince of Bevern on the 14th, at the moment of his retreat before the Austrians. On the approach of the Prussians, Daun occupied the heights stretching from the village of Chotzemitz towards Kolin; he placed his infantry on the flanks, which were supported by steep eminences, filled the villages in his front with detachments of infantry and irregulars, stationed the cavalry in the centre where they could act with effect, and made a skilful disposition of his formidable train of artillery.

In this situation Daun was attacked by the king of Prussia, who, directing all his efforts against the Austrian right, had almost succeeded in turning their flank, notwithstanding their superiority of number, the tremendous fire of the artillery, the skill of the general, and the bravery of the troops. Victory seemed to incline to the enemy, and Daun had even ordered a retreat; but the fortune of the day was changed by the impatience of two Prussian generals, who, disobeying positive orders, broke their line on the right to dislodge a party of Croats, and were repulsed with considerable loss. The Saxon cavalry instantly rushed into the interval, crying out at every stroke, "Remember Strigau!" and cut to pieces or dispersed all whom they encountered. Daun availed himself of this fortunate manoeuvre with equal skill and promptitude; he was seen flying from rank to rank, animating the soldiers by his voice and gestures; he had two horses killed

under him, was twice slightly wounded, and showed himself
the worthy antagonist of the great Frederic. In vain the
king of Prussia exerted all his skill and courage in this desperate conflict ; his cavalry charged six times, and were six
times repulsed ; Frederic again rallied them, and finding them
dispirited, exclaimed, " Would you live for ever !" They
were a seventh time led to the charge, and were again driven
back. Perceiving the battle lost, the king ordered two
regiments of cuirassiers to disengage the infantry ; but discouraged by the dreadful carnage of their companions, they
refused to advance. He then sullenly withdrew from the
field with a squadron of gardes du corps, and thirty hussars ;
and was repeatedly heard to cry out, "My hussars, my brave
hussars, will all be lost !" The troops also, for the first time
defeated, gave way to despondency, and in their retreat exclaimed, "This is our Pultawa !" Daun purchased the victory
with the loss of 9000 men ; but on the side of the Prussians
not less than 14,000 were killed, wounded, and taken prisoners ; and 43 pieces of artillery, with 22 standards, fell into
the hands of the Austrians.

Maria Theresa, who was anxiously waiting the event of an
engagement, which, if unfortunate, would have rendered her
situation more deplorable than that to which she had been reduced at the commencement of the former war, received the
account with a joy proportionate to her apprehensions.
Sumptuous feasts were given, medals struck, and presents
distributed ; the officers were rewarded a month's pay, and
the subalterns and common soldiers were gratified with donations. Anxious to display her gratitude to the general who
had first defeated her formidable antagonist, she conveyed, in
person, the news of this important victory to the countess
Daun, and instituted the military order of merit, or the
order of Maria Theresa, with which she decorated the commander and officers who had most signalised themselves,
and dated its commencement from the æra of that glorious
victory.

To give repose to the troops, and to replace the magazines
which had been destroyed by the Prussians, Daun remained
several days on the field of battle ; and as he advanced to
Prague, found that the Prussians had raised the siege on
the 20th of June, and were retreating with precipitation

towards Saxony and Lusatia. He joined prince Charles, who assumed the sole command, but continued to direct the operations, in consequence of the death of marshal Brown. Leaving a corps under Nadasti to watch the king, who had fallen back on Leutmeritz, the Austrian commanders directed their whole force against the body retreating into Lusatia, under prince Augustus William, brother of the king of Prussia. They turned his left flank, seized, after a desperate conflict, the post of Gabel, cut him off from his magazines at Zittau, and compelled him to take a circuitous route over the mountains to Bautzen, with the loss of his provisions and baggage. At this juncture the king himself hastened from Leutmeritz, and pushed forward to Zittau to give battle to prince Charles; but finding him too strongly posted, and being alarmed by his numerous enemies, who were preparing to attack him on all sides, he left the command of the army to the prince of Bevern, for the protection of Silesia, and marched with a body of troops against the French and imperial army in Saxony.

The total defeat of the Prussians at the battle of Kolin, and the retreat of Frederic from Bohemia, inspired the empress-queen with presumptuous hopes equal to her former apprehensions. The language of the court of Vienna was, to crush the king of Prussia and divide his territories; the house of Austria was to recover Silesia and Glatz; Magdeburgh and Halberstadt were to be assigned to the king of Poland; Cleves, la Marc, and Ravensberg to the elector Palatine, and Prussian Pomerania to the Swedes. Nor did these seem empty vaunts, as the arms of the confederates were equally successful on all sides.

Early in the spring the French had assembled two armies on the Rhine; one under Marshal d'Etrées, destined to act against the duke of Cumberland, and the other under the prince de Soubise to join the army of execution, and penetrate into Saxony. They rapidly overran the Prussian territories on the left bank of the Rhine; d'Etrées then crossed the Weser, spread his detachments over the southern part of the electorate of Hanover and the whole landgraviate of Hesse Cassel, defeated the duke of Cumberland at Hastenbech, and drove him to Stade in the vicinity of the Elbe. In this situation the English commander signed the

humiliating convention of Closter-Severn, under the mediation of the king of Denmark, on the 26th of July.   The
auxiliary troops were to retire to their respective countries,
while a part of the Hanoverian force was to be quartered in
Stade and the neighbourhood, and the remainder to cross
the Elbe.   In consequence of this reverse of circumstances,
the princes of the empire, who had joined with England and
Prussia, began to waver.   The duke of Brunswick seceded
from the alliance, and concluded a convention with France,
by which he yielded the possession of Brunswick and Wol-
fenbuttel during the war; he also recalled his troops, and
ordered his son the hereditary prince to quit the army of
the duke of Cumberland.   The landgrave of Hesse Cassel
was preparing to follow his example, and even made proposals to join the confederacy with his whole force.   The
French were thus enabled to direct their principal force
against the king of Prussia, and marshal Richelieu turned
towards Magdeburgh, and threatened that capital with a
siege, while his troops plundered the adjacent country.
Meanwhile the prince of Soubise penetrated to Erfurth,
and receiving considerable reinforcements from Richelieu,
had, on the 20th of September, joined the army of the empire
under the prince of Saxe Hilburghausen at Eisenach, and
was at the head of 80,000 men.

During these transactions in Germany the Swedes burst
into Prussian Pomerania; the Russians, under marshal
Apraxin, amounting to 100,000 men, in July commenced
offensive operations, and a corps of 30,000 men under general
Fermor, having bombarded and taken Memel, rejoined the
grand army, which spread into Prussia, and committed the
most dreadful devastations.   To this force marshal Lehwald
opposed only 22,000 men.   In obedience to the orders of
the king he risked a battle at Jagersdorf on the 30th of
August; but after a conflict, in which he obtained some
advantage, retired to Vehlau.

While the French, Russians, and Swedes, with the army
of the empire, were thus threatening the Prussian dominions,
prince Charles was equally successful.   The prince of
Bevern had occupied Gorlitz, in order to cover Silesia, and
the Austrians encamped at Aussig.   In this situation a
Prussian post on the Holtzberg was carried by Nadasti, on

the 7th of September, and Winterfield fell in the conflict. His loss was severely felt by the Prussians : Frederic had relied on his activity and skill for the defence of Silesia; and from the moment of his death the prince of Bevern was unable to make any effectual opposition to the superior forces of prince Charles. To complete this series of successes, general Haddick burst from Silesia, with 6000 horse, penetrated through the Marc of Brandenburgh, and laid Berlin itself under contribution ; and while the king hastened to the defence of his capital, the allied army burst into Saxony, and the prince of Saxe Hilburghausen, at the head of a considerable force, passing the Saale at Weissenfels, drove marshal Keith, who had been left to cover Saxony, into Leipsig.

But in this momentous crisis the extraordinary talents of Frederic unfolded themselves with peculiar energy; and he discovered resources which surprised his enemies. On the retreat of Haddick from Berlin, he rapidly returned into Saxony, delivered marshal Keith, drove the enemy across the Saale, and hastened to meet the army of Soubise, which, besides the troops under the Prince of Saxe Hilburghausen, had been strengthened with considerable reinforcements from Richelieu. The confederates having advanced to Micheln, the king occupied Schortau with the resolution of bringing on a battle, as the enemy had taken a defective position ; but Soubise moving in the night to more advantageous ground, Frederic relinquished his intended attack, and retired to the height above Rosbach, where his front stretched along a declivity overhanging the Schortau, and his flanks were covered by the villages of Bedra and Rosbach.

Despising the diminutive force of the Prussians, which scarcely exceeded a third of their numbers, the confederates deemed themselves secure of victory, gave signs of the most extravagant exultation, and were only anxious to prevent the escape of so easy a prey. They quitted their camp on the 5th of November, and at eleven in the morning moved in battle array, against the left flank of the Prussians.

Frederic availed himself of the nature of the ground to effect one of the most singular manœuvres which occurs in military history. The height on which he encamped was narrow, steep, and long ; it terminated abruptly above the castle of Rosbach, and on that side rose in a ridge more elevated than the other ; the infantry formed two lines at the extremity of this height, and the cavalry a single line in the rear. The king had taken up his quarters in the castle of Rosbach, and at ten in the morning ascended through an aperture made in the roof to examine the motions of the enemy. After an hour's observation, he ordered his repast, and dined quietly, and with a good appetite ; at one he again ascended, and in half an hour perceived the heads of the enemy's columns opposite to his left flank, and directing their march slowly towards his rear. He descended, ordered the tents to be struck, commanded Seidlitz to advance with the cavalry under cover of the ridge towards Reichenswerben, and the infantry to follow in divisions.

The generals of the combined army mistook the tranquillity of the Prussians for the effect of despair ; seeing the tents struck with an appearance of precipitation, they concluded that they were retiring, and hastened forward with the cavalry to intercept the retreat. On approaching Reichenswerben a tremendous cannonade was opened, and Seidlitz, descending from the heights with the cavalry, burst with irresistible fury upon the heads of their columns. The heavy cavalry and the celebrated gens d'armes were totally dispersed by rapid and successive charges, and driven in disorder on their infantry. At this moment the Prussian infantry advanced in order of battle and completed the overthrow by a tremendous fire of cannon and musketry. The discomfiture of the combined army was the consequence of these manœuvres, and in less than half an hour, the confederates were driven from the field. The loss on the side of the king, who had scarcely brought half his troops into action, was not more than 300 men ; while on the side of the allies, 4000 were killed and wounded, 7000, with eleven generals, taken prisoners, and 63 cannons, and 22 standards, fell into the hands of the conquerors. The approach of night prevented the king from pursuing his advantage, and the allied troops fled rather than retreated towards Erfurth, harassed by the Prussian detachments, who made numerous prisoners.

The king was prevented from pursuing his success by the rapid progress of the Austrians in Silesia, where the prince of Bevern, with only 25,000 men was opposed to a force of 90,000. He had been compelled by want of provisions to draw towards the centre of Silesia, and being followed by prince Charles, took shelter under the walls of Breslau on the south side of the Oder. The Austrian commander encamped behind the Lohe, opposite to the Prussians, and detached Nadasti to besiege Schweidnitz ; that fortress was invested on the 27th of October; on the 10th of November the third parallel was completed ; and two of the redoubts being carried by assault, the governor, with the garrison of 6000 men, surrendered prisoners of war on the following day.

Nadasti having rejoined the army, prince Charles, who was aware of the advance of the king, hastened to attack the prince of Bevern ; and, after a desperate engagement, in which the loss was equally severe to both parties, the Prussians retreated through Breslau during the night, leaving 6000 men in the town. On the ensuing evening the prince of Bevern was taken prisoner, while reconnoitring*, and general Kyauo, to whom the command devolved, led the remains of this gallant, but discomfited army, towards Glogau. This conflict cost the Austrians not less than 8000 men, and the Prussians lost 5000 killed and wounded, and 3600 prisoners, with 80 cannon and five standards. Two days after Breslau surrendered without resistance, and the Austrians thus recovered the greater part of Silesia. New regulations were issued for the government of the province ; many of the principal inhabitants took the oath of allegiance, and preparations were made to distribute the troops into winter quarters.

During these events the king of Prussia made a rapid progress through Lusatia, collected the remains of the prince of Bevern's army, and advanced towards Breslau, with

---

* To the prince of Bevern Maria Theresa displayed great humanity, which was the more commendable, as Frederic sullied his great qualities by a disdainful and rigid behaviour to those officers, who, by the fortune of war, were thrown into his power. The prince of Bevern was gratified with permission to write to the king of Prussia ; but as he received no answer, he required leave to pay his own ransom, that he might wait on his sovereign in person. Maria Theresa, with a magnanimity peculiar to herself, declined accepting a ransom, and restored him to his liberty without exacting any condition."

a resolution to try the fortune of another battle, notwithstanding the diminution of his force, and the severity of
the weather.   In this situation Daun urged prince Charles
to remain on the defensive, till the king was obliged to quit
Silesia by the want of provisions, and the lateness of the
season.   But as the Prussian army did not now exceed
30,000 men, so inconsiderable a force was despised by the
Austrians, who tauntingly called them the grand guard of
Potsdam.   The advice of Daun was therefore rejected, as
timid and disgraceful; and prince Charles, confident of his
superiority, wantonly exposed himself to an attack.   On
the approach of the Prussians, he quitted his camp at
Breslau, and advancing to meet them, took up a position
near Lissa; his left, stretching behind the villages of
Striegwitz and Sagschutz, occupied the space between the
rivulet of Schweidnitz, which ran at the rear of his camp,
and a commanding height above Leuthen; while his centre
and right extended down a gradual descent to the wood of
Nipern.

On the 4th of December the king made himself master of
Newmarkt, which was occupied by a corps of Austrian
irregulars for the guard of their bakery ; and early on the
morning of the 5th made arrangements for a battle.   The
advanced guard having routed a corps of Saxons posted at
Borne, Frederic put his troops in motion, and at the head of
his hussars rode to a chain of woody heights, running parallel to the front of the Austrians, from whence he reconnoitred
their position.   Being well acquainted with the ground, on
which he had frequently manœuvred his troops, he resolved
to direct his principal attack against the left of the Austrians,
which commanded the rest of their lines.   In an instant the
Prussian order was reversed, and their columns, which
hitherto had seemed to direct their march against the right
of the Austrians, suddenly verged towards the left.*

Prince Charles imagining that the attack was directed
against his right wing, had reinforced that part with additional troops, and even with the corps de reserve.   Daun
himself, though more cautious, mistook this evolution for a

* The king seems to have derived the idea of this fine manœuvre from
that of Epaminondas, at the battle of Leuctra, and he had rendered it
familiar to his troops by frequent practice.

VOL. III.   C C

retreat, and said to prince Charles, "The Prussians are retiring, let them go." But the king occupying with the hussars, the heights stretching before the camp of prince Charles, was enabled to observe the movements of the enemy, while he concealed his own, and his army had already gained the left flank of the Austrians before they were undeceived. Prince Charles now in vain attempted to reinforce his left; and Nadisti, who commanded that wing, after charging the Prussian cavalry with great spirit, gave way, and left the infantry exposed, and the Prussians carried the villages of Sagschutz and Striegwitz. The Austrian generals endeavoured to form a line parallel to the Prussians, but were prevented by the artillery, which was placed on the heights commanding their position. They repeatedly rallied the troops, and disputed the ground with great obstinacy; although the new regiments, led up to replace those who were repulsed, were broken by the impetuous and uninterrupted attack of the Prussians. They then made a desperate stand in the village of Leuthen, where they concentrated their efforts ; and as the place was strengthened with entrenchments, and the houses occupied by the fugitives, the post was contested with great obstinacy. The Austrians at length gave way, but rallied behind the ditches, with which the ground was intersected, when a part of the Prussian cavalry bursting on their right, threw them into irrecoverable confusion ; whole battalions were killed or made prisoners, and the remainder fled with precipitation over the bridges of the Schweidnitz.

Seven thousand were killed and wounded, 20,000, with three generals, made prisoners ; 134 pieces of cannon, and 59 colours, with the whole baggage and military chest, fell into the hands of the enemy. On the side of the Prussians the whole loss did not exceed 5000 men in killed and wounded. Breslau capitulated on the 10th, and 17,635 soldiers, 686 officers, and 13 generals, surrendered themselves prisoners of war. Lignitz soon afterwards fell into the hands of the enemy, and Schweidnitz, the only fortress which was held by the Austrians, was blockaded by the victorious troops. Thus by one imprudent action Maria Theresa lost 50,000 men, and what was of still greater consequence, the troops lost their confidence in their own bravery and numbers, which had been the cause of their late successes, and which it required all the prudence of Daun to restore.

The campaign was also finally unsuccessful on the part of the allies. The Russian forces, soon after their victory at Jagersdorf, suddenly quitted all their conquests, except Memel, and retired beyond the frontiers. The Prussians, delivered from this enemy, directed their efforts against the Swedes, and not only drove them from Prussian Pomerania, but forced them to take refuge under the cannon of Stralsund.

In the north of Germany also, the confederates suffered a sad reverse. On the victory of Rosbach, Richelieu hastily quitted Magdeburgh, and fell back into the electorate of Hanover. Soon after the convention of Closter Severn, the duke of Cumberland having retired to England, the command of the British auxiliaries was consigned to prince Ferdinand of Brunswick, who had been educated in the school of Frederic ; and the troops, animated by the victory of Rosbach, and the spirit and talents of the new general, panted for an opportunity to retrieve the honour which they had lost by the late reverses. The enormous exactions, and cruel devastations of Richelieu in the electorate of Hanover, and his attempt to disarm the Hanoverians and Hessians, furnished a pretext to break the convention, which had never been ratified by the kings of England and France. Prince Ferdinand disregarded the commands of his brother the duke of Brunswick to dismiss his troops, and by an affected compulsion afforded his nephew, the hereditary prince, an opportunity of indulging his military ardour, and re-entering the British service. The landgrave of Hesse Cassel also broke off his negotiations with France, and returned to his engagements with England and Prussia. The troops were accordingly again collected at Stade, and being reinforced by a body of Prussians, took the field with redoubled ardour, and drove the French from the duchy of Lauenburgh and part of the dominions of Brunswick ; but the lateness of the season prevented them from prosecuting their success, and both armies retired into winter quarters, the French into the electorate, and the auxiliaries into the duchy of Lunenburgh.

Thus terminated this bloody and singular campaign, memorable perhaps beyond any preceding period in the records of time, for the number of great and important actions, the stupendous exertions of military skill, the variety of events, and wonderful revolutions of fortune. The Austrians, at first baffled and overborne by the skill and energy of Frederic, seemed sunk beyond all hopes of recovery, and at the moment of their lowest depression, rose to a height of success surpassing their most sanguine expectations. Forty thousand Hanoverians and auxiliaries were reduced to a state of inaction, and only not prisoners of war; the French masters of all the country between the Weser and the Elbe; the king of Prussia totally defeated, his army hemmed in by a force six times their number; Silesia, the purchase of so much blood and treasure, wrested from him; his country invaded on every side, and his capital laid under contribution. But at the very moment of his seemingly inevitable downfall, the transcendant genius of Frederic effected a stupendous change in his fortune; the power of the French was humbled by a single effort; the Hanoverians, inspired by his success, resumed their arms; the Russians, though victorious, retreated as if vanquished; the Swedes were driven from all their conquests, and their country invaded; the Austrian army almost annihilated, and 17,000 men, the scanty and discomfited remains of 100,000, pursued by the victorious enemy into the heart of the hereditary dominions.

The army of Maria Theresa was to be new modelled, disciplined, and exercised, and again supplied with baggage, arms, and military stores. The enormous expense was severely felt by the empress-queen, who had drained her treasures for the preceding campaign, and had recently remitted considerable sums to St. Petersburgh, to obtain the co-operation of the empress Elizabeth. She was no longer assisted by the zeal and riches of England; the cause of the king of Prussia was more popular than that of the house of Austria at the commencement of the former war, and the British subsidies had been lavished with still greater profusion on her rival. An offensive and defensive treaty was concluded between the courts of London and Berlin, and to the king of Prussia was assigned an annual subsidy of 650,000l. almost double the sum which Maria Theresa had received at the time of her greatest distress.

Chap. CXIII.—1758.

In consequence of the ill success of the French at the commencement of the campaign, Maria Theresa did not derive the expected assistance from her new ally, and turned her views to the Russians, who had opened the year with considerable advantages. In January general Fermor took possession of Königsberg, and before the end of the month overran all Prussia and was preparing to penetrate through the electorate of Brandenburgh, and join the Austrians in Silesia or Saxony. But although the court of Vienna had made the most vigorous preparations to repair the losses of the preceding campaign, their funds were insufficient to replace the necessary stores and equipments; their troops were thinned by a dreadful sickness, derived from their fatigues and sufferings; and an efficient force was not brought into the field before the beginning of April.

On the other hand, the king of Prussia, assisted by the money of England, and his own wonderful resources, had already commenced the campaign. After taking Schweidnitz, which had been blockaded the whole winter, on the 16th of April, he suddenly directed his march into Moravia, and invested Olmutz. The siege of this place, which was defended by a garrison of 8000 men, was a fortunate event for the house of Austria. From its marshy situation and extent it could not be easily invested; and its distance from the Prussian magazines rendered the passage of convoys through a mountainous country extremely precarious and difficult. The operations of the siege were also unskilfully conducted; for by opening the first parallel at too great a distance, the Prussian batteries consumed their ammunition with little effect; and notwithstanding a continual fire for several days, the artillery of the place remained in full activity.

Prince Charles having resigned in consequence of the ill success of the preceding campaign, Daun, to whom the sole management of the war was intrusted, skilfully availed himself of the errors of his great antagonist: he had time to assemble 50,000 men; but as they were principally recruits, he judiciously avoided an action, by encamping at Leutomischel, fifty miles from Olmutz, from whence he encouraged the garrison by frequent succours, while his numerous light troops kept the Prussians in continual alarm. Having inured his soldiers to the sight of the enemy, he covered his operations by a cloud of irregulars, and breaking up his camp, advanced to Ivanovitz. Alarming the king with various movements, as if inclined to risk a battle for the deliverance of Olmutz, he sent generals Loudon and Ziskowitz to intercept a convoy of 3000 waggons by Troppau, from Silesia, without which the operations of the siege could not be continued. The two generals ably seconding the judicious plan of the commander, attacked, dispersed and destroyed the convoy, though protected by 12,000 men, and only 250 waggons reached their place of destination. In consequence of this loss the king raised the siege, and rapidly marching through Bohemia, succeeded in conveying his heavy artillery, with the sick and wounded to Glatz, and proceeded himself to Landshut.

Daun pursued the Prussians ; but instead of following the king into Silesia, where he expected to encounter great obstacles from the numerous fortresses and the disposition of the people, he turned his views towards Saxony, which was covered by prince Henry with only 20,000 men ; the re-conquest of which country would deprive Frederic of his principal resources, and open the defenceless part of his hereditary dominions. His hopes of success were justified by the posture of affairs ; the army of the empire, under the prince of Deux-Ponts, had already forced prince Henry to retire towards Dresden ; and the Russians had penetrated into the Marc of Brandenburgh, and laid siege to Custrin. Daun therefore, leaving general Harsch with 20,000 men as a corps of observation on the frontiers of Silesia, moved through Lusatia ; and despatching Loudon toward Francfort on the Oder wrote to general Fermor, urging him to avoid a battle with so artful an enemy, till the grand blow was struck in Saxony.* He then made preparations to cross the Elbe at Pilnitz, and fall on the rear of prince Henry, who was encamped at Gamig, near Dresden. The recovery of Saxony seemed now certain ; but at this critical moment, the rapid

* This letter was intercepted ; and, after the battle of Zorndorf, sent back by the King of Prussia.

advance of the king frustrated the judicious measures of the Austrian commander.

After his masterly retreat from Olmutz, Frederic, leaving the margrave Charles to cover Silesia, marched with 20,000 men against the Russians who were besieging Custrin, and were only opposed by count Dohna with an inconsiderable force. Having in twenty days traversed two hundred and seventy miles, he joined Dohna on the 12th of August, in the vicinity of Custrin, at the time when the town was almost reduced to ashes. Crossing the Older eight miles below, he advanced towards the Russians, compelled Fermor to raise the siege, attacked him on the 25th near the village of Zorndorf, and, after a desperate engagement, gained a decisive victory, which obliged the Russians to retreat towards the frontiers of Poland, with the loss of 19,000 men.

Leaving Dohna with a small corps to watch the motions of the enemy, Frederic returned with the same rapidity, was joined at Grossenhayn by a corps from Silesia under marshal Keith, and, on the 12th, encamped near Reichenberg, where he opened a communication with prince Henry. Having extricated his brother, his great object was to relieve Neiss, which was besieged by general Harsch, either by forcing marshal Daun to an engagement, or by advancing before him into Silesia. With this view he broke up his camp, and took the position of Schoenfield, opposite to that of Daun, who occupied the strong post of Stolpen. The Austrian commander, however, carefully avoided an engagement; and when Frederic turned his flank, removed to the neighbourhood of Liebau, and again blocked up the road to Silesia; his right rested on the Stromberg, his centre stretched along a chain of commanding heights, and his left reached the wood which commences near Jauernig; at the same time his reserve, under the prince of Durlach, occupied Reichenbach, which lay at a distance behind his right wing.

In consequence of this movement, Frederic despatched a corps to occupy Weissenberg, and encamped on the heights within three miles of the Austrians. His centre stretched from Hochkirchen as far as Radewitz, from whence the left, forming an angle, extended to Kitlitz near Weissenberg; the right, forming a similar angle on the opposite side, occupied a ridge of commanding heights, surmounted by the

village of Hochkirchen, and separated by a narrow valley
from the woods which covered the left of the Austrian camp.
This valley was watered by a rivulet, and the passage
obstructed by numerous fish-ponds, the dams of which were
commanded by the Prussian batteries. Hochkirchen, the
most elevated ground, was defended by six battalions, and a
battery of fifteen pieces of cannon; and at the foot of the
height a battalion was posted in a mill and some cottages to
guard the passage of the rivulet, which ran along the front,
and separated the two armies. But, as the Austrian irregulars under Loudon occupied the woody heights which
flanked the right of the camp, and as the troops posted on
the Stromberg threatened the Prussian detachment at Weissenberg, the position appeared so untenable with an inferior
force, that marshal Keith remarked to the king, "The
Austrians deserve to be hanged if they suffer us to remain
quiet in this post."—" True," replied Frederic, presumptuous
from his late successes, "but I hope they fear us more than
the halter."

This overweening confidence seems to have rendered him
negligent even of common precautions; and he was further
deceived by the artifices of Daun, who, by forming barricades,
and strengthening his front with numerous redoubts, seemed
as if anxiously employed to maintain himself on the defensive.
But the Austrian commander meditated a surprise; and on
the night of the 13th of October, carried his project into
execution. Leaving his fires lighted, and employing troops
of labourers to fell trees as if forming abbatis, he ranged his
army in three divisions, which were conducted by himself,
by Loudon, and by the duke of Aremberg. Loudon, with
the irregulars reinforced by four battalions, and the whole
cavalry of the left wing, was to emerge from the woods, and
fall on the rear and flank of the Prussians at Hochkirchen;
Daun himself led the infantry of the left, on the side of the
mills; the duke of Aremberg was to augment the confusion
by an attack on the Prussian left, while the prince of Baden
Durlach was to force the detachment at Weissenberg.

Every thing seemed to concur in favouring the enterprise.
Even at the moment when the columns were forming, the
king had been induced by the representations of Seidlitz and
Ziethen, and the reports of deserters, to order some brigades

and squadrons under arms, but towards break of day suffered
them to return to their tents. In the midst of this security,
the village clock of Hochkirchen struck five, the signal for
the attack. The bodies led by Daun and Loudon instantly
pushed forward ; favoured by darkness and the negligence of
the outposts, they burst upon the enemy's camp, seized their
batteries, and the first alarm which the Prussians received,
was from the flames of the village, and the fire from their own
artillery : in the midst of the confusion the Austrians rushed
into the tents, put to the sword all who were asleep or unable
to escape, and, before break of day, were formed in the
midst of the Prussian lines.

An army less inured to discipline than that of Frederic,
would have been totally discomfited ; but on the cry of alarm
the soldiers ran to arms, and were speedily formed in the
best order that the circumstances of the surprise and the obscurity of the morning would permit. The king put himself
at the head of three brigades, and wheeling round Hochkirchen, attempted to take his adversaries in flank ; but was
compelled to yield to superior numbers, and surrounded by
the Austrians, was only rescued by the bravery of his hussars.
His usual firmness, however, did not forsake him ; he was
every where present, and inspired his troops with an ardour
similar to his own. He was ably seconded by marshal Keith
and prince Maurice, who placing themselves at the head of
some battalions, attempted to force their way through Hochkirchen, and regain their battery ; but all their efforts failed
of success ; the marshal fell, pierced with a musket ball, and
prince Maurice was dangerously wounded. Hochkirchen,
however, became the scene of a desperate conflict; the
Prussians, after obtaining possession of the place, were again
driven out, and that important post was reoccupied by the
Austrians. The king prepared to make a final effort by
means of his left wing, but was prevented by the duke of
Aremberg, who, with the Austrian right, had fallen on that
part of his line, and made himself master of the redoubts.
The important post of Hochkirchen being irretrievably lost,
Frederic recalled the detachment at Weissenberg, which had
already repulsed the prince of Durlach, and descended into
the plain with the infantry and the remains of his baggage,
covered by his cavalry. He was repeatedly charged by the

Austrian cavalry, but made good his retreat, and occupied
the heights of Bautzen, scarcely two miles from the field of
battle.

This battle lasted five hours; the loss on the side of the
Austrians was not less than 8000 ; that of the Prussians
9000, with the greater part of their tents and baggage, 101
cannon, and thirty standards.   Most of the Prussian generals
were wounded; even the king himself received a slight contusion ; his horse was killed under him, and two pages fell
at his side.   His brother-in-law, prince Francis of Brunswick,
was killed in the action; but what most affected the monarch
was the loss of his friend, marshal Keith, whose body being
accidentally discovered by Daun in the church of Hochkirhen
was buried with military honours.   Notwithstanding this
brilliant victory, Daun did not abate his characteristic caution;
aware of the steadiness of the Prussian infantry, the inexhaustible resources of the king, and the rapidity of his
movements, he did not attempt to pursue his advantage, and
the same evening resumed his former position.

This victory filled the court of Vienna with the most
lively joy, and honours and emoluments were lavished on the
commander-in-chief.   The empress-queen expressed her
grateful acknowledgments by a letter written with her own
hand ; a statue was erected to his honour ; and the Austrian
states made him a donation of 300,000 florins, to repurchase
the lordship of Ladendorf, a family domain which had been
sold by his father : the empress of Russia also testified her
regard, by the present of a gold-hilted sword.

The defeat of the Prussians at Hochkirchen was not,
however, followed by any considerable advantage.   Frederic,
though foiled, was still formidable ; he drew prince Henry
from Saxony with 7000 men, and gaining a march on Daun,
hastened by Gorlitz and Lauban towards Silesia.   Daun
unable to intercept his progress, sent a detachment to harass
his march, and turned towards Saxony, which was evacuated
by the Prussian troops, except the garrisons; Leipsig was
besieged by the army of the empire ; Torgau by Haddick ;
and Daun himself invested Dresden.   But his views were
baffled by the promptitude and address of the Prussians.
General Wedel having driven the Swedes from the Marc of
Brandenburgh, hastened into Saxony, and relieved Torgau ;

at the same time count Dohna, who was equally successful
against the Russians, uniting with Wedel, between Torgau
and Dresden, relieved Leipsig ; and the king himself, having
forced general Harsch to raise the siege of Neiss, left
Fouquet to observe the Austrians, and returning through
Lusatia, on the 13th of November, had again reached
Bautzen. Daun therefore evacuated Saxony, and took up
his winter quarters in Bohemia, while the army of the
empire fell back into Franconia ; the Russians retired into
Poland and Prussia; and the Swedes to Stralsund.*

* During this campaign Daun had been ably seconded by Lacy and
Loudon, two foreigners of different characters and talents, who, as well
at this as at subsequent periods, highly distinguished themselves in the
service of the house of Austria.

Count Lacy was of Irish extraction, and son of marshal Lacy, who, in
conjunction with Munich, commanded with such distinguished success
the Russian armies against the Turks in the reign of the empress Anne:
He was born in 1718 ; and, after a polished education, learned the art of
war in the great school of marshal Munich.   At the accession of Maria
Theresa he entered the Austrian service, and by his behaviour, talents,
and courage, acquired the esteem of his commanders, and rose rapidly to
the rank of colonel.   His acquaintance with the theory of war and skill
in tactics, together with his activity and vigilance, recommended him to
the notice of Daun ; and he improved the good opinion of his general,
by his courtier-like behaviour and fascinating manners.   From the rank
of colonel, which he held at the commencement of the septennial war, he
soon rose to that of major-general, and owed his elevation to the protection and friendship of Daun, who consulted him on every occasion, and
employed him in the execution of the most important and delicate measures.   Though he was animated with a spirit of enterprise, and frequently urged the commander-in-chief to acts of vigour and decision,
yet he possessed equal coolness and presence of mind ; his ardour never
exceeded the bounds of prudence, nor hurried him into attempts which
might incur the censures of his cautious patron.   He was singularly
useful in disciplining the troops, and superintending the manœuvres of
which Daun was the inventor ; he was a strict friend to order, and introduced an extraordinary degree of economy in every branch of the military department.

Gideon Ernest Loudon, supposed to be descended from a noble family
of the county of Ayr, in Scotland, which in the fourteenth century settled
in Livonia, was born at Tootzen, in 1716; and, as soon as he was capable
of bearing arms, entered into the Russian service. He was present at the
siege of Dantzic ; and, in 1734, served in the army sent by the empress
Anne towards the Low Countries. But on the signature of the preliminaries, the troops, who had advanced as far as the Rhine, were marched
to the banks of the Dnieper, against the Turks and Tartars, who had

Chap. CXIV. — 1759.

Maria Theresa saw the new year open with the most sanguine hopes of success. Her armies, no longer incomplete, sickly, and dejected, were in high health and spirits; Daun

made an irruption into the southern provinces of Russia. During the campaigns from 1736 to 1739, Loudon served under marshal Munich, and raised himself from the rank of cadet to that of first lieutenant. After the peace he quitted Russia, with an intention of entering into the Austrian army; but in his way through Berlin, was persuaded by some officers, with whom he had served in the Turkish campaigns, to request an audience of the king, and to solicit the rank of captain. On being presented, Frederic contemptuously turned away, and said to his suite, "That man's physiognomy does not please me;" but the king had reason to repent this refusal, and the candour to avow his regret.

Repulsed at Berlin, Loudon obtained letters of recommendation from the imperial ambassador, and went, in 1742, to Vienna. While he was in the ante-chamber, a person accosting him, inquired his name and business: Loudon having mentioned his name, and explained his business, the stranger complacently offered his assistance, and passed directly into the cabinet. In a few moments he was summoned, and observed in his unknown protector the husband of Maria Theresa. Under such favourable auspices his request was granted; and he obtained a company in the Sclavonian free corps of Pandours, raised by Trenck, who had known Loudon in Russia, and was well pleased to retain under him so gallant an officer. In 1744, when prince Charles of Loraine forced his celebrated passage over the Rhine, Loudon led his company in the foremost boat, and first landed on French ground. In a subsequent skirmish, a musket-ball penetrated his right breast, the only wound which he ever received; he fell, was taken prisoner, and conveyed to a neighbouring village. A few days afterwards the Austrian army advanced, the Pandours drove out the enemy, Loudon was restored to liberty, and had the satisfaction of saving from pillage the house of the peasant where he had been placed, and by whom he had been benevolently treated. At the peace, Trenck's regiment being disbanded, Loudon with difficulty obtained the rank of major in a frontier corps, and was quartered in Croatia till the septennial war, when his enterprising spirit induced him to repair to Vienna, and solicit employment: but not having obtained leave of absence, he was on the point of being reprimanded, and sent back to Croatia, when he fortunately obtained the patronage of prince Kaunitz, through whose recommendation he was despatched into Bohemia, at the head of 800 Croats. He joined the army under marshal Brown, soon after the battle of Lowositz, and in the retreat escaped alone, out of 100 grenadiers, who were cut to pieces by the Prussian hussars. During the remainder of the campaign, he acquired, by his unwearied activity had gradually inured the troops to discipline, and by his judicious operations had taught them that the enemy was not invincible ; the troops placed the most implicit confidence in their commander, and panted for the opening of the campaign to add new laurels to those gained at Hochkirchen.

The cause of the house of Austria was supported by her allies with increasing zeal and vigour. The empress Elizabeth redoubled her preparations ; Sweden made as great exertions as the weakness of the government would permit ; the Catholic states of Germany vied in pouring forth their men and treasures, and even the army of the empire was reinforced and completed at an early period of the year beyond its usual numbers.

France above all devoted herself to the support of her ancient rival, now become her closest ally. The influence

and prudence, the love of the troops, and the confidence of the commander-in-chief.

In February 1757, a design being planned to seize the small fortress of Hirschfeldt, Loudon, who was despatched with 300 Croats to make a false attack, forced his way into the place : but the main body being repulsed, he retreated in order, with two pieces of cannon, the first which had for some time been taken from the Prussians. This action was the forerunner of his great reputation, and raised him to the rank of colonel. During the blockade of Prague, Loudon was foremost in various sallies, and continuing to distinguish himself at the head of the Croats, was intrusted with the command of 4000 light horse, and appointed major-general ; the patent which conferred this rank, falling into the hands of some Prussian hussars, Frederic despatched a trumpet with it, and expressed his satisfaction in being instrumental in the promotion of so gallant an officer. In April 1758, Loudon received the military order of Maria Theresa, and was the most active officer in the army. He greatly assisted in cutting off the Prussian convoy, which occasioned the delivery of Olmutz ; he planned the surprise of Hochkirchen ; and Daun, in his letter, announcing this victory to the empress queen, candidly attributed the success to the steadiness of the infantry and the manœuvres of the Croats under Loudon ; for this service he was promoted to a still higher rank, and, in 1759, he was intrusted with the command of a separate army, to act in conjunction with the Russians.

Unlike Lacy, Loudon was of a shy, reserved, and unassuming character. Plain and unpolished in his appearance, cold and awkward in his address, he was seldom animated, except in the field of battle. Long accustomed to lead irregular troops, he was often enterprising, even to rashness, and was more calculated for measures which required a rapid and vigorous execution, than for directing the complicated operations of a campaign.

of Austria was paramount in the court and cabinet; cardinal
Bernis, who had presumed to express his desire to terminate
the war, was dismissed in disgrace; Stainville, on his return
from Vienna, was created duke of Choiseul, and appointed
secretary of state for foreign affairs, and had effected, in
concert with the mistress, a new treaty of alliance, which
was signed with the empress-queen on the 30th of December.
In this second treaty of Versailles, the king of France
engaged to use all his efforts in procuring the restitution of
Silesia and Glatz to the house of Austria; agreed to furnish
the succours, either in men or money, according to the option
of the empress-queen, to pay the subsidy to Sweden, which
had hitherto been discharged conjointly with Austria, and
to maintain during the whole war 100,000 troops in Germany against the king of Prussia. He also guarantied to
the house of Austria all the conquests from the Prussian
territories on the Lower Rhine, and promised to concur in
raising the archduke Joseph to the dignity of king of the
Romans, and to assist in concluding a marriage between one
of the archdukes and the princess of Modena. In return
Maria Theresa confirmed the cession of Ostend and Nieuport
during the war, and renounced her right to the eventual
succession of the duchies of Parma and Placentia, as stipulated
by the peace of Aix-la-Chapelle.

Confident in the assistance of their allies, and elated by
their recent success, the court of Vienna even ventured to
issue a conclusum of the Aulic Council, threatening the
elector of Hanover, the landgrave of Hesse Cassel, prince
Ferdinand of Brunswick, and the other adherents of the
king of Prussia, with the ban of the empire, if they did not
abandon his alliance, dismiss their armies, and supply their
contingents of men and money according to the decree of
the diet.

Early in the year, Frederic and his allies were successful
in various expeditions against the Austrian, French, and
Russian magazines; and prince Ferdinand being reinforced
by a body of English troops, attacked the French at Bergen,
near Frankfort, but was repulsed with considerable loss.
These enterprises, however, only retarded the operations of
the Austrians and French. The latter, under Contades,
passed the Rhine at Cologne in the beginning of May,

united with a corps under Broglio at Giessen, overran Hesse, occupied Cassel and Minden, where they seized considerable magazines; while another corps, formed on the side of the Wesel, burst into the bishopric of Munster, and on the 25th of July took the capital with a garrison of 4000 men.

In consequence of his resolution not to act on the offensive until the approach of the Russians, Daun did not take the field till the beginning of May. Encamping between Schatz and Jaromitz in Bohemia, he continued seven weeks watching the motions of the king of Prussia, whose principal force was concentrated near Landshut; but on the advance of the Russians towards the Oder, he moved into Lusatia, and encamped at Mark Lissa, and the king retired to Schmuesseifen in the vicinity of Lauenburgh. No obstacle now seemed capable of retarding the long-expected junction of the Austrians and Russians. The Prussian forces were scattered in Saxony, Silesia, and on the Oder, and on every point overawed by superior armies: De Ville with 20,000 Austrians, threatened to penetrate into Silesia by the defiles of Landshut, which were guarded by only 10,000 Prussians under Fouquet; Daun, at the head of 70,000 men, hovering on the frontiers of Lusatia and Lower Silesia, was opposed by the king with only 40,000; on the side of Saxony, prince Henry was reduced to the defensive against the army of the empire, while Dohna, with less than 20,000, covered the Marc of Brandenburgh against 70,000 Russians under Soltikof.

In June, the Russians drove back the corps of Dohna, totally defeated them at Zullichau under Wedel, who had assumed the command, and directed their march to Frankfort on the Oder. This success was the signal for the co-operation of the Austrians: Loudon was detached from the main army with 30,000 men, and leaving Haddick with 12,000 at Guben to cover his march and maintain a communication with Daun, hastened with the remainder, who were principally cavalry, and joined the Russians at Frankfort.

To oppose this formidable force, Frederic collected his forces in the vicinity of the Oder. Leaving garrisons in Dresden, Leipsig, Torgau, and Wittemberg, to employ the

army of the empire, he drew the remainder of the troops to
Sagan, and reinforced them with a detachment from Silesia.
Having transferred the command in Lusatia to prince
Henry, he defeated the corps of Haddick at Guben, with the
loss of 2000 men, and 500 provision waggons ; on the 4th of
August, he was joined by Wedel, at Mulrose, crossed the
Oder on the 11th, between Lebus and Custrin, and, at the
head of 40,000 men, advanced to give battle to the combined
Austrians and Russians, amounting to 80,000. This extraordinary march, and his unparalleled exertions to bring
on an engagement, on the issue of which his fate seemed to
depend, arrested the attention of all Europe, and the combined army prepared for the conflict with a degree of precaution which their great superiority in numbers seemed to
render unnecessary. They occupied the heights on the left
bank of the Oder ; their front was covered by a marshy
plain, intersected by rivulets and drains, and their rear and
flanks by a line of formidable intrenchments, strengthened
with redoubts, and stretching from a height near the village
of Cunersdorf, beyond the Judenberg, or Jew's burying-
ground. The Russians were posted in the intrenchments;
and the Austrian cavalry under Loudon, with the Cossacs,
occupied the low ground between the front and the Oder,
but on the approach of the Prussians, marched to the left,
and formed in a small hollow crossing the camp at the foot
of the Judenberg.

Early on the 12th the king attacked this formidable
position. Masking his movements by means of the woods,
he suddenly enveloped the right flank, and from the surrounding eminences concentrated the fire of his artillery on the
redoubts and intrenchments. This fire soon rendered the
intrenchments untenable, and the Prussians advancing, stormed
the redoubts without much difficulty, took the Russians in
flank, drove them with a dreadful slaughter beyond the
village of Cunersdorf, and made themselves masters of 180
pieces of artillery. Still, however, the Austrian and Russian
troops on the left continued firm, and forming in several
lines, were protected by their artillery placed on the Judenberg.

In these circumstances, Seidlitz, and most of the other
Prussian generals, exhorted the king to be satisfied with his

advantage, which must compel the combined forces to retire during the night; they urged him to spare his troops, exhausted with the fatigues of an action which had already lasted seven hours, and burning with thirst from their march over a sandy soil, in an intense heat. Frederic paused for a moment, but was soon impelled by his natural ardour to pursue his success against an enemy almost defeated, and once more put his fortune to the stake. Animated by the example of their sovereign, the troops again advanced; the cavalry, in particular, attempted to break through the intrenchments near the Judenberg, but were repulsed with considerable loss, and Seidlitz himself wounded. The Russians, however, panic-struck with the impetuosity of the charge, abandoned their battery on the Judenberg, and the Prussian infantry instantly moved forward to seize the height, which would have decided the fortune of the day. At this critical moment Loudon, with his Austrians, rushed to the battery, and turned the cannon, loaded with grape shot, on the Prussians, who were advanced within a hundred and fifty paces. This unexpected discharge mowed down whole ranks; the Prussians repeated their desperate attack, but in vain; exhausted by the incessant fatigue of the action, and thrown into confusion by the destructive fire of the artillery, they began to give way. Loudon instantly burst upon them at the head of his cavalry, threw them into irreparable disorder, and in a few minutes these troops, already victorious, were dispersed and defeated.

Frederic, with a few pieces of cannon and a single regiment, exposed his person to protect the retreat of his troops; two horses were killed under him; his clothes were pierced with musket-balls; he received a slight contusion, and was only rescued by the exertions of the hussars. Favoured by the approach of night, he succeeded in saving the remnant of his army, and again took post on the same ground * which

* A Prussian officer, who was present in the action, thus describes the situation of the king early the ensuing morning:—"I saw the king the next morning stretched upon a little straw, reposing among the ruins of a farm-house, in the village of Oetcher, which had been destroyed by the Cossacs. He slept with as much soundness and tranquillity as if he had been secure from all dangers; his hat partly covered his face; his drawn sword lay by his side; and two adjutants were snoring at his feet —a single sentinel mounted guard."

he had occupied before the engagement, with scarcely more than 1000 men. During the action general Wunsch, with a detachment of Prussians, had crossed the Oder, and made himself master of Frankfort, with a view to intercept the retreat of the combined forces ; but on the defeat of the king, he abandoned his conquest.

In describing this battle, Frederic feelingly observes, " Qu'on voie à quoi tiennent les victoires ! " He himself was so confident of success, that in the middle of the action he wrote a billet to the queen :   " We have driven the Russians from their intrenchments; in two hours expect to hear of a glorious victory ! " But at the conclusion of the engagement he sent another despatch :—" Remove from Berlin with the royal family ; let the archives be carried to Potsdam, and the capital make conditions with the enemy." He lost in this desperate conflict 20,000 of his bravest troops with all his artillery, and most of his generals were wounded ; but the allied army had little reason to exult in their success, for not less than 24,000 men were killed and wounded, and Soltikof declared, that on such another victory, he must go alone with his truncheon in his hand, to carry the news to St. Petersburgh. As this loss fell almost entirely on the Russians, and as the Austrians gained the chief honour of the victory, without suffering from the heat of the action, the Russians were inflamed almost to madness, threatened to put Loudon to death, and he escaped the effects of this sudden frenzy, by not making his appearance till their fury had subsided.

This misunderstanding saved the hero of the house of Brandenburgh, who, after his prodigious exertions to raise the army which had just experienced so terrible a defeat, was now almost a fugitive. In vain Loudon pressed Soltikof to pursue the enemy, and offered to bring the king prisoner within three days ; the Russian general could not be roused to exertion, and suffered the decisive moment to escape. The representations of Daun were attended with no better success : and Soltikof replied,   " I have gained two battles, with the loss of 27,000 men ; I now expect two victories from you, as it is not just that the troops of my sovereign should act alone."

While the king had turned his efforts against the Russians

the army of the empire overran Saxony, took possession of
Torgau, Wittemberg, and Leipsig, and invested Dresden.
A temporary reconciliation also was effected between the
Austrians and Russians; and Daun, in a conference with
Soltikof at Guben, settled a plan for future operations; the
Russians were to remain in the Marc of Brandenburgh, on
the left bank of the Oder, and to be supplied with forage and
provisions; and on the capture of Dresden, which was on
the point of surrendering, the two armies were to co-operate
in the recovery of Silesia.   But it was now too late; the
inactivity of the Russians after the battle of Cunersdorf had
given the king time to recover from his dreadful discomfiture;
and he rose like the hydra with new strength from his defeat.
He collected his scattered forces; recalled general Kleist,
with 5000 men, from Pomerania; and supplied the loss of
his artillery from his fortresses.   In a few days he was again
at the head of 28,000 men, covered his capital and Brandenburgh, and even sent a detachment under general Wunsch to
restore his affairs in Saxony.

Daun had scarcely opened a communication with Soltikof,
when prince Henry marched to Goerlitz in his rear, compelled the detachment under De Ville to retire, and sending
parties into Bohemia, destroyed the Austrian magazines at
Boehmisch-friedland and Gabel.   In consequence of this
masterly manœuvre, Daun retired to Bautzen, to draw his
supplies from Dresden, which had recently surrendered.
The Russians being thus disappointed in their intended
junction with the Austrians, attempted to penetrate into
Lower Silesia; but were anticipated by the king, who
rapidly marching through Sagan, took post at Neustadtel,
and covered that country.   Meanwhile Daun approached
Goerlitz, with a view to attack prince Henry; but was baffled by that able general, who during the night made a
retrograde march to Rothemberg, as if returning to Silesia,
then changing his route, cut off an Austrian detachment at
Hoyerswerda, and directing his march by Esterwalda crossed
the Elbe, at Torgau, on the 25th of September.

These movements deranged the plan of operations concerted between Daun and Soltikof; the Russians had already
begun to experience great want of provisions, and the court
of Vienna, unable, from the destruction of their magazines,

to provide for the wants of their own army, offered an equivalent in money; but Soltikof laconically replied, " My
soldiers cannot eat gold." After some ineffectual attempts
to penetrate in Silesia, they continued their march towards
Poland, and Loudon retired with his corps to Olmutz. From
these disappointments Daun relinquished his designs on
Silesia and Brandenburgh, and turned all his views to the
affairs of Saxony.

The army of the empire, assisted by an Austrian force
under general Guasco, had invested Dresden on the 9th of
August; they had, however, neither made approaches nor
erected batteries, and notwithstanding a close blockade,
general Schmettau the Prussian commandant, held out with
great perseverance. General Wunsch was rapidly advancing to the relief of the place, and had arrived within two
German miles, when Schmettau capitulated, after a blockade
of twenty-seven days. The garrison were allowed to depart
with the honours of war, and to retain the military chest,
containing 5,000,000 crowns, with the baggage, artillery,
ammunition, pontoons and waggons; but the Austrians
secured considerable magazines of provisions, which enabled
them to maintain themselves in Saxony. Wunsch, disappointed in his endeavour to relieve Dresden, retired towards
Torgua, where he defeated the army of the empire, though
four times superior in number, and made himself master of
Wittemberg and Leipzig. In consequence of this success,
general Fink was despatched by the king with a more considerable corps, and their united forces again advanced towards Dresden.

This reverse of circumstances drew Haddick from Lusatia:
he passed the Elbe at Dresden, and, joining the army of the
empire, attacked the Prussians, but was repulsed with considerable loss; and prince Henry arriving with his whole
army at Torgau, the Prussian forces joined at Stroehlen, on
the 4th of October, and threatened Dresden. In consequence
of these movements, Daun marched into Saxony, passed the
Elbe at Dresden, compelled prince Henry to fall back, and
took post at Belgern. With a view to turn the position of
the Prussians, he detached the duke of Aremberg with a
considerable force to Domitsch, but this corps being defeated
with the loss of 1500 men, and general Hulsen arriving with

the army of the king, he fell back to Dresden, and encamped at Plauen. Frederic, who had been detained by illness at Glogau, having joined his army, with the hopes of forcing the Austrians to abandon Dresden, intercepted their convoys, made irruptions into Bohemia, and even detached general Fink, with a considerable corps, to occupy Maxen in their rear, and general Dielke with 3000 men to take post on the Elbe. By these bold movements the imperial army was prevented from entering into cantonment, straitened for forage, and Bohemia opened to the incursions of the enemy. In this situation Daun formed the bold plan of surprising the Prussian corps at Maxen, and conducted this delicate enterprise with equal judgment, celerity, and secrecy. Fink had no sooner taken post in the rear of the Austrians, than general Sincere was sent with a few regiments to watch his motions; and during the following days, detachments to the number of 40,000 men were drawn out to attack him in front, flank, and rear. Daun himself proceeded to Dippoldiswalda, from whence the main body of the Prussians had retired to the heights of Maxen; he reconnoitred their position, and arranged the different points of attack. After ordering the corps at Dippoldiswalda to march towards Reinhardsgrimma, he returned to Plauen to observe the motions of the king, and make the necessary dispositions, should Frederic discover the enterprise, and attack his camp, weakened by half its number. Observing, however, no sympton of alarm or preparation, he departed in the middle of the night, and rejoined the troops at break of day, as they were preparing for their march. His presence was highly necessary, as many of his officers were alarmed by the difficulties of the ground, and by a frost, accompanied with sleet, which rendered the steep ascents almost impracticable for the conveyance of cannon, or the march of cavalry. Having ordered the roads to be reconnoitred, Daun persisted in his enterprise, drove in the advanced post of the enemy at Reinhardsgrimma with little opposition, penetrated through a thick wood, and occupied the heights, commanding the Prussian camp, with formidable batteries; at the same time a body of light troops, passing by Rohrsdorf, came in their rear, and the corps of Dohna was attacked by the troops of the empire.

The success of these manœuvres being facilitated by the

unskilful dispositions of the Prussian commander, the well-
directed fire of the artillery, and the impetuous attack of
the Austrian grenadiers, overbore all resistance. The Prussians quitted the heights, and retired towards Bloschwitz,
with the resolution to cut their way through the enemy; the
approach of night suspended the engagement; but the Austrian general deprived them of all hopes of escape by occupying the surrounding defiles ; and in the morning they surrendered themselves prisoners of war, on the condition of
preserving their baggage. Thus the Austrians took 549
officers, including 17 generals, 14,900 men, and 17 pieces of
cannon ; and what rendered this action more remarkable, few
of either side fell on the field of battle, notwithstanding
the impetuosity of the attack, and the resistance of the Prussians.

So masterly were the dispositions, so secret was the enterprise, and so completely was the communication intercepted,
that the king was unapprised of the danger till it was too
late ; and Hulsen, who was detached to favour the retreat of
Fink, arrived only to be informed of his capitulation. The
corps also under general Dielke being greatly exposed on the
surrender of Fink, attempted to recross the Elbe; but as they
had removed their bridge in consequence of the frost, they
endeavoured to effect the passage in boats; in this situation
they were attacked, and 1500 men with the commander
made prisoners. Daun, however, was not too much elated
by these advantages to neglect his usual precaution ; he presented himself before the Prussian camp thus weakened and
discouraged with the loss of 20,000 men ; but perceiving the
king still formidable, he declined an engagement, and returned
to Plauen, where he was able to succour Dresden if attacked
and to maintain his communication witd Bohemia.

On the other hand, the French, after a series of successes,
experienced a fatal reverse at Minden, and prince Ferdinand
was enabled to send a reinforcement of 12,000 men to the
king, which joined him at Freyberg in the beginning of
December, and supplied the loss experienced at Maxen.

Leaving this body behind the Mulda to protect his rear,
the king made a final attempt to draw the Austrians from
Dresden, by turning their flank, and gaining Dippoldiswalda.
But Daun having reinforced that post, he dismissed the suc-

cour furnished by prince Ferdinand, left his tents standing in the camp at Wilsdruf, and cantoned his troops in the neighbouring villages, watching the moment when Daun should retire into winter quarters, to seize Dresden. The Austrian commander, however, maintaining his post with equal perseverance, followed the example of the king, and both parties vied in braving the rigour of the severest winter which had been long felt in Germany.

The loss experienced by both armies during this dreadful close of an arduous campaign may be easily conceived from the description of a Prussian officer, who was an eye-witness: "The winter was uncommonly severe, and the snow for several weeks covered the ground to the height of the knee. The army was distributed in the small towns and villages, and the troops were so straitened that only a part could shelter themselves under a roof: the houses were occupied by the officers, and the men dwelt in temporary cabins, lying about their fires day and night like a horde of Tartars. They employed the whole day in cutting and conveying fuel from a considerable distance; and from the extreme scarcity of provisions the soldiers were reduced to bread alone, of which they made a kind of soup with water.

"In addition to these hardships they were still further harassed in guarding the camp at Wilsdruf, which was performed by the whole army in turn, and which, from the number of sick, allowed them but a short interval for repose. Here the centinels had no fires, and officers sheltered themselves in huts formed of planks; the common soldiers, to give motion to their frozen blood, ran up and down like madmen, or, forgetting to dress their provisions, crowded together in the tents, and lay one on the other to warm at least a part of their bodies by the heat of their comrades. In this situation either attack or defence was impossible; and no regiment returned from this camp to their melancholy winter quarters, without seeing the number of their sick increase. They died in their cabins 'like flies,' and this winter campaign cost the king more than two battles; nor did the Austrians experience a better fate; for contagious disorders broke out in their army, and in the space of only sixteen days they lost 4000 men."

Chap. CXV.—1760.

After much difficulty in settling the plan of the campaign, it was agreed, that while the French were opposed to the British and Hanoverians, Soltikof and Loudon, with a combined army of Austrians and Russians, should invade Silesia; that the Swedes, under Ehrenswald, the troops of Wirtemberg under their sovereign, and another corps of Russians under Tottleben, should burst into Brandenburgh; that the united fleets of Russia and Sweden should besiege Colberg; while Daun and the army of the empire should achieve the conquest of Saxony.

The troops of Maria Theresa had proved victorious during the whole of the last campaign; they had recovered from the fatigues and sufferings of the winter; the regiments were complete, and the men animated by their recent success. On the contrary, the king of Prussia laboured under the greatest difficulties; he had experienced the most fatal defeats, and his losses were not to be estimated by the number of killed and wounded, but by the destruction and capture of whole armies. He had indeed recruited his troops; yet, to use his own words, "they were no longer veterans, or soldiers fit for service, but only for show. What could be done with an assemblage of men, half Saxon peasants, half deserters from the enemy, and led by officers who were engaged from necessity, and employed for want of others? Even of these, the regiments of infantry had only twelve instead of fifty-two, the regulated number." Yet with all his efforts he could only muster in the field 75,000 men, to act against a force of 250,000. Notwithstanding the English subsidy, he was distressed for funds to supply the enormous expense of the war, and was under the necessity of having recourse to the coinage of base money, and to other dishonourable expedients.

In April, Daun occupied the camp of Pirna, and observed the motions of the king, who, taking a strong position at Katsenhauser, near Meissen, cantoned the greater part of his forces in the neighbouring villages, to recover from the fatigues of the winter. In this state the two armies remained till they were called into action by the operations in Silesia.

Loudon, having quitted Olmutz in April, entered Lower Silesia, near Reichenbach, blockaded Glatz, and, after a series of masterly manœuvres, succeeded in forcing an intrenched camp, occupied by Fouquet, with 9000 men, to guard the defiles of Landshut, and made the commander and the greater part of the corps prisoners. After remaining a few days in the mountains to secure the passes, Loudon returned to Glatz ; on the 26th, the upper fortresses being taken by storm, the governor capitulated ; and, on the 30th, Breslau itself was invested.

On the first news of the blockade of Glatz, Frederic, with the greater part of his forces, crossed the Elbe at Zehren, and took the route to Radeberg, in order to penetrate into Silesia, and join the corps of Fouquet. Lacy retired on his approach ; but the king had no sooner reached Radeberg, than he was confounded with the intelligence of Fouquet's defeat and capture ; he received the account with extreme agitation, and his usual magnanimity seemed for a moment to forsake him. Striking his forehead, he exclaimed, " Such disasters happen to me alone !" He soon however recovered his presence of mind, and redoubled his efforts to reach Silesia. Leaving a corps at Meissen, he marched to Bautzen : but Daun having crossed the Elbe at the same time as the Prussians, hastened to Goerlitz, and thus anticipated the enemy, whose progress was harassed by the corps under Lacy. Frederic, perceiving that he could not reach Silesia, made a retrograde movement, turned against Lacy, drove him across the Elbe, forced the army of the empire to quit the camp at Plauen, and invested Dresden, with the hopes of obtaining an immediate surrender by the fear of a bombardment. But all his efforts were ineffectual ; though he set fire to different parts of the town, and actually made a breach in the wall.

Daun remained a few days to arrange with Loudon the plan of future operations in Silesia, and then turned towards Lower Saxony. He approached Dresden on the seventh day of the investment, threw a succour of 12,000 men into the town, and took post on the neighbouring heights. As at the siege of Olmutz, his views were directed to deliver the town by intercepting the convoys, and cutting off the communications of the enemy : with 70,000 men he himself

occupied the right bank of the Elbe ; Lacy, and the army of
the empire, at Gross Seidlitz and Dohna, threatened the
Prussians on that side, and the garrison of the town was
increased to 25,000 men.   The views of the Austrian commander were promoted by the capture of Glatz.   On receiving intelligence of that event, Frederic broke up his
camp in the night, resumed his former resolution of penetrating into Silesia, and passing the Elbe at Zehren, on the
1st of August, took the route of Upper Lusatia.   Daun,
aware of his design, advanced with equal activity ; and, to
prevent the king from again deceiving him by a retrograde
movement, marched in a parallel direction, while Lacy hung
upon the rear of the Prussians.   Such was the situation and
vicinity of the two armies, that, to use the expressions of the
king, " A stranger might have mistaken them for one, that of
marshal Daun like the advanced guard, the Prussians, the
main body, and the corps of Lacy, the rear guard." *

In the course of this march Daun learned that Loudon
had raised the siege of Breslau on the approach of prince
Henry, and that Soltikof with the Russians had advanced to
the right bank of the Oder.   He therefore avoided an engagement until he had effected a junction with Loudon and
Soltikof ; and on the 7th of August, after a march of eighty-
four miles in five days, encamped at Lowenburgh at the same
time that the Prussians reached Buntzlau.   He then succeeded in gaining a position behind the Katzbach, by which
he cut off the king from his magazines at Breslau and
Schweidnitz, and prevented his junction with prince Henry;
here he united with Loudon and the corps under Lacy, and
their troops occupied the left bank of the Katzbach from the
Oder to Cossendau.

Soltikof displaying an unwillingness to cross the Oder,
Daun resolved to attack the king with his own troops,
which did not amount to less than 90,000 men, while the
Prussians were scarcely 30,000.   Unable to withstand this
superior force, Frederic, like a skilful partisan, embarrassed
the Austrian commander by a continual change of position,
till, straitened for provisions, he was reduced to the necessity of attempting to force the passage of the Katzbach, in
order to open a way to his magazines at Schweidnitz.   The

* Œuvres Posthumes, tom. iv. p. 104.

vigilance and number of the Austrians, however, defeated all
his efforts ; and at length a corps of 20,000 Russians under
Chernichef, having passed the Oder at Auras, his last resource was, to attempt a junction with prince Henry. He
therefore took post near Lignitz, with the intention to cross
the Katzback, and push on to Parchwitz.

In this situation Daun hoped to repeat the surprise of
Hochkirchen, and overwhelm the Prussian monarch by the
great superiority of his force. His dispositions were skilfully arranged : Lacy was to turn the right flank of the
Prussians, and fall on their rear; Daun himself was to
attack their front ; and Loudon to cross the Katzbach,
occupy the heights of Pfaffendorf above Lignitz, and cut off
their retreat.

Frederic penetrated their designs, and unwilling to hazard
a battle with so superior a force, hastened to effect his intended retreat. He moved from his camp in the evening,
leaving some hussars to keep up the fires, and imitate the
cries of the patroles and sentinels, and during the night repassed the Katzbach at Lignitz. At the moment of his
departure his conjectures were confirmed by an adjutant of
O'Donnel's regiment, who had deserted, and informed him
that the Austrians were in motion for the attack. Having
reached the heights of Pfaffendorf, Frederic made preparations to receive the enemy; he posted his right on that part
of the eminence which overhangs Lignitz and the Schwartzwasser, and placed batteries to enfilade the only two roads
through which Daun could pass; he then formed his left
across the other part of the eminence on the side of Bautzen,
on the very ground which Loudon was to occupy, and established a formidable battery on a commanding height.

On the 15th of August, before break of day, Loudon passed
the Katzbach, and as he ascended the heights fell in with
parties of Prussian hussars which had been sent to discover
and harass his movements. Although aware that a change
had taken place in the position of the enemy, he did not
expect to encounter the whole Prussian army, and heading
himself one of the columns, continued to advance. At this
moment the hussars retired, and while he was preparing to
form and occupy the heights, he received a discharge from
the Prussian battery, which being only 800 paces distant,

occasioned great havoc among his troops, who were pressed together in close columns. The darkness augmented the confusion; but though taken unawares, Loudon formed his men as they came up, and did not give way until he had withstood five successive charges: during the carnage he rode from rank to rank, and repeatedly exclaimed, "Is there no ball for me!" At length his troops being mowed down by a destructive fire, cut to pieces by the Prussian cavalry, and unable to discern the position and evolutions of the enemy, he was compelled to relinquish his enterprise. In this action Loudon lost not less than 10,000 men, and 80 officers killed, wounded, and prisoners, with 23 standards, and 82 pieces of artillery; but he made a masterly retreat, and under cover of a battery on a height beyond the Katzbach, deliberately removed the pontoons, and ranged his troops on the opposite bank.

Daun and Lacy having passed the night at the head of their troops, advanced towards break of day, and were surprised to find the Prussian camp totally deserted. The wind being contrary, Daun did not hear the cannonade on the side of Bautzen, but a thick smoke seemed to announce that Loudon was engaged; and he perceived the right of the Prussians under Ziethen drawn up on the height above Lignitz. Surprised with these unexpected movements, he continued some time in suspense: at length determining to attack Ziethen, he despatched Lacy to cross the Schwartzwasser, and turn the flank of the enemy, while he himself advanced through Lignitz; but the instant the heads of the Austrian columns appeared, they received the fire of the Prussian artillery, and a feu de joye announced the total defeat of Loudon. His plans being thus deranged, Daun re-crossed the Katzbach, recalled Lacy, and the Prussians pursued their march to Parchwitz, which they reached the same evening, though incumbered with 6000 prisoners and 1100 sick and wounded.*

* Scarcely any battle has been more erroneously described than this of Lignitz. Most authors have supposed that the movements of the king, which led to the engagement, were the effect of design, whereas his intention was to secure his retreat to Parchwitz, and his junction with prince Henry, that his forces might not be cut off in detail; and he only determined on an engagement when he perceived that it could not be

Still, however, the situation of the king was extremely critical; he had only one day's bread in his camp, and Chernichef, with the corps of 20,000 men posted at Lissa, intercepted the communication with his magazines at Breslau, while general Beck was in full march to join the Russians, and was followed by Daun with the main army. But Chernichef, who had remained five days without intelligence from the Austrians, was alarmed by a letter sent from the king to prince Henry, for the purpose of being intercepted, announcing a glorious victory over the Austrians, and describing his preparations for an immediate attack on the Russians. He accordingly broke up his camp in great haste, and repassed the Oder; and the Prussians advancing to the neighbourhood of Breslau, supplied their wants from their own magazines. While the king was allowing his army to repose at Neumark after the extreme fatigue of the preceding operations, the Russians retired towards Poland, and were followed to Vinzig by prince Henry, who then returned and joined the king near Breslau.

Daun thus disappointed in his principal object, attempted to besiege Schweidnitz, and afterwards Glogau, but was again baffled by the king, and obliged to retreat to the mountains in order to preserve his communication with Bohemia. The campaign was drawing to a close, and was likely to conclude in a manner far different from the sanguine hopes which had been conceived at the commencement. The

avoided. On this subject I shall subjoin a letter from Sir Andrew Michael to the duke of Newcastle the day after the battle :—

" As I have been extremely indisposed for several days, and unable to ride on horseback, I was not in the action ; but the king of Prussia, when he marched his army from the field of battle, sent for me to ride along with him ; when I came up to him, and gave him joy of the victory, he was pleased to say very graciously, ' You have shared the fatigues with me, I want you should likewise rejoice with me.'

" He then entered into a detail of the battle, commended highly the behaviour of his troops ; and after making some excellent reflections on the imperfection of human foresight, he said, ' You see how I have laboured to no purpose to bring about the event that has now happened ; the victory I have gained is entirely owing to the bravery of my troops. Had I remained in the camp of Lignitz, I should have been surrounded on all sides; had I but arrived one quarter of an hour sooner on the field of battle, the event would not have happened, and a few days would have put an end to the whole affair.' "

forage of the mountains being wholly consumed, Daun could only detach small parties into the plain; and the bad state of the roads retarded the passage of his convoys from Bohemia. In this dilemma he succeeded in alluring the Russians with the hopes of plundering Berlin, and concerted with them an irruption into Brandenburgh, to draw the king from Silesia. Twenty thousand Russians, with fifteen thousand Austrians under Chernichef and Lacy, covered by the army of Soltikof, penetrated into Brandenburgh, and, after a march of six days, the vanguard of 3000 men appeared before the gates of Berlin. They were vigorously repulsed by the Prussian troops under general Hulsen and the prince of Wirtemberg, who had hastened from Saxony and Pomerania; but unable to defend an extensive town without fortifications, the Prussians, on the approach of Lacy, retired to Potsdam and Spandau, and the capital surrendered on the 9th of October.

The project of the Austrian commander had the desired effect; the king precipitately quitted Silesia to relieve his capital, and as the combined troops retired on his approach, he marched rapidly towards Saxony. Daun likewise leaving Loudon in Silesia, turned towards Saxony, crossed the Elbe at Tristowitz, and endeavoured to obstruct the passage of the enemy. The duke of Wirtemberg was posted at Dessau; the prince of Deux Ponts, with a considerable part of the army of the empire, at Wittemberg; and Daun himself was approaching Torgau. Frederic, however, with part of his forces, crossed the Elbe near Dessau, and compelled the imperial troops to retire to Leipzig; on reaching Kemberg he was joined by Ziethen, who with the remainder had passed at Wittemberg, and marched to prevent the junction of the troops of the empire with the main army.

During these movements the Austrian commander advanced to Torgau, and concentrated the greater part of his forces in the vicinity. As the winter was approaching, and the campaign drawing to a close, by maintaining his position, he might take up winter quarters in the Prussian territories; while the Russians, who were at Landsberg on the Wartha, might again penetrate into the heart of Brandenburgh, and the king would be pent up in the confined district between the Pleis, the Saal, the Elster, and the Unstruth, without magazines, and cut off from his resources. In this situation

Daun judiciously avoided a battle, and chose a position, which, defended by his powerful artillery, seemed almost impregnable. His left was supported by Torgau, and covered by fish-ponds and a small lake; the centre occupied the hill of Siptitz, and the right extended to an eminence which rises beyond the marshes of Grosswig; the Rohr, a marshy and almost impracticable rivulet, ran along the front; and the extensive wood of Domnitz enveloped the right. Lacy, with the reserve of 20,000 men, covered the high road to Dresden, and the fish-ponds before the right wing; and the camp was defended by four hundred pieces of artillery.

Frederic having in vain attempted to draw the Austrians from their advantageous position, by marching to Schilda, as if he meditated an enterprise against Dresden, again resolved to commit his desperate fortune to the hazard of a battle. He divided his army into two bodies; one of these commanded by Ziethen, took the road from Eilenberg to Torgau, with a view to establish a battery on the height of Grosswig, and attack the village of Siptitz; while the king himself, leading the other through the wood, was to fall upon the Austrians at the same time in the rear, and separate their army in the centre.

Daun, whose advantageous position was defended by a powerful train of artillery, and whose army was one-third superior to that of the enemy, did not expect an attack; but undeceived by the approach of the king, he ordered his second line to face about, and the artillery to be conveyed to the rear, which then became the front. He had scarcely ranged his troops before the body headed by the king advanced. Without waiting for his cavalry, or without being seconded by Ziethen, Frederic led on his grenadiers, and was received with such a tremendous fire, as induced him to exclaim to one of his adjutants, "Did you ever hear so dreadful a cannonade!" These troops being repulsed, he rushed forward with a second line, and, after a still more desperate resistance, was compelled to give way; he then ordered a third line to advance, which being seconded by the arrival of the cavalry, gained ground, and took several regiments prisoners.

At this juncture Daun, though severely wounded in the thigh, rallied his troops, and exposing himself like a common soldier, drove the Prussians, with a dreadful carnage, back into the wood. All the efforts of the king, who on this occasion seemed determined either to conquer or to die, were ineffectual; most of his generals were wounded; he himself received a violent contusion, and reluctantly retiring from the field, considered the day as lost. At the same time Daun, compelled to quit the field by the anguish of his wound, was conveyed to Torgau, leaving the command to general Buccow, and ordering Lacy to watch the motions of Ziethen. He despatched a courier to Vienna, to announce the total defeat of the enemy, and retired to repose in the arms of victory. But the night announced a fatal change. As the enemy had retreated, the Austrians lulled into security, neglected the usual precautions. Ziethen, harassed by the irregulars, checked by the cavalry of Lacy, and embarrassed by the difficulties of the ground, did not arrive in time to second the first assault; at length, however, forcing his way through all obstacles, he reached the point of attack, but finding the battle lost, marched towards Grosswig to favour the retreat of the king. At this time darkness had suspended hostilities. Passing near the village of Siptitz, which was in flames, he was informed that the heights were weakly guarded. On this intelligence two of his bravest battalions advanced through the village, and after a short but desperate conflict, gained the heights and seized the batteries; they were followed by the rest of the infantry, with the cavalry and artillery, and the whole body formed on the slope of the eminence.

This surprise changed the defeat into a victory. At the moment when the Austrians imagined the enemy were retiring, a tremendous cannonade from the heights of Siptitz, spread consternation through their ranks. In the darkness and confusion the troops knew not whom to resist, or how to form; in vain Lacy attempted to dislodge the Prussians; they were joined by the body under the king, and, after being twice repulsed, he retreated to Torgau.

Both armies being mixed together in the field, prisoners were taken on both sides, and the royal historian relates a singular instance of the confusion which reigned after this memorable day. During the night numerous fires were kindled in the forest, to which the scattered soldiers of both armies repaired as to an asylum; they passed the night together in perfect tranquillity, and agreed to deliver themselves to the victor on the ensuing morning. Even Frederic himself, in traversing the field, fell in with a party of Austrian carbiniers, who were dispersed by his escort; and almost at the same moment, a battalion of Pandours was made prisoners, with two pieces of cannon.

Lacy reached Torgau about ten in the evening, and Daun instantly gave orders to retire. Though weakened by his wound, he crossed the Elbe with part of the troops on three bridges which had been thrown over the river the day before the battle, and proceeded to Dresden; while Lacy covered his retreat, and ascending the left bank, joined his commander at the break of day.

In this engagement the Austrians lost 20,000 men killed, wounded, and prisoners; and the Prussians 13,000 of their bravest infantry. All Saxony, except Dresden and the vicinity, again fell into the hands of the Prussians; Frederic was enabled to relieve Brandenburgh, Silesia, and Pomerania, and to send a succour of 8000 men to prince Ferdinand. Loudon, who had invested Cosel, raised the siege, and retired to Glatz; the Swedes were driven back to Stralsund, and the Russians again took up their winter quarters in Poland.

The loss, however, of this battle reflected no disgrace on the Austrian commander, but rather increased his reputation; it was attributed to his absence from the field, and Frederic himself acknowledged that he owed his victory to the wound of his antagonist. Maria Theresa also, with her natural magnanimity, received Daun with greater honours than in the midst of his most brilliant successes; and on his return met him at the distance of two German miles from the capital.

This unfortunate termination of the campaign in Saxony was not compensated by any material advantage on the side of Westphalia. Notwithstanding the exhausted state of her finances, and the loss of her most important colonial possessions, France made prodigious exertions, and sent into the field a force of 120,000 men. The main army, commanded by Broglio, advanced on the side of the Upper Rhine; and a body of 30,000 men was intrusted to St. Germain on the Lower Rhine. The commencement of their operations was however retarded by disputes between the generals; and prince Ferdinand gained time to obtain reinforcements from England, which augmented his army to 70,000 men. But he was still so much inferior to the French that he was reduced to the defensive. In June, Broglio advanced into the landgraviate of Hesse; at the same time the corps on the Lower Rhine penetrated through Westphalia, joined the main army at Corbach, and Broglio assumed the sole command. On the approach of the French, prince Ferdinand removed to Calle, in order to cover Cassel; and when Broglio detached the Chevalier de Muy with 35,000 men to cut off his communication with the bishopric of Paderborn and Westphalia, he quitted Calle, and, after a desperate engagement, defeated the Chevalier de Muy at Warburgh, with the loss of 5000 men. But on the very day of the battle, Broglio entered Cassel, and prepared to overrun the electorate of Hanover; he took Gottingen, pushed his detachments towards Saxony to open a communication with the army of the empire, and prevented the march of a reinforcement sent by the king of Prussia. He was however baffled by the skill and vigilance of prince Ferdinand, who maintained himself on the frontiers of Hanover, and even made a diversion on the side of the Lower Rhine. The hereditary prince, at the head of 15,000 men, passed through Westphalia, drew forth part of the garrisons of Munster and Lippstadt, crossed the Rhine, took possession of Cleves and Ruremonde, and on the 10th of October laid siege to Wesel. In consequence of this irruption, Broglio detached the marquis de Castries, with 20,000 men, who crossed the Rhine, drew 10,000 men from Cologne and the garrisons of the Low Countries, advanced to Rheinberg, and occupied the strong post of Closter Camp. He was here attacked by the hereditary prince, but, after a desperate action, repulsed him with the loss of 1600 men, and forced him to repass the Rhine, and raise the siege of Wesel.

Meanwhile Broglio had occupied a strong post at Einbech, and sedulously avoided an engagement. At the close of the season he wintered in Hesse; and prince Ferdinand, after an ineffectual attempt to retake Gottingen, took up his head quarters at Paderborn ; the hereditary prince distributed his troops in the bishopric of Munster.

During these transactions George II. closed his long and auspicious reign on the 25th of October, by a sudden death, and was succeeded by his grandson, George III., a prince in the flower of youth, who, in habits, disposition, and political principles, totally differed from the late monarch. Born and educated in England, he gloried in the name of Britain, and had not imbibed those foreign prejudices, which had often involved his two predecessors in the chaos of German politics, and had occasionally interfered with the interests of Great Britain. Untrained in the military school, he was by habit and principle devoted to peace; and his resolutions were strengthened by the state of the public mind at the period of his accession.

The severe sufferings of the British troops during the preceding winter, and the enormous expense of the German campaigns, began to abate the national enthusiasm, and revived the aversion of the people to a continental war. The nation regretted the separation from the house of Austria, and inveighed against the continuance of hostilities, as solely calculated for the aggrandisement of the house of Brandenburgh, and for a prince, who, though nominally the head of the Protestant interest in Germany, was the great supporter of infidelity, both by his writings and conduct. The transcendent eloquence of Mr. Pitt, and the dangerous situation of affairs, had confounded all opposition in parliament, which rather assembled to obey his dictates than to debate on the propriety of his measures; the Leicester House party, whom he had alienated, availed themselves of the growing discontents, and in numerous pamphlets and periodical publications retorted with effect on the minister the arguments which he himself had used against German measures and German influence.

One of the first objects of the young monarch was to annihilate the distinctions of Whig and Tory, and to emancipate himself from that aristocratic influence, which had gradually increased during the reigns of his two predecessors, and held the crown in bondage. He retained, however, the former administration, and in his first speech declared his intention to prosecute the war with vigour, and support his allies as the sole means of obtaining a safe and honourable peace. But the pacific sentiments of the new sovereign, and the confidence which he reposed in the earl of Bute, whose aversion to continental connections was well known, gave new spirit and hopes to the party who were desirous of peace.

That nobleman, being appointed groom of the stole, was, in virtue of his office, introduced into the privy council, and though he held no responsible post, was considered as the source of royal favour; while Mr. Pitt, who had disdained to court a party, stood alone, with no other support than what resulted from his successful career and transcendent eloquence.

Maria Theresa beheld with pleasure this change in the British cabinet, and this revolution in the public sentiment; she anticipated the dismission or retreat of Mr. Pitt, as the period when England would again relapse into a lukewarm support of her inveterate enemy. Her hopes were also raised by the situation of the Spanish court. Charles III., less pacific than his brother, and recollecting the degrading neutrality which he had been compelled to sign when king of Naples, was inclined to preserve the family connection with France. He was also drawn towards the house of Austria, by the conciliating conduct of Maria Theresa, in not urging her pretensions to Parma, and acquiescing in the order of succession, which he had established for Naples and Sicily.* These amicable dispositions were strengthened by the marriage of his niece, the infanta Isabella, princess of Parma, with the archduke Joseph on the 7th of September, 1760; and the cabinets of Vienna, Madrid, and Versailles, thus firmly united by the ties of blood and political interests, were now concerting those arrangements, which terminated in a family compact between Spain and France, and gave to the house of Austria a new and powerful ally.

Chap. CXVI.—1761.

DURING the winter, Maria Theresa was employed in recruiting her armies, and in repairing the great loss she had sustained at the battle of Torgau. In the midst of these preparations overtures for peace, originating from France, were made at the court of London, through the medium of prince Gallitzin the Russian ambassador; and Maria Theresa, affecting the same inclinations, proposed a congress at Augsburgh. She was not unacquainted with the negotiations

* Memoirs of the King of Spain, ch. lix.

between France and Spain, and she was aware that the offers of the court of Versailles were merely intended to gain time, till Spain could be drawn into the quarrel. In proposing a congress, she therefore displayed an apparent readiness for peace, although she avoided engaging herself in any specific negotiation. France soon proved the insincerity of her proposals, by endeavouring to entangle the negotiation with the long-pending contests between England and Spain, relative to the restoration of ships captured during the war, the cutting of logwood, and the privilege of fishing on the banks of Newfoundland; while the German disputes, in which the house of Austria was solely concerned, were not even brought into discussion.

In the midst of these negotiations the campaign was opened; and Maria Theresa was again flattered with the hopes of crushing the Prussian monarch. Her principal efforts were directed against Silesia, where the sole command was intrusted to Loudon, who was to be joined by the Russians under marshal Butterlin, the successor of Soltikof. On the north of Prussia, a Russian and Swedish fleet, with a body of land forces under count Romanzof, was to besiege Colberg, and penetrate into Pomerania; and marshal Daun, with the main army, was to act on the side of Saxony, and support, by detachments, the operations of Loudon and Romanzof. At this juncture the French, after having baffled an attempt made by prince Ferdinand in the depth of winter, to break their chains of quarters, and drive them from Hesse Cassel, were preparing to co-operate with the forces of the house of Austria on the side of Saxony. The king of Prussia, hemmed in on all sides by this powerful combination, marched in person to defend Silesia; prince Henry was opposed to marshal Daun, and prince Eugene of Wirtemberg, with a small force, took post in an intrenched camp to cover Colberg against the attacks of the Russians.

This campaign exhibited a singular change in the operations of the field. The active and enterprising Frederic, overpowered by the multitude of his enemies, and exhausted even by his victories, seemed to have adopted the phlegm as well as the caution of Daun, and acted wholly on the defensive. Even Loudon, who had distinguished himself by a degree of intrepidity approaching to rashness, did not give scope to his natural spirit of enterprise. He was shackled

by instructions from the council of war; he was thwarted
by the cabals of his numerous enemies, who were jealous of
his rapid and unexampled rise; and he was unwilling to
risk an action which would wither the laurels he had acquired in the preceding campaigns; but above all he was
embarrassed by the capricious and dilatory conduct of the
Russians, derived from the uncertain state of the court and
cabinet of St. Petersburgh.

The empress of Russia, though gradually sinking into the
grave under a mortal disease, yet displayed a motley mixture
of that weakness, devotion, and voluptuousness. which had
been the grand characteristics of her life. Her favourite
was devoted to France, and some of her leading ministers
were devoted to England, or awed by the influence of her
successor the great duke Peter, who was smitten with an
enthusiastic admiration of the king of Prussia. The greater
part of the cabinet, swayed by their private interests, biassed
by national prejudices, or desirous of conciliating the heir
apparent, communicated the plans of the two powers to the
king of Prussia, and thwarted the operations of the field.
Marshal Butterlin was attached to this party, and was only
anxious neither to commit the honour of the Russian arms,
nor to assist in crushing the king of Prussia; hence, although
he durst not resist the specific orders of the empress, he
found continual excuses for delay, and either thwarted or
coldly supported every plan proposed by Loudon. It was
even a subject of public conversation among the Russian
officers, that they were not to attack the king of Prussia, but
only to defend themselves if attacked.

Loudon passed the early part of the campaign in different
manœuvres to seize Neiss, or some fortress on the frontiers
of Silesia, as a support to his line of operations; but he was
constantly baffled by the skill and activity of the king. At
length he overcame the indolence of the Russian general;
Butterlin crossing the Oder, on the 17th of August, near
Closter-Leubus, effected a junction with the Austrians
between Jauer and Strigau, and the combined troops formed
a body amounting to not less than 130,000 men. As the
whole army of the king did not exceed 50,000, he was unable
to make head against so superior a force; he took a strong
position at Bunzelwitz, in the neighbourhood of Schweidnitz,
which contained his magazines, and fortified it with all the

resources of art. From the nature of the ground, the situation of the hills, the course of the rivers, and the intervention of marshes, it was almost impregnable, and was defended with numerous intrenchments, a strong and intricate pallisade, 466 pieces of artillery, and even 182 mines. In vain Loudon exerted his efforts to dislodge the Prussians; he proposed to storm these intrenchments, but was thwarted by the unconquerable repugnance of the Russian general. In this inactive situation both armies remained till the 10th of September, when the Austrians being unable to furnish the Russians with subsistence, Butterlin left Chernichef with 20,000 men, and withdrew towards Poland. His retreat was hastened by the destruction of his magazines at Kublin, which was effected by a considerable detachment under general Platen.

Loudon thus deserted, retired in chagrin towards the mountains, and resumed his position at Kunzendorf. Deeply affected with the conduct of the campaign, his anxiety and disappointment brought on a severe cholic, to which he was occasionally subject; he did not, however, remit his activity and vigilance, and when want of provisions compelled the king to withdraw towards Neiss, he seized that opportunity of attacking Schweidnitz.

Schweidnitz, which from the extent of the works required a garrison of 7000 men, was only defended by 3000, many of whom were deserters, or peasants compelled to enter into the service. It likewise contained 500 Austrian prisoners, among whom was major Rocca, an Italian partisan, who being imprudently indulged with great liberty by the governor Zastrow, examined the fortifications, and remarked the negligence in the service of the garrison, which he found means to communicate to Loudon. In consequence of this intelligence, the Austrian general with twenty battalions moved in the night of the 1st of October, at two in the morning approached the fortress, and dividing his troops into four bodies, prepared to attack the gates of Strigau and Breslau, the Water-fort, and the fort of Benkendorf. At this juncture, the commandant, as if suspicious of some intended enterprise, ordered the garrison under arms, but omitted to send out patroles, or throw light balls in the vicinity. The Austrians, therefore, advanced unperceived to the palisades, and after a few discharges of cannon gained the outworks.

In one place alone they experienced a desperate resistance; the regiment of Loudon being twice repulsed, count Wallis, who led them to the assault, exclaimed, " Comrades, we must scale the fortress, or I will here perish! such was my promise to our commander ; our regiment bears his name, and we must conquer or die!" The soldiers, animated by this address, again leaped into the ditch, and by a desperate effort mounted the rampart. The other attacks were attended with more speedy success ; the confusion of the garrison was increased by the Austrian prisoners, who burst open the doors of the casemates, and possessed themselves of the bridges, and by break of day Schweidnitz, with all its garrison and magazines, was in the hands of Loudon. This important acquisition did not cost more than 600 men, many of whom were killed by the accidental explosion of a powder magazine. The capture of Schweidnitz deranged all the projects of the king ; to cover Neiss, Brieg, and Breslau, he fell back to Strehlen ; Loudon was enabled to take up winter quarters in Silesia, and the Russians, under Chernichef, in the county of Glatz.

On the side of Pomerania the prince of Wirtemberg maintained himself with great resolution in his intrenched camp ; but unable to resist superior numbers, he left Colberg to its fate, which, after a most obstinate and gallant defence, fell into the hands of Romanzof, on the 16th of December.

In Saxony marshal Daun contented himself with keeping prince Henry in check, and favouring the operations in Silesia ; but on the capture of Schweidnitz he drew 24,000 men from the army of Loudon, and endeavoured to dislodge prince Henry, without the risk of a battle. That able commander, however, maintained his ground ; and Daun, hoping that in the disastrous state of the Prussian affairs, the king would be unable to make head another campaign, confined his views to the possession of Dresden and the neighbouring part of Saxony, and at the close of the year drew his troops into winter quarters, and returned to Vienna.

Thus, without a single battle, the affairs of the empress-queen were more prosperous than during any preceding period of the war. The Austrians retained their position in Saxony, and by the capture of Schweidnitz were enabled to take up winter quarters in a part of Silesia ; by the possession of Colberg, the Russians obtained a port on the Baltic, where they could form magazines without conveying them through Poland; and Prussian Pomerania and Brandenburgh were open to their future incursions.

The sanguine hopes of Maria Theresa were equalled by the despondency of her rival. Frederic repaired to Breslau to hasten the completion of an intrenched camp which had been begun during the campaign, secluded himself from society to give vent to his grief, and seemed, in this last extremity, as if resolved to terminate his career of glory under the walls of the capital of Silesia. The despondency of the monarch pervaded his army; and even the remnant of his veteran troops, whom he had so often led to victory, declared that if attacked, they would lay down their arms.

On the side of Westphalia alone, affairs wore a less favourable aspect. Prince Ferdinand, by skill and resources equal to those of the great Frederic, baffled all the efforts of the French, with a far inferior force, prevented their intended co-operation with the imperialists, and at the close of the campaign confined them to the same ground which they occupied at the commencement of the year.

The cause of the house of Austria, however, seemed prosperous in every court of Europe. France had matured her plans of policy; and Spain, having temporised till her galleons from America were safely arrived in port, threw off the mask, avowed the signature of the family compact, which united all the branches of the house of Bourbon, and prepared to co-operate with Austria and France.

The changes which took place in the British administration furthered the views of France and Spain. On the resignation of the earl of Holdernesse, lord Bute had received the seals as secretary for the northern department, and his influence soon became predominant in the cabinet. Anxious to prevent the adoption of measures which might render the war more extensive, he listened to the delusive professions of the house of Bourbon, and endeavoured to avoid or protract the declaration of the hostilities against Spain. In vain Mr. Pitt represented the progress of the projected union; in vain he urged the necessity of intercepting the Spanish galleons: his counsels were rejected, and this great but imperious minister, disdaining to support measures which he could not guide, indignantly retired from the helm. The duke of Newcastle, instead of retiring with Mr. Pitt, was induced by a hope of regaining his influence, to continue in office; but he was unable to acquire either the confidence or favour of the sovereign.

The British cabinet thus forced into a war with Spain, and irritated by the prevarication of France, did not intermit their efforts either by sea or land; the impulse given by Mr. Pitt to the wheels of government had not subsided; war was declared against Spain, and hostile preparations urged with increasing vigour. But the new part of the ministry, as well as the young monarch, were not disposed to continue the enormous expense of a continental war. The term of the subsidiary treaty with the king of Prussia having expired, they delayed entering into new engagements, and urged him to make overtures to the court of Vienna. A coldness had accordingly arisen between the two powers; and the English ministry, embarrassed with hostilities against Spain, were anxious either to hasten an accommodation, or to turn their whole efforts towards the prosecution of a naval war.

Chap. CXVII. — 1762.

Such was the favourable aspect of the Austrian affairs at the termination of the year: and all the sanguine hopes conceived by the warm imagination of Maria Theresa seemed on the point of being realised.

A more striking picture of the distress of the great antagonist of the house of Austria cannot be drawn, than in his own words: "Prince Ferdinand alone, of all the allies, had terminated the campaign without loss; and the Prussians were unfortunate in every quarter. Prince Henry had retired from the mountains of Saxony, but the district in which he was confined scarcely furnished the daily subsistence of his troops; the superiority of the enemy enabled them to occupy the most advantageous posts; and every thing was to be apprehended for the winter and the ensuing campaign. The situation of the king was still more deplorable: the capture of Schweidnitz occasioned the loss of the mountains and half of Silesia; he possessed only the fortresses of Glogau, Breslau, Brieg, Neiss, and Cosel; he was master indeed of the course of the Oder, and of the districts beyond; but that territory, ravaged by the Russians at the commencement of the campaign, could furnish no subsistence; nor could he derive any supply from Poland, as 15,000 Russians, forming a cordon on the frontiers, intercepted all communication. The army was compelled to defend its front against the Austrians, and its rear against the Russians. The communication between Berlin and Breslau was precarious, but, above all, the loss of Colberg rendered the situation of affairs desperate; there was no obstacle to prevent the Russians from besieging Stettin, at the commencement of the spring, or even from seizing Berlin and the whole electorate of Brandenburgh. In Silesia the king had only 30,000 men; prince Henry had scarcely more, and the troops who had served in Pomerania against the Russians were totally ruined. The greater part of the provinces were overrun by the enemy, or laid waste; and the king knew not whence to draw recruits, where to find horses, accoutrements and subsistence, or how to secure the passage of the military stores to the army."

In the midst of these auspicious appearances in favour of the house of Austria, an event happened, which rescued the Prussian monarchy from impending destruction. Elizabeth, empress of Russia, died on the 5th of January, and was succeeded on the throne by her nephew, Peter III. With the empress expired the national antipathy which had been fostered against the king of Prussia: the new sovereign in his early youth had visited the court of Berlin, and, struck with the admirable discipline of the Prussian army, conceived an enthusiastic admiration of Frederic, which was raised almost to admiration by the splendid successes, the unshaken fortitude, and the heroism of that extraordinary man.

During the reign of his predecessor, Peter had not concealed his partiality, and had even communicated the secrets of the cabinet and the plans of operations to his favourite hero. But he now avowed his attachment without reserve; he bitterly censured the ingratitude of Maria Theresa towards England, inveighed against her ambition, and stigmatised Elizabeth for having exhausted the blood and treasure of her empire to exalt a rival, and depress a friend. He had scarcely received the oath of allegiance from his subjects, before he ordered his troops to abstain from hostilities against the king of Prussia, and to quit the Austrian army; he imparted this intelligence with a childish transport to the British minister, and soon afterwards secretly despatched his favourite Godovitz to conclude an alliance with the hero of his idolatry. With a servility unbecoming the sovereign of a great empire, he even sought an honorary rank in the Prussian army, and seemed to pride himself more as a lieutenant-general of Frederic, than as autocrat of all the Russias. The change of politics at St. Petersburgh occasioned a similar revolution in the court of Stockholm; an armistice was concluded between Prussia and Sweden, and Maria Theresa was deprived of another ally. The exultation of the king of Prussia at this fortunate and long-expected event was equal to his former despondency; he broke from his sullen retirement, showed himself again to his troops, appeared in public with every mark of joy, and again resumed his favourite amusements and ordinary course of life.

Maria Theresa, on the contrary, suddenly fell from her towering hopes of recovering Silesia, and subverting the Prussian power. In consequence of the successes of the last campaign, she had haughtily rejected the overtures of England to mediate an accommodation; from a principle of mistaken economy, she had disbanded 20,000 men, and this unseasonable diminution of her forces, in conjunction with the defection of Russia, was still farther augmented by a leprous disorder, which spread contagion among her troops, and rendered a considerable part of her army unfit for service. The Austrians seem to have been confounded at this sudden reverse of fortune; and although marshal Daun took the command of the Silesian army in May, he could not prevent the king from drawing his troops from Pomerania and Mecklenburgh to the neighbourhood of Breslau, and making preparations for the recovery of Schweidnitz. They were still farther disheartened by the conclusion of an offensive alliance between Russia and Prussia, and by the march of the corps under Chernichef, who, having separated from the Austrians, and taken the route to Poland, returned and joined the Prussians. By this accession of strength, the king became equal, if not superior, to Daun, and was enabled to pursue offensive operations.

Meanwhile Daun had exerted his principal efforts to preserve Schweidnitz, and to render it capable of sustaining a long siege. During the whole winter, peasants and soldiers were employed in repairing and strengthening the works, and a chain of intrenched posts was formed in the mountains, which would enable the army to maintain a communication with the town. The garrison of 12,000 chosen troops was commanded by Guasco, a distinguished general in the Austrian service, who was assisted by Gribeauval, an able engineer, and the place was provided with every requisite for maintaining a siege.

In May, Daun, with 60,000 men, had descended into the plain, and encamped at the distance of six miles beyond the Schweidnitz, with his right wing extending to the foot of Zobtenberg, and his left towards the Schweidnitz Wasser; while the king, who waited for the junction of the Russians, retained his troops in cantonments on the banks of the Lohe. Before their arrival, however, he sent a considerable body towards the frontiers of Upper Silesia ; and Daun was compelled to weaken his army by a detachment to cover Moravia. On the 1st of July, Chernichef passed the Oder, and the king put his army in motion. Daun, threatened by the Prussian detachments which hovered on his flanks, and alarmed for the safety of his magazines in Bohemia, retired successively to Boegendorf and Ditmansdorf; but although a corps of Cossacs penetrated into Bohemia, and pushed their incursions even to the gates of Prague, he still maintained a communication with Schweidnitz, by means of his intrenched posts, and rendered the siege impracticable. At this critical juncture, another revolution took place in Russia, which seemed likely to restore the ascendency of the Austrian arms.

Peter III., having disgusted his subjects by his attachment to the Prussian monarch, and displeased the army, nobility, and clergy, by his well-meant, but ill-timed innovations, a secret conspiracy was formed against him, and headed by his consort, whom he had alienated by his brutal and capricious behaviour. He was frequently apprised of these machinations ; but refused to listen even to the suggestions of the king of Prussia, and remained insensible of his danger until the insurrection broke forth, which deprived him of his crown and life.

Catherine II., whom this singular revolution placed on the throne of Russia, was a daughter of Christian Augustus of Anhalt Zerbst, a petty prince of Germany, in the service of Prussia, and was born in 1739, at Stettin, where her father was governor. At the age of sixteen, she was called into Russia, and espoused the great duke Peter, who, from person, character, and manners, was calculated rather to disgust than to please a princess of great beauty, cultivated talents, and extreme sensibility. His neglect and ill-usage alienated her affections; the dread of perpetual imprisonment induced her to head the discontented party; and by one of those sudden revolutions which are natural to arbitrary governments, she succeeded in wresting the crown from her husband, and placing herself on the Russian throne. On her accession she issued a manifesto, declaring the king of Prussia the enemy of the Russian name, ordered Chernichef to return to Poland, and the troops in Pomerania to re-occupy Prussia, and resume hostilities.

Chernichef related the account of this revolution to the king, and privately communicated his orders to withdraw from the army. Frederic, though confounded by an event, which, to use his own words, "overturned the projects of man," made no opposition to his departure, but prevailed on him to defer his march three days. The time was precious: the Austrian commander was ignorant of the revolution, and Frederic availing himself of this interval, attacked the two intrenched posts of Burkensdorf and Oehmsdorf, and, after a slight contest, dislodged the Austrians, who amounted to 8000 men, although covered by lines equally strong from nature and art. In consequence of this reverse, Daun removed his camp to Wursten Waltersdorf, and Tannhausen; while the Russians, who by their presence had contributed to his defeat, began their march towards Poland. Schweidnitz was instantly invested, the trenches opened on the 7th of August, and the operations of the siege were covered by the king on the side of Peterswalde, and by a corps under the prince of Bevern, which had been drawn from Upper Silesia, on the side of Reichenbach. After the departure of the Russians, Daun, foiled in the attempt to cut off the corps under the prince of Bevern, withdrew to Scharfenek, and left Schweidnitz to its fate. The town held out till the 9th of October, when the explosion of the powder magazine, which opened a breach in the rampart, compelled the governor to surrender, and the garrison were made prisoners of war, after a resistance of sixty-four days. The king himself paid a due eulogium to the gallant defender of the place; when Guasco, at the head of his officers, was presented, Frederic said, " Sir, you have given a noble example to those who are intrusted with the defence of fortresses; your resistance has cost me 8000 men."

Thus terminated the campaign in Silesia, by which the Austrians irrecoverably lost that valuable province. The king, leaving a body of troops under the prince of Bevern, hastened into Saxony, to co-operate with prince Henry; and Daun, having consigned to Loudon a corps opposed to the prince of Bevern, directed his march towards the same point; but before their arrival the fortune of the war was already decided. At the opening of the campaign, Serbelloni, the Austrian commander, covered the frontiers of Bohemia and Saxony with a chain of posts, which extended from Plauen and Dippoldiswalda, along the heights from Freyberg to Waldheim. Prince Henry, however, though inferior in force, passed the Mulda, penetrated this chain, and separated the Austrian troops from the army of the empire; he maintained his advantages in different skirmishes, and harassed Bohemia by continual incursions.

Serbelloni being recalled, and the command intrusted to Haddick, the new general formed a junction with the army of the empire, and drove prince Henry beyond the Mulda; but the prince having received considerable succours from Silesia, again attacked the army of the empire, who were posted at Freyberg, forced their intrenchments, and defeated them with the loss of 3000 killed and wounded, 4000 prisoners, twenty-eight pieces of artillery, and several standards. Prince Albert, of Saxony, who was detached from the army of Daun, arrived too late; Haddick was unable to resume offensive operations, and the discomfited remains of the imperial troops retired to Altenberg, on the frontiers of Bohemia. Prince Henry, pursuing his success, sent a corps by Einsedel into Bohemia, which reduced Egra to ashes, destroyed the Austrian magazines at Saatz, and penetrated to the walls of Prague. Another corps spread over Saxony, burst into the heart of the empire. levied contributions on every side, alarmed the diet of Ratisbon, and forced Nuremberg, with many of the towns and states, to sign a neutrality. Unable to check this torrent, Daun concluded an armistice for the winter, which comprehended Saxony and Silesia, and the two armies retired into quarters.

The allies of the house of Austria were not more fortunate. At the commencement of the year the French forces in the landgraviate of Hesse and the southern part of Hanover, assembled in June, and occupied the strong post of Stolpen; they were here attacked by prince Ferdinand, and, after a desperate engagement, defeated with considerable loss. The remainder of the campaign was almost a continued series of disasters; the French were harassed and baffled on all sides by prince Ferdinand, and at the close of the year possessed no other place in Hesse, except Ziegenhayn, which the allies were preparing to invest, when the signature of the preliminaries terminated hostilities.

The co-operation of Spain produced no essential advantage to the house of Austria; and the invasion of Portugal was attended with the ill success which so unjust a measure deserved. Animated by the genius of the count de Oeyras, afterwards distinguished by the title of Pombal, inspirited by the vigorous succours of the English, and directed by the military skill of count de la Lippe, the Portuguese made an unexpected resistance, and compelled the combined forces of the French and Spaniards again to evacuate the country. In fact, Spain was drawn into hostilities, only to become the victim of her weakness and duplicity; the isle of Cuba and the Manillas were taken; her marine weakened by the capture of twelve ships of the line, and, besides the enormous expense of the equipments for the war, she lost near four millions sterling, in treasure and valuable merchandise, which fell into the hands of the English cruisers.

France, unsuccessful both by sea and land, exhausted of her blood and treasure, and, in addition to her former losses, deprived of the valuable colonies of Martinico, with its dependencies, St. Lucia, Tobago, and Grenada, saw her commerce annihilated, and her ships pent up in her harbours, and was disappointed in her hopes from the co-operation of Spain. She therefore made overtures to England, with a sincerity natural to her desperate situation, and found a ready compliance from the British cabinet. England had nothing more to hope from a prolongation of the war; the people were satiated with victories, which added neither to their internal security nor external aggrandisement; the duke of Newcastle, under whose direction the war had commenced, had retired from the helm, and his place at the head of the treasury was filled by lord Bute, whose pacific sentiments were in unison with those of the sovereign and nation. As the two parties equally desired a peace, the conditions were adjusted without much difficulty; and a treaty was signed at Fontainebleau on the 5th of November, 1762, between England, France, Spain, and Portugal. The German disputes, which in the reigns of the two former monarchs, might have prolonged the war, became only a secondary consideration, to the unbiassed wisdom of the sovereign who filled the throne. The king of Prussia hastened the separation of England by his ambitious projects, which returned with returning success, and by his unqualified invectives against the ill faith of the British cabinet. Finding that his sole voice opposed the conclusion of peace, and aware, from past experience, that when he was delivered from the Russians and Swedes, his forces were equal, if not superior, to those of Austria, England had withdrawn the subsidy; and having bound France, by the 13th article of the preliminaries, not to furnish succours to the empress-queen, abandoned the discussion of the affairs of Germany to the courts of Berlin and Vienna.

Many motives contributed to bend the lofty spirit of Maria Theresa, and incline her to peace. She had been deserted by the Swedes, on the accession of Peter III.; and the expectations which she had formed from the recent revolution in Russia were equally disappointed. The first steps taken by the new empress indicated a hostile disposition towards the king of Prussia; but these measures were occasioned by her apprehensions rather than by her inclinations. At the commencement of a new reign, with so defective a title to the crown, she was unwilling to engage in foreign hostilities; and she had found among the papers of the late emperor unequivocal proofs that Frederic had disapproved the capricious conduct of Peter, and repeatedly urged him to treat her with mildness and humanity. In this disposition the behaviour of Frederic towards the troops under Chernichef conciliated her favour; she ordered the kingdom of Prussia to be restored, discontinued all acts of hostility and, during the remainder of the campaign, preserved an exact neutrality.

In addition to these disappointments Maria Theresa saw her hereditary countries exposed to the irruptions of the Prussians, and Hungary threatened by the Turks, who had been excited by the intrigues of the king of Prussia to meditate hostilities. Motives no less cogent were suggested by the dreadful devastations of the Prussians in Saxony, the panic of the German states, the defection of all her allies, the difficulty of finding resources and raising money, disgusts among her ministers, the declining health of the emperor, and dissensions in her family.

Urged by these motives Maria Theresa herself made overtures to Frederic, which being favourably received, conferences were opened at Hubertsburgh, a palace of the elector of Saxony, and after a short discussion relative to the restitution of the county of Glatz, and the succession to the margraviates of Bareuth and Anspach, the peace was signed on the 5th of February, 1763. The treaties of Breslau and Berlin formed the basis of that of Hubertsburgh. Maria Theresa renewed her renunciation of Silesia and Glatz, and both parties guaranteed each other's possessions. All places and prisoners taken during the war were to be restored; and Frederic by a secret article, promised to give his suffrage for electing the archduke Joseph king of the Romans. In this arrangement the empire was also comprised, and the peace of Westphalia, with the other constitutions of the Germanic body, renewed. A treaty was signed the same day between Augustus III. and the king of Prussia, for the evacuation of Saxony, and the restitution of the archives, and part of the Saxon artillery.

The pacification of Hubertsburgh, which terminated the seven-years' war, placed the affairs of Germany in the same situation as before the commencement of hostilities; and both parties, after an immense waste of blood and treasure, derived from it no other benefit than that of experiencing each other's strength, and a dread of renewing the calamities of so destructive a contest. Maria Theresa, however, had the mortification of seeing her friends suffer for their attachment to her cause. Saxony was exhausted almost beyond recovery; her allies in the empire were drained by excessive contributions; and France lost Louisiana, the province of Canada, Cape Breton, with all the islands in the gulph and river of St. Lawrence, Grenada, the Grenadines, St. Vincent's, Dominica, and Tobago. Spain yielded Florida, and all her other possessions on the continent of America, to the east or south-east of the Mississippi, and the British empire was thus consolidated in that quarter of the globe.

Chap. CXVIII. — 1762–1769.

The elevation of the archduke Joseph to the dignity of king of the Romans, was the immediate consequence of the peace. On the 27th of May, 1764, the election took place without opposition, at Franckfort, and this successful event secured to the family of Maria Theresa the imperial crown, and prevented the evils of an interregnum, in which the sudden death of the emperor Francis might otherwise have involved the empire.

Francis was at Inspruck in the Tyrol, where he had assisted at the marriage between his second son, the archduke Leopold, and Maria Louisa, infanta of Spain. He had been for some time indisposed, and threatened with an apoplexy, and he imagined that his disorder was increased by the heavy atmosphere in the valleys of Tyrol: like the emperor Albert I., he repeatedly expressed an earnest desire to return to Vienna; and on viewing the mountains with which Inspruck is surrounded, exclaimed, " Oh! if I could once quit these mountains of the Tyrol!"

In the morning of the 18th of August, being pressed by his sister Charlotte Marianne, abbess of Remiremont, to be blooded, he answered, " I am engaged this evening to sup with Joseph, and will not disappoint him; but I promise you I will be blooded to-morrow." At the opera in the afternoon, he felt himself disordered; went out, accompanied by his son, and in retiring through his valet de chambre's room to his own apartment, was struck with a fit of apoplexy. As he tottered for a few moments, Joseph caught him in his arms, but could not support him, and Francis falling on the floor, expired without a groan, in the fifty-eighth year of his age.

In his private deportment Francis was lively, polite, and affable; but he seemed rather formed for the situation in which he was born, than for that high rank to which he was elevated by his marriage with Maria Theresa. His honours sat awkwardly upon him, and he was uneasy under his dignities. Though appointed co-regent of the Austrian dominions, and seated upon the first throne of Europe, he possessed only the shadow of authority, and his opinion was without weight in things of consequence. Naturally indolent and unambitious, he never attempted to make the smallest struggle; but submitted without a murmur to be a cipher, contented only to be consulted by foreign ambassadors for the sake of form. He even affected to display his own insignificance, and to consider himself as subordinate to his consort. Being once at the levee, when the empress-queen was giving audience to her subjects, he retired from the circle, and seated himself in a distant corner of the apartment, near two ladies of the court. On their attempting to rise, he said, "Do not regard me, for I shall stay here till the *court* is gone, and then amuse myself with contemplating the crowd;" the ladies replying, "As long as your imperial majesty is present, the court will be here;" "You mistake," he added with a smile, "the empress and my children are the court; I am here only a simple individual."

Had Francis possessed more influence, the system of Europe would probably not have been overturned; for France was as odious to him as Prussia was to the empress-queen, and he seemed to have appreciated the necessity of preserving the strictest friendship with Great Britain. He did not, without great reluctance, consent to the alliance with the house of Bourbon; and among his papers was found a remark which confirms this observation: "The less connection with France the better; the god of the French is convenience; they have been often tried, and have been always found unfaithful."

The royal historian has recorded, that Francis, not daring to interfere in affairs of government, employed the sums which he drew from Tuscany in commerce. He established manufactories, or lent money on pledges, and undertook to furnish the imperial troops with uniforms, arms, and horses. Associated with count Botta, and a merchant named Schimmelman, he farmed the revenues of

Saxony; and in 1756, even supplied with forage the Prussian army, which was then engaged in hostilities with the
empress his consort; during the seven-years' war, he furnished the empress with large sums, but always took care
that they should be vested on good security; he was, in a
word, the court banker.   Francis left two chests of money;
one belonging to himself and the other which he adminis-
tered for the empress.   His own was supposed to contain
about 1,000,000 florins in money, and 19,000,000 in paper,
which his son Joseph inherited; but his love of amassing
treasure did not render him hard-hearted; on the contrary,
he was "open as day to melting charity," and distributed
100,000l. in annual donations to distressed persons.

He was extremely fond of natural philosophy, and endeavoured to make his skill subservient to his love of money.
With this view he attempted, by means of burning glasses,
to form several small diamonds into one large stone ; and
continually employed chemists in searching for the philosopher's stone.   He patronised men of letters, and made col-
lections of medals, natural history, and natural philosophy;
and to his care the capital owes a cabinet as rich in those
articles as any European cabinet can display.   Though his
abilities and acquirements were inferior, and his deportment
less dignified, in one respect he was far greater than Maria
Theresa ; he was more inclined to toleration, and always
recommended, in matters of religion, persuasion and argument rather than violence and persecution.

Among numerous instances of benevolence, which reflect
honour on his memory, two have been thought most worthy
of being handed down to posterity.   A fire having burst
forth in a magazine of saltpetre at Vienna, Francis hastened
to the spot, and as he advanced to give his orders, one of
his suite represented to him that he too much exposed his
person : "Do not," the emperor replied, "be alarmed for
me, but for those poor creatures whom it will be difficult to
save."   During the depth of winter a violent inundation
overflowed the suburbs, and the waters rising to an extraordinary height, many could only save themselves by taking
refuge on the tops of the houses.   For three days they remained in that dreadful situation without nourishment ; the
rapidity of the stream, and the floating masses of ice, rendering the passage so dangerous, that the most intrepid boat-

men could not be persuaded by any recompence to expose themselves. In this imminent peril Francis threw himself into a boat, and exclaiming, " I trust my example will not be lost," rowed over to the opposite shore ; his example had its due effect ; the boatmen no longer hesitated to encounter the same danger as the emperor, and the people were saved. If the study of history is useful, it is particularly so when it records examples of courage springing from humanity, and where the foremost in rank is the first to distinguish himself in braving danger or in acts of benevolence.

Maria Theresa bore the afflicting stroke of her husband's sudden decease with the utmost resignation. Though doatingly fond of him, and herself a pattern of conjugal attachment, she had supported his numerous infidelities without the smallest murmur, and even without appearing to be apprised of them.* In a letter to her daughter, she calls him by the endearing names of consort, friend, her heart's joy, for two-and-forty years ; she added, " brought up together, our sentiments have ever been the same, and all my misfortunes have been softened by his support." She derived a melancholy pleasure from the recollection of his amiable qualities, and even soothed her grief by preparing with her own hands the shroud which was to cover his body, but charged the confidential women of her court, who saw her employed in that dismal office, not to divulge it ; and the secret was not known till her death. To the time of her decease she constantly wore mourning ; her apartments were hung with black ; she frequently descended into the vault which contained his remains, and continued several hours praying by his sepulchre, and preparing for her own dis-- solution.

In consequence of his pre-election, Joseph succeeded to the title of emperor ; and Leopold, her second son, became great duke of Tuscany, in virtue of the act of succession promulgated by Francis in 1763.

The empress-queen was no sooner recovered from the first agonies of her grief, than she turned her attention with redoubled energy to the concerns of government and the establishment of beneficial regulations for promoting the

---

* Mr. Wraxall has recorded a striking proof of her magnanimity in her conduct to the princess of Auersberg, the mistress of Francis. — Memoirs, vol. ii. p. 353.

welfare of her subjects. She founded or enlarged, in different parts of her extensive dominions, several academies for the improvement of the arts and sciences; instituted numerous seminaries for the education of all ranks, and reformed the public schools. She particularly turned her attention to the promotion of agriculture, which, in a medal struck by her order, was intituled the " art which nourishes all other arts *," and founded a society of agriculture at Milan, with bounties for the peasants who obtained the best crops. She confined the rights of the chase, often so pernicious to the husbandman, within narrow limits ; and issued a decree enjoining all the nobles who kept wild game to maintain their fences in good repair, permitting the peasants to destroy the wild boars which ravaged the fields. She also abolished the scandalous power usurped by the landholders of limiting the season for mowing the grass within the forests and their precincts, and mitigated the feudal servitude of the peasants in Bohemia.

Among her beneficial regulations must not be omitted the introduction of inoculation, and the establishment of a smallpox hospital. On the recovery of her children from a disorder so fatal to her own family, Maria Theresa gave an entertainment, which displays the benevolence of her character. Sixty-five children, who had been previously inoculated at the hospital, were regaled with a dinner in the gallery of the palace at Schoenbrun, in the midst of a numerous court ; and Maria Theresa herself, assisted by her offspring, waited on this delightful group, and gave to each of them a piece of money. The parents of the children were treated in another apartment ; the whole party was admitted to the performance of a German play ; and this charming entertainment was concluded with a dance, which was protracted till midnight.

Perhaps the greatest effort made by the empress-queen, and which reflects the highest honour on her memory, was the reformation of various abuses in the church, and the regulations which she introduced into the monasteries. She corrected the evils attendant on mortmain, or pious legacies bequeathed to the church, as an expiation for sin, by forbidding all ecclesiastics from being present at the making of a will ; she diminished the number of monks and nuns,

* Arti artium nutrici.

F F 4

by ordering that no persons should be admitted to take the vows who had not attained the age of twenty-five; and she abolished a burdensome impost of ten per cent., which every new abbot had extorted from his vassals, under the pretence of furnishing an equivalent tax on collateral succession, to which abbey lands had been declared subject. She took away the pernicious right which the convents and churches enjoyed, of affording an asylum to all criminals without distinction; she suppressed the inquisition, which, though curbed by the civil power, still subsisted at Milan, and abolished throughout all her dominions the no less odious than inhuman custom of forcing confession by torture. She suppressed the society of Jesuits, although her own confessor was a member of that order; but did not imitate the unjust and cruel measures adopted in Spain and Portugal, and softened the rigour of their lot by every alleviation which circumstances would permit.

Chap. CXIX.—1769-1777.

It is a melancholy task to turn from these salutary and benevolent acts to a series of ambiguous negotiations and unjust encroachments, which again changed the whole system of Austrian policy, occasioned a temporary union with the king of Prussia, and ended in the partition of Poland, a transaction which disgraced the reign of Maria Theresa.

Notwithstanding her memorable declaration in 1756, that no consideration on earth should induce her to enter into an alliance of which the king of Prussia was a party, the empress-queen forgot that apprehension of his ambition which had hitherto been her ruling principle, and not only relinquished all hopes of recovering Silesia, but contributed to consolidate and extend the power and influence of her natural enemy. This change in the conduct of the court of Vienna was principally owing to the predominance which Russia began to assume in the scale of Europe, and particularly to the despotic ascendency which Catherine had acquired in Poland.

Poland, which formed a barrier between Austria, Prussia, Turkey, and Russia, had sunk from the first to the most inconsiderable power of the north, in consequence of intestine commotions and the diminution of the regal authority. The neighbouring sovereigns fomented these internal discords, in order to preserve their influence in the government, and prevent the nation from recovering its former ascendency; and the constitution was calculated to promote their views. It was a republican form, presided by an elective monarch, who was chosen by the nobles or gentry, and extremely limited in his authority. The great body of the people were in a state of feudal vassalage, and the nobles * were the sole proprietors of land in fee, or descendants of those proprietors, consequently numerous, and in general needy. Among these, the most powerful and opulent, like the feudal barons, maintained large bodies of retainers, and were supported by those of their own order, who hoped either for protection or advantage. Hence factions were formed, and the higher nobles, perpetually at variance either among themselves or with the crown, were assisted and encouraged by foreign states.†

From the death of John Sobieski the house of Austria had maintained a considerable influence in Poland, and, in con-

---

* A noble, as designated by the laws of Poland, was a person not engaged in trade or commerce, either possessing land, or the descendant of a family which formerly possessed land. Every noble was capable of being a candidate for the throne.

† The supreme legislative authority resided in the three estates of the realm, the king, senate, and equestrian order assembled in a national diet. The senate consisted of the bishops, palatines, or governors of provinces, castellans or lieutenants of the palatines, and the sixteen ministers of state; all these were appointed by the king, but when nominated could not be deprived of their charges, except by the consent of the diet.

The equestrian order, or lower house, was composed of nuntios chosen by the nobles or gentry in the respective dietines, and no qualification was required either in the electors or elected. This assembly exhibited a disgraceful scene of faction, tumult, and bloodshed, and was incapable of concluding any business of state; because the most important questions could not be decided without unanimity of suffrages, as each nuntio, by his liberum veto, or negative, had the power of suspending, or even of dissolving the diet. To obviate the evils arising from this dreadful privilege, the Poles had recourse to diets of confederacy, which, though composed of the same members, and conducted with the same forms, were capable of deciding by plurality of voices. Still, however, the evil was only remedied in part, as the diets of confederacy could not decide on many affairs of state, nor make regulations which might lead to a radical change in the constitution.

currence with Russia, had raised Augustus, elector of
Saxony, to the throne. The late emperor had sacrificed
some of his fairest provinces to support the son of Augustus,
and Maria Theresa was equally desirous to promote the interest of the house of Saxony, which had displayed so warm
an attachment, and undergone such sufferings in her cause.
On the death, therefore, of the king of Poland, which happened on the 5th of October, 1763, she prepared to exert all
her influence in favour of his son Christian Frederic ; but
that prince dying soon after his father, leaving a minor son,
who was ineligible to the vacant dignity, she encouraged his
brother, prince Xavier, to become a candidate.

On this vacancy Poland became a scene of faction and
disorder ; several natives offered themselves as candidates,
among whom the most conspicuous were prince Czartorisky,
his nephew count Stanislaus Poniatowski, high standard-
bearer of Lithuania, count Branisky, and prince Lubomirsky.
Of these count Branisky was supported by prince Radzivil,
and by those independent magnates who deprecated the interference of foreign powers ; but all the other competitors
yielded to count Poniatowski, who was assisted by the influence of Russia.

This amiable and accomplished nobleman was son of count
Poniatowski, castellan of Cracow, by the princess Czartoriska,
and had captivated the affections of Catherine when grand
duchess. The vanity of the empress was flattered by the
prospect of conferring a crown upon her favourite ; and her
ambition was no less gratified in securing the election of a
king who seemed likely to become wholly dependent on his
benefactress. She lavished her treasure to bribe the venal
nobles, assembled an army on the frontiers, and, in order to
exclude all foreign candidates, restricted the Poles to the
choice of a piast or native.

The empress-queen saw with concern the attempts of
Russia to exclude the house of Saxony, and gain the preponderance in Poland ; she published a spirited manifesto, declaring her resolution to maintain all the rights, prerogatives,
and possessions of the Poles, particularly their privilege of
appointing a sovereign by a free and voluntary election, and
being seconded by a declaration equally strong on the part
of France, prepared to assert the pretensions of the house of
Saxony by arms.

To counteract the opposition of Maria Theresa, Catherine gained the king of Prussia: the two sovereigns entered into a treaty to secure the election of Stanislaus; and being joined by the Porte, the three powers issued similar declarations, exhorting, or rather commanding the Poles to elect none but a piast for their king. Soon afterwards a corps of Russian troops entered Poland, defeated prince Radzivil and his party, and, in conjunction with a Prussian force on the frontiers, awed the diet of election, and secured the nomination of count Poniatowski, who was chosen on the 7th of September, and crowned by the title of Stanislaus Augustus. Maria Theresa, ill seconded by France, and opposed by Turkey, Prussia, and Russia, was too prudent to follow the example of her father, at a time when her subjects were yet bleeding with the wounds of the septennial war. She did not, therefore, openly oppose the election of Stanislaus: but, recalling her minister from Warsaw, strove, in concert with France, to diminish the preponderance of Russia, by fomenting the intestine troubles and assisting the malecontents with money. She thus prepared to avail herself of the first opportunity to interfere with effect in the affairs of Poland, and this opportunity soon presented itself.

Stanislaus, though solely indebted to Catherine for his elevation, beheld with regret the total dependence of his country on the court of Petersburgh. He was anxious to emancipate himself from the Russian yoke, to abolish the liberum veto, and reform other glaring defects in the constitution, which furnished a perpetual pretext for foreign interference. But his character and abilities were not equal to this great design; without military talents he could not direct or awe his turbulent subjects; and he was too deeply immersed in gallantry and pleasures, to undertake an enterprise which required the greatest exertions of body and mind. Some salutary regulations introduced into the finances, the army, the courts of justice, and the further reforms which he meditated, gave umbrage to Russia, and roused those turbulent spirits who were desirous to retain their country in a state of anarchy. Catherine and Frederic fomented these discontents, and revived the religious disputes, by declaring themselves protectors of the dissidents, under which denomination were comprised all Christian sects who dissented from the Roman Catholic religion. The dissidents had been originally indulged with the free exercise of their worship, admitted to seats in the diet, and had participated in all the privileges of the Catholics ; and these rights were confirmed by the celebrated treaty of Oliva. In process of time the Catholics, acquiring the ascendency, gradually deprived the dissidents of their privileges, and, in 1733, excluded them from the diet. Soon after the election of Stanislaus, the dissidents appealed to England, Russia, Prussia, and Denmark, as mediating powers in the treaty of Oliva, and obtained their recommendation to the diet ; but these applications were unfavourably received, the exclusion was confirmed, and with great difficulty they even obtained the free exercise of their worship. The king himself, though inclined to toleration, concurred with the Catholics, and thus excited still farther the resentment of the empress of Russia. Catherine remonstrated against the proceedings of the diet, encouraged the dissidents to form confederacies, and even strengthened them with a body of troops. Religious disputes were soon blended with political cabals ; the dissidents were joined by bodies of discontented Catholics, and a confederacy of Catholics was formed under the appellation of malecontents, and headed by prince Radzivil.

A national diet, assembled to consider the claims of the dissidents, was awed into compliance by a Russian force ; the most violent of the Catholics were arrested and imprisoned, and the diet dissolved, after appointing a committee to adjust the contested points. This committee was induced by bribes and threats to arrange a body of articles, which not only restored the privileges of the dissidents, but perpetuated the elective monarchy, the liberum veto, and the other abuses in the constitution ; and these articles were sanctioned by an extraordinary diet held at the commencement of 1768.

Such arbitrary proceedings roused the majority of the nation ; bodies of Catholics assembled on the frontiers of Turkey and Hungary, seized the fortress of Bar in Podolia, and formed an union which was called the Confederacy of Bar. The royal troops were either defeated, or joined the insurgents ; additional forces from Russia poured into Poland, and the country became a scene of bloodshed and devastation ; while the king, without a shadow of authority, was a mere puppet in the hands of the Russian party.

In one of these conflicts a party of Russians pursued the Poles into the Turkish territory, and burnt the small town of Balta. This accidental incursion was construed as a violation of territory; the Porte was instigated by France to publish in October, 1768, a declaration of war against Russia, and by this diversion enabled the confederates to protract hostilities.

The rapid success of the Russians against the Turks, and particularly the conquest of Moldavia, alarmed the court of Vienna, and disposed the empress-queen to listen to the overtures of the king of Prussia, who was himself jealous of his new ally. That wily monarch had long coveted Polish or Western Prussia, which formed a communication between the disjointed parts of his dominions, but could not expect to realise his views without the concurrence of Austria and Russia. He therefore projected the partition of Poland; and the distracted state of that country, and the relative situation of the neighbouring powers, seemed to offer a favourable moment for the fulfilment of his plan. Aware that Russia was interested to oppose a dismemberment, he endeavoured first to secure the concurrence of Austria, and, by their joint influence, to extort the acquiescence of Catherine while she was involved in a Turkish war.

As early as 1765 he had proposed an interview, which had been eagerly accepted by Joseph, at that time an enthusiastic admirer of his great rival; but he was disappointed by the jealousy of the empress and her minister. The Austrian cabinet, however, being now alarmed by the success of the Russians, the emperor himself, with the consent of Maria Theresa, offered to visit Frederic in Silesia. The interview took place at Neiss, on the 25th of August, 1769, and seemed likely to remove that enmity which had long divided the two houses. Frederic addressed the emperor by declaring he considered that day the happiest of his life, as it became the epoch of an union between two families too long hostile, but whose real interests consisted rather in seconding than destroying each other. Joseph replied, " Silesia no longer exists for the house of Austria." He then proposed to maintain a neutrality in Germany, in case of a war between England and France; and the king acceded to this proposal, a convention was signed by the two monarchs themselves, and by an additional article they engaged to observe a neutrality, in their respective dominions, should any unforeseen troubles arise; they likewise agreed to maintain a private correspondence, and settle their respective disputes without the intervention of ministers.

In the ensuing year the Turkish fleet being destroyed at Tchesme, Bender taken by count Panin, and Wallachia added to the Russian conquests, the court of Vienna was still more alarmed with the progress of these new and dangerous neighbours; magazines were formed in Hungary, reinforcements of troops despatched towards the frontiers, and the empress-queen did not affect to conceal her resolution of taking part in the war.

In these circumstances a second interview took place; the emperor, accompanied by prince Kaunitz, repaired to a camp formed at Neustadt in Moravia, where he received the visit of the Prussian monarch. Frederic and his generals were habited in the uniform worn by the Austrian recruits, and, on meeting the emperor, the king addressed him with the delicate compliment, " I have brought your imperial majesty many recruits." The two sovereigns treated each other with the utmost cordiality; and the business for which the meeting had been arranged was transacted between Frederic and the Austrian minister. Kaunitz pressed the king to join the house of Austria, in opposing, by force of arms, the ambitious projects of Russia; and urged that such an union was the only barrier to resist that torrent from the north which threatened to overwhelm all Europe. Frederic artfully evaded this overture, but tendered his intervention to conciliate the courts of Vienna and Petersburgh, and offered to procure from the Porte the acceptance of the Austrian mediation: at the same time he reiterated his former assurances of amity, and, at the request of the emperor, promised to communicate any overtures which might be made to him by France.

These professions were confirmed by the arrival of a messenger from Constantinople, with letters requesting the mediation of Austria and Prussia, and declaring the resolution of the Porte to accept no proposals which were not made by their intervention. This mediation was gladly accepted by the emperor and his minister, and the rival houses of Austria and Brandenburgh seemed cordially united in their views and interests.

At this interview Frederic held forth the partition of Poland as a bait to the Austrian court, and represented the policy of persuading or compelling Russia to concur in the dismemberment, instead of retaining Moldavia and Wallachia. The map of Poland was laid before the two sovereigns, the limits of the respective portions were adjusted, and the plan of operations arranged.*   The consequences of these interviews were soon manifest; the Austrian and Prussian troops had already entered Poland, under the pretence of preventing the progress of the plague; and Maria Theresa brought forward vague claims on some Polish districts, of which she affected to postpone the discussion till the return of peace, and declared that she would protect the territories in question from all insults, either on the part of the Russians or the confederates.

Notwithstanding this union with the king of Prussia, and the arrangements for the partition, a singular change suddenly took place in the conduct of the court of Vienna. Maria Theresa, in a letter to Stanislaus, written with her own hand, gave the strongest assurances that her friendship for him and the republic was firm and unalterable; that she had never entertained a thought of seizing any part of his dominions, and would suffer no dismemberment. At the same time she concluded a treaty with the Porte, by which she agreed to declare war against the Russians, if they did not relinquish all their conquests, and desist from their enterprises in Poland. In return she was to receive an annual subsidy of 10,000 purses, or 720,000 pounds, by four instalments, the first of which was to be paid as soon as the Austrian troops were put in motion; and she flattered herself with the hopes of regaining, from the gratitude of the Turks, those provinces which had been ceded at the peace of Belgrade. The troops were accordingly put in motion; the first instalment was paid; promises of assistance were

---

* I have little hesitation in asserting that the plan of this partition originated with the king of Prussia; but so infamous was this transaction, that each of the three powers endeavoured to fix the blame on the others. We need however only read the king of Prussia's own account, in " La Politique depuis 1763 à 1775," Œuvres Posthumes, tom. 5., to be convinced that he was the prime mover of this partition, and that he obtained his end by fomenting and availing himself of the jealousy between the courts of Vienna and Petersburgh.

lavished on the confederates; immense preparations made in Hungary; and the imperial minister at Berlin pressed the king to remain neuter, should the Austrians attack the Russians in any other country except Poland.

Frederic had now matured the plan at which he had laboured with unceasing assiduity. He therefore rejected the proposal of a neutrality, endeavoured to prevent the jealousy of the two powers from breaking out into open hostilities, and despatched his brother prince Henry to St. Petersburgh, to negotiate a peace with the Turks, and to effect an accommodation between Austria and Prussia, which was to be cemented by the partition. Catherine, intoxicated with her success, demanded as the price of a peace with the Turks, the cession of the two Cabardias, Azof and its territory, the independence of the Crimea, the free navigation of the Black Sea, an island in the Archipelago, and the sequestration of Moldavia and Wallachia, for twenty-five years. In imparting these extravagant proposals to the court of Vienna, Frederic artfully softened their resentment, and endeavoured to protract the negotiation; but finding prince Kaunitz dazzled with the expected advantages of the Turkish alliance, he exerted all his endeavours to secure the concurrence of Russia. He succeeded in alarming Catherine with the dread of an Austrian war, and at length persuaded her to accept a portion of Poland, as an indemnification for restoring Moldavia and Wallachia.

In the midst of these negotiations, a corps of Austrian troops entered Poland, and occupied the lordship of Zips, as an ancient dependency of the kingdom of Hungary. This usurpation furnished an additional argument to the king of Prussia, and facilitated his views. Catherine declared to prince Henry, that if the court of Vienna presumed to dismember Poland, the neighbouring powers must follow the example. Frederic took advantage of this hint, excited her apprehensions, and at length extorted her consent to the partition; the respective portions were specified in a convention signed at St. Petersburgh, in February, 1772, between the empress and the king of Prussia.

Having thus succeeded at the court of Russia, Frederic again applied to the cabinet of Vienna; he expressed the approbation of Catherine at the seizure of Zips, urged them to occupy the districts which they wished to appropriate, and insinuated that himself and Russia would follow the example. Unwilling, however, to relinquish the advantages which they expected to derive from their connection with the Porte, they hesitated in adopting the proposal, and Kaunitz in particular dreaded lest the dismemberment of Poland should occasion a breach of the alliance with France. But by the same artifices which Frederic had employed in Russia, he alternately alarmed and lured the court of Vienna, and even made warlike preparations as if he designed to enforce the partition. His schemes were attended with success. Maria Theresa listened to the overtures of the Prussian monarch, and preferred a share in the plunder of Poland to an uncertain and burdensome war.   She felt or affected to feel, indeed, great scruples of conscience, in participating the disgrace of this infamous transaction; but she was not the less exorbitant in her demands, and extended her claims almost to the half of Poland.   After a long discussion, the dread lest the secret should be divulged, and the instances of Prussia, induced her to lower her pretensions, and the final treaty of partition was signed at St. Petersburgh on the 5th of August.

During the negotiations for the partition treaty, Poland had been torn by intestine feuds, and sunk into a dreadful state of anarchy ; the confederates had made a considerable progress, and with the animosity natural to such contests, both parties had committed the most daring acts of licentiousness and cruelty. The unfortunate monarch was solely maintained on his throne by a Russian army, and resided at Warsaw as a kind of state prisoner, in the midst of a Russian garrison; in this situation he was seized in his capital by a daring band of confederates, and was only rescued from assassination by an escape almost miraculous. *

At length the time approached for the execution of the treaty, which had been arranged with such consummate art and profound secrecy. The three powers throw of the mask, by publishing a manifesto asserting their respective claims, and with an insulting mockery, urged those very disorders and miseries in which they had contrived to plunge the unfortunate Poles, as motives for their glaring violation of the rights of nations.   On the publication of this manifesto, they made a specification of their intended acquisitions, and

* For an account of his escape, see Wraxall's Memoirs, vol. ii. p. 56.

the respective districts were instantly occupied by their troops.

Both parties were equally confounded by these proceedings. The king and the royalists found themselves betrayed by the empress of Russia, whom they had considered as their protectress; and the confederates had even flattered themselves that the Austrian troops were advancing to their assistance. The nation now felt the fatal effects of faction and discord; but the two parties were unable to form a coalition; the king was a state pageant in the hands of the Russians; and the confederates, threatened on all sides, were soon routed and dispersed.

The king and nation published refutations of the pretended claims; issued counter declarations and memorials; and appealed to all the other states who had guaranteed the integrity of Poland. But neither this appeal, nor the sentiments of justice and humanity made the smallest impression on the three courts, and they hastened to complete the partition, lest the rising spirit of the nation should be supported by the other states of Europe. The empress-queen, who had hitherto acted a secondary part, now came forward, and her minister at the court of Warsaw peremptorily required the king to assemble a diet, in order to hasten a definitive arrangement between the republic and the three powers, " who would not expose their pretensions to the hazard of future contingencies, and of those troubles with which Poland had been always agitated." The same declaration was delivered by the ministers of Russia and Prussia, and Stanislaus issued circular letters for the convocation of the general diet.

The diet assembled on the 19th of April, 1773; but such was the disposition of the nation, that in the lower house the majority of the nuntios long opposed the dismemberment; and they were encouraged by the king, who exhibited the firmest resolution to preserve the integrity and independence of his country. The ambassadors of the three courts now had recourse to terror : the king was menaced with deposition, his family with imprisonment and ruin, and the capital itself was threatened with pillage; bribes and promises were lavished among the members of the diet, and every engine employed to obtain the fulfilment of their views. At length the Poles, without hope from abroad, and without strength at home, indignantly yielded to their fate. Still, however, the king continued firm, and threatened to abdicate rather than dishonour himself by sanctioning the dismemberment of his kingdom; he demanded an asylum in England, and stretching forth his right hand to the British plenipotentiary, exclaimed, " I will suffer this hand to be cut off rather than sign the act of Partition." But Stanislaus, though buoyed up by the enthusiasm of the moment, did not possess sufficient energy to endure the extremity of his fortune : his feeling mind was alarmed for the fate of his family; and he had not spirit to disdain a crown held only by the sufferance of his oppressors. He yielded to the menaces of the Russian ambassador, and gave his assent to that fatal instrument, which finally blotted the name of his devoted country from the nations of Europe.

The partitioning powers were too prudent to trust their unjust acquisitions to the forbearance of an indignant nation; they extorted an act for the immediate dissolution of the diet, and the appointment of a committee of delegates to adjust their respective claims, and to accede to a new constitution which they had prepared for that unhappy country. The delegates entered on their humiliating office ; and, before the month of September, concluded the treaty of partition in conformity to the dictates of the three courts.

The Russian district formed the north-eastern part of Poland, and consisted of Polish Livonia, parts of the palatinates of Witepsk, Polotsk, and Minsk, and the whole palatinate of Micislaw, containing a population of 1,500,000 souls; and Frederic obtained the district called Royal or Western Prussia, with a population of 860,000 souls.

The declaration published by Maria Theresa founded her right to a large portion of Poland on obsolete claims of the crowns of Hungary and Bohemia ; but she advanced as a favour, that although she could prove her incontestible right to Severia, Podolia, Volhynia, Pokutia, Red Russia, and Little Russia, and other considerable districts, yet she would content herself with a moderate equivalent. This equivalent was, a large territory in the south of Poland, comprising Red Russia, Gallicia, and parts of the palatinates of Cracow, Sandomir, Lublin, Bezk, Volhynia, and Podolia, containing a fertile and extensive country, with a population of 2,500,000 souls, and the valuable salt works of Vielitzka,

which brought to the republic an annual revenue of 90,000*l.*
This district was consolidated and annexed to the Austrian
territories, under the ancient appellation of the kingdoms of
Gallicia and Lodomeria.

The partitioning powers did, however, less injury to the
republic by dismembering its fairest provinces, than by establishing a form of government, which gave still further
scope to the exorbitant liberty of the nobles. They excluded
all prospect of reform, by perpetuating the elective monarchy,
the liberum veto, and the other inherent defects of the constitution ; and still further circumscribed the authority of the
crown, by taking from the king the appointment of bishops,
castellans, palatines, and ministers of state, and the patronage
of the starosties, or royal fiefs, and by vesting the executive
power in a permanent council chosen by the diet and presided by the king.

The avidity of Austria and Prussia was not gratified by
these acquisitions, and the treaty of partition was scarcely
signed before the courts of Vienna and Berlin began to make
new encroachments. The two courts connived at each other's
encroachments, and, from the situation of affairs, seemed
likely to succeed in extending their acquisitions.

The good fortune which had hitherto attended the arms of
Catherine had deserted her in the campaign of 1773, and her
generals were defeated in their attempts to carry the war
beyond the Danube. At the same time the rebellion of
Pugatchef, who assumed the character of Peter III., shook
her throne ; and the Turks, encouraged by this diversion,
obstinately refused to listen to overtures for peace. But in
the ensuing year the Russian arms again became successful ;
Romanzof passed the Danube, and hemmed in the Turkish
army in the mountains of Bulgaria, and the Grand Vizier
was compelled, by a mutiny of his troops, to accede to the
terms dictated by the Russian general. By this treaty,
signed at Kagniardji, the Russian head-quarters, Catherine
secured the independence of the Crimea, the free navigation
of the Turkish seas, and obtained the forts of Kertsch,
Yenikale, Kinburn, and the surrounding district, Azof, and
the cession of the Great and Little Cabardias. She restored
all her other conquests to the Turks ; but in the restitution
of Moldavia and Wallachia, exacted such stipulations relative
to their privileges and religion, as afforded her a pretext to

interfere in the affairs of those provinces. In consequence of this glorious peace, she was enabled to crush the rebellion of Pugatchef, and to turn her attention to the affairs of Poland.

The court of Vienna was extremely mortified at this sudden pacification. Even during the whole negotiation for the partition of Poland, the empress-queen had not intermitted her intrigues with the Porte. She had beheld with jealousy the recent success of the Russians, and saw with great regret and apprehension the conclusion of a peace, which rendered the empress of Russia the protectress of Moldavia and Wallachia, and which so greatly increased her territories and ascendency in the east of Europe, and enabled her to turn her attention to the affairs of Poland.

The fears of the empress-queen were not ill-founded. Catherine authoritatively required both Austria and Prussia to desist from their encroachments, and abide by the treaty of partition ; she even reproached the court of Vienna for the exactions of their troops in Poland, and extorted from the emperor an humiliating disavowal of their conduct. These spirited remonstrances were attended with effect. Maria Theresa first declared her readiness to oblige the empress of Russia by restoring the territories of which she had taken possession ; and the king of Prussia, was compelled to follow her example. Still, however, the final conclusion of this nefarious transaction was retarded by various negotiations ; representations, remonstrances, and threats succeeded each other, and it was not till 1777, that the three powers, influenced by mutual jealousy and fear, desisted from their projects of aggrandisement, and nearly adopted the limits which had been assigned by the first treaty of partition.

Chap. CXX.— 1777.

At the conclusion of the partition of Poland, the situation of Maria Theresa was highly flourishing, and her great accessions of strength and influence excited jealousy among the European powers. She possessed a well disciplined army, exceeding 200,000 men, which could be considerably augmented ; the finances were restored to order, and notwith-

standing the numerous expenses of the military establishment,
the treasury was enriched by an annual saving of 2,000,000
crowns. From inclination and principle she was averse to
the horrors of war, and desirous of closing her days in peace;
but her son the emperor, a prince of an aspiring and
ambitious temper, was eager to augment his dominions, and
panted for an occasion to signalise his name. Some time
after the death of Francis, the council of the conference
which had for so long a period directed the administration,
was abolished, and prince Kaunitz, as prime minister,
acquired unbounded influence in the conduct of foreign
affairs. He adapted himself with consummate address to
the discordant characters and views of the mother and son;
but he exerted his principal attention to preserve the alliance
with France, which during the events of the preceding years
had been repeatedly threatened with dissolution.

On the death of Louis XV., sanguine hopes were entertained by the court of Vienna, that their ascendency at
Versailles would be secured by the influence of the young
queen*, and that Choiseul would be placed at the head of a
new administration formed under their auspices. But in
these expectations they were grievously disappointed; the
young king, though warmly attached to his queen, restrained
her interference in political concerns, and placed his whole
confidence in the count de Maurepas, who had been strongly
recommended by the dauphin his father, and whose principles were adverse to Austrian politics. The resolution of
the king was also strengthened by a memorial presented to
him, by the order of his deceased father, on the day of his
accession. This paper designated the house of Austria as
the natural enemy of France; displayed in strong colours
the evils which had been derived from the treaty of Versailles: and inculcated the necessity of establishing a new
system of policy.

By the advice of Maurepas, the duke d'Aiguillon was
dismissed, and the conduct of foreign affairs intrusted to the
count de Vergennes, a man of a cool head, penetrating
judgment, and refined address, who had highly distinguished
himself in his embassies at Constantinople and Stockholm,
and who, from gratitude and principle, was zealous in promoting the views of Maurepas. Vergennes pursued the

* The archduchess Maria Antoinetta, daughter of Maria Theresa.

same system of policy with consummate skill; he maintained
a private and constant correspondence with Louis XVI., unknown to the queen; he secretly renewed the friendly intercourse with the king of Prussia; and at the very moment
when by lures and promises he governed in essential points
the court of Vienna, he inculcated in the mind of the king
the necessity of supporting the Prussian power, and of
counteracting the further aggrandisement of the house of
Austria, as the means of perpetuating the influence of
France in Germany, and isolating England from the states
of the continent. In a memoir privately submitted to the
king, he earnestly inculcated this grand principle of his
political system: "What would have become," he says, "of
France, if the enormous efforts made during the septennial
war had been attended with the expected success? The
king of Prussia crushed, and his power annihilated, France
would have been reduced to the degrading alternative of
having no ally in the empire, or of submitting to the law
imposed by so precarious a friend as the house of Austria.
It is to the dread inspired by the king of Prussia, that
France owes the alliance of the court of Vienna. By preserving, therefore, the power which is the object of that
dread, we can alone hope to perpetuate that alliance." He
adds, "I dare to assert, that we ought not to hesitate in pre-
ferring the preservation of the Prussian power in Germany,
to that of the branches of the house of Bourbon in Italy.
Although the kingdom of Naples, in the hands of the emperor, would give him many advantages, those advantages
have no positive weight in the balance of Europe: but it is
far different with regard to Prussia; her consolidated power,
particularly since the acquisition of Polish Prussia, renders
her of considerable importance in the balance of the empire,
and, by a necessary consequence, in that of Europe."

Louis adopted this principle, and in most instances made
it the grand rule of his conduct. He maintained the alliance
with the house of Austria, from a regard to treaties, from
affection to the queen, and from a sense of the advantages
derived from that connection; but he no less secretly and
sedulously cultivated a friendly intercourse with Prussia
and the secondary powers. He justly appreciated the pacific sentiments of Maria Theresa, for whom he entertained
an almost filial affection, and he was equally convinced that

prince Kaunitz was sincerely disposed to maintain the alliance on terms of reciprocal advantage to both nations.   He entertained, however, an unfavourable opinion of his brother-in-law, the emperor, and attributed to his sole interference the alliance with Russia and Prussia, the partition of Poland, and the seizure of the Bucovina, the possession of which had been lately confirmed to her by Russia.   His prejudice against Joseph strikingly appears by a secret letter written to Vergennes, on the invasion of Venetian Dalmatia by the imperial troops, under the pretence of a dispute relative to the limits : " The measures," he says, " which the Austrian cabinet have for some time pursued are equivocal and fallacious.   The invasion of the Venetian territories by the troops of the emperor, denotes his ambitious and despotic temper, which he has not concealed from the baron de Breteuil ; he has doubtless fascinated his mother, as she was by no means pleased with his usurpations, and did not at first conceal her dissatisfaction.   It appears, also, by the despatch of Thugut, that Kaunitz disapproved all that had passed, but his opinion was overruled.   We have nothing at present to do, but to watch carefully, and be on our guard relative to everything that comes from the court of Vienna ; civility and reserve must be the rule of our conduct."

These motives, and this refined policy, explain the whole conduct of the French cabinet, and display their apparent inconsistency in supporting the petty interests of the house of Austria, while they opposed all her attempts for further aggrandisement.

The court of Vienna exhibited strong marks of disappointment and uneasiness, on the nomination of the French ministry, without their knowledge or intervention ; the emperor displayed* the strongest aversion to the French court and nation ; even prince Kaunitz did not refrain from sarcastic reflections on the characters and measures of the new administration, and the whole cabinet testified a returning partiality to England.   During the transactions for the partition of Poland, the court of Vienna had maintained a

---

* I passed the winter of 1777 and 1778 at Vienna, and had frequently the honour of meeting the emperor, in private societies, where he visited without ceremony.   On these occasions he did not affect to conceal his Anti-Bourbon sentiments, and seldom failed of uttering some severe sarcasms against the French.

stately reserve towards that of Versailles; but the partition
was no sooner completed, than their jealousy of Russia revived in consequence of her increasing preponderance, and
perpetual encroachments on the side of Turkey. To resist
so formidable a power, they endeavoured to regain the confidence of France, and in 1777, baron Thugut was despatched
to Paris to propose a defensive league against Russia, in
favour of the Turks. The French ministry, however,
anxious not to offend the empress of Russia, declined the
proposal, under the pretence that such an alliance would
alarm Europe, and that it would be sufficient to conclude the
league when the Ottoman empire was actually threatened
with an invasion.

In consequence of the ill-success of the minister, the
emperor himself, who was desirous to ascertain the real
sentiments of the French cabinet, and to exert his influence
over his sister, paid a visit to Versailles. He had long
meditated this journey, but had been prevented by the secret
opposition of the French ministry, and by the repugnance of
the king, whose prejudices against his brother-in-law had
rather increased than diminished. Vergennes encouraged
these prejudices; he artfully expatiated on the ambitious
projects of the emperor, insinuated that the purpose of the
journey was to gain the support of France to his views of
aggrandisement, and endeavoured to fortify the mind of his
master against the influence of the queen. The anti-Austrian party also were loud in their clamours; they accused
the emperor, not only of an intention to wrest Servia and
Bosnia from the Turks, Friuli from the Venetians, and to
seize Bavaria, on the death of the elector, but to covet
Loraine and Alsace, the patrimony of his ancestors. The
prejudices of the king, therefore, were not effaced by
all the blandishments of the queen, and were still further augmented by the incompatible characters of the two
sovereigns.

In these circumstances, the visit of the emperor did not
tend to revive the harmony between the two houses. He
was indeed received with the most flattering marks of respect
and attention; but the king and ministers viewed their illustrious guest with jealousy and alarm, and in all political
matters he experienced the utmost coolness and reserve.
The vanity of Joseph was mortified by his disappointment;

he returned to Vienna still more disgusted with the French, whom he affected to consider as a trifling and frivolous people ; and he accused the cabinet of Versailles of being jealous of his talents, fearful of his future ascendency in Europe, and hostile to the interests of the house of Austria.

Chap. CXXI.—1777-1779.

Joseph had scarcely returned from France, when the death of the elector of Bavaria, without issue male, on the 30th of December, 1777, opened a new prospect of aggrandisement to the house of Austria, and again kindled the flames of war in Germany.

On this event, Charles Theodore, elector Palatine, was generally considered as rightful heir to all the Bavarian territories which were not female fiefs or allodials.

The elector of Saxony, in right of his mother, who was sister of the deceased elector, claimed the allodial property, which he valued at 47,000,000 florins.

The duke of Mecklenburgh Schwerin contended for the possession of the landgraviate of Leuchtenberg, in virtue of an investiture granted to his ancestor Henry by the emperor Maximilian, in 1602.

But these petty pretensions were lost in those of a more powerful claimant. The house of Austria had long coveted the possession of Bavaria, and Joseph had even espoused Cunegunda, sister of the deceased elector, a princess who possessed no personal attractions, with a view to secure the allodial property ; her death without issue having frustrated these expectations, the court of Vienna brought forward other pretensions to almost one half of the succession.

Maria Theresa, as queen of Bohemia, claimed those fiefs in the Upper Palatinate which had been conferred by the kings of Bohemia on the Bavarian line since the convention of Pavia ; and as archduchess of Austria, and representative of Albert, she founded her pretensions to Lower Bavaria in virtue of the investiture granted by Sigismond. She claimed also the lordship of Mindelheim in Suabia, in consequence of a reversion granted to the house of Austria by Matthias, in

1614, and confirmed by succeeding emperors ; and she even
asserted a prior title to the allodials, by what was called a
right of regredience, or in virtue of her descent from Anne,
great grand-daughter of Albert and wife of Ferdinand I.,
and also from Mary Anne, daughter of William, fifth elector
of Bavaria, and wife of Ferdinand II.

Joseph, as emperor, claimed the landgraviate of Leuchtenberg, the counties of Wolfstein, Haag, Schwaabeck, Halss,
and a few inconsiderable districts, as male fiefs reverting to
the empire.

In consequence of these pretensions, and the views which
they had long entertained of appropriating Bavaria, the
court of Vienna had anxiously watched the health of the
elector ; and he was no sooner seized with the small-pox than
they put their troops in motion towards the frontiers.
Having secured the Bavarian ministers, the gates of Munich
were shut on the death of the elector, and for five days the
Austrian envoy alone was permitted to forward an express ;
the imperial troops instantly entered the electorate, and occupied those parts which were claimed by the house of Austria.
The elector Palatine, however, issued letters patent, remon-
strating against the encroachment, prepared to take possession of the inheritance, and repaired to Munich to receive the
homage of his subjects.   But it soon appeared that he had
consented to previous arrangements ; for, on the 3rd of
January, his minister signed a convention, acknowledging
the legitimacy of the Austrian pretensions, which was ratified
on the 15th by the elector himself.   In fact, the court of
Vienna had purchased his acquiescence by promising to provide for his natural son ; and as he had no legitimate issue,
he sacrificed, without scruple, the interests of his presumptive
heir, the duke of Deux Ponts, who was descended from a
collateral branch of the Rhodolphine line.

On the 20th of January Kaunitz delivered a circular note
to the foreign ministers, briefly specifying the pretensions of
the emperor and Maria Theresa ; and, from the situation of
affairs, the court of Vienna deemed themselves secure of their
object.   Their troops were in possession of the country, and
they expected the co-operation of France ; Russia, embarrassed by the disputes relative to the Crimea, did not seem
willing or capable of opposing their claims ; England, involved in the war with the American colonies, could not turn

her attention to the affairs of the continent; and the imperial cabinet hoped that the king of Prussia, who was alone capable of interposing with effect, was too much broken with age and infirmities to encounter the dangers and fatigues of the field, or to engage the whole power of the house of Austria, assisted by France. They were strengthened in this opinion by the apparent inactivity of Frederic; but that wily monarch had secretly incited the duke of Deux Ponts to oppose the dismemberment of his future inheritance*, and made private overtures to France and Russia.

France, true to her system of policy, would not openly oppose, but was anxious to obstruct, the aggrandisement of the house of Austria; and Frederic succeeded in convincing the empress of Russia that she was interested to prevent any change in the German empire. Thus encouraged, he persuaded the duke of Deux Ponts to appeal to Prussia and. France, and to protest before the diet against the dismemberment of the Bavarian territories. The elector of Saxony followed this example, and being thus furnished with a pretext for his interference, Frederic opened a negotiation with the court of Vienna. A paper war ensued; and on both sides notes and memorials were issued, refuting and enforcing the validity of the Austrian pretensions.

The king of Prussia urged that the whole of the Bavarian succession was an inalienable and indivisible patrimony, as well from the principles of the feudal system as from the convention of Pavia, renewed by subsequent family compacts, in two of which the elector Palatine himself was a party, and confirmed by the Golden Bull and the peace of Westphalia. He reprobated with peculiar energy the private arrangement with the elector Palatine, without the consent of his presumptive heir, the duke of Deux Ponts, as contrary to the laws and constitutions of the empire, and as a precedent that would expose the smaller states to be swallowed up by the larger. He also charged the emperor with a breach of his capitulation, in authorising so illegal a transaction, and in occupying with the Austrian troops some integral

---

* The duke of Deux Ponts had even been induced by the elector Palatine to accede to the convention with the house of Austria, from the apprehension of losing Juliers and Berg; but was dissuaded by count Goertz, the Prussian ambassador, at the very moment when he was about to sign. I received this information from count Goertz himself.

parts of the duchy of Bavaria, without the consent of the empire.

The court of Vienna replied with all the ingenuity which the discussion of these intricate questions prompted.

Arguments on both sides were continually repeated in different forms in the course of the controversy, and were urged with all the subtlety and acuteness which marked the fertile imaginations of Kaunitz and Hertzberg, and supported with all the chicane and cavil which German jurists could invent, and with all the authorities which could be drawn from the doubtful records of antiquity.*

During this discussion, which gradually increased in acrimony, and was at length carried before the diet of the empire, active preparations were made for hostilities; troops were assembled in Saxony, Silesia, Bohemia, and Moravia; and the emperor and Frederic repaired to take the command of their respective armies.

At this juncture the emperor, disappointed in his hopes of assistance from France, opened a correspondence with the king of Prussia, and the two sovereigns wrote to each other as private individuals. In the first letter he proposed a project of a convention, by which the king was to acknowledge the validity of the agreement between the empress-queen and the elector palatine, and to make no opposition to any future arrangement relative to the exchange either of a part or the whole of the Bavarian territories, provided the acquisitions of the house of Austria did not border on the Prussian dominions. In return, he promised not to oppose the incorporation of the margraviates of Anspach and Bareith, with the territories of the reigning house of Brandenburgh, or any exchange which might suit the convenience of the king of Prussia, provided likewise that his acquisitions did not border on the Austrian territories.

These propositions were founded on the same principle of spoliation which had characterised the partition of Poland; but circumstances were changed. The king of Prussia was more interested to prevent the aggrandisement of the house of Austria in the empire than to make any new acquisition. He therefore rejected these propositions, affecting great ab-

* The reader who is desirous to examine this controversy may consult the papers on both sides in Hertzberg's Recueil des Deductions, Traités, &c.

horrence of thus parcelling out the states of the empire for political convenience and mutual aggrandisement; and the discussion which had already exercised the ingenuity of the ministers, was again renewed by the two sovereigns. But Joseph seemed more desirous to display his own talents and power, than to offer reasonable terms of accommodation. Proud of the army, which was far more numerous, better disciplined, and more abundantly supplied with artillery than at the beginning of the war, and anxious to cope with the great Frederic, his thirst for military glory burst forth in terms of defiance, notwithstanding his affectation of humility and love of peace.

After stating the claims of Austria, and reasserting the validity of the agreement with the elector Palatine, he concluded: " I expect with tranquillity whatever your majesty is pleased to answer or to do. I have already learned so many useful things from your majesty, that were I not a citizen, and were not the welfare of several millions of human beings concerned, I would almost add that I should not be averse to learn also from you the part of a general. Nevertheless your majesty may be convinced that the maintenance of peace, particularly with a person like you, whom I truly reverence and love, is my sincere desire, and that 400,000 brave soldiers ought not to be employed in destroying each other, for no good reason and to no purpose." The answer of Frederic was no less distinguished by his characteristic irony. " Your imperial majesty has the goodness to banter; no, sire! you need no master, so great are the talents which Heaven has conferred on your imperial majesty, that you are capable of acting any part. You will recollect that Lucullus had never commanded an army when the Roman senate sent him into Pontus; he had scarcely arrived before he defeated Mithridates. I shall be the first to applaud your imperial majesty's victories, provided they are not obtained at my expense."

This correspondence was continued with little effect from day to day, until the king, suspecting that the emperor was only desirous of gaining time, transferred the discussion to his ministers; and count Cobenzl was despatched to Berlin, in April, on the part of the empress-queen, with full powers to continue the negotiation. But as the proposals of the Austrian plenipotentiary were exactly similar to those of the emperor, the negotiation was attended with no better success, and Cobenzl returned to Vienna. At length the imperial court brought the controversy to a conclusion, by declaring, that if the king of Prussia refused to adopt the propositions which had been offered, as the basis of a preliminary treaty, all amicable arrangement was impossible, and all farther explanations superfluous.

In March the respective armies had assembled ; Joseph, accompanied by marshal Lacy with 100,000 men, occupied the celebrated position of Konigsgratz, above the confluence of the Adler and the Elbe, which was rendered almost impregnable by works and inundations ; and marshal Loudon, with an army of 50,000 men, defended the frontiers of Saxony and Lusatia. The king of Prussia commenced hostilities by invading Bohemia on the 5th of July ; he took possession of Nachod, penetrated to the banks of the Elbe, between Konigsgratz and Jaromitz, and encamped opposite to the emperor. Another army of Prussians and Saxons under prince Henry entered Bohemia, near the town of Zittau, forced the post of Gabel, and took 1500 men prisoners. By this manœuvre Loudon was compelled to retreat ; but taking a strong position at Munchengratz, behind the Iser, he secured his communications, and covered the flank of the emperor. To draw him from this important post, a Prussian detachment under general Platen penetrated into his rear, and spread such consternation to the gates of Prague, that the archives were removed, and the garrison evacuated the town ; Loudon, however, maintaining his post, the Prussian detachment retreated, and the king was baffled in his attempts to dislodge the Austrians. After ravaging the country and destroying the forage, Frederic, in September, fell back towards Silesia, and prince Henry, evacuating Bohemia, retired into Saxony and Lusatia. Thus this singular campaign, in which so numerous an army was brought into the field, headed by a young sovereign panting for military glory, and eager to signalise himself against his great and formidable rival, passed without a siege or a single action of importance.

The principal cause of this inactivity was derived from the repugnance of Maria Theresa to continue hostilities, and her determined resolution to conclude peace on reasonable terms. When the account of the elector of Bavaria's death was first brought to Vienna, she received it with the deepest emotion, and passed several days in deep anxiety; she entreated the emperor and prince Kaunitz to weigh her pretensions with calmness and deliberation, and to be convinced of her right to any part of the Bavarian territories before they took possession. But though her pacific sentiments were overborne by the impetuosity of Joseph, yet when she was persuaded to send an army into the field, she persisted in her determination to conclude peace on the first opportunity. During the discussion with Prussia, she was frequently in tears at the prospect of a war; and when the correspondence between the emperor and Frederic had closed, and the Prussian army had actually entered Bohemia, she made an extraordinary effort by opening a correspondence without the knowledge of her son. She despatched baron Thugut, under a feigned character, and enjoined him, among other expressions, to testify her regret that Frederic and herself were going to tear the grey hairs from each other's head. Her letter to the king on this occasion announced the pacific sentiments by which she was actuated: " From the recall of baron Riedesel, and the entrance of your troops into Bohemia, I perceive, with extreme sensibility, the breaking out of a new war. My age, and my earnest desire for maintaining peace, are well known, and I cannot give a more convincing proof than by the present proposal. My maternal heart is justly alarmed for the safety of two sons and my son-in-law, who are in the army. I have taken this step without the knowledge of my son the emperor, and I entreat, whatever may be the event, that you will not divulge it. I am anxious to recommence and terminate the negotiation, hitherto conducted by the emperor, and broken off to my extreme regret. This letter will be delivered to you by baron Thugut, who is intrusted with full powers. Ardently hoping that it may fulfil my wishes, conformably to my dignity, I entreat you to join your efforts with mine to re-establish between us harmony and good intelligence for the benefit of mankind, and the interests of our respective families." In a postcript, she added, " Having just received the intelligence of the approach of your army towards that of the emperor, I am the more anxious to despatch this letter, lest some accident should change the present situation of affairs. I purpose also to send a courier to the emperor, to prevent, if possible, any hasty measure on his part, and sincerely hope I shall succeed."

This letter inclosed a proposal for a suspension of arms, and for restoring all the possessions occupied by her troops, except an extent of territory which would yield an annual revenue of 1,000,000 florins, and which should not be contiguous to Ratisbon, nor divide Bavaria into two parts as the district she then held. She offered to unite her endeavours with those of the king of Prussia to negotiate a just and equitable accommodation between the electors Palatine and Saxony relative to the allodial possessions.

The king was conciliated by these moderate proposals; his answer bore an honourable testimony to the motives of the empress-queen, and equally evinced the sincerity of his pacific professions.

" Baron Thugut has delivered to me your imperial majesty's letter, and no one is or shall be acquainted with his arrival. It was worthy of your majesty's character to give these proofs of magnanimity and moderation in a litigious cause, after having so heroically maintained the inheritance of your ancestors. The tender attachment which you display for your son the emperor and the princes of your blood, deserves the applause of every feeling mind, and augments, if possible, the high consideration which I entertain for your sacred person. I have added some articles to the propositions of baron Thugut, most of which have been allowed, and others will, I hope, meet with little difficulty. He will immediately depart for Vienna, and will be able to return in five or six days, during which time I will act with such caution, that your imperial majesty may have no cause of apprehension for the safety of any part of your family, and particularly of the emperor, whom I love and esteem, although our opinions differ in regard to the affairs of Germany."

The additional propositions were, that the house of Austria should restore the whole of Bavaria to the elector Palatine, except part of the district of Burghausen, and in return should gratify the elector of Saxony with 1,000,000 crowns, and the investiture of the principality of Mindelheim and the district of Rotenburgh, and guaranty the reversion of the remainder of the Bavarian inheritance to the house of Deux Ponts; that the emperor should cede to the elector of

Saxony the rights which he pretended to exercise over certain fiefs in Saxony; should confer on the duke of Mecklenburgh a vacant fief of the empire, as an indemnification for
his claims; and should not oppose the future incorporation
of the margraviates of Anspach and Bareith with the possessions of the crown of Prussia, nor prevent the exchange
of those districts for Lusatia, with the consent of the elector
of Saxony.

The empress-queen expressed extreme regret at her inability to accede to all these demands; but, as a final attempt
to prevent a cruel and destructive war, proposed to restore
all her acquisitions in Bavaria, if the king would relinquish
his intention of incorporating the margraviates of Anspach
and Bareith as long as there existed a younger branch of his
family, in conformity with the ancient compact established
by the house of Brandenburgh, and confirmed by the emperors and empire. The king, however, rejected all proposals
relative to the renunciation of these claims, and resumed
with new vigour the operations of the field, which he had
hitherto suspended. The empress-queen appeared in the
deepest affliction at this second rupture of the negotiation,
and still more at the inflexible spirit of her son, who thwarted
all her endeavours to terminate hostilities. To conquer his
obstinacy she sent his confidential servant, count Rosenburgh,
with a new plan of pacification; but Joseph peremptorily
refused to concur in the renewal of the negotiation, while
the armies were in the field. He did not conceal his disapprobation of the concessions made by his mother, which
he stigmatised as disgraceful; and even declared, that should
the Prussian propositions be accepted, he would retire to
Aix-la-Chapelle, and re-establish in that city the ancient
seat of the emperors. Nor was the mission of the archduke Leopold to the army attended with better success; and
his interference only contributed to disunite the two brothers,
who had hitherto lived in harmony.

The empress-queen was no less thwarted by prince Kaunitz.
He deemed her repeated attempts to renew the negotiation
neither well timed nor consistent with the dignity of the
house of Austria. Aware of the king of Prussia's desire of
peace, he censured the extreme anxiety of his mistress for
the termination of hostilities with unusual freedom, and contended, that a firm and vigorous conduct would procure more

advantageous terms. Hence, in drawing up the counter propositions to the Prussian offers, he introduced new conditions, and threw in captious and obscure expressions, which tended to embarrass the negotiation. The empress, impelled by the opposition of her son, and seduced by the persuasive eloquence of her minister, acted against her own judgment in suffering the continuance of the war; yet she never intermitted her efforts, and when the campaign was closed renewed her attempts with perseverance and address, and applied for the mediation of France and Russia.

Her efforts were favoured by the disposition of the courts of Versailles and Petersburgh. France was bound by the treaty of 1756 to assist the house of Austria, if attacked, with a considerable body of forces, and had been repeatedly summoned to comply with this engagement. The French ministry were greatly embarrassed with this demand: in furnishing the stipulated succours, they would have contributed to the aggrandisement of the house of Austria, and involved themselves in a continental war; in continuing to delay the fulfilment of the treaty, they were apprehensive of disgusting the court of Vienna, and of occasioning the renewal of the alliance with the maritime powers. They therefore eluded the demand under various pretences, exhorting the empress to effect an accommodation, and tendered their mediation between the belligerent powers. While Maria Theresa had entertained hopes of assistance, or of effecting a separate accommodation, she had declined the intervention of France; but foiled in those expectations, she again turned to the court of Versailles, and France eagerly accepted the office of pacifying Germany, and agreed to support the conditions which had been already offered.

The empress of Russia was equally willing and interested to terminate the troubles of Germany. She had continued to receive a subsidy of 500,000 crowns from Prussia, and was bound in return to assist the king as soon as her contest with the Porte was terminated. She had therefore no sooner entered into negotiation with the Turks than she came forward as an armed mediatrix, declaring, that unless the empress-queen gave satisfaction to the princes of the empire, by removing their just causes of complaint, for the occupation of any part of the Bavarian territories, she would assist the king of Prussia with the corps stipulated by treaty. She followed this declaration by despatching 20,000 men under prince Repnin through Poland, towards the frontiers of Gallicia.

This unexpected declaration astonished Maria Theresa, and disconcerted Kaunitz; but Joseph received the challenge with no less satisfaction than spirit. As the disputes with the Turks were not finally settled, he hoped that the empress of Russia would be unable to take an active part in the affairs of Germany; he therefore extorted from his reluctant mother an order for recruiting the army with 80,000 men, and entertained the most sanguine hopes that he should again take the field. Maria Theresa, however, acted with more prudence and humanity: she sighed after the termination of the public troubles; and conscious that her people, loaded with taxes, were incapable of supporting additional burdens, deemed no concessions beneath her dignity, which could secure the continuance of peace.

Before the Russian declaration had been delivered at Vienna, she had implored the good offices of Catherine, and requested her to join her mediation with that of France, which she had already accepted. She exerted all her efforts, therefore, to conciliate France and Russia, and strengthened her interest at the court of Petersburgh by a strain of flattery which almost equalled eastern adulation. Having paid her acknowledgments for the readiness with which Catherine had accepted the proffered mediation, she said, she " embraced with zeal this opportunity of testifying her esteem, her friendship, her confidence, and her deference." She attempted to explain and apologise for her conduct in taking possession of the Bavarian territory, and expatiated on her moderation in offering to restore her acquisitions, provided Frederic would recede from his illegal pretensions on the margraviates of Anspach and Bareith. After detailing her endeavours to induce the king of Prussia to accept reasonable terms of accommodation, she added, " I confide in your known equity, and leave to your imperial majesty the choice of adopting those means of reconciliation, which, in conjunction with France, shall be proved to be the most equitable and proper for the speedy re-establishment of peace, fully persuaded that I cannot place in better hands my interests and my dignity."*

* MS. Letter from the empress-queen to the empress of Russia, which I procured at St. Petersburgh.

These adulatory, and even humble expressions from the first sovereign in Europe, and from a court distinguished for their arrogated pre-eminence, flattered the vanity, and conciliated the favour of Catherine. She did not support her imperious and peremptory declaration, and gradually receded from the resolution which she had at first adopted, of entering into all the views of the Prussian monarch.

Meanwhile, Frederic, who had been buoyed up with the hopes of being assisted by the whole force of Russia, and by the secret encouragement of France, increased his demands, and even required the unequivocal cession of the whole of Bavaria, and the payment of 40,000,000 crowns to the elector of Saxony. But he was disappointed in his expectations; France, though desirous to prevent the aggrandisement, was anxious to save the honour of the house of Austria; and the empress of Russia, softened by the address of Maria Theresa, refused to support his new proposition. Encouraged by these favourable appearances, the court of Vienna indignantly rejected his proposal, and declared that they would rather sacrifice their whole army than submit to conditions more humiliating than those which had been already offered. This difference of opinion seemed likely to occasion the continuance of the war, and partial hostilities were renewed on the frontiers of Bohemia and Silesia. But the king perceiving that he was not countenanced by France and Russia, receded from his demand, and submitted to the French ministry a plan of pacification nearly similar to the last conditions offered by the empress-queen. This plan being approved by Maria Theresa, was digested by the mediating powers, and preparations were made to open a congress at Teschen.

During this negotiation, Joseph had opposed every obstacle in his power to the arrangement of the preliminaries; and when an armistice was nearly concluded, and the ministers nominated for the congress, he in February sent a detachment of 10,000 men to bombard Neustadt, with the hope of provoking the Prussians to continue hostilities. But his views were frustrated by the pacific inclinations both of Frederic and the empress-queen. Notwithstanding this insult, the king consented to an armistice; the congress was opened on the 10th of March at Teschen, a small town in Austrian Silesia, by the plenipotentiaries of the belligerent and mediating powers, and those of Saxony, the elector

Palatine, and the duke of Deux Ponts. Baron Breteuil, who was protected by the queen of France, and attached to the house of Austria, dictated, in conjunction with the Russian minister, the terms of peace. Still, however, Maria Theresa was thwarted by the intrigues of Joseph; nor did he desist till the accommodation between the court of St. Petersburgh and the Turks alarmed him with the prospect of an immediate attack from Russia. From that moment his attempts to embarrass the conferences ceased; the solicitations of Maria Theresa hastened the negotiation, and a peace was concluded on the 13th of May, the birth-day of the benevolent princess who thus restored tranquillity to Germany.

Maria Theresa was often heard to declare, that no event in her whole reign ever inspired her with such heartfelt and permanent satisfaction as the treaty of Teschen. Her joy was adequate to the recollection of the difficulties she had encountered, and the consciousness of the blessings which she had conferred on her people, by delivering them from the horrors of war. When the news was conveyed to Vienna, that the king of Prussia had acceded to the conditions, she exclaimed, "I am confounded with joy. I am not partial to Frederic, but I must do him the justice to confess that he has acted nobly and honourably; he promised me to make peace upon reasonable terms, and he has kept his word. I am inexpressibly happy to spare the effusion of so much blood." She repaired immediately to the cathedral, and rendered public thanks to God for the termination of hostilities.

The principal management of the whole transaction relative to Bavaria had been intrusted to prince Kaunitz, and both the emperor and empress had expressed the highest satisfaction with his zeal and ability. But although gratified with the approbation of his sovereigns, he had been much embarrassed by the discordance of opinion between the mother and son, which occasioned frequent and violent altercations. The peace was therefore no sooner concluded than he requested permission to resign; but he was prevailed upon by the importunities of his sovereigns to continue in office, on condition that a vice-chancellor should be appointed to assist him in the business of his department. His request being gratified, he recommended count Philip Cobenzl, who had acted as plenipotentiary at the congress of Teschen, and who possessed the favour and confidence of the emperor.

CHAP. CXXII.—1779, 1780.

ALTHOUGH France had mediated the peace of Teschen, and assisted in procuring honourable terms for the house of Austria; yet her refusal of the succours stipulated by the treaty of Versailles, and her secret opposition to the dismemberment of Bavaria, had greatly irritated the court of Vienna. The imperious spirit of Joseph was roused to the highest pitch of indignation; he inveighed against the perfidy of the French cabinet, and asserted that from an alliance of almost thirty years, his family had reaped neither honour nor advantage. He drew a striking comparison between the political principles of England and those of France, and seemed desirous to renew the connection with the maritime powers. Maria Theresa was more calm and temperate in her resentment, though scarcely less dissatisfied; her fondness for her daughter induced her to overlook the duplicity of her ally, and she dreaded to detach herself from the Bourbon family, with five of whose branches her children had intermarried. Kaunitz likewise could not avoid lamenting the artifices of France, and at particular times detailed the evils of the French alliance; yet he was not willing to overturn a work which he had long considered as the pride of his life, and as the criterion of that esteem which he was to expect from posterity. Influenced by these discordant and opposite sentiments, the court of Vienna acted with uncertainty and inconsistency; but though they were not inclined to break with France, their resentment against her conduct during the Bavarian war, and the renewal of her connection with Prussia, induced them to court England and Russia.

From the peace of Paris, England had been incessantly distracted by feuds and party contests, which rose to an unusual degree of acrimony, and occasioned continual changes of administration. Lord Bute, though a nobleman of sound sense, elegant learning, and high integrity, was ill calculated to direct the helm of government in a country like England,

subject to the storms of faction. The plan which he carried
into execution of delivering the crown from the shackles of
the aristocracy, had alienated that powerful party, and deserted by those whom he had brought into office, he resigned
in disgust in 1763.

During the short period of six years which followed his
resignation, the helm of state had been directed by five
successive administrations, each of which did little more
than annul the measures pursued by their predecessors. But
in nothing was this fluctuation of counsels, and continual
change of measures, more fatal, than in the conduct of
government towards the American colonies.

From the first symptoms of the American troubles, France
had been guilty of extreme duplicity, as well as impolicy.
During an affected neutrality, she had secretly fomented the
commotions in the colonies, encouraged the malcontents by
promises of support, and finally entered into a formal treaty
to acknowledge their independence. Having gradually matured their plans for depriving Great Britain of this source
of commercial wealth and naval power, the French ministry
threw off the mask, and sent an auxiliary force to support
the insurgents. On this occasion they had acted with such
extreme caution, as to deceive the court of Vienna ; and
Kaunitz had frequently pledged himself for the sincerity and
good faith of France. But when the conduct of the French
ministry belied their professions, and war had actually commenced, the Austrian cabinet affected to declare their
abhorrence of the cause of rebellion ; they refused to receive
the agents of America in a diplomatic capacity, and even
prohibited all commerce between their subjects in the Low
Countries and the rebel colonies. Joseph said to Sir Robert
Keith, who expressed the king's satisfaction at this proof of
friendship — " In issuing this proclamation, and rendering it
as effectual as possible, her imperial majesty has followed
the impulse of that regard which she and all her family
always felt for his majesty ; as to myself, I am extremely
concerned for the difficulties which embarrass the king's
government. The cause in which England is engaged, is
the cause of all sovereigns, who have a joint interest in the
maintenance of due subordination and obedience to law, in
all the surrounding monarchies. I observe with pleasure the
vigorous exertions of the national strength, which the king

is employing to bring his rebellious subjects to submission, and I sincerely wish success to the measures."

Maria Theresa also expressed herself with equal warmth.*

During the Bavarian war, the conduct of France had increased this real or affected inclination towards England; the peace of Teschen was no sooner concluded, than prince Kaunitz, in the most amicable terms, proffered the intervention of his sovereign to effect an accommodation between France and Great Britain; and though this offer was declined, he continued to court the British cabinet with the hope of obtaining their assistance in conciliating the friendship of Russia. In thus endeavouring to conciliate Catherine, Maria Theresa had two objects in view; the first to gain her concurrence in securing for the archduke Maximilian the coadjutorship of Munster and Cologne, and the other to annihilate the influence of the king of Prussia.†

* " I am sensible," she said, in an audience which she gave to the British minister, "of every fresh proof of the king's kind attention to my welfare and prosperity ; I am happy to find that my amicable intentions in issuing the prohibition against any intercourse between my subjects and the rebel colonies, have made a due impression on the king's mind. I have a high esteem for his majesty's principles of government, a sincere veneration for his personal character, and a hearty desire to see the restoration of obedience and tranquillity in every quarter of his dominions. My friendship for the king, and my hereditary affection for the royal family have never abated ; though a difference in political opinions (the source of which I cannot avoid attributing to the king of Prussia) has diminished the opportunities of an interchange of good offices between the two crowns. I have endeavoured to settle the Ostend affair in the manner most agreeable to the king. The business indeed is of a trifling nature ; but his majesty will do me the justice to believe that he would have found me equally well disposed in matters of much higher importance."

† The empress-queen had succeeded in procuring establishments for all her younger children, except the archduke Maximilian. Leopold was great duke of Tuscany ; Ferdinand governor of Milan, and by his marriage with Maria Beatrix, daughter of the duke of Modena, had secured the reversion of his father-in-law's dominions. Maximilian had entered into holy orders, and was candidate for the coadjutorship of the archbishopric of Cologne and the bishopric of Munster, which would entitle him to succeed to those valuable sees with the electoral dignity. But in the attainment of this object, Maria Theresa experienced great opposition. The electorate of Cologne having hitherto been held by a member of the house of Bavaria; France, to whom the electors of Cologne had generally been attached, was interested to oppose the views of the house of Austria, and vest that reversion in a prince of a less power-

As Russia possessed great weight in the Germanic body, and considerable influence in the chapter, her concurrence was of the utmost importance; but the empress-queen was still more interested to deprive the king of Prussia of that influence at St. Petersburgh which he had exerted with such effect during the Bavarian contest. Such, however, were the situation and principles of the Russian court, that this task was attended with extreme difficulty.

Catherine II. was distinguished for a masculine force of mind, and an intrepidity above her sex, added to great personal attractions, affable manners, and graceful deportment. She possessed in a no less degree the failings derived from an ardent and sensitive imagination; she wanted forbearance in prosperity, and accuracy of judgment; she was impetuous in her resolutions, and tenacious of her opinions. But vanity was her predominant foible; puffed up by uninterrupted prosperity, and by the applause lavished on her character and actions from every quarter of Europe, her love of flattery was almost insatiable; she considered herself equally pre-eminent in talents and in power, expected to be addressed in a strain of Oriental adulation, and to be approached with all the deference due to a divinity.

From her recent successes against the Turks, the ardent imagination of Catherine conceived the romantic project of reviving the ancient name and power of the Greeks, and establishing a new empire at Athens or Constantinople. Inspired with this splendid vision, she gave to her second grandson the name of Constantine, clothed him in a Greek dress, procured Greek nurses to instruct him in the language of the people over whom he was to reign, and struck a medal representing on one side the head of the young prince, and on the other a cross in the clouds, from which a flash of lightning demolished the mosque of St. Sophia.

The person who had the greatest influence at St. Petersburgh, and who possessed the most extensive power over the empress, was prince Potemkin. He first introduced himself to the notice of Catherine at the revolution, became

---

ful family. Maria Theresa, however, had succeeded by means of her daughter, in gaining the acquiescence of Louis, notwithstanding the opposition of Vergennes; but the advancement of the young archduke was no less opposed by the king of Prussia, who exerted his powerful influence in the chapter to prevent the election.

afterwards her favourite, and though supplanted, contrived to retain his ascendency over her mind. Intimately acquainted with the temper and disposition of his sovereign, he made her weaknesses, her desires, and her passions subservient to the accomplishment of his views. With an imagination as romantic as that of his mistress, Potemkin promoted and even suggested her most visionary projects, and was the soul of all her schemes. He flattered her ruling passions, fostered the jealousy she entertained of her son the great duke, and found means to represent himself as the only person who, by extensive connections and interest, was capable of discovering and thwarting any project to place that prince on the throne wrested from his father. He counteracted the influence of count Panin, by representing him as the adherent of the great duke, and, by his sarcasms and ridicule, diminished the credit of prince Orlof, who, during the early period of her reign, had principally swayed the counsels of Russia.*

Count Panin, who had been governor of the great duke, was raised to the post of prime minister, from the opinion which the empress entertained of his integrity, and from his services in the revolution which placed her on the throne. He possessed, however, no personal influence over his sovereign, but was enabled to thwart or change the measures of government, by his acquaintance with the routine of office, and by the method he adopted of retarding or altering the public and private communications with foreign courts. He was cold and formal in his manners, indolent in business, and

---

* He was equally rapacious and extravagant, and though he held the chief command of the army, and was loaded with more honours, titles, and emoluments than ever before fell to the lot of a subject, he at one time aspired to become duke of Courland, at another hospodar of Moldávia and Wallachia, and even turned his views to the throne of Poland. He possessed great acuteness of understanding, versatile talents, desultory rather than extensive knowledge, and almost irresistible powers of ridicule. He was the slave of caprice, levity, interest, and vanity, and though naturally indolent and voluptuous, was roused by the impulse of the moment to uncommon deeds of activity and exertion. He followed no regular system of policy, but was wrought upon by the suggestions of fancy or interest, to adopt those of every country: he was by turns a partisan of England and of France, and during the Bavarian war, had been gained by the king of Prussia, who lured his ambition by offering to assist him in acquiring the duchy of Courland, and to negotiate a marriage between him and a German princess.

dissipated in society; but he was capable of almost impenetrable dissimulation, indefatigable in intrigue, and swayed most of the inferior agents of the court and cabinet. He was inveterate in his enmity to England and the house of Austria, and devoted to the king of Prussia, and by his means to the cabinet of Versailles.

Since the peace of Hubertsburgh, Frederic had paid assiduous court to the empress of Russia, and by the most unbounded flattery and affected deference, had conciliated her esteem and friendship. To consolidate his influence, his brother prince Henry had twice visited St. Petersburgh, and had effected a marriage between the great duke and the princess of Wirtemberg. He likewise confirmed the great ascendency which the king had gained over the prime minister Panin, who became so subservient to his views, as to consider the continuance of the Prussian influence necessary to the maintenance of his own.

For a considerable period of her reign, Catherine had adhered to the long-established friendship between England and Russia. She possessed too acute an understanding not to perceive that the interests of the two countries were inseparably connected; but she had been alienated and mortified by the frank and unbending spirit of the British cabinet, who would not condescend to gratify her insatiable desire of flattery, or concur in promoting her schemes of Oriental grandeur. The court of Versailles, with their usual address, had taken advantage of this alienation, had flattered her ruling passions, and affected to enter into all her schemes. She knew and despised the spirit of intrigue and duplicity which distinguished the French cabinet; but their adulation was so grateful to her feelings, and the partisans of France were so numerous in her court, that she was often led into measures which were contrary to her judgment and her interests. The king of Prussia, the bitter enemy of England, warmly promoted the designs of the French cabinet, and he was ably seconded by his creature count Panin. Their great object was, to draw the empress into a close connection with the house of Bourbon; with that view they concerted, directly or indirectly with Vergennes, the measures to be pursued by France, and Panin even sketched out the papers which were sent from the cabinet of Versailles, in a manner calculated to please and allure his imperial mistress. By these artifices

Catherine had not only been prevented from coming forward to the assistance of England during the American war, but had even been induced to publish the declaration which occasioned the armed neutrality : a measure calculated to introduce a new code of maritime law, hostile to our dearest interests, and tending to deprive us of the advantages derived from our naval superiority.

Such being the character of the Russian court, the views of Maria Theresa could not be effected by a common emissary, and Joseph himself undertook this important task. Availing himself of the intention of Catherine to visit her new acquisitions in Poland, he testified to prince Gallitzin, the Russian minister at Vienna, his earnest desire to be personally acquainted with so renowned a princess, and requested permission to pay his court to her during her journey. This mark of attention from the first sovereign in Europe flattered the vanity of Catherine. Sensible that without the assistance of Austria she could not realise her views on the side of Turkey, she blushed with joy when she received the intelligence, sent a cordial and friendly answer, fixing on Mohilef as the place of meeting, and at the particular request of Joseph, consented to wave all parade, etiquette, and superfluous ceremony.

The emperor reached Mohilef on the 23d of May, and on the 25th, the day of the empress's arrival, was presented to her by the imperial minister, count Cobenzl, under the title of count Falkenstein. The meeting of the two sovereigns was most cordial and friendly : Catherine, already prepossessed in his favour, was struck with his animated countenance, easy manners, agreeable behaviour, and lively conversation ; Joseph on his part took uncommon pains to strengthen this favourable impression ; he conformed himself entirely to her character and disposition, treated her with freedom mingled with respect, displayed that apparent candour which he knew how to assume, and, by the most delicate and artful flattery, wrought up her admiration of his character almost to enthusiasm. He likewise artfully affected to applaud her romantic schemes, and without giving a positive promise, succeeded in persuading her that he was inclined to promote her plans of Oriental aggrandisement. He at the same time gained prince Potemkin, by humouring his caprice, flattering his ambition, and luring him with a promise to

promote his views of becoming hospodar of Moldavia, and
even to assist his advancement to the throne of Poland.
Potemkin, who was jealous of Panin, eagerly received these
overtures, and promoted the designs of the emperor with all
his influence.

Catherine warmly pressed the emperor to prolong his stay,
and Joseph followed her to St. Petersburgh, where he continued till the latter end of July. This favourable reception
confounded count Panin and the Prussian party. In vain
they had attempted to prevent his visit, and they now as
vainly endeavoured to alarm their mistress, by representing
him as a prince wholly actuated by ambition, and who, under
the mask of candour and simplicity, concealed the most dangerous designs. Besides flattering and conciliating the empress and her powerful favourite, Joseph omitted no opportunity and neglected no means of securing the preponderance
he wished to gain in the cabinet of Russia. Aware that
France was attempting to counteract his efforts, he artfully
courted the friendship of the British cabinet, by promising to
exert his ascendency in favour of England, when he had
overthrown the Prussian party. The emperor found them
warmly inclined to concur in his views : fully sensible of the
inveterate enmity of Frederic, and of the disadvantages which
they had experienced from his intrigues, they eagerly seized
an opportunity which seemed likely to lower the influence of
so dangerous a rival, and to renew the connection with the
house of Austria. Fortunately the British minister at the
court of St. Petersburgh, Sir James Harris, afterwards earl
of Malmesbury, was well calculated to co-operate in so delicate an undertaking.

Aided by these means, and by his own consummate address, Joseph succeeded in annihilating the Prussian interest,
and in establishing his own on a permanent footing ; and thus,
by a singular combination in politics, the house of Austria,
the intimate ally of France, was supported by the British
ministry ; while the Prussian party was espoused with equal
warmth by the French minister, M. de Verac.

From the first interview at Mohilef the admiration which
Catherine had formerly expressed for Frederic II. rapidly
subsided. She talked of him as superannuated, rapacious,
wholly devoted to his own interests, and actuated by a perfidious and crooked policy ; while she launched forth into new

praises of the unaffected ease, openness, and amenity of
Joseph, and extolled him as one of the first characters of
the age.

Having fully succeeded in the grand object of his journey,
the emperor quitted St. Petersburgh in the latter end of July,
and the manner in which he took leave of his imperial
hostess will evince the affected candour, address, and flattery
by which he captivated her esteem.   " I have shown myself
as I really am, and have used neither art nor fallacy to your
imperial majesty; you are, therefore, in a situation to judge
of my character and merits, and as I am well aware that
from the moment of my departure attempts will be made to
calumniate and blacken me, I entreat you, before you give
implicit credit to such representations, to consult your own
judgment, and establish your opinion in consequence.   I am
no flatterer," he added, " but I will sincerely avow that your
imperial majesty has exceeded the high reputation you enjoy,
and shall always consider the few weeks I have passed in
your company as the most agreeable and profitable of my
life."   The empress, strongly affected with these expressions
of his esteem, which were heightened by his candid, yet dignified manner of delivery, shed tears, and, when he stooped to
kiss her hand, embraced him with great emotion.*

The absence of Joseph did not obliterate the favourable
impression which he had made on the mind of the empress,
and which was strengthened by a regular and intimate correspondence.   To regain his lost ascendency, Frederic sent his
nephew, the prince of Prussia, to St. Petersburgh; but in
this critical attempt the foresight of the wily monarch seems
to have failed.   The habits, character, person, and talents of
Frederic William were ill calculated to eclipse those of his
imperial rival; he was unwieldy in person, awkward in deportment, embarrassed in conversation; he did not, like
Joseph, come incognito, but as prince of Prussia; and his
establishment was formed by his uncle, with a singular mixture of rigid parsimony and affected pomp, which rendered
his mission ridiculous.   The empress received this visit with
extreme reluctance, and was as much prejudiced against the
prince as she had before been prepossessed in favour of the
emperor.   She detained him several days at Riga and on the
road, and, under various pretexts, delayed the interview till

* From private information.

the 27th of August. The manners and person of the prince did not remove her prejudices ; and she listened with pleasure to the railleries of prince Potemkin and the prince de Ligne on Prussian economy, as well as on the whimsical and motley appearance of the prince's attendants.

The interview was conducted with great pomp and etiquette, but was little satisfactory to either party ; the prince appeared to Catherine heavy and reserved, and her reception struck him as cold, formal, and unpromising. She could not conceal her disgust whenever her princely visitor was present, and though unusually affable to others, treated him even in public with scarcely common civility or attention. The nobility imitated the example of their sovereign ; the prince, unlike the emperor, was neither followed nor courted ; he was every where coldly received ; and these repeated mortifications rendered him still more embarrassed, awkward, and reserved. Notwithstanding his numerous and powerful friends, he did not succeed in any object of his mission ; the empress even hastened his departure by intimating to count Panim that his stay was irksome and disagreeable ; and he quitted St. Petersburgh displeased and disgusted, after having confirmed instead of diminishing the high opinion which Catherine entertained of the emperor, and sunk still lower the interest of his uncle.

All the attempts of Frederic to induce her to oppose the elevation of the archduke Maximilian to the coadjutorship of Munster were ineffectual. She not only gave a peremptory refusal to his instances, but expressed her resolution to assist the empress-queen with all her influence, and wrote to all her ministers in the empire to promote the election, which was accordingly carried into effect. This refusal publicly proclaimed the final overthrow of the Prussian ascendency ; and thus, in the last year of her reign, Maria Theresa had the satisfaction of re-establishing the ancient and important connection of the house of Austria with Russia.

CHAP. CXXIII. —1780.

THE peace of Teschen and the renewal of the connection with Russia were the last great acts of the reign of Maria Theresa. She had for some time suffered from an induration of the lungs, which at length became mortal ; and after a gradual decline, she was seized on the 19th of November with the illness which soon terminated her life.

During her grievous sufferings, which affected all who beheld her, she never uttered a single complaint, and scarcely gave signs of impatience ; and although inclined from education and habit to a minute observance of the ceremonies of the church, she did not discover the most trifling weakness in her devotions. Fully submissive to the decrees of Providence, and only apprehensive lest her frame should be unequal to support the pains of a mortal disease, and that the motives of resignation which she had drawn from reason and religion might lose their effect, should her understanding be impaired, " God grant," she exclaimed, " that these sufferings may soon terminate, for otherwise I know not if I can much longer endure them." With the same spirit she said to her son Maximilian — " My firmness and constancy have not yet abandoned me ; address your prayers to heaven, that I may preserve my tranquillity to the last moment." On recovering from a violent attack, which took away her senses, she was affected with the sight of the emperor, who had burst into tears. " I entreat you," she said, " to spare me ; my own sufferings do not appal me ; but the. consciousness of your affliction will take away all my firmness."

Having received the sacraments, she summoned her family into her presence, and thus addressed them : — " My dear children, I have just received the sacraments, and am satisfied that I have no hope of recovery ; you cannot forget the anxious solicitude with which the late emperor your father and myself have superintended your education ;" then turning to the emperor, " my son," she added, " as after my death all my possessions in this world belong to you, I cannot dispose of them ; my children alone still are, and will always be mine ; I deliver them to you, be to them a father. I shall die contented if you promise to take that office upon you ;" then, turning to the others, she said — "consider the emperor as your sovereign ; obey him, respect him, follow his advice, confide in him, love him sincerely, and you will be secure of his friendship and affection." She gave to each of them her blessing ; and, observing that they were all deeply affected, she calmly added — " retire into another apartment, and recover your spirits."

Each time that she was relieved from fits of suffocation
and fainting, and even on the evening which preceded the
day of her dissolution, she employed herself in explaining to
the emperor the state of affairs, and in dictating and signing
despatches. She wrote a letter to prince Kaunitz, expressing,
in the most obliging terms, her gratitude for his faithful
services ; she commissioned count Esterhazy, chancellor of
Hungary, to thank his countrymen for their fidelity and
zeal, which had secured her throne; and to entreat them to continue the same to her successor. During the night she held a
long conversation with the emperor, who perceiving her
exhausted state, entreated her to take some repose ; but she
replied — "In a few hours I shall appear before the judgment seat of God, and would you have me sleep ? "

In her last moments she regretted life, not for the loss of
worldly honours and regal power, but from an anxious
solicitude lest those numerous persons whom her secret
bounty had relieved, should be deprived of subsistence, when
the hand that supported them was no more ; and almost her
last words were — "I would wish for immortality on earth, for
no other reason than for the power of relieving the distressed."
She preserved a calm tranquillity, and even serenity of mind,
which seemed almost above the powers of human nature, and
could only be derived from an awful sense of religion, and
the recollection of a well-spent life ; she expired on the 29th
of November, 1780, in the sixty-fourth year of her age, and
the forty-first of her reign.

To the character of Maria Theresa, as exhibited in the
preceding pages, it is only necessary to add, that she was
easy of access to all her subjects, affectionate to her family,
kind to her domestics, and unboundedly charitable, but without ostentation. She combined private economy with public
liberality, dignity with condescension, elevation of soul with
humility of spirit, and the virtues of domestic life with the
splendid qualities which grace a throne. But it must not be
concealed that she was subject to the failings of human
nature, from which the best characters are not exempt. She
readily gave ear to spies and informers, encouraged tales
of private scandal, and indulged an unwarrantable curiosity
in prying into the secrets of families. From a spirit of unlimited devotion to the Roman Catholic faith, she was
superstitiously minute in her religious exercises, and her

zeal often degenerated into a culpable excess, and hurried her into acts of intolerance, which cast a shade on her memory.] Her death, however, was a general loss to the people, who adored her; her reign is considered as the best and most glorious æra of their history; and the halcyon days of Maria Theresa are still proverbial throughout the whole extent of the Austrian dominions.

Maria Theresa had by Francis six sons and ten daughters; of whom nine survived her.   Her sons were :

1. Joseph, who succeeded her.
2. Leopold, great duke of Tuscany, and afterwards emperor.
3. Ferdinand, who was appointed governor of Austrian Lombardy; and, in virtue of his marriage with Maria Beatrix, daughter and heiress of Hercules Rinaldo, duke of Modena, obtained the reversion of the duchies of Modena, Mirandola, and Reggio.   Before the departure of Ferdinand from Vienna to take possession of his government, several entertainments were given on that occasion.   Among others it was proposed to have a grand illumination at the palace of Schonbrunn; but, when the plan was presented to the young prince, he seemed thoughtful, sighed, and at length burst into tears.   The empress, observing his emotion, anxiously inquired the cause; " My dearest mother," he answered, " after so many feasts given for me, surely this illumination is unnecessary; it is expensive, and the pleasure will be only transitory. The dearness of bread, and the pressure of the times, have reduced many respectable families to extreme distress, and the money will be better employed in relieving the most indigent." Maria Theresa tenderly embraced her son, joined her tears with his, and gave him a considerable sum to distribute in charity.   The young prince passed the whole day in secretly relieving distressed objects, and the next morning he entered the empress's apartment with a countenance sparkling with delight, embraced her with transport, and enthusiastically exclaimed, " Oh, my mother, what a feast !"

4. Maximilian, grand master of the Teutonic order, coadjutor of Cologne and Munster, and elector of Cologne, April 15. 1784.   He died 1801.

Her surviving daughters were :

1. Mary Anne, abbess of Prague and Clagenfurth.
2. Mary Christina, married to Albert of Saxony, son of Augustus III., king of Poland.   He received on his marriage the principality of Teschen as an appanage; they were appointed joint viceroys of Hungary, and, on the death of prince Charles of Loraine, governors general of the Netherlands.   She was the favourite daughter of Maria Theresa, and inherited her personal attractions.
3. Maria Elizabeth, abbess of Inspruck.
4. Maria Amelia, who espoused Don Ferdinand, duke of Parma.
5. Caroline, queen of Ferdinand, king of Naples.   She owed her ele-

vation to the premature deaths of her two elder sisters, Joanna and Josepha. Joanna was betrothed, at the age of twelve, to the king of Naples, but died of the small-pox. Josepha was destined to supply her place, and in the bloom of youth and beauty, was affianced to Ferdinand, on the 8th of August, 1767. She was to have been married by proxy on the 14th, and preparations were even made for her departure. But she testified the deepest regret at quitting her family, and descended into the vault of the Capuchins, to enjoy for the last time the melancholy pleasure of weeping over the ashes of her father. In this agitation of mind she was seized with the small-pox, which in less than a week hurried her to the grave, on the very day appointed for the commencement of her journey.

6. Maria Antoinetta, married to Louis, dauphin, and afterwards king of France.

Chap. CXXIV.—REIGN OF JOSEPH II. —1780–1784.

The eyes of Europe were fixed upon the successor of Maria Theresa, as upon a sovereign in the prime of manhood, whose personal qualifications, as well as civil and military talents, seemed capable of raising the house of Austria to a greater height of splendour and power than had yet been attained.

Joseph II. born in 1741, was in the fortieth year of his age when he ascended the throne of his ancestors. He was endowed by nature with a lively disposition, quick parts, and an ardent temper ; but his education had been greatly neglected, and those who were placed about his person were wholly unfit for the purpose of forming a young prince to fulfil the important duties of his exalted station. His youthful mind, trained by dull pedagogues, who rendered learning distasteful, or instructed by bigoted monks, contracted an aversion for science ; and he did not discover the smallest inclination for any branch of literature. From this narrow mode of education he gave no early indication of that active and penetrating mind which he really possessed.

Towards the sixteenth year of his age he was roused from this state of apathy, by the great events of the seven years' war ; the exploits, resources, and victories of Frederic seemed to engross his mind, and inspired him with a desire of emulating the great rival of the house of Austria. Animated by this spirit, he desired to serve against the Prussians ; but this first display of energy being imprudently repressed, and his request rejected, he relapsed into his former apathy, and seemed only anxious to avoid exciting the jealousy of his parents.

In the twenty-fourth year of his age, being called by the sudden death of his father to the possession of the imperial dignity, appointed co-regent of the Austrian dominions, and intrusted with the command of the army, the activity of his character began to develop itself.

The long reign of his mother, the death of a beloved wife, the little share which he was allowed to enjoy in the administration of public affairs, and the leisure of a long and almost uninterrupted peace, left him at liberty to gratify his passion for useful knowledge. Europe saw and admired an emperor of Germany travelling without pomp, ostentation, or etiquette, affecting the frankness and simplicity of a private individual, examining with the minutest attention the naval and military establishments, the arts, manufactures, courts of justice, and charitable institutions, and exhibiting an example of indefatigable perseverance and rational observation, which no sovereign had displayed since Peter the Great. To these valuable qualities he joined an intense application to business, easiness of access, cheerfulness in society, vivacity in conversation, politeness in demeanour, sobriety and temperance, a contempt of fatigue, and disregard of danger. During his frequent journies in the Austrian territories he examined the situation of his subjects, particularly that of the lower classes; he visited the cabin of the shepherd, and the hut of the peasant, inquired into their wants, relieved their distresses, appeared anxious to abolish their servitude, and publicly declared that his greatest honour would be to rule over freemen.*

* Many instances of his attention to the distress of his subjects were recorded before his accession; two of which give striking proofs of benevolence and humanity. Hearing of an old officer, who had a large family without the means of providing for them, he unexpectedly called at his house, and finding eleven children, said, " I know you have ten children, but whose is the eleventh ?" " It is an orphan," replied the veteran, " whom I found exposed at my door, and I could not suffer it to perish for want of assistance." Joseph, struck with this act of humanity, said, " Let the children be in future my pensioners, and do you continue to give them examples of virtue and honour ; I settle upon each of them 200 florins a year, of which you shall receive the first quar-

To a benevolent temper Joseph united an aspiring mind, and was not deficient in that ardour for military glory which had distinguished the most illustrious of his ancestors. During the Bavarian war he displayed more eagerness to engage than Frederic himself; he shared the hardships,

ter to-morrow: I myself will take care of your eldest son, and, as an earnest of my future intentions, give him the commission of a lieutenant."

Another time, as he was passing through the streets of Vienna, he saw a young woman with a bundle in her apron, seemingly plunged in the deepest affliction. Struck with her youth and distress, he delicately inquired into the cause of her grief, and learned that the contents of her bundle were some clothes of her mother, which she was going to sell as their last resource. " I never expected," she added, sobbing, " that we should be reduced to such extreme penury, as my mother is the widow, and I the daughter, of an officer, who served with distinction in the army of the emperor, but without meeting the recompence he had a right to expect."

" You ought," replied Joseph, " to have presented a memorial to the emperor; have you no friend or acquaintance, who could recommend your case to him?" She then named a courtier who had repeatedly promised to do it, but whose recommendation had failed of success; and she did not conceal her opinion of the emperor's want of generosity. " You have been deceived," he replied, suppressing his emotion; " had the emperor known your situation, he would not have withheld his assistance; he has been misrepresented to you; I know him well, and his love for justice; prepare a memorial, and bring it yourself to-morrow to the palace; if your circumstances are such as you describe, I will present you and your memorial, and second your request: nor will my interference, I trust, be ineffectual." The young person, overcome by this unexpected kindness from a stranger, broke forth into expressions of gratitude, which Joseph interrupted by saying, " In the mean while you must not sell your clothes; how much do you expect to get for them?" She answered, " Six ducats;" " Allow me to lend you twelve," replied the emperor, "until we know the success of our application." He then took his leave; and, having informed himself of the truth of her story, expected her at the appointed time and place, but, on her not appearing, despatched a messenger for her and her mother.

When the young woman returned home, her description of the person and manners of the stranger convinced her friends that he was the emperor, and she was so much shocked at her freedom in censuring the conduct of her sovereign, that she had not courage to appear before him. Being at last prevailed upon to repair to the palace, she fainted in his presence. On her recovery, the emperor sent for her and her friends into the closet, and delivering to her a pension for her mother, equal to the appointments of her father, he said, " I entreat you and your mother to excuse the delay which has been the cause of your embarrassment. You are convinced, I trust, it was on my part involuntary; and should any one in future speak ill of me, I only require you to be my advocate."

fatigues, and dangers of the soldiers*; slept on the bare ground, skirmished with the advanced posts, led reconnoitring parties, and the whole army joined in the exclamation of a grenadier, — "Why should I complain of dangers, when I see the crown of my sovereign as much exposed as my cap!"

With the advice and assistance of marshal Lacy, he new-modelled the army, and introduced that wonderful system of order and economy which so highly distinguishes the military constitution of Austria. His accession was hailed as the commencement of a golden age, which was to surpass the glory of ancient periods, and shame the boasted exertions of modern times. With such omens of greatness and splendour did the new sovereign begin his auspicious reign; but these flattering predictions were not realised; nor does any instance occur in history of a prince who more disappointed the expectations of mankind, and who died less esteemed, and less regretted, than Joseph II.

In tracing the reign of Joseph, which, though a period of only ten years, contains a multiplicity of events that materially affected the interests of the house of Austria, we shall first direct our attention to his plans of reform.

Before we attempt to sketch a detail of these numerous and complicated plans, it will not be improper to review the situation of his vast empire at the time of his accession. The Austrian monarchy, comprising an extent of 180,000 square miles, and peopled with 24,000,000 of inhabitants, was composed of as many nations as provinces, differing from each other in language, religion, government, laws, customs, and civilisation. The greater part formed one large and compact body; others, as the Netherlands, Lombardy, and the possessions in Suabia, were separated from each other, and without communication either among themselves or with the great mass of the hereditary countries. The feudal system generally prevailed; in some parts modified by written laws, or local customs; in others, as in Hungary, existing in all its primeval absurdity and oppression. The clergy and nobles were all-powerful, the citizens in little estimation, and the peasants, except in the Netherlands Tyrol, and Austria Proper, in a state of vassalage. The

* " His toilette," observes his biographer, " is that of a common soldier, his wardrobe that of a sergeant, business his recreation, and his life perpetual motion."

Roman Catholic was the dominant religion, and the clergy possessed enormous riches, power, and influence. Each province was represented by an assembly of states, composed of the nobility and clergy, and a few deputies from the free and royal cities, who divided with the sovereign the right of administering justice and imposing taxes, which principally fell upon the lower class of people. A monarchy so constituted could not acquire that vigour which ought to result from its extent and population. Every province was divided from the others; all the bonds which connect the subjects of a large empire were broken; and the only tie which preserved their union was the sovereign. Poverty, wretchedness, and oppression were the lot of the greater number; ignorance, pride, and corruption formed the character of the smaller body.

Maria Theresa, at an early period of her reign, had turned her attention to the deplorable situation of her subjects. She had abridged the enormous privileges of the nobility and clergy, and lightened in many instances the yoke which oppressed the peasants. Her innovations were moderate and gradual; but the progressive mode was ill-suited to the sanguine temper and impatient spirit of Joseph, who, not content with following his mother's example, in sowing the seeds of improvement and suffering them to grow up to maturity, was anxious to reap the harvest before it was ripe.

He formed the grand but impracticable plan of abolishing all distinctions of religion, language*, and manners, by declaring that in future there should be no more provinces, but one nation, one family, and one empire. He purposed to unite all these different kingdoms and nations into one great body, governed by one simple system of administration, and actuated by one common interest, both moral and political; he purposed to deliver the peasants from feudal oppressions, to annihilate superstition, and encourage industry, agriculture, arts, commerce, and manufactures; to infuse into the great political mass a force proportionate to its size, and adapted to its situation in the midst of Europe, surrounded by powerful enemies and jealous neighbours.

In the Austrian dominions ten principal languages are spoken; German, Hungarian, Sclavonian (including the Polish, Bohemian, and Illyrian dialects), Latin, Wallachian, Turkish, modern Greek, Italian, Flemish, and French.

In conformity with these views, Joseph first abolished the numerous and separate jurisdictions, and divided the Austrian monarchy into thirteen governments*, each of which was subdivided into a certain number of circles or districts, proportionate to its extent.   Over each circle presided a magistrate called captain of the circle, who superintended the execution of the laws, and protected the peasants from the oppression of the feudal system.   In the capital of each government was established a court of justice, divided into two tribunals, one for the nobles, and the other for the lower classes, from the decision of which an appeal lay to a second, then to a third court, and finally to the supreme tribunal at Vienna.   To a subordinate magistrate was intrusted the care of the police; over him were placed a military commander and a governor general, who presided in the tribunals.   Thus the whole administration was composed of four departments, political, economical, judicial, and military.   All these respective officers were subordinate to the councils or chanceries of state at Vienna, whose resolutions were delivered to the sovereign for his final ratification or rejection.

Although Joseph simplified the form of government, and abolished many useless tribunals, and feudal offices, which were dilatory and oppressive, he yet introduced a still greater evil, by making the basis of the administration the absolute will of the sovereign, from which there could be no appeal. In the prosecution of this scheme he committed many violent and arbitrary acts of authority.   The provincial states, which limited the power of the crown, were either entirely suppressed, or rendered inefficient by various modifications. Although he had acknowledged the rights and privileges of the Hungarian states by his circular letter on the death of his mother, yet he declined the ceremony of coronation, from an unwillingness to confirm those rights and privileges by a solemn oath.   He wantonly ordered the crown, sceptre, and other emblems of royalty, which the nation cherished with superstitious reverence, to be forcibly carried from Pres-

---

* 1. Gallicia.   2. Bohemia.   3. Moravia, with Austrian Silesia. 4. Lower Austria.   5. Interior Austria, or Styria, Carinthia, and Carniola.   6. Tyrol.   7. Exterior Austria, or the possessions in Suabia. 8. Transylvania.   9. Hungary, with the Bannat of Temeswar.   10. Croatia.   11. Lombardy.   12. The Low Countries.   13. Goritz and Gradisca, with the city of Triest.

burgh, and deposited at Vienna. By abolishing the use of the Latin and Hungarian tongues in all the public offices, and substituting the German (for the acquisition of which only two years were allowed), he not only introduced great confusion into the departments of state, but justly alarmed the natives, lest the abolition of those languages, in which their statutes, charters, and capitulations were composed, should lead to the suppression of their privileges. In new-modelling the courts of justice in Hungary, he totally changed the forms, usages, and times of assembling, and introduced so much disorder, that it was thought necessary by his successor to re-establish the ancient tribunals with all their imperfections.

Joseph declared the Roman Catholic the dominant religion; but, at the same time, diminished the exorbitant authority of the pope ; he forbad the bishops to carry any bull into execution, unless confirmed by government, subjected monastic establishments to the jurisdiction of their respective diocesans, and exempted them from all obedience to their chiefs resident at Rome. He lessened the revenues of the largest bishoprics, suppressed some, and created others ; and, for the purpose of facilitating access to public worship, established four hundred new parishes. He suppressed many monasteries, and all the nunneries except the Ursulines and the Salesians, which were preserved for the purpose of education ; but the number of the members permitted to remain was considerably reduced.* The suppressed convents were converted into hospitals, universities, barracks, or military magazines. In abolishing the monasteries he was guilty of great injustice, by not allowing sufficient pensions for the maintenance of those who were ejected ; and many nuns, who from education and long habit were incapable of providing for themselves in the world, were reduced to the lowest state of indigence and distress.

With the laudable view of purifying religion from the dregs of superstition, pilgrimages were forbidden, many of the churches were stripped of their images and ornaments, and reduced to their primitive simplicity. A politico-moral catechism† was composed for the use of schools, and intro-

* In 1780, were 2024 convents in the Austrian dominions, which were diminished to 700 ; and 36,000 monks and nuns to 2700.

† As a specimen of many of the childish and ridiculous regulations of Joseph, we submit to the reader a few extracts from this poli-

duced in the instruction of youth.   In making these alterations, Joseph did not duly reflect that, in abolishing the
forms, he injured the substance of religion, among a people
long accustomed to consider the essence of adoration as consisting in external ceremonies, and not sufficiently enlightened
to appreciate a more simple form of worship.   Primogeniture
was abolished, and marriage degraded almost to a state of
concubinage, by declaring it a civil contract, facilitating
divorces, and rendering bastards capable of inheriting.
Funeral honours were forbidden; and because all are reduced
to a level in the grave, all were to be interred with the same
ceremonies, without distinction of birth or situation; thus
imprudently checking one of the first affections of the human
mind, the display of virtuous respect to the memory of deceased relations, which, though often carried to excess by
useless pageantry, has never been productive of the smallest
inconvenience to the state.

But the wisest and best digested part of his plan, and
which continued longer than his other innovations, was the
edict of toleration, issued on the 13th of October, 1781, and

tico-moral catechism, which was intended for the common people, and in
which the references are profanely made to his acts in the same manner
as to the Bible in the ordinary catechism :

" Thou shalt not send any money into foreign countries for masses."

" Thou shalt not appear at processions with costly flags, nor dressed
with sashes, or high feathers in thy hat, nor with music."

" Thou mayest purchase and read the Catholic Bible, which is approved by the imperial censors."

" Thou mayest obtain from thy bishop a dispensation for marriage,
where there is no natural or religious order to the contrary."

·" Thou shalt not seek for any dignity of the court of Rome, without
the permission of thy sovereign."

" Thou shalt not bring into the land any foreign breviary, missal, or
psalter, or other similar work or paper."

" Thou shalt forbear all occasions of dispute relative to matters of
faith ; and thou shalt, according to the true principle of christianity,
affectionately and kindly treat those who are not of thy communion."

" Thou shalt not hold in thy house any private assembly for devotion."

" Thou shalt not in anywise use the crown of St. Christopher, or other
superstitious supplications."

" Thou mayest marry the woman whom thou has ravished, if she is
willing to marry thee when she is out of thy power."

" Thou shalt not transport out of the land, hares' skins, or hares' fur."

" Thou shalt not keep any useless dogs."

" Thou shalt not plant tobacco without the permission of thy lord."

afterwards enlarged at different intervals. By this edict he
granted to all members of the Protestant and Greek churches,
under the denomination of Acatholici or Non-catholics, the
free exercise of their religion. He declared all Christians
of every denomination, equally citizens, and capable of holding all charges and offices in every department of state ; he
permitted every community consisting of 3000 souls, resident
in any town, to build a church, provided they could establish
a permanent fund for the support of a preacher and the relief
of the poor ; and he ordered a new translation of the Bible to
be made in the German tongue. On the Jews he also conferred many liberal privileges, and granted to them the right
of exercising all arts, and trades, following agriculture, and
freely pursuing their studies at the schools and in the
universities.

These innovations introduced with such precipitancy by the
first sovereign of Europe, whose ancestors had evinced so
warm an attachment to the Catholic faith, alarmed the see of
Rome, and occasioned the memorable journey of Pius VI. to
Vienna. After an intimate but ineffectual correspondence,
the pope, who was vain of his eloquence, hoped by his personal interference, to arrest the progress of these dangerous
reforms. The unbending spirit of Joseph did not brook this
interference, and he declared that the presence of the pope
would not change his resolutions. Pius, however, persisted,
and notwithstanding his advanced age, weak state of health,
and the severity of the season, commenced his journey on the
27th of February, 1782.

The head of the church was received with every mark of
exterior homage and veneration : the emperor met him at
some distance from the capital, alighted on his approach,
and, after the most respectful salutations, conveyed him in
his own carriage to Vienna. Attended by prince Kaunitz,
Joseph accompanied the pope to the private chapel, where a
Te Deum was sung in honour of his arrival ; and the
venerable guest was lodged in the apartments which had
been occupied by Maria Theresa. The pontiff, however,
obtained only these and similar marks of distinction ; his
exhortations and remonstrances were received with coldness
and reserve, and he was so narrowly watched, that the back
door of his apartments was blocked up to prevent him from
receiving private visitors without the knowledge of the em-

peror. Even his presence at Vienna did not for a moment suspend the progress of the ecclesiastical reform ; the arch-bishop of Goritz, who had distinguished himself by his opposition to the imperial edicts, was sent in disgrace to his diocese, and several convents in Lombardy were suppressed.

Pius, chagrined with the inflexibility of the emperor, and mortified by an unmeaning ceremonial, and an affected dis-play of veneration for the holy church, while it was robbed of its richest possessions, and deprived of its most valuable privileges, quitted Vienna at the expiration of a month, equally disgusted and humiliated, after having exhibited himself as a disappointed suppliant at the foot of that throne which had been so often shaken by the thunders of the Vatican.

The abolition of feudal vassalage formed another part of the general reformation. Joseph issued in 1780 the cele-brated edict for the regulation of taxes, which, by altering the impost on land, was intended to give full liberty to the peasants, and effect the abolition of slavery. Having ordered a measurement of all the estates in his hereditary countries, he abolished in his German dominions all feudal distinctions and manorial rights, such as tithes, heriots, and corvées, or task works, due from the peasants to the lord. And as one of the pretences that attached the peasants to the soil was the responsibility of the landlords for the payment of the land-tax to the crown, he exempted the lord from that responsibility, empowered the peasants of every village to choose among themselves a representative for the purpose of collecting the land-tax, and paying it into the exchequer ; and rendered the whole village accountable for the regular discharge of the amount. Although reason and humanity may vindicate this attempt to diminish the evils of feudal vassalage, yet justice must condemn the mode of proceeding ; because sufficient precautions were not taken to indemnify the landholders for the loss they sustained, and because the new land-tax was raised in some instances to the enormous amount of sixty per cent. Hence this decree failed of producing the effects which the monarch designed, and prevented the introduction of the same regulations into Hungary and the annexed provinces.

In one particular Joseph surpassed his rival Frederic II.; though illiterate himself and not affecting to honour or patronise men of letters, he encouraged the arts and sciences, and contributed more to the advancement of learning, during his short reign, than any other sovereign in Europe. In every province he instituted or improved an university, academy, or seminaries, founded or augmented public libraries, created establishments for the study of medicine, surgery, and botany, natural philosophy, and natural history, and built numerous observatories and laboratories. He took away from the priests the power of censuring books, a power which they had hitherto exercised with such rigour, that on subjects of religion, morality, and government, a valuable and a prohibited publication were almost synonymous terms; this office he vested in a committee of men of letters at Vienna, whose liberal views were directed to encourage the freedom of the press. Yet the same sovereign who affected to give full scope to the liberty of the press, and declared that he wished to reign over free men, checked the improvement of the human mind; he set bounds to inclination and curiosity, by decreeing that no one should travel into foreign countries before the age of twenty-seven. He did not consider that talents are developed in some sooner than in others; and that unless every person is allowed to follow the mode of instruction congenial to his peculiar disposition and habits, the delightful enthusiasm of letters will be ill supplied by the most perfect theoretical rules which despotism or pedagogues can invent.

Joseph was highly attentive to the encouragement of manufactures and the improvement of commerce. Large sums were lent to merchants; poor artists were supplied with money, either without, or at a low interest, or were assisted in erecting buildings and machinery. From a well-meant but erroneous system of policy, the importation of foreign manufactures was forbidden, except on the payment of an enormous duty, which amounted to a prohibition; domestic fabrics were supported, and others of cotton, wool, and glass established. He removed all obstacles to a free circulation of trade, by suppressing the provincial custom-houses, and by permitting the import and export of the native productions which had been hitherto prohibited. New roads were made at an enormous expense *; canals dug or improved; Triest

* The new road from Carlstadt to Carlobago did not cost less than 2,000,000 florins, or 200,000*l.*

and Fiume declared free ports; and a harbour formed at Carlobago, in Austrian Dalmatia.

But among his numerous attempts to extend the commerce of his subjects, Joseph was peculiarly attentive to encourage the trade of Hungary, whose productions, consisting chiefly of wines, grain, forage, and heavy commodities, could not be transported by land to any considerable distance. The ports of Fiume, Segnia, and Carlobago being too distant, and the canal of Morlachia too tempestuous, the Danube, which, dividing Hungary and receiving all the navigable streams, forms an outlet to the Black Sea, afforded the only means of opening so valuable a trade. And as that river, from the confines of the Bannat, flows through the Turkish territories, he obtained from the Porte, in 1784, the free navigation of the Danube, the Black Sea, and the Dardanelles; and granted to a company of Italian merchants an exemption from all duties, and a bounty on grain exported from Hungary and the annexed provinces. In 1786 the first effort was made ; twenty vessels, freighted with corn, descended the Danube to its mouth, the grain was then embarked in ships which had sailed from Triest and Fiume, and landed at Genoa and Marseilles. But in 1787, this valuable trade was annihilated by the impolitic war with the Turks, which terminated at once the aspiring views of Joseph and the hopes of the Hungarian nation.

CHAP. CXXV. — 1781–1785.

THE connection with France which Joseph inherited as a legacy from Maria Theresa, and which, under her prudent management, had been of considerable advantage to the house of Austria, proved the source of the principal embarrassments in his reign. The dislike which he had formerly manifested, seems to have increased on his accession ; and during the first months of his reign he openly declared his aversion to the French court and French principles ; but before the close of the year, a second journey to Paris effected a total change in his sentiments. This change was occasioned by his eagerness to execute a project he had long meditated for abrogating the Barrier Treaty, which his family regarded

as an humiliating tie of dependence on the maritime powers.
The court of Versailles availed themselves of the ardour of
Joseph in prosecuting his favourite schemes to effect the
abolition of a treaty which formed the only bond of the
ancient union between the house of Austria and England,
and to secure the influence which the emperor had acquired
in the councils of Russia. Instead, therefore, of the reserve
which they had maintained during his former journey, they
received him with marks of the highest confidence and cordiality, gave him hopes that they would encourage and promote all his projects, and succeeded in persuading him that
the power of England was hastening to its decline.   The
queen likewise furthered the views of the ministry, by all the
arts of insinuation which she possessed in so eminent a
degree; and by exerting her powerful influence over the
mind of her brother, she succeeded in eradicating the prejudices he had fostered against her husband.   Flattered by
these attentions, and buoyed up by the assurances of the
French court, Joseph peremptorily declined an invitation of
George III. to extend his journey to England, a country
which he had been long anxious to visit; and returned to
Vienna full of confidence in the alliance with France, and
with new resolutions to hasten the abrogation of the Barrier
Treaty.

From the conclusion of the peace of Aix-la-Chapelle to
the commencement of the seven years' war, the empress-
queen had been engaged in continual disputes with the Maritime Powers, relative to the repairs of the fortifications and
the payment of the annual subsidy; and her refusal to fulfil
all the conditions was the principal cause which occasioned
the rupture of the long-established friendship between Austria and Great Britain, and the connection with France.
The alliance between Austria and France rendered the
Barrier Treaty an empty name, and virtually, though not
formally, annulled its influence. But Maria Theresa, too prudent to throw herself wholly into the arms of France, firmly
resisted all the solicitations of her son to drive the Dutch
garrisons from the Netherlands, and to abolish the Barrier
Treaty by a formal act.

Joseph was too sanguine and impetuous to forego present
advantages from the apprehension of uncertain and distant
inconveniences. Aware that the fortifications of the barrier

towns were nearly dismantled, and that great expense would
be requisite to place and keep them in repair, he saw no
medium between their total demolition and total restoration.
He had not sufficient sagacity to appreciate that in the grand
scale of comprehensive politics, the Barrier Treaty was in-
trinsically advantageous to the house of Austria ; for as long
as it remained in force, the French could not overrun the
Netherlands without involving themselves in a war with the
Maritime Powers.   In fact, he considered his alliance with
France as permanent, beyond the possibility of change ; and
his sentiments were expressed by Kaunitz, in a conversation
with count Wassenaar, plenipotentiary from the United Provinces : — " The emperor will hear no more of barriers, for
they no longer exist ; every treaty of which the basis is overturned, loses its effect : the Barrier Treaty was concluded
against France, but now our connections with France render
it null, and afford a more secure barrier than the other, which
was chimerical."   To the observation of Wassenaar, that in
this world systems are apt to change, Kaunitz replied, " The
connections which the house of Austria has formed are the
consequences of a fixed and premeditated system ; they are
not calculated to last only for a short time, but will at least
continue in force a hundred years.   Even should a minister
start up in the cabinets of Versailles or Vienna, sufficiently
insane to attempt breaking these connections, he will be sent
to the madhouse, instead of succeeding in abolishing so firm
and well cemented a system.   The emperor acts for your advantage, nor have you any cause of apprehension either from
him or from France."

Such was the haughty and peremptory answer which
Joseph, by the mouth of Kaunitz, gave to the remonstrance
of the United Provinces ; and such was the weak and misguided policy of a sovereign, who in less than seven years
beheld his connection with France dissolved, and the Netherlands separated from the Austrian dominions.   It did not
escape the penetration of Joseph that the war between Great
Britain and Holland presented an opportunity which might
never again occur, to facilitate the execution of his designs.
He had therefore scarcely returned from France, in November, 1781, before he issued orders to demolish all the fortifications of the Netherlands except Luxemburgh, Ostend, and
the citadels of Namur and Antwerp ; and this decree was

followed by a requisition delivered to the States General, requiring them to recal their garrisons from the barrier towns. After an ineffectual remonstrance the states submitted, and the Dutch troops evacuated all the places in the Austrian Netherlands.

The facility with which Joseph carried this point induced him to enlarge his views, and to demand that the limits of Austrian Flanders should be re-established, as they had been fixed by the convention of 1664, between the king of Spain and the United Provinces. He began by asserting his new pretensions in an extraordinary manner; in November, 1783, a Dutch soldier of the garrison of Leifkenstock, a small fort on the Scheldt, being, as it was customary, buried in the village of Doele, the sovereignty of which was claimed by the house of Austria, a detachment from the garrison of Ghent dug up the body and threw it into the ditch of the fort. Another corps marched from Bruges, and occupied the Dutch forts of St. Donat, St. Paul, and St. Hiel, and some other districts. In the beginning of the following year also, a detachment from Antwerp surprised Old Lillo, a fort near New Lillo, where the Dutch ship which guarded the entrance of the Scheldt was stationed.

With a view to terminate these disputes, conferences were held at Brussels, between the imperial and Dutch plenipotentiaries, in April, 1784; and Joseph increasing his demands, brought forward numerous claims besides that of re-establishing the ancient limits of Flanders.

While the plenipotentiaries were discussing these claims, the negotiation suddenly took a new aspect. In August, 1784, Joseph had declared that he would desist from all his pretensions, under the sole condition that the navigation of the Scheldt should be opened, and that his subjects of the Netherlands should be permitted to carry on a direct commerce with the East Indies; he peremptorily added, that from that moment he would consider the navigation of the Scheldt as open, and regard any opposition on the part of the States General as an immediate declaration of hostilities. During these transactions, an imperial brigantine from Ostend, attempting to enter the Scheldt, was on the 5th of October taken by the Dutch at the mouth of that river, and conducted to Flushing; and another vessel from Antwerp was stopped at Saffinguen by a Dutch brig, and after refusing to return, was fired at and forced to strike.   The emperor little expected such acts of firmness and vigour ; for at this moment the Netherlands were unprovided with troops and magazines. • He was in fact convinced that the Dutch would not venture to stop the imperial vessels, and in reply to the remonstrances of prince Kaunitz to take the necessary precautions should they fire, he repeatedly answered, " they will not fire !" When the account of their resistance reached Vienna, Joseph was in Hungary ; and Kaunitz accompanied the despatches from Brussels with the brief remark " but they have fired!"   Instantly the conferences at Brussels were broken up ; the imperial ambassador recalled from the Hague, and orders issued for a large body of troops to march to the Netherlands, and attack the United Provinces.   The Dutch on their part made the most vigorous preparations ; and the two powers appealed to the other nations of Europe. The United Provinces were secretly instigated by offers of succour from the king of Prussia ; the emperor confided in the hopes of assistance from Russia and France, and these petty disputes seemed on the eve of exciting a general war.

Suddenly, however, Joseph listened to the remonstrances of Holland ; he receded from his demand of opening the navigation of the Scheldt, and all other claims excepting the cession of Maestricht ; but he required exemplary satisfaction for the insult offered to his flag, as an indispensable preliminary to the renewal of any negotiation.   This sudden change in the sentiments of so impetuous and inflexible a sovereign as Joseph, was owing to the opposition of France, on whose effectual assistance he had fondly established his expectations of success.

Hitherto the cabinet of Versailles had appeared to act in conformity with the wishes of the emperor ; they had encouraged him to abrogate the Barrier Treaty, and even affected to concur in his attempts to extend the limits of Austrian Flanders.   But they were unwilling to alienate the Dutch, with whom they were on the point of concluding an alliance, the object of which was to weaken the British power in the East Indies.   They therefore opposed the opening of the Scheldt, and the king, in a note to the court of Vienna, declared his resolution to support the Dutch by force of arms ; while he offered his mediation to compose the dispute.   At the same time orders were given to form two armies of ob-

servation in the neighbourhood of Luxemburgh and on the
Rhine, and the French court even complied with the request
of the Dutch in sending the count de Maillebois as generalissimo of their forces in the place of prince Louis of Baden,
who had been compelled to resign.

This intervention was equivalent to a command. Joseph
saw too late the folly of throwing himself into the hands of
France, and had no other alternative than to retract in the
manner least injurious to his dignity and honour. He now
endeavoured to compensate in solemnity and show for what
he lost in substance, and to impose upon Europe by imperious
language, while in fact he relinquished the principal points
from which he had publicly declared his resolution never to
recede. His honour was apparently saved, and his pride
gratified by the arrival of the count de Wassenaar and the
baron de Leyden, two deputies from the United Provinces,
who apologised for the insults offered to the imperial flag.
At the conclusion of this mock ceremony, the negotiation
was renewed at Versailles under the auspices of France.
The emperor, after changing his ground from the free navigation of the Scheldt to that of the Maes, and from the
cession of Maestricht to the demand of an indemnity, finally
limited his claims to a sum of money as a compensation for
his pretensions, and an indemnification for the damages
suffered by his subjects, from the inundations made by the
Dutch in the environs of their fortified places. This sum,
after long debates, was fixed by the emperor at 10,000,000
guilders, and the 21st of September as the term which should
decide on peace or war. But as the Dutch plenipotentiaries
were not authorised to agree to the payment of more than
8,000,000, and as the imperial ministers were bound by
express orders, the negotiation was on the point of being
broken off, when France agreed to disburse the additional
two millions. The preliminary articles were concluded at
Paris, September 20. 1785, and the definitive peace signed at
Fontainbleau, on the 8th of November, under the guaranty
of France. By this treaty the emperor renounced all right to
the free navigation of the Scheldt, beyond the limits of his
own territories, which ended in the county of Saffinguen,
and his pretensions on Maestricht and its dependencies. In
return he received 9,500,000 guilders as an indemnity for
Maestricht, and its adjacent territories, and 500,000 as a

compensation for the damages caused by the inundations ; he also acquired the forts of Lillo and Liefkenstock, and the limits of Dutch Flanders were reduced, according to the convention of 1664. During the course of the negotiation, the Dutch required the renovation of the treaty of 1731, which excluded the Flemings from the commerce of the East Indies ; but Joseph resisted this demand, and exacted that no mention should be made of the navigation of his subjects to the East, and that each power should be at liberty to form its own regulations of commerce.

Thus ended a dispute which at first seemed to threaten the peace of Europe ; but which after the most violent threats and pompous discussions terminated in a pecuniary accommodation, and in a manner predicted by Frederic II., who during the negotiation, said to general Bouillé, " Vergennes will compel the most serene republic to purchase an accommodation with our brother Joseph, by giving him drink money." *

Chap. CXXVI. — 1784–1786.

WHILE the attention of Joseph appeared to be solely engrossed by his contest with Holland, he was involved in two projects no less difficult ; to extend his dominions on the side of Turkey, and to obtain Bavaria in exchange for the Netherlands. With a view to secure the assistance of Catherine in his meditated plan of aggrandisement, he zealously promoted her projects for the extension of her power in the East, and directed his principal attention to increase the ascendency which he had gained at St. Petersburgh.

The overthrow of the Prussian influence was completed by the disgrace of count Panin, and a closer and more intimate union was formed between the two imperial courts. No formal treaty was indeed concluded, because Catherine insisted on an alternate signature of the respective copies, as sovereigns of equal rank. Joseph could not make a concession so derogatory to the imperial dignity ; he urged that he held his right from the electors, to whom he was responsible for its preservation, and that no sovereign in Europe

* Alluding to the custom of giving postilions money to drink.

had hitherto refused to give precedence to the imperial crown. Catherine asserted her claim with equal obstinacy, and declined purchasing even his desired alliance at so humiliating a price. At length the difficulty was adjusted; a compromise, proposed by Catherine, was accepted by the emperor, and instead of a specific treaty, the stipulations were comprised in a secret convention, drawn up in the form of letters, which were respectively addressed and signed by the two sovereigns. The conditions were, a defensive alliance and general guaranty of their respective dominions; and the stipulated succours, as well as the period of its duration, were limited.

Encouraged by this prospect of assistance, the empress hastened to execute her plans for the acquisition of the Crimea. The independence of that peninsula was in fact only another name for its dependence; and its separation from the Ottoman empire a prelude to its subjugation. Catherine, availing herself of the article in the peace of Kagnardji, which stipulated that the khan should be confirmed by Russia as well as by the Porte, obtained the election of her creature Sahim Gheray, and supported him in his dignity in opposition to the Porte, and to a party of his own subjects, who chose another sovereign. He was scarcely seated on the throne before he was prevailed upon or compelled to abdicate and cede the Crimea to his protectress. Repenting of this act, he made his escape, and attempted to put himself at the head of the Turkish party, but was arrested and sent a prisoner to Voronetz, and the Russian generals took possession of the Crimea in the name of their mistress. The Porte preparing to avenge this infringement of the neutrality, and to recover so important a territory, the renewal of hostilities seemed inevitable.

Catherine made the most vigorous exertions, and claimed the promised assistance of the emperor. Nor did Joseph belie his engagements; his internuncio at Constantinople declared to the Porte that the two imperial courts would act in perfect concert; and at the same time an Austrian army advanced towards the Turkish frontiers. In his private correspondence, likewise, with Catherine, he evinced extreme ardour to promote her views, and declared that he was not only ready to fulfil his duty as an ally, but she might employ him to the whole extent of his faculties; she might consider him as her general, and his army as her own. To his zealous co-operation the empress owed her success; for the Porte, awed by the formidable preparations of the two imperial allies, shrunk from the contest, and concluded, on the 9th of January, 1784, the convention which transferred to Russia the sovereignty of the Crimea and of the Kuban.

The conduct of Joseph in this transaction appears extremely impolitic, and even almost without a motive; for he affected great disinterestedness, and expressed his resolution to accept no compensation for himself, while he assisted in securing so great an acquisition to Russia. In reality he was eager to share in the spoils of the Ottoman empire; and he had coveted Moldavia and Wallachia; but finding the empress averse to his acquisition of those countries, he grasped at the recovery of the Ultra-Danubian provinces, and was secure of the support of Catherine, who expressed her readiness to repay the essential service he had rendered in the conquest of the Crimea.

In these views he was again thwarted by the secret interposition of the French cabinet, who had acted with their usual address and duplicity: they had encouraged the Turks to resist the encroachments of the two imperial courts; sent engineers to fortify the strong places on the side of the Danube, and endeavoured to form a coalition with England for the protection of the Ottoman dominions. Their proposals being rejected, they consented to the acquisition of the Crimea by Russia; but turned their efforts to obstruct the aggrandisement of the house of Austria on the side of Turkey. They expostulated with the emperor, threatened him with the formation of a confederacy with the kings of Prussia and Sardinia, and seemed resolved to throw all Europe into combustion rather than permit any further dismemberment of the Turkish empire. Joseph, apprehensive for the safety of his Italian dominions, as well as for that of the Netherlands, which he had rendered totally defenceless, and failing in his attempts to engage the support of England, relinquished his schemes of conquest, and again sullenly yielded to the peremptory mandates of the court of Versailles.

Notwithstanding his disappointment and disgust at being thus doubly foiled after his extensive preparations, he did not break off his connection with France, but fondly hoped for her concurrence in another object of greater importance, which he had long meditated, and which was the secret motive of all his recent transactions in the Netherlands. This project was to obtain Bavaria in exchange for the Austrian Netherlands.

Bavaria contained a population of 1,200,000 souls, whose number might, under an able administration, be soon doubled, and yielded a revenue of 60,000,000 florins, capable of considerable increase by the augmentation of the taxes, and by the suppression of several convents, whose annual income exceeded 2,000,000 florins. The possession of Bavaria would unite the German dominions and Hungarian provinces into a compact and solid mass, and extend the Austrian territories and influence, in a continued line from the confines of Poland and Turkey to the frontiers of Alsace and the shores of the Mediterranean. Foiled in his attempts to acquire Bavaria by force of arms, he now endeavoured to obtain his object by different means.

He maintained that influence over the cabinet of Munich which he had acquired during the negotiations for the peace of Teschen, and finally persuaded the elector to exchange Bavaria for the Netherlands (Namur and Luxemburgh excepted), to be erected into a kingdom, with the revived title of Austrasia or Burgundy. He was well aware that as the acquisition of Bavaria would render him the virtual sovereign of all the south of Germany, the exchange would meet with a decided opposition from the king of Prussia; from the princes and states of the empire; from Great Britain and Holland, without whose concurrence as joint guarantees of the Barrier Treaty, the Netherlands could not be alienated; from the king of Sardinia, who could not without a jealous eye behold the house of Austria connecting Bavaria with the Tyrol, and thus obtaining a free access into Italy; and from his subjects in the Netherlands, who would object to the transfer of their country, as an infringement of their liberties.

Joseph foresaw these obstacles, and did not neglect the necessary precautions to render them ineffectual. By co-operating against the Turks he had already secured the assistance of Russia; he had gained France by the offer of Namur and Luxemburgh, and looked forward with confidence to her zealous concurrence. He considered Great Britain as not yet recovered from the distresses occasioned by the American contest, and as both unable and unwilling to enter into a continental war in support of the Barrier Treaty. He hoped to gain the United Provinces by offering to relinquish his demands for the free navigation of the Scheldt, and for the cession of Maestricht, and by lowering his claims; or if mild and conciliating measures failed of success, he resolved to extort their consent by an army of 80,000 men, who were marching towards the Low Countries.

But he principally founded his hopes of success on the active assistance of Russia, and Catherine prepared, with unabated zeal, to promote the meditated exchange. In January, 1785, count Romanzoff, her minister at Frankfort, made a verbal proposal to the duke of Deux Ponts, requesting his concurrence, as presumptive heir of Charles Theodore, to the cession of Upper and Lower Bavaria, the Upper Palatinate, the duchy of Neuburgh, the principality of Sultzbach, and the landgraviate of Leuchtenberg; in return, the elector was to receive the Austrian Netherlands, except Namur and Luxemburgh, with the title of king of Burgundy. The consent of the elector, he added, had been already obtained, and France and Russia would guaranty the exchange. On the score of population, revenue, and local situation, he magnified the advantages on the side of the elector, requested the duke to give an answer within eight days, and peremptorily declared that his opposition would not prevent the exchange.

But this deep-laid scheme of policy was again thwarted by the great rival of the house of Austria, who, at the advanced age of seventy-four, still retained the spirit and vigilance which had distinguished his early years. He again privately offered his protection, and encouraged the duke of Deux Ponts to reject the proposal. By his advice the duke publicly appealed to France, Prussia, and Russia as guarantees of the peace of Teschen; by his suggestion, also, the states of Bavaria presented a strong remonstrance against the projected exchange; by his representations the princes and states of Germany were roused by an exaggerated list of grievances, and the precipitate and arbitrary conduct of Joseph was delineated in the most glowing colours. Frederic expatiated on the unjust claims of the emperor to the Bavarian succession, exposed his total disregard to treaties by the

resumption of the Barrier towns, and the proposal for opening the navigation of the Scheldt, and excited a serious
apprehension lest the same principles should be extended to
the affairs of Germany. He at the same time made a spirited
remonstrance to the court of Versailles, accused them of
being bribed by the offer of Luxemburgh and Namur to acquiesce in so flagrant a violation of public law and the constitutions of the empire, and testified his resolution to spend
his last moments in asserting the liberties of Germany
against the tyranny of its chief.

A general alarm was thus spread from one part of the
empire to the other, and the elector of Bavaria, in consequence of a demand made by the states of the duchy, delivered a notification, asserting that the reports of a convention
between him and the emperor were unfounded ; and that the
only treaty which he had concluded, related to an adjustment of limits, which he communicated to them.

Joseph had now reduced himself to a critical dilemma.
He appeared as much astonished at this sudden and decided
opposition as if he had not foreseen the smallest obstacle, and
had expected an unlimited obedience to his dictates. He
first preserved a sullen silence ; but, at length, disavowed any
intention of extorting the acquiescence of the duke of Deux
Ponts, while he asserted the legality of the exchange, if made
with the consent of all parties. He insinuated that he had
not authorised the proposals of the Russian minister ; and
Catherine endeavoured to save the honour of the emperor,
by declaring that she had ordered count Romanzoff to suggest
the exchange, from a conviction that the advantages to both
parties would be reciprocal ; but as the duke of Deux Ponts
had declined acceding, she had no intention to enforce its
execution. France also made the same declaration.

This disavowal did not satisfy either the king of Prussia
or the princes and states of Germany ; for, as it appeared, as
well from the manifestos of France and Russia, as from the
declarations of the emperor, that the plan had been relinquished, not from any conviction of its injustice or impro-
priety, but because the duke of Deux Ponts had withheld his
consent, it followed, that should, on any future occasion, the
house of Austria be enabled to obtain the concurrence of that
branch of the Palatine family, the exchange might yet be
effected, notwithstanding the stipulations of the peace of

Teschen. The king of Prussia therefore proposed to revive
the league of Smalkalde, and formed the Germanic Union,
or confederacy of the princes and states, for maintaining the
indivisibility of the Germanic body in general, and of the
respective states in particular. This union, signed at Berlin
on the 23rd of July, 1785, between the king of Prussia, the
king of Great Britain, as elector of Hanover, and the elector
of Saxony, was afterwards joined by the elector of Mentz, the
margrave of Anspach, the duke of Deux Ponts, and other
princes; and under the ostensible pretext of preserving the
constitution of the empire, became a formidable bar to the
encroachments of the house of Austria.

Filled with resentment and alarmed with apprehensions of
this league, Joseph in vain represented it as founded on the
ambitious and interested views of the king of Prussia, whom
he contemptuously styled Anti-Cæsar, as tending rather to
disturb than promote the peace of the empire, and as imposing
shackles on the princes and states ; he also attempted to form
a counter-confederation, and prepared for immediate hostilities. But the general disapprobation of the German states, the
vigorous preparations of Prussia, the firm countenance of the
confederate princes, the indecision of the elector of Bavaria,
the conviction that France would not engage in a war to
support his pretensions, that Holland was neither to be intimidated by menaces nor lured by promises, and that Great
Britain was resolved to oppose the transfer of the Austrian
Netherlands, the rising discontents in Hungary, and an insurrection in Transylvania, scarcely quelled, compelled him
to adopt pacific views, and finally to relinquish the projected
exchange.

CHAP. CXXVII.—1786–1788.

THE Germanic League, the last hostile act of Frederic II.
against the house of Austria, was effected under the pressure
of those infirmities which soon afterwards hurried him to the
grave. He had been some time afflicted with the dropsy and
a complication of disorders ; but preserved the vigour of his
administration and exerted the powers of his mind almost to

the last moment. He died on the 17th of August, 1786, in the 75th year of his age and in the 47th of his glorious reign.

It is needless to dwell on the character or exploits of a prince so well known in history; it will be sufficient to observe that his acquisitions added a population of 2,000,000 souls to his paternal inheritance, that he almost doubled his revenues, that he left a treasure of 8,000,000 sterling, and an army of 200,000 men, the best disciplined troops in Europe. He thus raised and consolidated a power which had long been a thorn in the side of the house of Austria, and which under his reign began to divide the German empire, and to be a counterbalance to the influence arising from the vast extent and numerous population of the Austrian territories.

The death of the king of Prussia was followed by an essential change in the system of European policy. Before that event the ascendency of France had for some time been paramount in Europe. During the American contest she had consolidated a confederacy which almost isolated England from the powers of the Continent, and had finally succeeded in severing the colonies from the mother country. But she derived no cause of exultation from her success; her navy was almost annihilated, her commerce nearly ruined; above all, her finances were reduced to an alarming state of dilapidation, and an annual deficit of nearly three millions sterling threatened a national bankruptcy. This deficiency had been long felt; but the secret had been confined to the principal members of government, and its effects concealed; while the evil itself was aggravated by the delusive system adopted by Necker of anticipating the revenue.

To these embarrassments were added the rising spirit of republicanism, which was naturally derived from the interference of France in the American contest, and a just punishment for her impolicy and ill faith in fomenting and supporting rebellion. Although the French cabinet, by their confident boasts, and by the activity and address of their agents, endeavoured to maintain their ascendency, they could not wholly conceal their real situation, and sunk in influence and credit, while England, on the contrary, began to rise in the scale of Europe.

After a period of twelve years, the administration of lord North was dissolved by its own weakness and the ill success of the contest in America, and a new ministry formed of which lord Rockingham was the head, but of which Mr. Fox, who principally directed the department of foreign affairs, was the efficient leader. At this juncture the brilliant victory of Rodney in the West Indies, revived the spirit of the nation, while it disabled the marine and baffled the hopes and plans of the house of Bourbon. But as it was now too late to recover America, the British cabinet testified an inclination for peace ; relinquished those lofty demands of unconditional submission which the late administration had so weakly supported ; and agreed to acknowledge the independence of the colonies as the basis of a negotiation. They again accepted the proffered mediation of Austria and Russia ; but instead of implicitly trusting to the interference of lukewarm friends or treacherous allies, they despatched Mr. Grenville to Paris to open a direct negotiation with the French minister.

In the midst of these transactions the death of lord Rockingham occasioned a partial change in the ministry. Mr. Fitzherbert (afterwards lord St. Helens), who was in consequence deputed to Paris in the room of Mr. Grenville, fulfilled his delicate office with great ability and address : while he treated with Vergennes, he succeeded in alarming Franklin, Adams, and Jay, the three American commissioners, and prevailed on them to sign separate and provisional articles, which severed America from France.* Vergennes, thus baffled

---

* Although this negotiation was carried on at Paris, even Vergennes, with all his penetration, was ignorant of the transaction until the articles were signed. The following incident induced the American commissioners thus to contravene the treaty with France, by which it was stipulated that neither of the contracting parties should conclude a peace, or even a truce, except by mutual consent. The French cabinet, however, exulting in the separation of the colonies from England, were apprehensive lest the formation of an independent republic in America might ultimately prove prejudicial to France, and occasion the loss of their West India Islands. Vergennes therefore sent to Marbois, French minister at Philadelphia, a long list of questions relative to the most effectual means of preventing the internal growth, and checking the external power of the new republic. The answer to these questions formed a voluminous report, containing a regular and systematic plan for exciting such a spirit of discord, not only in the several states, but even among different classes of individuals, as would have almost reduced the country to its state of original wildness and barbarism. This despatch being intercepted by a British cruiser, was shown to the American com-

and unable to prosecute hostilities, acceded to the terms of
peace, and a treaty was concluded at Versailles on the 3rd of
September, 1783. Great Britain acknowledged the independence of the American colonies, and ceded East Florida
and Minorca to Spain. To France she restored the river
Senegal, with several forts on the African coast, a small
accession of territory in the East Indies, and the island of
Tobago in the West Indies; to which were added the full
sovereignty of the islands of St. Pierre and Miquelon on the
coast of Newfoundland (before possessed by France), under
certain restrictions, together with a more advantageous
arrangement of the respective fisheries. England also consented to abrogate the article of the peace of Utrecht, which
related to the demolition of the fortifications of Dunkirk.

The trifling advantages which France had procured for
herself and Spain were greatly inadequate to the enormous
expenses of the war ; but she exulted in having wrested the
colonies from the mother country*, and anticipated the advantages expected to be derived from the diminution of the
British commerce and power. The same opinion prevailed
throughout the Continent ; and the court of Vienna in particular prophesied that England would ultimately sink in the
unequal contest with the house of Bourbon. Nor were there
wanting even in England persons of enlightened minds, who
regarded this peace as the ruin of their country, and who
predicted that "the sun of Great Britain was set for ever."
But such persons did not appreciate the energy of the British
constitution, the resources of the country, the character of
the people, and their spirit of commercial enterprise.

By the equivocal conduct of the emperor, England had
been alienated from the house of Austria. After assiduously
courting the British cabinet, he had betrayed their con-

missioners. The indignation of Adams and Jay was roused at this instance of perfidy ; they thought themselves justified in acceding to separate articles with England; overruled the opposition of Franklin, who
was inveterate in his animosity to the mother country, and by threats
deterred him from disclosing the secret to the French minister.

* It was a singular coincidence of events that this treaty, the source
of so much triumph and exultation to Louis XVI. and his court, was
signed on the 20th of January, and that on that very day ten years, the
unfortunate monarch was sentenced to the scaffold, the fatal consequence
of the republican spirit which had been introduced and fostered by his
impolitic interference in the American contest.

fidential communications to the court of Versailles, had exerted his influence at St. Petersburgh in favour of France, and to gratify the empress, had even acceded to the armed neutrality. The breach was widened by the abrogation of the Barrier Treaty. Notwithstanding his professions at the commencement of the war, Joseph had countenanced the American agents, and connived at the clandestine trade which his subjects of the Netherlands carried on with the rebellious colonies. When the British cabinet accepted his mediation in conjunction with that of Russia, he proposed such terms as could only have been dictated from Versailles; and affected to prophesy that the issue of the contest would be fatal to England. The indignation naturally excited by such unfriendly conduct, had been still further heightened by the recent attempt of Joseph to exchange the Netherlands for Bavaria. The British cabinet therefore at length relinquished those hopes, which had been too fondly cherished, of renewing the ancient connection ; they turned their whole attention to gain the king of Prussia, who, except in his inveterate enmity to the house of Austria, was guided by principles totally contrary to those of his predecessor ; and by his assistance succeeded in overthrowing the French influence in Holland. Since the peace of Aix-la-Chapelle, France had gained a considerable ascendency in the councils of the United Provinces, and was supported by the party adverse to the house of Orange. During the seven years' war the states had maintained a neutrality, and in the American contest had displayed such an evident partiality towards France and the rebellious colonies, as involved them in hostilities with England. This war promoted the ascendency of France ; the conclusion of the disputes with the emperor led to a formal alliance, which was signed at Fontainbleau, November 10. 1785, and soon afterwards the anti-Orange party, or patriots, succeeded in overthrowing the authority of the stadtholder.

The prince of Orange being supported by numerous adherents, endeavoured to recover his authority by force of arms, and the country was threatened with the horrors of a civil war. Attempts were made by the mediation of France and Prussia to appease these troubles; but as France was anxious to maintain the patriot party, and as Frederic was lukewarm in his support of the prince of Orange, who had espoused his niece, their intervention failed of success.   The new sovereign, Frederic William, who was warmly attached to his sister, was anxious to adopt a more efficient line of conduct, and was easily instigated by England to take a part in the affairs of Holland.   The arrest of the princess by the patriots, in her journey towards the Hague, furnished a pretext for hostilities, and the Prussian troops, led by the duke of Brunswick, made the conquest of Holland with a rapidity and success which astonished Europe.   The states were compelled to rescind their resolutions, and the prince of Orange was restored to his former authority.

During these events France had evinced a resolution to support the patriot party by arms ; but awed by the hostile preparations of England, and checked by the increasing embarrassments in her finances, she shrunk from the contest, and yielded the preponderance in Holland to her rival.   This revolution was followed by an alliance between the Maritime Powers and Prussia, and their united influence baffled the ambitious projects of Joseph for aggrandisement on the side of Turkey.   France, thus deserted by Prussia, threatened by England, and deprived of her influence in Holland, began to turn with warmth and sincerity towards the court of Vienna. The death of Vergennes, which happened at the commencement of 1787, had diminished that systematic jealousy which had been fostered against the house of Austria.   The new minister, Montmorin, and afterwards de Brienne, archbishop of Thoulouse, courted the emperor as their only stable and powerful ally ; and he seemed equally desirous to avail himself of their favourable disposition.

In consequence of these hopes, Joseph received the news of the death of his great rival Frederic with perfect indifference; and instead of attempting to execute his usual threat, that he would seize that opportunity to recover Silesia, he sent assurances of his pacific inclinations to Berlin, received the Prussian minister with great complacency, and testified an earnest desire to live on terms of amity with the new monarch.

Chap. CXXVIII.—1787–1790.

ALTHOUGH Joseph had privately encouraged the patriots of Holland, and gave to the adherents of France an asylum in the Netherlands, he took no public part in their favour; but considered the contest simply as the means of employing the arms of Prussia, while he pursued his plans for sharing with Russia the spoils of the Turkish empire.

The acquisition of the Crimea having rather increased than satisfied the ambition of Catherine, she displayed on every occasion a resolution to subvert the Ottoman empire. She had secured the support of Joseph; she had gained the friendship of France by concluding, in January, 1787, a league of amity and commerce, and by refusing to renew the former treaty with England. She revived the ancient Greek names in her new territories on the Black Sea; her consuls and agents were employed in exciting discontents among the Greeks and other Christian subjects of the Porte; and with a view to awe or conciliate the Tartar hordes bordering on the Turkish empire, she made a progress into the southern provinces of European Russia, with a pomp and magnificence suitable to the grandeur of her projects. Accompanied by the principal persons of her court, as well as by the Austrian, English, and French ministers, she took her departure at the commencement of the year, travelled by land to Kiof, and on the approach of spring 1787, embarking on the Dnieper, descended to Cherson. In the first part of this journey, pioneers preceded to level the way; the road was illuminated by bonfires, and lined with crowds of spectators; a flotilla of magnificent barges was prepared for her voyage*; the inhabitants of whole villages, with numerous flocks and herds, were removed to the banks of the river; and a desolate and inhospitable region assumed the appearance of felicity, population, and industry. Large bodies of troops were also collected at different places: at Krementschuck 14,000 men, dressed in new uniforms, exhibited the manœuvres of a battle; and at Pultawa the empress was gratified with an exact representation of the celebrated

* One of these vessels is said to have contained seven apartments, and a saloon where forty persons might dine.

victory gained by her predecessor Peter the Great over Charles XII.

Joseph availed himself of this journey as a pretext for paying another visit to his ally, that they might in person complete arrangements for partitioning their intended conquests. He reached Lemberg in the middle of April, and after waiting twenty days, proceeded towards Cherson, the place appointed for the interview. He arrived there on the 14th of May, and, eager to display his respect towards his ally, hastened to meet her on the journey. His impatience occasioned some embarrassment. The courier who conveyed the news of his departure, found the barge aground; and Catherine, unwilling to be surprised in that situation by her imperial visitor, instantly disembarked, and with the greater part of her suite proceeded by land. On the approach of Joseph she alighted, and after the accustomed salutations, the two sovereigns pursued their journey in the carriage of the empress. At Kaidak a singular scene took place. In consequence of Joseph's precipitancy, no preparations could be made for his reception. Prince Potemkin, who was waiting the arrival of the imperial flotilla, had already finished his repast, and the autocrat of all the Russias, with the emperor of Germany, could not without difficulty procure even a scanty meal. But this disappointment afforded matter of mirth, and gave to Catherine an opportunity of displaying her ease and hilarity. Joseph, who from his usual mode of travelling, was not unaccustomed to similar privations, bore his part with equal spirit and good humour; the wit and raillery of Potemkin contributed to enliven the scene, and the two sovereigns condescended to assist in preparing their scanty meal, of which they partook with more enjoyment than they had before derived from the greatest luxuries of the table.

From Kaidak they proceeded to Cherson, where Catherine made a magnificent entry, passing under a triumphal arch, on which was inscribed in the Greek tongue, "The way to Byzantium." After a stay of four days, distinguished by exhibitions of uncommon magnificence, she continued her progress through the Crimea, which she had recently distinguished by the Greek appellation of Taurida.

In this journey every species of splendour, which the fertile and romantic genius of Potemkin could invent, was exhibited to grace the presence of his sovereign. At Batcheserai, the capital of the peninsula, she was lodged in the ancient palace of the Khans, and entertained with the spectacle of a burning mountain, artificially illuminated; at Sebastapol she viewed with pride and exultation a powerful navy, her own creation, riding in the finest harbour of the Black Sea.

Joseph accompanied the empress during this progress, although he had previously received notice of the rising discontents in the Netherlands, and his presence was required at Vienna. But it was observed that he had lost much of that native vivacity which marked his first visit to Russia, and was absorbed in continual reflection, brooding over his various projects of reform and the increasing embarrassments of his reign. On his return to Perislaf, on the bank of the Dnieper, he took leave of his imperial hostess and hastened to Vienna.

The specific arrangements made during this journey have never been divulged. But the encroachments and intrigues of Russia, the petty warfare on the Turkish frontier, the hostile preparations of the two imperial courts, and the circumstances of this ostentatious journey, drew from the Porte a sudden declaration of war against Russia on the 15th of August; and a Turkish squadron appearing at the mouth of the Dnieper, commenced hostilities by bombarding Kinburn.

Confounded at this unexpected and vigorous measure, Catherine affected to temporise; and offered terms of accommodation through the mediation of France. At the same time she accelerated her preparations, published a vindication of her conduct, and called for the stipulated assistance of the emperor.

By this summons Joseph was reduced to a critical situation. Mortified at witnessing the importance of those acquisitions which he had contributed to secure to Catherine without obtaining an equivalent, he was eager to make amends for his former disappointment. But his alarms were awakened by the close union between the courts of London and Berlin; he was embarrassed by the efforts of the French court to prevent the dismemberment of the Ottoman empire; and above all he was unwilling to engage in a Turkish war, while so considerable a part of his military force was required to quell the insurrection in the Netherlands. He therefore endeavoured to temper the ardour of his ally, and protract the commencement of hostilities. By his internuncio at Constantinople he declared that he would succour Russia, if attacked ; yet proffered his mediation to prevent the effusion of blood. Like Catherine, however, he did not intermit his military preparations; and bodies of troops, with large magazines, and a numerous train of artillery, covered the Danube, or filled the roads from the capital to the Turkish frontier. He pursued this dubious line of conduct till he had effected a temporary suspension of the troubles in the Netherlands ; and while his internuncio was acting the part of a mediator at Constantinople, he attempted to surprise the fortress of Belgrade.

A considerable force, collected in the neighbourhood of Semlin, prepared in the night of the 2nd of December to cross the Danube and the Save in two columns; one led by Alvinzy, the other by Gemmingen. Their march being obstructed by the badness of the roads and darkness of the night, and the passage of the rivers impeded by a thick fog, the vanguard alone of the first column reached the place of rendezvous, which was a neck of land on the Turkish territory, under the walls of Belgrade. In this situation they were discovered at the approach of dawn, and exposed to inevitable destruction had they been attacked by the garrison. But the governor affecting to be satisfied with the apologies of Alvinzy, permitted them to withdraw, and they repassed the Save with great precipitation.

This flagrant violation of public faith did not, however, provoke the Turks to commence hostilities. They made a dignified appeal to the gratitude of the emperor ; they reminded him of the inviolable faith with which they had observed the treaty of Belgrade by rejecting all the allurements of France and Prussia on the death of Charles VI., when the very existence of the house of Austria was endangered. Such motives had little influence on the mind of so ambitious a monarch as Joseph, eager to signalise his arms, and to share in the spoils of a feeble enemy. He accordingly published on the 10th of February, 1788, a declaration of war, in which he did not even attempt to varnish pis aggression with the slightest colour of equity ; he did not charge the Turks with a single infraction of the peace ; he only justified his attack by pleading his engagements with the empress of Russia, and inveighing against the obstinacy of the Porte in rejecting her demands.

When Joseph made this declaration, he not only meditated the recovery of Bosnia and Servia, but grasped at the possession of Moldavia and Wallachia, and flattered himself with the hopes of extending the boundaries of his empire to the Dniester. Instead, therefore, of acting as a mere auxiliary, he came forward as a principal in the war. He had already assembled an army of 200,000 men, with a train of 2000 pieces of artillery, on the Turkish frontier, and impatiently waited the approach of spring to take the field.

The two imperial allies prepared to direct their force against the whole extent of the Turkish frontier from the Adriatic to the Black Sea. The main body of the Austrians was assembled on the borders of Sclavonia, to open the campaign with the siege of Belgrade, and to direct its progress on the side of the Danube; the principal force of the Russians, under prince Potemkin, was collected on the Bog, to pursue the advantages gained the preceding year; and a considerable corps uniting with an Austrian force under the prince of Coburgh in the Bucovina, was to reduce Chotzim, and co-operate with the main armies on the Sereth, the Pruth, or the Dniester. Besides these three armies, other bodies were stationed in Transylvania, the Bannat, Sclavonia, and Croatia, to connect or support the principal attacks. An armament was to be despatched to the Archipelago, to favour the progress of Potemkin; and Joseph not only persuaded the bashaw of Scutari to raise the standard of revolt, but even hoped to draw the Venetians into the war.

The most sanguine expectations prevailed that the war would be conducted with spirit and success equal to the magnitude of the preparations, and the vast designs of the sovereign. But the plans of the allies were frustrated by unexpected obstacles. The equipment of the naval armament was prevented by the opposition of England and Holland, who forbade their seamen to enter into the service of Russia; and an attack from the king of Sweden, equally sudden and daring, called the whole attention of Catherine to the preservation of her capital. The greater part of her troops who were marching to the scene of action were countermanded, and instead of a formidable force the prince of Coburgh was joined by Soltikof with only 10,000 men.

Joseph experienced a new disappointment from the resolution of the Venetians to maintain a neutrality, notwithstanding all the promises and threats of the two imperial courts. The bashaw of Scutari also, discouraged by the embarrassments of the allies, massacred the Austrian officers whom he had received at his court, and made his peace with the sultan; and his example was followed by the neighbouring bashaws, who were wavering between their duty and dread of his power.

Instead of compensating for the weakness of his ally by his own strenuous exertions; instead of pressing the siege of Belgrade before the enemy were capable of interrupting his operations, Joseph wasted the early part of the campaign in inaction, vainly waiting for the advance of the Russians, and dreading lest he should draw on himself the whole force of the grand vizier. At length the consciousness that his indecision had dishonoured his character in the eyes of his army, his people, and Europe, impelled him to undertake the siege; bridges were thrown over the Save, and a train of battering artillery drawn from Semlin and the neighbouring garrisons. But his tardiness exposed him to the very danger which he had so anxiously endeavoured to avoid. At the commencement of the campaign the grand vizier Yusuph assembled his army in Bulgaria, as a central point from which he could equally make head against the Austrians or Russians. By a judicious system of defence, he baffled and harrassed the Austrians, by desultory attacks he inured his troops to the sight of the enemy, and by a series of trifling successes inspired them with unusual confidence. Being relieved from all apprehensions of the Russians, he turned his whole force against the Austrians. He advanced towards Belgrade, and as the emperor precipitately retired behind the Save, he threw bridges over the Danube at Cladova, broke the Austrian cordon by defeating a corps under Wartensleben posted on the heights of Meadia, spread alarm and devastation through the neighbouring districts of the Bannat, and threatened to pour his victorious troops into Hungary.

The affairs of the emperor were now in the most alarming situation. He had fallen from his towering hopes of subverting the Ottoman empire, and in the middle of a campaign commenced with the most powerful army which the house of Austria had ever brought into the field, and with preparations which almost exceeded belief, saw the war carried into his own dominions. His troops were disheartened by ill success, and confounded at the desperate courage of the enemy. The army was thinned by an epidemic malady, and the population of the hereditary countries drained for recruits to supply the vast deficiency derived from disease and the sword ; the treasury was exhausted, and the populace of the capital, irritated by the dearness of provisions, broke out into tumults.

In this perilous situation Joseph left 30,000 men at Semlin, and hastened with 40,000 to support Wartensleben and cover Hungary. To divert the tide of misfortune he also transferred to Loudon, whom he had hitherto neither employed nor consulted, the command of the army in Croatia, with distinguished marks of honour.

The people and the army were equally gratified by this appointment. The journey of the veteran general from the capital to the frontier was a triumphal procession, and the soldiers received their commander near Berbir with as much enthusiasm as if they had gained a decisive victory.* Loudon did not suffer this ardour to cool, and commenced offensive operations, so congenial to his character and talents, on the 26th of August. The very day after he joined the army, he defeated the Turks under the walls of Dubitza, and soon reduced the fortress to capitulate. He threw bridges over the Save, dispersed a corps of observation encamped near Berbir under the bashaw of Travnic, and pushing into the heart of Bosnia, invested Novi. The trenches were opened on the 11th of September, the second parallel completed the third day, and the siege prosecuted with the greatest activity ; a body of 7000 Turks who attacked the Austrian lines were repulsed ; two assaults were made against the place, and on the 3rd of October, the garrison surrendered prisoners of war. The approach of winter alone retarded the successful progress of this active commander.

During these operations the prince of Coburgh, in conjunction with Soltikof, had laid siege to Chotzim, which from the exposed situation of the works was expected to

* Loudon had always disapproved of a defensive war, and his constant axiom was, that more men are lost by sickness or desertion in inaction, than fall by the hand of the enemy in the most bloody campaign.

prove an easy conquest. The batteries were opened on the 20th of July; but notwithstanding an incessant fire, which laid the town in ashes, and ruined the principal magazine, the heroic governor, with his half-famished and intrepid garrison, did not surrender till the 20th of September, when he was allowed to depart with the honours of war. This obstinate and almost unparalleled defence wasted the season of action, and prevented the allies from undertaking any other important enterprise during the remainder of the campaign.

While Loudon and the prince of Coburgh were thus retrieving the honour of the Austrian arms, the emperor was exposed to new disgrace. After his junction with Wartensleben he took post near Slatina in the valley of Caransebes. The clamours of the troops and the representations of his officers having induced him to summon a council of war, all the generals, except Lacy, declared for an immediate engagement: but the emperor, affecting to adopt the opinion of his confidential adviser, remained on the defensive. His caution, however, was of little avail against his enterprising antagonist: for the Turks, encouraged by his indecision, with incredible labour formed batteries on the neighbouring hills, and made a continual attack on his camp for two days and nights. Joseph succeeded indeed in repulsing the enemy; but surrounded with difficulties, and apprehensive of another assault, he broke up his camp during the night of the 20th of September, and fell back to Temeswar. This retreat completed the disgrace of his arms. Indignation, confusion, and dismay, pervaded the ranks. The night was dark, and a false alarm having put the troops in motion, all who were attached to the baggage took to flight, and the soldiers fired on each other. The emperor, who was in an open chaise at the head of one of the columns, mounted a horse, and attempted to rally the fugitives at a bridge, but was hurried away by the crowd, and separated from his suite. In this situation he rode alone the distance of a German mile before he was able to rejoin his troops.* In this confusion part of the baggage and artillery fell into the hands of the enemy, and 4000 men were lost in a march of only four days.

* Joseph reproached his aid-de-camps for having deserted him. One of them sarcastically replied, " We used our utmost endeavours to keep up with your imperial majesty, but our horses were not so fleet as yours."

Fortunately for the emperor, general Fabris kept the Turks in check by defending the passes of Transylvania, and the commencement of the rainy season compelled the vizier to withdraw from the Bannat. He placed a strong garrison in Viplanka, and marching towards Belgrade, was followed by the emperor, who resumed his former position at Semlin. No important operation, however, took place, except the capture of Viplanka by a detachment under general Harrach, and in November the campaign was closed by an armistice of three months for Sirmia and the bannat of Temeswar.

Thus terminated a campaign in which 30,000 men fell in desultory skirmishes, and 40,000 were swept away by pestilence ; losses but poorly compensated by the capture of Szabatch, Chotzim, Dubitza, and Novi. Joseph himself, afflicted with a disorder derived from fatigue and chagrin, returned to Vienna, brooding over the loss of his military reputation, and the distress and disgrace which he had brought upon his people and his army.

In 1789 the Turks anticipated the Austrians, by re-commencing hostilities at an early season. The grand vizier, leaving troops on the lower course of the Danube to observe the Russians and Austrians, crossed the river in March, 1789, at Ruschuk, with 90,000 men, and rapidly advanced towards Hermanstadt, with the intent to penetrate into Transylvania, break the Austrian line, and carry the war into the hereditary countries. His progress was suddenly arrested by the death of the sultan Abdelhamen and the accession of Selim, for he was recalled and disgraced by the new sovereign, assassinated in his way to a place of exile, and his post given to the bashaw of Widdin, a man of a rash and presumptuous temper, and deficient in military skill.

By this fortunate revolution, the allies were enabled to recover their ascendency. Early in the year the prince of Coburgh, proceeding with 18,000 men from Chotzim to Adjud, was joined by 7000 Russians under the celebrated Suwarof. On the 31st of July they defeated, at Fotzani, a body of Turks who had advanced from Brachilow to prevent their junction, with the loss of their camp, baggage, magazines, and artillery. They then suddenly directed their march against the main army, under the grand vizier, who had ascended the Alt to Rimnik, and gained, on the 22nd of

September, a stupendous victory over a vast and ill organised multitude. The whole army was dispersed or put to the sword, and the camp, baggage, and artillery, with no less than one hundred standards, fell into the hands of the conquerors.

This great victory opened a similar career of success to the main army, and Loudon, on the 3rd of September, invested Belgrade. He pressed the siege with his usual activity, carried the suburbs by assault, and completed the third parallel. On the 6th of October, the governor proposing an armistice for fifteen days, Loudon briefly replied, " Not for fifteen hours." He ordered the cannonade to be resumed with redoubled vigour, and within three days the garrison of 7000 men surrendered prisoners of war.

Joseph, sinking under the disorder which carried him to the grave, was revived by this series of successes. The sick and exhausted monarch rose from his bed to receive the joyful tidings, and attend a Te Deum at the church of St. Stephen. A festival was proclaimed for three days ; the capital was illuminated, the theatres opened gratis to the people, and, in allusion to the christian name of Loudon, the streets resounded with the triumphal song of Gideon. The successful commander was also nominated generalissimo with the same uncontrolled authority which had been formerly intrusted to prince Eugene.

The victory of Rimnik and the capture of Belgrade were the harbingers of greater success. Hassan Pasha, the Turkish high admiral and celebrated conqueror of Egypt, whose confidence in his good fortune had encouraged him to assume the command of an army, was totally defeated at Tobac, in Bessarabia, by prince Potemkin, and his discomfiture was followed by the surrender of Bender, Akerman, Kilia Nova, and Isatza, and with the investment of Ismael. At the same time the prince of Coburgh took Bucharest and Hohenlohe, forcing the passes which lead into Wallachia, made himself master of Rimnik and Crajova. Loudon also reduced Semendria and Cladova, and blockaded Orsova, which, being situated in an island of the Danube, was inaccessible to regular attacks. By these conquests the allies became masters of the whole line of fortresses which covered the Turkish frontier ; the three grand armies, originally separated by a vast extent of country, were rapidly converging to the same point, and threatened, by their united force, to overbear all opposition, and in another campaign to complete the subversion of the Ottoman empire in Europe.

But in the midst of this successful career, the increasing ferment in the hereditary countries, the rebellion in the Netherlands, and, still more, the interposition of the Maritime Powers and Prussia, checked the hopes of Joseph at the very moment when his projects of aggrandisement seemed hastening to their completion. Justly alarmed at the successes of the two imperial courts, the three combined powers emancipated Poland from the domination of Russia; they delivered the king of Sweden from the Danish invasion, and laid the foundation of a general alliance for reducing the overgrown power of Austria and Russia. The king of Prussia even encouraged the rising discontents in Hungary, fomented the troubles which the impolitic innovations of Joseph had excited in the Netherlands, and, in the commencement of 1790, opened a negotiation with the Porte for the conclusion of an offensive alliance, intended not only to effect the restoration of the dominions conquered during the existing war, but even of the Crimea, and the territories dismembered by the two imperial courts from Poland.

The only power to which Joseph might have turned as a counterpoise to this combination was France, from whose recent change of system he had flattered himself with hopes of a cordial support, and from whom he had even received private largesses to a considerable amount. But in the short interval of the two preceding years a fatal alteration had taken place both in the court and kingdom. The spirit of republicanism, excited by the American contest, had increased to an alarming height, and, with the growing embarrassments of the revenue, contributed to weaken the energy of government. The indecisive character of Louis, and even his virtues, furthered the projects of the republican. Without a discriminating judgment or force of mind, his great passion was to introduce beneficial reforms into the different departments of administration. Hence, he became the dupe of artful or misguided men, and adopted every plausible innovation, however injurious to his prerogative.

At this period France was in a state of great ferment. The concessions of the king encouraged new demands, and not only the magistracy, but even the greater part of the nobility and clergy, joined the prevailing clamour for what was called a new order of things. The populace, instigated by their demagogues, and encouraged by the duke of Orleans, rose tumultuously, seized the magazines of arms, and stormed the Bastille.

Concessions were only the prelude to still greater degradations ; the princes of the blood and many of the nobles, who ought to have formed the bulwark of the throne, emigrated from France, and the National Assembly triumphantly decreed the abolition of all privileges, published a theoretical rhapsody, which they called a declaration of the Rights of Man, and voted themselves permanent. An alarming scarcity of provision inflaming the general discontent, a sanguinary mob from Paris forced the palace of Versailles, massacred the guards, and dragged the degraded king and queen as prisoners to the capital. At the same time the National Assembly removed to Paris, and continued by their resolutions and debates to inflame the public mind, and heap new insults on the head of the unfortunate monarch and his amiable queen, Marie Antoinette.

This being the unfortunate situation of the country, Joseph saw the impending dissolution of the alliance on which he had so confidently relied, and the revival of that hostile spirit which had formerly menaced the downfall of Austria. He had reason to apprehend the loss of those very Netherlands for the security of which he had made great and incessant sacrifices.

Chap. CXXIX. — 1787–1790.

That rich and fertile territory, usually known by the synonymous appellations of the Netherlands and the Low Countries, formed past of the vast dominions which had been attached to the Spanish monarchy. Conquered by the joint forces of the Maritime Powers, it was transferred, at the peace of Utrecht, under their guaranty, to the house of Austria, on condition that the ancient laws, customs, and constitutions should be inviolably preserved. The late emperor, Charles VI., was inaugurated on these terms. His daughter, Maria Theresa, entered into similar engagements on her accession ; but during her reign some changes, with the consent, if not at the request, of the states, were introduced in the mode of representation in Brabant, and in the system of taxation. Joseph gave the same solemn sanction to the existing constitution.

Perhaps there was no country on the surface of the globe so small in extent, under the government of one prince, of which the component parts differed so widely in manners, government, and laws. Each of the provinces not only formed a separate sovereignty, enjoying a peculiar constitution, but the same variation extended to the cities and districts. In most of the provinces the rights and privileges were founded on tradition or prescription; but in Brabant and Limburgh they were detailed in a charter called La Joyeuse Entrée*, which contained fifty-nine articles, a collection of ancient usages and immunities granted by the former dukes of Brabant. The sovereign was restrained from conferring charges on any except natives, no inhabitant was to be tried out of the country, and full liberty of speech was to be allowed in the assembly of the states, with many other privileges; the charter was also concluded with a declaration similar to the celebrated clause in the coronation oath of Andrew II., king of Hungary, that if the sovereign should cease to observe the articles, his subjects should also cease to obey him, until the breaches in the constitution were repaired, and the immunities restored.

The power of the clergy was almost unbounded; the hierarchy consisted of one archbishop and seven bishops; there were also a hundred and eight abbeys, each endowed with annual revenues from 60,000 to 300,000 florins, numerous convents, and the number of religious persons, regular and secular of both sexes, amounted to above 30,000. The clergy possessed a considerable part of the landed property, and being the first order of the states, were enabled to relieve themselves from a considerable part of the public burdens, by fixing the land-tax at a low rate, and throwing the imposts on articles of consumption.

Their predominant influence was extended by the system of public education, which was subjected to the immediate control of the hierarchy. The university of Louvain had

* It was so called because the charter on which it was founded was promulgated on the *entry* of Philip the Good into Brussels.

long been celebrated for its numerous and richly-endowed colleges, and was formerly distinguished for learning and discipline. It possessed extraordinary privileges, with the patronage of numerous benefices, both in the Netherlands and in the bishopric of Liege; and above all, its academical honours were indispensable qualifications for the possession of every civil and ecclesiastical office. The members devoted to the papal see, maintained a blind adherence to the system of the ancient schoolmen, and proscribed all innovations adopted in other seminaries.

In this country, and among a people so tenacious of their customs, liberties, and religion, Joseph did not merely attempt to reform abuses and lop superfluous branches, but even laid the axe to the very root of the constitution itself. He purposed to force on the natives what he termed a simple and efficient form of government, and to establish nearly the same system of ecclesiastical polity, finance, and jurisprudence, as he had introduced into his hereditary countries. He commenced his innovations at an early period of his reign by abolishing several convents, prohibiting processions, jubilees, and confraternities, and removing statues, images, and offerings from the churches.

But in 1786 his plans were fully developed. He reformed the system of public education, by abrogating the privileges of the university of Louvain, and instituting a new seminary for the study of theology, over which he placed foreigners as directors, independent of the control of the bishops, and at which he ordered all youths destined for the church to pursue their studies. The innovation was vehemently opposed, and in December, 1786, gave rise to a tumult among the students, which was not suppressed without a military force. The archbishop of Mechlin, who took an active part, was summoned to Vienna, and the papal nuncio, who had countenanced the opposition to the imperial decrees, was abruptly ordered to quit the Netherlands. This attempt was followed by similar changes in the civil government.

The abolition of their venerated constitution excited universal indignation and alarm among the people of the Netherlands. The clergy and laity formed a common cause for mutual security. Brabant became the focus of opposition; the states, in the terms of their constitution, refused to grant the customary subsidies. until their grievances were redressed ; they forbade the collectors of the revenue to acknowledge the authority of the new intendants, and presented a spirited remonstrance to the governors-general. They suppressed also the new seminary at Louvain, dismissed the foreign professors, invited the other states to form a general confederacy, and claimed the guaranty of foreign powers, particularly of France. Their example was followed by the other provinces. Tumults burst forth in different places, the populace assumed the national cockade in imitation of the French, and the aspect of the whole country portended an insurrection.

On the 28th of May, 1787, Joseph received the first account of the tumults at Pereslaf, as he was preparing to cross the Dnieper. But infatuated with his plans, despising the danger, and employed in paying court to Catherine, he slighted the intelligence, and gave orders that no letters should be forwarded to him during the journey. He determined, however, to pursue rigorous measures, and in answer to strong representations in favour of lenity and caution, replied, " the flame of rebellion can only be extinguished by blood." On his return to Pereslaf, he learnt with astonishment and agitation the progress of the insurrection ; and after taking a hasty leave of Catherine, returned to Vienna in the beginning of July. New mortifications awaited his arrival. He was thunderstruck with the intelligence that the Flemings, instead of awaiting the repeal of the obnoxious edicts, had risen in arms, and obtained concessions from the governors-general; and that prince Kaunitz had not only approved these lenient measures, but pledged himself for the acquiescence of his sovereign.*

Joseph highly reprobated the conduct of the governors-general, and of his minister, as feeble and pusillanimous, and expressed his inflexible resolution to enforce the execution of his plans. He ordered troops to march to the Netherlands, summoned the governors-general and count Belgioioso to Vienna ; and at the same time despatched an angry mandate to the contumacious states, commanding them, as a mark of

---

* Sir Robert Keith to Lord Caermarthen, Vienna, Aug. 3. 1787. Prince Kaunitz was so much displeased with the violent proceedings of Joseph, and his refusal to ratify the concessions made to the people of the Netherlands, that he offered to resign, and for a time discontinued to countersign the mandates of the emperor.

obedience, to submit their complaints, and apologise for their misconduct at the foot of the throne.

The states did not refuse to give the required proof of obedience, but charged their deputies to express the loyalty of the nation and represent its grievances. On the 15th of August they were admitted to an audience, and their chief addressed the emperor in a speech replete with professions of loyalty, accompanied with firmness and spirit; and, at the conclusion, were permitted to read the list of their grievances.

The emperor, who had scarcely restrained his indignation during the recital, replied sternly : " The great dissatisfaction which I feel from all the late proceedings in my Belgic provinces cannot be effaced by a vain parade of words : nothing but a series of actions can prove the sincerity of your professions. I have charged prince Kaunitz to communicate to you in writing, for the information of the states, certain articles, the execution of which must precede any deliberation. Your instant and entire obedience is not only necessary to restore all things to their proper order, but to put a stop to the present interruption of commerce. I give you daily proofs that the good of my subjects is the sole object of all my actions, and you must be convinced that I have no thought of overturning your constitution, as in the moment of your greatest outrages, and when you have deserved my utmost indignation, with all the power which I possess, I only reiterate to you my assurances that I will preserve your liberties."

The conditions announced with this parade of liberality, comprised the restoration of all innovations, the payment of the subsidies, and the revocation of all orders issued by the states contrary to the views of the sovereign. In case of an immediate compliance, the emperor promised that the ancient tribunals and administration of justice should be restored, that the intendances should not be established, nor the abbeys deprived of their privileges. He promised also that the territorial impost of forty per cent., and the military conscription should not be introduced into the Netherlands.

Promises so vague, accompanied by demands so contradictory, did not satisfy the Belgic states, and they announced their resolution not to comply with the preliminary articles without full security for the redress of their grievances. But while the people were expecting the march of the imperial troops, and were making preparations for resistance, a sudden change took place in the conduct of Joseph. As he could not venture to drive his subjects of the Netherlands to desperation while embarrassed with the Turkish war, he endeavoured to attain by artifice what he could not effect by force. He therefore treated the deputies with the greatest condescension, and affected a willingness to accede to most of their demands. These concessions produced the desired effect, and the objects in dispute were amicably arranged. The states announced their compliance with the wishes of their sovereign, the volunteers laid down their arms, and, in return, the march of the imperial troops was countermanded. Count Murray issued the edict which suppressed the new ordinances, and promised that conferences should be held with the states, to adjust the subjects remaining in dispute.

These measures occasioned a temporary restoration of tranquillity. But it was soon evident that Joseph only suspended his projects to deceive his subjects. He dismissed count Murray, who had tranquillised the minds of the people. The army in the Netherlands was silently augmented, and the command intrusted to general d'Alton, a man of an undaunted and inflexible temper, united to the spirit of a rigid disciplinarian. Count Trautmansdorf was appointed minister plenipotentiary ad interim, with instructions which prove the views and insincerity of the emperor. He was ordered to consider the declaration of count Murray as extorted by fear, and consequently invalid; to hold no conference with the states on the subjects in dispute; to remove gradually all disaffected persons from their employments; but above all, to effect a complete reform in the supreme council of Brabant, "without which," to use the words of the emperor, "nothing could be done." He was no less positively enjoined to commence his administration with the re-establishment of the general seminary at Louvain.

On the arrival of Trautmansdorf at Brussels, in October, 1787, he found the people in a state of general agitation, and with suspicions naturally inspired by the prevarications of the sovereign, watching all his proceedings with a jealous eye. He therefore suspended the execution of the decree for the suppression of the university during three months, and gained great popularity by this act of indulgence. The other demands were obtained without difficulty, and the subsidies which had been refused unanimously voted, with a declaration that this compliance was a testimony of gratitude for the appointment of a minister so agreeable to the nation.

Joseph, too ardent and arbitrary to listen to the dictates of prudence or justice, disapproved the suspension, and issued peremptory orders to establish the general seminary, whatever might be the consequence. His views were warmly supported by general d'Alton, who was eager to bring the military force into action, and boasted that he could subjugate the whole Netherlands in six weeks. Trautmansdorf reluctantly fulfilling an order of which he deplored the fatal consequences, commanded the rector and other members of the university to submit to the plan of reform. The whole body appealing to the council of Brabant, he required the latter to enforce the imperial decree, allowed only two hours for deliberation, and threatened, in case of refusal, to employ force, and revoke the recent concessions. At the same time d'Alton drew out a body of troops, with artillery, near the house in which the council was assembled, and sent a detachment through the streets to awe the populace. The states, however, still undaunted, disdained to return an answer, and only ordered the message to be entered on their journals. The detachment which patroled the streets being insulted, fired on the populace : a tumult ensued, in which six persons were killed and several wounded, and d'Alton poured a body of troops into the Town-house. But at this awful crisis Trautmansdorf again suspended the rising commotion by ceasing to press his demands, and by declaring that the general had drawn out the troops without his concurrence.

Intelligence of these proceedings being transmitted to Vienna, the emperor rewarded the officer who had ordered the troops to fire, and encouraged d'Alton to persist in coercive measures ; yet, with the same duplicity as before, he held forth to the natives the offer of a general amnesty and complete restitution of his favour. The governors-general, who returned at this juncture, found the country in a state of apparent tranquillity, and the people impressed with hopes that Joseph had at length relinquished his impolitic designs. But within a few days after this public declaration, the university was again closed, the rector banished for three years, and the refractory members expelled ; while a body of troops stationed in Louvain slaughtered many of the inhabitants, who assembled to deplore the overthrow of that university which had been their pride and support. The general seminary was re-established; the colleges of Mechlin and Antwerp, celebrated for the education of youth destined to the ecclesiastical profession, were likewise closed, and the same measures of coercion employed against the inhabitants.

Soon after these violent proceedings, the states of the different provinces assembled to grant the ordinary subsidies, and notwithstanding the causes of dissatisfaction, all complied with the usual custom except those of Hainault and Brabant. Their refusal drew from the emperor a severe address, in which he threatened to revoke the amnesty, to prosecute all who had taken part in the late troubles, to annul their privileges, and to abrogate the Joyous Entry. The states of Brabant, alarmed by these threats, sent on the 26th of January, 1789, a petition to deprecate the anger of the sovereign, and procured the suspension of the impending punishment. Those of Hainault, persisting in their resolution, their assembly was dissolved on the 31st by the military force, their chiefs arrested, and their constitution abolished. Confident that this severe example would intimidate the refractory states of Brabant, Joseph announced his intention to make a change in their government, which should prevent a repetition of their contumacy, and secure the regular grant of a permanent subsidy, by extending the right of representation to other towns and districts.

In the present temper of the country such an arbitrary project excited general indignation ; and the whole province became a scene of civil commotion.

While Brabant was thus divided by internal feuds, Joseph seized the opportunity to overthrow the constitution. By his command, Trautmansdorf summoned an extraordinary meeting of the states, and required their concurrence in the proposition for increasing the third order, and establishing a permanent subsidy. The deputies, however, boldly refused their consent, exclaiming with one accord, " though the emperor may dissolve us, we will not violate a constitution which we have solemnly pledged ourselves to preserve." In consequence of this refusal, the edict was enforced, the assembly dissolved, and the Joyous Entry annulled. The deputies repaired to the hall of the council of Brabant, and protested against these proceedings ; but their protests were disregarded, and on the ensuing morning three imperial edicts proclaimed the dissolution of the ancient constitution, the new arrangement for the administration of justice, and various alterations in the imposition and collection of the taxes.

Joseph fondly considered this event as the termination of the struggle ; and d'Alton re-echoed his sentiments when he said, " the 18th of June is a happy epoch for the house of Austria ; for on that day, the victory of Kolin saved the monarchy, and the emperor became master of the Nether-lands." But neither the infatuated monarch nor his sanguine general were acquainted with the resolution and sentiments of a free nation. Although the presence of the military pre-vented an immediate tumult, this apparent tranquillity was the calm which precedes the storm. The licentious spirit, which at this time agitated France, spread like an electric shock among a people who were provoked by repeated insults and oppressions ; the patriots daily augmenting in numbers exulted in the hope of being assisted by their neighbours, and of forming a similar constitution on the ruins of the Austrian government. Vengeance and retaliation were denounced against the royalists ; the walls, churches, and houses were covered with placards, calling on the people to imitate the example set by the citizens of Paris.

Trautmansdorf, who had before averted the danger by prudence and lenity, was now anxious to meet it with firm-ness. Conscious that the imperial troops, who scarcely amounted to 20,000, were too few to awe a whole nation, he earnestly requested an accession of force. His apprehen-sions were ridiculed by d'Alton, who boasted that after send-ing a battalion of each regiment to the army in Hungary, he should still be able to maintain internal tranquillity ; and Joseph reluctantly despatched only a single regiment, " not because he deemed it necessary, but to encourage a timid government." The forebodings of the minister were too soon realised. Scarcely a month elapsed after the dissolution of the ancient constitution, before the people tumultuously rose, in various districts, released the arrested persons, attacked the military, and plundered the houses of the magis-trates. In these commotions many lives were lost at Tirlemont, Louvain, Antwerp, and Mons, before tranquillity could be restored ; and at Diest, the patriots led on by the monks, expelled the imperial troops and the magistrates. Brussels being likewise the scene of a momentary effervescence, the minister proposed to disarm the citizens ; but this measure was rejected by d'Alton, who presuming on the force of military discipline, contemptuously exclaimed, " If they want arms, I will supply them."

At this period many young men of Brussels, who had uttered seditious speeches, were sent without trial to serve in the army of Hungary ; and in the agitated state of the public mind, this arbitrary act spread through the nation indignant and sullen despondency. Emigrations took place from all quarters ; the fugitives repairing to the frontiers of Holland and Liege, joined those who had quitted their country in the preceding troubles, and formed a numerous body, ready to act offensively against the government. They found an able chief in Van-der-Noot, a factious advocate of Brussels, who had taken an active part during the troubles, and at whose instigation the third estate had refused to grant the annual subsidy. Being arrested and condemned for treason, he had in 1787 escaped into England. After ineffectually endeavouring to obtain for his countrymen the protection and assistance of the British cabinet, he repaired to Berlin. Receiving from the king of Prussia only dubious promises, he went to Holland, where he was permitted to reside under a feigned name, by the connivance of the Dutch government, which on this occasion imitated the conduct of Joseph towards the exiles in the late revolution. He returned in 1789 to Breda, whither he drew the archbishop of Mechlin, the abbot of Tongaloo, Crumpiper, the chancellor of Brabant, many of the nobility of Brussels, almost all the members from the states, and Van Eupen, canon of Antwerp. By their efforts, the emigrants were disciplined, distributed in different parts of the neigbouring country, arms and ammunition secured, and a force amounting to 10,000 men organised and appointed. A committee was established at Breda for the regulation of their proceedings, and their views seconded by another secret committee at Brussels.

In the midst of this ferment, the emperor strangely blending conciliation and severity, published a decree re-establishing the university of Louvain, in all its rights and privileges.

This ridiculous versatility excited contempt instead of giving satisfaction, and produced no effect in allaying internal disaffection, or checking the efforts of the party in Holland. A regular plan of hostilities was digested by the chiefs of the insurgents, and Van-der-Mersch, an officer who had signalised himself in the imperial service during the seven years' war, was appointed commander. Van-der-Noot assumed the title of plenipotentiary agent of the people of Brabant, and a manifesto, under his signature, was published "in the name of the clergy and third estate of Brabant, in union with many of the nobility, renouncing their allegiance, and declaring that they no longer considered Joseph as their sovereign." This manifesto, as a declaration of war, was sent to the government, and followed by the march of the patriot army into Brabant.

With a view to counteract its effects, the government of Brussels ordered it to be burnt by the common executioner, and published a long vindication of the emperor ; urging that although he had abrogated the Joyous Entry, yet he had confirmed the essential principles of the constitution, the security of persons and property. To awe the disaffected within the walls, many persons of the first rank were arrested on a charge of conspiracy, the gates were shut, palisadoes planted on the fortifications, the citizens disarmed, and active preparations made for defence.

Meanwhile hostilities commenced. A party of patriots marching from the neighbourhood of Breda, surprised, on the 25th of October, the forts of Lillo and Liefgenshoek, on the Scheld, made the scanty garrison prisoners, and conveyed the guardship to Bergen-op-Zoom. Another body of 3000 men, under the command of Van-der-Mersch, penetrated to Turnhout, and though many were armed only with bludgeons, pitchforks, and staves, and without cannon, they repulsed the imperial general Schroeder, who attacked them with 1500 men. This unexpected victory, proclaimed a miracle by the monks, increased the spirit and numbers of the insurgents, while it disheartened the royalists. But on the approach of general d'Arberg with 7000 men, the patriots retired within the Dutch territories, and concealing their arms, as usual, dispersed themselves in Dutch Brabant and the neighbouring districts of Liege, waiting for a more favourable opportunity to renew their incursions.

While the imperial general remained at Hogstraten, the insurgents made a new and more effectual attempt on the side of Flanders. A body despatched by Van-der-Mersch approached Ghent, seized two of the gates, and forcing their way into the town, were joined by the burghers with cannon and ammunition; the garrison of 1200 men was overpowered by numbers, driven across the Scheld, and blockaded in the barracks of the fort of St. Pierre. D'Arberg with 3000 men hastened to the scene of action, and occupied the citadel; but he was unable to stem the torrent of revolt. Bruges and Courtray declared for the rebels; new succours poured into Ghent; the fort of St. Pierre was stormed, the troops in the barracks made prisoners, and d'Arberg himself forced to retire in the night to Brussels. All Flanders was instantly emancipated; the states assembling at Ghent, in November 1789, published a declaration of independence, and invited the other provinces to form a general alliance. Terror and despondency spread to the seat of government, the governors-general quitted Brussels; d'Alton and Trautmansdorf, whose disputes were increased by the impending dangers, acted without concert; d'Alton concentrated his troops to make a last effort for the preservation of the capital, Trautmansdorf liberated the arrested persons, restored arms to the citizens, and issued no less than twenty-two declarations in the name of the emperor, hoping to conciliate the people by suppressing the seminary at Antwerp, re-establishing the Joyous Entry, and declaring an amnesty.

Of this confusion and alarm the patriot chiefs availed themselves with equal vigour, skill, and promptitude. Vander-Mersch assembling a body of insurgents, made a new irruption into Brabant, seized Diest, and advancing to Tirlemont, threatened Louvain. D'Alton instantly marched against the rebels, but pressed by the insurgents of Flanders, and unwilling to risk a battle which, if unfortunate, would have left him no hope of retreat, he suddenly concluded, with the acquiescence of Trautmansdorf, an armistice for ten days, which was to be provisionally extended, with the consent of the states of Brabant. In this interval he hoped to turn his forces against Flanders, but every moment of delay was fatal to the imperial cause; the patriots anticipated his designs, seduced whole troops of his soldiers, augmented their party by new accessions of force, and organised an insurrection at

Brussels, which terminated the struggle. On the 8th of December the women and children endeavoured to demolish the intrenchments, and tore up the palisadoes. The people assumed the national cockade ; the streets resounded with the cries of "Long live the patriots! Long live Van-der-Noot!" The soldiers began to desert, and two companies of the regiment of Murray at once joined the patriots.

On the 11th, an officer imprudently attempting to snatch a cockade from the hat of a burgher, a tumult ensued, and the inhabitants flew to arms. The imperial troops, separated and discouraged, were attacked by different bands of the populace, assisted by the deserters, and, after a conflict which continued the greater part of the night, were driven into the upper town. D'Alton, fallen from his former presumption, dreading the approach of Van-der-Mersch on one side, and the Flemish army on the other, doubtful of his troops, who were reduced to 5000 men, surrounded by secret and declared enemies, was happy to secure his retreat by a capitulation. He quitted Brussels on the evening of the 12th, leaving the cannon, military chests, and stores in the hands of the insurgents, and took the route to Luxemburgh, pillaging, plundering, and wasting the country as he passed. The example of the capital was followed by the other towns ; the imperial troops successively retired from Antwerp, Louvain, and Mechlin into Luxemburgh, and the governor, general Bender, assuming the command, prepared to defend that duchy which alone continued faithful to the house of Austria.

The news of the revolution affected Joseph to an alarming degree, and made a deep impression on his mind, already weakened by bodily and mental infirmities. He burst into tears, complaining bitterly that he had been deceived by the intelligence from Brussels ; he acknowledged his total inability to devise measures for the recovery of those valuable dominions, and demanded the advice of Kaunitz, whom he had yet scarcely deigned to consult on these momentous events. By his suggestions he consented to adopt conciliatory measures, and count Philip Cobenzl, who was supposed to possess great influence in the Netherlands, was despatched to Brussels to tranquillise the people, by revoking the late edicts, and restoring their privileges. These measures were, however, adopted too late. When Cobenzl reached the frontier, all the provinces, except Luxemburgh, were in the possession of the insurgents, the congress was convoked to form a new constitution, and his overtures were rejected with disdain.

In this moment of distress Joseph found no resource. He in vain appealed to the empire; he in vain obtained a circular letter from the pope to the prelates of the Netherlands recommending them to return to obedience. Embarrassed by the Turkish war, deriving no assistance from the courts of Versailles and Petersburgh, his sole allies on the Continent, he was reduced to the alternative of courting the interposition of Prussia, his inveterate enemy, England, whom he had betrayed and insulted, and Holland, whom he had despised and humbled. His haughty spirit was broken by calamity and disease; he grasped even at the shadow of a hope, and was eager to embrace any measure, however degrading, for the recovery of the Netherlands, even though he should reduce them again to that dependence on the Maritime Powers from which it had been his boast to emancipate them. He hoped to conciliate Prussia by cessions on the side of Poland; he trusted that England would gladly tender her assistance to obtain the renewal of the Barrier Treaty; he relied on the jealousy which the independence of the Netherlands would excite in Holland; he flattered himself that the chiefs of the different provinces would return to their allegiance, and accept a free constitution under the guaranty of the triple alliance. But he was again deceived. England refused to interfere in a cause which was opposed by her great continental ally; Holland beheld his distress with indifference, if not with satisfaction; Frederic William, who was maturing a grand system for the reduction of Austria, fomented the discontents in the Netherlands, and exerted all his efforts to inflame that hostile spirit which pervaded every part of the hereditary dominions, and was rising against Joseph in the different courts of Europe.

CHAP. CXXX. — 1789, 1790.

THROUGHOUT the hereditary countries the same ferment prevailed as that which had preceded the explosion in the Netherlands. Addresses poured from all quarters against the innovations of Joseph; and the principal members of the civil government represented in terms equally strong the difficulties which occurred in collecting the new land-tax. In Hungary the discontents rose to an alarming height, and were inflamed by the severities used in enforcing the military levies. These unprecedented acts of authority were universally stigmatised as oppressive and unconstitutional; and many of the counties refused to comply with requisitions which they declared illegal and beyond their ability to fulfil. The Hungarian nobles also, in the same haughty tone in which they had formerly dictated to their kings, demanded the confirmation of their rights, the permission to resume their national dress, and the revival of their native language in the acts and records of the kingdom.

In the midst of these public distresses, the declining spirit of Joseph was troubled with domestic feuds. He had offended his brother Leopold, by an imprudent partiality to his nephew the archduke Francis, who had been brought up under his auspices, and by an unjustifiable attempt to secure for him the reversion of the imperial crown. This impolitic attempt to raise the son above the father created an incurable jealousy between the two brothers; and Leopold not only censured every part of his conduct, both in internal and external policy, but sedulously avoided even an interview or any species of communication which might implicate him in the transactions or embarrassments of his brother.

Joseph sunk under the struggle of contending passions, the weight of accumulated calamities, and the effects of disease. The same languor which prevailed in the chamber of the sick monarch, was, for a time, diffused through every department of state: although a war with Prussia seemed inevitable, he neither formed magazines nor made the necessary augmentations of the army; equally unable to avert, and unwilling to encounter the danger, he displayed the extremes of anxiety, alarm, and irresolution. But as the storm approached, his mind regained a portion of its pristine activity, and, in the commencement of February, 1790, he ordered the requisite preparations for impending hostilities. He felt also the necessity of conciliating his subjects to frustrate the designs of Prussia, which were founded on their growing disaffection, and accordingly revoked many of his unpopular edicts, and prepared to rescind many others. He

received the haughty demands of the Hungarians with condescension and complacency, restored their constitution as it
existed at his accession, promised speedily to solemnise the
ceremony of his coronation, and as an earnest of his intentions, sent back the crown of St. Stephen.

The rapture with which the crown was received proved
the precipitation and folly of wantonly choking the feelings
of a people so susceptible of national prejudice, and so awake
to national honour. Triumphal arches were erected in its
passage; every town was a scene of festivity; numbers
flocking from all quarters swelled the cavalcade, and at Buda
exulting multitudes crowding to the cathedral welcomed the
precious palladium of their national splendour and freedom.

At night the crown was removed into the chapel of the
palace, and guarded by two magistrates with drawn sabres.
The whole city was illuminated, the streets resounded with
songs of joy and exultation, and on every side was heard
the exclamation, "Long live the liberties of the Hungarian
people!"

But Joseph did not live to experience the good effects of
this change of conduct; for at this awful crisis his reign and
life were hastening to a close. Though naturally robust
and hardy, his incessant exertions of body and mind had
worn down his frame; and his last campaign accelerated his
decay. He exposed himself to the sultry heats of the summer, and to the noxious air which exhaled from the marshes
in the vicinity of the Danube, where he often slept on the bare
ground. He was his own minister and general; by day he
encountered the fatigues of a common soldier, and regulated
the complicated affairs of the army; at night he scarcely
allowed himself more than five hours for repose, conducting
with his own hand the extensive correspondence relative to
all the affairs of his vast empire.

In December, 1788, a fever, derived from anxiety, hard-
ship, and fatigue, compelled him to retire to Vienna. During
several months he was in considerable danger, and was afterwards long confined by an asthmatic complaint. With extreme care and attention he seemed to recover gradually;
but his incessant restlessness, and the fatal revolution in the
Netherlands, occasioned a relapse, and he finally sunk under
accumulated disorders of body and mind.

Joseph closed his life with great marks of piety and contrition. Finding himself rapidly declining, he assembled his physicians, and exhorted them to inform him whether there were any hopes of amendment. He received their prognostic of his impending dissolution with the greatest firmness, and despatched a letter, requesting the immediate presence of his brother Leopold. He then prepared himself for his approaching end, by performing all the ceremonies of the church, and received the holy sacrament, and extreme unction.

But the activity of his mind did not forsake him, and he never discontinued the use of his pen. After a violent attack of his disorder, one of the physicians inculcating the necessity of repose, he replied, I have been so much accustomed to business that it will be irksome to be unemployed, especially at a time when the welfare of my subjects requires all my attention. He therefore continued, almost without intermission, to direct the affairs of government, though in the midst of the most excruciating torments.

He made his last declaration to the army, through count Haddick, president of the council of war. "Feeling," he said, "the approach of death, I should deem myself highly ungrateful did I not express my entire satisfaction at the fidelity, bravery, and promptitude which my army has displayed on all occasions. To be a soldier, was ever my warmest desire; to promote the honour and welfare of my troops my principal care. As a sovereign, I have directed my chief endeavours to that end; and as a companion in war, I vied with them in sharing their hardships and dangers. Whatever could assist in the recovery of the sick and wounded, or contribute to their comfort and preservation, was never omitted, and every soldier was to me an object of regard.

"The last campaign has fully answered my most sanguine wishes for the honour of my arms; and my troops have acquired that fame throughout Europe which they highly deserved. I shall carry with me to the grave the consoling conviction that they will continue by their actions to merit so just a reputation."

Enfeebled by incessant sufferings, his dissolution was accelerated by the unexpected death of his beloved niece, the archduchess Elizabeth, a princess of the house of Wirtemberg, and sister to the great duchess of Russia. He had himself chosen this amiable princess to be the consort of his favourite nephew Francis, and loved her with paternal fondness, while she looked up to him with filial reverence and affection. On receiving the melancholy intelligence, the emperor smote his forehead with his hands, remained for some time absorbed in grief, and at length exclaimed, " Oh God, thy will be done !"

In the midst of his agony he had the courage to support an interview of three hours with his nephew; but although his firmness of mind did not give way, his bodily strength could not resist so awful a shock. Feeling the approach of death, he summoned his confessor at three in the morning, and devoutly heard the prayers ordered by the church for persons in the last agonies. Though his sight failed, his senses remained unimpaired till the last moment, and he expired on the 20th of February, 1790, with perfect composure, and almost without a groan, in the forty-ninth year of his age, and the tenth of his reign.

His testament contained only a few lines, by which he declared Leopold his universal heir; but a codicil annexed proved a grateful and affectionate disposition, for he ordered that all employed about his person should receive their whole salary during their lives.

On the table in his cabinet were found several letters written the preceding day, which equally displayed the calmness of his mind, and the warmth of his feelings. One of them, in a trembling hand, was addressed to some ladies of high distinction, whose society he had long frequented.

" To the five ladies * who bore with my society.

" The moment draws near in which it is time to take a last farewell, and to thank you for the patience and kindness you have shown me for so many years, during which I have never regretted one day passed in your company. The idea of quitting it is the only act of resignation that gives me pain. In regard to myself, I cannot be sufficiently grateful for the decrees of Providence, relying on whom, I wait my dissolution with perfect resignation. Remember me, and think of me also in your prayers. You will see by my writing the state I am in. Once more adieu !"

Joseph undoubtedly possessed many great and amiable qualities, but they were counteracted by a restlessness of tem-

* Princesses Frances and Charles Lichtenstein, countesses Clary, Kinski, and Kaunitz.

per, and a rage for innovation, which were with difficulty controlled even in his youth, by the calm judgment and wary circumspection of his mother; defects aggravated by a spirit of despotism derived from his high birth, and fostered by his confined education.* To these may be added, an habitual duplicity, and a disregard of the most solemn engagements, which sunk him in the opinion of Europe, and deprived him at once of the love of his subjects, and the confidence of his allies.

A wise statesman will always consult the genius and temper of his people, and make even prejudice and superstition subservient to the general good. Joseph, unfortunately for himself and for Europe, acted in direct contradiction to this plain rule, he attempted to abolish deep-rooted institutions, and to extirpate prejudices and opinions which had been consecrated by ages. He expected that to be the work of a moment which could only be the gradual operation of successive years; he never distinguished what was just or specious in theory, from what was reducible to practice. To use the words of his rival Frederic, "his head was a confused magazine of despatches, decrees, and projects." With the most thoughtless precipitation, he made laws before he had removed the obstacles to their execution, or could discover and remedy their defects, and changed them with the same precipitation as they were made. Hence he issued an amazing number of ordinances and rescripts, many of which being ill-digested or ambiguous, were seldom carried into execution. Couriers were despatched upon couriers counteracting preceding orders, and every new edict was modified or limited by additional decrees.

* His mother bore testimony to his inflexible character when she said to a celebrated artist, " I teach my son to love the arts, which may tend to soften his mind, for he has a hard heart." She no less regretted his restlessness of temper, and rage for innovation. " My son," she said to a lady of her court, "desires me to dismantle the fortifications of Vienna. I am an old woman; I almost remember when Vienna was besieged by the Turks, and that unless the capital had been capable of withstanding a blockade until it was relieved by John Sobieski, the Ottoman hordes would have ravaged the hereditary dominions, and even overrun the empire. I have myself twice seen Vienna almost the frontier of my dominions. Let Joseph act as he pleases when I am dead, but while I live, Vienna shall not be dismantled."

With these principles, it is no wonder that his reign was a continued scene of agitation and disappointment. He himself bore witness to the folly, the inconsistency, and the impracticability of his schemes, when at the close of his life, he said, I would have engraven on my tomb, " Here lies a sovereign, who with the best intentions never carried a single project into execution."

Joseph was twice married. His first wife was Elizabeth Maria, daughter of Philip duke of Parma, a princess of great beauty and accomplishments. She died in November 1763, in the prime of youth, of the small pox, and left a daughter who survived her only seven years. Joseph was long inconsolable for her loss, and always cherished the warmest affection for her memory.

His second wife was Maria Josepha, princess of Bavaria, daughter of the emperor Charles VII., whom he espoused in 1765. Joseph was reluctantly induced to conclude this marriage by the importunities of his parents, and the prospect of obtaining the allodial inheritance of her brother. But as the princess was deficient in personal charms and mental accomplishments, she never acquired his affection, and he treated her with coldness and neglect. Death dissolved this ill-assorted union before the close of the second year, and in May, 1767, the young empress fell a sacrifice to the same disorder, which had proved fatal to her predecessor.

Joseph did not again enter into the bands of wedlock, and dying without issue, was succeeded by his brother Leopold.

Chap. CXXXI. — REIGN OF LEOPOLD II. — 1790.

LEOPOLD II. ascended the tottering throne vacated by the death of his brother in the forty-third year of his age. Wherever he turned his eyes, he saw himself surrounded by dangers ; his monarchy was shaken to the very foundations ; all parts of his vast dominions were either agitated by intestine commotions, or the scene of open rebellion. The Netherlands erected into an independent republic, seemed irrecoverably torn from his empire. In Bohemia and Lower Austria the states presented a remonstrance

against the new land tax, and purposed to follow this appeal
with a general representation of their numerous grievances,
and an earnest demand of redress. In Hungary the ferment
had risen almost to rebellion, notwithstanding the restitution
of the privileges, extorted from the late sovereign. It was
urged by the disaffected that as Joseph was never crowned
and had violated the fundamental laws of the realm, his despotic conduct had abrogated the rule of succession; that
Leopold had therefore no hereditary claim to the throne, and
that the ancient right of electing the monarch reverted to
the nation. In the full confidence of their strength, they
anticipated the exercise of this darling privilege: "Hungary," they exclaimed, "has no need of an Austrian king."

Nor was the aspect of Europe in general more favourable
to the house of Austria.

The English had been driven by repeated acts of insult
and duplicity, and by the intimate connection of the court
of Vienna with France, to abandon the hope too long
cherished, of renewing the ancient league which had rescued
the house of Austria from the brink of destruction, and
maintained the safety of Europe. As a counterpoise to the
union of Austria and France, they had formed a strict alliance with Frederic William, king of Prussia, which placed
at their disposal the first military power of Germany. They
had also rescued Holland from the trammels of France, and
were preparing measures to render their political and commercial regulations independent of Austria and Russia, and
to resume their former ascendency on the Continent. They
had rescued the king of Sweden from the dangers of a
Danish invasion, and purposed to force the two imperial
courts to relinquish their conquests from the Porte; they
had assisted in liberating Poland from the domination of
Russia, and promoted the re-establishment of the hereditary
monarchy as the means of restoring that degraded country
to its pristine splendour. They were opening new channels
for the transport of naval stores, and other necessary commodities hitherto exclusively drawn from Russia; and by
assisting Prussia to obtain Dantzig and Thorn from the
Poles for equivalent advantages, they hoped at once to unite
the two powers in promoting the interests of their trade,
and to gratify a prince whose agency had contributed to
their ascendency.

Frederic William, king of Prussia, from habit, interests, and personal feelings hostile to the house of Austria, was concentrating all his efforts to secure that preponderance in Germany which had been so long and so ably contested by his predecessor. Besides the engagements which he had formed in common with the Maritime Powers, he had concluded, on the 29th of January, 1790, an alliance with the Porte for obtaining the restitution of the Crimea, and the provinces lost during the existing war, as well as for wresting Gallicia from Austria. He fomented the internal troubles in every part of the Austrian dominions, suffered his officers to assist the insurgents in the Netherlands, permitted a committee of disaffected Hungarians to hold their meetings at Berlin, and was ready to engage in a war against the house of Austria, if he could not otherwise realise his views.

To resist this great combination, Leopold had no other ally except Russia, who was too much employed in the war with Turkey, to afford him effectual assistance. The French Revolution had burst asunder the bands of amity formed by the treaty of Versailles, and the most powerful party in the nation not only inflamed the commotions in the Netherlands, and grasped in imagination so valuable a territory, but endeavoured to animate the people with that political antipathy which in preceding times had given rise to the bloody contests between the houses of Austria and Bourbon.

The important points which demanded the immediate attention of Leopold were, to compose the discontents in the hereditary countries, to recover the Netherlands, to secure a speedy and honourable peace with the Turks, to effect a reconciliation with Prussia, and to obtain the imperial crown.

Well aware that the success of all his endeavours would ultimately depend on an accommodation with Prussia and the Maritime Powers, he had scarcely reached Vienna before he opened a direct correspondence with Frederic William, in which he justified the continuance of the war against the Turks, expressed his alarm at the recent alliance with the Porte, and offered to conclude peace, on the condition of retaining the territories secured to Austria by the treaty of Passarovitz. Yet while thus earnestly courting peace, he did not act with indecision or weakness. He hastened to repair the losses of his army, and assembled a considerable force in Bohemia and Moravia, to resist any sudden attack on the part of Prussia. He intrusted to Loudon the command of this force, but to avoid the slightest pretext for aggression, he ordered him to form a cordon from Leutmeritz to Jablunka, at a considerable distance from the Prussian frontier.

In his letters to the king of Prussia, he apologised for these precautions. "In the present crisis," he said, "prudence will not allow me to omit proper measures for the defence of my states in case of attack. Your majesty, I am convinced, would have taken the same precautions on a similar occasion; it is in your power to stop these armaments, and confer a great obligation on me, by explaining your intentions and removing all my doubts."

After announcing his resolution to solicit the imperial dignity, and requesting the concurrence of Prussia, he added, "In future I solemnly protest no views of aggrandisement will ever enter into my political system. I will doubtless employ all the means in my possession to defend my country, should I unfortunately be driven to such measures; but I will endeavour to give no umbrage. To your majesty, in particular, I will act as you act towards me, and will spare no efforts to preserve perfect harmony. I will use my utmost endeavours to acquire the confidence of my co-estates of the empire, and in regard to the Germanic association, I protest, that should I be invited I would not hesitate to accede, provided its stipulations were rendered common and reciprocal."

Overtures so candid met with a suitable return. In reply, Frederic William proposed to adopt as the basis of a general pacification either the *status quo* before the war, which was suggested by Great Britain, or a general arrangement adapted to the interests of the respective powers, by proportionate exchanges, equivalents, and compensations, which he himself preferred. In proposing this alternative, his object was to acquire Dantzic and Thorn, by extorting from the house of Austria a considerable part of Gallicia, as an indemnification for Poland, and repaying this cession by procuring from the Turks the provinces ceded to Charles VI. at the peace of Passarovitz. To secure the acquiescence of Leopold, he promised not to oppose the recovery of the Netherlands, and offered to support his pretensions to the imperial crown.

Some modifications were respectively brought forward by both parties, and an armistice with the Turks suggested by England. But Leopold, anxious to push his success before the king of Prussia could take part in the contest, rejected an armistice, and redoubled his efforts for the prosecution of the war. The grand vizier having been strangled for his defeat at Rymnik, was succeeded by Hassan Pasha; and the prince of Coburgh was intrusted with the direction of the Austrian army on the Danube, in consequence of the removal of Loudon to command the troops on the Prussian frontier. After a long blockade, the garrison of Orsova being alarmed by an earthquake, abandoned the place, and the Austrians hastened to besiege Widdin and Giurgevo. But the threats of the king of Prussia prevented the prosecution of the siege of Widdin ; while at Giurgevo they were attacked by the Turks, and after a desperate engagement driven from their lines. This was the last action of the war ; because the transactions on the Prussian frontiers soon occasioned the conclusion of an armistice.

Reinforcements had continued to pour into Bohemia and Moravia ; while Frederic William, after detaching a force on the side of Poland, led a considerable army into Silesia, and took up his head quarters between Frankenstein and Reichenbach. During the pause which the approach of the two armies occasioned, the negotiations were renewed, and a congress formed at Reichenbach by the Austrian, Prussian, English, and Dutch plenipotentiaries. The king of Prussia seemed determined not to recede from his purpose of acquiring Dantzic and Thorn, and Leopold was equally resolved not to yield the fertile and populous district of Gallicia, with the valuable salt mines of Vielitza, for what he termed the barren districts possessed by the house of Austria at the peace of Passarovitz. During this fruitless discussion Leopold artfully opened a separate communication with Great Britain, on whom the decision of this important contest ultimately depended ; and fortunately England still fostered a predilection for Austria, which all past provocations had not obliterated. Unwilling to lessen her territories, they did not approve the proposed restoration of Gallicia as a compensation to Poland for Dantzic and Thorn, and were no less anxious to prevent any dismemberment of the Turkish dominions. They endeavoured therefore to promote a separate

peace between Leopold and the Porte, on the condition of
restoring all conquests made during the war, and hoped
afterwards to extort the acquiescence of Russia in similar
terms.   They were equally anxious to effect the restoration
of the Netherlands to the house of Austria, with the revival
of the Barrier Treaty, and the re-establishment of the ancient
constitution under the joint guaranty of Great Britain,
Prussia, and Holland.

Leopold, acquainted with the sentiments of the cabinet,
gained their confidence, and turned their assistance to the
promotion of his own views with consummate address.   He
expressed to the British minister at Vienna his conviction,
that from the character of the sovereign, the wisdom of the
administration, and the national influence, England was the
only power which could restore general tranquillity ; he declared his readiness to accept the terms proposed by the
king, requiring a trifling extension of frontier, necessary for
the maintenance of peace and security.   This extension
was, the town and territory of Old Orsova, and a similar
district in Croatia, which gave the Turks a footing beyond
the Danube and the Una.   He expressed also his readiness
to receive the Netherlands with their ancient constitution,
and to revive the Barrier Treaty ; but he artfully hinted,
that an unsuccessful war would drive him to the necessity of
relinquishing a part of those countries to France, to purchase
her assistance in recovering the remainder.   By this conduct, and these lures, he drew from the Maritime Powers a
public declaration that they would not co-operate in the re-
establishment of peace with the Porte, except on the basis
of the *status quo*, or actual possession before the war, and
that they should not deem themselves bound to take part in
a contest which might ensue from the perseverance of the
king of Prussia in his demand of Dantzic and Thorn, and
the cession of Gallicia.

Frederic William, thus unsupported by the Maritime
Powers, alarmed lest the Turks should be alienated by his
proposal to dismember their territories, and aware that the
Poles could not be induced to cede Dantzic and Thorn, the
two barriers of their country, without a proper equivalent,
adopted more pacific sentiments.   His decision was hastened
by the artful threat of Leopold, that he would not hesitate
to purchase a peace from the Turks by the restitution of all

his conquests, in order to turn his whole force against Prussia. The discussion was therefore soon brought to a conclusion, and a convention signed on the 5th of August, 1790, at Reichenbach, by which Leopold agreed to enter into an armistice with the Turks, to open a negotiation for peace under the mediation of the Maritime Powers, on the basis of the *status quo,* and to give an equivalent to Prussia, should he obtain any advantage or acquisition from the Porte. He also engaged not to assist Russia, should the attempts to conclude a peace between her and the Porte fail of success; and he consented to restore to the Netherlands their ancient constitution and privileges, under the guaranty of the three allied powers.

On the signature of this convention, the two armies withdrew from the frontiers ; and by the intervention of Prussia an armistice was concluded between Austria and the Porte, at Giurgevo, on the 19th of September, for nine months. A congress of plenipotentiaries from Austria, Turkey, and the mediating powers was soon afterwards assembled at Szistova, and all the subjects of contention seemed on the point of being arranged by an amicable compromise. The negotiation was, however, suspended by a dispute relative to the cession of Old Orsova and the district on the Una, which Frederic William considered as a breach of the convention, and required an equivalent. Leopold persisting in his demand, asserted that those cessions were trifling in themselves, and necessary for the security of his frontier ; he argued that they had been usurped by the Turks in contravention to the peace of Belgrade, and, in June, 1791, his plenipotentiaries, suspending the conferences, even retired to Bucharest. But at this crisis the divisions of the allied powers favoured the views of Leopold.

During the proceedings of the congress, the allies were preparing to fulfil their original design, by prescribing to Russia the same conditions which they had already prescribed to Austria. With this view the king of Prussia hastened his military preparations, sent a force into Poland, and took possession of Dantzic and Thorn, while England fitted out naval armaments for the Baltic and the Black Sea.

Catherine, sensible of the straits to which the emperor was reduced, no sooner received intelligence of the convention concluded at Reichenbach, than she accelerated a peace with Sweden, that she might be prepared to resist the threatened attack. She redoubled her efforts against the Turks, and gained considerable advantages; but must have been ultimately reduced to relinquish her acquisitions, had the allies continued to act with vigour and unanimity.

The genius of Mr. Pitt, who had conceived and matured the new plan of continental policy, was shackled by the disinclination of parliament to enter into a war with Russia, for interests in which England was not immediately concerned. He reluctantly suspended his armaments, abandoned the engagements which had been contracted with Prussia, and was forced to recur to the feeble offices of negotiation. This failure was a fatal blow to the ascendency which had been gained by England in the Prussian cabinet. Frederic William, indignant at being thus deserted, inveighed against the wavering policy of the British government, and endeavoured to extricate himself from his dangerous situation by relinquishing the grand objects of the alliance and conciliating those powers to whom he had vainly purposed to dictate terms of peace.

Leopold skilfully profited by a schism which had saved his ally from humiliation. He exerted the same address to amuse and gain Prussia, which he had before employed to conciliate England, and he found little difficulty in securing a prince who was deeply mortified at the failure of all his projects, and who had no resource but to hasten the conclusion of peace. A secret and intimate correspondence was opened between the courts of Vienna and Berlin; the conferences at Szistova were resumed; the principal conduct of the negotiation was thrown into the hands of the Prussian minister Lucchesini, who even negotiated the cession of those districts which had before nearly caused a rupture; and the memorable treaty of Szistova, which restored peace, and suspended the rivalry between Austria and Prussia, was signed on the 4th of August, 1791.

Leopold relinquished all his conquests, retaining only Chotzim and its territory as a deposit, until the conclusion of a peace between Russia and the Porte; and he promised not to afford any assistance to the empress against the Turks. By a convention which was signed separately to save the honour of Prussia, the Porte ceded to Austria Old Orsova with its territory, on the condition that it should not be fortified, with a small district in the mountains of Croatia, stretching along the left bank of the Una.

This negotiation and the consequent union between Austria and Prussia, produced an important change in the interior of the two courts, and was followed by the attainment of the other objects to which the views of Leopold were directed. On the 30th of September, 1790, he was unanimously chosen king of the Romans, made a solemn entry into Frankfort on the 4th of October, and on the 9th was crowned emperor by the elector of Mentz. The articles of the capitulation were not different from those of his predecessors; but a clause which had been omitted in the preceding capitulation was revived, to secure his interference with the new French government, for the preservation of the rights reserved by preceding treaties to the German princes in Alsace, Loraine, and Franche Comté. This clause was a declaration that he would execute the resolutions contained in the memorials of the electoral college, and a memorial to this effect was accordingly presented immediately after his coronation.

Chap. CXXXII.—1790, 1791.

HAVING traced the conduct of Leopold in restoring external peace and obtaining the imperial crown, we call the attention of the reader to the prudent measures which he adopted for tranquillising the internal commotions of the hereditary countries.

The new land tax was the principal cause of the discontents. Leopold had scarcely reached Vienna before he gratified the ardent wishes of his subjects by suppressing the board for carrying this impost into execution, suspending two of the principal projectors who had rendered themselves obnoxious to the landholders, and finally by re-establishing the ancient mode of taxation. He abolished also the general seminary for education, which had been instituted by Joseph, and restored the revenues appropriated to the maintenance of the episcopal schools; but he accompanied this restoration with salutary reforms, and made great improvements in the German schools; restored to each kingdom, province,

and district the form of government which existed under
Maria Theresa, amended by salutary modifications.   He removed the shackles with which the injudicious policy of
Joseph had fettered the commerce of his subjects with a
view to prevent the importation of foreign commodities* ;
he retained and even extended the edict of toleration, and
improved the regulations which had been introduced for the
relief of the Jews.

By these wise and lenient measures he gained the affections of his subjects, and soon restored tranquillity in
most parts of his extensive dominions except Hungary.

The Hungarians considered the restoration of their privileges by the late emperor as an act of compulsion ; and they
were therefore not pacified by the lenient measures which
distinguished the commencement of the new reign, nor by
the promises of Leopold to restore all their privileges.   Encouraged by the intrigues of Prussia, and the prospect of
assistance from the Turks, they hoped to revive many
obsolete rights, and extort additional concessions.   In the
provincial assemblies the most violent language was held,
and the turbulent spirit displayed in an address from the
people of Pest, proved that a considerable part of the nation,
with the style, had adopted the sentiments and principles, of
the French demagogues.†

---

* Joseph had even prohibited the importation of salt fish, a regulation
which in a Catholic country was attended with extreme inconvenience.

† " The fame, august sovereign, which has preceded you, has declared
you a just and gracious prince.   It says that you forget not you are a
man ; that you are sensible the king was made for the people, not the
people for the king.   The violent commotions which have agitated our
country after so many acts of injustice are thereby somewhat allayed.
Scarcely therefore could we trust our eyes, when in your first rescript to
us of the 14th instant, we found not those securities for the safety of our
constitution, which our hereditary rights, and the inflexible patience of
the people under the lawless reign of the late emperor demanded ;
securities which your majesty has fully granted to the Belgians, an act
which will remain as a proof of your sentiments throughout all ages.

" From the rights of nations and of man, and from that social compact
whence states arose, it is incontestible that the sovereignty originates from
the people.   This axiom our parent Nature has impressed on the hearts
of all ; it is one of those which a just prince (and such we trust your
majesty ever will be) cannot dispute ; it is one of those inalienable im-
prescriptible rights which the people cannot forfeit by neglect or disuse.
Our constitution places the sovereignty jointly in the king and people, in

Without attending to these lawless declamations, Leopold calmly proceeded to summon a general diet, for the ceremony of his coronation, which was the more remarkable, as no similar assembly had been convened since the inauguration of Maria Theresa, a period of almost fifty years. The majority of the nobles, proud of having compelled Joseph to revoke his reforms, and flattered with the hope that their concurrence was necessary for the prosecution of hostilities against the Turks and Prussia, flocked to the meeting full of confidence, and prepared a new inaugural act, which would have reduced the sovereigns of Hungary to the same state of weakness and degradation as the kings of Poland.

The judicious and undaunted conduct of Leopold triumphed over licentiousness and faction. Though involved in dangers which appeared almost insurmountable, he refused to make the slightest change in the coronation oath taken by Maria Theresa. At this critical juncture, when the spirit of opposition was spreading rapidly through the country, by the active efforts of the disaffected, he had the address to conciliate the whole body of Illyrians. These people, amounting to no less than 3,000,000, were principally attached to the Greek religion, and settled in the Bannat and the adjacent regions; but were considered as aliens by the proud Hungarians. Their repeated solicitations to be represented in the diet having been rejected with scorn, they laid their request at the foot of the throne, and Leopold permitted them to form a national diet at Temeswar. By this concession he won their gratitude and support, and thus encouraged and strengthened the loyal party, which his firm and temperate conduct had gained in Hungary.

Still, however, the spirit of the malcontents was unshaken, and the opposition rose to so high a pitch that the state sent envoys to the congress of Reichenbach, claiming the privilege

such a manner that the remedies necessary to be applied according to the ends of social life for the security of persons and property, are in the power of the people. We are sure, therefore, that at the meeting of the ensuing diet, your majesty will not confine yourself to the objects mentioned in your rescript; but will also restore our freedom to us, in like manner as to the Belgians, who have conquered theirs with the sword. It would be an example big with danger to teach the world that a people can only protect or regain their liberties by the sword, and not by obedience."

of attending the conferences for conclusion of peace, and insisting that their deputies should in every future negotiation be admitted with the same authority and powers as the royal plenipotentiaries. They no less peremptorily demanded the revocation of various immunities which had been granted to those who did not profess the Catholic religion. The disaffection spread among the military. Several Hungarian regiments proposed to swear allegiance to the nation, and even the officers in addresses to the states announced their resolution of sending deputies to the diet. All these and still farther demands were comprised in the new inaugural act, which was formally presented to Leopold at Vienna.

He gave a firm and dignified refusal to these imperious requisitions*, and his language was supported by measures equally firm and decisive. The convention of Reichenbach being concluded, the hopes entertained by the disaffected of receiving assistance from Prussia and Turkey were annihilated, and Leopold awed his rebellious subjects with the force collected in Moravia and Bohemia. Sixty thousand men were drawn to the vicinity of Buda; and the officers who had signed the addresses were transferred to other regiments and replaced by Germans. The states in vain attempted by various modifications of their demands to overcome or elude the firmness of Leopold; he persisted in his resolution of receiving the crown on no other terms than were contained in the inaugural acts of Charles and Maria Theresa, and fixed the place of his coronation at Presburgh instead of Buda.

The crown and regalia being accordingly sent to Presburgh, the states assembled on the 3d of November, and on

---

* In a rescript sent through the chancellor, count Palfy, he declared, "I will maintain inviolate the constitution of the kingdom as it descended to me from my grandfather and mother, in the hope that a constitution guaranteed by the Pragmatic Sanction will also be received by the states. According to that constitution the legislative authority is jointly vested in me and the diet; but I alone am charged with the executive and judicial powers, and with the distribution of honours and favours, in conformity to the laws and customs of the country. I will abide by the Pragmatic Sanction. I will never suffer the right of succession, belonging to me and my heirs, to be taken into consideration. I will never acquiesce in any innovation in the military or executive power, nor will I ever consent to the smallest infraction of the privileges granted to the non-catholics."

the 10th the king, accompanied by his five sons, made his solemn entry. His presence awed his enemies, and animated his friends; the whole diet seemed to be actuated by principles of loyalty, and selected the archduke Leopold from among the candidates for the office of palatine, which was vacant by the death of prince Esterhasy. On this occasion, when the primate at the head of the states returned thanks to the king for having yielded to the wishes of the nation by giving them the archduke as their palatine, Leopold replied, " I expected to find myself in the midst of a faithful nation; but you have even exceeded my warmest wishes. I am now in the bosom of my family." Turning to his son, he added, " The duties and obligations of the palatine are specified in the laws of the country. We therefore order you as a father and as a king to fulfil those obligations, and never to suffer your filial affection to divert you from your duty. We declare in the presence of these faithful states and orders, that we shall estimate your affection to us as a son by the exemplary discharge of your office." Then presenting the palatine to the states, he concluded, " I offer you my son, as a pledge of my sincere regard, to become a distinguished mediator between us, and to promote our mutual affection."

A people highly susceptible of strong emotions, were touched with these noble sentiments; every heart beat with rapture; some burst into tears of loyalty and affection; and the speech was ordered to be inserted in the public records as a counterpart to the memorable exhortation of the national darling, St. Stephen, to his son Emeric.

Having ratified an inaugural act in the same terms as those of Charles and Maria Theresa, Leopold received, on the 15th of November, 1790, the crown from the hands of his son the new palatine. After the public dinner he gave a new proof of his earnest desire to conciliate the nation. Rising from his seat he made a short address to the assembly, and announced his consent to the establishment of a law obliging every future king to be crowned within six months after his accession. This unexpected declaration, which removed the fears of the Hungarians lest any sovereign, in imitation of Joseph II., should evade the coronation oath, in order to infringe their liberties, raised a general transport of enthusiasm, and all vied in displaying the warmest proofs of loyalty, gratitude, and affection. The diet increased the usual honorary of 100,000 florins to 225,000. And to exculpate themselves likewise from the imputation of having reduced their sovereign to the necessity of signing the humiliating convention of Reichenbach, they offered the whole strength and treasure of the country to secure an honourable peace with the Turks. " Let these wicked rumours," said the primate in an address to the king, " be dissipated ; may the hopes of your august house revive ; may your friends exult and your enemies tremble. The Hungarian nation is united with the king ; the king with the nation."

The enthusiasm which animated the assembly was still further heightened by his answer; and the affection of the lower orders captivated by his liberal attention to their welfare. " We accept," he said, " this honorary from our faithful states with a grateful mind; and it acquires additional value in our estimation, because it is not extorted from the people. We shall also hereafter appreciate the efforts of the states in proportion as they endeavour to extend their care to every class of citizens. We are not desirous to increase the royal authority, but to confine it within the bounds of law and beneficence ; we are convinced that the states will be actuated by the same spirit of patriotism, and far from limiting their affection to one order or class of citizens, will extend it equally to all. Convey, I entreat you, into all your districts, this our earnest wish ; and announce this message, that your sovereign is desirous to rule by the laws, yet still more anxious to rule by love."

Leopold, after taking an affectionate leave of the states, returned to Vienna, and the diet continued their sittings under the presidency of the palatine, to arrange the important business submitted to deliberation. Their decisions in general coincided with the wishes of the sovereign ; and such beneficial changes were made in the existing laws and customs as redounded to the welfare and happiness of the nation.

CHAP. CXXXIII.—1790,1791.

THE recovery of the Netherlands was the next object to which Leopold directed his attention ; and his views were furthered by the party contests natural to all popular govern-

ments, as well as by a change which had taken place in the
sentiments of the people.

Without any systematic plan, united only by indignation
against the arbitrary measures of their late sovereign, roused
by the exhortations of the priests, and, above all, encouraged
by unexpected success, all ranks and orders had cordially
co-operated in overthrowing the Austrian government. But
fortune had no sooner crowned their efforts than cabals and
factions agitated the new government, the army, and the
people. The chief power was appropriated by Van-der-Noot
and Van Eupen, whose efforts had principally contributed to
the revolution. Their influence soon became obnoxious to
the nobles and clergy, who were excluded from authority,
and the opposition arising from this schism rendered their
administration more jealous, oppressive, and arbitrary. The
country was therefore overwhelmed with all the horrors of
a revolutionary government, and loaded with greater evils
than had been experienced under the despotic rule of Joseph.
Tumults took place, and the two parties of aristocrats and
democrats struggled for superiority; the one under Van-der-
Noot and Van Eupen supported the existing congress as the
engine of their own power, the other, headed by Walchiers,
a rich banker, joined with the duke of Aremberg and Ursel,
and the count de la Mark, clamoured for the establishment
of a national assembly similar to that of France.

In these contests the heads of both parties endeavoured to
gain the countenance and support of foreign powers; Van-
der-Noot applied to England, Prussia, and Holland, and
offered to purchase their recognition of the new republic, by
renewing all the treaties of commerce and alliance. The
king of Prussia, whose principal view was to prevent the
re-establishment of the Austrian sovereignty, was not dis-
inclined to the proposal; but the Maritime Powers, with
equal justice and policy, rejected the overture, pressed the
congress to return to their allegiance, and offered to concur
in the re-establishment of the ancient constitution. On the
other hand, the democrats made application to the popular
party in France, from the chiefs of which they received the
strongest assurances of support, and swarms of agents from
the Jacobin clubs excited the people against the congress.

These dissensions spread into the army. The troops who
had nominated by acclamation Van-der-Mersch generalissimo

of the Belgic forces, were dissatisfied with the refusal of the congress to confirm their appointment, and espoused the popular cause. A representation was also made by the officers, supporting the nomination of the troops, and peremptorily requiring the reformation of abuses, and the establishment of a new form of government. Six deputies who were sent by the congress to displace the general, being arrested under the charge of attempting to disorganise the army, the congress despatched Schonfield, a Prussian officer, with 6000 men, to enforce their authority. Van-der-Mersch, on his part, made preparations for defence; but he had no sooner drawn his troops out of Namur than the inhabitants detained his artillery and ammunition; and the army refusing to act against their fellow-citizens, he was compelled to surrender, and confined in the citadel of Antwerp. This arrest and imprisonment of a general, whose military services had greatly contributed to the revolution, occasioned general discontent, and alienated the people of Flanders, of which country he was a native. These disputes not only enabled the troops at Luxemburgh, whose number did not exceed 12,000, to maintain themselves against the insurgents, but even to recover Limburgh, by the assistance of the peasants, who still preserved their loyalty to the Austrian government.

Such was the situation of the Netherlands when the signature of the convention of Reichenbach enabled Leopold to avail himself of the divisions in the government, and of the revolution which had taken place in the sentiments of the people.

Conciliation being hopeless, Leopold made preparations to reduce the Netherlands by arms, sent gradual reinforcements to the troops at Luxemburgh, and had no sooner concluded the convention than he despatched a succour from the hereditary dominions, which augmented the army to 30,000 men. During the march of the troops he renewed his offers of reconciliation, and requested the mediation of the allied powers. A congress was accordingly formed at the Hague, in September, by count Mercy, the Austrian plenipotentiary; lord Auckland, the British ambassador; count Keller, the Prussian envoy; and Van-der-Spiegel, the grand pensionary of Holland. Soon after their meeting the emperor published a second manifesto, promising to govern each of the provinces according to the constitutions, charters, and privileges in force during the reign of Maria Theresa under the guaranty of the allied powers, and to revoke all the unconstitutional regulations introduced by Joseph. He offered a general amnesty; and, at the instances of the three plenipotentiaries, fixed the term of submission on the 21st of November.

These offers made a sensible impression at Tournay, Ghent, Ostend, and other parts of Flanders; but the people of Brussels displayed a decided aversion to the Austrian government, and some of the most violent publicly tore in pieces and burnt the imperial manifesto. Deputies from the states were, however, despatched with full powers to the Hague, to negotiate the terms of submission. They were charged with an answer from the congress to the imperial manifesto, conceived in strong terms, and urging that the constitution offered by Leopold was not the ancient and legal constitution; claimed the confirmation of that established by the inaugural act of Charles VI.; at the same time demanded a prolongation of the armistice for eight days to summon the states, and elect deputies for the arrangement of a final accommodation. They claimed also the interference of the mediating powers, particularly recommending themselves to the British Court, to whose good faith and consistency they bore an honourable testimony, who, they observed, " had never encouraged the insurrection in the outset, nor fed them with false promises in the progress; but had, on every occasion, exhorted them to return to their allegiance, and expressed an earnest desire to assist them in recovering and securing their ancient and legal constitution."

The demands of the Belgic deputies being both equitable and agreeable to the stipulations of the convention of Reichenbach, were warmly supported by the ministers of the mediating powers. But all endeavours to procure a prolongation of the armistice, or to enter into farther negotiation, were peremptorily rejected by count Mercy, who declared that the mediation of the allies terminated with the expiration of the term fixed by themselves; that they had no farther right to interfere in the affairs of the Netherlands; that the very name of an armistice was disgraceful in a discussion between a sovereign and his rebel subjects; and that the army, which had been augmented to 45,000 men, would commence its march the very first hour after the expiration of the 21st of November.

The insurgents suffered the 21st of November to elapse without the required submission, and the imperial troops, under general Bender, passed the Meuse, entered Namur amidst the acclamations of the people, seized the artillery, drove back the Belgic forces, and, on the 30th of November, appeared before Brussels. Bender summoned the congress to submit, and allowed twenty-four hours for deliberation. The people and members of the government, who were encouraged by the arrival of general Koehler with 7000 patriots, at first determined to resist; but being left without leaders, by the flight of Van-der-Noot, Van Eupen, and other chiefs, Koehler retired again into Flanders; and, on the 3rd of December, a corps of Austrian troops entering the town, were received as the heralds of peace and security. At the same time detachments took possession of Tirlemont, Mechlin, Louvain, and Antwerp, and before the close of the year all the provinces were again subjected to the Austrian power.

The refusal of Leopold to prolong the armistice for so short a term, and the rejection of all interference from the three mediating powers, excited the most lively indignation, particularly at Berlin and the Hague. The grand pensionary declared that he would throw up his commission and instantly return to Holland; and the king of Prussia commanded count Keller to remonstrate against this conduct as a breach of the convention, to claim the revival of the ancient, not the new-fangled, constitution, and to exhort the natives not to conclude an accommodation with the house of Austria, except with the concurrence and under the guaranty of the Maritime Powers.*

* He followed these orders by a still stronger remonstrance written to the emperor himself in his own hand. " I cannot," he said, " suppose that your majesty approves the proceedings of your plenipotentiary, or that your intention is to obtain possession of the Netherlands by force of arms. My declaration accepted by your majesty at Reichenbach, and guaranteed by the Maritime Powers, authorises the allies to concur in restoring the Netherlands, to secure to them their ancient constitution, and to settle with your majesty the terms and the epoch for the re-establishment of that ancient constitution, on the true sense of which so much difference of opinion has existed during the late reigns." He bitterly censured the conduct, the prejudices, and the arbitrary resolutions of count Mercy, " who ought not," he added, " to have preferred force to conciliation, and who, by yielding to the urgent demands of the other plenipotentiaries for a prolongation of the armistice, would have prevented the effusion of blood, and perhaps the ruin of those fine provinces."

This dispute might perhaps have involved Europe in a new war, had not the British cabinet been guided by more moderate and pacific motives. They joined, indeed, in the remonstrances of Prussia and Holland, while they soothed the resentment of Frederic William, and despatched lord Elgin to Vienna, to persuade the emperor to adopt more conciliatory measures. At the congress lord Auckland seconded the views of his court with equal spirit and address. The conferences being renewed on the 8th of December, by the consent of the emperor, count Mercy, with much reluctance, was induced to retract his declaration, and to conclude the convention of the Hague. By this act, which passed on the 11th of October, the emperor was to receive the homage of the Belgic provinces in the usual form, and to confirm their respective constitutions, privileges, and customs, in the same manner as they had been confirmed by the inaugural acts both of Charles VI. and Maria Theresa.

This convention being provisionally signed by Mercy, was transmitted to Vienna for the approbation of his sovereign. Leopold, however, again disappointed the expectations of the mediating powers. Instead of ratifying the agreement concluded by his minister, he adhered to his former declaration, and confirmed the constitution, privileges, and customs existing at the close of the reign of Maria Theresa, before the innovations of Joseph. As the three mediating powers could not depart from the principle of the convention concluded at Reichenbach, nor break their solemn promises to the Belgians, to procure the revival of the constitution which subsisted when the Netherlands were transferred to Charles VI., they withheld their ratification, and Leopold recovered these provinces without subjecting himself to foreign interference.

The impolicy of Leopold in refusing to gratify the people of Brabant with the renewal of their ancient constitution, excited general dissatisfaction, and gave a colour to the complaints of the disaffected. Unfortunately, other popular pretexts for opposition were afforded, by the removal of five

He concluded with exhorting the emperor, "in conformity with his assurances at Reichenbach, to bring back the Belgic nation under his dominion by peaceable means, without having recourse to arms; and secure to them a constitution which might restore tranquillity and reunite the interests of the sovereign with those of his subjects."

obnoxious members of the council of Brabant. Against this measure the States presented a violent protest, and not only withheld the customary subsidy, but refused their assent to a proposal for liquidating the debt contracted during the revolution, and remedying the damages sustained by individuals, notwithstanding the proposal had been agreed to by all the other provinces. The suspension of their sittings, the erasure of their protests from the journals, and the arrest of four of their members, increased the ferment. To prevent the interference of the Dutch, Leopold concluded an alliance with the States-general, and procured the expulsion of Van-der-Noot and Van Eupen from Holland. But in spite of all his precautions the discontents continued to augment; the revolutionary spirit spread like contagion over the land; the democrats were incited and encouraged by the Jacobins of France; corps of emigrant insurgents were formed in French Hainault; plots were daily formed, insurrections organised, and the most vigorous measures scarcely maintained the tottering authority of government.

The conduct of Leopold throughout this whole transaction seems to have been the result of a deep-laid but mistaken plan of policy. Notwithstanding repeated instances of political jealousy given by the French government, he was no less firmly attached to the fatal alliance of the house of Bourbon than his two predecessors. In spite of the increasing ferment in France, he still fondly entertained sanguine hopes that his brother-in-law would recover his authority, and that a renewal of the treaty of Versailles would again secure the safety and tranquillity of the Low Countries. Above all, he had inherited a rooted dislike of the Barrier Treaty, and was averse to rivet the shackles which England and Holland had formerly imposed on his predecessors. From these motives he employed every art to evade their guaranty, and still more that of Prussia, which would have afforded a pretext for the perpetual interference of an inveterate rival.

Although Leopold recovered the Netherlands on terms which he deemed more consistent with his honour and interests than by owing their restoration to the agency of the Maritime Powers, yet, by eluding their guaranty, he relinquished the advantages which he might have derived from their support in case of hostilities with France. To this erroneous system of policy, and this mistaken point of honour, may be attributed the subsequent loss ⸱of the Netherlands, and, with that loss, the stupendous ascendency of France and fatal degradation of the house of Austria.

CHAP. CXXXIV. — 1790–1792.

THE accommodation with Prussia, the armistice with the Porte, the recovery of the Netherlands, and the restoration of internal tranquillity left Leopold at liberty to turn his attention to the affairs of France, and to direct his efforts to the relief of his unfortunate relatives. A pressing and additional motive for his interference was derived from the encroachments of the National Assembly on the rights of the Germanic body.

In France the delirium of liberty had continued to spread, and a people at once emancipated from all the restrictions of ages were wild for new systems, and disdained the bounds of reason and moderation. Tne National Assembly, instead of introducing prudent and gradual reforms or remedies for existing evils, razed the constitution to its very foundations, to rebuild it according to abstract theories and systems of fancied perfection. They stripped the crown of its prerogatives, changed the very title of their monarch, abolished all titular distinctions, as well as the privileges of the nobility, suppressed the parliaments, divided the kingdom into departments, and divided all religious establishments, converting the estates and revenues of the clergy into national property, allowing the ministers of religion only a scanty and temporary salary, and imposing on them an oath contrary to the principles of the Catholic church.

The unfortunate king, with his characteristic meekness and resignation, beheld the progress of anarchy and licentiousness, the alienation of the people, the gradual seduction of the army; and though confined within the precincts of the Tuileries, and subject to the daily insults of the populace, he seemed to forget his own miseries in those of his family and subjects. At length the exhortations of the insulted queen, the danger of his family, and the increasing tide of evils which hourly swelled with accumulated force, roused even his patient and forbearing spirit, and impelled him to devise

some means for averting the dangers with which he was surrounded, and for stemming the torrent of calamities and
crimes which threatened to overwhelm his country.   Several
plans for escaping from the capital, for placing himself at the
head of the army, dissolving the assembly with the assistance of foreign powers, acquiring popularity, and rallying
round the ruins of the throne the remnant of those who were
yet friends to government and order were proposed ; but
were all marred by the reluctance of the ill-fated monarch,
who was determined not to engage in a civil war, nor to
desert his country ; two errors to which he attributed the
ruin of our Charles I. and James II.   He at length, however, acquiesced in a scheme which was proposed by Mirabeau, and who was preparing to make a last effort in support
of the crown.   The king was to quit Paris, to escape to
Montmedi, one of the frontier towns, and place himself at the
head of the few regiments which still continued faithful, and
which had been drawn to that quarter by the marquis de
Bouillé, commandant of the district.   Mirabeau was to awe
the Jacobins, to increase his party by bribes and promises, to
obtain from the people a petition for the convocation of a
new national assembly ; and it was hoped that this plan
would rally and strengthen the friends of order, and enable
them to crush the faction which was rising on the ruins of
every institution.

The sudden and fatal death of Mirabeau prevented the
execution of this design ; the king, without a single person
of efficient character and influence in whom he could confide,
fluctuated in still greater uncertainty than ever.   From an
apprehension for the safety of the nonjuring clergy, and
from aversion to receive the sacrament at the hands of a constitutional priest, he was induced by the persuasion of La
Fayette, once the popular idol and the chief of the constitutionalists, to pass the season of Easter at the palace of St.
Cloud.   But this journey, which was expected to flatter the
nation by the pretext of proving to all Europe that the king
was at full liberty, was opposed by the populace ; and, notwithstanding the interference of La Fayette, Louis was
drawn back to the Tuileries, amidst the menaces, reproaches,
and insults of the mob.   Overwhelmed with confusion and
despair, the degraded monarch threw himself into the power
of the constitutionalists, and, by their advice, published the

celebrated letter addressed to the foreign ministers, in which
he declared himself at full liberty, and notified his approbation of the revolution.

The letter excited a momentary applause in the National
Assembly, but the very next day was stigmatised as a proof
of deceit and hypocrisy; and while it humbled the king in
the eyes of Europe and of his turbulent subjects, disgusted
those who were warmly attached to his cause and devoted to
the principles of the ancient government.

Such was the state of France and the distress of the royal
family when the instances of the German princes and the
machinations of the factious forced Leopold into a contest
with the government and nation.

In the abolition of all ecclesiastical and territorial rights
within the limits of France, the National Assembly had also
comprehended those of the German states in Alsace, Franche
Comté, and Loraine, and the other provinces ceded to Louis
XIV.; although those rights had been solemnly confirmed
by the peace of Westphalia, as well as by subsequent treaties,
and were respected amidst all the wars which for above a
century agitated Europe. The princes and states remonstrated against this infraction at an early period of the revolution, and laid their grievances before the government; yet
their application, though supported by the influence of the
king, drew from the assembly only a vague and inadequate
offer of indemnification in national property for the rights
abrogated in Alsace, while the claims relating to the other
provinces were passed over with contemptuous silence. The
states accordingly renewed their appeal to the German diet,
and obtained the introduction of a clause in the capitulation
of the new emperor, which bound him to interpose for the
preservation of their rights.

In compliance with this engagement, Leopold himself, on
the 14th of December, 1790, addressed a letter to the king,
containing strong professions of amity, and requiring as a
proof of reciprocal friendship the re-establishment of the
rights secured to the German princes. By the impulse of
the ruling party, the king in his answer was compelled to
adopt a style of presumption scarcely surpassed by that of
Louis XIV. He expressed surprise that the proprietors of
fiefs in the French territories should apply to the emperor in
an affair which did not regard the empire, but solely related

to themselves as French feudatories; he at the same time
urged the emperor to withhold his support, and induce the
claimants to accept the equitable compensation proposed by
France. As a proof of a decided resolution to support this
refusal, the assembly voted a large augmentation of the military force.

Thus treated with contempt and injustice, the princes
again laid their complaints before the diet, and called on
their chief for a more effectual interference : the pacific
representations of the emperor were drowned in the clamour
for redress, and a decree was passed, in July, 1791, for the
renewal of their demands, in their own name and in that of
the empire.   While this discussion was pending, the forcible
occupation of Avignon, which, notwithstanding its transfer
to the Roman see, had still maintained a nominal connection
with the empire, inflamed the general indignation.

Such being the system pursued by the assembly, and such
the melancholy situation of the royal family, it raised the
wonder of all Europe that Leopold still continued to maintain
an apparent indifference to the sufferings of his sister and
brother-in-law, as well as to his own insulted dignity. But
he was influenced by prudential motives. He well knew the
benevolent weakness of the king, who rejected with horror
any decisive measure, from a dread of involving his country
in a civil war. He was also aware that charges were levelled
against his sister as the patroness of an Austrian committee
in the palace for effecting a counter revolution; and he was
sensible that he should expose her, who was considered by
the violent party as a public hostage for his pacific conduct,
to the vengeance of an enraged nation.

Yet during this momentous interval he was far from be-
holding with real indifference the state of his royal relatives,
and was fully awake to the danger which threatened every
crowned head from the violence and diffusion of the Jacobin
principles. He anxiously watched the progress of events,
and at an early period seems to have approved a plan suggested by Montmorin for the relief of his unfortunate brother-in-law. Its object was to combine the principal powers
of Europe in a feigned attack against France, as a pretext
for enabling the king to assume the command of an army, to
recover his former authority, and to regain the love and confidence of the people by appearing as the restorer of peace
and tranquillity.

But this frivolous scheme being abandoned in consequence of the king's formal approbation of the constitution, another was arranged at Mantua, in concurrence with the count d'Artois and count Alphonso d'Urfort, a confidential agent sent by the king, who met Leopold during his journey in Italy. In May, 1791, 35,000 Austrians were to march towards the frontier of Flanders and Hainault; 15,000 troops of the circles towards Alsace; 15,000 Swiss were to threaten the Lyonnois and Franche Comté; 15,000 Sardinians to assemble on the frontier of Dauphiné, and 20,000 Spaniards in Catalonia. To these were to be joined the regiments still remaining loyal, the volunteers whose fidelity was unquestionable, and all the royalists and constitutionalists of the provinces. A declaration was to be published under the signatures of the kings of Spain and Naples, the infant of Parma, and all the princes of the blood who were at liberty, as members of the house of Bourbon. It was hoped that this vast combination would awe the democrats, and enable the royalists to regain the ascendency. The emperor engaged to conduct the negotiation with the king of Prussia, and announced the accession of the king of England as elector of Hanover. Aware, however, of the extreme desire of the king and queen of France to relieve themselves from the indignities to which they were hourly exposed, Leopold exhorted them not to attempt their escape, but to use their endeavours in acquiring popularity, that the people, alarmed at the approach of foreign armies, might find their safety only in the king's mediation and in submission to his authority. "This," it was added, "is the emperor's opinion. He depends solely on this plan of conduct for the success of his measures, and he shudders with apprehension of the fatal consequences, should the king and queen be arrested in their flight. Their surest dependence is on the movements of the armies, preceded by threatening manifestoes." In delivering this plan to the count d'Urfort, he added, "Tell my brother and sister that I will assist them, not by words but by deeds."*

This plan, which was scarcely less chimerical than the

---

* Some persons have questioned the authenticity of this plan as too chimerical; but Bertrand de Moleville, from whom we give it, has fully proved its authenticity by declaring that the original is still in existence with marginal corrections in the hand of the emperor.

former, was rejected by the king and queen; and notwithstanding the instances of the emperor, they attempted to escape from Paris.* Being arrested at Varennes, the whole scheme was deranged, all hopes of escape were totally cut off, the royal family were carried back in barbarous triumph, the king was threatened with a public trial and deposition, and the axe was laid to the root of the declining monarchy.

The imminent danger of the royal family induced the emperor to abandon his temporising conduct, and on the 6th of July he published at Padua a solemn appeal to the other powers of Europe. He called on them to join in a common declaration, demanding of France the immediate liberation of the king and royal family, and requiring for them the inviolability and respect due by the laws of nature and of nations from subjects to their sovereigns. He urged them to declare that they would unite in avenging every future attempt committed against the liberty, honour, and safety of the king and royal family, that they would acknowledge as constitutional laws legally established in France, those alone which should have the voluntary acquiescence of the king,. being at liberty, and if these commands were not complied with, that they would concur in employing all the means in their possession to put a stop to the scandalous usurpation of power, which bore the appearance of open rebellion, and of which the example threatened the safety of other governments.

Conscious that without the co-operation of England, the Netherlands could not be preserved, and that all hostile efforts against France would be fruitless, he sent the draught of this declaration to the king, accompanied with a private letter, which indisputably proves his views and sentiments at this important crisis.†

* It has been asserted by persons of great authority, that the emperor even arranged the plan of this escape; and some documents in my possession corroborate the opinion. But there is other evidence equally strong for the account given in the text. The only means of reconciling these discordant assertions is by recurring to the cautious character of Leopold, and supposing that he often acted from the impulse of the moment, and therefore frequently wavered between opposite extremes. Doubtless we cannot have better authorities for the account of this memorable flight than those of Bouillé and Bertrand.

† I am persuaded," he said, " that your majesty is not unacquainted with the unheard-of outrage committed by the arrest of the king of

New and repeated proofs of hostility displayed by the ruling faction, with the sanguine declarations and urgent instances of the emigrants, confirmed the resolutions of Leopold. His determination was still farther strengthened by the king of Prussia, who was equally interested to oppose the progress of that fanatic enthusiasm which threatened the overthrow of every throne. With a view to settle a specific plan of conduct, a confidential interview was arranged between Leopold and Frederic William at Pilnitz, a palace belonging to the elector of Saxony in the neighbourhood of Dresden.

But in the short period which elapsed before the meeting, the sentiments of Leopold underwent a considerable change. Notwithstanding he received favourable answers from the different powers to whom he had appealed, his hopes were frustrated by a decisive and unequivocal refusal on the part of England to depart from a strict neutrality. His disinclination to engage in measures which might lead to hostilities was increased by the representation of his principal

France, the queen my sister, and the royal family, with the same surprise and indignation as myself; and that your sentiments accord with mine on an event, which, threatening more atrocious consequences, and fixing the seal of illegality on the preceding excesses, concerns the honour and safety of all governments. Resolved to fulfil what I owe to these considerations, and to my duty as chief of the German empire and sovereign of the Austrian dominions, I propose to your majesty in the same manner as I have proposed to the kings of Spain, Prussia, and Naples, as well as to the empress of Russia, to unite with them in a concert of measures for obtaining the liberty of the king and his family, and setting bounds to the dangerous excesses of the French Revolution. The most obvious plan seems to be that we should unite in sending a declaration, either jointly or separately, by our ministers in France, which may restrain the chiefs of the violent party and prevent desperate resolves, still leaving open the means of an honourable amendment and pacific establishment of such a state of things as may preserve the dignity of the crown, and maintain the essential points of general tranquillity. I submit, therefore, to your majesty the draught annexed, which appears to me most likely to fulfil these views; but as the success of such a declaration is uncertain, and must depend on the support of efficient measures, my ambassador shall receive immediate instructions for entering with your ministers into such a concert as circumstances require; and I will not fail to communicate to your majesty the answers which I may receive from other powers. The favourable disposition which they all manifest for the re-establishment of peace, tranquillity, and concord bids fair to remove all obstacles to an union of views and sentiments, in a situation of affairs which so nearly interests the good of all Europe."

ministers, particularly of Lacy, who united in decrying a war, urging that it would occasion the immediate loss of the Netherlands, which were left defenceless by the demolition of the barrier fortresses, and of which the majority of the natives only waited for foreign support to throw off the Austrian government. The exhortations of the king, his brother-in-law, decided the resolution of Leopold, if he yet retained any inclination to engage in a war with France.

The meeting, however, took place on the 27th of August 1791, and Bouillé was summoned by the king of Prussia to arrange a plan of attack. While the two sovereigns were employed in private discussions, they were interrupted by the sudden arrival of the count d'Artois, accompanied by Calonne, who came with the hope of persuading them to engage in immediate hostilities. The king of Prussia was easily inflamed by their representations; but no arguments could overcome the caution of Leopold, or draw him into specific engagements; and he was with difficulty induced, by the importunities of the French princes, to sign the celebrated declaration.*

It is no wonder that a vague declaration, intended merely to satisfy the importunities of the French princes, the fulfilment of which depended on a contingency never likely to happen in the common course of events, should not be followed by any important consequences. Leopold, who yet hoped by temperate measures to disarm the rage or baffle

* "The emperor and king of Prussia, having heard the representations of Monsieur the king's brother, and the count d'Artois, declare, that the present situation of the king of France concerns the interest of every sovereign in Europe. That interest they hope will be acknowledged by the powers whose assistance is required, and consequently those powers will not refuse to unite with their majesties in employing the most efficacious means to place the king of France in a situation to establish in perfect liberty the foundations of a monarchical government, equally agreeable to the rights of sovereigns and the welfare of the French nation. Then, and in that case, the emperor and the king of Prussia are determined to act promptly, and by mutual concert, with the forces and vigour necessary to obtain the desired end. In the mean time they will give orders for their troops to be ready for actual service."

Reports were industriously circulated that a regular treaty for the partition of France was arranged at this meeting. But the whole conduct of Leopold, and particularly his subsequent measures, prove that he had formed no offensive designs. The secret articles which have been produced bear the strongest marks of forgery.

the designs of the Jacobins, was resolved not to engage in hostilities. He therefore seized the first favourable opportunity to annul his engagements, and on the acceptance of the constitution by Louis, and his temporary restoration to liberty, he received the French ambassador, who had been forbidden to appear at court, revoked his circular letter from Padua, and was the first sovereign in Europe who admitted the tri-colour flag into his ports. He rejected all plans of hostile aggression, received with coolness the expostulations of the empress Catherine; and scarcely deigned to listen to the chivalrous projects of the king of Sweden, who even offered to lead an army of Swedes and Russians to the gates of Paris, while the Austrians and Prussians were to invade France on the side of the Netherlands.

Leopold did not abandon these hopes of preserving tranquillity until he was driven from his pacific system by the continual provocations of the Jacobins.

On the return of the king from Varennes, the leaders of the Jacobins endeavoured to raise against him the popular indignation, and exerted themselves to bring him to a public trial. But their views were thwarted by the royalists, the constitutionalists, and the moderate of every description, who were encouraged by the concert of powers, and who felt that their own safety was connected with that of the monarch. After a desperate struggle, Louis was restored to the exercise of his authority, and, on the 14th of September, accepted the constitution, an event which was followed by the voluntary dissolution of the National Assembly, whose functions had expired.

The king hoped that the establishment of the constitution would remove the principal causes of discontent, and that the new representatives wonld be animated with sentiments less hostile to the regal authority. But these frail hopes were disappointed. The Constituent Assembly having, by a disinterested though absurd decree, declared themselves incapable of being re-elected in the legislative body, by this vote excluded those who were animated by moderate sentiments, and who, as framers of the constitution, were interested in its preservation, and enabled the Jacobins to obtain the preponderance. The new members, therefore, were principally drawn from the middling and lower classes of society, visionary projectors, men of ruined fortunes, the most furious declaimers in the political clubs, all animated by the boldest spirit of enterprise, and breathing the fury of revolutionary principles. They were headed and directed by a few chiefs, who, for the scourge of Europe, united superior talents with a courage exalted to fanaticism. The faction which thus gained the ascendency received the appellation of Girondists*, from the department for which the leaders were principally chosen; and Brissotines from the name of their chief.

The object of these demagogues was to establish a republic on the ruins of the throne. They laboured to realise the plans of a Richelieu and a Louvois, by extending the limits of France to what they termed her natural boundaries, the Pyrenees, the Alps, the Rhine, and the Ocean. From this centre, they traced, in imagination, the limits of an empire as stupendous as that of ancient Rome; from a territory in which the bounty of nature or the ingenuity of man had comprised every requisite for defence and every advantage for attack, they purposed to extend their power and to diffuse the contagion of their principles over the whole habitable world.

Their active and sagacious spirit equally employed the most frivolous artifices, and the most specious motives, to revive the hostile spirit of their nation against Austria, a power whose territories were the first object of their cupidity, and who, from proximity, strength, the ties of blood and alliance, was the most able, as well as the most interested, to check the diffusion of their principles, and to oppose the execution of their designs. They maligned the conduct of the queen, exaggerated her levities into crimes, found no calumnies too black, no charge too atrocious, to render her the object of popular odium. Their papers and journals were filled with declamations on the evils entailed on their country by the alliance with Austria. Not only the clubs, the streets, and the squares resounded with invectives against the emperor; but the members of the National Assembly gave vent to the most virulent accusations against his conduct, character, and principles. They feigned a committee of Austrian adherents, as sitting in the very capital, under the auspices of the queen, deceiving the king,

* The history of this remarkable faction is admirably given by Lamartine in his recent work.

forging fetters for the people, and arranging, in conjunction with the court of Vienna, a plan to deliver up the nation to that house, which they depicted as invariably a fatal friend or inveterate enemy.

Such a series of insults and provocations, such a systematic plan of hostility, would have justified immediate aggression on the part of Leopold. But he dreaded to aggravate the misfortunes of a beloved sister, or to expose the life of his brother-in-law ; and he was apprehensive of again plunging his country into a war, from which he had recently delivered it with so much difficulty. Hence, he had no sooner reco-vered the Netherlands, than he recalled the greater part of his troops, reduced his army, and refused to march an Aus-trian corps towards the French frontier, even as a means of affording a pretext for Bouillé to form a camp at Montmedy, in order to favour the escape of the king. Hence, he revoked the vigorous measures which had been dictated by necessity, as soon as they had begun to produce their effect ; yet in the midst of changes which indicated want of decision, he still held forth equivocal threats or distant insinuations, which at once discouraged the royalists and inflamed instead of awing the Jacobin faction.

This conduct, therefore, only hastened the danger which Leopold was so anxious to avert. Besides the dispute rela-tive to the feudal rights of the German princes, new subjects for invective were soon discovered by the sagacity of the Brissotines; new pretences were devised for precipitating the nation into that conflict to which they looked forward as the means of establishing their darling republic, and extend-ing the empire of their baneful principles.

Leopold anxiously laboured to remove all causes of com-plaint. He repeated his instances with the elector of Treves and the other princes on the frontier to suspend the military armaments and disperse the French emigrants. But from the menacing aspect of France, the warlike preparations and hostile language of the ruling party, he began to be appre-hensive of an attack. He therefore concluded the prelimina-ries of a defensive treaty with Prussia for the maintenance and guaranty of the empire ; and to unite the princes of Ger-many in a common cause, he ratified the conclusum of the diet relative to the contested feudal rights. He announced these measures to the king of France, and in dignified language declared his decided resolution to give all the aid required by his imperial authority in support of these just claims. His example was followed by the king of Prussia.

The machinations and violence of the Brissotines overbore all the pacific measures of Leopold. They impelled the king to order preparations for assembling an army of 150,000 men, and forced him to adopt their own language and indecorous menaces for the immediate dispersion of the emigrants. Brissot roused the assembly and nation by a violent harangue, in which he proved that France had no danger to dread, and every advantage to hope, from a war. After adverting to the situation of the European powers, he turned the force of his invective against Leopold.*

He was followed by the principal members of his party, who all enforced and exaggerated his declarations; and the result of their efforts was the celebrated manifesto, published in December, 1792, which, amidst the cant of affected moderation, was conceived in similar language, displayed the same sentiments, and denounced vengeance against all who should support the emigrants, or presume to interfere in the internal concerns of the nation.

The situation of Leopold hourly assumed a more serious aspect. It was necessary to secure so important a territory

---

* " What have we," he said, " to fear from the emperor of Germany? Augmentation of debt, diminution of taxes, frequent insurrections in Hungary, inveterate hatred among the people of the Netherlands, all presage the most imminent danger to the house of Austria. Throughout the Austrian territories the people are harassed with that passion for aggrandisement from which nothing but misfortunes can be expected. Everywhere the soldier, whom princes endeavour to render the enemy of the people, refuses to separate his interest from that of the people, among whom are his friends and his parents. The resolutions of the emperor are feeble : he desires, he seeks what is just, but he wants energy to resist the machinations and perfidious counsels of those ambitious men by whom he is surrounded. The ties of blood, no less than prudence, may have induced him to affect in his letters amicable expressions : he can gain nothing by attacking us, on the contrary, he has every thing to fear. The political variations of the cabinet of Vienna ought not to inspire you with alarm. As a prince, the emperor desires peace, though as chief of the Germanic empire he appears to desire war. But away with the politics of the court of Vienna ! What have we to do with the politics of courts, we who *will* to be free, we who only wish to defend our liberty, we who possess the means of doing it. France desires peace, yet fears not war ; she seeks no new allies, she has twenty-five millions of souls devoted to the support of her cause."

as the electorate of Treves, which opened a way into Germany, and cut off the communication between the Upper Rhine and the Netherlands. While he therefore redoubled his instances for hastening the dispersion of the emigrants, he ordered his commander in the Netherlands to take measures for succouring the elector of Treves if invaded or threatened with invasion. An official communication of these precautions was, on the 21st of December, made to the French ambassador at Vienna, in terms which were calculated to remove the impression of any hostile design. Prince Kaunitz, after stating the compliance of the elector with the request of the imperial court for the dispersion of the emigrants, added, that he had claimed the assistance of the emperor, should his territory be threatened with attacks, which he had reason to apprehend, and that the emperor had ordered general Bender, his commander in the Netherlands, to furnish prompt and effectual succour, should the electorate be invaded or threatened with invasion. He professed a firm conviction that the king's moderate sentiments justified his order by alluding to the want of subordination in the distant departments of France, and concluded with deprecating a war "*from the infallible consequences which it would produce, as well to himself and to the German empire, as to the other sovereigns who had united in concert for the maintenance of public tranquillity and the safety and honour of crowns.*"

This communication furnished new fuel to the flame. These vague and mysterious expressions were artfully seized by the demagogues, and the *concert of powers* instantly became the war-whoop of the party. Gensonné presented the report on this paper with a speech calculated to give full effect to the spirit of hostility which had been raised against Austria. He argued that the emperor had broken the treaty of Versailles, for which France had lavished her blood and treasures ; that his whole conduct had been hostile to the liberties of the French nation ; that under the show of force and a concert of powers, his real object was to procure the adoption of a congress, and insidiously to subvert the constitution. He appealed to the Assembly, and in that ardent language which was now become popular, called on the members to apprise the nation of its danger, and urged them to vindicate their liberty, by anticipating the alarming projects of the imperial court. The ardour of the Assembly was still more inflamed by Guadet, the vice-president, who darting to the tribune, poured forth a torrent of glowing invective; the whole body rising at one and the same moment by the impulse of enthusiasm, amidst tumultuous shouts and cries of " the Constitution or Death," sanctified by oath a declaration stigmatising as a traitor to the country any Frenchman who should take part in a congress to modify the constitution, who should mediate with rebel emigrants, or enter into composition with the German princes relative to the feudal rights in Alsace. Some of the ministers who were present, were borne away by the general ardour, and the unfortunate monarch himself was necessitated to sanction a decree which precluded all hopes of amicable accommodation.

The hostile faction did not allow this burst of enthusiasm to subside. Even at the moment when the minister apprised the assembly of the total dispersion of the emigrants, they renewed their invectives against the emperor. On the second report of the diplomatic committee relative to the communications with the imperial court, Brissot himself rose to address the assembly. " The mask," he exclaimed, " is fallen; your real enemy is known; the order given to general Bender tells you his name. It is the emperor! The electors were but his puppets, the emigrants but his instruments! Despise the emigrants : the national court of justice will punish the rebellion of those mendicant princes. Nor are the electors more worthy of your anger; fear has prostrated them at your feet, and a free people will not crush its humbled enemies. The emperor! I repeat, the emperor, is your true enemy. Him you must combat ; him you must either conquer or force to renounce the confederacy he has formed against you. He intended either to alarm or attack you. If you are to be attacked, it behoves you to anticipate him ; if he means to force you to an unworthy capitulation, you must realise what you have a hundred times sworn, The Constitution or Death."

We spare the reader a further detail of these insults and invectives so offensive to humanity, so degrading to the nation, so hostile to good faith and justice. In spite of frequent communications from the ministers, proving the pacific disposition of Leopold, the king was required to demand of

him whether, as head of the house of Austria, he would live
in peace with France, and renounce all treaties and con-
ventions directed against the sovereignty and safety of the
nation. The refusal of full satisfaction before the 1st of
March was to be considered as a declaration of war ; and
orders were given for putting the troops in a condition to
take the field on the first signal. The king in this, as in
former instances, was swept away by the torrent, and the
fatal and peremptory demand was transmitted to the French
ambassador at Vienna.

The emperor now perceived that all his attempts to maintain peace were vain. He therefore signed the alliance with
the king of Prussia, by which the two monarchs mutually
guaranteed their respective territories, and agreed to act in
concert for the preservation of peace ; and reserved to themselves the power of inviting Russia, England, Holland, and
the elector of Saxony to unite in similar defensive engagements.

Leopold also, by his minister prince Kaunitz, gave a becoming answer to the arrogant demands of France, and
assumed that language which became his dignity and feelings. He justified the orders given to marshal Bender, by
his duty as chief of the Germanic body, to succour a co--
estate when menaced with unjust attacks, and he proved on
facts admitted and acknowledged by the French themselves,
that the promised succour to the elector of Treves depended
on a previous compliance with the demand for the dispersion
of the emigrants.

He entered into an enlarged view of the question relative
to the concert of powers. He justly considered such a concert as warranted by the situation of his brother-in-law, and
ally, before the acceptance of the constitution, "forced by
atrocious violence to fly, protesting solemnly against an
acquiescence to which he had been compelled, and with his
family arrested and imprisoned by his own subjects." He
declared that he had himself invited the powers to suspend
their concert, which was not to resume its activity till the
same dangers should revive ; but he enforced the necessity
of maintaining such a provisional alliance by dwelling on
the disordered state of France, developing the intrigues of
the Jacobins for the propagation of their principles, and in-

stancing, in particular, a recent conspiracy to foment a revolt in the Low Countries.

This declaration was followed by a note from the Prussian minister at Paris, announcing the perfect agreement of the court of Berlin with the views of the court of Vienna.

The dignified language of the imperial declaration, and the clearness with which it developed the plots and designs of the dominant party, inflamed their fury, and gave new scope to their machinations. The minister by whom it was read was frequently interrupted with bursts of laughter and indignation. The name of the emperor was treated with every mark of insult, contempt, and indignity; the exclamation of "War! War!" resounded on every side. The cry of war was re-echoed from house to house, and from street to street, and a head of some recent victim to popular rage, designated as that of the emperor, was carried in barbarous procession, and held up to the windows of the queen's apartment in the palace of the Tuileries. The emotions raised by these artifices were not suffered to subside; the demagogues obtained the expulsion of the ministers attached to the king, on whose moderation rested the last hope of peace, and with peace the last barrier of the monarchy.

Within a few days, Brissot again harangued the Assembly. He threw a veil over the outrages and aggressions of which the court of Vienna so justly complained, and artfully reduced the dispute to the simple question of foreign interference. He grossly accused the unfortunate Louis of premeditated falsehood, and closed an harangue replete with uncommon acrimony against Leopold, by denouncing de Lessart, the minister for foreign affairs. This denunciation was enforced with all the virulence of the Jacobin journals, and the declamations of popular clubs; and the ill-fated minister, without the privilege of being heard in his own defence, was sent for certain condemnation to the criminal tribunal at Orleans*. Such a dreadful example terrified all the friends of peace ; the other ministers either resigned, or were dismissed ; and the Jacobins gained a fatal and uncontrolled ascendency in the cabinet and the nation.

While this tempest was gathering in France, Leopold himself was no more. He was seized, on the 27th of February, with a malignant dysentery, and in three days was

* He was among the victims massacred on the 10th of September.

hurried to an untimely grave, in the forty-fifth year of his age, leaving his dominions in a state of more serious danger than even when he assumed the reins of empire. From the suddenness of his decease, the critical state of affairs, the recent assassination of the king of Sweden, and the savage principles professed by the Jacobins, his death, though without any apparent foundation, was attributed to poison.

Leopold is known rather as great duke of Tuscany, which country he ruled twenty-five years, than as sovereign of the Austrian dominions and emperor of Germany, because he did not move long enough in this elevated sphere to fix the public opinion. But we cannot withhold great praise from a sovereign, who, within the short space of a single year, relieved his country from foreign war and internal commotion, who baffled a great combination which threatened the independence of his house, and established a throne which at his accession was tottering to its very foundations.

Maria Louisa, daughter of Charles III. of Spain, was born in 1747, and espoused Leopold in 1765. The decease of a beloved husband, who expired in her arms, made so deep an impression on her feeling mind that she did not recover from the shock, but followed him to the grave in the ensuing May. She bore him sixteen children, of whom all except two survived her.

Francis, the eldest, was born in 1768, succeeded his father in all the hereditary dominions in the twenty-fifth year of his age, and obtained the imperial crown in the July subsequent to his father's death. The checkered events and wonderful revolutions of his reign are too near the present times to be traced with accuracy or impartiality.

The second son, Ferdinand Joseph, received the great duchy of Tuscany as an independent sovereignty; but being deprived of his territory by the arms of France, he obtained as a compensation the electorate of Saltzburgh, and afterwards that of Wurtzburgh, a mere nominal sovereignty. — The third son, Charles, is too highly distinguished as a warrior, and as the great supporter of his family, to need any other notice than a bare mention of his name. — The fourth, Leopold Alexander, was chosen palatine of Hungary, and being accidentally burnt to death, was succeeded in that dignity by the fifth son, Maximilian Joseph. — The other sons were Joseph Anthony, John Regnier, Louis, and Rhodolph. — The daughters, Maria Theresa, Mary Anne, Maria Clementina, and Maria Amelia.

INDEX.

THE END.

LONDON :

SPOTTISWOODE and SHAW,
New-street-Square.